Broadcasting, Cable, the Internet, and Beyond

An Introduction to Modern Electronic Media

Sixth Edition

Joseph R. Dominick
University of Georgia, Athens

Fritz Messere
State University of New York, Oswego

Barry L. Sherman

Mc
Graw
Hill

Boston   Burr Ridge, IL   Dubuque, IA   Madison, WI   New York   San Francisco   St. Louis
Bangkok   Bogotá   Caracas   Kuala Lumpur   Lisbon   London   Madrid   Mexico City
Milan   Montreal   New Delhi   Santiago   Seoul   Singapore   Sydney   Taipei   Toronto

Higher Education

Published by McGraw-Hill, an imprint of The McGraw-Hill Companies, Inc., 1221 Avenue of the Americas, New York, NY 10020. Copyright © 2008. All rights reserved. No part of this publication may be reproduced or distributed in any form or by any means, or stored in a database or retrieval system, without the prior written consent of The McGraw-Hill Companies, Inc., including, but not limited to, in any network or other electronic storage or transmission, or broadcast for distance learning.

This book is printed on acid-free paper.

1 2 3 4 5 6 7 8 9 0 DOW/DOW 0 9 8 7

ISBN: 978-0-07-313580-9
MHID: 0-07-313580-1

Editor in Chief: *Emily Barrosse*
Publisher: *Frank Mortimer*
Sponsoring Editor: *Suzanne Earth*
Editorial Assistant: *Erika Lake*
Marketing Manager: *Leslie Oberhuber*
Developmental Editor: *Craig Leonard*
Project Managers: *Christina Thornton-Villagomez and Carey Eisner*
Design Manager: *Srdj Savanovic*
Art Editor: *Emma Ghiselli*
Manager, Photo Research: *Brain J. Pecko*
Production Supervisors: *Carol Bielski and Tandra Jorgensen*
Composition: *10/12 Palatino by Aptara*
Printing: *PMS 646, 45# New Era Matte Plus, R.R. Donnelley & Sons, Inc.*

Cover: *Nick Koudis/Getty Images.*

Credits: The credits section for this book begins on page C-1 and is considered an extension of the copyright page.

Library of Congress Cataloging-in-Publication Data

Dominick, Joseph R.
  Broadcasting, cable, the Internet, and beyond: an introduction to modern electronic
  media/Joseph R. Dominick, Fritz Messere, Barry L. Sherman. —6th ed.
      p. cm.
  Includes index.
  ISBN-13: 978-0-07-313580-9 (pbk. : alk. paper)
  ISBN-10: 0-07-313580-1 (pbk. : alk. paper)
    1. Broadcasting—United States. 2. Cable television—United States. 3. Internet—United
  States. 4. Telecommunication—United States. I. Messere, Fritz. II. Sherman, Barry L.
  III. Title

HE8689.8.D66 2008
384.0973—dc.22

                                                                        2006046968

www.mhhe.com

Once again, to Candy, Eric, and Jessica, and to the memory of Barry L. Sherman

About the Authors

Joseph R. Dominick received his undergraduate degree from the University of Illinois and his PhD from Michigan State University in 1970. He taught for four years at Queens College, City University of New York, before coming to the College of Journalism and Mass Communication at the University of Georgia, where from 1980 to 1985 he served as head of the Radio-TV-Film Sequence. Dr. Dominick is the author of three books in addition to *Broadcasting, Cable, the Internet, and Beyond* and has published more than 40 articles in scholarly journals. From 1976 to 1980, Dr. Dominick served as editor of the *Journal of Broadcasting*. He has received research grants from the National Association of Broadcasters and from the American Broadcasting Company and has served as media consultant for such organizations as the Robert Wood Johnson Foundation and the American Chemical Society.

Fritz Messere received both his undergraduate degree (1971) and his master's degree (1976) from State University of New York. He is chairman of the Communication Studies department at Oswego State University and professor of broadcasting and telecommunications. In addition to *Broadcasting, Cable, the Internet, and Beyond*, Professor Messere is the coauthor of four books on media and media production. He has broad experience in radio and TV production. He has served as external assistant to FCC Commissioner Mimi Wayforth Dawson, as senior fellow of the Annenberg Washington Program in Communication Policy, and on the National Experts Panel on Telecommunications for the Rural Policy Research Institute.

Barry L. Sherman (1952–2000) was a professor in the Grady College of Journalism and Mass Communication at the University of Georgia. From 1986 to 1991 he served as chair of the Department of Telecommunication. Dr. Sherman was named director of the George Foster Peabody Awards in 1991, a position he held until his death. In addition to *Broadcasting, Cable, the Internet, and Beyond,* Dr. Sherman was the author of *Telecommunications Management: The Broadcast and Cable Industries* and *The Television Standard.* His writings also appeared in a variety of scholarly and professional publications. Dr. Sherman was active in many professional organizations, including the Broadcast Education Association, the International Radio and Television Society and the Museum of Broadcast Communications.

Preface

The title of the sixth edition of *Broadcasting, Cable, the Internet, and Beyond* is the same as that of the fifth edition, but this edition contains more information about the "Beyond" part. The past few years have provided some clues about what is on the horizon for the electronic media, and we hope the sixth edition helps instructors and students prepare for what lies ahead.

First, it's obvious that the future will be a digital one. The Internet is already digital; television will go all digital in 2009; and radio will eventually follow. In addition to changing the basic electronic media technologies that have been around for the last 80 years or so, the new digital environment opens up new opportunities for programmers, advertisers, and audience members. It also raises new issues for lawmakers, media executives, and researchers.

Second, the electronic media will be available on more and more multiple platforms. People can now watch TV on their big screen at home, a medium screen on their computers, and a small screen on their iPods or cell phones. Radio arrives via a conventional radio, a satellite radio, live over the Internet, or recorded in podcasts. The Internet is available on desktop computers, laptop computers, personal digital assistants, and cell phones.

Third, consumers will have increased control over their media exposure. It was not that long ago when if a person wanted to watch *Seinfeld,* he or she had to be in front of a TV at 9 P.M. on Thursday (or be competent enough to program a VCR to record it). In the future it will be common for people to make their own TV viewing schedules thanks to easy-to-use digital video recorders (DVRs) such as TiVo. Those people who forgot to set their DVRs might be able to download episodes of their favorite programs from iTunes or network Web sites or view them via video-on-demand. Those interested in news can choose among traditional broadcast and cable network newscasts or check out CNN.com or other news-oriented Web sites. Radio listeners can choose from more than a hundred music formats thanks to satellite radio or choose to listen to podcasts about their favorite topics.

Finally, audience members will be supplying more of the content of electronic media. Traditional newscasts often carry video of news events taken by individuals with camcorders or cell phone cameras, but the main channel of distribution, of course, will be the Internet. Thousands of user-created blogs on a huge variety of topics now populate the Web. The social networking site MySpace.com has more than 47 million members who spend significant amounts of time checking out what others have posted. Podcast.net lists more than 36,000 available podcasts, some by traditional media outlets but most of them by individuals, that can be downloaded. The slogan of YouTube.com is "Broadcast Yourself," and the site hosts an amazing variety video clips provided by members.

These are just some indications of what lies in the "Beyond" part of the electronic media that we hope will be reflected in the pages of this edition.

New and Improved

Chapter 1 ("History of Broadcast Media") has been updated to include the recent round of corporate restructuring and realignments and includes a new discussion of the business strategies of diversification and vertical integration. In response to user suggestions, we have pruned some of the Internet history from Chapter 2 ("History of Cable, Home Video, and the Internet") and have expanded the discussion of the history of digital video recorders (DVRs) and DVDs.

Chapter 3 ("Audio and Video Technology") has received a major overhaul and now contains an extended discussion of digital TV, satellite radio, and terrestrial digital radio, along with information about multiple delivery channels, including iPods. The newest trends in radio formats are discussed in Chapter 4 ("Radio Today"), while Chapter 5 ("Broadcast and Cable/Satellite TV Today") looks at the most recent changes in the structure of the television industry. Chapter 6 ("The Internet and New Media Today") contains updated information about Internet usage, the growth of Google and iTunes, as well as a discussion of the growth of online advertising.

Chapter 7 ("The Business of Broadcasting, Satellite, and Cable") has been updated to reflect the latest trends in cable and Internet advertising. Chapters 8 ("Radio Programming") and 9 ("TV Programming) now include a discussion of the most recent strategies in program development and scheduling.

The revised Chapter 10 ("Rules and Regulations") discusses the continuing effects of the Telecommunications Act of 1996, including the increasing competition between telephone and cable companies along with the latest legal developments in the struggle by media companies to combat illegal file sharing on the Internet and the recent crackdown by the FCC on indecency. Chapter 11 ("Self-Regulation and Ethics") discusses the broadcast industry's advertising campaign to popularize the V-chip.

The changing and challenging world of audience measurement is the subject of Chapter 12 ("Ratings and Audience Feedback") that now includes an expanded discussion of the local People Meter and the current methods of measuring the Internet audience. Chapter 13 ("Effects") has been updated to reflect the latest research about video games and the impact of the media on politics. Finally, Chapter 14 ("The International Scene") now reflects the major changes that have taken place in the BBC and in the media in China and Canada.

Boxed Inserts

The sixth edition continues the use of thematically organized, boxed inserts in every chapter to present extended examples of topics mentioned in the text or interesting snapshots of industry leaders. Dozens of new boxes have been added. For example:

- A new box in Chapter 1 ("History of Broadcast Media") profiles Robert Adler, the often unsung hero who invented the remote control.

- Chapter 10 ("Rules and Regulations) contains an Issues box that details some of the regulatory problems that go along with the shift to digital TV.

- An Issues box in Chapter 11 ("Self-Regulation and Ethics") examines the ethical problems brought on by using video news releases.

- A new box in Chapter 4 deals with the growth of Hispanic radio formats and listenership.

- Chapter 9 includes an Issues box that looks at the changing guard in network news.

- A Profiles box in Chapter 6 examines the successes and failures of technology wizard Steve Jobs.

Web Support

As with the fifth edition, each chapter of the book is supported by an interactive Web site that students can use to supplement the material found in the text. The site has been updated and includes a study guide, practice tests, chapter summaries, key terms, and links to other relevant sites. For more information, see the McGraw-Hill Web site at www.mhhe.com/dominick6.

Something Familiar

The sixth edition continues to use the same organizational structure that was introduced in the fifth edition.

- Part One ("Foundations") examines the history of the electronic media and introduces audio and video technology.

- Part Two ("How It Is") is an overview of the electronic media: radio, television, cable, and the Internet. Each of the three chapters in this section follows a common organization. Each surveys the structure of the media, looks at economic and social forces that influence their operation, examines current issues, and closes by outlining various career options.

- Part Three ("How It's Done") opens with a chapter that describes business aspects of each medium. Subsequent chapters concentrate on programming and how broadcasters and cablecasters select and schedule content that appeals to audiences that advertisers want to reach.

- Part Four ("How It's Controlled") looks at the regulatory process. The first chapter in this section discusses the rationale behind regulation, examines the FCC and other forces that shape electronic media regulation, and reviews the key federal and local laws that influence the day-to-day operations in the industry. The next chapter looks at self-regulation and examines how industry practices and ethics influence what the audience sees and hears.

- The final section, Part Five ("What It Does") focuses on the audience. The first chapter in this section explains how ratings are determined, while the following chapter examines the social impact of the electronic media. The last chapter in this section surveys international electronic media and examines the media structure in four selected countries.

Moreover, every chapter has been updated and revised to reflect changes to this dynamic area. Charts and tables contain the most-recent data available.

As has been our goal in the previous editions, we continue our attempt to create a book that is concise but still contains sufficient depth of coverage. Again, as before, we have tried to maintain a conversational writing style that students will find interesting. Finally, we reiterate our hope that the sixth edition fulfills the goal we first set when the first edition appeared: to produce a textbook that is informative and that captures some of the excitement, exhilaration, and immediacy that go with this industry.

Acknowledgments

There are many people who have provided statistics and insights into the current state of the electronic media industries and we'd like to thank them. In no special order, thanks to Frank Palumbo—ACNielsen; Lou Borrelli—NEP Supershooters; Steve LeBlanc at FX Network; Terry Ottina at the National Association of Broadcasters; John Krauss of the WRVO group of stations; Jamie Schopflin—Apple Computer; Andi Sporkin—National Public Radio; Lee Vanden Handel at Premiere Radio; Thom Moscarsky—Arbitron Research; and to our families, who continue to provide snacks, support, and good counsel.

And, of course, thanks to all those who reviewed the previous edition for their helpful suggestions:

Virginia Becheler, SUNY Brockport
Craig Breit, Cerritos Community College
Mu Lin, University of North Florida
Carol J. Richardson, St. Louis Community College at Meramec
Susan Salas, Pepperdine University
George E. Whitehouse, University of South Dakota
Brad Yates, University of West Georgia

We sincerely thank the McGraw-Hill production team who helped make this edition possible: Christina Thornton-Villagomez and Carey Eisner, production editors; Srdj Savanovic, designer; Brian J. Pecko, photo research; and Carol Bielski and Tandra Jorgensen, production supervisors.

Finally, this is the second edition to be published after the untimely death of our friend and coauthor, Barry Sherman. Once again, we hope we have produced a book that Barry would be proud of.

Joseph R. Dominick
Fritz Messere

Brief Contents

Detailed Contents

Part Two
How It Is

Part Three
How It's Done

7
The Business of Broadcasting, Satellite, and Cable   151

8
Radio Programming   172

9
TV Programming   195

Part Four
How It's Controlled

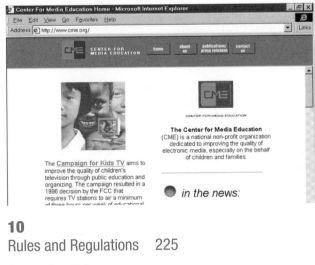

10
Rules and Regulations   225

11
Self-Regulation and Ethics   253

Part Five
What It Does

12
Ratings and Audience Feedback   271

13
Effects   287

14
The International Scene   311

List of Boxes

Part One Foundations

Introduction

Keeping up with the fast-changing world of the electronic media continues to be a challenging task. In the few years since the last edition of *Broadcasting, Cable, the Internet, and Beyond,* the following are just some of the things that have occurred:

- Satellite radio became a serious competitor with terrestrial radio by increasing its subscriber total to more than 12 million and signing big names such as Howard Stern, Martha Stewart, and Bob Dylan to provide programs.
- For their part, terrestrial stations introduced "high-definition" radio, a digital service that promised much better sound quality.
- Apple introduced the iPod, which spawned "podcasting" and prompted the legal downloading of more than a billion tunes from its iTunes service.
- Telephone companies such as AT&T introduced video services; cable companies such as Comcast introduced phone service over the Internet.
- The government set a firm date for the television industry's transition to a digital format.
- High-definition TV sets went down in price and up in popularity.
- The WB and UPN networks merged into the new CW network; Rupert Murdoch started yet another service: My Network TV.
- AOL and others offered TV over the Internet.
- People could watch TV programs on their iPods and cell phones.
- The Federal Communications Commission got tough on indecent television content and levied millions of dollars in fines.
- The ratings of TV news programs continued to decline as more and more people turned to the Internet for their news.

This list could be extended but by now the point is probably clear: All of the developments mentioned above suggest that the world of the electronic media will continue to change and have a great effect on society. This, in turn, suggests that it is important for students to appreciate these changes and what they mean for the future.

Students will note that all of the chapters in this book end with a section called "Suggestions for Further Reading." This introduction is different. We will end it with some suggestions for reading further—reasons why you should keep reading the rest of the book.

To be specific:

- Many of you will go into careers in the electronic media. This book presents a foundation of information for you to build on as you pursue your professional goals.
- For those of you who do not intend to become media professionals, knowledge of the electronic media will help you become intelligent consumers and informed critics of radio, TV, and online media. The electronic media are so pervasive in modern life that everyone should know how they are structured and what they do.
- Finally, all of you will spend the rest of your life in the Information Age, an age in which the creation, distribution, and application of information will be the most important industry. The electronic media are at the core of the Information Age. Everybody benefits from the scholarly study of an industry that will be a crucial part of business, education, art, politics, and culture.

In sum, the authors hope that what you learn from this book will be liberating in the traditional sense of a liberal education: We hope that the knowledge that you acquire will free and empower you in this new era.

History of Broadcast Media 1

Quick Facts

 First radio broadcast: Reginald Fessenden, Christmas Eve, 1906

 First radio network company: NBC, 1926

 First "Top 40" radio broadcasts: 1952

 First public demonstration of TV: 1939 World's Fair

 Cost of first TV commercial: $4 (1941)

 Cost of commercial minute in 2006 Super Bowl: $5.0 million

"What hath God wrought?"

That was the message sent by wire from Washington, D.C., to Baltimore one spring day in 1844. Using a code made up of dots and dashes, Samuel Morse had demonstrated the potential of his new communication device—the telegraph. For the first time in history, it was possible to send a message across long distances almost instantaneously.

"Come here, Watson. I need you."

Thirty-four years after Morse's invention, Alexander Graham Bell uttered those words into a telephone, a device that could send the human voice through a wire, making it even easier to communicate at a distance. Both the telegraph and the telephone are radio's ancestors, and their evolution anticipated many of the factors that would shape radio. Specifically:

- Both the telegraph and the telephone businesses supported themselves through commercial means.
- Big corporations came to dominate both industries.
- Both the telephone and the telegraph were point-to-point communication media. They sent a message from one source to one receiver.

Radio started off as a point-to-point medium until people discovered the advantages of broadcasting—sending the same message to a large number of people simultaneously. But we're getting ahead of the story.

THE INVENTORS

In the late nineteenth century, efforts were under way to liberate electronic communication from the wire. Physicists such as James Maxwell and Heinrich Hertz demonstrated the existence of electromagnetic radiation, energy waves that traveled through space. Other researchers investigated the nature of these mysterious waves. None of them, however, was able to perfect a system of wireless communication. The creation of such a system—radio—was due to the efforts of many inventors. There are three, however, whose contributions bear special mention: Marconi, Fessenden, and De Forest.

Marconi and Wireless

Guglielmo Marconi, who came from a wealthy and cultured Anglo-Italian family, had seen a demonstration of the mysterious radio waves while a college student. Enthralled with the new discovery, a young Marconi started experimenting with radio transmitters and receivers. Eventually he was able to send a radio signal more than a mile.

Marconi was aware of the commercial possibilities of his experiments. He realized that the biggest potential use for his wireless communication system would be in situations where it was impossible to use traditional wire telegraphy: ship-to-ship and ship-to-shore communication. Accordingly, he traveled to Great Britain, the leading maritime country of the period, and applied for a patent. The British granted him a patent for his wireless telegraphy system in 1896, and Marconi formed his own company to manufacture and sell his new device.

As his company became successful, Marconi turned his efforts toward increasing the range of his signals. In December 1901, he successfully transmitted a wireless signal—three short beeps, the letter S in Morse code—across the Atlantic, a distance of more than 2,000 nautical miles. The age of radio was dawning.

Fessenden and the Continuous Wave

Keep in mind that Marconi was sending wireless telegraphy—dots and dashes. No one was yet able to send the human voice via radio waves. For this to occur, someone had to develop a new way of generating radio signals. Marconi used a technique that generated radio waves by making a spark jump across a gap between two electrodes. This was fine for Morse code, but the human voice was another matter. To transmit voice, or music or other sounds, what was needed was the generation of a continuous radio wave that could be transformed to carry speech.

Reginald Fessenden, a Canadian-born electrical engineer, came up with the solution. Working with the General Electric Company, he built a high-speed alternator, a piece of rotating machinery much like those used to generate alternating current for household use.

Fessenden tested his alternator on Christmas Eve, 1906. Wireless operators on ships up and down the eastern coast of the United States were amazed when through their headphones they heard a human voice speaking to them. It was Fessenden explaining what was going on. After some violin music and readings from the Bible, the inventor wished his audience a merry Christmas and signed off.

Guglielmo Marconi was able to build a lucrative communications empire on his wireless invention. Here a successful Marconi listens to radio signals in the wireless room of his personal yacht, *Electra.*

This first "broadcast" caused a mild sensation and marked a major technological breakthrough. As dramatic as the change from typewriter to word processor, the shift from the spark gap to the continuous-wave transmitter ushered in a new age for radio. Radio waves could now carry more than just dots and dashes.

De Forest and the Invisible Empire

Around 1910, the most popular way of receiving radio signals was to use something called a **crystal set.** Scientists had discovered that some minerals, such as galena, possessed the ability to detect radio waves. Moving a tiny wire, called a cat's whisker, over a lump of galena allowed the listener to hear the faint sounds of wireless telephony, as radio broadcasts were called back then. Crystal sets were cheap and easy to assemble, but they had one big drawback: They couldn't amplify weak incoming signals.

If radio was to become a mass medium, something better was needed: a receiver that would boost the level of weak signals and make radio listening easier.

Lee De Forest found the answer during his experiments with something called a Fleming valve. This device looked like an ordinary light bulb. It consisted of a plate and a thin wire and was used to detect radio waves. De Forest discovered that the insertion of a small wire grid between the plate and the wire acted as an amplifier that boosted weak radio signals until they were easily detected. Hooking together two or three such devices could amplify signals millions of times. De Forest, realizing the potential of his invention—which he named the **audion**—for radio, wrote in his diary that he had "discovered an Invisible Empire of the Air." De Forest's invention made galena obsolete. The audion moved radio into the electronic age.

The inventor tried to create a market for his audion by using publicity stunts such as broadcasting phonograph records from the Eiffel Tower in Paris and a performance from the New York Metropolitan Opera. These early demonstrations had few listeners, but they did show that broadcasting was possible. It would take a few more years, however, before that idea gained wide acceptance.

De Forest's invention also got him into legal trouble. The Marconi company sued him, claiming that his audion infringed on their patents to the Fleming valve. Another patent battle over the audion dragged on for more than 20 years before reaching the Supreme Court. De Forest eventually sold rights to the audion, for a modest $50,000, to AT&T, who wanted to use it to amplify the signal of long-distance phone calls, and he turned his attention to other areas.

The audion contributed to improvements in transmission as well as reception. It subsequently was refined into the vacuum tube and formed the basis for all radio transmission until the 1950s, when it was replaced by the transistor and solid-state electronics.

BOARDROOMS AND COURTROOMS

Now that radio had been successfully demonstrated, the next step was to refine it and make it commercially rewarding. Accordingly, the next phase of broadcasting's evolution is marked by the activities of corporations more than of individuals. It's a tangled story, complicated by legal feuds, conflicting claims, politics, and war. It's also an important phase: Decisions made during this period permanently shaped radio's future.

Legal Tangles

To begin, let's review the situation as of 1910. Radio was still thought of as a point-to-point communication device—much like the telegraph and the telephone. Despite De Forest's demonstrations, broadcasting, as we know it today, did not exist. Radio's main use was still ship-to-ship and ship-to-shore communication.

Although Marconi's company (British Marconi) and its American subsidiary (American Marconi) dominated the business, there were other companies interested in radio: General Electric, AT&T, and Westinghouse. Each of these companies held patents on certain elements necessary to manufacture radio transmitters and receiving sets but no one company had patents that covered the entire process.

Predictably, each company produced its own version of the inventions patented by the others so that it could enter the business. The result was a long and costly legal battle over patent infringements. Had something drastic not happened, radio's evolution might have been severely hindered.

Radio Goes to War

Something drastic—World War I—was not long in coming. The military benefits of radio were apparent from the start of the conflict. The U.S. Navy had equipped all of its warships with radio and operated three dozen coastal radio stations. When the United States entered the war in 1917, the government, in the interests of national security, gave the Navy complete control over all radio operations, including all commercial stations.

This move had two important consequences for radio. First, the Navy assumed responsibility for patent infringement. This meant the various companies involved could pool their discoveries to improve radio communication. This is exactly what happened, and by the war's end in 1918, the technology was vastly improved. Second, during the war the Navy had taken control of 45 coastal radio stations and eight high-power transmitters owned by American Marconi. When the war ended, the Navy was reluctant to give them back because it was convinced that such an important function as international radio communication should not be controlled by a company (American Marconi) that was in turn controlled by a foreign power (Britain). In fact, bills were introduced in Congress to give the Navy exclusive control over radio's future. Obviously, some important decisions had to be made.

Birth of RCA

The first decision was what to do about the Navy. Commercial interests in the United States were opposed to any governmental intrusion into the free enterprise system and did not want the Navy controlling a potentially lucrative business. Consequently, the bills giving the Navy control over radio were never brought to a vote. Unlike some other countries, the United States chose not to put radio under direct governmental control.

The second problem was what to do about American Marconi and a possible British monopoly. To make matters even worse, with the Navy out of the picture, all of the prewar patent problems immediately resurfaced. The ultimate solution to the problem was suggested by the Navy: Buy out American Marconi and start a new company. Representatives from the U.S. government went to General Electric, the company with the most resources and financial clout, to handle the deal. After much tough negotiating, the management at Marconi agreed to the plan. Marconi would sell its American subsidiary to a new company—the Radio Corporation of America (RCA). Note that RCA would still be in the business of point-to-point communication and planned to make its money by sending wireless telegraphy and telephony to U.S. and international customers.

The next step was to solve the patents problem. Ultimately, RCA entered into a cross-licensing agreement with GE, AT&T, and Westinghouse that enabled each company to use the others' discoveries. The companies also agreed to divide the market: GE and Westinghouse would manufacture radio equipment, and RCA would sell it. AT&T would build the transmitters.

Ironically, just as these new agreements were falling into place, it became clear that the real future of radio would not be in point-to-point communication but in broadcasting—providing news and entertainment to the general public. Because of this, all of the agreements that were negotiated among these companies would soon fall apart as radio headed in a new direction.

BROADCASTING'S BEGINNINGS

Radio burst on the scene in the 1920s and soon became a national craze. There were several cogent reasons for the incredible growth of this new medium:

1. An audience of enthusiastic hobbyists, thousands of them trained in radio communication during the war, was available and eager to start tinkering with their crystal sets.
2. Improvements during the war gave radio better reception and greater range.
3. Big business realized that broadcasting might make money.

Its beginnings were modest. In 1920, Frank Conrad, an engineer for Westinghouse, began experimental broadcasts from his Pittsburgh garage. Conrad's programs, consisting of phonograph recordings and readings from the newspaper, became popular with listeners who were picking up the broadcast on crystal sets. Westinghouse noticed the popularity of Conrad's program and began manufacturing radio sets that were sold by a local department store. As sales of radio sets increased, Westinghouse moved Conrad from his garage to a studio on the roof of the company's tallest building in Pittsburgh. This new station was licensed by the Department of Commerce and given the call letters of KDKA (it's still on the air today, making it the oldest operating station). Conrad had established that there was a market for radio broadcasting.

Westinghouse quickly started other stations in Chicago, Newark, and other cities. RCA, GE, and AT&T also started radio stations. As the year 1922 began, there were 28 stations actively broadcasting; 6 months later there were 378; and by the end of the year, 570. Receiving sets were selling quickly; by the end of the decade almost one-half of the homes in America had a working radio.

The tremendous growth brought problems. For the listener, the biggest annoyance was interference. There were only a few frequencies available that gave good reception, and many stations were operating on them, which caused great difficulty for the listener as the competing signals interfered with one another.

At the corporate level, the problem was money. The cross-licensing agreement did not anticipate broadcasting. In 1923 RCA made $11 million from selling radio sets and only $3 million from its wireless telegraphy operation. AT&T, prohibited from manufacturing radio sets by the agreement, was obviously displeased. Friction soon developed between the members of the cross-licensing agreement over who had the right to do what. After a 4-year imbroglio, the parties finally agreed to a plan that ultimately solved the problem. AT&T left the broadcasting business and sold its assets to the other companies involved in the agreement. In return, AT&T would be granted a monopoly over the wire interconnections that were used to link stations together into a network (see "Radio Networks" section). RCA won the right to manufacture radio sets and acquired WEAF, the powerful New York City station formerly owned by AT&T.

RADIO'S FAST TIMES: THE 1920s

Things happened quickly for radio in the 1920s. In 8 years, from 1920 to 1927, radio went from a fad to a major industry and a major social force. We have

The control room and studio of KDKA, Pittsburgh, generally considered to be the oldest broadcasting station in the nation. Note that early broadcasters had to be careful about loose wires.

already noted how big business got involved with early radio. The three other major developments of this period that helped to shape modern radio were the development of radio advertising, the beginning of radio networks, and the evolution of radio regulation.

Advertising

When broadcasting first started, nobody thought too much about how it was supposed to make money. Most of the early broadcasters were radio and electronics manufacturers. For these companies, radio was simply a device to help sell their products. Other businesses that owned large numbers of early radio stations were newspaper publishers and department stores. For these companies, radio was a promotional device; it helped sell more newspapers or attracted people to the store. Nobody envisioned that it might be possible for a radio station to make money.

In time, however, costs started building up. To compete successfully, stations required reliable

equipment, special studios, and technicians and professional talent who had to be paid for their labor. Rising costs forced many stations off the air. Those that were left scurried to find some way to produce revenue.

It was the phone company that came up with the answer. Considering broadcasting an extension of the telephone, AT&T developed a system whereby anyone who had a message to deliver would come to their station, pay money, give the message, and leave (just as people did when they came to a phone booth and made a call to a single person). AT&T called the arrangement "toll broadcasting." It wasn't long before advertisers began to appreciate the potential of this new arrangement. The Queensboro Corporation, a New York real estate company, was the first to buy time on WEAF. Others quickly followed.

Although it may seem odd today, this early experiment in commercial broadcasting was resented by many listeners. There was even talk of a bill in Congress to prohibit it. By 1924, however, enough stations had followed WEAF that it was obvious the public did not object to radio ads. If anything, the audience liked the improved programming that came with advertising. By 1929, advertisers were spending more than $20 million on radio advertising and the new medium was on solid financial ground.

Radio Networks

There were three main reasons for the development of chain or network broadcasting in the mid-1920s. The first stemmed from the broadcasters themselves and was primarily economic. It was less expensive for one station to produce a program and to have it broadcast simultaneously on three or four stations than it was for each station to produce its own program. The second reason came from the audience. The listeners of local stations in rural areas—far from the talent of New York, Chicago, or Hollywood—wanted better programs. Networking allowed big-name talent to be heard over small-town stations. A third reason was the desire of advertisers to increase the range of their programs beyond the receivers of local stations and thus multiply potential customers. Given the pressure from these three sources, the development of networks was inevitable.

After AT&T pioneered the interconnection of stations using their long-distance phone lines, RCA, headed by David Sarnoff, set up a new company in 1926 to separate the parent company from the broadcasting operation. The National Broadcasting Company (NBC) was to oversee two broadcasting networks. The "Red" network consisted of the stations acquired from AT&T when the phone company left the broadcasting business, and the "Blue" network comprised stations originally owned by RCA, Westinghouse, and GE. By 1933, NBC had 88 stations in its network.

A competitor came on the scene when the Columbia Broadcasting System (CBS) was formed in 1927. Under the direction of William S. Paley, CBS started with 16 stations, but by the end of 1933 the younger network had 91 members. Another network, the Mutual Broadcasting System, began operation in 1934. The radio networks would be the controlling force in broadcasting for the next 20 years.

Radio networks forever changed American society. First they stimulated national advertising. With one phone call, advertisers could procure nationwide exposure for their products. Second, radio networks brought to rural areas entertainment previously provided to urban areas. Now everybody could hear the same comedians, big bands, Hollywood movie stars, and political commentators. Network radio stimulated the beginnings of a truly national popular culture. Finally, the networks changed American politics, as campaigns became truly national in scope. Politicians who mastered the new medium, such as Franklin Roosevelt did in his fireside chats, had a distinct advantage over their competitors.

Rules

Attempts to regulate the new medium can be traced back to 1903, when a series of international conferences was called to discuss the problem of how to deal with wireless communication. The result of these efforts for the United States was the Wireless Ship Act of 1910, requiring certain passenger vessels to carry wireless sets. Two years later, the pressure for more regulation increased when amateur wireless operators were interfering with official Navy communications. In the midst of this, the *Titanic* struck an iceberg and sank. Hundreds were saved because of wireless distress signals, but the interference caused by the many operators who went on the air after knowledge of the disaster spread hampered rescue operations. As a result, the public recognized the need to develop legal guidelines for this new medium. The Radio Act of 1912 required sending stations to be licensed by the Secretary of Commerce, who could assign wavelengths and time limits. Ship, amateur, and government transmissions were to be assigned separate places in the spectrum.

The problem with this law was that it envisioned radio as point-to-point communication and did not anticipate broadcasting. Consequently, as more stations went on the air, broadcasting for long periods at a time, interference became a severe problem.

By 1926 the interference problem had become so bad that it was obvious to all that some form of federal control was needed if radio was to avoid being suffocated in its own growth. In response to requests from the radio industry for legislation, Congress passed the **Radio Act of 1927.** Its key assumptions were the following:

- The radio spectrum was a national resource. Individuals could not own frequencies, but they could be licensed to use them.

- Licensees would have to operate in the public interest.

- Government censorship was forbidden.

In addition, a five-member **Federal Radio Commission (FRC)** was established to enforce the new law. Within 5 years the FRC had solved the interference problem and laid the groundwork for an orderly system of frequency sharing that would obtain maximum benefit for the public. In 1934, in an attempt by President Franklin Roosevelt to streamline government administration, Congress passed the **Communications Act of 1934,** which replaced the FRC with a seven-member **Federal Communications Commission (FCC).** The basic philosophy of the 1927 law, however, was not changed.

RADIO DAYS, RADIO NIGHTS: 1930–1948

The years from 1930 to 1948 can be termed the radio years. The new medium grew at a phenomenal rate, became an integral part of American life, developed new forms of entertainment and news programs, and ran into a few problems along the way.

Growth

Table 1–1 documents the skyrocketing growth of radio. Other statistics are equally impressive: from $40 million spent on radio advertising in 1930 to $506 million in 1948; from 131 network affiliates in 1930 to 1,104 in 1948. Keep in mind that this growth occurred despite a worldwide depression and another world war.

With growth came new problems. One had to do with questionable radio content. The FRC, with backing from the courts, was able to shut down radio broadcasts by quacks and swindlers, such as John R. Brinkley, who used his station to promote bogus patent medicines, and Norman Baker, who touted his homemade cancer cure over KTNT in Iowa.

Table 1–1	The Growth of Radio		
Year	Number of Stations	Percentage of Homes with Radio	Number of Employees
1930	618	46%	6,000
1950	2,867	95	52,000
1970	6,889	99	71,000
2005	13,599	99$^+$	130,000

Another problem concerned FM (frequency modulation) broadcasting. Invented by Edwin Armstrong (see boxed material), FM transmission was first publicly demonstrated in 1933. FM had two big advantages over AM (amplitude modulation): FM was less prone to static and had better sound reproduction quality. Armstrong took his invention to his friend David Sarnoff, now chief executive at RCA, who had supported the inventor's work in the past. Unfortunately for Armstrong, the time was not right for FM. Conventional AM radio was doing fine; it didn't need additional competition. In addition, RCA had made a major investment in AM and was more interested in getting a return on this money than in developing a new radio service. Finally, Sarnoff was committed to another developing technology, television, which he saw as more important. Consequently, RCA would not back the new radio technology. Dismayed, Armstrong built his own FM station but World War II intervened and halted its development. Nonetheless, at the end of the war there were about 50 FM stations in operation. The FCC dealt it another blow, however, by moving FM to a different spot in the radio spectrum, thus rendering obsolete about 400,000 FM receiving sets. Although its ultimate future would prove to be bright, FM struggled along for the next 20 years.

The last problem concerned NBC's two networks and the FCC. After a lengthy study of monopolistic tendencies in network broadcasting, the FCC ruled that NBC had to divest itself of one of its two networks. NBC sold its Blue network to Edwin Noble, who had become rich by selling Life Savers candy. Noble renamed the network the American Broadcasting Company (ABC).

Impact

By now, radio had become part of the country's social fabric. It was the number-one source of home entertainment, and the stars of early radio were familiar to the members of virtually every household in America. Radio news reports had a sense of immediacy that set them off from items in the newspaper. People trusted and depended on radio.

The social power of radio was demonstrated several times during this period. Franklin Roosevelt used his informal fireside chats to help push his legislation through Congress. In 1938, Orson Welles used a quasi-newscast style in a radio adaptation of

Profile: Edwin Armstrong

In his early years, Edwin Howard Armstrong was fascinated by two things: radio and heights. In 1910, when he was 20, Armstrong built his own antenna to aid his experiments with radio. Armstrong liked to hoist himself to the top of his 125-foot tower to enjoy the view.

A few years later, while climbing a mountain, Armstrong worked out a method by which De Forest's audion could be modified to amplify incoming radio signals as well as detect them. Armstrong's invention, the regenerative circuit, would become part of almost every piece of radio equipment.

Armstrong's inventions were not overlooked by the radio industry. In 1913, David Sarnoff, chief inspector for the Marconi company, visited Armstrong's labs for a demonstration of his equipment. The two quickly became friends.

Armstrong's success in the laboratory, however, was not matched by success in the courtroom. Beginning in 1914, Armstrong became embroiled in a complicated legal struggle with Lee De Forest over who had actually first discovered the principle of regeneration, a battle Armstrong eventually lost.

Armstrong served in the Army during World War I and spent some time flying over France in rickety biplanes. While in the Army, Armstrong continued to invent devices that improved the quality of radio transmission and reception.

Armstrong's inventions brought him money and fame. In 1922, David Sarnoff, then head of RCA, signed a deal with Armstrong that brought the inventor more than a quarter-million dollars in cash and stocks. A few months later, Armstrong, perhaps symbolizing his new on-top-of-the-world status, scaled the radio antenna atop the 21-story building owned by RCA. Armstrong even sent photographs of his feat to his friend Sarnoff. Sarnoff was not amused.

In the next few years, however, several events brought Armstrong back to earth. After some initial victories in his court fight with De Forest, Armstrong had a setback. The Supreme Court, operating more from technical legal rules than from scientific evidence, ruled against him in 1928.

For most of the next 5 years, Armstrong devoted his time to perfecting FM, an invention he hoped would bring him to new heights of fame and prosperity. When Sarnoff refused to back the new technology, their friendship began to evaporate.

Undaunted, Armstrong set up his own FM transmitter for demonstrations. By 1940, Armstrong was on top again. Other radio set manufacturers were impressed and paid Armstrong for the rights to manufacture FM sets. The FCC set aside part of the electromagnetic spectrum for commercial FM broadcasting. Even Sarnoff had changed his mind about FM and offered Armstrong $1 million for a license to his invention. Armstrong, probably remembering the earlier incident with Sarnoff, refused.

Word War II interrupted the development of FM. After the war ended, optimism for the new medium flourished again. This confidence, however, was short-lived. The FCC moved FM out of its former spectrum slot, and Sarnoff announced that RCA had developed its own FM system, one that did not rely on Armstrong's inventions.

The break between the two old friends was now total. Armstrong sued RCA for patent infringement and RCA martialed its massive financial and legal resources against him. The lawsuit lasted 4 years and drained Armstrong physically, financially, and emotionally. By 1954, Armstrong was near bankruptcy, depressed, estranged from his wife, and convinced that his creation of FM was destined to be a failure.

More than 50 years in the future, looking back, we, of course, know that Armstrong was wrong. Despite the initial hardships, FM flourished. In early 2006, FM commanded more than two-thirds of the listening time of Americans. The inventor, however, would never see his invention succeed. In 1954, Edwin Armstrong, the man who was fascinated by heights, committed suicide by jumping out of the window of his 13th-floor apartment.

War of the Worlds that featured Martians invading the United States. Many people thought the program was real and panicked. Finally, singer Kate Smith stayed on the air for 18 straight hours during a pledge drive for war bonds. She eventually raised more than $39 million.

Moreover, radio took advertising revenue away from the newspaper and magazine industries and radio newscasts effectively killed the "extra" editions of the newspaper. Radio also had an impact on the sound recording industry. The early radio networks refused to play recorded music, and the

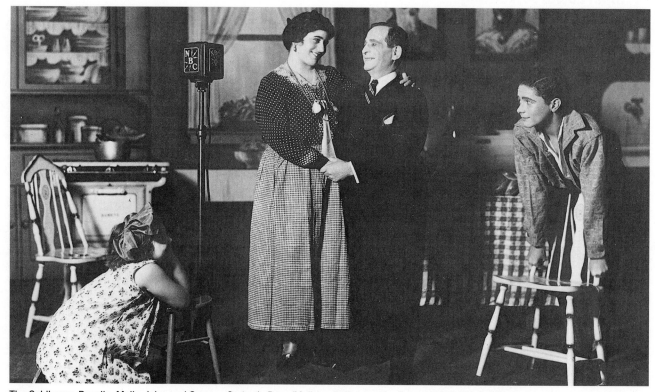

The Goldbergs: Rosalie, Molly, Jake, and Sammy. Gertrude Berg (Molly) was the creative force behind *The Goldbergs*, a radio situation comedy that premiered in the early 1930s and moved to TV in 1949.

recording industry was reluctant to permit their records to be played on radio. As more and more people turned to radio for music, the recording industry nearly died during the economic downturn of the 1930s; it survived thanks to better marketing efforts and the popularity of the juke box, a coin-operated phonograph found in most drug stores, restaurants, and bars. Interestingly, the idea that playing records on the radio would be helpful to both industries had yet to catch on.

Programs

Radio programs during this time period were quite diverse. In fact, almost every program genre now available on contemporary television first appeared on the radio. Situation comedies were numerous; *The Goldbergs* premiered in 1929, as did the biggest comedy hit of the period, *Amos 'n' Andy*. Although it would be considered racist today, almost the entire nation stopped to listen to it during its 7:00 to 7:15 time slot. Other situation comedies, including *Burns and Allen* and *Jack Benny,* quickly followed.

Crime shows, such as *Law and Order* and *CSI*, can trace their ancestry back to 1930s radio programs, such as *Gangbusters* and *Mr. District Attorney.* The roots of dramatic shows such as *ER* and *West Wing* can be found in *Dr. Christian* (1937) and *Mr. President* (1947). *American Idol* is a more ambitious version of *The Original Amateur Hour* from 1934. *The Hedda Hopper Show* and *Walter Winchell*, both from the 1930s, were earlier versions of *Entertainment Tonight* and *Inside Edition*. And, of course, modern TV soap operas, such as *The Guiding Light*, owe their heritage to radio soaps, such as *The Guiding Light* (radio version in 1938) and *Ma Perkins* (1933).

Radio news got off to a slow start, but by 1930 the networks were carrying regular newscasts. The events of the 1930s gave radio news a boost as reporters and commentators described and analyzed events leading up to World War II. An impressive array of reporters, including Eric Sevareid, Edward R. Murrow, and William Shirer reported regularly from Europe. Millions of people in the United States would huddle around their radios to hear timely reports on the war's progress. The amount of network time spent on news more than doubled from 1940 to correctly reasoned that if the elements of a visual scene could be scanned and broken down into a series of tiny electrical signals able to be transmitted and reassembled in a receiver, a viewable television picture would result. It took a while, however, to put this principle into practice.

After a series of false starts with mechanical scanning systems, two inventors, Vladimir Zworykin and Philo Farnsworth, were able to perfect a method of electronic scanning that would eventually become the basis for modern television. Working at RCA's research labs, Zworykin developed the "iconoscope," the eye of an electronic TV camera. Farnsworth grew up in Idaho and, working mainly by himself, developed an "image dissector," which, with a different design, accomplished much the same thing as Zworykin's iconoscope. The Depression of the 1930s forced Farnsworth to turn for financial support to the Philco Corporation, a radio set manufacturer and rival of RCA. Even at this early date, it was clear that corporate America would be behind future TV growth. It was also clear that the existing radio industry would be a major force in shaping the new medium. Consequently, TV came into being with an organized pattern (networks and local stations) and a support system (commercials) already in place.

Improvements in TV continued during the 1930s. Experimental TV stations went on the air. RCA and Farnsworth settled a patent suit, and RCA was permitted to use Farnsworth's invention to further enhance its TV system. By 1939, the new invention had improved enough to be ready for its public debut at the World's Fair.

The development of a commercial TV system was interrupted by the war. Station construction was halted, and all but a handful of stations went off the air. On another front, however, World War II accelerated the technology behind TV. Scientists involved in perfecting TV went into the military and studied high-frequency electronics. Their work greatly improved the U.S. system of radar and also advanced the technical side of TV. As the war neared its end, it was apparent that TV would be back, stronger than ever.

When the war ended, the broadcasting industry made immediate preparations to shift its emphasis from radio to TV. Assembly lines that had been used to turn out war materials were retooled to produce tubes and TV sets. Returning soldiers, skilled in radar operation, were hired by many stations that were eager to use their electronics knowledge. Set manufacturers made plans to advertise their new, improved products.

David Sarnoff standing in front of a TV camera as he opens the RCA pavilion at the 1939 New York World's Fair. This was the first time a major news event was covered by television.

1945. There were some notable individual achievements, including Murrow's dramatic accounts of the bombing of London. All in all, radio news reached its high point during the war.

After the war, the future for radio never looked brighter. It was America's number-one source of news and entertainment. Advertising revenue was increasing, and more and more people were listening. Radio's future, however, was about to be drastically changed.

TELEVISION

Nine miles from Manhattan, in Flushing Meadows, Queens, a mosquito-infested swamp underwent a magical transformation. At a cost of $156 million, the New York World's Fair opened on that site in April 1939. RCA, NBC's parent company, had chosen this event to make a public demonstration of its latest technological marvel—television. David Sarnoff, the head of RCA, called the invention "a new art so important in its implications that it is bound to affect all society." He was right.

The idea of TV goes back to the 1880s. Early TV pioneers such as Paul Nipkow and Boris Rosing

The two figures who most dominated the development of American network broadcasting—William S. Paley and David Sarnoff—could not have been more different. Sarnoff, from an emigrant Russian family, began his career as a wireless operator for the Marconi company. Paley came from an affluent family and after his college graduation became an executive in the family-owned Congress Cigar Company. Following his purchase of the struggling radio network, Paley became president of CBS.

Sarnoff gained national attention when he was one of several telegraph operators who relayed messages about the sinking of the *Titanic*. Marconi took note of the young man who was quickly promoted into the managerial ranks of American Marconi and later RCA. Popular history suggests that in 1916 Sarnoff wrote a prophetic memo to his superiors at Marconi, predicting that radio would become a mass medium. Recent research suggests that the memo might have been written some years later, making it less prophetic. In any case, Sarnoff eventually became chief executive officer at RCA and managed the company until 1969. It was Sarnoff who made NBC a force in radio broadcasting and who was a firm believer in the potential of television. Sarnoff also championed color TV.

Paley was more interested in the programming side of the business. He signed Bing Crosby and Kate Smith to contracts at CBS. In 1948, he scored a programming coup when he lured a number of big stars—Jack Benny, Edgar Bergen, and others—from NBC to CBS. Paley's achievements extended into news broadcasting as well. Under his leadership, CBS assembled a crew of reporters that began a tradition of outstanding journalism at CBS. It was Paley who persuaded Edward R. Murrow, the famous war correspondent, to take an executive position at CBS.

Rivals most of their careers, Paley and Sarnoff left their own personal marks on American broadcasting.

By 1948, television was clearly on its way; network programming was introduced; popular radio shows made the transition to TV; and the new medium created its own stars. When Milton Berle's program came on Tuesday night at 8 P.M., it seemed the whole country stopped to watch. Ed Sullivan, a newspaper columnist with no discernible TV talent, hosted a variety show that quickly followed Berle's show to the top of the ratings charts.

Freeze

The growth of TV during 1948 was phenomenal. Set manufacturers couldn't keep up with the demand. More stations were going on the air and many more were seeking to start. It seemed as if every town wanted a TV station. Things got so hectic that the FCC declared a freeze on new TV station applications while it studied the future of TV.

The TV industry, however, was not in a state of suspended animation during the freeze. Stations whose applications were approved before the freeze were allowed to go on the air. By 1950, 105 TV stations were broadcasting. Further, the networks, using AT&T land lines, were able to complete a coast-to-coast hookup, which enabled live network broadcasts to reach 95 percent of the homes then equipped with TV. Despite the freeze, TV had grown to nationwide proportions.

The freeze thawed in 1952 when the FCC produced a document called the **Sixth Report and Order,** which addressed several issues:

- A table of channel assignments was constructed, structuring the provision of TV service to all parts of the United States.

- To accommodate the hundreds of applicants seeking a TV license, the FCC opened up new channels (14–69) in the **ultra-high frequency (UHF)** part of the electromagnetic spectrum to join the channels (2–13) already in use. (Most TV sets couldn't get the UHF channels without a special antenna, so the new channels started off with a technical disadvantage that would slow their development for years to come.)

- Anticipating the future, the commission set standards regarding color TV.

- Finally, thanks to the efforts of Frieda Hennock, the first woman FCC commissioner, 242 channels were set aside for noncommercial TV stations.

Television programming developed and flowered during the freeze period. This was the golden era of TV as high-quality plays authored by such notables as Rod Serling and Paddy Chayefsky were key parts of the prime-time schedule. The *Today* show, still going strong at this writing, premiered in 1952. The most significant situation comedy of the era was *I Love Lucy,* starring Lucille Ball, a comedienne who would appear on TV in one form or another in four different decades. *I Love Lucy* was significant not only for its popularity but also because it was filmed in Hollywood, marking the beginning of the Hollywood involvement in TV, a trend that would grow over the next three decades.

RADIO'S PERIOD OF ADJUSTMENT

Faster than most people imagined, TV became the dominant news and entertainment medium. Although some people thought that radio might go the way of the blacksmith and the ice box, it managed to adjust and prosper.

At the risk of oversimplification, the coming of TV had four main effects on radio. First, it completely changed network broadcasting. After the freeze was lifted, mass-market advertising moved to TV. By 1955, network radio was taking a financial beating, with revenues dropping by about 58 percent from 1952. As major radio stars like Jack Benny and Bob Hope shifted to TV, network radio programs lost audiences to the new medium. Pretty soon the once-powerful radio networks were reduced to providing 10-minute newscasts on the hour and some daytime programs. It would take network radio nearly 30 years to recover.

Second, television made radio turn to specialized audiences through the development of particular formats. Local stations, faced with more hours to fill since the networks cut back on their programs, looked for an inexpensive way to fill the time. They found it with the disc jockey (DJ) and recorded music. Abandoning the long-standing antagonism against playing records on the air, stations chose music that would appeal to a specialized audience. Some rural stations concentrated on country-and-western music, while some stations in urban markets developed a rhythm-and-blues format. Many FM stations played classical music. The most influential format developed in this period, however, was called Top 40. Capitalizing on the growing popularity of rock-and-roll and the growth of the "youth" culture, Top 40 appealed to teens by playing a relatively small number of popular songs over and over. By 1960, hundreds of stations had adopted the format.

Lucille Ball and Desi Arnaz starred in *I Love Lucy.* From 1951 to 1957, the show was always among the top three most popular TV programs.

Third, the advent of TV brought the radio and record industry closer together. Contrary to past thinking, radio airplay helped sell records. The record companies kept radio's programming costs to a minimum by providing the latest hits free to the station. In return, the radio stations gave the record industry what amounted to free advertising. Record sales nearly tripled from 1954 to 1959.

Finally, television forced radio to become more dependent on local advertising revenue. Since they were no longer conduits for material produced by the networks, local stations became more responsive to their markets. They could play regional hits; DJs could make special appearances at local events; stations could provide more local news. All of this increased radio's appeal to local advertisers. In short, radio redefined its advertising base. In 1945, less than one-third of radio advertising came from local ads. Ten years later that proportion had nearly doubled.

To sum up, over the course of about a dozen traumatic years, radio made the necessary adjustments that enabled it to prosper in an era that was to be dominated by TV.

Frieda Hennock always valued education. Born in Poland, she moved to the United States when she was 6. After graduating early from high school, she took law classes at night and finished her degree at the age of 19. She was admitted to the bar 2 years later and, not surprisingly, became the youngest woman lawyer in New York City. During the late 1920s she distinguished herself as a criminal lawyer but eventually her interest turned to corporate law. Her expertise and ability earned her a position at one of New York's leading law firms.

During the 1940s, Hennock became active in politics and raised money to support several prominent Democrats, including Harry Truman. In 1948, when all political experts were predicting a Truman loss in the upcoming election, Truman repaid Hennock for her past support by nominating her to the Federal Communications Commission. This gesture, however, may have been more symbolic than substantive since, at the time, Republicans in Congress were blocking all new presidential appointments until after the election, when, presumably, a Republican would hold the office. Hennock, nevertheless, displayed impressive political skills and gained support from both Democrats and Republicans. To almost everyone's surprise, her nomination was approved by Congress, making her the first woman on the commission and the only one out of 800 Truman appointees to be confirmed. (Truman, of course, also surprised everybody and won the 1948 election.)

Hennock joined the FCC at the start of "the freeze," the period when the commission refused to consider new applications for TV stations while it worked out technical rules and regulations for the new medium. Her interest in education came to the surface. In the early days of radio, many educational institutions acquired broadcasting licenses only to give them up later after coming under pressure from commercial broadcasters who saw an opportunity for profit. When FM came on the scene, the FCC reserved 15 percent of the frequencies for use by educational institutions. The commercial broadcasters didn't object to this, since they didn't think FM would amount to much.

Hennock believed that a similar reservation should be made for educational TV stations, a position that immediately put her at odds with commercial broadcasters who wanted the frequencies for themselves. As they had done during the early days of radio, the broadcasters argued that they were the ones who could best provide educational programming through sustaining, or commercial-free, programs. Hennock's colleagues at the commission favored the broadcasters' position.

Despite the odds against her, Hennock mobilized support from educators, private foundations, and the media. In 1951 she was rewarded with a partial victory when the FCC proposed reserving about 10 percent of available TV channels for noncommercial educational broadcasting. Hennock, however, campaigned for 25 percent. Despite her efforts, when the freeze was lifted in 1952, only 12 percent of the channels available were set aside for noncommercial broadcasting. Hennock voiced her dissatisfaction with the ruling and continued to campaign for greater educational access to television.

Hennock's remaining years on the commission often found her at odds with her colleagues and the establishment. She opposed the proposed merger of ABC with Paramount Theaters. She argued against rate increases for AT&T. Since many of the new educational stations were in the UHF band, she spent her last days on the commission campaigning to make UHF stations more competitive with VHF stations.

Hennock completed her term in 1955, and Republican president Dwight Eisenhower did not reappoint her. She resumed her successful law practice until her death in 1960. Today's noncommercial broadcasters can be thankful that Frieda Hennock's determined efforts gave education a permanent place in the television spectrum.

TV'S GROWTH CURVE: 1953–1962

The next 10 years saw an incredible surge in the fortunes of TV (see Table 1–2). In 1952, some 34 percent of households had TV. Ten years later 90 percent were equipped. There were 108 stations broadcasting in 1952. Ten years later there were 541. In the same period, the amount of money spent on TV advertising quadrupled. By any yardstick, TV was booming.

New Wrinkles

On the technology side, the Ampex Corporation introduced videotape recording in 1956. This invention made it possible to store TV programs in a high-quality format that could be used again and again. Tape also made program production cheaper and would ultimately replace film in the production of many situation comedies. Finally, tape helped kill off

Table 1–2	The Growth of Television		
Year	Number of Stations	Percentage of Homes with Television	Number of Employees
1950	98	9	9,000
1970	862	95	58,400
2005	1,749	99	180,000

live drama on TV. Before long, only news and sports were broadcast live; most other shows were either taped or on film.

RCA introduced color TV sets in 1954 and, after a slow start, color TV eventually caught on. By 1962, about a half-million color sets were sold and RCA announced it was finally making a profit from their sales.

As mentioned earlier, UHF TV stations got off to a slow start because their signals did not go as far as **very high frequency (VHF)** signals and TV sets were not equipped with the special antenna needed to pick up UHF broadcasts. In 1961, the FCC persuaded Congress to pass the All-Channel Receiver Bill, which required all television sets to be able to receive all TV channels, not just VHF. Even so, UHF grew slowly.

Two other technological milestones occurred during this period that were to prove highly significant for the future of TV. The significance of the first was immediately apparent. A rocket roared off Cape Canaveral in July 1962 carrying *Telstar,* the first active communication satellite capable of relaying signals across the Atlantic Ocean. Only 25 years after Marconi's death, wireless signals were crossing the Atlantic in a way he had never imagined.

The ultimate significance of the second event was overlooked by virtually everybody. A new idea, introduced in the early 1950s, was gaining ground. People who lived in mountainous areas could not get good over-the-air TV reception. Residents of these areas hit upon a novel solution. They would put an antenna on top of one of the tall peaks and run wires down to the homes in the valley. The residents would pay a fee to receive their programs over a cable. This system was called **community antenna TV, or CATV.** Later CATV would come to stand for cable TV. Conventional broadcasters thought that transmitting signals by cable was a clever idea but that it would have little general application. As the next chapter illustrates, they were mistaken.

Hollywood and New York

Although Hollywood had been a major center in the production of radio programs, it was not a significant force in the development of early television programming. Hollywood's lack of influence is somewhat surprising given that the major motion picture studios had the experience, talent, and facilities that could have easily been adapted for TV. Two factors were mainly responsible for Hollywood's lack of influence. First, the Federal Communications Commission indicated that post-freeze applications for TV stations from movie studios would not be favorably received. This prevented the studios from starting their own networks to compete with the established networks in New York. Moreover, if they couldn't compete directly against the existing TV industry, the studios were not going to cooperate with it by providing content. Hollywood saw television as a threat to its profitability; the more people who stayed home watching TV, the fewer who went to the movies. Consequently, the major studios refused to release their current films to the TV networks and prohibited their biggest stars from appearing on TV shows.

Eventually, however, economic conditions brought the two industries closer together. The struggling DuMont Network, lacking stations in many of the major cities, went out of business in 1958. The ABC network was also having financial problems but found a new source of cash when it merged with Hollywood-based United Paramount Theaters in 1953. Thanks to its improved financial condition, ABC became more competitive during the late 1950s.

The merger also marked the beginning of a trend toward closer cooperation between Hollywood and the New York–based TV industry. The major film studios discovered that they could make money by producing series for the new medium. ABC again led the way when it signed a contract with the Walt Disney studios for a 1-hour weekly series called *Disneyland.* The show was a big hit, and in short order other mainstream Hollywood companies, such as Warner Brothers and MCA Universal, followed suit. By 1960 about 40 percent of network programming was produced by big movie studios. Hollywood's desire to compete directly with the established TV networks was finally fulfilled in the late 1980s when Twentieth Century Fox established the Fox Network. A few years later Paramount and Warner Brothers debuted their own networks, and Disney got back into the network TV business when it acquired ABC in 1995.

Programming

Big-money quiz shows, such as *The $64,000 Question* and *21*, were popular at the end of the 1950s but quickly died out after a major scandal revealed that some of the shows were rigged. Adult westerns, such as *Wyatt Earp* and *Gunsmoke*, also became popular; by 1959, there were more than 20 western series on the air. Television news grew slowly during these years, as nightly network newscasts were only 15 minutes long.

STABILITY FOR TV: 1963–1975

The next dozen years or so marked a fairly stable period in the history of broadcast TV. The networks were the dominant force of entertainment and news and enjoyed more or less steady financial growth. In any given minute of prime time, around 90 percent of the sets in use were tuned to network shows. Programming, while sometimes innovative, basically followed the formats from the 1950s. True, there were some events within the industry that ruined the placid mood, but compared with what was to come, these years seem almost tranquil.

Technology

On the technological side, the slow but steady growth of cable TV began to capture the attention of the broadcasting industry. The early developments of this new medium are detailed in the next chapter. For now, the main thing to note is that cable grew slowly during this time period, reaching only 10 percent of all TV homes in 1974.

Interestingly, UHF stations got a boost from cable. Cable systems had to carry all of the local stations in a market, including UHF. Once on the cable, the signal strength disadvantage of UHF no longer mattered, putting UHF and VHF stations on an equal footing and helping UHF increase its audience reach.

Finally, communication satellites became more important to TV. Those that followed *Telstar* were placed in a geosynchronous orbit, which meant that the satellites maintained their position relative to a point on earth and could serve as relays for ground stations. Satellites would eventually replace wires as the preferred medium for sending much of the content of broadcast TV.

Public TV

Noncommercial TV progressed slowly during the early 1960s, growing to 100 stations in 1965. A major development occurred in 1967 when a study sponsored by the Carnegie Foundation recommended a plan for what it called "public" TV. The term **public broadcasting** came to include a wide range of station owners: universities, school boards, state governments, school systems, and community organizations. Indeed, some of the problems that were to plague public broadcasting were in part caused by its heterogeneous nature. In any case, one of the important things about this report was a shift in philosophy: Noncommercial TV would no longer be limited to programs stressing formal instruction and education. Instead, it would provide an alternative to commercial programming. With amazing rapidity (just 8 months later), Congress passed the **Public Broadcasting Act of 1967,** which created the Corporation for Public Broadcasting (CPB). The main function of CPB was to channel money into programming and station development. Two years later, CPB created the Public Broadcasting Service (PBS) to manage the network interconnection between the public stations.

Unfortunately, Congress never provided enough funds for public TV, making it difficult for public TV to establish any long-range plans. Nonetheless, the service presented some award-winning programs: *Masterpiece Theater; Upstairs, Downstairs; Black Journal; Sesame Street;* and *The Electric Company.* By the late 1970s, however, its future was somewhat cloudy.

New Regulations

In 1971, after much debate about the harmful effects of cigarette smoking, Congress passed a law prohibiting the advertising of cigarettes on TV. Despite initial complaints from broadcasters that the new law would cost them more than $200 million in revenue, other advertisers quickly replaced the tobacco companies and TV ad revenues continued to increase.

Around this same time, the FCC was concerned that the networks were dominating TV. Accordingly, the commission announced the **Prime Time Access Rule (PTAR)** in 1970. In effect, this rule gave the 7:30–8:00 P.M. (EST) time period back to the local stations to program. The rule encouraged the growth of syndicated programs, such as *Wheel of Fortune,* and

The cast of *All in the Family*, a show that brought a harsh edge of realism to the situation comedy format.

made the syndication market an important one in TV programming.

Programming

There were several overlapping trends in TV programming during these years. In the early 1960s, programs containing violent content, such as *The Untouchables*, were becoming popular and began a controversy—that continued into the next century—over the effects of TV violence. At the same time, CBS was successful with a number of rural comedies, such as *The Beverly Hillbillies* and *Green Acres*. Escapist programs were also popular; *I Dream of Jeannie* and *Star Trek* both premiered during this period. Another notable trend in programming was the maturation of the situation comedy. *All in the Family* and *M*A*S*H* injected a new style of realism into the situation comedy. Finally, this period also marked the coming of age of TV news. The networks expanded their nightly newscasts from 15 to 30 minutes in 1963. In addition, audiences for local news shows were also increasing. At some stations, revenue

from news programming was the station's most important source of income.

CHANGES FOR TV: 1975–1999

The period from 1975 to 1999 heralded great changes in the TV industry. New technologies emerged to compete with traditional TV, increased competition lessened network domination of audience viewing, and the industry itself was reshaped by changes in the economic and business climate.

Competition

The growing popularity of cable TV, discussed in the next chapter, siphoned viewers away from broadcast TV networks. Premium channels, such as HBO, specialized cable channels, such as ESPN and MTV, and **superstations,** such as WTBS, became increasingly popular. Broadcast audience shares declined as more people opted for other viewing choices. Moreover, videocassette recorders (VCRs) became increasingly common in American households. From only a handful in operation in 1978, VCRs were in more than 80 percent of homes by the end of 1999. Some people used VCRs to tape network shows and play them back at more convenient times, but many others used them to watch rented theatrical movies on tape, which also ate into the broadcast networks' audiences. In addition, a fourth network—the Fox Broadcasting Company—premiered in 1987, dividing the audience into even smaller segments. By the mid-1990s, thanks to its acquisition of the rights to major-league baseball and professional football and some innovative programming such as *The Simpsons*, *Ally McBeal*, and *The X-Files*, Fox had emerged as a major network player. Three other networks, WB (owned by Warner Brothers), UPN (owned by Paramount), and the Pax network, also entered the scene.

Additionally, cable channels, the Internet, video games, and prerecorded videocassettes siphoned off more of the audience of broadcast TV. Not surprisingly, the share of the audience that tuned to the four major networks continued to decline, dropping to about 50 percent in 2000.

The **Telecommunications Act of 1996** (see Chapter 10) made the television business even more competitive by allowing telephone companies to offer TV services. As the 21st century began, however, the phone companies were moving cautiously in this area and had yet to make a significant impact on broadcast TV. The 1996 act also relaxed the limits on television station ownership and made it easier for TV stations to own cable systems.

Mergers

From 1975 to the present, mergers and acquisitions have periodically reshaped the broadcasting landscape as companies jockeyed for market superiority and competitive advantage. Two main strategies behind mergers and acquisitions are **diversification** (branching out into other businesses) and **vertical integration** (expanding into related businesses at different points in the production process). In 1985, Capital Cities Broadcasting, a big group owner of TV stations, bought the ABC television network. Over the next few years the new Capital Cities/ABC diversified into cable TV by gaining control of ESPN. Ten years later, in an example of vertical integration, the Walt Disney Company acquired Capital Cities/ABC. The films and TV programs from Disney's production division were guaranteed an outlet over ABC's network of TV stations and cable channels.

Another example of diversification occurred in 1986 when, in an example of history coming full circle, GE, one of RCA's original owners back in 1919, acquired RCA and NBC. GE, one of the nation's biggest companies with interests ranging from defense systems to home appliances, was now firmly entrenched once again in the broadcasting business. A few years later, Westinghouse, another broadcasting pioneer, acquired CBS. In the late 1990s, Westinghouse spun CBS off from the rest of the company, and, in another example of vertical integration, the network merged with media conglomerate and content producer Viacom.

The biggest deal of the period, however, was the $166 billion megamerger in 2000 between America Online and media conglomerate Time Warner. The new company had interests in a wide range of media including the Internet, cable TV, publishing, and moviemaking.

The competitive maneuvers continued during the first half of the new decade as Rupert Murdoch's News Corporation—a conglomerate that includes newspapers, a movie company, and a film studio—acquired satellite broadcaster DirecTV, another example of vertical integration. In addition, new business strategies continue to emerge. In an effort to focus its operations and improve its stock price, Viacom announced in 2005 that it was splitting into two companies: the CBS Corporation, which would include all the broadcasting operations, and Viacom, consisting of the film and cable divisions. Finally, in 2006 Warner Brothers and CBS announced plans to merge the UPN and WB television networks into a single network called CW, and Fox started a new network called, appropriately enough, My Network TV.

Many critics have argued that continued mergers will severely limit the number of diverse social and cultural voices. They suggest that as the number of competitors decreases, so does the number of different viewpoints, types of artistic expression, and alternative information outlets, resulting in a society whose knowledge, tastes, and attitudes are homogenized. On the opposite side are those who say that in the age of the Internet, bloggers, satellite radio, and 500-channel cable systems, it is impossible for any small group of media companies to dominate the public's information and cultural outlets.

Public TV: Searching for a Mission

Public TV's recent history has been marked by two main themes: a general lack of money and a search for a purpose. A second Carnegie Commission Report, dubbed Carnegie II, was released in 1979. The report reviewed the problems that had plagued PBS from its inception: a lack of long-range funding from Congress, the lack of insulation of public TV from political squabbles, a clumsy managerial structure, and a need to define its mission.

Regarding the debate of public broadcasting's basic mission the following questions arose: Should public TV return to its original purpose during its inception in the 1950s and become an educational service? Or should it provide more general-appeal programming as an alternative to commercial broadcasting? But what exactly was an alternative? "High-brow" programming for the culturally elite or programs such as *Austin City Limits*? Should it compete with the major networks or become a service for minority interests? Which minorities? Such questions are still being asked today.

To make matters more complicated, cable networks were providing some of the material that had previously been the province of public TV and public TV was beginning to look more like a commercial network; The Discovery Channel, the Arts and Entertainment Network, and the Learning Channel presented educational and prestige programming that siphoned away some PBS viewers. And public TV stations, in an attempt to raise more money,

Profile: Robert Adler, Unsung Hero

Most people know that Alexander Graham Bell invented the telephone and Guglielmo Marconi constructed the wireless, but almost no one knows whom to thank for developing one of the most important and ubiquitous devices that totally reshaped the modern television viewing experience: the remote control.

Some early TV sets were equipped with a wired device that changed stations, but the real breakthrough came with development of a wireless remote control. Technicians at the Zenith Radio Company developed an early version which used photo cells and light beams, but the device never gained popularity because a beam of sunlight could strike the TV and set off a flurry of channel switching. Another prototype changed channels using radio waves, but radio waves traveled through walls and might affect TV sets in the next room or apartment. In 1956, a Zenith engineer, Robert Adler, found a method that got around these problems. Adler's remote control, called the Space Command, used ultrasound, sounds at frequencies that were inaudible to the human ear, to change channels and turn the set on and off. The inside of the Space Command contained four aluminum rods (no batteries needed). When the viewer pushed the appropriate button, it struck one of the rods and generated a tone that the TV receiver translated into the appropriate action.

The early remote controls were generally sold along with expensive, high-end TV sets, which limited their popularity. Moreover, since there were only two or three channels available to most viewers, the remote control was not that much of a help. It was only with the advent of cable and satellite services in the 1970s and 1980s and the drastically increased number of channels available that the remote control became a truly useful device.

Modern devices have made great strides since the Space Command. They use infrared light and UHF radio waves to transmit their signals and can perform dozens of different TV tuning and selection tasks. Today almost every TV set in the United States comes equipped with a remote control device.

As for Robert Adler, he served as director of research for Zenith until 1982 and was eventually awarded a total of 180 U.S. patents for his innovations. Adler received an Emmy in 1998 for his development of the remote control. He also earned the gratitude of millions of couch potatoes.

adopted a policy of "enhanced underwriting," announcements from companies that helped underwrite the costs for programming and that sounded suspiciously like commercials.

Despite its problems, PBS still produced programming that garnered critical praise and loyal fans. Ken Burns's 1990 documentary on the Civil War was the highest-rated program in the history of PBS. *Sesame Street* celebrated its 35th year on PBS in 2004. *The Antiques Roadshow* sent many Americans rummaging through their attic in search of forgotten treasures. Regularly scheduled news and public affairs programs such as *Frontline* and *Newshour with Jim Lehrer* score steady if not spectacular numbers in the ratings.

Programming

One of the biggest programming trends of the late 1970s was the emergence of the prime-time continuing episode series, also called prime-time soaps, such as *Dynasty* and *Dallas*. Another significant trend was the shift back to warm and wholesome family situation comedy as exemplified by *The Cosby Show* and

The Wonder Years. News programming continued to expand both on cable and on broadcast TV. The Cable News Network (CNN) began in 1980 and prompted the broadcast networks to expand their own news programming by adding late-night and early-morning programs. By the mid-1980s, the networks were providing about 40 hours of news every week.

The 1990s were notable for the growth of the news magazine program, such as *60 minutes, 48 Hours,* and *Dateline NBC.* In 1995, the networks scheduled 8 hours per week of these programs. Part of the reason for their popularity was economic. News magazines cost less to produce than sitcoms and dramas. Despite their production costs, sitcoms were also popular and NBC led the way with *Seinfeld, Cheers,* and *Friends.*

Television programming in the first decade of the new century was dominated by two genres: "reality" programming, such as *Survivor* and *Amazing Race,* and procedural dramas, such as *CSI* and *Without a Trace.* The fall 2004–5 prime-time schedule, for example, had 14 hours of reality shows. The reason for this proliferation was simple: Reality shows got good ratings and were relatively cheap to produce. By

2006, however, the reality movement began to show signs of cooling off. On the other hand, procedural dramas, which usually started off with a crime and followed the procedures used to solve it, remained popular. In early 2006, 7 of the 15 top-rated TV shows were procedural dramas.

Technology

In the 1970s TV production equipment became smaller and easy to carry. One of the results of this was the development of **electronic news gathering (ENG),** which revolutionized TV coverage. Using portable cameras and tape recorders, reporters no longer had to wait for film to be developed. In addition, ENG equipment was frequently linked to microwave transmission, which allowed live coverage of breaking news.

The 1980s saw the development of **satellite news gathering (SNG).** Vans equipped with satellite uplinks made it possible for reporters to travel virtually anywhere on earth and to send back a report. Local stations sent their own correspondents to breaking news events in Europe and Asia for live reports. Stations also formed satellite interconnection services that swapped news footage and feeds.

The backyard satellite dish, or **TVRO (TV receive-only),** popped up in many rural and suburban areas during the 1970s and 1980s. Initially, those with TVROs could receive broadcast and subscription programming for free. The TVRO business ran into hard times, however, after many programmers scrambled their signals and consumers had to pay a monthly fee to receive the channels.

A more promising development, the **direct broadcast satellite (DBS)** made its appearance during the 1990s. DBS uses high-powered communication satellites to send programming to umbrella-sized dishes mounted on rooftops. After a slow start, the DBS services grew in popularity. About 15 million homes were receiving DBS signals as the new century began.

The emergence of the Internet and the growth of the World Wide Web during the 1990s posed both challenges and opportunities for broadcasters. Stations and networks were quick to establish Web sites. These Web sites functioned primarily as promotional devices for their traditional services and as a handy source of audience feedback about programming. Broadcasters were concerned, however, that their Web sites might siphon off viewers from their programs. They feared, for example, that audience members might get their local news from the Web site and skip watching the station's newscast. Moreover, broadcasters were searching for ways to make their Web sites profitable for their companies. Maintaining a mutually beneficial relationship between the Web site and the traditional broadcast service continued to be a problem into the new century.

RADIO IN THE VIDEO AGE

Since 1960 the TV set has pushed radio from center stage. Television now dominates news and entertainment, and radio has carved out a new niche for itself. This section will examine the more significant trends that have shaped modern radio.

High Tech

Radio became portable during the early 1960s because of the **transistor,** a tiny device that took the place of the vacuum tube. This made it possible to produce small, lightweight, and inexpensive radios. The invention of printed and integrated circuits shrank radio sets even further. Taking advantage of these and other developments, the Sony Corporation marketed the Walkman, a miniature radio–cassette player that produced high-quality sounds through lightweight earphones. Radio had become a truly personal medium.

FM

Perhaps the most significant event in the radio industry since 1960 has been the evolution of FM to being the preferred service among radio listeners. After a slow start, the number of FM stations nearly tripled from 1960 to 1980. The number of FM radios increased from 6.5 million in 1960 to 350 million in 1980. Listening patterns had totally changed: In 1972, FM held only 28 percent of the audience's total listening time and AM held 72 percent, but by 2000 the figures were reversed—72 percent FM and only 28 percent AM. Why the change?

First, FM was able to broadcast in stereo. This enhanced sound gave it a distinct advantage over AM among the many consumers who valued improved audio quality. Second, AM stations were hard to come by. Those wishing to go into broadcasting during this time period were almost forced to start FM stations because all of the AM frequencies were taken. Third, the new FM stations developed new formats, such as progressive rock and easy listening,

Conservative Rush Limbaugh hosts a radio program that is carried by about 600 radio stations, reaching more than 15 million listeners each week.

that drew listeners. Faced with declining audiences, AM stations searched for a format that would be successful. Many went to an all-talk format, while others switched to golden oldies.

Radio Networks

The 1960s were dark days for network radio. Advertising revenues dropped, and fewer stations were network affiliates. Looking for some way to rebound, ABC split its original network into four specialized services that complemented the new specialized formats on local stations: Entertainment, Information, Contemporary, and FM. The idea worked, and ABC had doubled the number of its affiliates by 1970. NBC, CBS, and Mutual soon followed suit. Network radio bounced back, and by 1980 there were more than a dozen nets in operation.

This growth was accompanied by changes in network ownership. In 1987, Westwood One took over the NBC network. Consolidation in the radio network business would continue into the 1990s as Infinity Broadcasting took over Westwood One and eventually merged with CBS.

Coupled with this trend was the growth of radio **syndication** companies. Syndication companies, much like networks, send programming to local stations. The growing popularity of syndicated talk shows, such as those of Rush Limbaugh and Howard Stern, helped build the audiences of many AM stations.

Fine-Tuning Formats

The increased number of radio stations has made radio a highly competitive business. In an effort to attract an audience segment that is of value to advertisers, many radio stations have turned to audience research to make sure that the station's programming reaches its target audience. This research has produced a set of highly refined **formats** that have sliced the radio audience into smaller and smaller segments. For example, there are several subvarieties of the country format; album-oriented rock attracts 18- to 24-year-old males; and news-talk is geared for the over-45 male audience. In 2000, *Broadcasting Yearbook* listed 70 different formats, ranging from "alternative" to "Vietnamese." In the larger markets, a radio station that attracts only 10 percent of the listening audience will usually rank at or near the top of the ratings.

Consolidation

The 1996 Telecommunications Act lifted the national ownership limits in radio stations, prompting an unprecedented wave of consolidation in the inudstry. By the start of the new century, Clear Channel had emerged as the biggest radio company, owning more than 1,200 stations in 190 markets. Other large group owners included Viacom, Cox, Entercom, and ABC Radio. The top 25 radio companies account for about 80 percent of the advertising money spent on radio.

BROADCASTING IN THE TWENTY-FIRST CENTURY

The current state of the radio and television industry is discussed in Chapters 4 and 5. This section lists the major highlights of the last few years that have shaped and will continue to shape the current situation.

- *Advances in technology.* Two satellite radio services, Sirius and XM, offered talk and music in a digital format that is beamed directly to car and home receivers equipped with a special antenna

The 2006 season finale of *American Idol* drew more than 36 million viewers.

and receiver. Subscribers to the two services increased have steadily from their launch in 2001–2 to a combined total of about 10 million in 2006. The addition of radio shock jock Howard Stern to Sirius's lineup promised to send those numbers even higher.

Faced with this competition, terrestrial radio broadcasters introduced high-definition (HD) radio, a digital service whose sound quality is a tremendous improvement over the traditional analog service. As of mid-decade, HD radio was growing slowly; only 300 of the nation's approximately 13,000 radio stations were broadcasting HD.

The trend toward digital broadcasting was moving faster in the television industry. As of 2006, about 85 percent of television stations were broadcasting a digital signal along with their traditional analog signal (see Chapter 3). The FCC set a target date of December 31, 2006, for a transition from analog to digital, but this date could be extended if fewer than 85 percent of the homes in an area do not have TV sets that can receive the digital signals. A measure introduced in Congress in late 2005 set February 17, 2009, as a final date for this transition to digital.

High-definition television (HDTV—see Chapter 3 for details) was also growing in popularity. As of mid-decade, about 10 million homes, about 9 percent of all TV households, were equipped with HDTV sets. Analysts expect this number to rise to about 60 million homes by 2009.

- *Mobile media.* Television and radio broadcasters were moving to news mobile platforms to distribute their content. Several companies were experimenting with cell phone video. ESPN, for example, offered phone subscribers highlight clips, news, interviews, and access to analysis and statistics. NBC Mobile provided news, weather, and sports clips, as well as live coverage streamed from MSNBC and CNBC.

  The introduction of Apple's iPod opened the way for podcasts, specially prepared programs that can be downloaded to a user's iPod and played back when convenient. NPR, for example, offers podcasts of many of its favorites. The video iPod opened up additional possibilities. Music videos can be downloaded from Apple's iTunes for $1.99 per video. Thanks to a deal between Apple and ABC, consumers could download popular ABC programs, such as *Lost*, the day after they were broadcast, also for $1.99. The overall profit potential of these ventures is still unclear.

- *The Internet.* The impact of the Internet on traditional broadcasting is still evolving. A few developments, however, are easy to see. Since most people log on to the Internet in the evening, they watch less TV. In addition, almost all radio and TV stations have started their own Web sites, most functioning as promotion tools for the station and its programming. Third, the Internet has opened up new territory for audio broadcasting. As of mid-decade, there were about 2,000 Internet-only radio stations, broadcasting a diverse range of music. Many television and radio station personalities have started Web logs, or blogs, that allow more interaction with station audiences.

Experiments using the Web are continuing. In late 2005, for example, AOL announced that it was going to launch In2TV, a free Internet TV service that would be supported entirely by advertising. Since AOL is part of Time Warner, AOL has more than 4,800 episodes of series produced by Warner Brothers, including such classics as *Welcome Back, Kotter* and *Growing Pains*, that it could air via the Internet.

- *Convergence.* The move toward convergence continued into the new century. As digital movies on DVD and digital television programs become more common, they will ultimately combine with video games, Internet video, and digital music to form one standardized stream of digital content. In like manner, the current channels of distribution—cable, satellite, and the Internet—will converge into one high-speed broadband connection. Consumers will ultimately have one big screen in their homes where they will watch TV, play back digital movies, surf the Internet, send e-mail, play video games, and run their usual computer software . . . but we're getting ahead of ourselves. This chapter is about history, not the future.

Speaking of the past and of the future, remember that Fessenden made his first radio broadcast in 1906. What if Fressenden were alive today? It is doubtful that he or any of the other early inventors could envision how radio and TV would evolve over the next hundred years or so. By the same token, it is unlikely that you or anybody else reading this book will be able to imagine what TV and radio will be like a hundred years from now.

SUMMARY

- Marconi, Fessenden, and De Forest were early inventors who helped radio develop. General Electric, Westinghouse, and AT&T were companies that were interested in early radio. Each company held patents needed by the others, and, as a result, many legal battles hampered radio's early development.

- During World War I, the Navy took responsibility for patent infringement, which allowed for significant technical improvements in the medium. When the war was over, a new company, RCA, was formed and quickly became the leading company in American radio.

- The 1920s were a significant period for radio. Early stations were experimental, and the notion of broadcasting was discovered more or less by accident. The new fad grew quickly, and soon there were hundreds of stations on the air. Radio networks and radio advertising were developed, and the federal government took charge of radio regulation.

- The period from 1930 to 1948 was the "golden age of radio," as the medium was the prime source of news and entertainment for the nation. This situation changed as television came on the scene in the 1950s.

- Developed by Zworykin and Farnsworth, TV was first unveiled in 1939. After its development was interrupted by World War II, television quickly became popular, and by the mid-1950s it had taken radio's place as the number-one medium in the country.

- The FCC froze applications for TV stations from 1948 to 1952 while it determined standards for the new medium. After the freeze was lifted, TV growth skyrocketed. Networks dominated TV until the 1970s when cable emerged as a formidable competitor.

- Radio reacted to TV by becoming a localized medium that depended on formats to attract specific segments of the listening audience.

- Television's Fox network premiered in the 1980s, which caused ABC, CBS, and NBC further audience erosion. The ownership of all three major networks changed hands during the 1980s and 1990s. The Telecommunications Act of 1996 prompted a wave of consolidation in the radio industry.

- The Internet and the shift to digital technology will have an impact on the future of radio and TV broadcasting.

KEY TERMS

crystal set   7
audion   7
Radio Act of 1927   11
Federal Radio Commission
    (FRC)   12
Communications Act of 1934   12
Federal Communications
    Commission (FCC)   12
Sixth Report and Order   16
ultra-high frequency (UHF)   16

very high frequency (VHF)   19
Telstar   19
community antenna TV (CATV)   19
public broadcasting   20
Public Broadcasting Act of 1967   20
Prime Time Access Rule
    (PTAR)   20
superstations   21
Telecommunications Act
    of 1996   21

diversification   22
vertical integration   22
electronic news gathering
    (ENG)   24
satellite news gathering (SNG)   24
TVRO (TV receive-only)   24
direct broadcast satellite (DBS)   24
transistor   24
syndication   25
formats   25

SUGGESTIONS FOR FURTHER READING

Abramson, A. (2003). *The history of television, 1942 to 2000.* Jefferson, NC: McFarland.

Archer, G. (1938). *History of radio to 1926.* New York: American Historical Society.

Barnouw, E. (1966). *A tower in Babel.* New York: Oxford University Press.

——— (1968). *The golden web.* New York: Oxford University Press.

——— (1975). *Tube of plenty.* New York: Oxford University Press.

Douglas, S. (1987). *Inventing American broadcasting.* Baltimore, MD: Johns Hopkins University Press.

Eberly, P. (1982). *Music in the air.* New York: Hastings House.

Hilliard, R., & Keith, M. (1992). *The broadcast century.* Stoneham, MA: Focal Press.

Lewis, T. (1991). *Empire of the air.* New York: HarperCollins.

Stashower, D. (2002). *The boy genius and the mogul: The untold story of television.* New York: Broadway Books.

Sterling, C., & Kittross, J. (2001). *Stay tuned: A concise history of American broadcasting.* Belmont, CA: Wadsworth.

Udelson, J. (1982). *The great television race.* Tuscaloosa, AL: University of Alabama Press.

White, L. (1947). *The American radio.* Chicago: University of Chicago Press.

INTERNET EXERCISES

Visit our Web site at www.mhhe.com/dominick6 for study-guide exercises to help you learn and apply material in each chapter. You will find ideas for future research as well as useful Web links to provide you with an opportunity to journey through the new electronic media.

History of Cable, Home Video, and the Internet

2

Quick Facts

 Cost of monthly cable service, 1950: $3.00

 Cost of monthly cable service, 2006: $73 (includes high-speed Internet access)

 First satellite TV broadcast: NBC, 1962

 Cost of first home satellite dish: $36,000 (1979)

 Cost of DirecTV satellite system, 2006: $0 (But you have to sign-up for a year of service)

 First consumer VCR: 1975

 Development of the Internet: 1986

 Development of the World Wide Web: 1991

As we discussed in the last chapter, a sea change occurred in the radio business in 1978, when the majority of radio listening in America shifted from the AM band to FM. In 1998, a similar moment of significance took place, when ratings revealed that more Americans were watching cable programming in the evening than were watching one of the over-the-air broadcast networks. In scarcely a generation, cable has moved from a small-time adjunct to broadcast TV, to a huge and influential media business. This chapter traces the growth of cable and other alternatives to broadcast television, including satellites, DVRs, and the "new kid on the block"—the Internet and its network, the World Wide Web (WWW). Like many mass media today, cable's beginnings were modest and its early steps were halting. What follows is a small part of the cable success story.

DEMANDING WIVES AND POWERFUL ALLIES: THE STORY OF CABLE TELEVISION

On Thanksgiving Day 1949, KRSC in Seattle became the first operating TV station in the Pacific Northwest. Up in Astoria (near Portland), Oregon, there was at least one family with a television set. Back in 1947, Ed Parsons and his wife, Grace, were at a convention in Chicago, where they first saw TV. Grace wanted one in her home, so Ed bought one by mail order. He tried to tell his wife they were too far from any TV stations to get any channels. "She figured I was an engineer; so there was no reason why she shouldn't have television," he later said. For months, the set sat idle. Ed thought it would end up as an interesting-looking table.

But the new station in Seattle kindled Ed's interest and inventiveness. He put together a system of antennas, amplifiers, and converters and tried to pull in a signal from Seattle. He took the rig all around town and even flew it in his own airplane. Ultimately, he found he got the best test signal from Seattle (where KRSC was testing its tower) from the top of the Astoria Hotel, just across the street from Ed and Grace's apartment.

Working out of his small radio repair shop, he built the antenna array and amplifiers needed to pull in KRSC, and he stretched antenna wire over to his apartment. As the new station signed on, the Parsons—and more than a dozen friends and relatives who crammed into their apartment—were the only people in Astoria who could watch it. Soon, however, Parsons was stringing antenna wire all over town for $125 per household. Grace was happily watching "Uncle Miltie," as were millions of other new TV viewers.

Back east, a big union boss was planning a brief trip. John L. Lewis was a man who usually got what he wanted. As president of the United Mine Workers, one of the nation's most powerful unions, he wielded enormous power. It was difficult to say no to Mr. Lewis, or to his legion of large, loud, and loyal "friends." One day in 1950, one of those friends—an executive secretary in the union—was expecting a weekend visit from Mr. Lewis. There was one major problem, though. The secretary lived out in Lansford, Pennsylvania, about 70 miles from Philadelphia, too far to receive a decent TV signal. And Mr. Lewis liked to watch TV, especially the Friday night boxing matches.

On the edge of town, near Summit Hill (the next town over), Bob Tarlton, a young veteran of World War II, was working at the radio and appliance store he and his father owned. Summit Hill was about 500 feet higher than Lansford. Fuzzy pictures from Philadelphia could be seen on the new TV sets the Tarltons had just started to sell. But they wanted to improve the picture (and sell some TV sets as a result). So they strung antenna wire from their store to a radio antenna in Summit Hill. The picture was greatly improved.

One day, a well-dressed but rather swarthy and brusque man appeared in the Tarltons' shop. It was the union secretary from Lansford. He wanted that crisp, clear picture in his home for Mr. Lewis. It was an offer the Tarltons couldn't refuse. They ran a cable from a hilltop in Lansford, down to the union secretary's home. Mr. Lewis and his friend were pleased.

Soon, the Tarltons' other customers wanted to get on the antenna to improve their reception, especially those who had just bought a TV set from them. The Tarltons borrowed money from a local bank, improved their antenna system, and replaced common antenna wire with the newfangled coaxial cable the telephone company was using to promote long-distance service. They began charging customers $100 for installation, and a monthly fee of $3.

Through the early 1950s, in Astoria, Oregon, Lansford, Pennsylvania, and dozens of other small communities on the fringes of good TV reception, community antenna TV (CATV, or more commonly, **cable TV**) was catching on. By the end of the famous TV freeze in 1952, 70 cable systems were serving about 15,000 homes in the United States. Five years later, 500 systems brought improved TV signals to about 350,000 homes. As President Kennedy took office in early 1961, about 650 systems served just under 700,000 subscribers.

Broadcasters weren't sure how to regard the new industry. At first they welcomed the fact that their signals were reaching homes that otherwise couldn't receive them. On the other hand, broadcasters planning on starting up new UHF stations might find that they could not make a profit unless they were carried on the cable. Their prosperity would be under the control of the cable operator, a situation broadcasters did not find appealing.

The FCC was reluctant to get involved. In 1958, the commission decided that it did not have the authority to regulate cable because cable was not broadcasting and used no spectrum space.

Meanwhile the cable industry continued slow but steady growth. By 1964 a thousand cable systems were in operation, mainly serving small- to medium-sized communities. Two years later the number grew to more than 1,500. At about this same time, the concept behind cable was changing. In addition to carrying local stations, cable systems began to import the signals of distant stations that previously were not available to the community. This development alarmed the broadcasting community. If several new stations were all of a sudden available in a market, the audience shares and the advertising revenues of the existing stations would decline, perhaps forcing some local broadcasters off the air. Particularly disturbed were the owners of UHF stations, whose operations were not very profitable to begin with. The broadcasting lobby asked the FCC for some protection.

A few years earlier, the FCC had committed itself to the development of UHF broadcasting to encourage the expansion of broadcast television. The growth of cable posed a threat to its policy. Accordingly, from 1965 to 1966, the FCC reversed itself by claiming jurisdiction over cable and issued a set of restrictive rules that protected over-the-air broadcasting. (The prevailing philosophy at the FCC at this time envisioned cable as merely an extension of traditional TV signals. Thus it is not surprising that any challenge to broadcasting by cable's development would be curtailed by regulation.) Cable systems had to carry all TV stations within 60 miles and couldn't carry shows from distant stations that duplicated those offered by local stations. In 1968 the commission ruled that CATV systems in the top 100 markets had to get specific approval before they could import the

signals of distant stations. Taken together, these rules effectively inhibited the growth of CATV and made sure that any growth would be limited to smaller communities. While all of these rules were being made, CATV systems were quietly improving their technology so that by the late 1960s many systems could carry as many as 20 different channels.

In 1972 the FCC, pressured by both traditional broadcasters and the cable industry, issued yet another set of rules. Among other things, these rules specified the following:

1. Local communities, states, and the FCC were to regulate cable.

2. There would be 20-channel minimums for new systems.

3. There would be carriage of all local stations.

4. More regulations on the importation of distant signals, including the nonduplication provision mentioned earlier, would be implemented.

5. Pay cable services would be approved.

Once again, the major impact of these rules was to discourage the growth of cable in urban areas. Cable was insignificant to city residents, who already received good reception from a number of local stations. Cable system operators were not encouraged to bring service to urban areas, since the stringing and installation of cable was expensive in densely populated areas, and once cable was installed the operators would have a big job making sure that no imported signal duplicated local programs. To top things off, a major cable company nearly went bankrupt. Cable did, however, grow in midsized markets, and by 1974 it had penetrated a little more than 10 percent of all TV homes. On balance, its future did not look promising. As we shall see in the next section, however, things changed.

Pay TV: An Idea ahead of Its Time

Early on, a number of entrepreneurs had the notion that cable could be used to control what programs went into any individual household. Specifically, they thought that one or more channels on a TV set could be used to send movies and sports, for a one-time or extra monthly fee. As early as 1953, Paramount Pictures built a cable system in Palm Springs, California, and offered movies like *Forever Female* with Ginger Rogers, for $1.35. They also offered the Notre Dame–USC football game for $1.00. Only about 75 homes signed up for "pay as you look" service, and it ended—amid strenuous objections from TV broadcasters and fearful theater owners—less than a year later. Though similar pay-TV ventures were tried in Oklahoma, Los Angeles, and elsewhere, the idea was tabled for nearly 20 years.

Cable Growth

There were two basic reasons for the explosive growth of cable in the late 1970s, one technological, the other regulatory. In 1975, a then little-known company in the pay-TV business, Home Box Office (HBO), rented a transponder on the communications satellite *Satcom I* and announced plans for a satellite-interconnected cable programming network. Cable systems could set up their own receiving dish and HBO would transmit to them first-run movies, which the operators could then sell to their subscribers for an additional fee. Although pay TV was not a new idea, HBO's new arrangement meant wider coverage of cable systems at a lower cost. Further, the new programming service provided a reason for people in urban and suburban areas to subscribe to cable. Now the big attraction was no longer better reception of conventional channels but content that was not available to regular TV viewers, including movies, sports events, and musical specials. In a few years other cable-only channels were also distributed by satellite—Showtime, The Movie Channel, Christian Broadcasting Network—as well as independent local stations, dubbed "superstations," such as WTBS in Atlanta and WGN in Chicago. Other specialized cable networks—ESPN (sports), CNN (news), and MTV (music videos)—soon followed. Cable now had a lot more features to attract customers.

The second reason for growth came from the FCC. By the mid-1970s the commission realized, with some help from the courts, that its 1972 rules were stifling cable's growth. Consequently, the FCC postponed or canceled the implementation of many of its earlier pronouncements and changed its philosophy: It would henceforth encourage competition between cable and traditional TV. Eventually, as the Reagan administration advanced its deregulation policies, the FCC dropped most of its rules concerning cable. In 1984 Congress passed the **Cable Communications Policy Act.** The law, which was incorporated into the 1934 Communications Act, endorsed localism and set up a system of community regulation tempered by federal oversight. The FCC was given definite but limited authority over cable. The local community was the major force in cable regulation, which it exercised through the franchising process. The act gave cable operators, among other things, greater freedom in setting their rates and released them from most rules covering their program services.

Taken together, these two factors caused a spurt of cable growth that attracted the interest of large media companies such as Tele-Communications, Inc. (TCI), which in turn invested in cable. This in turn caused cable to grow even faster. In fact, the growth was so great that many cable companies in a rush to get exclusive franchises in particular communities promised too much and had to cut back on the size and sophistication of their systems. Nonetheless, although the growth rate tapered off a bit in the mid-1980s, the statistics are still impressive. From 1975 to 1987, the number of operating cable systems more than tripled. The percentage of homes with cable went from about 14 percent in 1975 to 50 percent in 1987. Even the urban areas shared this growth and at least parts of many big cities were finally wired for cable.

Ted Turner used cable TV to take a struggling Atlanta UHF station and turn it into superstation WTBS.

Table 2–1	The Growth of Cable TV		
Year	Operating Systems	Subscribers (millions)	TV Homes (%)
1960	640	0.7	1.4%
1965	1,325	1.3	2.4
1970	2,490	4.5	7.6
1975	3,366	9.8	14.3
1980	4,048	15.5	20.5
1985	6,600	37.3	43.7
1990	10,200	54.0	58.0
1995	13,000	60.0	63.0
2000	9,947	73.1	70.0
2005	7,926	73.4	66.0

Source: Compiled by the authors from various industry publications.

subscribers. In this same year, cable passed the "magic number": More than one-half of all households in the United States were cable subscribers.

The growth of cable (detailed in Table 2–1) continued through the 1990s and 2000s. At mid-decade, cable was available to more than 98 percent of American homes. About 66 percent of all TV homes subscribed to some form of cable. Annual revenue from these subscribers amounted to about $45 billion in 2005. There were signs, however, that the cable boom was cooling off. Subscriber growth was flat, and cable was losing subscribers to satellite broadcasters such as DirecTV and Dish Network. One bright spot was the continued growth of cable advertising revenue, up nearly 14 percent from 2004 to 2005.

ALTERNATIVES TO CABLE

It should come as no surprise that the rise of cable led other innovators and entrepreneurs to get on the multichannel bandwagon. Leading the way were satellite; multichannel, multipoint distribution service (MMDS); and a huge consumer favorite: playback devices, such as VCRs, DVDs, and DVRs. (See Table 2–2.)

By 1988 the cable industry had become dominated by large multiple-system operators (MSOs). The era of a locally owned "mom-and-pop" cable system was over. The top-10 MSOs controlled more than 54 percent of the nation's subscribers, and the largest MSO, TCI, alone had more than 10 million

Profile: From Cottonseed Salesman to Cable King—Bob Magness and TCI

The media world was shaken in 1998 with the announced merger of two of its largest companies: telephone giant AT&T and cable power Tele-Communications, Inc., also known as TCI. The combined company, valued at nearly $50 billion, is a world leader in local and long distance telephone, cable television operations, and entertainment and information programming. It may be hard to believe, but global powerhouse TCI wasn't even founded until 1965. And it probably wouldn't have even existed if a young cottonseed salesman hadn't stopped to pick up a couple of hitchhikers whose truck had broken down one day in Paducah, Texas.

A native of Oklahoma, Bob Magness had served in a rifle platoon under General George Patton in World War II. After the war, he got a business degree from Southwestern State College in Texas and went to work selling seed to farmers and ranchers. One day, after visiting a cattle rancher near Paducah, Magness stopped to help two workmen whose truck was stalled at the side of the road. He was amply rewarded for his Good Samaritan gesture.

It turns out the hitchhikers had been constructing a cable system in Paducah. Over lunch at a hamburger stand, they boasted how good a business cable television was getting to be. Magness was bitten by the cable bug. In 1956, with money he got by mortgaging his ranch, Magness built his first cable system in Memphis, Texas. Two years later, he moved to Bozeman, Montana, to build a system there. In 1965, he brought his cable operations to Denver, and he renamed his company TCI in 1968. A short time later, he brought in John Malone to help run his operations. For the next two decades, Magness and Malone grew the company into a cable and media superpower. At the time of his death in 1996, Bob Magness was Colorado's second-richest resident, with a net worth greater than $1 billion.

It makes one rethink the old notion that picking up hitchhikers is a bad idea.

Table 2–2	Growth of Satellite TV
Year	**Number of Subscribing Households**
1995	2,200,000
1998	8,700,000
2001	17,000,000
2004	20,000,000

Source: Compiled by authors from industry sources.

The Satellite Sky

In 1945, science fiction writer Arthur C. Clarke wrote an article in *Popular Science* describing the elements of a satellite communications system. He theorized that global communications could be possible by reflecting signals off three satellites parked in orbit at equal distance from one another. It took a little over 20 years for this dream to become a reality, spurred by the "space race" between the Soviet Union and the United States.

In 1962, the first satellite TV transmission was made using *Telstar I*. Commentator David Brinkley reported from France to eager audiences in the United States that "there was no big news." He was mistaken. Satellite TV was on its way. By the early 1970s, Western Union had successfully launched the *Westar I* and *Westar II* satellites. The industry took its first major step into the entertainment field in 1976, when Home Box Office used satellite TV for the "Thrilla in Manila" heavyweight championship fight between Muhammad Ali and Joe Frazier. That same year, Ted Turner put his Atlanta station WTBS on satellite, and the Christian Broadcasting Network (later to become The Family Channel) became the first satellite-delivered basic cable network.

Proof that satellite TV had arrived came in 1979, when Neiman Marcus featured a home satellite dish on the cover of its famous Christmas catalog. Price: $36,000. Throughout the 1980s, the price began to drop and dishes began to proliferate, aided by crucial decisions in Congress and at the FCC. In 1984, the Cable Communications Policy Act (cited earlier) legalized the private reception of satellite TV programming. Hardware prices dropped below $5,000, and more than half a million home dishes could be seen dotting the American landscape, especially in rural areas unlikely to be served by cable TV due to low population density. The act also permitted program services, like HBO and Showtime, to scramble their signals and to require dish owners to subscribe (like cable customers) to these services.

TVRO: The Big Dish   By the late 1980s, direct-to-home satellite (DTH, in industry parlance) became a growth industry. The backyard satellite dish was dubbed TVRO (TV receive-only), and sales of the 3-meter dish eclipsed first 2 million (1988) and then 3 million (1990) consumer households. But these dishes were too big and cumbersome to supplant cable TV in suburban homes. Some neighborhoods considered them unsightly and developed local codes restricting their use. The anti-piracy provisions of the cable act allowed for prosecution of those receiving program services illegally. Sales peaked, then plummeted. By 2005, only about 2 million TVROs could still be seen strewn across the American landscape. To take off, satellite TV would have to become physically smaller, and cheaper; that development didn't take long.

Direct Broadcast Satellite   A new alternative to cable TV took the nation by storm in the mid-1990s. High-powered **direct broadcast satellite (DBS)** service provided for nationwide distribution of TV programming from a new generation of orbiting satellites to compact (18-inch) home dish receivers. The dishes were aimed at one of three satellites launched by Hughes Communications. With use of digital compression (see Chapter 3), these satellites could beam over 200 channels to subscribing households; the channels were offered in different packages by four competing organizations: DirecTV, United States Satellite Broadcasting (USSB), Echo Star, and the Dish Network. In the 1990s, the new dish, mounted on a window ledge or near the chimney, became a new TV status symbol, not unlike the rooftop antennas of the 1950s.

The number of households that subscribed to DBS grew from 2.2 million in 1995 to more than 20 million by 2006. This growth was fueled by two factors: (1) DBS systems dropped in price (see the Quick Facts at the beginning of this chapter) and (2) Congress softened existing regulation governing satellite TV and allowed DBS systems to include local channels in their offerings. Mergers and acquisitions resulted in just two companies, DirecTV and

The event that brought HBO into national prominence was the "Thrilla in Manila," a heavyweight championship match between Muhammad Ali and Joe Frazier that was distributed by satellite and cable.

Dish Network, dominating the field. Clearly, cable had a new competitor.

Wireless Cable

As we have seen, because of construction costs, utility problems, and franchise disagreements, cable service lagged in the inner cities. In major urban areas satellite dishes, even the smaller ones now available, remain impractical. There is simply too little space. Yet people in major urban areas also want cable services, especially movies.

One solution is wireless cable, also known as **multichannel, multipoint distribution system,** or **MMDS.** MMDS makes use of short-range microwave transmissions to beam channels of video programming from a central transmitter location, such as the top of a tall office building. Receiving households use a small microwave antenna to pick up the signals and a special decoder called a **downconverter** to turn them into TV channels.

MMDS service has been slow to catch on. By 2006, there were fewer than a million wireless cable households. Though this figure represented fewer than 1 in 100 TV homes, this segment of the industry was optimistic about future growth, particularly as an alternative to cable modems and telephone hookups for the delivery of high-speed data and Internet services.

HOME VIDEO

For nearly half a century, Peter Goldmark was one of the true visionaries in telecommunications. From his laboratory at CBS had come high-fidelity sound recording, the long-playing phonograph record, and some of the basic research that resulted in color TV. Regarding home video, Goldmark made this prediction in 1976 (cited in *Videography,* July 1986, p. 61):

> I doubt that packaged video programs for home entertainment would be economically justifiable. It's speculative in so many ways, and basically a question of cost. Will people pay . . . for a first-rate entertainment program they know they may view only once or twice?

In fairness, Goldmark was talking about buying movies for home viewing. Nobody had yet conceived the idea of video rentals. However, the statement does reveal the speedy germination of a new industry that would have immediate and long-term impact on American TV. In less than 20 years the home video market exploded onto the media scene. Today broadcast, satellite, and cable TV are just part of a total "home video environment." Wedded to many home screens is a range of attachments and accessories, including VCRs, DVD players, video game consoles, DVRs, and surround sound, that have helped transform the way we watch TV. This revolution began with the introduction of the **videotape recorder (VTR).**

The history of videotape recording is intertwined with the history of television provided in Chapter 1. Before the videotape recorder became a mainstay in the American home, it first had to be perfected in production studios, networks, and TV stations. Few inventions in media history have been as significant. After all, for more than six decades—from early inventors tinkering in the 1880s to the battle between CBS and NBC over color in the early 1950s—TV was *live.* What you saw was what was actually going on—in the studio or in the "great outdoors"—in front of the camera.

The Kinescope Recorder

Until the mid-1950s, there was only one way to record TV programs. The **kinescope recorder** was a film camera especially equipped to shoot an image from a TV screen. The quality of a kinescope recording (or "kinny" as it was affectionately called) was

poor. The images were fuzzy, the picture was too dark, and since the film frame was different from the TV frame, the kinny sometimes cut off heads, feet, and other parts of the picture. After a single replay, the kinescope was generally discarded, which explains why so few of TV's early programs are around today.

The Videotape Recorder (VTR)

On November 30, 1956, the videotape recorder (VTR) made its debut. A short time later, the Ampex Corporation introduced a color VTR. In fact, an impromptu debate between U.S. vice president Richard Nixon and Soviet premier Nikita Kruschev was captured on videotape at an exhibition in Moscow in 1959. One highlight of this encounter (dubbed the "Kitchen Debate," since the exhibit also included a demonstration of a modern U.S. kitchen), had the future U.S. president sheepishly admitting that the Russians were ahead of America on certain things, such as space travel, but that "we are way ahead on other things, like color TV."

Events: Life in the Kinescope Days

Before the videotape recorder, video recording meant kinescope. Since were so many problems with this process, it was no wonder that the networks eagerly welcomed a substitute. In addition to their poor quality, kinnies used expensive film stock. In 1954, American TV operations used more raw film for kinnies than did all the Hollywood film studios combined. NBC alone used more than 1 million feet of film a month to feed programs to stations in the different time zones.

Kinescope recording was also troublesome and a little nerve-racking. At CBS Television City in Hollywood, recording started at 4:30 P.M. to pick up the shows broadcast live at 7:30 in the East. Engineers recorded a 35-millimeter kinescope along with a 16-millimeter backup copy. When the first 34-minute kinny reel was done, a switch was made to a second kinescope machine. Then a courier grabbed the exposed reel and rushed it to a nearby film lab. Meanwhile, another courier took the 16-millimeter copy and, using a different route to minimize the chances that both reels would get caught in a traffic jam, rushed it to the same lab.

As the film came out of the dryers, it was spooled onto reels and packed into cans. The waiting couriers then rushed it back to the CBS projection room. These films were called "hot kinnies" because at airtime they were still warm from the dryer. At the same time, another set of couriers was heading back to the lab with the second kinny reels to be developed. If traffic was bad or if the film lab had problems, things could get tense. Veteran engineers recall several times when they were threading up a reel only a minute or so before airtime, and there were other occasions when they had to use the 16-millimeter backup copy. Despite these hardships, CBS never lost a show because of a kinescope processing problem. Nonetheless, everyone was relieved when magnetic recording was perfected.

For 20 years, however, from its debut in 1956 to the eve of the nation's Bicentennial birthday celebration in 1976, the video recorder was for TV stations, networks, and production facilities, not for home viewers. It was too cumbersome, large, and above all, expensive.

TV Recording Comes Home: The VCR

The **VCR (videocassette recorder)** revolution began with the introduction of the Betamax VCR by Sony in 1975. Crude by today's standards, the table model machine could record up to 1 hour of video. However, the machine touched off a fiery court battle between Sony and Universal Pictures. Shockingly (at least to the movie studios and their major clients, the broadcast networks, for whom they produced the majority of programs seen on prime-time TV), Sony was promoting the machine's ability to tape broadcasts off the air! "Piracy!" claimed the studios. After a much-publicized legal battle, which came to be known as the "Betamax case," in 1984 the U.S. Supreme Court ruled that home taping did not violate copyright law. Not that they needed further encouragement, but this ruling essentially gave Americans a green light to tape TV shows.

Sony's Betamax machine did not have the home video market to itself. Another Japanese firm, Matsushita, introduced a competing format, VHS (for video home system), in 1977. The two formats were incompatible; VHS tapes would not play on a Betamax machine and vice versa. Although Betamax produced better picture quality, the VHS format had a longer recording capability. The two formats battled for marketplace superiority during the late 1970s and early 1980s. Eventually, VHS won the battle and became the standard home recording medium and playback medium for the next 20 years.

In 1978 there were 175,000 VCRs in use in the United States. By 1982 nearly 5 million units were in use, representing about 9 percent of TV homes; in 1985, some 26 million homes had VCRs—about one-third of all households; and by 1988 the figure had doubled: 52 million VCRs were in use, representing just under 60 percent of homes. Today 95 million households own a VCR, representing about 9 in 10 homes in the United States. As we shall see, most of these machines are rapidly becoming obsolete, thanks to the rising popularity of DVD players and DVRs.

At first, all home VCRs were table models, designed mainly to record TV shows off the air for later playback (a phenomenon known as **time-shifting,** the term reportedly coined by Sony executive Akio Morita). However, in a few short years technological development had reduced the size of the VCR and had made home color TV cameras practical realities. A second growth industry was created: home video moviemaking. Weddings, confirmations, bar mitzvahs, and other cultural rites are captured by camcorders (portable combination camera and VCR units), which have replaced 8-millimeter film as the medium of record. The proliferation of home camera equipment has been almost as spectacular as the rise of the VCR itself. In 1985 about half a million homes had portable video equipment. By 2005, there were over 40 million camcorder units in use, about one in every four homes! Many newer camcorders use

Akio Morita, a co-founder of the Sony Corporation, the company that pioneered the development of the VCR.

digital technology to record their content not on tape but on a DVD or hard drive.

DVDs and DVRs

Perhaps the most significant trend in home video over the last decade has been the growth of the **digital video disc (DVD)** or *digital versatile disc,* which has replaced videotape as the dominant home video medium. Using the same digital technology as the audio CD, the DVD has several advantages over tape: The DVD contains more content, has better picture and audio quality, and doesn't wear out after repeated plays. In 1998, there were only 1 million DVD households in the United States. By 2001, that number had grown to 18 million. Five years later, thanks to falling prices, there were more than 60 million households with a DVD unit.

Hollywood movies that were previously released on videocassettes were replaced by movies on DVDs. In addition, a new revenue stream for production companies emerged with the advent of DVD boxed sets of TV programs. The boxed sets of the first two seasons of *Seinfeld,* for example, generated more than $95 million in revenue.

As the new century opened, digital video recorders (DVRs), such as TiVo, made their debut. These machines record content not on tape or a DVD but on a hard disk drive, similar to what is found

Issues: Format Wars—History Repeating Itself?

As mentioned in the text, when videocassette players were first introduced, there were two competing and incompatible formats: Beta (championed by Sony) and VHS (short for video home system, championed by JVC). Consumers faced a problem because they had to choose one system over the other. Although many experts thought that the picture quality was better on the Beta system, it was VHS that eventually won out in the marketplace. The big deciding factor was recording length. The Beta cassettes could hold only an hour of video; the VHS tapes could hold about 3 hours. If a consumer wanted to record a 2-hour movie, it would take two Beta cassettes but only one VHS. As the film rental business began to blossom in the early 1980s, most of the early stores stocked their shelves with VHS cassettes. Sony eventually gave up the fight and by 1988 began to produce VHS machines.

Another format war began brewing in 2006—this time over the format for high-definition DVDs. Once again there are two incompatible systems vying for marketplace domination, and once again the consumer is caught in a dilemma. The two formats are Blu-ray, backed by Dell, Panasonic, Pioneer, and Sony, to name a few, and HD-DVD, backed by Toshiba, NEC, Sanyo, and several big movie studios.

Engineers who have seen the two formats side by side agree that both formats produce excellent high-definition images. Both formats are also what technicians call "backward compatible," which means that both formats will be able to play all your old standard-definition DVDs as well as high-definition DVDs.

Blu-ray discs can hold more information than HD-DVDs and will be able to pack more special features and bonus content onto a single disc. HD-DVD does possess a significant economic advantage: HD-DVDs can be manufactured with only slight changes to existing machinery that creates the standard DVD. On the other hand, the Blu-ray system requires that manufacturers install totally new equipment. Any disc manufacturing company that chooses the Blu-ray format faces a huge expense in retooling. In addition, HD-DVD was the first out of the gate, appearing on the market in mid-2006, while Blu-ray made it to retailers' shelves months later.

Of course, there are many other factors that will be important in determining which format eventually wins out. Consumers will carefully weigh the prices of new high-definition DVD players and discs. Advertising and marketing will play a major role, and the format that gets the best movies from the major studios will have a big advantage. Once again, the marketplace will decide, but in the meantime, consumers in the 2000s who want to invest their money in a new technology will face the same dilemma as consumers in the 1980s: Which one will succeed and which one will be passed by?

inside a computer. They make it possible to record up to 300 hours of programs and pause live TV. Initial sales were slow, but household penetration was expected to grow to about 20 percent by 2007.

The Video Store

In scarcely 10 years a new commercial establishment, the video store, became a fixture at neighborhood shopping malls. By 1984, about 20,000 specialty video stores were operating. VHS tapes dominated the sales and rental market until the turn of the century, when they were replaced by the DVD. As of 2004 there were about 25,000 video outlets in operation. Renting and selling DVDs is a big business. In 2005, consumers spent more than $16 billion to buy DVDs and more than $5 billion renting them.

The outlook for video stores is cloudy. Revenue growth slowed in 2005. Moreover, video stores faced competition from pay cable and pay satellite channels that can offer a choice of more than 50 movies at a price that is equal to or less than a DVD rental. Cable and satellite providers are also experimenting with video on demand, a system that would allow subscribers to choose from hundreds of movies and to view their choices at their convenience. Faced with this competition, the traditional video store, such as Blockbuster, diversified its offerings and now stocks video games and movie paraphernalia on its shelves.

Finally, audiences are spending less time with their television sets (and radios) and more and more time with their computers. A new media competitor has burst upon the scene: the home computer. And it has its own "network," the Internet and the World Wide Web (WWW). We close our brief history of electronic media with the story of the Web.

THE INTERNET AND THE WORLD WIDE WEB

The term **Internet** refers to the global interconnection of computer networks made possible by using common communication protocols. The **World Wide Web** is just one service available on this global network. Other Internet services we use, including Gopher, FTP, and e-mail, may function within a Web browser, but they are really separate network technologies. There are others, too, and more are in development. But our book is about sending sounds and pictures, mainly. So our discussion will focus on the development of the Internet and its primary audiovisual component: the World Wide Web.

Cold War and Hot Science: The Birth of the Internet

The Internet, like television, was in development for decades. Like radio, the Internet was developed out of concern for military preparedness and assurance that the military could communicate in times of emergency.

The main impetus behind the Internet's development was the Cold War struggle between the United States and the Soviet Union, which marked the period from the end of World War II in 1945 until the fall of the Berlin Wall in 1989.

In 1957 the Soviet Union astounded the world by launching *Sputnik,* the earth's first man-made satellite. This event would have a huge impact on U.S. technology, planting the seeds for the Internet. Many people began to question how it was possible for the Soviet Union to completely surprise the United States with a new, possibly threatening technology. President Dwight D. Eisenhower called the nation's top military advisors and scientists to form a new agency called the **Defense Advanced Research Projects Agency (DARPA).** On January 7, 1958, DARPA was created to ensure that America would never again be taken by surprise by new technologies.

Post–Nuclear War: Would There Still Be a Dial Tone?

In the wake of the Cuban missile crisis in October 1962, when the United States and the Soviet Union stood on the brink of nuclear war, military commanders became convinced that it was going to be necessary to develop a communication system that could survive a missile attack. A lot was already known about building sophisticated voice and video networks. AT&T had interconnected the country with telephones by 1914, and the first coast-to-coast hookup for television was completed in 1951. But computer networks were relatively new and consisted mostly of using modems on a standard phone circuit to make an interconnection. Telephone switching centers were located near major cities, and

When Joseph C.R. Licklider wrote *Man–Computer Symbiosis* in 1960, his work inspired many to seriously consider the relationship between computer science and psychology. In 1962, DARPA's attention turned toward computers and "Lick," as he was known, was chosen to head up DARPA's behavioral science office. **Cybernetics,** the study of the interrelationship between man and machines, was a new field of study, and Licklider was keenly interested in it. His ideas that a computer could serve as a problem-solving partner to humans, in real time, sounded like science fiction to many. Licklider even talked about creating an "Intergalactic Network" of interconnected computers and of a new concept called **time-sharing.** The notion of connecting computers together to function in some kind of an interconnected network was a radical idea. Though many computers had been interconnected into networks, the process was cumbersome and expensive; usually one communicated with computers using punch cards and "dumb" terminals.

Cold War tensions between the United States and the Soviet Union prompted America to embark on research into many different technologies simultaneously. Computers and communication systems became a priority, and the military's SAGE project inspired Licklider to see computing in a new light. He reasoned that it didn't make sense to have many different computers using different operating systems, all of them unable to communicate with one another. The Intergalactic Computer Network should have a standardized connection, he thought. Soon after, Licklider began pulling together some of the nation's brightest young researchers to work on the project, among them Bob Taylor of Dallas, who by 1963 headed up DARPA's Office of Information Processing Techniques. Taylor had three terminals in his office at the Pentagon. One was connected to the University of California at Berkeley, another to the main computer at the Strategic Air Command in Santa Barbara, and the third to Lincoln Labs at MIT. Unfortunately, none of the computers could communicate with the others and they all required different log-in procedures. Taylor found the lack of interconnection frustrating.

Computers weren't small and they certainly weren't cheap, Taylor thought. Why not fund a networking project that would try to link them together? With networking, researchers at MIT could use resources at UCLA and vice versa. Taylor called on Larry Roberts, a brilliant 29-year-old scientist at MIT to help make this happen. The rest, as they say, is history. But Licklider's influence on DARPA and network computing in indisputable. "Lick was among the first to perceive the spirit of community created among the users of the first time-sharing systems," said Taylor. "In pointing out the community phenomena created, in part, by the sharing of resources in one time-sharing system, Lick made it easy to think about interconnecting the communities, the interconnection of interactive, online communities of people."

they were sure to become targets of Soviet missiles. To make the nation's emergency communication system less vulnerable, a new approach to networking was necessary.

The Air Force hired the Rand Corporation to figure out a way to bolster American communication systems in case of war. Paul Baran of Rand had been pondering some hypothetical questions about the capabilities of different types of computer networks. He reasoned that, in order to make a communication system less vulnerable to attack, that system would need to take many paths to send messages. This concept was similar to the way neural networks work inside the human brain. If one brain cell is damaged, an alternate neural route around the damaged area can be found because of the millions of neural connections that exist. Baran was convinced that a computer network could mimic a neural network, but his ideas were so revolutionary few people in the telecommunications industry believed they were possible. It took Baran nearly 5 years to convince people that such a network could work. Meanwhile a British physicist named Donald Davies, working independently, had come to the same conclusion: A distributed network of information could provide redundancy of information. Davies thought that data should be broken up into small strings of bits that could be enclosed in "electronic packets," which would be able to move quickly within a communications network having many different connections. The notion of **packet switching** was born.

Packet switching provided the ideal solution to the problem of data loss during emergencies. Data packets were small, and, if a packet was lost, it could be sent and resent over the networks easily. With many interconnected computers, packets had several possible paths they could travel to reach their final destination. This distributed system could provide survivability in case of a missile attack, because, if one part of the network was destroyed, there would be other paths available.

ARPANET: Forerunner of the Internet

Bob Taylor at DARPA decided to build the network that could survive nuclear war. In 1968, the ARPANET project was born.

Twelve different companies bid on the project. Bolt, Beranek, and Newman (BBN), a small engineering firm in Cambridge, Massachusetts, got the contract to begin development work on the basic network computer called the Interface Message Processor (IMP) machine.

Early work in computer interactivity was going on at several separate geographical locations simultaneously. How could all of the various universities and research labs working on DARPA projects communicate with one another? The solution was to build an interactive computer network that could share data quickly. Engineers realized that to make this happen they would have to devise a way of controlling network message traffic. The **Network Control Program (NCP)** was a scheme devised to provide this control. NCP became the forerunner of today's **Transmission Control Protocol (TCP),** the switching system that controls modern communication networks.

In the fall of 1969, UCLA and Stanford became the first of many links in this distributed network. Success of the network was not immediate. Researchers at UCLA wanted to connect their new machine with another computer at Stanford. Sitting at a computer terminal at UCLA's computer lab, undergraduate Charlie Klein typed an "L." Stanford called back on a standard telephone and confirmed the computer had received an "L." Then Klein typed an "O," and again the researchers at Stanford confirmed an "O." Feeling more confident, Klein typed a "G," hoping to gain remote access to the Stanford computer. He hit the carriage return, and both computers crashed, perhaps the first (but definitely not the last) time an attempted log-in failed!

Later that day, the bugs were ironed out of the login process and the first computers designed for networking were connected. Soon more nodes (sites) were added to the network. In 1970, the University

of California at Santa Barbara and the University of Utah were connected; then MIT, Harvard, Carnegie-Mellon, and other major research universities were added. **ARPANET** became the first fully interconnected nationwide computer network.

Where It's @: The Rise of Electronic Mail

While designers of the ARPANET system had originally envisioned its primary use for the exchange of missile telemetry information and had planned for large database transfers using file transfer protocol (FTP), most users were actually using the network to send personal communications to their colleagues. In 1972, Ray Tomlinson of BBN, the company that designed the network, had invented the first practical network e-mail program. Tomlinson and all ARPANET users had their own specific computer accounts, but each user needed a way to separate his own name from the name of the computer system he was using. Looking at his teletype terminal, Tomlinson saw mostly letters and numbers. However, when he saw the @ sign, Tomlinson thought it could be used to combine one's personal user name with the name of his host computer system. Today, the @ has become one of the lasting symbols of our interconnected world!

The 1970s were pivotal for the development of ARPANET. Several public demonstrations of the network's capabilities convinced DARPA to extend packet-switching capability through the use of communications satellites and ground mobile radio transmitters. These efforts, known as **interneting,** began a research initiative designed to solve the problems associated with linking different kinds of networks together. Also, nodes connecting England and Norway broadened the international scope of the network. By 1976, Web pioneers Vinton Cerf and Robert Kahn had developed Transmission Control Protocol/Internet Protocol (TCP/IP) to replace Network Control Program. With TCP/IP, the delivery of a message was the same, regardless of what information was contained inside the packet. A file sent over the network could just as easily be a document, a picture, or a set of numbers. This change in protocol now made it easier to send photographs, sounds, and other material over the network. With new nodes being added every month, ARPANET grew from its original 2 connections to more than 200 by 1981. Eventually it encompassed more than 1.5 million miles of interconnected telephone lines. While

ARPANET's success was well known to many, its usage was still limited to people with high-level military clearance. It was still not a medium available to the masses.

USENET: Bringing Computer Networking to the Masses

By the late 1970s, many large corporations and most universities had the ability to connect to a computer network. In 1976 Steve Bellovin, a graduate student at the University of North Carolina, created **USENET,** a system that enabled groups of computer users to send messages between the UNC campus at Chapel Hill and nearby Duke University in Durham. USENET operated like a bulletin board. A topic area was created, and computer users on the network could post their opinions on the topic. At first, most bulletin boards featured postings on computer-related topics. It wasn't long until politics (mostly liberal), music (mostly contemporary), and sex (mostly recreational) became popular topics on the system.

In the late 1970s, Matt Glickman, a high school student, and Mark Horton, a graduate student at the University of California at Berkeley, rewrote the USENET program to extend its capacity. Through USENET, faculty and students at dozens of universities, who were not previously authorized for ARPANET accounts, now had access to the network. USENET grew rapidly. Starting from just three sites in 1979, USENET grew into thousands of different newsgroups. As might have been expected, the ARPANET administrators objected to USENET's carrying discussions about drugs, sex, and rock-and-roll over the network's computers (this was a military project, after all). As a result, an alternative routing system was created to route USENET newsgroup messages around the main ARPANET network. The bulletin boards would carry the prefix "alt," to distinguish these messages from the more traditional research, military, and computer science traffic.

Today, USENET newsgroup topics range from hip-hop music to collecting Barbie dolls to soap operas to weird sexual behaviors. Alt, indeed.

The various interconnected computer networks grew as users realized TCP/IP would provide greater flexibility than the many different proprietary systems that existed. There was no single initiative to create a vast, worldwide interconnected network, yet that's exactly what seemed to be happening. One innovation, called **TELNET,** gave users the ability to connect to and control various computers from remote locations. Another innovation, Bob Metcalfe's Ethernet, allowed an array of computers to be connected into a single **local area network (LAN).** Now it was possible for all kinds of computers to be linked together, both in the same office and literally around the world. These network innovations gave rise to widespread usage of e-mail and electronic bulletin boards, and they provided remote access to unique scientific databases. Government funding allowed more and more universities to join the network. By the early 1980s, a flourishing research community was interconnected.

Personal Computing: The New Mass Medium

The contribution of the personal computer to the growth of networking cannot be overestimated. Personal computers made it affordable for businesses to provide workers with individual computers instead of teletypes or "dumb" terminals, and, when Apple Computer introduced the Macintosh computer in 1984, the desktop publishing revolution began. This revolution in desktop computers and the growth in networking capability allowed individuals to access networked materials, use e-mail, and develop materials for publication. Many people were beginning to predict a closer relationship between computers, communications, and a social usage for the network with Compuserve, America Online, Genie, and other services providing individual accounts.

To meet the growing demand for interconnection, domain name servers such as ".gov" for government, ".edu" for educational institution, and ".mil" for military unit were developed. It was no longer necessary to memorize numerical IP addresses. Now it was possible to send a message to a person's name at a particular institution (<yourname> @hostinstitution.edu.country).

With the success of interconnection came a realization that problems associated with speed and bandwidth would eventually grind the network to a halt. A highly influential report, "Towards a National Research Network," issued by the National Research Council spurred then-senator Al Gore to sponsor legislation to fund a super high-speed network using fiber-optic technology. This set the stage for the development of the **information superhighway**

An early Macintosh computer.

concept. **NSFNET** would be a high-speed backbone that linked supercomputer centers at Cornell, San Diego, Illinois, and Pittsburgh. Instead of carrying messages at 56kps (kilobits per second), the new network could transmit messages at 1.5Mbps (megabits per second).

The Internet at Last!

The Internet was officially born in 1986, when NSFNET replaced the aging ARPANET with a faster network providing 30 times more bandwidth. Using TCP/IP technology, NSFNET allowed universities to link together in a "daisy chain" arrangement ultimately connecting to one of the supercomputer centers. For the first time, faculty at smaller institutions had the ability to run experiments on the nation's largest and fastest research computers. At the same time, commercial vendors recognized the importance of the developing trends and started work on commercial products that could take advantage of the unique networking characteristics of TCP/IP. As the 1990s arrived, private **Internet service providers (ISPs),** such as America Online (AOL), gave consumers access to the Internet, while large telecommunications corporations, such as MCI and AT&T, provided new backbone capability. Public access to the Internet was occurring at libraries and universities around the country, too. During just a 5-year period, between 1987 and 1992, the speed of the Internet backbone increased a remarkable 400 percent, while traffic on the Net increased exponentially.

In Search of Search Engines: Sorting Out the Internet

By now, a tremendous amount of information was available on the Internet and most of it was free. But how could Internet users organize and sort out all these data? The answer to the question came from university researchers and computer companies who started to develop numerous tools for utilizing information available on the Internet. One of the first Internet crawlers was Archie, a robotlike program that checked FTP (file transfer protocol) sites to catalog which databases were publicly available. Gopher programs, available on most publicly accessible networked computers, provided a menu system that allowed the user to access resources on the Internet. And WAIS (wide-area information servers) systems were distributed by Apple Computer and others to provide users the ability to search many Internet servers simultaneously. With the capability of very-high-speed data access, affordable computers, and free databases available for searching, the stage was set for the introduction of the World Wide Web.

The Birth of the World Wide Web (WWW)

In March 1989, Tim Berners-Lee, while working at CERN, Europe's high-energy particle physics laboratory, circulated a paper that called for the creation of a program that used a graphical interface (pictures, as opposed to text) for requesting information available on networked databases. After the paper kicked around for more than a year, CERN gave Berners-Lee the job to write the program. He dubbed his concept the "World Wide Web." Here's how his revolutionary concept worked.

Nearly 60 million people per week visit Yahoo's Web site.

The vast majority of information on the Internet consisted of text: words in documents, and lines of letters and numbers. Berners-Lee's idea was to insert a system of **hyperlinks,** packets of computer commands, within the texts. By clicking a link, the program makes a request to the server. The server determines the location of the link through the use of a **URL (uniform resource locator)** address, gets that information, and sends it back to the computer that requested it. Since the data inside the requested packets could be anything (text, video, audio, etc.), the Internet was now capable of displaying text, video, audio, or any combination, and the user did not need to know elaborate computer code to find it. The WWW was WWWonderful.

By the fall of 1991, the World Wide Web began running experimentally on several different computer systems in Europe and the United States. During the next year, various versions of the CERN browser were installed on some 26 different computers around the world for testing. In January 1993, Marc Andreesen, working at the National Center for Supercomputer Applications (NCSA), released the first version of Mosaic, the forerunner of Netscape Navigator. This revolutionary program made it even easier for computer users to find text, sound, and pictures on the Internet. At this point, World Wide Web traffic was still minuscule, roughly 0.1 percent of all the traffic on the Internet. That would soon change.

Mosaic and the World Wide Web together formed the "killer application" that was needed to make the Internet really take off among all sorts of people. The World Wide Web became an overnight sensation. Within 6 months the number of Web-based servers jumped from a few to over 200, and traffic increased tenfold as well. People outside of the research community began to take a real interest in the WWW. Everywhere newspapers, television, and magazines were talking about the new phenomenon. In 1994 Andreesen left NCSA to form Netscape Communications and the World Wide Web saw its first commercial applications.

The usage statistics for the Web are staggering. Between 1993 and 1995, the number of Internet users more than tripled, from about 12 million to 40 million worldwide. By 2005, that number had skyrocketed to more than 900 million. Although that is a huge number, it only represents about 15 percent of the total world population.

There are more than 100 million Web sites. The total number of Web pages on the Internet is hard to determine. Yahoo, a widely used search engine, scans about 20 billion pages, but some experts suggest that the total number is probably much higher, maybe around a trillion pages. Internet traffic has slowed a bit since the beginning of the decade, but it is still increasing at a rate of about 100 percent a year.

CABLE, SATELLITES, HOME VIDEO, AND THE INTERNET IN THE TWENTY-FIRST CENTURY

As of mid-decade, the following developments had occurred:

- The cable TV industry continued to consolidate. In 2002, Comcast acquired the cable assets of AT&T Broadband. Three years later, Comcast teamed up with Time Warner to announce plans to acquire Adelphia's cable systems.

- Cable continued to draw audiences away from the traditional TV networks. In 2005, about 60 percent of the prime-time audience were watching cable. That number might increase thanks to a 2005 deal that would move *Monday Night Football* from ABC to ESPN.

- Cable companies began using their lines to provide other services to their subscribers, including high-speed Internet access, video-on-demand, and local telephone service.

- Speaking of telephone service, the Telecommunications Act of 1996 paved the way for competition between telephone companies and cable companies. After a slow start, competition heated up in 2005. Thanks to a technology called **Voice over Internet Protocol (VoIP),** cable companies began offering phone service to their subscribers. VoIP was cheaper than traditional phone service and was popular with consumers. By mid-decade, about 75 percent of all cable systems offered telephone service.

Since many of the subscribers who turned to VoIP canceled their traditional phone service, the phone companies fought back by offering video. The major phone companies announced plans to spend more than $20 billion to upgrade their systems in order to provide TV service. Verizon, for example, intended to offer 100 channels of TV to its subscribers in 2006 or 2007.

- More and more consumers are turning to high-speed broadband Internet connections, such as DSL telephone lines and cable modems, that make it easier to receive audio and video. At the start of 2006, more than 40 million households had broadband.

- The Internet allowed everyone a chance to be a mass communicator. Web logs, or **blogs,** are personal journals that are kept by private individuals and periodically updated. They may discuss politics, art, education, or society, or they may contain introspective comments. Although the exact number is hard to pin down, it was estimated that as of 2006, about 10 million blogs existed on the Web. Another development is **podcasting** (the name is derived from Apple's popular iPod). Podcasting is the production and distribution of audio or video files that are available on the Web. Podcasting allows an individual to put together self-produced radio or TV shows. Figures for 2006 suggest that about a million podcasts were available on the Web.

SUMMARY

- Cable television began in the late 1940s and early 1950s, as viewers in mountainous and rural areas strove to be a part of the "TV craze." At first, the FCC was reluctant to regulate the cable business, but under pressure from broadcast TV, a set of restrictive regulations was put in place that stymied the growth of cable for over 20 years.

- Cable's period of explosive growth began in the 1970s, spurred by the adoption of new FCC rules, the spread of satellites for program distribution, and the rise of innovative programming services. Two important program concepts, pay TV (led by Home Box Office) and the "superstation" (developed by Ted Turner), were

developed at this time. By the 1980s, more new program services appeared, like CNN and MTV, making cable increasingly attractive to TV households. Cable boomed, as more than half of all TV homes decided to subscribe to the service. Today, cable TV reaches more than 6 in 10 TV households and delivers a range of services to consumers, including video, data, and even telephone service.

- Cable's growth created competition, including direct broadcast satellite and the consumer favorite: the videocassette recorder (VCR). The first home satellite dishes were large, cumbersome, and expensive. Nevertheless, TVROs dotted the landscape in the 1980s. A new generation of smaller and more affordable satellite dishes appeared in the 1990s and have taken the video industry by storm. Other alternatives to cable, including MMDS, or "wireless cable," have been less successful.

- The rise of the VCR and DVD has been spectacular. The home video business exploded on the scene in the 1980s, fueled by a landmark Supreme Court case legalizing home video recording, the arrival of affordable video recorders, and the rise of video rental shops. The video sales and rental business tops $20 billion in annual revenues.

- The newest of the so-called new media is the Internet and its video/audio segment known as the World Wide Web (WWW). The Internet is a by-product of the Cold War between the Soviet Union and the United States, arising from an initiative to link major universities and civil defense sites to avert (or survive) nuclear war. It arose from the creation of the Defense Advanced Research Projects Agency (DARPA) in 1957, following the successful launch by Russia of its *Sputnik* satellite.

- By the 1970s, most users of ARPANET were not using the system to exchange missile guidance information. Instead, researchers and college professors were using the system to exchange electronic messages. The concept of e-mail was taking shape. By the end of the decade, USENET, a simplified bulletin board system, and TELNET, a means of dialing into large computers from remote locations, were growing in popularity.

- Sales of personal computers skyrocketed in the 1980s. The Apple and IBM PC brought a new class of entrepreneurs, experimenters, and enthusiasts to the field of computing. Individual computer users in universities and businesses could now connect to one another to exchange data (and e-mail). In response to the growing demand, the National Science Foundation replaced the aging ARPANET infrastructure with a faster network that had much higher bandwidth. Hundreds, then thousands, of universities and schools soon logged on to the network. They were followed in the early 1990s by millions of home computer enthusiasts, using commercial gateways like Prodigy and America Online (AOL).

- The last piece of the puzzle was provided by Tim Berners-Lee, who coined the term *World Wide Web*. His innovative idea was to connect data on the Web via *hyperlinks,* packages of computer commands that computer users could execute with a simple click of the mouse. As a result, text, sounds, and pictures could be transmitted and received on the Internet virtually anywhere in the world, without the need for sophisticated or technical commands.

- Today, the Internet is taking its place alongside radio, broadcast TV, and cable television as a means of sending and receiving media content. Time will tell if the new Web replaces such "ancient" networks as CBS, NBC, and ABC.

KEY TERMS

SUGGESTIONS FOR FURTHER READING

Bartlett, E. R. (2000). *Cable television handbook.* New York: McGraw-Hill.

Hafner, K., & Lyon, M. (1996). *Where wizards stay up late: The origins of the Internet.* New York: Simon & Schuster.

Hillstrom, K. (2005). *The Internet revolution.* Detroit, MI: Omnigraphics.

Ovadia, S. (2001). *Broadband cable TV access networks.* Upper Saddle River, NJ: Prentice Hall.

Parsons, P. R., & Frieden, R. M. (1998). *The cable and satellite television industries*. Boston, MA: Allyn and Bacon.

Randall, N. (1997). *The soul of the Internet: Net gods, netizens, and the wiring of the world*. Boston: International Thomson.

Reid, R. H. (1997). *Architects of the Web: 1,000 days that built the future of the Web*. New York: Wiley.

Robichaux, M. (2002). *Cable cowboy: John Malone and the rise of the modern cable business*. Hoboken, NJ: Wiley.

Salus, P. H. (1995). *Casting the net: From ARPANET to the Internet and beyond*. Reading, MA: Addison-Wesley.

Southwick, T. (1999). *Distant signals: How cable TV changed the world of telecommunications*. Denver: The Cable Center.

Sterling, C. J., & Kittross, J. (2001). *Stay tuned: A concise history of American broadcasting*. Belmont, CA: Wadsworth.

Winston, B. (1998). *Media technology and society: A history*. New York: Routledge.

INTERNET EXERCISES

Visit our Web site at **www.mhhe.com/dominick6** for study-guide exercises to help you learn and apply material in each chapter. You will find ideas for future research as well as useful Web links to provide you with an opportunity to journey through the new electronic media.

3 Audio and Video Technology

Quick Facts

 Bandwidth of an FM channel: 200 kilohertz

 Bandwidth of a digital television channel: 6 megahertz

 First high-definition TV broadcasts: 1998

 Cost of 51-inch digital HDTV projection TV, 1999: $5,000

 Cost of 51-inch digital HDTV projection TV, 2006: $1,699

 Percent of dads hoping for a consumer electronics gift on Father's Day, 2006: 42

Watching TV and listening to radio are the easiest things in the world to do. Just twist that dial, flip that switch, or punch that button and poof: Vivid sounds and picturesque images are yours (unless, of course, you're watching a test pattern). Surfing the Internet requires a bit more interactive work, but not too much. The ease with which we command TV and radio reception hides the incredibly difficult problems and complex technical processes involved in moving sound and pictures from their source to you. This chapter attempts to demystify the magic of radio and TV technology. We describe how the process works and, more important, why it matters. In many ways understanding the technology behind electronic media helps you understand their history, legal status, social and political power, and future.

BASIC PRINCIPLES OF MEDIA TECHNOLOGY

It's helpful to begin a discussion of technical aspects of radio and TV with some basic principles.

Facsimile Technology

All modes of mass communication are based on the process of **facsimile** technology. That is, sounds from a speaker and pictures on a TV screen are merely representations, or facsimiles, of their original form. We all learn and practice facsimile technology at an early age. Did you ever use a pencil or crayon to trace the outline of your hand on a sheet of blank paper? That's an example of facsimile technology. Having one's face covered by plaster of Paris for a mask or sculpture is facsimile technology; so are having your picture taken and photocopying a friend's lecture notes.

In general, the more faithful the reproduction or facsimile is to the original, the greater is its **fidelity.** High-fidelity audio, or hi-fi, is a close approximation of the original speech or music it represents. And a videocassette recorder marketed as high fidelity boasts better picture quality than a VCR without hi-fi (known as H-Q, to distinguish video high fidelity from its audio counterpart). Indeed, much of the technical development of radio and TV has been a search for better fidelity: finding better and better ways to make facsimiles of the original sounds or images. Today's developments in digital technology are yet another example of our quest for higher-fidelity pictures and sound.

The second point about facsimile technology is that in creating their facsimiles, radio and TV are not limited to plaster of Paris, crayon, oils, or even photographic chemicals and film. Instead, unseen elements such as radio waves, beams of light, and digital bits and bytes are utilized in the process. Although you cannot put your hands on a radio wave as you can a photo in your wallet, it is every bit as much there. The history of radio and TV is directly linked to the discovery and use of these invisible "resources," from Marconi's early radio experiments in the 1890s to the newest forms of audio and video digital transmissions of today.

In the technical discussion that follows, bear in mind that the engineer's goal in radio, TV, and cable is to create the best possible facsimile of our original sound or image, to transport that image without losing too much fidelity (known as signal loss), and to re-create that sound or image as closely as possible to its original form. Today, engineers use both analog and digital systems to transport images and sounds, but more and more we are switching to digital transmission.

Transduction

Another basic concept is **transduction,** the process of changing one form of energy into another. When the telephone operator says "the number is 555-2796" and you write it down on a sheet of notepaper, you have transduced the message. Similarly, when you slip on your earbuds and turn on an iPod while you stroll through the mall, you are transducing—although some around you will surely wonder what you're listening to.

Why does this matter? Well, getting a sound or picture from a TV studio or concert hall to your home usually involves at least three or four transductions. At each phase loss of fidelity is possible and must be controlled. With our current system of broadcasting, it is possible that with each phase the whole process may break down into **noise**—unwanted interference—rendering the communication impossible. Although breakdowns due to transduction rarely occur, they do happen. Technicians were embarrassed when the sound went out during the 1976 presidential debate between Gerald Ford and Jimmy Carter. Closer to home, a VCR with dirty heads can make a Tchaikovsky ballet look like a snowy outtake from *The Ring*.

Today, the United States is in the midst of a digital revolution. In fact the DVD player has become the fastest-selling consumer electronics device of the decade. And television stations are converting over to a digital television (DTV) system that includes high-definition transmission and surround sound. New radio systems, including satellite radio and digital HD radio stations, are providing greatly improved fidelity with reduced noise. Today it's common to see digital televisions and radios side by side with standard broadcast receivers on store shelves, but more and more digital technology is replacing analog equipment.

Television and radio signals begin as physical energy, commonly referred to as light waves or sound waves. When you hear a bird chirping in a tree, your brain directly perceives the event by processing the sound waves that enter your ears and vibrate your eardrums. You see the bird as your brain processes the reflections of light that have entered the eye and fallen on the retina. This is direct experience: no transduction, no signal loss; true high fidelity. To experience the bird's chirping on radio, however, the following translations or transductions occur.

As we stand there with a microphone attached to a digital recorder, the bird's song is first changed into mechanical energy. Inside a dynamic microphone, the various sound wave pressures cause a small coil to vibrate back and forth in a magnetic field. This sets up in the coil a weak electrical current that reproduces the pattern of the original sound waves. Next, this current is fed into a digital converter and held in the recorder's memory for a fraction of a second while the signal is sampled, or, in other words, converted into a series of digital bits and bytes. Thus the bird's song is translated into patterns of zeros and ones as the sound has been converted into a series of digital samples. How well the transduction occurs is based on the quality of our facsimile. In other words, the higher the sample rate, the higher the quality of the recording. Next, we'll write that sampled information into a file (like a .WAV or .MP3 file) and then store it for playback later. Our digital recorder might store the sound file on a small flash drive or a miniature hard drive.

Now we have a facsimile of the chirping, stored as a series of digital bits in an electronic file. Next, we need to transduce that sound file into electrical energy. When we hit the play button on our recorder, it transfers the stored *binary digits* (bits) back into the recorder's memory. From there the data are sent to a digital-to-analog converter that reads the data files

and converts them back into electrical energy pulses. The amplifier detects the pulses, boosts them, and sends them to the output jack. And as stereo buffs know, the quality of our facsimile is now based on the quality and bandwidth of our amplifier. We are now halfway to hearing the chirp through the radio.

Next, we transduce the electrical energy into electromagnetic energy. At the radio station we feed the amplified sound from the recorder to the transmitter. Here the signal is superimposed, or "piggybacked," onto the radio wave (channel) assigned to that station through a process called modulation (examined in detail later). The fidelity of the signal is based on the station's power, its location, its channel, its bandwidth, and all sorts of other factors.

At home we turn on the radio and tune to the appropriate channel. Our antenna detects the signal and begins to reverse the transduction process. The electromagnetic energy is conducted from the antenna to the radio's circuits where it is transduced into electrical impulses as it enters the detector; then it is filtered and sent to the radio's amplifier. Next, the amplified signal vibrates the diaphragm of the radio's loudspeaker. At long last it is transduced back into its original form, physical energy, as we hear the chirp in the form of vibrations on our tympanic membrane (eardrum). Note the many transductions in this process.

What's the point of all this? Why does the transduction process matter?

Signal and Noise: Analog versus Digital

First, the recording example we discussed took a sound and converted into a digital file. Digital technology has many advantages over older analog recording techniques. Assuming that the original sound was faithfully sampled and properly stored, then the quality of the sound will always be the same as long as the integrity of the digital file is kept intact. You can make many copies of the sound file and they'll all sound as good as the original. This is one of the real benefits of digital technology: consistent sonic quality.

However, imagine if we tried to record the bird chirping using a handheld cassette recorder. The analog recording and playback process would be quite different. In analog audio, the bird chirping goes through many translations, with the possibility (and likelihood) of losing some information or adding some unnecessary data at each phase. (Ever notice that cassettes have some noise called *hiss* mixed in with the audio?) It's rather like playing the game "telephone," where several people whisper a simple message in turn. By the time the message gets to the last person, a lot of the original information has dropped out and some irrelevant information has crept in. In electronic terminology, losing information in the transduction process is known as signal loss, and the unwanted interference is known as noise. Now you can understand a term found in many advertisements for stereos: the **signal-to-noise ratio.** In common terms, this is a numerical representation of the amount of "pure" picture (in video) or sound information (in audio) when compared to the unwanted noise acquired during the transduction process. The higher the signal-to-noise ratio, the higher the fidelity; the lower the ratio, the "noisier" the sound or picture. Digital technology produces much higher signal-to-noise ratios (and better sound and pictures) than analog technology.

Analog and Digital Signals: The Real Lowdown

How information is converted from one form of energy to another is an important aspect of transduction. Until the 1990s, broadcast transmissions utilized analog signals. This means that to change the energy from physical to electrical impulses, an "analogy" to the original sound or image replaced the matter itself. It sounds tricky, but the concept is really pretty simple. By their nature, analog transmissions and recordings are subject to a great deal of signal loss and noise. They merely represent the original signal, itself a major limitation since the transmissions can never include all the information present in the original sound or picture. And analog signals tend to decay over time and space. Think of older snapshots you've taken: Over time photographs blur, tear, and fade.

Most of the excitement in broadcasting, home audio, and video today concerns digital recording and transmission: Rather than creating an analog to the original sound or picture, the signal itself is transduced into digital form. Each element of the audio or video signal is converted into its digital equivalent—that is, a series of numbers—using a binary code. A binary code is one with only two values, such as "on-off," "yes-no," "open-shut," or 0 and 1. Computers use strings of binary codes, called *bytes* (digital words comprised of bits of information), to process information. In digital recording, each sound is a unique sequence of binary numbers: 0101 (binary for the number 10), 1110 (the number 14), 10011 (the

number 19), and so on. The digital words used for recording audio are quite long. They comprise information about the frequency (pitch) and the amplitude (loudness) of each sound in the recording.

To record a picture or music, the signal is electronically sampled and converted into strings of digital bytes. It could be stored in digital form on a flash drive, or your computer's hard drive, on a CD or a DVD, but let's assume that we want to store the information on a CD. When we want to record information on a CD, we send digital pulses to a laser (*l*ight *a*mplification by *s*timulated *e*mission *r*adiation). The blank CD is made up of a light-sensitive layer protected by clear plastic. As it turns at a high speed and as pulses are sent to the CD burner, the laser beam alters the light-sensitive CD layer. The laser burns a pattern of reflective and nonreflective areas that correspond to the zeros and ones in our binary files.

In the playback process the digital information on a CD is transduced by a beam of laser light, the same way the bar codes on your groceries are at the supermarket checkout. There are no needles, no friction, no wear, no scratches. More important, if the sampling rate is high enough, there is virtually no opportunity to introduce noise. When the signal is transmitted and played back, what we hear through the speakers is a virtual duplicate of the original signal with very high fidelity and excellent signal-to-noise ratio, meaning it is virtually noise-free.

A frequent topic of this text is the transition from analog to digital. Radio, TV, cable, and recording have all moved to digital means of production. As a result, they are merging with the computer and newer wireless digital devices. This phenomenon has received its own industry buzzword: **convergence.**

Oscillation and the Waveform

Another basic principle to both audio and video signal processing is the concept of **oscillation.** Recall that we hear sounds and see images as variations, fluctuations, or vibrations detected by our ears and eyes and interpreted by our brain. Remember too that every vibration has a unique signature or "footprint"; every sound and image has its own characteristics. How well we see, how acutely we hear, and how well we can re-create these signals as sounds and pictures depend on our ability to identify, store, and re-create those vibrations. In electronic terms, the vibration of air produced by our mouths, the instruments we play, and objects in our natural environment, as well as the vibration of light

Figure 3–1

Principle of Oscillation and the Common Waveform

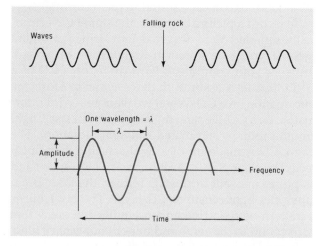

that accounts for every color and image our eyes can see, is known as oscillation. The footprint or image of an oscillation we use to visualize the presence of the invisible is known as its **waveform.** Figure 3–1 demonstrates the phenomenon of oscillation and the common waveform.

The most common way we can visualize oscillation is by dropping a small rock into a pail of water. You know that the result will be a series of circles or waves, radiating outward from the spot where the rock fell, until dissipating some distance from the center (depending on the size of the bucket and the height from which we drop the rock). All audio and video signals produce a pattern like this, except that they are invisible to the naked eye. However, while we can't see the patterns with the naked eye, by using the appropriate electronic equipment (such as an oscilloscope and a waveform monitor), we can detect them, use them, even create them ourselves.

Frequency and Amplitude

A major way in which we describe a wave is by its **frequency,** the number of waves that pass a given point in a given time. Originally measured in cycles per second (cps), frequency is more commonly measured now in **hertz (Hz),** in homage to early radio pioneer Heinrich Hertz.

In our example with the rock, depicted in Figure 3–1, the frequency is simply the number of waves that pass a given point in a single second.

Note also from the bottom of Figure 3–1 that the distance between two corresponding points on a wave is called the **wavelength.** Also note that frequency and wavelength are inversely related. High frequency means a short wavelength; low frequency means a long wavelength. In the early days of radio, U.S. stations were classified by their wavelengths. Today we identify them by their frequencies.

A wave may also be described by its height or depth, from its normal position before the rock is dropped to the crest created by the splash. This is known as its **amplitude.** When choosing a section of beach to swim in, families with small children are likely to select those with slow, low, undulating waves—waves of low amplitude or, to use a radio term, long waves. Surfers will select a wild stretch of shoreline with frequent, mammoth-sized (high-amplitude) waves capable of picking the swimmer up and depositing her anywhere on the beach. In radio terms, these are the high-frequency short waves.

What's the significance of all this? For one thing, this is precisely how radio and TV work. As we examine in detail later, local radio stations wish to blanket their area with a strong local or regional signal. That's why AM signals use medium-length waves. International broadcasters like the BBC and Radio Moscow seek to spread the word about their countries around the globe. Hence they use short waves to hopscotch around the world. The services of these and other shortwave broadcasters are traced in detail in Chapter 14.

Frequency Response

Consider a final point about oscillation and the waveform. How well we can record and play back music or pictures depends on the range of frequencies that our radio or recorder is capable of receiving or reproducing. This is known as the unit's **frequency response.** A radio set that can only reproduce frequencies below 10,000 cycles and above 1,000 cycles will simply exclude very low and very high sounds. At the same time, a receiver with the best speakers, with a frequency response from 20 to 20,000 hertz, will be able to reproduce all the sounds the human ear can hear. It's the difference between hearing a symphony orchestra on a good stereo or through the tiny speaker on your cell phone. This is critical since the history of the popular arts is directly linked to the frequency response of the prevailing methods of signal processing.

In the recording industry the early success of banjo-playing minstrel-type performers, who frequently whistled in their acts, was in large part due to their audibility on 78-rpm records of limited, mainly high-frequency capability. Early recording stars such as Al Jolson, Rudy Vallee, and Eddie Cantor fall into this class. Similarly, in retrospect, Elvis Presley's limited tonal range seems to have directly fit the limitations of the cheaply produced 45-rpm record popular in the 1950s, which was meant to be heard on a teenager's much-abused "personal" record player (certainly not on dad's hi-fi in the den). In fact, early rock-and-roll record producers frequently listened to the final mix of a song on small car speakers instead of big studio monitors! Is it any surprise that the orchestrations, sound collages, and other experimentations ushered in by the Beatles' *Sergeant Pepper's Lonely Hearts Club Band,* the Beach Boys' *Pet Sounds,* and other groups in the late 1960s were aided by the developments of high-fidelity studio recording and FM stereo broadcasting? Today the complexities and acoustic calisthenics of rap and hip-hop performers (such as Busta Rhymes and Black Eyed Peas) are made possible by the extended range of frequencies available with new audio components, such as digital recording consoles and CD players.

STEPS IN SIGNAL PROCESSING

Having mastered the basics of media technology, let's turn to how it's actually done. All electronic signals—radio, TV, cable, satellite, and computer—follow the identical path from their inception to our consumption. These steps are depicted in Figure 3–2.

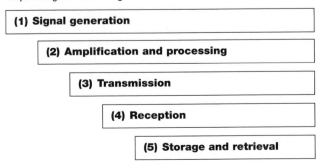

Figure 3–2

Steps in Signal Processing

(1) Signal generation

(2) Amplification and processing

(3) Transmission

(4) Reception

(5) Storage and retrieval

STEP 1: SIGNAL GENERATION

This step involves the creation of the necessary oscillations, or detectable vibrations of electrical energy, which correspond to the frequencies of their original counterparts in nature. In plain language, signal generation involves getting the sound vibrations into a microphone, or the bits and bytes onto a CD, a DVD, or an MP3 player.

Audio Signal Generation

Sound signals are generated by two main transduction processes: mechanical and electronic. Mechanical methods, like microphones, phonograph records, and tape recorders, have been in use for many years. Records and tapes have been largely replaced by digital electronics, such as CDs, DVDs, and MP3 players. First, let's briefly review how mechanical methods work.

Mechanical Methods Mechanical generation uses facsimile technology to create an analog of the original signals (by now you should be able to understand that technical-sounding sentence). That is, mechanical means are used to translate sound waves into a physical form, one you can hold in your hand, like a phonograph record or an audiocassette.

Inside the microphone One place where speech or music is mechanically re-created to produce electrical signals is inside a microphone. There are three basic types of microphones: dynamic, velocity, and condenser. Each produces the waveforms required for transmission in a different manner.

In a dynamic microphone a diaphragm is suspended over a electromagnet. In the center of the microphone is a coil of electrical wire, called a *voice coil.* Sound pressure vibrates the diaphragm, which moves the voice coil up and down between the magnetic poles. This movement induces an electrical pattern in the mike wire analogous to the frequency of the entering sound. Thanks to durable and rugged design similar to a sturdy kettle drum and good frequency response with voices and most music, dynamic mikes are frequently utilized in radio and TV productions, particularly news gathering.

There are other types of microphones that use different principles. For example, velocity microphones, also known as ribbon microphones, replace the voice coil with a thin metal ribbon. There is no diaphragm; the oscillations of the ribbon suspended

We live in an interconnected world. Certainly the evening news shows us that world events have intertwined our lives with the lives of others from around the globe. But beyond the ramifications of the global media, perhaps no other device is doing more to change our culture than the cell phone.

According to a poll conducted by the Pew Research Center, the cell phone has become the most important communication device available for many under the age of 25. Some of the implications are undeniable, some amusing and some disturbing. For example, more than one in four users admit that they talk on the phone when driving and do not always drive as safely as a result.

The Pew study provides a detailed picture of how cell phones are being used in everyday life. Many say that the device has changed their lives in some ways. Youth are more likely to use their phones to make spontaneous calls when they have free time or when they want to kill time. (They're also more likely to get sticker shock at the end of the month when the bill comes.) A third of all youth say they cannot live without their cell phones, compared with only 18 percent of the general population. Interestingly, people under 29 are not always truthful about where they are when they're on the phone.

In an interview with the Associated Press, one college student from Tennessee said that he used his phone to do everything: talk, play video games, and use as an MP3 player. Almost 90 percent of all people polled said that they've encountered annoying people using cell phones, conversely only 8 percent said that they had ever been rude talking on their cell phone.

---

between the electromagnetic poles produce the necessary electric signals. Velocity mikes produce a lush sound and were very common in the "golden age" of radio. (You can see one on David Letterman's desk on *Late Night*.)

Condenser microphones use an electrical device known as a capacitor to produce electronic equivalents of sound pressure waves. The capacitor is comprised of two electrically charged plates. The pattern of electricity in the plate (its amplitude and frequency) varies in relation to its distance from its stationary backplate. That distance is affected by the pressure of the incoming sound waves. While this might seem complex, the process is quite similar to the workings of your own ear. Without touching the volume knob on a portable stereo, you can vary its loudness simply by moving the headphones closer to or farther from your eardrums.

Inside the phonograph record and tape recorder
Phonograph records now seem archaic, but they were an important means of mechanical transduction of audio signals. Because they've been around for more than a century and are an important part of broadcast history, we're going to spend a moment discussing them. In recorded music, the sounds produced by musicians and singers are transduced into cuts made on each side of the central groove on the record (this is probably why songs on an album are known as

"cuts" in the popular music business). This process is known as *lateral cut recording*. As the turntable rotates, the stylus (needle) vibrates laterally as it follows the record groove, creating the vibrations corresponding to the original words and music.

Early 1900s record reproduction ranged from 200 hertz (G below middle C, for you musicians) to around 1,500 hertz (second G above middle C), making the sound tinny, but a typical high-fidelity LP record ranges over nine octaves, from 50 to 15,000 hertz, which pretty much includes most of the sounds that are produced by voice and musical instruments.

Another way we begin sound signal processing is by converting sounds into electromagnetic pulses or "blips" on a piece of audiotape. Under a microscope, a piece of audiotape can be seen as a concentration of millions of metallic particles suspended in a plastic base. When a small electrical signal is fed into the recording circuit, an electromagnetic field is emitted by the tape head. As the tape passes the head, its microscopic metal filings are charged (arranged magnetically) into an exact replica of the electrical patterns moving through the tape head. We have now created an analog signal, just like the grooves on a record or the oscillations in a microphone. Playing back is simply the reverse of the recording process. The signals recorded on tape induce a magnetic field in the playback head, which is then amplified and sent to speakers.

The tiny electret condenser is the preferred microphone in TV news due to its small size and rugged design.

Professional audio recording facilities use tape that is 1 or 2 inches wide, capable of recording 8, 16, and even 24 or 48 separate sets of signals on one piece of tape. Consequently, such machines are known as multitrack recorders. Broadcast stations use ¼ inch wide tape recording in stereo.

For many years radio stations also used audiotape cartridge players, or "carts," for their music, commercials, and station identifications. These machines use a special tape cartridge with only one reel. The tape winds past the heads and back onto itself. This allows for the musical selections to arrive quickly at their original starting point (in radio jargon, they are fast-cued).

Cassette tape recorders use a miniaturized reel-to-reel configuration enclosed in a small plastic housing. Because of their small size and portability they were popular with news reporters. The tape is only ⅜ inch wide, and, as we all know from our home and car stereos, the tape can be recorded and played back on both sides. Thus there are up to four tracks of information crunched onto the small tape area. This is why cassette stereo units produce some noise and hiss and why the better ones allow for noise-reduction options (such as Dolby B and Dolby C).

Why is it useful to know how phonographs and tape recording works? A basic understanding of audio technology adds much to our study of the radio industry. Our entire broadcast history was preserved on records, audio-, and videotape. These older analog technologies are frequently referred to as "legacy" devices, and you may still see them in radio and television stations.

Digital Electronics As a trip to the nearest electronics store confirms, there has been a revolution in audio in recent years. Recordings and magnetic tapes have given way to compact discs (CDs), audio DVDs, MP3 players, and the minidisc (MD).

Digital audio was made possible by the development of a new means of signal generation, known as **pulse code modulation** (PCM). This and other modulation methods are seen in Figure 3–3. At the top of the figure is the original waveform: the shape of the original sound we seek to record and reproduce. Let's say for this example, it's the sound of a guitar string being plucked. Below the waveform is its shape, transduced into an AM signal. Like a surfer on a wave, its new shape is a series of peaks and valleys, or changes in amplitude. In essence, the amplitude of the carrier changes with the variations of the plucked guitar string. Below that is the same waveform transduced into an FM signal. Now the message is in the form of a series of changes in the number of times it occurs over a period of time (in this case let's say in 1 second)—that is, its frequency. At the bottom is the waveform translated into a digital signal. By sampling the amplitude of the wave many thousands of times each second (by turning a laser beam on and off

Figure 3–3

Modulation Methods

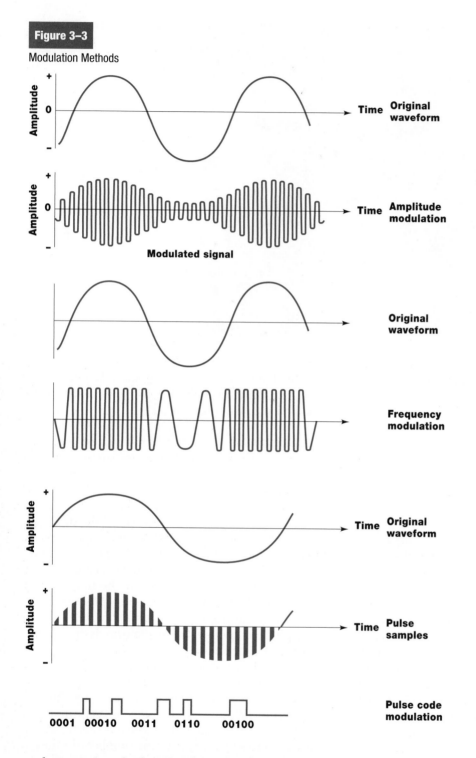

and measuring the length of the light beam at each interval), a digital version of the wave could be produced. This process is called pulse code modulation.

Foremost, unlike an analog signal, a digital wave is virtually constant—it is the identical shape on recording, on transmission, going into the amplifier, and coming out of the speakers. Second, unlike tapes and standard phonograph records, if the digital device can "read" the file successfully, all the original information will be preserved and the original sounds will be reproduced in a noise-free environment.

CDs As we mentioned previously, the information on a compact disc (CD) is carried beneath the protective acrylic coating in a polycarbonate base. In the base is a series of pits and flats. The pits vary in length in precise correspondence to the waveforms they represent. The flats represent no waveforms: utter silence. As the disc rotates, a laser beam is focused on the disc. Like a mirror, when the beam "sees" a pit, it reflects back a light wave that contains data about the original sound wave. Now, using a digital-to-analog converter and other electronics, the data are collected and transduced into an electrical signal through amplifiers and into speakers. The result is a clean, nearly perfect sound. In technical terms, the frequency response for CDs ranges from 20 to 20,000 hertz (remember, the best LP record ranges from 50 to 15,000 hertz), and CDs have a signal-to-noise ratio of 90 decibels (compared with about 60 decibels for records), the common measure of the intensity of sound, which is pretty darn good.

Unlike with records and tapes, there is no friction or wear. Discs are comparatively immune from damage in routine handling and storage, but they can

Ethics: Negativland—Digital Artists or Rip-Off Artists?

Digital sampling techniques allow virtually any sound or image to be reproduced and rerecorded, thereby raising a critical ethical dilemma. Is it ethical to borrow musical phrases from one song and then combine them with pieces of other songs without the original copyright owner's permission? Most performers and musicians argue that their work should be protected from such digital manipulation. Others argue that the technology has created a new art form. Composers should be free to use sounds and images from other works to create new ones, especially those that use the expropriated images for comedic or satirical purposes.

Negativland is one of those groups of new "composers." The "band," if you can call it that, exists by purloining the work of other artists and turning compilations of those bits of work into their own songs. Their albums make use of hundreds of digital samples—from familiar rock guitar riffs to snippets of conversations from TV talk shows to slogans and jingles from radio and TV advertisements. The results are mixed (pun intended), but when it works, the effect can be insightful and interesting.

Negativland spent nearly 25 years as part of San Francisco's vibrant underground, running a free-form radio show on Berkeley's edgy KPFA-FM. Things changed when the Irish supergroup U2 sued Negativland over the release of an album titled *U2*, which included a vicious parody of the supergroup's "I Still Haven't Found What I'm Looking For." The lawsuit has been detailed by Negativland in their book entitled *The Story of the Letter U and the Numeral 2.* Issues related to fair-use statutes in U.S. copyright law have been a concern for the group, and they have consistently advocated for reforms.

Never ones to shy away from issues related to modern culture, their CD *Dispepsi* made use of samples of dozens of soft drink ads to satirize the leading cola companies. Apparently Coke and Pepsi are too busy with their "Cola Wars," and have thus far failed to file suit.

Negativland caused quite a stir in late 1998 with the release of its CD with the not-so-clever title of *Over the Edge Volume 3—The Weatherman's Dumb Stupid Come-Out Line.* According to the band's co-leader Mark Hosler, five CD-pressing plants refused to manufacture the disc, apparently under pressure from the Recording Industry Association of America, and Disctronics, a plant in Texas, said it was refusing to make the CD since it might contain unauthorized sound clips.

In 2005 the group issued *No Business*, a CD/book that manipulates trademarked icons like Mickey Mouse, SpongeBob, Batman, and Starbucks. Still, despite mixed reviews from critics, the group performed a shortened version for the Duke University Conference on the Public Domain. Don Joyce, co-founder of the band, has said that *No Business* is certainly illegal with packaging that has a variety of trademark infringements all over it. Today's digital technology makes it easy to capture and manipulate the works of others. The question is whether groups like Negativland should be able to bend the law to make social statements about it. What do you think?

become scratched. With proper care, they should never warp, unwind, or jam in the player, and they cannot get accidentally erased.

Writable compact discs (CD-Rs), developed for the computer industry, have become standard features today on home computers and have the added ability to record audio signals. As peer-to-peer file sharing became popular on the Internet, CD-Rs came into their own. CD-Rs have helped popularize the MP3 format, which we'll discuss in a moment.

Digital versatile discs and Super Audio CDs   Digital versatile discs (DVDs) have become remarkably popular since their introduction in 1997. Most people think of DVDs for playback of movies, and prerecorded discs are capable of reproducing from one to six channels of audio or Dolby 5.1 surround sound (a theaterlike, multichannel sound experience). This makes it possible to playback movies encoded with Digital Theater Sound (DTS). However, a new audio format, DVD-A, has been established that allows multichannel audio playback and fidelity greater than the current CD format.

Fidelity greater than CDs? Some audiophiles claim that CDs are incapable of producing harmonics above the range of human hearing and that the sampling rate for CDs is inadequate, imparting a coarse, almost clinical sound. The new DVD-A format allows a wider band of frequencies to be recorded and with greater fidelity, 24-bit recording as opposed to 16 bits as currently used on CD (remember the bigger the digital word—24 bits as opposed to 16—the more data about the original signal is recorded). DVD-A discs are not compatible with older DVD players, and they won't play back on a standard CD player.

Super Audio CD (SACD) is another new format that has been developed in recent years. Like DVD-A discs, SACDs promise the highest-quality sound format, and they use a brand-new audio technology called Direct Stream Digital (DSD) encoding. Unlike DVD-A, CDs, and other digital technologies, SACDs do not use pulse code modulation. Instead, these new CDs use 1-bit sampling at amazingly high sample rates (more than 2.8 million samples per second). Some experts claim this new sampling technology gives SACDs a more realistic sound quality.

SACDs, like DVD audio discs, are capable of playing back DTS 5.1 multichannel sound. SACDs were invented by Sony and Philips, the two companies that originally invented the CD. While it's too early to tell whether there will be widespread acceptance of the

new audio format in the consumer marketplace, new high-definition (HD) radio may use these technologies to broadcast surround sound and multichannel audio.

Moving Picture Experts Group—Audio Layer III (MP3)
MP3 is the name for a recording compression technology that grew for file sharing and exchange on the Internet. It has quickly spread from college campuses to home audio systems. MP3 uses compression technology to eliminate inaudible frequencies as a way of shrinking the file size of an audio recording. This compression scheme, which made it possible to share audio files via the Internet, grew to be very popular by the year 2000. Compression technology makes it possible to squeeze thousands of songs onto tiny MP3 players. Today, many DVD players and personal CDs can play back the MP3 format. MP3 files come in a variety of quality standards, but the highest-quality MP3s (such as Apple's iTunes files) nearly equal the sound of CDs.

Some broadcasting stations have encoded music on computer drives using MP3 technology. The result is that it is possible to store hundreds of hours of music on several large computer hard drives. Today most stations use computers for music playback since special programs allow the program director to order music selections in accordance with the station's format.

Minidisc   In 1993, Sony introduced a compact digital replacement for cassettes called the **minidisc (MD).** The minidisc is about 2½ inches in diameter, just about one-quarter the size of a standard CD. Designed mainly as walkabout stereos, the MD eliminates the problem many portable CD players have had: skipping as a result of laser mistracking. MDs can record up to 74 minutes of music, and HD-MD discs can record up to 13 hours on one disc. Some minidisc machines can also read out text (liner notes, song titles, and so on), and they can be reused for recording numerous times. Like MP3s, minidiscs use compression technology for recording and playback.

While minidiscs have become fairly common in broadcasting stations as substitutes for analog cart machines and for radio news gathering, the minidisc has never really been accepted in the home marketplace.

Video Signal Generation

Television's ability to transmit images is based on the technology of scanning. The TV camera scans each element of a scene line by line; the picture tube

Figure 3–4

Examples of Scanning

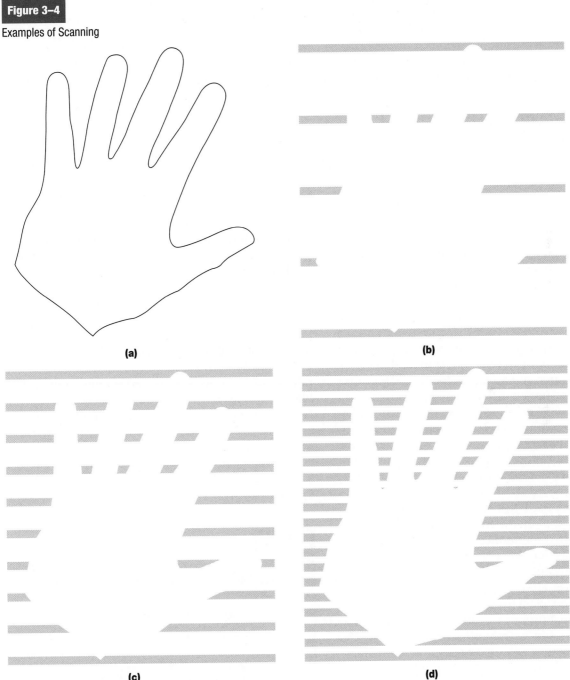

(a)

(b)

(c)

(d)

in your TV set retraces the scene. Earlier in the chapter we said tracing the outline of your hand is a way to create a facsimile representation of the hand on the sheet of paper, like the illustration in Figure 3–4(*a*). Let's change the game a little bit. Instead of drawing one continuous line, suppose we trace the hand by using a series of five parallel lines, as depicted in Figure 3–4(*b*). We move the crayon straight across. We lift it when it encounters the hand and return it to the paper when it passes by a "hand" area. The result is the rough facsimile of the hand in Figure 3–4(*b*). Now, let's use 10 lines instead of 5.

This tracing will provide a fairly good representation of the hand, as in Figure 3–4(*c*). Just for fun, let's alternate the tracing by doing every odd-numbered line first, then each even-numbered line. After two passes, top to bottom, the result is Figure 3–4(*d*). In this exercise we have actually demonstrated the workings of TV technology.

When done invisibly by the TV camera, the tracing process is called *scanning*. The process of alternating lines is known as the *interlace method*. And the process of replicating the scan on the picture tube to produce the image at home is known as *retracing*. The process originates in the TV camera and is re-created at home on the picture tube.

The Importance of Scanning

At this point you may feel saturated by needless technical information. Actually there are excellent reasons why this information is critical to understanding modern telecommunications.

Standardization

First is the issue of standards. There are a number of different television systems, and the number of lines utilized in the scanning process varies throughout the world. The United States now has several different standards for television. Our analog system uses a 525-line system adopted in 1941 by a group known as NTSC (National Television Systems Committee). The complete picture consists of a composite of two separate scans or **fields,** each consisting of 262½ horizontal scanning lines. The two fields combine to form a single picture, called the **frame.** In the United States, the AC power system we use oscillates at 60 hertz. Thus, our TV system uses a 60-hertz scanning rate. Since two fields are needed to produce one frame, 30 complete pictures are produced every second.

Much of European TV uses a system known as PAL (for phase alternating lines), adopted several years after the U.S. system. Based on the AC power available there, European TV uses a shorter scanning rate (50 hertz), but with more scanning lines (625). Many Americans are startled to see how clear European TV is; that's due to the fact that it has 100 more lines of resolution. However, European television is subject to some flicker, since the two picture fields are refreshed fewer times per second. France and Russia use yet a third system.

Beyond better picture quality, the issue of standardization involves a lot of other important matters. Televisions and VCRs produced for one system will not work on the other. The same is true for prerecorded videotapes; you can't bring a tape recorded in the United States to Europe and expect it to play.

Digital television and high-definition television

The scanning process is also directly involved in many of the newest technical innovations occurring in television today. Digital television (DTV) is the new standard being adopted by television stations around the country. DTV is actually a multiple-standard system that was devised through the collaboration of broadcasters and set manufacturers. There are 18 different formats that can be transmitted, but essentially most new DTV televisions convert them into either standard definition or high definition. **High-definition television (HDTV)** is the moniker for digital television utilizing either 720 or 1,080 scanning lines, producing an image rivaling 35-millimeter film in quality. But the new digital television system can transmit a *scalable* picture. That means that the quality of the transmission can be varied from 480 lines to 1,080 lines of resolution. DTV can also change the aspect ratio (the ratio of screen width to screen height) of conventional TV. In standard TV the screen is 4 units wide and 3 units high. In wide-screen, the ratio is 16:9 (16 units wide and 9 units high), much like the frames of a motion picture (see Figure 3–5). Television stations are able to change the resolution of the picture and the width of the screen to meet the needs of the programs transmitted.

As we trace in the "Television Today" chapter (Chapter 5), TV stations, networks, cable, and satellite systems are in the process of converting from the

Figure 3–5

The new wide-screen TV sets have an aspect ratio of 16:9 compared to an aspect ratio of 4:3 for tradional sets. The new aspect ratio is closer to the dimensions of a theater screen.

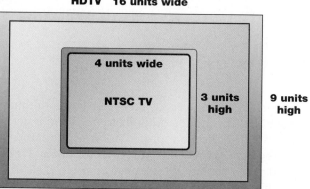

60-year-old 525-line system to the new digital system. Many TV stations across the nation have already begun the transition to DTV. NFL games, the *Tonight Show, 24, CSI,* and many prime-time TV shows are already being transmitted in the digital format. Mark your calendars: The FCC has called for a complete transition to DTV by February 17, 2009.

The switch to DTV is actually quite complex and involves three standards for resolution (number of lines), several sets of frames, and two scanning methods. The new DTV sets are able to tune in TV signals using 480, 720, and 1,080 lines, all of which have much higher fidelity than traditional analog 525 NTSC (because there's less noise in the picture). And the picture can be scanned in 24, 30, or 60 frames per second. Finally, the new TV signals can be sent every other line (the traditional interlace method) or line by line—an alternative scanning method known as progressive scan, which most computers use.

So what difference does this make? Plenty. Using 480 lines (and only a portion of the channel allocation) allows TV stations to *multicast;* that is, they can send more than one program over the same channel allocation at the same time but not in high definition. One station might actually transmit as many as four or five different programs on one 6-megahertz television channel. Broadcast TV is touting this multicasting feature so it can compete more successfully with its cable competitors, which have made multiple versions of their channels available for some years now (like ESPN, ESPN2, and ESPNews). A local television station could start its own all-local news program service, for instance, and still broadcast the network program feed on the same channel. And using the progressive scan method brings TV much closer to the computer business, which has used progressive scan on its monitors for years now. Some large, flat-screen displays would be able to be used for both progressive scan television and computer images.

Beyond the picture quality, DTV is capable of broadcasting in surround sound and could also provide the home user with a data stream information channel, providing both picture and interactivity. And consider this: Now that the new TV system can use progressive scanning and is a digital signal, it may be possible to marry the home computer and the home entertainment center into one unit in the future.

Closed captioning   Closed captioning is a technology that uses the blanking period between scans (called the *vertical blanking interval*) to send additional

Wide-screen (16:9) HDTV sets are now becoming more commonplace in the home.

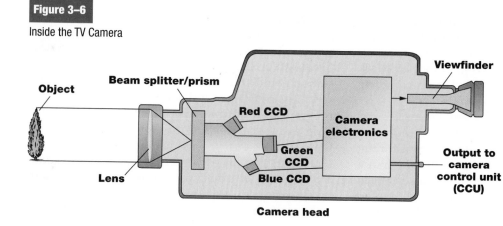

Figure 3–6

Inside the TV Camera

information with the TV signal. Appropriate decoders provide captions for deaf viewers or specialty text services, such as news capsules or stock market reports, to specially equipped TV sets.

Inside the Camera: Pickup Device   We already know that the purpose of scanning is to transduce physical light into electronic signals. The process occurs inside the TV camera, as depicted in Figure 3–6.

The first step in creating TV is the collection of an image by a lens. Inside the TV camera the image is captured by a beam splitter and prism that break down the image into the primary colors of red, green, and blue. Attached to the prism are light-sensitive wafers called *charge-coupled devices (CCDs)*. Each of the red, green, and blue chips can sample 1 million picture elements in a manner not unlike the way a printing press uses dots to produce a color newspaper photo. The CCDs rasterize the red, green, and blue components of the picture by turning them into rows of individual dots that we call *pixels.* Here's how it works: When light passes through the beam splitter and hits the red (or blue or green) chip, it creates a charge that's proportional to the amount of light that strikes it. Each point that becomes charged becomes a pixel of information. Combining circuits in the camera overlay the red, green, and blue information to produce a full-color picture. These signals are extremely weak and need to be amplified by the camera electronics. A black line is added after each horizontal line and after each complete scan to allow the image to burn into our retina. These are known as the blanking pulses. The signal that exits the camera thus contains two sets of information: picture information plus blanking. At the camera control unit (CCU) or in the switcher, a third

signal (sync) is added. The synchronization pulse enables the output of two or more cameras and other video sources to be mixed together and allows all the scanning processes to take place at the same time, from camera to receiver.

In analog television, the complete TV picture of red, green, and blue scan lines, picture plus blanking plus sync, is known as the *composite video signal.* Digital television and DVDs frequently provide separate outputs of the color channel signals, known as *component video.* This provides better picture fidelity.

STEP 2: SIGNAL AMPLIFICATION AND PROCESSING

Now, we've successfully transduced sounds and pictures into electronic analog or digital signals. The next step is to boost those signals so that they can be transported from one place to another and to mix them with other sounds and images so we can hear more than one musical instrument or see a great football catch from many different angles. In engineering terms, we're talking about signal amplification, mixing, and processing.

Audio Amplification and Signal Processing

An **amplifier** is a device that boosts an electrical signal. Typically, in electrical circuitry the voltage or current of an input is increased by drawing on an external power source (such as a battery or an AC or DC transformer) to produce a more powerful output signal. Devices to perform this function range from the original vacuum tubes like De Forest's audion (which made radio and sound movies practical in the 1920s), to transistors (which emerged in the 1950s to enable manufacturers to reduce the size of radios and TVs), and finally to integrated circuits in the 1970s (which permitted "microelectronics").

Modern amplifiers may perform functions beyond increasing the power of the sound (or video) source. An **equalizer** is a special kind of amplifier that is frequency-dependent. This means that it can work to boost or reduce a specified range of frequencies while leaving others unaffected. Equalization, referred to as EQ by sound engineers and music trendies, enables a sound signal to be fine-tuned for its best tonal quality. For example, equalizers can be used to make bass (between 60 and 250 hertz) sound more fat, thin, or "boomy." An equalizer can also be used to boost vocal sections out of the "soup" of an orchestrated passage and even to isolate, diminish, or remove poor-sounding sections or mistakes in vocals or music. Once limited to expensive studios, EQ is now available in many home and car stereo systems. In fact, a tiny iPod has several equalization settings on it allowing you to change the tonal balance of the playback.

Rock bands may use amplification circuitry that allows for electronic special effects to be added.

These include reverberation, which is simply an echolike effect. Special amplifiers can create all sorts of effects, from echoes to "sing-along" doubling or tripling. They can even create artificial choruses and deep echo chambers. Other devices are available to play tricks on audio signals. Phasers (not the kind used by Kirk and Spock) and distortion boxes on guitars (for example) manipulate the phase relationship between frequencies to create fuzz tones, pitch changers, or other effects. Today computers can be manipulated to record sounds backward and to speed up or slow down recordings. In the 1950s and 1960s it was common practice for radio stations to use speeded-up recorders to rerecord popular songs so that they played more quickly, allowing for more commercial and promotion time.

Mixing Consoles and Control Boards   The next link in the audio production chain is the audio console, which combines sound sources into a single signal. In radio and TV stations the console is generally referred to as an *audio board*. In recording studios and motion picture sound studios, it is commonly known as the *mixing console*. Regardless of its name, the console is the central nervous system of the audio

Modern radio production boards use slide faders to control audio levels from various input sources.

facility. Today consoles are likely to be either analog or digital. It is the place where all audio signals are inputted, selected, controlled, mixed, combined, and routed for recording or broadcast transmission. Let's examine each of these phases individually.

The first function of the board is to accept (input) sound sources. A major-market radio station may have several computers for playing back music and commercial messages, several CD players or digital cart machines, and perhaps five or more microphones spread among several studios but capable of being interconnected. A recording studio is even more complex.

The board usually consists of a number of sliding faders that control the sound level. Ten-, 12-, and 24-input boards are common. Some inputs correspond to one and only one sound device. Others use select switches and routing devices to allow for a single input to control as many as four or five different sound signals.

Each input is controlled by a sliding bar called a *fader.* By using the fader, the board operator can adjust the sound level of each studio input. More elaborate boards allow for equalization and special effects to be controlled at this stage as well. Consoles also allow for each source to be measured or metered and for the outputs of various signals to be amplified similarly.

Sitting at one location, the audio person can combine and compose the overall sound of a performance, which is called the *mix.* All the various audio sources are combined together, sometimes in a single (monaural) mix for AM radio but more commonly in a two-channel (stereo) mix where the different instruments are placed left, right, or in the middle of the sound field. Today a five- or six-channel mix may be done for a surround sound high-definition program or a movie soundtrack. The resulting mixes are recorded on a computer using special audio recording software or broadcast live to viewers and listeners at home.

Desktop Audio   As you might have guessed, today's high-memory, fast computers can perform the same audio tricks as can the largest, most sophisticated mixing consoles. With a microphone, a sound card, and a fast hard drive, many home computers can be turned into fully functional sound studios. In fact, computers are probably the most common recording device in radio and television today.

The result is a revolution in audio signal processing. Many radio executives have converted their

stations into "tapeless" radio stations, where the announcing, music, amplification, and mixing are done on a desktop computer.

One company, Radio Computing Services (RCS) of Scarsdale, New York, calls its desktop system Master Control and touts it as the "paperless, tapeless, all-digital studio." In its system, all audio signals—jingles, commercials, musical selections, even telephone calls from listeners—are stored on computer hard drives. There are no tape machines, CDs, or turntables. In essence, an entire radio station is converted into a network of desktop computers. The jock doesn't even have to be in the same city as the radio station since the system can send and receive the voice tracks as sound files over the Internet.

Video Amplification and Processing

You're watching a live newscast, but before the TV signal travels from the camera to the transmitter, several things happen. First, the electrical signal is amplified—increased in electrical intensity—and carried along a wire to a monitor, within a video control room where it is viewed by the director and other production personnel. In most TV programs the cameras and other video input sources (tape machines, video servers, computers, the graphics generator, and so on) are mixed together before they are transmitted. The **switcher,** a device used for mixing TV signals, is probably the first thing a visitor to a TV control room notices. The advanced models are impressive-looking devices consisting of several rows of buttons and numerous levers. A television director uses a switcher to put the desired picture on the air. If camera 3 shows what the director wants to see, then pushing the appropriate button on the switcher puts camera 3 on the air. If video server 4 has the desired instant replay, then pushing another button puts it on the air.

The switcher also lets the director choose the appropriate transition from one video source to another. Simply punching another button generates what's known as a *cut*—an instantaneous switch from one picture to another. By using a fader bar the director can dissolve from one picture to another or fade an image to or from black.

If a special-effects generator is added, a host of other transitions is possible. One picture can wipe out another horizontally, vertically, or in many other patterns. A split screen with two or more persons sharing the screen at the same time is possible, as is **keying,** an effect in which one video signal is electronically cut out or keyed into another. The most common use of this process is **chromakey.** A specific color (usually blue or green) drops out of one picture and another picture is seen everywhere that color appeared in the original picture. Weathercasters, for example, usually perform in front of a blue background, which is replaced by keyed-in weather maps or other graphics. (Performers must be careful not to wear clothing that is the same color as the chromakey blue, or they will appear transparent on screen.)

Digital Video Effects   As might be expected, digital technology has had an immense impact on video processing. Each TV signal can be converted into a series of binary code numbers that can be manipulated and then reconverted back into a TV signal. There are numerous types of digital video effects, or DVE, in industry parlance. They include freeze-framing, shrinking

images in size and positioning them anywhere on the screen (as happens when an anchor talks to a field reporter and both pictures are kept on screen), stretching or rotating a video picture, producing a mirror image, and wrapping the picture into a cylindrical shape.

Desktop Video   Until the late 1980s, generating video special effects required large, expensive processing equipment. Only a few big-city TV stations and production centers had the capability to produce digital video (DV).

In the early 1990s computer companies merged the video signal with the personal computer. As if to underscore the low cost and simplicity of these new technologies, one common setup was known as a "video toaster."

Today, the digital revolution is in full swing. Video can even be produced on powerful laptop computers; Apple Computer's Final Cut Pro and Avid's Express

Video inputs are mixed together in the television control room.

As soon as the Web became popular, an interesting voyeuristic technology took off: the webcam. The concept was simple. You simply hooked a video camera to your computer and streamed the output directly to the Web.

Soon a number of sites took off showing people living their lives in front of the camera. Some sites were free, and others, ones with more prurient views, charged a fee. Since their invention webcams have become part of the Internet world, allowing us views into exotic as well as fairly mundane places. WebCam Central allows you to search by category or location or choose random sites. You might find a webcam showing a view of the great pyramids or another illuminating a computer lab at some university, a view of Sydney's Harbor or the view of a mall's foodcourt in Newark, New Jersey (really). Amazing webcams allows you to search by continent. (There are actually seven webcams for Antarctica!)

Finally, technology has allowed us to make the webcam mobile. Suncam TV broadcasts live views from an SUV in Florida, even during hurricanes. As mobile technology improves, it's likely we'll see more webcams and phone cams showing us more of the world. Some of it is bound to be mundane, but some of it will provide us with unique views.

software provide professional video editing capabilities in systems that interact with DV camcorders and other production devices. Advances in high-speed, high-capacity hard disks and DVD drives allow the storage and retrieval of still and moving images. Other software can be used to produce dazzling titles and graphics. As a result, the kind of spectacular visuals once reserved for music videos with huge budgets, or for the promotional messages of the major networks, can now be produced by anyone with a broadcast-quality camcorder linked to a PC.

STEP 3: SIGNAL TRANSMISSION

We've now succeeded in selecting sounds and pictures, changing them from physical energy into electronic signals, and amplifying and mixing them. The next step is to take them from point A to point B. Broadcasting is really the process of signal transmission. As we read in the history chapter, the modern age of broadcasting began when scientists and inventors became able to do this over the air, without wires. Ironically, as we move comfortably into the new century, we are now trying to do it all over again by wire (over cable and the Internet) and by wireless (using wireless local area networks to mobile devices). But let's not get ahead of the story.

Audio Transmission

As Chapter 1 described in detail, the radio pioneers found that electrical signals created by human beings could be transported across space so that buttons pushed here could cause a buzz over there.

They soon replaced signals and buzzes with a voice at both ends.

The Electromagnetic Spectrum   This magical process was made possible by the discovery and use of the **electromagnetic spectrum,** the electromagnetic radiation present throughout the universe. Figure 3–7 is a chart of the spectrum. A fundamental component of our physical environment, electromagnetic radiation is traveling around and through us at all times. We can see some of it (the narrow band of frequencies corresponding to visible light and color, or the "heat waves" that radiate off a parking lot in the summertime). But most of the spectrum is invisible to the naked eye and must be detected by human-made devices (like radio and TV receivers).

In the past century we have learned how to superimpose, or "piggyback," our own electronic signals on the electromagnetic waves that exist in nature, a process known as **modulation.** This is done by generating a signal that is a replica of the natural wave. This signal, produced by a radio station on its assigned frequency, is called a **carrier wave.** It is "heard" on our radios as the silence that comes just before the station signs on in the morning or after the national anthem at sign-off. The radio signal is created by varying the carrier wave slightly, in correspondence with the frequencies of the signals we mean to transmit. Our tuner, tuned to the precise middle of the carrier, interprets these oscillations and reproduces them as sounds in the speaker system. If this process seems hopelessly complex, consider this metaphor. Suppose there is a natural rock formation in the shape of a bridge. Adding a bed of concrete atop the formation,

The Electromagnetic Spectrum

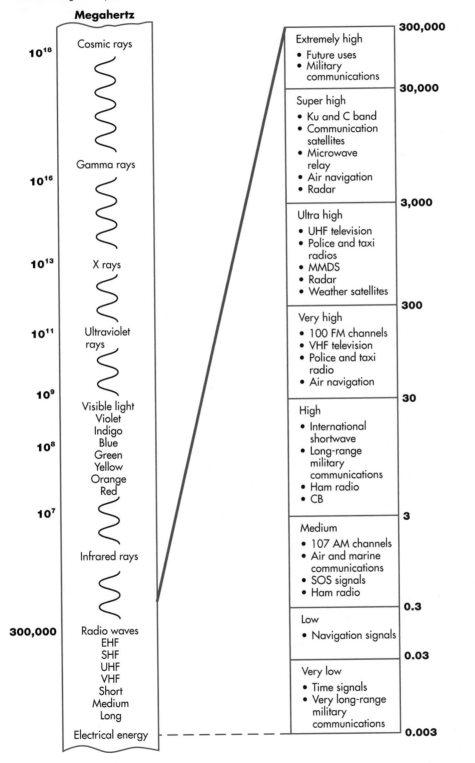

we have propagated a carrier wave. When we ride a car across the bridge, we have superimposed a signal, or modulated the carrier wave.

Radio Frequencies   Only a small part of the electromagnetic spectrum is utilized for AM and FM broadcasting and related transmissions. This range spans from long waves of very low frequency to extremely short waves of relatively high frequency. In general, the higher one goes in the spectrum, the more sophisticated the electronics needed in the modulation process. Unlike AM and FM, new satellite radios use very high frequencies beamed from a geostationary satellite to your car or home. Pretty amazing.

Each new development in electronic media has taken us higher in the spectrum. Radio broadcasting began toward the low end of the spectrum, in the area ranging from 0.3 to 3 megahertz (mega = million), a region known as the medium waves. Included in this region is the range of 550 to 1,605 kilohertz (kilo = thousand), which is the range of the AM radio dial. In fact, in many countries AM is still referred to as the medium-wave (MW) band.

The high frequencies (which, with satellite and infrared communications, actually aren't so high anymore) range from 3 to 30 megahertz. These waves are utilized for long-range military communications, CB, and ham radio. Since high-frequency waves can be used to transmit signals over greater distances than can medium waves, this part of the spectrum has been used for over 50 years by international shortwave stations such as the BBC and the Voice of America. The shortwave band on a radio is sometimes labeled HF, for high frequencies.

The next group of radio waves used for telecommunications applications is the very high frequencies, or the VHF band. VHF ranges from 30 to 300 megahertz. Television stations operating on channels 2 to 13, FM radio stations, police radios, and airline navigation systems are located in this band.

Above the VHF channels are the ultra-high frequencies, or the UHF band, spanning the region from 300 to 3,000 megahertz. This part of the spectrum is used for TV stations 14 to 83, including most of the new digital TV stations, police and taxi mobile radios, radar, and weather satellites. In addition, it is UHF radiation that is modulated to cook our food in microwave ovens.

Much of recent telecommunications development has occurred in the next two radio bands: super-high frequencies (SHF) and extremely high frequencies (EHF). SHF spans from 3,000 to 30,000 megahertz and EHF from 30,000 to 300,000 megahertz. Commercial satellites—which deliver pay cable channels, superstations, advertiser-supported cable networks, and satellite news—emanate from these bands, as do new developments in digital audio broadcasting, military radar, and air navigation.

Spectrum Management   Keeping track of all these uses of the electromagnetic spectrum is difficult and requires substantial domestic and international regulation, a process known as *spectrum management.* In the United States, decisions regarding which services operate in which regions of the spectrum, and at what operating power, are handled primarily by the Federal Communications Commission (FCC) and, to a lesser extent, the National Telecommunications Information Administration (NTIA). Here's how broadcast radio and TV service is administered in the United States.

Radio channel classifications   At the latest count more than 13,700 radio stations were on the air in the United States. Yet there are only 117 AM channels and 100 FM channels. How is this possible? The answer is spectrum management. By controlling operating hours, power, antenna height and design, and other factors, the FCC squeezes all radio stations into the 217 channels. If you can imagine 13,700 cars competing for 200 parking spaces (kind of like the first day of classes), you have a sense of the task at hand.

- *AM channels and classifications.* The 117 AM channels are divided into three main types: 60 are clear channels, 51 are regional channels, and the remaining 6 are local channels. Here's how the system works: The clear channels are frequencies that have been designated by international agreements for primary use by high-powered stations. Such stations use ground waves in daytime and sky waves at night to reach a wide geographic area, often thousands of miles. The United States has priority on 45 clear channels. Stations on these frequencies include some of our oldest and strongest. Class A stations, like WABC in New York at 770 kilohertz, WJR in Detroit at 610 kilohertz, KFI (640 kilohertz) in Los Angeles, and KMOX (1120 kilohertz) in St. Louis, have the exclusive right to the clear channel after sunset. They operate at high power, from 10,000 to 50,000 watts. Class B stations use either clear channel or regional channel frequencies, but many must operate at reduced power at night to avoid interference. Their power outputs range from 5 to 50 kilowatts. Class C stations are designated as local stations. Ranging in power from 250 to 1,000 watts, Class C's must share channels with numerous other stations. To do this they generally use directional antennas and strategic placement to blanket their main population areas. Over 2,000 Class C stations share six local channels. These stations are mostly at the right or top end of the dial (above 1,230 kilohertz).

- *FM channels and classifications.* In 1945 the FCC set aside the region from 88 to 108 megahertz for FM. This allowed room for 100 channels, each 200 kilohertz wide. This means that when your FM radio is tuned to 97.3 the station is actually radiating a signal oscillating from 97.2 to 97.4 megahertz. Of the 100 channels, 80 were set aside for commercial use. The remaining 20 channels, located from 88 to 92 megahertz, were reserved for educational and noncommercial stations.

To facilitate the development of commercial FM, the FCC divided the United States into three regions. Zone I includes the most densely populated area of the United States: the Northeast. Zone I-A covers the southern California region. The rest of the country composes Zone II. FM stations also use A, B, and C designations. Class A FM stations operate in all zones, Class B's in Zone I, and Class C's only in Zone II.

Each class is defined by its effective radiated power (ERP), the amount of power it is permitted to use. Class C FMs are the medium's most powerful. They can transmit up to 100,000 watts (ERP). They may erect transmitters with a maximum height above average terrain (HAAT) of 600 meters. Class B's can generate up to 50,000 watts ERP at 150 meters HAAT, and Class A's are authorized to a maximum of 3,000 watts ERP at 100 meters HAAT. Unlike AM radio, both FM and television signals must have a line of sight in order to be received. As a result, the height of the transmitter above average terrain is an important consideration for how far the signal will travel. At maximum power and antenna height, Class C's can cover about 60 miles, Class B's about 30, and Class A's up to 15. In January 2000, the FCC created a new low-power service, limiting stations to a maximum of 100 watts ERP with an antenna height of 30 meters HAAT. These new low-power stations have a coverage radius of approximately 3.5 miles and are available only as a noncommercial service.

Sidebands and subcarriers The bandwidth of FM (200 kilohertz) allows these stations to transmit more than one signal on their channel. Such signals use the area above and below the station's carrier frequency, known as the *sideband.* The most common use of the sideband is to disseminate separate signals for the left and right channel to broadcast stereo. This is called **multiplexing.** If you have an old FM stereo receiver, it may be labeled "FM multiplex."

FM station operators may use additional spectrum space to send multiplex signals, which can be tuned only by specially designed receivers. To do this, stations apply to the FCC for a subsidiary communications authorization (SCA). Such services include the "background" music one hears in malls and elevators, a Talking Book service for the blind, telephone paging, data transmission, and special radio services for doctors, lawyers, and some others.

Although technically the process is not the same, AM stations can use their carrier waves for other purposes as well. Many AM stations transmit a subaudible tone used in utility load management. A subscriber, such as a business, rents a special receiver. During peak electric use hours the station transmits a tone that turns off the subscriber's appliances. When the peak load period is over, another subaudible tone turns them back on.

Digital radio In 2003, a new hybrid digital radio was approved for general broadcasting. Digital AM and FM radio transmissions are encoded within the sidebands of the radio channel. These new services allow a radio station to send entirely different analog and digital programs to listeners. And because the program is digital, like CDs, it is unaffected by static and other problems that plague analog transmission. Digital AM broadcasts will be closer to full fidelity than current analog AM signals and digital FM will be equal to satellite radio–quality broadcasts. Both AM and FM digital broadcasts will be able to show data information such as song titles and artists. This will allow local broadcasters to compete more effectively with satellite radio.

Video Transmission

As might be expected, the TV signal, with its complex set of information (including picture, sound, color, blanking, and synchronization signals), requires enormous amounts of space in the electromagnetic spectrum. More than any other reason, this explains why there are over 13,000 radio stations but only about 1,700 TV stations on air in the United States.

The Television Channel   Each TV station, both analog and digital, requires a bandwidth of 6 megahertz. This is equivalent to enough space for 30 FM radio stations and 600 AM stations!

The NTSC system was perfected in the 1930s and 1940s when amplitude modulation (AM) techniques were considered state-of-the-art. For this reason it was decided to transmit the TV picture information via AM. Two-thirds, or 4 megahertz, of the TV bandwidth is used for picture information. Interestingly enough, interlace scanning was chosen as a way to conserve bandwidth. The sound signal is essentially a full-range FM, or frequency-modulated, signal, oscillating at 25 kilohertz above and below its center (carrier) frequency. The remainder of the video channel is occupied by protective guard bands that keep the various encoded signals from interfering with one another.

TV Allocations   The complexity of the TV signal and its vast need for space caused the FCC in the 1940s and 1950s to assign it a place higher in the electromagnetic spectrum than any that had been utilized in prior years.

Channels 2 to 13 are located in the **very high frequency (VHF)** portion of the spectrum, the area ranging from 54 to 216 megahertz. Interestingly, a sizable portion of the VHF band is not used for TV purposes. The area between channels 6 and 7 includes the space for all FM radio stations as well as aircraft-control tower communication, amateur or "ham" radio, and business and government applications.

Channels 14 to 83 lie in the **ultra-high frequency (UHF)** portion of the band, the region between 470 and 890 megahertz. There is another gap, this time between channels 13 and 14, which is reserved for government communications.

VHF stations 2 through 6 can achieve excellent coverage transmitting at a maximum of 100 kilowatts. Channels 7 to 13 require power up to a ceiling of 316 kilowatts. However, channels 14 and above need power up to 5,000 kilowatts to generate an acceptable signal (the UHF maximum is 10,000 kilowatts). In addition, more sophisticated antenna arrays are required. So viewers often have difficulty locating UHF stations on their dial, and, once stations are located, tuning and maintaining a clear signal can also be problematic. The FCC's freeze on

new stations from 1948 to 1952 (discussed in Chapter 1) also hurt UHF's development. The existing stations were all VHFs and had established loyal audiences before UHF even got started.

For these technical and historical reasons VHF stations have tended to travel "first class" in the TV business, while UHF properties have typically been relegated to the "coach" section.

From NTSC to ATSC: Digital TV Channels   The end is near for analog! In 2006, Congress told the FCC to finalize its plans for the transition from analog to digital television broadcasting. Previously, each existing TV station had been given a second UHF channel, 6 megahertz wide, to use for its new digital broadcasts, and most broadcasters are now broadcasting in both analog and DTV. The new digital channel allocations are 2 through 36 and 38 through 51. Once the conversion takes place, the old remaining TV channels 52 through 69 will be auctioned for other purposes.

The transmissions standards that we discussed earlier in this chapter were set by an industry group—the Advanced Television Standards Committee (ATSC)—in the mid-1990s. (For engineering and computer fans, the standard uses the MPEG-2 video compression format and the 8-VSB modulation format.) To speed the transition to DTV, the FCC mandated that all new televisions manufactured after March 1, 2007, must be able to receive digital television signals, even if the television is standard-definition TV. In addition, a timetable was set for TV stations to move from analog to digital. Congress set February 18, 2009, as the deadline when all full-power television stations will cease broadcasting an analog signal; however, low-power television stations will be converted to digital transmission at a later date.

Satellite Transmission

A common sight on lawns, homes, and businesses is the satellite dish, which has become an important means of radio and television transmission. These dishes are all pointed up to the sky to one or more of the dozens of communications satellites in orbit about 22,000 miles above the earth. These satellites are launched into an orbit that moves at the same rate as the earth rotates, a technique known as **geosynchronous orbit.** For all intents and purposes, the satellites are "parked" in their unique orbital slots.

Satellite Terminology Satellite technology has introduced a new vocabulary into telecommunications. Because of the complexity of their operations, the amount of information they carry, and the power needed to send a signal through the earth's atmosphere and back, satellites operate in the **super-high frequency (SHF)** portion of the electromagnetic spectrum. Technically speaking a satellite is a *transponder.* Satellites receive their signals from a ground station, which is called an *uplink.* The satellite then amplifies the signal and rebroadcasts it to a downlink (like a TV station or cable head-end) or in the case of DBS to a home receiver. Just as new developments led radio and TV to move up the spectrum, the same has happened in satellite communications. The first geosynchronous satellites were assigned to the area ranging roughly from 4 to 6 gigahertz (gHz, or billions of cycles) in an area known as the *C band.* Newer, more-powerful satellites operate from 12 to 14 gigahertz, a region known as the *Ku band.*

Direct Broadcast Satellite The year 1994 saw the launch of a new form of communications, known as **direct broadcast satellite (DBS).** DBS makes use of higher-powered satellites with a much larger footprint than traditional C- and Ku-band "birds" (as satellites are sometimes called). In addition, rather than needing a 3-meter dish (the size you see in some backyards),

DBS receivers are only 18 inches wide. They can be made to work successfully on a rooftop or window ledge, much like the TV aerials of yesteryear.

DBS satellites use MPEG-2 and MPEG-4 compression to send signals to home receivers. Data rates are fairly high, enabling a home to have several receivers tuned to different channels simultaneously.

Marketed by such firms as DirecTV and The Dish Network, DBS has enjoyed widespread consumer acceptance. Today DBS reaches one in four TV households. One of the newest wrinkles in DBS technology is the use of spot beams to deliver local television channels to satellite viewers. Newer DBS systems can receive signals from several satellites simultaneously, making reception of both standard-definition and high-definition signals possible.

Digital Audio Broadcasting If we can get direct satellite-to-home TV, why can't we also get direct satellite-to-car radio? Well, we can. **Digital audio broadcasting (DAB)** combines the technique of digital compression (advanced audio compression, or AAC), which made MP3 audio practical and popular, with super-high-frequency transmission (such as that used for satellites and microwaves). The result is CD-quality sound from a home or car radio without the need for records, tapes, discs, or your local radio station.

Modern computers can function as digital workstations.

In 1997, the FCC auctioned off part of the spectrum to two companies, and five years later they began beaming digital audio to cars and homes. XM and Sirius Radio transmit all-digital radio services to subscribers across America, and both services offer nearly 150 channels of unique programming and traffic information. XM beams its signals to customers from two geosynchronous satellites (appropriately named *Rock* and *Roll*), while Sirius uses three satellites that rotate in an elliptical orbit. The satellites transmit in the 2.3 gigahertz digital audio radio service (DARS) band. A small car-phone-sized antenna that fits unobtrusively on the roof of an automobile is used to receive the services.

Back to the Future: The Return to Wired Communications

As we traced in Chapter 1, the modern era of broadcasting began with the liberation of the telegraph by Marconi's wireless. Ironically, a century later, much of the change in contemporary telecommunications is due to the return to prominence of wired communications. This trend is led by the phenomenal growth of cable television and the rise of the Internet.

Cable Transmission   Shortly after World War II a new type of cable, called *coaxial cable,* was developed to support the burgeoning telephone industry. In addition to handling thousands of simultaneous telephone conversations, this cable was soon found to be an excellent conduit for disseminating TV signals. Since then, cable TV has become an increasingly widespread and important means of TV signal carriage.

Coaxial cable, or "coax" for short, consists of two electronic conductors. At the center is a copper wire shielded by a protective insulator called the *dielectric*. Outside the dielectric is a wire mesh, typically made of copper or aluminum. This conductor is shielded by a durable plastic coating, the outer body of the cable. This design gives the cable some special properties. The shielding keeps the signals within a confined space, reducing the electrical interference common in normal wiring (like that in household appliances) and extends the cable's life. Coaxial cable can also carry its own power source, which allows signals to travel comparatively long distances with little signal loss or noise.

Over the years, as the materials used to make coaxial cable improved, the number of TV signals transmittable by cable increased. In the 1950s cable TV systems could carry only three to five TV signals. Transistorized components and new cable materials raised cable channel capacity to 12 channels. The cable explosion in the 1970s came about as further technical refinements allowed cable systems to carry as many as 60 TV channels, as well as a range of other services (FM radio to data, text, and so on).

As you can see, local cable operators can exert a kind of media power that broadcasters cannot. Within certain limits (see Chapter 5), they—not the FCC—can control where a given TV station is placed on the cable. In addition, cable systems can reuse their own frequencies simply by installing two cables side by side. Moreover, a cable company can construct a system that allows communication from the receiver to the headend, enabling two-way, or interactive, communication. Newly introduced digital cable uses digital compression techniques to increase the channel capability of coaxial cable even more, making on-demand, pay-TV options and multiple programming sources (HBO1, ESPN2, etc.) a reality. Digital cable systems boast more than 200-channel capacity, although the technology is capable of providing even more channels in the future.

Another advantage of cable is addressability, the ability of a cable system to send a program to some houses that request it and to not send it to those that don't. Addressability is important in the development of pay-per-view TV, where only a portion of subscribers are willing to pay extra to watch a recent movie or sports event.

This flexibility accounts for cable's great expansion in recent years. Originally a source of improved reception of only three or four nearby TV stations, the cable has become a broadband source of local and regional broadcast stations, distant superstations, sports, movies, and other special-interest channels to more than two-thirds of the nation. The introduction of high-speed cable modems allowed cable to offer high-bandwidth Internet service in addition to cable programming, and now many cable systems are offering bundled telephone service (Voice over Internet Protocol, or VoIP).

For nearly half a century, two different wires connected most homes, for communications purposes. The common "twisted pair" brought telephone calls into and out of the home. The "coax" connected subscribing households to a cable television company. However, both telephone companies and cable systems are now installing a new kind of cable that allows the telephone companies to provide video service and the cable companies to handle telephone calls. Battle lines are forming due to this new means of video signal distribution.

Fiber Optics   Fiber-optic cable is a kind of "wireless wire." Instead of the copper and aluminum elements found in coaxial cable, fiber-optic cable contains strands of flexible glass.

Fiber-optic technology makes use of digital communications. That is, the electrical signals normally transmitted through conventional wire are converted into light pulses transmitted by a laser light source. These on-off (binary) pulses are decoded at the receiving source by a photodiode, a small, light-sensitive device. The process is similar to the way DVDs produce high-quality pictures and sound.

Fiber-optic cable has excellent potential in its applications to telecommunications. Electrical interference is nonexistent since there is no real electricity in the wire. Fiber is thinner and more flexible than coax, and perhaps most important, the bandwidth is

virtually limitless. On the downside, amplifying fiber-optic signals is hard to do, as is connecting and switching fiber-optic transmissions.

Fiber-optic technology is at the center of the struggle now emerging between the telephone and cable industries. Regional telephone companies are replacing their copper wires with fiber optics and have announced their intentions to offer video services in competition with cable. Cable companies have also been busy installing fiber in their operations. The benefits of fiber over the traditional copper cable are significant: clearer video and audio, low maintenance costs, and a virtually unlimited capacity for video and Internet services.

The pure, noise-free digital signal passing through the fiber connection into the home can be a telephone call, a radio show, a modem connection to the Internet, or a TV program. It should not be a surprise to the reader, then, that TV, cable, and telephone companies are in the process of entering each other's businesses to one degree or another.

STEP 4: SIGNAL RECEPTION

We've now modulated, amplified, mixed, and transmitted an audio or a video signal. The next step is reception: capturing that signal on a receiving device, such as a radio or TV set. As you might expect, the once-simple task of tuning a radio or dialing in a TV station has become quite complex. Just think of how many different remote control devices you own, or how many different entertainment boxes are connected to your TV set. Let's trace trends in some common audiovisual reception devices.

Radio Receivers

AM (MW) Band Receivers   The location of AM radio in the medium-wave part of the spectrum has several advantages. Long telescopic antennas are normally not needed, and a good signal may be received even when the radio is in motion. This makes AM ideal for car radios. AM radios can take almost any form, from microscopic transistor versions to large tabletop models. At night AM signals can travel hundreds of miles. While good reception should only be a matter of moving the receiver slightly for best tuning, the sad fact is that most AM radios are fairly inferior in design, making the radios sound worse than they should.

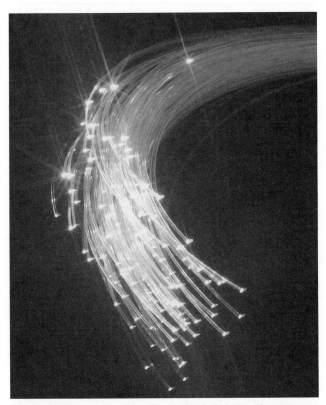

A fiber-optic bundle. Eventually fiber optics will replace the copper wires that now carry TV and telephone signals.

In addition, consider some of the disadvantages associated with AM: A check of the spectrum chart shows that the MW band is precariously close to the bandwidth of electrical energy. Thus AM radios are prone to interference and noise, heard mostly as static. In cars, energy produced by engines and electrical systems can often be heard on AM. At home, one can "hear" vacuum cleaners, lights turned on and off, and so forth. Buzzing and whining are often present as a result of carrier wave interactions with other AM stations. These distractions make AM difficult for serious listening.

Another limitation of AM reception has to do with its limited frequency response. As you know, AM stations generate signals in a bandwidth only 10,000 hertz wide. Recall that the human ear can hear a bandwidth about twice that. As a result, you may have noticed that AM sounds somewhat thinner or tinnier than FM (with a 15,000-hertz response). AM is best suited to speech and music of limited orchestration. Hence news/talk and sports tend to be popular AM formats; however, new high-definition digital AM transmission may bring quality music back to AM in the future.

FM Receivers The evolution of the FM receiver has followed an interesting path. From the beginning, the noise-free dynamic range of FM made it a natural element for the hi-fi enthusiast's home audio system. Thus many early FM tuners that had to be plugged into Dad's hi-fi system in the den. However, when FM stereo boomed in the late 1960s, consumers demanded FM in forms they had become familiar with in AM: in cars, transistor radios, table models, and so on. Thus most radios manufactured after 1970 were capable of both AM and FM reception. As a result, FM moved from an "add-on accessory" to the most important part of the radio receiver.

Since the FM signal requires a line of sight from transmitter to receiver, there are some potential pitfalls in signal reception. First, FM normally requires a long antenna, in the shape of a telescoping rod or a wire. The antenna needs to be directed for best results. FM signals tend to be blocked by buildings or moving objects with signals fading in and out in rural areas or in dense, city environments. Reception can also be improved by attaching the radio antenna to a TV antenna and in some areas by hooking the receiver to the cable TV system.

Moreover, multipath distortion is commonly experienced in cars when a station's signal is reflected off buildings or tall objects. Unlike the AM signal, this type of signal distortion is seldom heard as static. Instead, the distortion manifests itself as a blurring of the sound, sibilance, or a brittle sound. To solve this problem, the FM antenna needs to be redirected to minimize multipath.

Multiband Receivers Today virtually all radios offer both AM and FM bands. Recently the National Association of Broadcasters began pushing digital terrestrial radio, and we are beginning to see AM/FM HD radios being marketed by several manufacturers. Other receivers can monitor channels used by police and fire services, and some radios feature a weather band, capable of tuning in to the nearest government weather station. Weather radios can automatically turn themselves on to announce a weather alert and are very popular in the Midwest, where residents are subject to tornado warnings. Also popular are radios with "TV sound": These allow listeners to keep up with "soaps" and sports while at the beach or at work. Finally, many car radios are now being made with satellite reception capability in addition to AM and FM.

"Smart Radios"—Radio Broadcast Data Systems Digital technology makes possible a new generation of "smart" FM radio receivers. Using their subcarrier frequencies, FM stations can send information signals to the receivers. On such radio sets, a small display can provide a readout of the station's dial location, call letters, format, and even the name of the program.

These new smart radios are known as **radio broadcast data systems (RBDS)**. Advertisers are excited by one new feature called "coupon radio," which allows the listener to record information from the RBDS screen (such as a secret password) and use that information when making a purchase.

Satellite Radios Most automotive radio manufacturers now offer either XM or Sirius radios as options. As we noted in earlier chapters, satellite radio has about 13 million listeners and is growing. New models of satellite receivers can be used in boom boxes and in the home, extending the usefulness of the two services. XM has even introduced a satellite radio/MP3 player that allows the user to download favorite channels and then play them back on a music player about the size of an iPod.

TV Receivers

Improvements in our media devices usually are confined to making the items either grossly large or incredibly minute. For example, consider the contrast in radios between nearly piano-sized boom boxes and personal stereos custom-fit to the human ear canal. Changes in size and shape head the list of new developments in TV as the industry embraces HDTV.

Large-Screen TV In the early 1970s wall-sized TV screens began appearing in bars, nightclubs, and conference facilities. Today they are slowly creeping into the home video environment.

Large-screen TVs come in two main types. The first is the projection TV systems that beam the red, green, and blue elements that compose the color signal through special tubes to a reflecting screen suspended at a distance from the video unit. This is the type of system most commonly seen in sports bars.

The second type of large-screen TV that is rapidly gaining in popularity is the slim wall-mounted TV. These TVs are either plasma or LCD televisions. Unlike standard TVs, which are bulky and heavy, LCD or plasma TVs may be only a few inches thick, but they can produce startlingly excellent-quality pictures with extremely high resolution and vivid color. Both LCD and plasma TVs can act as computer monitors because they accept both digital and analog inputs. While they are way cool, they're also pricey.

Plasma screens are illuminated using tiny red, green, and blue fluorescent lights to form the image. Just like a standard television, the plasma display varies in intensity of color and brightness; however, plasma screens are made of thousands of tiny fluorescent lights that vary in proportion to the picture being displayed. Each fluorescent element is a plasma, a gas made from charged ions and negatively charged particles (electrons). When a signal is applied, the ions and electrons collide, releasing energy in the form of light.

Liquid crystal displays (LCDs) are different yet! Two thin membranes hold millions of liquid crystals in place, and as electric signals pass through the membranes, the liquid crystals interpret the signal as in either an ON or OFF state. In an ON state, they allow light to pass through them, and fluorescent tubes behind the membranes illuminate the image corresponding to the electrical signal.

Small-Screen TV For some TV enthusiasts smaller is better. These folks like to take the TV with them to the ball game, the beach, the office, or elsewhere. To satisfy this demand, manufacturers have introduced the visual equivalent of Sony's revolutionary Walkman radio design. Sony and its competitors, Casio and other Japanese manufacturers, have merged microprocessor technology and display expertise to produce smaller and smaller TV sets.

A couple of major problems have hindered the diffusion of this technology. For one thing, the screens are so small, they tend to produce very low light levels. Hence they can get drowned out by bright sunlight (a big limitation if you're at a day baseball game or the beach). Another fault is inherent in the medium: Unlike radio, a TV must be watched (at least some of the time) to be enjoyed. For obvious reasons the Watchman thus has limited success.

However, small DVD players have become popular additions to family minivans. Personal viewing screens are mounted behind the front console or on the ceiling, allowing families to watch their favorite movies while traveling along the highway. Also, portable DVD players are very popular with teenagers and frequent air travelers. These small players usually have a 7- or 8-inch screen and can play several DVDs on one battery charge.

Digital TV Sets How many times have you tried to watch two or three TV programs simultaneously? Using a remote control or nimble fingers, you flip continuously from one to the other—playing a sort of TV musical chairs—and end up missing the important parts of all programs. Well, if you're an inveterate flipper (like the authors), the digital receiver is for you. The integrated microchips that make tubeless cameras and micro-TVs practical have made it possible for the TV screen to display more than one channel at a time. The technique is known as *picture-in-picture (PIP)*.

Digital TVs also perform other electronic tricks. Suppose, when watching a baseball game, you decide to try to see the catcher's signs to the pitcher. Zoom allows you to fill the entire picture with just one small detail you would like to see, in this case the catcher's hands. To really get the sign, you can stop the picture momentarily, a technique known as *freeze frame*.

New midsized LCD screens are making an impact as well. These sets can be used for computers or as televisions. Perhaps one of the most striking aspects of LCDs is that they're only a few inches wide and can be easily mounted on your wall. LCDs come tailored for the 16-by-9 format, meaning you can watch TV or DVD movies in the wide-screen format, as they were meant to be viewed. Not all LCD televisions are high definition; however, some LCD TVs are called EDTV (meaning enhanced television). New sets by Sharp and Samsung come in sizes up to 40 inches wide, and some can actually display a split screen, half television and half computer. LCD prices have dropped dramatically in the last two years. The price ranges for LCD TVs start at $500.

STEP 5: STORAGE AND RETRIEVAL

The final step in audio and video technology is the storage and retrieval of sounds and moving images. As we all know, old programs never die: They live on forever in reruns. Some of the great growth industries in mass media in recent years are based on improved means of storing and accessing images, including the video store, nostalgic TV networks like Nick at Night, TV Land, and, yes, the Nostalgia Network. In fact, one of the benefits of the World Wide Web is that the content of all the memory of all the computers connected to the Internet is accessible to any single user. Increasingly, that content includes sounds and pictures, not merely text. Yet, not too long ago (in the 1940s and 1950s), radio and TV programs were still "live," as recording methods were noisy and inefficient. Even today, the complex signals involved in speech, music, motion pictures, and TV tax the storage and processing capacity of even the fastest microcomputers, so we're still a bit away from dialing up on our PC any movie ever made. Let's see where things stand with respect to radio and TV storage and retrieval.

Audio Storage

Phonograph Recording   The old standby, the phonograph record, has been around since the turn of the century. From that time, the sizes and speeds have been changed, but the basic design has remained consistent. Today, the most common record format is the 33⅓ revolutions per minute (rpm), 12-inch, high-fidelity recording. Few new records are issued each year, but many people still have record libraries.

Magnetic Tape Recording   The development of magnetic tape recording was revolutionary for both radio and TV. Unlike earlier recording methods, such as disc and wire recordings, magnetic tape was of very high fidelity. For all intents and purposes, radio and TV programs recorded on magnetic tape sounded just like they were "live." Tape recorders became the heart and soul of radio and TV operations.

Digital technology has all but replaced analog magnetic tape as the recording media of choice in broadcasting. However, some high-quality cassette recorders are still used by radio reporters to record meetings and to do interviews in the field.

While most manufacturers have pretty much abandoned production of analog tape recorders, many musicians and audio engineers prefer their rich, full sound when compared with the crisp, clean sound of digital recordings. Thus, reel-to-reel and cassette audio recorders promise to remain in use in recording studios for some time to come.

Video Storage

Magnetic Video Recording   As we stated in Chapter 2, the videotape recorder (VTR) made its network debut with *The CBS Evening News with Douglas Edwards* on November 30, 1956. But it hardly resembled today's tabletop VCR. (Pardon us as we romp through a brief Jurassic tape history.) For nearly 20 years, TV's tape machines were the size of a refrigerator-freezer and required four hands (two people) to operate them. The reels of tape, as big as 35-mm film canisters, were 2 inches across (thus, these were called 2-inch recordings). But they produced excellent, long-lasting copies of TV programs.

The next revolution in videotape recording was started by the Japanese. At the forefront of the emerging field of microelectronics, Sony technicians, in the late 1960s, perfected a means of storing the complex video signal on narrower tape, moving at slower speeds.

The idea was to stretch the magnetic tape around the revolving recording head so that there was virtually continuous contact between the tape and the recording head. For an analogy, imagine that instead of taking a single piece of chalk to one blackboard at the head of the class, your instructor had a piece of chalk in each hand and foot and was surrounded by a huge cylindrical blackboard. This technique became known as helical-scan tape recording, since the heads are positioned obliquely to the tape and the lines of picture information produced on the tape form the shape of a helix.

The birth of a standard: ¾-inch VTR

The helical-scan recorder had many advantages. Tape width shrank from 2 inches to ¾ inch, which had financial as well as technical advantages. The tape could be packaged in a protective case; thus the videocassette became popular. Most important, the size of the tape recorder shrank. In the early 1970s it became practical to send cameras and recorders into the field for coverage of breaking news and live sporting events. Although a number of helical-scan recorders had been introduced, by 1975 the industry had standardized. The 2-inch machine gave way to the ¾ -inch VTR.

The VTR was soon a fixture in TV production. After its introduction, recorders became small, portable, and usually dependable. Editing from one machine to another became easy, especially with the development of computer-assisted editing equipment. And the entire field of broadcast news changed: The era of electronic news gathering, or ENG, was launched.

Home video

In 1976 Sony introduced its first Betamax videocassette recorder (priced at a hefty $1,200); today the $49 home VCR has become the centerpiece of a revolution in the way we view TV.

The key was the development of high-density recording. Basically, the difference between broadcast-quality ¾-inch VTR and the ½-inch system introduced in the late 1970s is that the new system eliminated guard bands on the videotape, providing more room to store the picture signal on a reel of magnetic tape. Essentially, the VCR sacrificed some picture quality for smaller, lighter, and cheaper recorders with longer recording times. Clearly, the compromise was worth it: By 2002, more than 93 million U.S. homes (about 90 percent of all households) had acquired VCRs.

Initially there were two competing varieties of ½-inch helical-scan VCRs. Sony and its licensees used the Beta format; machines produced by Panasonic, JVC, and other manufacturers used VHS. For 10 years, a debate raged about which system was best; however, in the interim the American consumer had decided on the standard. Since more prerecorded tapes were available in the VHS format, by the mid-1980s the home market had more or less standardized in the VHS format.

Beta videotape didn't die off, however. A high-fidelity version, Beta-SP, became a vital part of professional TV production. At home, ½-inch tape was shrunk even further, into a compact version of VHS (VHS-C) and another popular Sony format, only 8 millimeters wide for small handheld camcorders.

Digital Video Recording

It should come as no surprise that the digital revolution sweeping the audio industry soon spread to television recording. The first wave of digital video recording was the appearance in the early 1990s of digital videotape. Today, many TV studios boast camera and editing systems that utilize digital videotape. Sony's system is easy to spot: Its equipment uses the DV prefix to denote digital videotape. DVC-Pro is the line of machines in widest distribution.

In a way, digital videotape is a hybrid recording system, combining the analog system of putting images on magnetic tape with the new digital sampling techniques. With the increasing processing and storage capacity of today's computers, it's possible to go all-digital. Why have tape at all? Why not store all the TV sounds and images on a computer server or a DVD or Blu-Ray recorder? More and more TV facilities, from CNN International to large-station newsrooms, have no VCRs in sight. Systems like Final Cut Pro and Avid Express have moved TV news and entertainment programming production from linear editing suites to nonlinear desktop computer consoles.

Digital Versatile Disc (DVD) and DVD Recording

The DVD playback format has become enormously popular since its introduction. Movie studios put extra features on DVDs and frequently release new movies on DVDs first, since the cost to produce DVDs is lower than videotape. It is no wonder that DVD recorders have being introduced into the marketplace by consumer electronics manufacturers. The recording devices are capable of better picture resolution than VCRs and provide a stable storage environment too. Videotape can become old and brittle over time, but DVDs should last forever (provided the format is not made obsolete by some other technical advance).

Recently two new competing DVD formats have been introduced, and the real performance benefit is that they can record and play back HD (high-definition) content. One system is called HD-DVD (logically), and the other is called Blu-ray Disc (BD), so called because it uses a blue laser.

Both formats promise huge storage capacity (for both the playback of HD movies and as storage

No, that's not a newspaper headline from the eighteenth century. It's a modern, global problem. Today's digital technology and the widespread popularity of VCRs, audiotape recorders, and now recordable CDs have made illegal copying of music, movies, and recordings a worldwide growth industry. To make matters worse, some of the illegal activity may actually be . . . well, almost legit. According to Ken Hansen of Canada's Royal Canadian Mounted Police, organized crime is getting involved in these activities because it is seen as a low-risk, high-reward activity.

It is common today for illegal copies of first-run movies to be available on DVD from street-corner vendors, whose wares may also include audiotapes and CDs, and fake name-brand cosmetics or leather goods. In fact, in Russia, illegal DVDs of popular movies like *Spider-Man 2* were available on the street within a few days after its theatrical release! The economic impact of this phenomenon is staggering. The Justice Department puts losses of intellectual property in the $250 billion range.

Illegal copies are being made and sold all over the world. In the United States, the Recording Industry Association of America (RIAA) and record companies won a major victory over Napster and Grokster, but new peer-to-peer file-sharing programs have replaced the defunct file-sharing services.

In Hong Kong, customs inspectors smashed a pirate recording factory in the To Kwa Wan district that had been producing more than 40,000 video discs each day. All the seized discs contained illegal copies of American movies, some still in the theaters. In Britain the Federation against Copyright Theft (FACT) shut down a major bootlegging ring at one of London's largest open-air markets. While these individual raids make headlines, thousands more pirated CDs and DVDs, particularly from mainland China and Russia, escape detection. And it's a big problem. Some estimate that 300 million pirated DVDs were produced in Russia alone in 2005.

In what may be a groundbreaking precedent, some entrepreneurs have taken advantage of Russian law and created an illegal music downloading service that may be legal. Allofmp3.com is a Russian online music store with a fancy Web site (in both English and Russian), offering music downloads for as little as 7 cents. *Pet Sounds,* the Beach Boys' masterpiece album, is offered for $1.11! In contrast, iTunes Music Store charges $9.99 for the same album. The company says that it's in compliance with Russian copyright, governed by the Russian Mulitmedia and Internet Society and general laws, which unlike the U.S. regulations do not cover individual downloading of music files. But here in the United States, Allofmp3.com is at the top of the office of the government's list of the world's most notorious piracy markets. There is a fierce debate going on currently between record companies and Allofmp3.com. The British Phonographic Industry (BPI) has won approval to serve proceedings against the Web site, and U.S. trade negotiators have warned Russia that the Web site could jeopardize Russia's entry in the World Trade Organization. According to Russia's 1933 copyright law companies that collect royalties for use of foreign artistic works are not obligated to pass them on to the International Confederation of Societies of Authors and Composers. At the moment, it seems perfectly legal to use this illegitimate music service.

---

devices for the next generation of computers). Still it is not clear which technology consumers will embrace. Microsoft has said it will incorporate HD-DVDs as an accessory, while Sony will add Blu-ray technology to PlayStation 3 consoles. At this time (2006) Blu-ray has more studios promising HD movie releases, but it also a more expensive technology. While the initial sets are priced high: $500 for HD-DVD and $1,000 for Blu-ray, consumer electronics become more affordable over time.

Digital Video Recorder (DVR)   The DVR is a video recorder that uses a computer hard drive as the main storage device. The recorder, marketed under such trade names as TiVo and Replay, connects to your cable box and telephone. It has the ability to record and play back television shows via a remote control, but its ability does not stop there. The TiVo is essentially a set-top computer that collects information about what television shows are on and when. You can tell the device what you like, and it will record programs for you. For example, you could program the TiVo to record every episode of *House* for an entire season. And because the machine allows instant record and playback access, you could skip through the commercials on a program or pause live TV. (Skipping

The digital versatile disc player is rapidly replacing the VCR.

through commercials gives some advertising executives pause to embrace this technology.) While TiVo and Replay both require a monthly fee to get access to the program guides, penetration has been rising since their introduction in 1999, particularly among DBS homes where the satellite companies have been packaging them with the service. However, the real growth has been in the cable arena, where cable companies are now marketing generic DVRs built into cable set-top boxes. While DVR penetration was only about 12 percent of all U.S. households (in 2006), some researchers predict that number will rise to 30 percent penetration by 2010. Some analysts wonder what the impact of DVR usage will be on American television viewing habits.

WEBCASTING: AUDIO AND VIDEO STREAMING

We close this section on audio and video technology with a technique that's blurring the lines between computers, TV sets, and radio receivers. The technique, called **streaming,** allows sounds and moving pictures to be transmitted on the World Wide Web and other computer networks. It allows these complex, high-memory transmissions to travel on high-speed cable modems or digital subscriber line (DSL) connections and even on slower, comparatively low-capacity bandwidths, such as 56K modems.

Streaming audio and video makes use of two nifty shortcuts called **buffering** and **compression.** To put a complex radio or TV signal on the Web, the signal is first "shrunk" and then transmitted in a much simpler form, using techniques of digital compression. Essentially, the complex signal is sampled, and redundant, nonessential information is stripped away, to be added back later (in decompression).

MP3 audio streams from SHOUTcast.com and RealAudio streams from NPR.org are just two examples of real-time feeds over high-bandwidth cable and DSL modems. CNN.com, ABC, NBC, and FOX are now podcasting prime-time programming using iTunes technology. Even so, music and moving video images are sometimes still too complex to transmit in real time over narrow bandwidths, like telephone lines. The solution is to stop playback for a short time so the computer hard drive can store the necessary information. It then begins playback, all the time replenishing the drive with new, incoming signals. This technique is called buffering.

Playing sounds and moving images on the Web requires special software. Featuring brand names like Quicktime, RealAudio, RealVideo, Shockwave, and Windows Media Player, these programs allow desktop computers to become more like radio and TV receivers. The software display controls are similar to a radio or TV set (with tuning buttons and volume controls). There are now literally hundreds of audio channels and radio and TV stations that can be heard and seen on any computer hooked to the Net (so long as it has a sound card, speakers, and the appropriate media player software).

The success of Apple's iPod has spawned new technology and new terminology over the past few years. The iTunes Music Store allows users to download daily or weekly news and entertainment shows. Individuals can post their own programs on podcasting Web sites, and new software programs like iLife have made the creation of personal audio and video programs extremely easy. We discuss this in greater detail in Chapter 6.

SUMMARY

- Broadcasting, cable, and new media make use of facsimile technology, reproducing sound and sight in other forms. The better the correspondence between the facsimile and the original, the higher the fidelity.

- Transduction involves changing energy from one form to another; it is at the heart of audio and video technology. Transduction can be analog—the transformed energy resembles the original—or digital—the original is transformed into a series of numbers.

- Audio and video signal processing follow five main steps: signal generation, amplification and processing, transmission, reception, and storage/retrieval.

- *Signal generation.* Audio signals are generated mechanically, by using microphones and turntables; electromagnetically, by using tape recorders; and digitally, by using laser optics. Television signal generation involves the electronic line-by-line scanning of an image. An electron beam scans each element of a picture, and the image is then retraced in the TV receiver.

- *Amplification and processing.* Audio and video signals are amplified and mixed by using audio consoles and video switchers. Today's digital technology enables sophisticated signal processing and a variety of special effects.

- *Transmission.* Radio waves occupy a portion of the electromagnetic spectrum. AM radio channels are classified into clear, regional, and local channels. FM stations are classified according to power and antenna height. The wide bandwidth of an FM channel allows for stereo broadcasting and other nonbroadcast services. There are two types of digital radio: satellite-based and terrestrial radio, encoded within the AM and FM signals. The traditional systems of transmit-

ting a TV signal are (1) over-the-air broadcasting utilizing electromagnetic radiation on channels located in the VHF and UHF portions of the spectrum and (2) by wire through a cable system using coaxial cable that can carry more than 100 channels of programming. New distribution technologies include fiber optics, satellite transmissions, and digital distribution using computer networks.

Television and radio are moving to new forms of digital distribution. On the TV side, the FCC has mandated a switch to digital high-definition television by 2009. That process is currently under way at the nation's TV stations and networks.

- *Signal reception.* Radio receivers pull in AM, FM, and other signals, in monaural or stereo. New digital multiband receivers are becoming more prevalent. In TV, large- and small-screen receivers have attained record sales in recent years, abetted by new digital capabilities and "smart" remote control devices.

- *Storage and retrieval.* New technology is reshaping audio and video storage and retrieval. Phonograph records, compact discs, and videotapes are being supplemented and may ultimately be replaced by digital storage media, such as recordable CDs, digital versatile discs (DVDs), and high-capacity disk drives on computers. A comparatively new phenomenon, audio and video streaming, permits radio and TV stations to send their complex signals onto the Internet. Today, any home computer with a sound card, a CD-ROM drive, and a microphone can produce and distribute its own radio and TV programs. The impact of this development on traditional radio, TV, and cable is unclear.

KEY TERMS

facsimile   49
fidelity   49
transduction   49
noise   49
signal-to-noise ratio   51
convergence   51
oscillation   51
waveform   52
frequency   52
hertz (Hz)   52
wavelength   52
amplitude   52
frequency response   52
pulse code modulation   55

MP3   58
minidisc (MD)   58
fields   60
frame   60
high-definition television (HDTV)   60
amplifier   62
equalizer   63
switcher   64
keying   64
chromakey   65
electromagnetic spectrum   66
modulation   66
carrier wave   66

multiplexing   69
very high frequency (VHF)   70
ultra-high frequency (UHF)   70
geosynchronous orbit   70
super-high frequency (SHF)   71
direct broadcast satellite (DBS)   71
digital audio broadcasting (DAB)   71
radio broadcast data systems (RBDS)   74
streaming   79
buffering   79
compression   79

SUGGESTIONS FOR FURTHER READING

Austerberry, D. (2004). *The technology of video and audio streaming* (2nd ed.). Amsterdam: Focal Press.

Bertram, H. N. (1994). *Theory of magnetic recording.* New York: Cambridge University Press.

Cicora, W.; Farmer, J.; Large, D.; & Adams, M. (2003). *Modern cable television technology* (2nd ed.). San Francisco: Morgan Kaufman.

DeSonne, M., ed. (1996). *International DTH/DBS.* Washington, DC: National Association of Broadcasters.

Luther, A. (1997). *Principles of digital audio & video.* Norwood, NJ: Artech House.

Menin, E. (2002). *The streaming media handbook.* Englewood Cliffs, NJ: Prentice Hall.

Hausman, C.; Benoit, P.; Messere, F.; & O'Donnell, L. (2007). *Modern radio production* (7th ed.). Belmont, CA: Wadsworth.

O'Leary, S. (2000). *Understanding digital terrestrial broadcasting.* Boston: Artech House.

Paulsen, K. (1998). *Video & media servers: Technology and applications.* Woburn, UK: Butterworth-Heinemann.

Persson, C. (1999). *Guide to HDTV systems.* Clifton Park, NY: Delmar.

Pohlmann, K. C. (1992). *The compact disc: Handbook of theory and use* (2nd ed.). Madison, WI: A-R Editions.

Robin, M., & Poulin, M. (2000). *Digital television fundamentals.* New York: McGraw-Hill.

Weise, M., & Weynand, D. (2004). *How video works.* Amsterdam: Focal Press.

Whitaker, J. (2001). *DTV: The revolution in digital video.* New York: McGraw-Hill.

Zettl, H. (2003). *Video basics 4.* Belmont, CA: Wadsworth.

INTERNET EXERCISES

Visit our Web site at **www.mhhe.com/dominick6** for study-guide exercises to help you learn and apply material in each chapter. You will find ideas for future research as well as useful Web links to provide you with an opportunity to journey through the new electronic media.

Part Two How It Is

Radio Today 4

Quick Facts

 Number of commercial AM stations on the air (2006): 4,759

 Number of noncommercial FM stations on the air (2006): 2,746

 Number of country radio stations (2006): 2,126

 Average number of radio stations available in most U.S. markets: 25

 Number of commercial stations in the United States playing a polka format: 4

 Number of different versions of "Danny Boy" in the XM Music Library: 200

More wondrous far than legends' figments wrought
By the ingenious bards of long ago. . . .
I feel like a spirit medium that can bring
The listener what'er he wishes from the void.
Do you want multitudes of thoughts, all types?
Full measure comes with the revolving dial;
The masters wait to pour out symphonies
That rock the world and set your soul on fire. . . .

　　　　　　Robert West, "My Name Is Radio!" (1941)

We'll be looking for caller number 10 but first you've got a lock
on a 30-minute block of rock direct from stereo compact disc on
the hot new Z-93 . . . Hot . . . hot . . . hot . . . hot.

　　　　　　DJ on large-market FM station (1999)

You're on Deep Tracks, Channel 40. With the best rock ever,
all commercial free.

　　　　　　XM Satellite Radio (2002)

Satellite radio! Video downloads! High-definition TV! Podcasting! . . . Amid the furor of today's communications explosion it's easy to overlook persistent, enterprising, unassuming radio. If nothing else, radio is resilient. It has withstood frontal attacks from an array of new media services, each promising to sound the death knell of the radio business. But in every instance, from the introduction of sound pictures in the late 1920s to the arrival of TV in the 1940s, from the birth of music TV in the 1980s to the surprising growth of podcasting, radio has rebounded, reformulated, and, most important, remained.

Radio today is as vital as ever. It is chameleonlike in form: from the supertiny Walkman to the new high-definition digital radios. It is omnipresent: Most households have five radios or more. It fills the air: There are nearly 14,000 stations on the air in the United States alone, not counting new low-power FMs. And it seems to meet our needs: Somewhere on that dial there can be found almost every form of music, all kinds of advice, hundreds of ball games, and special music events. Perhaps most important of all, in the face of an unprecedented flow of competition from within and outside the industry, radio remains economically viable.

Why do we continue to tune in to radio? As we pointed out in Chapter 1, radio has been around longer than any other electronic medium. Like baseball, hot dogs, and apple pie (to borrow an old commercial slogan), radio has become a part of our culture and tradition.

Radio has always been the most intimate of the mass media. It's portable—and personal. For many years, Walkmans provided youth with portable means to listen to their latest tunes, but now we are seeing a growing number of youth listening to iPods. What does that mean for the future of radio?

And as communications grow more global in nature (see Chapter 14), at its heart, radio continues to be an individualized service medium. In the aftermath of the terrible flooding during Hurricane Katrina, thousands of people in the Gulf Coast relied upon radio to get information about weather and disaster relief and to hear a reassuring voice. But radio's changing too. Now we can drive across the country and listen to an all-blues channel from XM satellite radio or dock an iPod to our car stereo. What will these changes mean for good ole radio?

Sometimes in our rush to credit TV for almost everything good or ill in our culture, there is a tendency to overlook radio. Let's not make that mistake. To borrow from some of its supporters, let's remember: Radio is red hot! In fact, "heat" is the appropriate metaphor. Everything about radio—from its competitive policies to its flamboyant personalities to increasingly large indecency fines—tends to be intense. Let's don our insulated gloves and delve into the radio business.

THE "THREE C'S" OF RADIO TODAY: COMPETITION, CONSOLIDATION, AND CONTROL

Over the past decade radio has been marked by three major trends, which we call the "three C's." These trends are **competition, consolidation,** and **control.** With many thousands of stations on the air, and consumers faced with many attractive alternatives to radio (like TV, MP3 players and DVD players, VCRs, and computers), radio competes vigorously for listeners. With radio deregulation (discussed more fully in Chapter 10) has come radio consolidation, the ownership of more and more stations by fewer and fewer large corporations. The combination of competition and consolidation has led to enormous control in the radio business, including the development of narrower, intensively researched radio formats, voice-tracking, and the rise of satellites and computers in radio operations, the meat of the material in Chapter 8. For now, let's see about the "three C's."

Competition in Today's Radio Business

Any discussion of the radio business must begin with one word: competition. Radio is arguably the most competitive of contemporary media. By almost every criterion there is more "radio" than anything else. There are more radios than there are TVs (about three times as many). There are five times as many radio stations as there are daily newspapers and nearly six times as many radio stations as TV stations. About the only thing there is less of in radio is advertising revenue. To understand commercial radio today, we must begin with its economics.

For some reason many people have difficulty with economic terminology, but few fail to understand the intricacies of pizza. So imagine you and a group of friends have just been served two pizzas at your favorite restaurant. As usual, the pies have been sliced. Let's see where the cuts are.

Advertising Revenue   Pie 1 (Figure 4–1) is apportioned on the basis of advertising revenue. In 2004 advertisers spent over $260 billion trying to convince the American public to buy their products. The bulk of that spending, nearly $68 billion, went to the television and cable. Newspapers and magazines got the second biggest slice with about $63 billion, or about 23 percent of all advertising dollars. A lot went to direct mail ($52 billion); about 13 percent went to other media, like billboards, bumper stickers, and blimps.

Look at the paltry radio slice: 7 percent of total advertising expenditures, representing about $19.5 billion. Lesson number one, then, for radio, is that if this pizza party were given in honor of America's leading advertising vehicles, you would leave comparatively hungry. What's even more worrisome is that radio revenue as a share of total advertising expenditure seems to be on the decline. In 2000, radio advertising represented about 9 percent of all ad dollars.

The Station Universe   Pie 2 (Figure 4–2) is divided on the basis of radio station type. There are about 13,700 radio stations on the air. Almost 4 in 10 stations (35 percent) are commercial AM stations. Although many of these are powerful stations emanating from large cities, the majority of AM stations are relatively low-powered, local operations serving the small and midsized communities that constitute the essence of "middle America." A larger proportion (45 percent) of radio stations are commercial FM operations. Because of their relatively late arrival on the scene and their technical requirements (described in detail in Chapter 3), the majority of the FMs are currently

Figure 4–1

Advertising Expenditures 2004

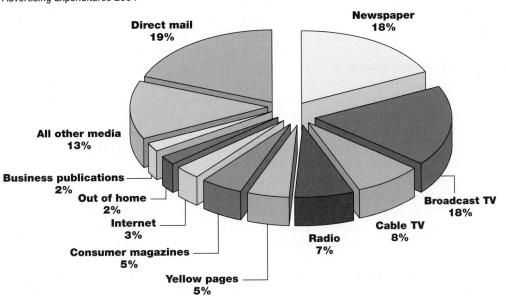

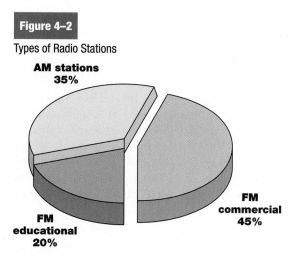

Figure 4–2

Types of Radio Stations

AM stations
35%

FM
educational
20%

FM
commercial
45%

allocated to midsized and large cities. In recent years, however, the Federal Communications Commission (FCC) allocated new FM stations to small communities.

The remainder of radio stations, about 2,700, or 20 percent, are designated as noncommercial stations. Most noncommercial stations are FMs.

The point of this pie is that radio today is largely a locally based medium. Many stations are commercial AMs, trying to operate on the advertising revenue available from local advertisers in the smaller markets. Large cities are often dominated by FM commercial stations, where major advertisers call the shots. Within the noncommercial environment the pressure is on to find funding: from the federal government, from religious organizations, from foundations, from university administrations or student fees, or from individual listeners.

Share of Audience   The point of both pies becomes clearer with one more statistic in view: share of audience. Today, almost 80 percent of all radio listening is to FM stations. In some cities, like Terre Haute, Indiana; Tallahassee, Florida; and Johnstown, Pennsylvania, FM share of audience is above 90 percent. In fact, many radio listeners, especially younger ones, rarely, if ever, tune to the AM band.

To sum up the competitive battleground, commercial radio is a business where more than 13,700 stations compete for a comparatively small percentage of national advertising expenditures. More than half of all stations serve the largest 300 cities in the United States (about three-fourths of the population lives in these cities).

In commercial radio, approximately 4,800 AM and 6,200 FM stations compete for audiences, though most radio listeners prefer the FM band. It should not be surprising, then, that the most profitable radio stations are the big FM music stations in the major cities and the powerhouse AM news/talk stations that cater to older listeners, and that many smaller stations, both AM and FM, report modest profit at best or are in a constant struggle to survive.

Added to this mix is satellite radio's growing listener base and new digital services, and it's easy to see competition to survive is fierce.

Consolidation: The Big Radio Groups

The increasingly competitive nature of the radio business is reflected in the kinds of companies now involved in the medium. For nearly one-half century, radio was generally a small business. Owners were also operators and lifelong residents of the community in which the station operated. Many owned other businesses in the area, such as automobile dealerships, restaurants, and even local newspapers. Reflecting this ownership pattern and the "homespun" environment in which they operated, such stations were commonly referred to as "mom-and-pop" stations.

Today, mom-and-pop radio has largely disappeared. Why? The competitive situation traced in the previous section was not lost on the radio business. Led by the National Association of Broadcasters—the industry's largest lobby group and trade association (see Chapter 11)—throughout the 1990s the radio business successfully lobbied Congress for regulatory relief. Their argument was that radio had become so competitive, with so many stations competing for such a small advertising segment and with so many stations losing money, that radio group owners should be able to own more stations. In addition, the argument went, a single owner should be able to operate more than the two stations (an AM and an FM) it was permitted to own.

For many years, radio group owners were restricted to owning only 14 stations total (7 AM and 7 FM). In addition, they could not own more than two stations in a single market (one AM, one FM); within one market they could not own more than one station in the same band, such as two AMs and two FMs. After some modification in the early 1990s, the passage of the **Telecommunications Act of 1996** literally changed the rules of the radio business, and in a few years the entire radio landscape shifted.

The new rules allow a single radio group to own as many stations as it wants. There are no national ownership caps. Even within markets, groups can amass more stations. For example, in cities with more than 44 stations, one company can own up to 8 stations (no more than 5 AM or FM). In cities with 30 to 44 stations, a single company can own 7 stations (up to 4 AM or FM). In midsized communities (15 to 30 stations) a single company can control 6 stations. Even in smaller towns (with up to 15 commercial stations), a single group can control 5 stations (up to 3 AM or FM).

These new rules have changed the radio business radically, at least in ownership. As the 1990s ended, local ownership gave way to the rise of the radio **supergroup.** By this, we do not mean rock-and-roll bands like Maroon 5, the Dave Matthews Band, or Red Hot Chili Peppers. The supergroups we refer to are radio's largest companies, which control most of the listening—and therefore most of the revenue—in radio today.

Table 4–1 lists the largest radio groups by overall revenue. Leading the pack is Clear Channel Radio, with 1,150 stations and revenue of more than $3.3 billion.

Like the big fish gobbling a school of smaller ones, Clear Channel emerged in the new millennium after purchasing many smaller radio groups. In 2006, Clear Channel announced that it would be selling more than 450 of its stations, nearly all of them in smaller radio markets around the country. While the sale marks an end to Clear Channel's consolidation of

Table 4–1	America's Largest Commercial Radio Group Owners	
Rank	**Group**	**Stations**
1	Clear Channel	1,150
2	Cumulus Broadcasting	306
3	Citadel Broadcasting	224
4	Infinity Broadcasting	179
5	Entercom	106
6	Salem Broadcasting	104
7	Cox Broadcasting	78
8	Regent Communications	74
9	ABC Radio	73
10	Univisions	70

Source: *Annual Report on American Journalism 2006*, Journalism.org.

Table 4–2	Largest Radio Group Owners by Revenue		
Rank	**Group**	**Revenue ($000)**	**% Total Revenue**
1	Clear Channel Communications	$3,570,650	18.2
2	Infinity Broadcasting (Viacom, Inc.)	2,223,700	11.4
3	Entercom Communications	487,775	2.4
4	Cox Radio	485,800	2.4
5	ABC Radio Networks (Disney)	454,850	2.3
6	Citadel Broadcasting	412,782	2.1
7	Radio One, Inc.	377,200	1.9
8	Univision Communications	338,875	1.7
9	Cumulus Media	325,700	1.6
10	Emmis Communications	311,175	1.5

Source: Center for Public Integrity revenue estimates for 2004.

radio, it will still keep control of all its larger and more profitable stations in the top 100 markets.

Based in Atlanta, Cumulus Broadcasting owns about 306 stations in 61 medium and small markets around the United States and is the second largest group owner. Citadel Communications comes next with 224 stations, followed by Infinity Broadcasting with 179 stations. Rounding out the top five is Entercom, which owns 106 stations.

The number of stations is not the only way to gauge the size and scope of some group operations. Table 4–2 shows the largest group owners by revenue. This chart tells a somewhat different picture.

As Table 4–2 shows, the power of radio groups is not measured solely by the number of stations owned by the group; how much advertising the group amasses is also significant. For example, Clear Channel, which owns about 10 percent of all commercial stations, takes in 18 percent of all revenue. Infinity Broadcasting, which is 80 percent owned and operated by Viacom, owns fewer than 200 radio stations. Yet it is ranked second in overall revenue, with more than $2.2 billion. Simple arithmetic reveals that the typical Infinity station earns more than $10 million in annual advertising revenue. In fact, Infinity owns many of the nation's highest-billing radio stations, including all-news power-houses WCBS-AM and WINS in New York, KNX-AM and KFWB-AM in Los Angeles, and WBBM and WMAQ in Chicago. As morning man Don Imus is fond of pointing out, Infinity's WFAN in New York, an all-sports station, is one of the nation's most profitable radio stations, with annual advertising revenue above $50 million.

The list of radio group owners is filled out with a number of other influential and respected names. Third on the revenue ranking is Entercom, followed by Cox and Disney's ABC Inc., a fleet of 73 stations. All three companies reported revenues above $450 million. ABC has been a leader in radio since the 1950s, and its list of radio assets includes talk radio leaders WABC in New York, KABC in Los Angeles, WLS and WZZN in Chicago, and WJR in Detroit. In Atlanta, ABC owns the two largest country radio outlets, WKHX-FM and WYAY-FM. At the beginning of 2006 Disney announced that it would sell its radio stations and programming networks to Citadel Communications. When the merger is complete Citadel will become the third largest group owner, in terms of revenue.

Other groups known for effective management, innovative programming, and profitable radio operations include Emmis and Susquehanna Radio. Cumulus, the second largest group owner, ranks ninth in overall revenue.

Mel Karmazin, one of the most influential people in radio, is CEO of Sirius Satellite Radio. Karmazin shook up the radio world in 2005 by hiring Howard Stern.

Howard Stern is perhaps the most infamous and controversial radio personality, but he's certainly not the only one who has stretched the boundaries of good taste. That distinction may now belong to Opie and Anthony. Increasing competition for advertising, especially in the nation's largest markets, has led to an unprecedented series of incidents that have stretched the bounds, some observers say, of good taste and fair play. Outrageous radio is also known as "raunch radio," and its air personalities are often called "shock jocks."

In 2002, when Greg Hughes (known as Opie) and his sidekick, Anthony Cumia, were fired by Infinity Broadcasting after the duo broadcast a live account of a couple having sex in the entrance of St. Patrick's Cathedral in Manhattan, many thought that outrageous radio would be reined in. The incident wasn't the only time Opie and Anthony were in trouble. Two years earlier the duo was fired from their Boston gig for a hoax in which they claimed the mayor of Boston had died in a car crash.

However, it appears that the desire for ratings and to shock the audience may sometimes be too much for radio personalities to resist. In St. Louis, a radio station aired phone messages from a well-known TV weatherman talking about a love affair and played an interview with a woman who claimed the weatherman was harassing her. The next day, the weathercaster died in a fiery plane crash that appeared to be a suicide.

In Columbus, WLVQ hosted "Toys for Ta-Tas," where strippers flashed people who donated toys for poor children, while another station in town hosted a contest where the winning listener had sex in a helicopter while flying over the house of a former spouse. In Denver, two disc jockeys kicked off their new show with a half-page newspaper advertisement that resembled the popular "fold-in" section in *Mad* magazine. When properly folded, the ad produced an attack on a competing station, complete with a four-letter expletive not normally seen in a family newspaper.

Today, things may become more subdued. That's due in part to the new fines that the FCC can now dispense when it finds that a broadcasting station has been egregiously indecent. In 2006 Congress gave the FCC the authority to raise indecency fines to $325,000 per incident, and the president signed the measure, making it law (see Chapter 10). Tom Taylor, editor of *Inside Radio,* said the effect of the new law will definitely be to change the way stations behave. Back in Columbus, Ohio, the morning host for WBZX was quoted as saying that the new rules would end the Holiday Hooters contest where the morning crew gave away breast jobs for Christmas.

A New Kind of "Doo-wop": Duopoly and LMAs   It is kind of ironic (or at least coincidental) that the medium of radio, built in part on early rock-and-roll music known as "doo-wop," has given new meaning to that shop-worn bit of slang. Where once doo-wop referred to the sound produced by harmonizing street-corner singers (Frankie Lymon and the Teenagers, the Coasters, and the Drifters, for example), today its homonym "duop" refers to the in-market control of radio listening and revenue by a few large group owners.

As we have seen, the FCC now permits a single company to own as many as eight stations in a single radio market. In addition, the FCC permits one company to manage the assets of another in the same market without being in violation of ownership rules. Known as a **lease management agreement** or **local market agreement (LMA),** the arrangement permits one station or group to control the programming, operations, and sales of additional radio stations in the same marketplace.

A review of the industry shows a pattern of consolidation since 1996. For example, since 1996 the average number of radio owners in each market has dropped from about 13.5 to 10, and consolidation continues in both large and small radio markets. In the top 50 markets, including New York, Boston, Los Angeles, and Miami, the top group owner controls approximately 36 percent of the market revenue, and the next largest firm controls 25 percent of radio station revenue. The four largest group owners generally control more than 85 percent of the revenue in these markets. In the smallest 100 markets the top two firms control more than 75 percent of the radio revenue in those markets. Duopoly is big business.

Is ownership consolidation in radio a good thing? Advocates of this trend maintain that group ownership allows for economies of scale (more efficient programming, better news gathering) to keep big-city radio exciting and interesting. Critics charge that group owners lack the sensitivity to community concerns that mom-and-pops have. With the sale of

Disney stations and Clear Channel's buyout, the face of corporate radio is changing. However, large conglomerates continue to dominate the landscape, owning the most powerful stations. If you're planning a radio career and favor local independent ownership, you may wish to consider small-market radio (although as we've seen, small markets have group owners too). If you're heading for New York, Chicago, Los Angeles, or other large markets, the corporate culture is no doubt in your future.

Control: Radio Programming and Promotion

The last "C" of radio today is *control*. With increasing competition and consolidation has come a desire on the part of radio managers to gain more and more control of the programming, promotions, and marketing of their stations. Radio today is marked by the kind of rigorous product and consumer research used to sell all kinds of consumer products, such as soap, automobiles, and cheese. Like all consumer items, the process begins with a full understanding of the attributes of the product. In the case of radio, the product is its programming. Let's examine the major trends in radio programming today.

RADIO PROGRAMMING TODAY

At the risk of sounding stereotypical, a snapshot of radio listeners today might include a teenager "tuned in" to a personal stereo on a school bus, a middle-aged executive listening to satellite radio in a luxury automobile, a city youth blaring music from a tricked-out funny car stereo, a trucker listening to a ballgame while traveling the highway in an 18-wheel rig, and a secretary listening to a desktop radio while at a computer workstation. It is highly unlikely that each is listening to the same type of station.

With more than 13,700 stations on the air and more than 25 local stations typically available for most listeners, and while competing for audiences against iPods, CD players, TV, the Internet, movies, and even live entertainment like concerts and theater, radio has become a focused and highly targeted medium. That is, rather than programming to meet the broadest tastes of the largest numbers of people in their listening areas, most stations today cater to a narrow market segment, the core of listeners who prefer a certain type of programming. The two key components of this trend are **target audience** and **format.**

The concept of target audience emerges from advertising research, which shows that the majority of purchases of a given product are made by a minority of the public: the target market for that product. For example, the overwhelming majority of beer is purchased by men between the ages of 21 and 49, teenagers account for most movies attended, and adults over 45 take the most European trips and antacids (although we're not saying they're related). In developing their campaigns, advertisers try to identify the target market for a product and then to develop appeals that meet the needs of this group.

Commercial radio today, particularly in the largest cities, is programmed in precisely the same fashion. Reflecting this trend, in fact, cities themselves are known in the business as "markets." Management identifies a target audience by its age, gender, music preferences, lifestyle, and other information, and it develops a program strategy to satisfy that group. The program strategy is known as the radio station's format. A successful radio station consistently delivers its intended target audience, in both aggregate size (quantity) and lifestyle preferences (quality). Its listeners are an identifiable subgroup, largely similar in age, gender, income, habits, leisure pursuits, and other characteristics. This makes the station attractive to advertisers: the name of the game in commercial radio.

Tables 4–3 and 4–4 list the top 16 radio formats and top 10 commercial formats, respectively, in terms of number of stations. Chapter 8 details how a format evolves from conception to execution. Until then, let's identify the major formats and their typical target audiences.

Country

Today, country radio is king. There are about 2,000 commercial radio stations playing country music, representing about one in six stations. As a radio format, country music has decided advantages. Its appeal is broad. While people of all ages listen to country, it's not a cradle-to-grave experience. Listenership is highest in the 25- to 49-year-old range. Listenership is predominantly white. Like most of the preferred formats, it delivers more women than men. Even so, large audiences of both sexes respond to the music. Country fans are loyal: They tend to listen to a single favorite station for long periods of time, making these stations a prime target for advertisers.

The growth in popularity of country music in the 1980s and 1990s led to the development of various

Table 4–3	Top 16 Radio Formats in the United States*				
Format	**Total**	**AM**	**FM**	**Commercial**	**Non-commercial**
Country	2,126	635	1,491	2,095	31
News & news/talk	2,032	1,319	713	1,437	595
Adult contemporary	1,758	281	1,477	1,648	110
Christian	1,209	297	912	488	721
Oldies	1,113	467	646	1,083	30
Sports	944	838	106	931	13
Religious	834	391	443	442	392
Talk	767	605	162	691	76
Spanish	698	376	322	633	65
Classic rock	637	21	616	594	43
Contemporary hit/top 40	634	36	598	540	94
Gospel	627	434	193	532	95
Rock/AOR	546	12	534	396	150
Classical	511	14	497	51	460
Jazz	365	18	347	60	305
Urban contemporary	361	62	299	298	63

*Stations may be using several formats within the broadcast schedule.

Source: *Broadcasting and Cable Yearbook 2006.*

derivatives. "Traditional" or "classic" country stations consider themselves the purest players of the format. The emphasis in music is on the country-and-western standards of 20 or 30 years ago.

"Contemporary" or "modern" country stations concentrate on current hits on the country charts, particularly the most up-tempo or upbeat tunes. Strong airplay is usually given to the "superstars" of country, like Faith Hill, the Dixie Chicks, Tim McGraw, and Brooks and Dunn. Some experts say that many country stations now target women almost exclusively.

Regardless of the music orientation, most country stations are "full-service" operations. Announcers tend to be friendly and helpful, directly involved in community events. Unlike some of the other contemporary formats, most country stations provide news, weather, and other information to their listeners. Remote broadcasts are common, from concerts and fairs to shopping malls and drive-ins.

Part of the continuing appeal of country music is its success on both AM and FM. Country is the number-one FM format and number two for AM. This means that the format has participated in the FM boom but also remains viable in AM. Like rock-and-roll, country radio is here to stay.

By the late 1990s, however, there were some chinks in country radio's armor. After a decade of growth, the country radio boom leveled off. The number of country stations peaked at nearly 2,600 stations in 1996; by 2002, the number had slipped below 2,200. Too, while country radio represents

Table 4–4	Top Full-Time Commercial Formats (May 2006)	
Rank	**Format**	**Station Total**
1	Country	2,032
2	News & news/talk	1,340
3	Oldies	732
4	Spanish	698
5	Adult contemporary	654
6	Sports	532
7	Top 40	488
8	Classic rock	458
9	Classic hits	422
10	Hot AC	376

Source: *Inside Radio* (M Street Publications).

Singer Faith Hill had hits on both country and adult contemporary radio stations.

20 percent of commercial stations, its strength is concentrated in medium and smaller markets in the South and Midwest. Though popular, country stations do not lead listening in the nation's most populous markets. For example, in 2006 New York City did not have a country station in the top 25 stations, and in Los Angeles, country format KZLA-FM was ranked 21st in the market.

News/Talk and Sports

News and talk is a broad radio format on more than 1,300 commercial stations. At one end of the scale are all-news operations, usually AM stations in major metropolitan areas that program 24 hours a day of news, sports, weather, and traffic information. Examples are WINS and WCBS in New York, WBBM in Chicago, and KNX and KFWB in Los Angeles. At the other end of the scale are all-talk stations, which rotate hosts and invite listeners to call in on a

range of topics—current affairs, auto mechanics, and counseling in every area, even sex. Examples are New York's WOR, KABC in Los Angeles, and KSTP-AM in Minneapolis. Between these extremes there are many news and talk stations, some of which mix play-by-play sports and occasional musical segments into the format. However, even the "hybrids" center their programming on information services.

About 500 stations are all-sports operations. Most are in large cities, particularly the cities that boast teams in the four major professional sports leagues: Major League Baseball, the National Football League, the National Hockey League, and the National Basketball Association. All-sports stations typically frame play-by-play action of these professional teams and major college games with nonstop discussion, analysis, and debate about sports teams, athletes, and coaches.

Whatever its unique interpretation, talk radio is the most popular format on the AM band and gaining popularity on FM as well. In fact, more than half of all AM listening today is to news/talk and sports stations. Part of the appeal of news/talk and sports is its audience composition. The news format attracts "big numbers," particularly during important drive time in the morning and afternoon. It follows that people who listen for news, traffic, and weather information are on their way to jobs. This makes them an ideal target for advertisers. The news format saw increased listenership as a result of the attacks on the World Trade Center and the Pentagon, the wars in Afghanistan and in Iraq, but it has the highest listener age among the top formats.

As we move through the second half of the decade, news/talk and sports are among commercial radio's most popular formats, accounting for more than 1,800 stations. Nationally syndicated personalities like Rush Limbaugh, Don Imus, Michael Savage, Dr. Joy Browne, and Dr. Laura Schlessinger, are reaching millions of listeners each day. At the local level, news, talk, sports, and information stations are rife with acerbic commentators, smart-talking "jocks," computer gurus, cigar aficionados, and gabbers of all political stripes.

Adult Contemporary and Oldies

Also in the top five commercial formats is adult contemporary (AC). Adult contemporary runs along a continuum from "soft hits" to "oldies." AC/soft

Podcasting provides broadcasters with new opportunities to connect with listeners.

stations emphasize current music with a soft, lyrical, and melodic beat. Sheryl Crow, Kelly Clarkson, Celine Dion, and Faith Hill are typical female artists played often on modern AC stations; their male counterparts include superstars like Paul McCartney and Elton John, as well as younger male artists like Keith Urban and Rob Thomas.

AC stations that take the "oldies" route play soft, nonmetallic, rock-and-roll hits from the 1970s to the late 1990s. Some oldies stations focus on music of the 60s, 70s, and early 80s. These stations usually label themselves something like "Oldies 97." The songs played were usually big hits in their day by the best-known bands of their time. Elvis, the Beach Boys, the Beatles, the Supremes, the Stones, and other mainstays of the rock-and-roll charts are featured. Other stations play a wide range of oldies but are more contemporary in their playlist (e.g., "music of the 70s, 80s, and 90s on Lite 104.3").

In AC, announcers are generally pleasant, friendly, innocuous, and noncontroversial. In fact, many listeners would be hard put to name the announcers at their favorite AC station (aside from a funny morning team), since the main reason they listen is for the music (such as the 9 A.M. at-work music hour).

AC stations are popular because they tend to attract the audience most in demand by advertisers and marketers: women between the ages of 25 and 54. The appeal of AC is wide: from urban areas to rural, from college-educated to grade school, from upper income to the poverty line. But AC is particularly strong "where it counts" to many advertisers: among middle- and upper-income housewives and working women in urban and suburban areas.

AC's strength in the bigger markets and attractive suburbs accounts for its large listenership. Today, about 14 percent of all radio listening is to some kind of AC station. As with country, however, the news is not all good for AC. The number of AC stations has been declining lately due to a rebound among both news/talk and the growth of Hispanic and urban format stations. The target audience of women, particularly younger women, is attracted to other formats, especially contemporary hit radio and black urban contemporary (discussed in a later section). Older audiences prefer oldies to the more contemporary AC formats. Still, AC remains a well-known and highly profitable radio format.

Contemporary Hit Radio

Targeting a younger audience than AC is the contemporary hit radio (CHR) format. Contemporary hit radio and Top 40 formats fall into this category. These radio formats are like an audio jukebox. The emphasis is placed on the most current music, the songs leading the charts in record sales. The music played is almost always bright or up-tempo. With a strict format, slow songs, long songs, and oldies (even those only a few months old) are avoided. Songs play again quickly (a program strategy known as **fast rotation**) and are removed from the playlist as soon as there is evidence that their popularity is declining.

Disc jockeys (DJs) tend to be assertive, high-energy personalities who sprinkle their shifts with humor, sound effects, and gimmickry. Contemporary hit radio stations sound "busy" compared with ACs: The air is filled with contests, jingles, jokes, buzzers, whistles, and, above all, hits. Currently about 10 percent of all listening is to this format; the majority of stations using the format are FM stations in large markets. Contemporary hit radio is most popular with those in the under-25 age group who are avid Web surfers looking at radio stations, movie sites, and other entertainment venues. They include preteen, teen, and young adult women. This is the group in recent years that has made mammoth stars of Greenday, Goo Goo Dolls, and Gwen Stefani.

Once thought to be a format in decline, CHR has rebounded remarkably in recent years, with about 12 percent of all listeners. There are numerous reasons for this turnaround. First, a spate of new artists appeared on the scene. Many were solo female performers, whose songs of independence, emotional turmoil, and love found and lost resonated with the core audience of young adult women. Such artists include Anna Nalick and Sheryl Crow, as well as Pink, Missy Elliot, and longtime torchbearers Mariah Carey and Madonna. In addition, a new kind of CHR called "hot adult contemporary" (hot AC) found success with older women (ages 25–49), moving these women away from their allegiance to oldies and soft rock standards. Some singers like James Blunt got their first exposure on AC formats. Groups such as Dave Matthews, Goo Goo Dolls, and 3 Doors Down appealed to this segment with melodic tunes that sounded very much like the mellow rock of the 1970s and early 1980s. Some CHRs in large cities are slanting their playlists toward specific music genres such as rock. In some instances, contemporary radio also

began to merge with the sounds of America's inner cities, giving rise to two important formats: Hispanic and black/urban contemporary.

Ethnic Formats: Hispanic and Black/Urban Contemporary

Next in share of listening are the so-called ethnic formats, those radio stations that target minorities in major cities. The leading ethnic formats are Hispanic and black/urban contemporary. Together these formats can be heard on 900 stations, and they account for about 16 percent of all radio listening. In fact, "ethnic" may be a misnomer: Their growing popularity indicates that people of many cultures enjoy these stations, mostly because of the attractive beat and rhythms of their music.

Hispanic Radio   Hispanic radio is the growth format of the day, with the number of stations more than doubling as we entered the twenty-first century. Nearly 700 stations consider themselves Hispanic and garner about 10 percent of radio listening. There are several different formats housed under this category: Mexican regional is popular in the Southwest and in large urban centers such as Los Angeles and Denver. Spanish contemporary is growing in acceptance, particularly in the Mid-Atlantic states.

The rise of Hispanic radio is due to two factors. The first is the growing population and economic clout of the Hispanic community. Today, the Hispanic population in the United States exceeds the total population of Canada. Advertisers spend more than $1 billion each year to reach this important group, more than $300 million in radio advertising.

The format also benefits from the rising popularity of its music. Subgenres within Hispanic formats such as reggaeton (a mixture of Latin and urban dance beats, sometimes with very explicit lyrics), Mexican, and salsa have attracted large and loyal followings and made stars of such artists as Don Omar, Shakira, Enrique Iglesias, Primavera, Intocable, Marc Anthony, and Grupo Innovacion. Many of these subgenres tend to do well in urban settings on both coasts. Arbitron reported that contemporary formats within these subgenres have been gaining listener share over the last few years.

Black/Urban Contemporary   The black or urban contemporary (UC) format refers to the percussive, up-tempo sounds of the stations in America's major

For the past few years revenue for radio has been flat, with little prospect of increasing given the growth of competitive services such as satellite radio, Internet radio, and podcasting. In some market sectors, however, this is not the case. Billboard's *Radio Monitor* reported that one of the two most significant trends in 2005 was the growth of Hispanic-targeted formats, which in many cases posted double-digit growth for 2005.

The rise in Hispanic radio probably comes as little surprise as the Hispanic population in the United States has exploded and now constitutes the largest single minority group in the United States. Current census estimates peg the population at nearly 40 million, or roughly 14 percent of the total population. Of that number, roughly 29 million are Spanish-speaking.

It's no wonder then that radio has turned to serving this growing population. Since the mid-1990s there has been a huge increase in Hispanic radio. M Street's *Inside Radio* lists 821 stations in the United States having some form of Hispanic programming, making it the fourth most popular format in the United States by numbers of stations. Formats run the gamut from reggaeton to Mexican regional to Latin to Hispanic urban. At the moment Mexican regional is the most popular of all the Hispanic formats. While the vast majority of stations are along the corridor bordering Mexico, you can also find the format doing well in Chicago, Denver, and Phoenix. Arbitron notes that there are stations in Wichita, Charleston, and Chattanooga programming Mexican regional. However, other programming is beginning to gain in importance. In 2005, New York's all-sports station WFAN launched *The Latin Beat,* a weekly three-hour program with baseball legend Roberto Clemente. The show covers Mets and Yankees games, discussing the sport's impact on New York's Latino listeners. In San Francisco, typically all-music KLIK-AM broadcasts Giants games in Spanish. This trend is likely to continue as Hispanic listenership grows.

Looking at Arbitron's 12+ trends shows that there has been a 50 percent gain in share points since 1998 in large radio markets. Demographics show that the audience composition is young, mostly in the 18- to 44-year-old range, with more male (58 percent) listeners. Half of the listenership has not completed a high school education, and 56 percent of the listeners earn less than $25,000 a year. Mexican regional listeners are most likely to have children at home and are least likely to go online.

Some broadcasters think that the market for Hispanic radio is growing so quickly that there's an actual lag between listenership and revenues. If that's true, look for Hispanic radio revenue to keep outpacing the radio industry generally.

cities. Black is actually a misnomer for the format: People of all racial and ethnic backgrounds enjoy the music, but the music skews toward listeners under 35. Urban contemporary arose out of the disco craze of the mid-1970s, when a gyrating John Travolta captivated the culture and sent a new generation to the dance floors. By the 1990s, rap music had emerged to create a new force in UC. Today variations of the format range from rap, hip-hop, and "house" music to more traditional rhythm-and-blues and soul music stylings. Hot urban contemporary artists in recent years include Eminem, Black Eyed Peas, Destiny's Child, Mary J. Blige, Usher, Ludacris, and LL Cool J. Like Hispanic radio, the urban format is played on stations in major cities with large African-American populations and garners about 9 percent of the listening audience in various formats such as urban contemporary, urban AC, urban oldies, and R&B.

Soft Adult Contemporary (Adult Standards and Easy Listening)

If Hispanic and urban radio is growing, the format known variously as "adult standards," "beautiful music," and/or "easy listening" may be losing audience. Beautiful music, or easy listening, refers to the stations that program "wall-to-wall," "background," or "elevator" music. One of the stalwarts of FM (which stood for "fine music" in its early days), easy listening has evolved into the soft adult contemporary format. Where once the "rules" called for only instrumental music (Mantovani, 101 Strings, Tony Matola, and so on), today it is common to hear Rod Stewart, Barbra Streisand, Jewel, Billy Joel, and Phil Collins in the format.

The primary reason for this change is the aging audience for the format. Beautiful music appeals mainly to older listeners, those above 45 years of age.

Today's mature audiences grew up after the dawning of the age of rock-and-roll. They are more likely to relax and unwind to pop tunes as opposed to lush instrumental orchestrations.

"Lite" music stations tend to have unique program elements. Music is generally played continuously; breaks for commercial announcements and news segments, if used, are kept to a minimum. Announcers have pleasant, low-key styles. They will never shout at you. Contests and other aggressive promotions are eschewed in favor of image-enhancing station events (sponsorship of appropriate music performances, for example).

The success of the format is not based on audience size, although in many markets lite music stations boast big audiences. Rather, these stations attract a high-quality audience of professionals and managers. In addition to being high earners, this audience tends to listen to the radio for long periods of time and to be loyal to a single station or to very few stations.

Album Rock: Modern and Classic

Album rock is a long-lasting legacy of the progressive rock movement of the late 1960s and early 1970s. At this time, rock artists began to experiment with the form, producing theme albums (such as the Beatles' *Sergeant Pepper,* the Who's *Tommy,* and *Dark Side of the Moon* by Pink Floyd). The length of songs played on the radio began to increase, from 2 minutes to 5 minutes or more. Like classical and jazz before it, album rock developed a core of informed, dedicated, loyal listeners: most of them young adult males. In fact, of all the major formats, album rock is most heavily targeted, or skewed, to male listeners. Over 60 percent of the album rock audience is male.

There are two main types of album rock stations. Those attracting younger males (teenagers and young adults in the 12- to 34-year-old age group) are known as alternative or modern rock stations. This is the group that has made superstars in recent years of such artists as Cake, Green Day, Franz Ferdinand, Foo Fighters, and Wheezer and older groups like Stone Temple Pilots, Pearl Jam, and Nirvana.

Those stations seeking aging male baby boomers (like the authors of this text) are known as classic rock stations. Their core audience of 25- to 54-year-old listeners is loyal to the music of the supergroups of the 1960s, 1970s, and early 1980s, including the Rolling Stones, the Doors, the Eagles, U2, the Allman

Brothers, Led Zeppelin, and others. Proof of the enduring appeal of older rock artists to both older and younger males is the fact that the most successful tours in recent years have been mounted by such aging rockers as the Stones, Pink Floyd, Aerosmith, Kiss, the Eagles, and Black Sabbath, giving new meaning to the phrase "long live rock."

Together, classic and modern rock stations number more than 500 and represent about 10 percent of all radio listening.

Other Formats

Together, the formats just described account for almost 90 percent of radio listening in the United States. The additional 10 percent is filled out by a number of other formats.

Religious stations appeal to a variety of faiths, but Christian stations are most plentiful. In addition to delivering inspirational talks, many religious stations include music in their format. Those targeting the black audience are generally known as gospel stations. Religious stations tend to be most popular among women 35+. The majority of religious stations (65 percent) can be found on the FM dial, with contemporary Christian stations making up more than half of all religious FM stations. Contemporary Christian stations feature upbeat Christian rock artists like MercyMe, Jeremy Camp, and Amy Grant, and their audiences skew younger than most other religious stations.

In 2005, there were more than 1,800 commercial and noncommercial stations playing some form of religious format. Despite their proliferation, religious stations lag in listenership, generally less than 3 percent of the listening audience. At any given point in time, fewer than 2 in 50 radio listeners are tuned to religion.

While classical music and jazz are the backbone of public radio stations (see the discussion that follows), some 300 or so commercial operations play each of these formats. Classical stations attract a very upscale listener in the 55+ demographic, typically college-educated and professional. The jazz enthusiast reflects a younger profile with listenership in the 35-and-above age groups. Although the number of classical and jazz aficionados is small (compared, say, with the audience for adult contemporary), the "high quality" of their listeners makes these stations potentially attractive advertising vehicles.

It sometimes appears that there are almost as many other formats as there are radio stations. Filling out the dial, there are Portuguese, Greek, Polish, Italian, and other foreign-language stations. Over 73 stations report that they carry ethnic programming. Clearly, commercial radio is in an era of expanding format diversity.

Noncommercial Radio

The bulk of America's radio stations seek profits through advertising sales, but about one in six stations does not. Into this class fall more than 2,100 noncommercial radio stations. There are three main types of noncommercial stations: community, college, and public.

Community stations are those that are licensed to civic groups, nonprofit foundations, local school boards, or religious organizations. There are about 500 of these stations, which operate in the FM band (between 88 and 92 megahertz), providing a range of services including coverage of local issues, study-at-home classes in conjunction with local schools, religious services, niche music programming, local talk shows, and other "home-based" activities.

WMNF-FM is a good example of one of the many successful community stations operating in the United States. The Tampa Bay station programs an eclectic variety of music throughout the day that reflects the interests of its many volunteers and station members. For example, there's a 1960s hippie show on Tuesday nights, but on Thursdays the music turns goth and industrial. Sunday mornings you'll find Native American music. Many volunteers share the mic to bring an amazing assortment of specialty shows to listeners.

The station is supported by donations, memberships, and the annual Heatwave concert, which has become one of the most popular annual concerts in the Tampa Bay area. Over the years the famous and not so famous have played in Tampa's famous Ybor City district in support of the station.

College radio is a broad category comprising about 800 stations licensed to universities and some secondary schools. About 650 of these stations are members of the Intercollegiate Broadcasting Society (IBS).

College stations are a diverse group. However, most of them share a similar programming pattern. The musical mix is eclectic and "progressive," featuring program blocks of new wave, new age, reggae, metal, jazz, and other alternatives to standard formats. Many college stations operate as training

sites for students planning broadcast careers. Thus, in addition to announcing, staffers gain experience in news, play-by-play sports, public affairs, programming, and promotions.

Public radio stations are also known as CPB-qualified stations. These stations meet criteria established by the Corporation for Public Broadcasting (CPB), enabling them to qualify for federal funds and to receive programs from National Public Radio (NPR). Today there are approximately 800 stations affiliated with NPR or carrying programming.

In 1998, standards for CPB-qualified stations were tightened. Today's public radio stations must have a professional staff of at least five full-time members; must operate at least 18 hours per day, 7 days a week; must operate at full power (250 watts AM and 100 watts FM); and must demonstrate sufficient local financial and listening support to justify federal grant monies. Research studies on public radio audiences suggest that NPR listenership has been growing over the past two decades, and while federal appropriations seem secure for the foreseeable future, there are critics who claim that public radio should not receive federal tax dollars to support radio programming.

As one might expect, the audiences for public radio tend to be comparatively smaller than those for commercial stations, but that does not mean the numbers are insignificant. Nationwide, public radio averages about a 2 percent share of audience at any given time. This compares with shares of 6 to 15 percent for highly ranked commercial radio outlets. However, in some cities public radio attracts sizable audiences. For example, KQED (San Francisco) and WRVO (Oswego–Syracuse, New York) regularly garner a 5 to 8 percent audience share. Sometimes it's useful to point out that while the numbers seem low, in reality, almost 30 million people listen to NPR programming every week.

The public radio audience is somewhat highbrow. Studies have shown that two-thirds of listeners to public radio stations have college degrees and many listeners have advanced and professional degrees. Male listenership is slightly higher than female, and on average 70 percent of public radio listeners are at least 45 years old. You may recall that this profile overlaps the target audience of some commercial radio formats, such as advertiser-supported classical and jazz stations and beautiful-music operations.

Among the most-popular programs in public radio are NPR's leading news programs *Morning Edition* and *All Things Considered;* the entertaining call-in

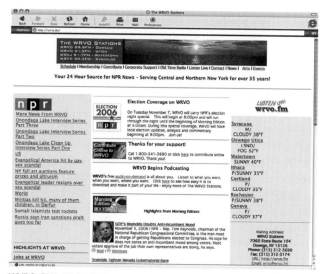

WVRO-FM's Web site.

program *Car Talk;* and the entertaining news quiz *Wait, Wait, Don't Tell Me.* In addition to NPR programming, most public radio stations carry programs from other suppliers, including American Public Media and Public Radio International. Popular shows such as *A Prairie Home Companion,* hosted by Garrison Keillor, attract a large and loyal following.

Some public stations have formed regional networks and program consortiums to develop programming that serves the needs of the region. Wisconsin Public Radio and Alabama Public Radio are examples of regional networks that develop programs for their specific listening audiences.

Low-Power FM   In 2000, the Federal Communications Commission approved **low-power FM** (LPFM) services. These news stations have power levels from 10 to 100 watts and serve small listening areas (approximately a 4-mile radius or less). Noncommercial entities such as colleges, religious groups, and nonprofit groups serving their local community are eligible to apply for a LPFM license. As of 2006, the FCC had granted more than 700 licenses for this new service.

Small community stations like Portsmouth Community Radio, WSCA-FM, and Radio Sausalito (which has no call sign) provide small communities with new opportunities for developing local content. While Sausalito's station is all jazz, Portsmouth has a much more diversified format including an obscure rock show called the *Split Brain Experiment.*

Whether these stations will flourish over the next several years will likely determine whether more communities apply for low-power stations.

SATELLITE RADIO TODAY

In Chapter 3 we profiled the technology behind the two national satellite radio services operating in the United States: XM Satellite Radio and Sirius Radio both offer consumers more than 160 channels of music, news, sports, and talk. The two companies bet that there were a substantial number of Americans willing to pay extra for radio service that surpassed what you could get on AM and FM. But were they right?

Critics of satellite radio point to the current diversity of the American radio landscape (nearly all Americans can receive almost 25 AM and FM signals). But a 2002 study by the Carmel Group indicated a number of reasons why these services are likely to succeed. First, the sound quality of digital radio is better than FM. In addition, the research suggests that the sheer diversity of listening opportunities from either XM or Sirius would trump traditional radio services. Since November 2001, when satellite radio began, nearly 12 million Americans have decided to pony up about $13 a month to listen to one of the two services.

XM Satellite Radio currently leads in the subscriber race, but in 2005 Howard Stern surprised the broadcast community by announcing that he would take his highly controversial radio program to Sirius Radio in early 2006. Some estimate that as many as 1 million people bought the Sirius service so they could continue to listen to Stern.

Initially, the future of satellite radio appeared to be skyrocketing, with Kegan Research projecting that the two services would have more than 45 million subscribers and annual revenues of nearly $8 billion by 2014. However, in early 2006, satellite radio subscriptions began to slow and by the end of the year, both XM and Sirius had revised their projected listenership goals downward. Whether this slowing of growth is temporary or the result of other forces, such as the amazing growth of iPod usage, remains to be seen.

Programming on the two services is very much niche-oriented. While some of the programming easily fits within the mold of the formats we discussed earlier in this chapter, much of satellite radio's offerings are simply beyond the scope of what a commercial radio station could program. Full-time raggae, blues, movie soundtracks, Broadway standards, and underground dance are just a few of the specialized channels available. Just as cable television began to grow as it offered a diverse array of programming, satellite radio is betting that it can offer programming that appeals to specific audiences that, while

In 2003, the FCC authorized all radio stations in the United States to broadcast in HD (high-definition digital) in addition to the stations' current analog channel. Currently more than 13,000 radio stations compete for listeners every day, and now that number could double. Each radio station in the country could immediately start broadcasting a second channel in high-definition sound.

There are some real issues. There are almost no digital radios out there that can receive the new signal, and the few radios that are on the market are fairly high priced, usually $300 and above. But if previous technology adoption is any indicator of what is likely to happen, then within a few years HD radios will be very cheap, and they will be built into cars by auto manufacturers. At the moment many cars are already equipped with AM/FM and satellite receivers, which brings us to an interesting question: Is there too much radio in the United States?

At the beginning of this chapter, we discussed the fact that radio advertising revenues were likely to remain constant at approximately 7 percent of all advertising expenditures. If there is no real increase in the amount of money spent on radio advertising, how will radio stations make money on HD radio?

The obvious answer is that as more and more listeners switch from analog to digital, advertising dollars will shift as well. But that would mean that AM and FM analog services would decline as revenue streams decline. Also, if forecasts for satellite are accurate, more and more people will switch from terrestrial radio to satellite. The lack of commercials and the amazing diversity of programming are strong attractions for some people. Then, too, 60 million Americans own iPods, and these devices are capable of downloading podcasts, representing another level of programming, not subject to FCC rules about indecency (or any other rules for that matter).

While terrestrial broadcasting and the National Association of Broadcasters have been touting HD radio as the next great innovation, the facts suggest that as the number of stations increase, the more radio will find it difficult going in an increasingly competitive market for listeners.

small from one market to another, will become large enough in the aggregate at the national level. This gamble is expensive; both XM and Sirius have bet nearly a billion dollars that they're right.

RADIO STATION ORGANIZATION

Regardless of their size, radio stations tend to share an organizational pattern. Figure 4–3 illustrates the flow of managerial control common to radio stations. The illustration is typical of a radio station in a midsized market, such as those described earlier in the section on radio economics.

There are typically four core departments at each station: operations, programming, sales, and engineering. **Operations,** also known as the *traffic department,* has the responsibility of placing advertising on the station in accordance with the contracts signed with advertisers. This is a difficult task: At any given time dozens of different contracts are in force, each with varying schedules for airtime, length, position, and so on. For this reason most radio stations have automated their traffic departments with computer systems that track commercial placement and billing. The operations director or traffic manager heads this important department.

The **program department,** headed by the program director, has overall responsibility for the sound of the station, including music, news, and public affairs. Stations with a music format may also employ a music director to oversee the development and implementation of the format; news/talk stations may appoint a news director to handle the logistics of news and public affairs coverage.

The **sales department** is very important. Sales personnel are fond of pointing out that theirs is the only department that makes money; all the others spend it. Led by the sales manager, this department is responsible for the sale of commercial time to local, regional, and national advertisers. Depending on the size of the station (and the size of its commercial client list), stations may employ both a local sales manager to oversee local sales and a national sales manager to handle spot advertising accounts. Today's commitment to research and promotion makes these important functions of this department, prompting many stations to value highly a promotions director and research manager.

Figure 4–3

A Radio Station Table of Organization

In public radio, the sales department is replaced with a fund-raising unit, typically led by the **director of development.** This staff plans, organizes, and executes the station's fund-raising efforts, including pledge drives, grant applications, program underwriting, and related activities.

The **engineering department,** headed by the chief engineer, basically has one function: to keep the station on the air with the best signal possible. Many radio stations once had large engineering staffs, with as many as 5 to 10 full-time employees, but relaxed federal regulations, improved electronic equipment, and competition from other businesses for engineering talent led to the streamlining of engineering departments. Some stations retain the services of a consulting engineer, who works part-time, as needed, to keep the station in prime operating condition.

Top-level management of, and responsibility for, a radio station is in the hands of the general manager (GM) or station manager. The GM is responsible for business and financial matters, including station revenues and expenses, short- and long-term planning, budgeting, forecasting, and profitability. The GM must run the station in accord with local, state, and federal regulations. The GM is responsible for maintaining and representing the station's image in the community. General managers also hire the major department heads, establish their goals, and monitor their performance.

Some large stations, particularly those in large markets and those owned by station groups, have both a GM and a station manager. In this case, the station manager has responsibility for the day-to-day operations of the radio station, such as hiring and firing, making sure the bills are paid, and keeping up employee morale; the GM reports to the "home office," representing the station to its corporate ownership, to the community, and to federal, state, and local regulatory bodies.

Traditionally, the route up the corporate ladder into the management of radio stations starts in sales; most radio GMs have a background as account executives, promotion directors, or research managers. However, it is not unheard of for GMs—even station group owners—to come from the music or announcing ranks. At a radio management meeting one will hear many well-modulated announcer voices; a very high percentage of owners and operators are former DJs.

Radio consolidation is leading to new management structures. In most markets, groups operating multiple stations have consolidated sales by using one sales staff to sell commercials on as many as eight stations. The engineering and traffic departments have been similarly streamlined. However, most duopolies prefer to keep programming and general station management decentralized. As radio is still primarily a local service medium, it makes sense to maintain local control of what the station sounds like, as well as what it's like to work there.

GETTING A JOB: RADIO EMPLOYMENT TODAY

The consolidation of radio due to rising competition, increasing group ownership, duopolies, and LMAs has had a measurable effect on radio employment. Total radio employment has dropped since duopoly rules went into effect.

With consolidation continuing, voice-tracking has become a popular option at group-owned radio stations. With modern technology it is possible to prerecord an entire 4-hour airshift and have a board operator or computer software correctly insert all the voice tracks in their appropriate places within the show. Some jocks do shows in different cities this way. While this practice allows group owners to more effectively use their highly paid talent, others see it as taking the spontaneity out of radio.

The news is not all bad. Opportunities for women and members of ethnic minority groups have been increasing in radio in recent years. For example, in 1977 the percentage of women in radio jobs was 28, and ethnic minorities accounted for only 10 percent of employees. By 1990 almost 40 percent of the radio workforce was female, and the percentage of ethnic minorities had risen to 15. Today, the radio workforce is about 17 percent ethnic minority and about 42 percent female.

Most of the new opportunities for ethnic minorities and women have occurred in sales and announcing positions. Today the majority of salespeople at many large stations are women. Whereas in 1985 black and Hispanic announcers were virtually unheard of (and unheard) outside of "ethnic" stations, radio today has an increasingly multiethnic and multicultural sound.

The FCC estimates that about 70,000 people work in the radio business. The majority work at commercial radio stations. Noncommercial radio employs about 4,000 people. The remainder of radio jobs are at corporate headquarters and networks.

Radio Salaries

Salaries in the radio business are largely a function of the size of the market. Overall, the average radio salary is low—only about $25,000 per year. In smaller markets most people, especially announcers, earn at or slightly above minimum wage. A salary of about $15,000 is typical for most small-market air personalities. However, in larger markets, top personalities—particularly the popular DJs in the lucrative early-morning time period—can earn seven-figure salaries.

In radio, the better-paying jobs are in sales. Account executives in large markets exceed $150,000 in annual income. The nationwide average is over $110,000 per year for radio sales managers. This trend is also apparent in smaller markets. For example, a general sales manager averages about $97,000 per year in earnings, nearly $25,000 more than the average salary for the program director. In fact, in some markets a successful sales manager might even make more than the station's general manager.

Talent is still sought after and rewarded in radio. The morning personality in a large market will command more than $150,000 per year; a highly rated morning team can earn as much as a million dollars.

SUMMARY

- Judging by the number of radio stations on the air and by the number of radios in homes, there is no doubt that the medium has survived the threat of TV. However, radio receives only 7 percent of total advertising expenditures. This means that radio is arguably the most competitive of the electronic media businesses.

- Radio stations, once family-owned operations, now are merged into groups of stations owned by corporations. Fueled by relaxed ownership regulations, these corporations have consolidated the radio business. Duopolies allow a single owner to operate as many as eight stations in a single community.

- Because of intense competition, most stations have turned to format radio, targeting their programming

toward specific factions of society. Some fear these trends are resulting in the franchising and depersonalization of the medium.

- Country, news/talk, contemporary hit radio, and album rock tend to monopolize commercial radio. Talk formats frequently rely on syndicated programming, such as Joy Browne and Rush Limbaugh. Black and Hispanic radio stations are growing in popularity.

- Three kinds of noncommercial radio stations— community, college, and CPB-qualified—compete for audiences with their commercial counterparts. Affiliates of National Public Radio (NPR) are the most influential in this group, though they are subject to the uncertainty of federal funding and face increasing technical, employment, and programming requirements.

- Satellite radio is the newest form of the medium. The service started in 2002 and has grown rapidly. XM and Sirius satellite radio beam hundreds of channels to listeners.

- Most radio stations have four major departments: operations, programming, sales, and engineering. The GM is responsible for all the executive decisions at a station.

- Radio consolidation has caused considerable shrinkage of the workforce. However, opportunities continue for women and minorities, and positions in sales, promotion, and programming can lead to lucrative careers in senior management.

KEY TERMS

competition   84
consolidation   84
control   84
Telecommunications Act
   of 1996   86
supergroup   87
lease management agreement   89

local market agreement
   (LMA)   89
target audience   90
format   90
fast rotation   94
community stations   97
college radio   97

public radio stations   97
low-power FM   98
operations   99
program department   99
sales department   99
director of development   99
engineering department   100

SUGGESTIONS FOR FURTHER READING

Adams, M., & Massey, K. (1995). *Introduction to radio: Production and programming.* Madison, WI: Brown & Benchmark.

Dempsey, J. (2006). *Sports-talk radio in America: Its context and culture.* Binghamton, NY: Haworth Half-Court Press.

DiTingo, V. (1995). *The remaking of radio.* Boston: Focal Press.

Engleman, R. (1996). *Public radio and television in America: A political history.* Thousand Oaks, CA: Sage.

Gross, L.; Gross, B.; & Perebinossoff, P. (2005). *Programming for TV, radio, & the Internet* (2nd ed.). Boston: Focal Press.

Hausman, C.; Benoit, P.; Messere, F; & O'Donnell, L. (2007). *Modern radio production* (7th ed.). Belmont, CA: Wadsworth.

Keith, M. (2000). *The radio station* (5th ed.). Boston: Focal Press.

Laufer, P. (1995). *Inside talk radio.* Secaucus, NJ: Carol Publishing Group.

Looker, T. (1995). *The sound and the story: NPR and the art of radio.* Boston: Houghton Mifflin.

Lynch, J. (1998). *Process and practice of radio programming.* Lanham, MA: University Press of America.

MacFarland, D. (1997). *Future radio programming strategies* (2nd ed.). Mahwah, NJ: Erlbaum.

McCoy, Q., & Crouch, S. (2002). *No static: A guide to creative radio programming.* San Francisco, CA: Backbeat Books.

Norberg, E. (1996). *Radio programming: Tactics and strategy.* Boston: Focal Press.

INTERNET EXERCISES

Visit our Web site at **www.mhhe.com/dominick6** for study-guide exercises to help you learn and apply material in each chapter. You will find ideas for future research as well as useful Web links to provide you with an opportunity to journey through the new electronic media.

Broadcast and Cable/Satellite TV Today 5

Quick Facts

 Network share of audience (prime time), 1975: 90 percent

 Network share of audience (prime time), 2005: 45 percent

 Number of TV networks, 1975: 3

 Number of TV networks, 2006: 7

 Number of homes in the United States with one or more TVs, 2006: 110,600,000

 Percent of TV homes with digital video recorders, est. 2006: 18

 Cable penetration of TV households, 2006: 66.3 percent

One word sums up the television industry today: transformation. Traditional broadcast television is transforming itself as TV stations spend millions of dollars to upgrade to digital TV. Broadcasters can now transmit high-definition signals or multiple standard-definition signals. At the beginning of 2006, CBS and Warner Brothers decided to shutter the WB and UPN TV networks and form the CW network. As if local stations did not have sufficient competition already, the viewing audience has discovered intriguing new options for their home leisure, including TiVos, cable, DVDs, video games, and the Internet. Now the networks distribute their programming via iTunes and other new media technologies like cell phones. This chapter takes a brief look at the dynamics of television today, particularly the broadcast and cable businesses. The next chapter presents a snapshot of the new media, especially the World Wide Web.

TELEVISION NOW

Watching TV is one of America's favorite pastimes. More than 98 percent of the homes in America—more than 110 million homes—have at least one TV. Of the homes with TV sets, 98 percent have a color set. Three-fourths of the homes in the United States have more than one set. More than a decade ago the census reported that American homes had more TVs than indoor toilets; that disparity continues to grow.

According to the ACNielsen ratings company, the average American home has the TV set on more than 7 hours each day. Those viewers have a lot of choices. About 66 percent of all homes subscribe to cable, and the typical TV household today receives 82 different channels of programming. And in just 10 years, 26 million Americans have subscribed to a DBS service.

TYPES OF TELEVISION STATIONS

There are over 1,700 TV stations in operation today. The various types of stations are depicted in Figure 5–1.

Commercial and Noncommercial Stations

The stations depicted in Figure 5–1 can be divided into two categories: commercial and noncommercial. The primary distinction between the two is the way in which each type of station acquires the funds to

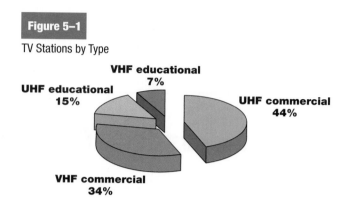

Figure 5–1

TV Stations by Type

stay on the air. Commercial stations—78 percent of the total number of TV stations—make their money by selling time on their stations to advertisers. Noncommercial stations are not allowed to sell advertising. These stations, which were set aside by the FCC for educational, civic, and religious groups, must adhere to the FCC mandate not to sell advertising time. They survive strictly through donations from individuals, businesses, and the government.

VHF, UHF, and DTV Stations

Another way to categorize stations is by the channels on which they broadcast. Stations that broadcast on channels 2 to 13 are called **VHF,** or **very high frequency,** stations. Those stations that broadcast on channel 14 and above are called **UHF,** or **ultra-high frequency,** stations.

VHF frequencies have historically been the preferred channels for broadcasters. During the 1950s and most of the 1960s, TV sets often did not have the capability to receive UHF signals. The quality of the UHF signal was also judged to be inferior to that of a VHF signal.

In 2009, by congressional mandate, all analog TV channels will be replaced by digital channels, and these distinctions will disappear; however, cable technology has erased many of the distinctions between VHF and UHF broadcasting already. Cable TV provides the subscriber pictures of equal quality whether the station is VHF or UHF. Cable has also made selecting a UHF station as easy as selecting a VHF. On some cable systems local UHF stations are reassigned to a lower channel.

Figure 5–1 reveals that the most common type of TV station today (more than 750 stations, or 44 percent) is a commercial UHF facility. About 570 stations

(34 percent) are commercial stations operating in the VHF band. There are about 250 noncommercial UHF facilities (15 percent) and about one-half that number of noncommercial VHF stations.

There were about 1,600 digital television stations (DTV) on the air in 2006, some on an experimental basis. Approximately 350 of these stations are noncommercial. Stations in the top 30 markets have nearly completed the transition to DTV, and most medium and small markets have at least some DTV service on the air.

Of course, like the situation in radio today, the commercial stations do not share equally in TV revenues. And noncommercial TV faces the same problems of funding that public radio faces.

The broadcast TV business is actually two businesses in one. There is **network television,** a system in which ABC, CBS, NBC, FOX, and some smaller networks develop program schedules for their affiliate stations. The networks sell most of the advertising in those programs (a process traced in detail in Chapter 7), which is how they make most of their money.

Then there is the **local television** business, which revolves around scheduling programs and selling advertising in the many cities and towns in which TV stations can be found. Managers of these stations earn their revenue primarily through the sale of advertising in their community and region.

Let's first take a look at the network TV business.

NETWORK TELEVISION

For many years the TV business (like the U.S. automobile business) was dominated by three giant companies. At the peak of their power in the 1960s and 1970s ABC, CBS, and NBC dominated the viewing habits of the nation. That dominance was especially acute in prime time: the evening hours during which the overwhelming majority of American households were watching TV. On the East Coast and in the far West, prime time ran from 7:00 P.M. to 11:00 P.M.; in the Midwest and certain parts of the Rocky Mountain region, prime time spanned 6:00 P.M. to 10:00 P.M.

At the height of their prime-time power the three major networks commanded more than 9 in 10 of all TV homes with the TV set on. With competition from new sources—most notably Fox, cable, and home video (see Chapter 2), the 1980s saw the beginning of a significant decline in the networks' audience share.

For example, the three networks drew 91 percent of U.S. TV households in prime time in 1978. By 1986, their share had slipped to 75 percent. By 1992, the network share for ABC, CBS, and NBC had slipped to 60 percent. The 1997–98 TV season saw even lower ratings for the networks. Combined, ABC, CBS, and NBC attracted only 47 percent of TV households.

Today the viewing shares for the major four networks (ABC, CBS, NBC, and FOX) hover around the 45 percent range.

Fox Broadcasting Company

The Fox Broadcasting Company (FBC) was launched in 1986 by Australian media magnate Rupert Murdoch. Murdoch had purchased the former Metromedia stations and was interested in using his newly acquired TV studio (Twentieth Century Fox) to produce programs for these stations. The decision was made to introduce programming slowly—first, one day of the week (Sunday), then gradually extending it throughout the week.

Today Fox network programming is available seven nights per week. Many successful shows now attract audiences and advertisers to Fox, including *American Idol, 24, The Simpsons, Family Guy,* and *House.*

New Networks Come . . . and Go

Motivated by the success of Fox and the revenue potential of the network TV business, two big players entered the network game in the mid-1990s.

The United Paramount Network (UPN), owned by media heavyweight Viacom, debuted in January 1995, anchored by *Star Trek: Voyager.* Like Fox, UPN began with two evenings of programming, with plans to expand beyond prime time to other days and other day parts. By 1999, UPN was broadcasting five nights per week. However, its ratings were low, compared with Fox and the Big Three networks. *WWE Smackdown!* led the ratings for the network.

Another network called the WB was backed by multimedia conglomerate Time Warner. WB Network launched in 1995 with comedies at its core, including *Father Knows Nothing* and *Unhappily Ever After.* If these programs seem suggestive of Fox series, perhaps this is because the WB Network was led at launch by two of Fox's founders: Jamie Kellner and Garth Ancier. Since then, WB found some success with shows like *7th Heaven* and *Smallville.*

In 2006 the FCC levied a heavy fine against the CBS television show *Without a Trace* for the portrayal of a teenage orgy. The FCC said that the portrayal was gratuitous to the show's plot. CBS and many critics of the fines responded that the material portrayed is often discussed in much more explicit detail during the daytime talk shows.

Regardless of whether you think the FCC acted appropriately, there appears to be some evidence that discussion and portrayal of sexual situations are on the rise in American television. According to a Kaiser Family Foundation report issued in 2005, the percent of shows with sexual content has been increasing substantially since 1998, when the first study was conducted.

According to the findings, nearly 8 out of every 10 prime-time shows during the 2005 season included a fair dose of sexual content in the plotline. The study concludes that among the top 20 shows watched by teens, nearly half of the shows included sexual behavior within the story. Further, when intercourse on TV is depicted or strongly implied, it is casual sex being depicted—30 percent of the characters involved appear to have just met.

Television programming has certainly changed from the 1950s when CBS would not let Lucy and Ricky share a bed in their New York apartment. In *I Love Lucy*, the couple had twin beds in their TV bedroom!

Does this statistic counting actually mean something? The study's lead researcher, Dale Kunkel, says yes. In the survey three out of every four teens aged 15–17 said that portrayal of sex on television influenced the behavior of kids their own age. Another study conducted by the Rand Corporation found that African-American youth who watched more TV shows with storylines about safe sex were less likely to initiate intercourse during the subsequent year.

What should the responsibility of networks be regarding the portrayal of sexual situations on television? Or should the responsibility for viewing choices remain in the home?

By the close of the 1990s, WB seemed to be outpacing UPN, propelled primarily by the success of two shows with followings (especially among teenagers)—*Buffy the Vampire Slayer* and *Dawson's Creek*. However, neither network attracted more than 5 percent of the prime-time TV audience overall, and both reported to their shareholders that they were losing money. But that wasn't enough to keep another competitor from entering the fray.

Pax TV, founded by longtime TV station owner Lowell "Bud" Paxson, launched in fall 1998. Unlike WB and UPN, which aggressively courted the teenage, inner-city crowd, Pax TV targeted older, more conservative audiences (perhaps because Paxson was an evangelical Christian and proponent of "family values"). The anchor programs for Pax TV were reruns of the popular CBS shows *Dr. Quinn, Medicine Woman; Diagnosis Murder;* and *Touched by an Angel.* Early ratings for the new network were meeting their projections. That's the good news; the bad is that these projections called for only 1 in 100 TV households (a rating of 1).

In early 2006, CBS and Time Warner announced that they were pulling the plugs on the two money-losing ventures and decided to jointly create CW (C for CBS and W for Warner Brothers). Some analysts speculated that both networks lost more than $500 million trying to make a go of the ventures. The new CW will target the 18–34 demographic, pulling some currently successful shows from both UPN and WB. Plans call for CW to program 13 hours in prime time plus program the Kids' WB shows on Saturday mornings.

Both UPN and WB had a large number of affiliated stations and combining the two left some stations, many owned by News Corp and Sinclair, without a network affiliation. Then Rupert Murdoch stepped forward and announced the creation of MyNetworkTV, a companion network to Fox. MyNetwork debuted in the fall 2006 season, programming 2 hours a night, Monday through Saturday.

The End of Network Television?

With seven networks competing for audiences (especially in prime time) and with growing attention paid by viewers to cable, home video, and the Internet, some observers have speculated that network television is a dinosaur business. Through

Shot from *CSI*—CBS Television's hit series. Procedural crime dramas have been among TV's top rated shows for the last few years.

the 2000s, audiences shrank, program costs rose, and advertising revenues have been lackluster. The result is that a TV network is no longer the steady source of corporate profits it used to be. For example, the Television Advertising Bureau says that the combined revenue of the seven networks was about $25 billion in 2005. But profits are a different story. The four major networks sold about $16.8 billion in spots for 2005 but generated few profits. Fox, the number-one network in ratings in 2004, lost about $140 million. CBS network posted a positive cash flow of about $400 million for 2005, while ABC posted a huge profit of $2.7 billion, but those numbers are largely on the revenues of ESPN and Disney channels, though *Lost* and *Desperate Housewives* added to the bottom line. The television network business is complicated and fickle.

Will network TV go away? Unlikely. Even at their worst, network programs still attract larger audiences than do most cable networks, the VCR, and the Internet. Think of the size of the audience for the Super Bowl—or for an episode of *American Idol, Grey's Anatomy,* or *CSI.* It's many times larger (usually by a factor of 10 or more) than the number of people watching wrestling on cable or reading their e-mail on AOL. But with escalating production costs and talent fees, reducing overhead as a way of maximizing revenue has become a way of life at the TV

networks. Look for this trend to continue apace in the new millennium.

LOCAL TELEVISION

The major networks seem to get all the attention in the TV business, even though they account for only half of all the advertising revenue spent on the medium. This section looks at where the rest of the dollars go—to about 1,300 commercial TV stations.

Figure 5–2 rates the various types of TV stations in economic terms. The rankings range from "five-star" stations, which traditionally have been the most

Figure 5–2

Rating the TV Stations

	VHF	UHF
Network O&Os	★★★★★	★★★★
Big Four network affiliates	★★★★	★★★
CW/Pax affiliates	★★★	★★
Independents	★	★
Low-power TV	½★	½★

profitable, to "one-star" stations, which have faced considerable financial hardship and even apathy among America's TV households.

Television's Cash Cows: Network Owned-and-Operated Stations

At the top of the rankings of commercial TV stations there are those that are owned outright by the corporate parents of the four established TV networks—ABC, Fox, CBS, and NBC. In industry parlance, these are owned-and-operated stations, or O&Os, for short. These are the five-star stations in Figure 5–2.

Network O&Os have traditionally been the most profitable of all TV stations. Located primarily in the VHF band, O&Os are considered the flagship stations of their networks. Situated in the largest TV markets, they often boast the call letters of their networks. In addition to owning NBC, General Electric is the parent of WNBC and WNJU in New York and KNBC in Los Angeles, plus stations in Chicago, Philadelphia, Boston, Miami, and Washington, D.C. CBS owns WCBS in New York and KCBS and KCAL in Los Angeles, as well as other stations in Boston, Minneapolis, Chicago, and Miami. Disney/ABC O&Os include WABC (New York), KABC (Los Angeles), plus TV stations in Chicago, San Francisco, Philadelphia, and Houston. Purchasing its own stations has been a cornerstone of the Fox strategy to achieve parity with the other major networks. It has invested hundreds of millions of dollars to purchase such stations as WNYW in New York, KTTV and KCOP in Los Angeles, WTTG in Washington, KRIV in Houston, and WFLD in Chicago. Most of the networks own more than one station in New York, Los Angeles, and Chicago, the three largest television markets in the country.

Ownership by a major network guarantees a steady supply of programming to these stations and a high profile for potential advertisers. Owned-and-operated stations are typically local news leaders in their marketplace. The fact that they emanate from the corporate or regional headquarters of their networks permits economies of scale and access to programming and personalities that other stations can't match. Extended local news shows generate quite a bit of cash for these stations.

For these reasons network O&Os have traditionally been the most profitable of all TV stations. Annual profit margins above 50 percent have been commonplace. Even as the ratings of their parent networks decline, O&Os remain cash cows for their companies,

returning, on average, more than 30 cents in profit for each dollar of sales. So while NBC, CBS, ABC, and Fox may lose money producing programs for the networks, they make money showing them on their O&O stations.

Cash Calves? Major Network Affiliates

The second-most-profitable class of TV facilities are those stations affiliated with a major network but owned by a different entity. In industry parlance, such stations are network-affiliated stations, or **affiliates** for short. Traditionally, the best affiliation to have was with one of the three "old guard" networks, ABC, CBS, and NBC. Like O&Os, most of these affiliates have been leaders in local news and public service in their communities. Many have been in operation since the dawn of TV (the early 1950s), and over the years they have cultivated enormous goodwill among their viewers.

But the world of TV affiliation has changed dramatically in recent years. In 1994, for example, Fox invested $500 million in New World Communications, a group of 12 stations, 8 of which were longtime CBS affiliates. The terms of the deal included switching the affiliations, naturally, from CBS, NBC, and ABC to Fox, in such cities as Dallas, Detroit, Atlanta, Cleveland, Tampa, and St. Louis.

In the wake of this bombshell, viewers across the country were unsure where to find CBS shows, as they moved to new channels (including some high-band UHFs). In response, CBS and the other traditional networks tried to shore up relationships with longtime allies to prevent further Fox defections. For example, CBS signed an unprecedented 10-year joint-venture agreement to keep its programs on KPIX-TV in San Francisco and KDKA in Pittsburgh. As part of the deal, NBC affiliates WBZ (Boston) and KYW (Philadelphia) switched to CBS. Interestingly, the 10-year deal lasted only a short time: In 1995 Westinghouse acquired CBS, which in turn was acquired by Viacom.

Today, about 200 stations each are aligned with CBS, NBC, ABC, and Fox. Many group owners such as Gannett, Hearst-Argyle, and Cox Broadcasting own large numbers of network-affiliated stations.

CW, MyNetwork, and i Affiliates

Affiliates of these newer networks are next in our hierarchy of TV station profitability. Each new network launched in 1995 with about 100 affiliated stations, but by 2000 each network boasted sufficient affiliates to reach more than 90 percent of America's TV homes. Pax TV, which launched in late 1998 with about 90 affiliates and covered about 75 percent of U.S. TV households, changed its name to Ion Media in 2006. As this edition went to press, it was not determined how many affiliates the new CW network and MyNetwork would have. Tribune Company, which owned 22 percent of the old WB, signed its 16 stations to the new CW, and Fox stations naturally signed up for MyNetwork.

In Figure 5–2 , we grant three stars for operating revenue and ratings potential to VHF affiliates of these new networks, and two to those that broadcast on the UHF band. Indeed, the overwhelming majority of old WB, UPN, and *i* (fomerly Pax) affiliates are located on the higher band. But viewers will find their shows regardless of where they are, especially if they attract the kind of following that *Gilmore Girls, Smallville,* and other popular shows do.

Independents: A Vanishing Breed

An **independent TV station** is one that does not align itself with a major network. With seven networks from which to choose, independent TV stations appear to be a vanishing breed. With each new edition of this book fewer and fewer stations have been relying on their libraries of movies, syndicated programs, and local professional sports to fill their program schedules. In 2005, fewer than 50 stations were not affiliated with either ABC, CBS, NBC, Fox, or one of the newer networks; however, that figure will change as the network scene shifts.

Unlike affiliated stations, independent stations have to develop programming for the entire broadcast day, seven days a week, Also, while affiliates get a boost from shows with high network ratings (*CSI,* for example). Indies have to do much more promotion in the local market. For this reason, we assign one star to independents. In major markets, an independent station (especially one on a low-band VHF frequency) can be a strong competitor. Los Angeles's KCAL (channel 9), with strong news programming, had revenues of over $100 million in 2004. And, if the indie is the home broadcaster of a local baseball or basketball team, revenues can be quite good. However, in smaller markets, where the stations are likely to be located on high-band UHF channels, remaining independents struggle for viewers and advertising support.

Low Power to the People: LPTV

Low-power television (LPTV) stations are a relatively unknown force in TV. The FCC authorized this service in 1982 to create openings for minority ownership of TV stations and to increase the number of broadcast offerings in a community. To promote minority investing in these stations, the FCC promulgated rules that would show preference for minority applicants. The FCC hoped that LPTV would increase broadcast offerings to communities by increasing the number of TV stations that served those communities or would provide niche service to small communities that cannot sustain a full-power TV station.

To restrict coverage to the community to which an LPTV station is licensed, the FCC placed limits on the power of LPTV stations. An LPTV station is limited to 3,000 watts effective radiated power for VHF and 150 kilowatts for UHF. Regular TV stations can be assigned transmitter powers 1,000 times more powerful than these. This low power (hence the name) limits the signal to a fairly small coverage area. The station may operate as long as its signal does not interfere with that of another station on the same channel. And while there are fewer program-related regulations, the FCC still enforces a ban on obscene material.

Today, more than 2,000 LPTV stations are in operation, mostly in the UHF band. Located mainly in rural areas (Alaska has the most LPTV stations), LPTV has faced financial hardship to date. In most cases LPTV operations have been unable to compete with affiliates and full-power independents for attractive programming. Their limited broadcast range has made it difficult for LPTV to interest advertisers in the medium. This is why we place LPTV at the bottom of our rankings of TV stations, with only one-half star.

However, LPTV still holds promise as a venue for special-interest and minority programs. Spanish-language services like Univision and GEM align with LPTV stations. Recently the FCC announced that LPTV stations would need to convert to digital transmission, and although the commission has not set a timeline for the transition to take place, it is not likely that LPTV stations will need to meet the same February 2009 deadline that full-power broadcasters will have.

TV STATION OWNERSHIP

Generally, one wouldn't ask "who" owns a TV station but would ask "what." Television stations are so expensive that few individuals can afford to own them. Instead, most TV stations are owned by companies that own other stations and networks or by investment groups.

For many years, TV station ownership was strictly regulated, with the number of stations a group could own limited to 12, to prevent concentration. Recent years have seen significant streamlining of TV station ownership. Today, a single TV group can own as many TV stations as it likes, as long as the total number of U.S. TV homes reached by those stations does not exceed 39 percent (actually UHF coverage is discounted some by the FCC). However, even that restriction may be relaxed in coming years. The leading TV group owners are listed in Table 5–1.

Today, CBS is the largest station owner, with 35 stations reaching the cap of 38.9 percent of TV households. The leading CBS-owned stations include New York's WCBS, Los Angeles's KCBS and KCAL, and Chicago's WBMM. CBS also owns stations in Philadelphia, Boston, Dallas, Atlanta, Detroit, and even Green Bay, Wisconsin, and Austin, Texas.

Table 5–1	Television's Top 25 Group Owners			
Rank	**Group Owner**	**Number of Stations**	**FCC Limit**	**Total Coverage***
1	CBS	35	38.90%	43.35
2	Fox TV	35	38.27	44.97
3	NBC Universal	30	33.99	39.08
4	Paxson	52	31.59	63.18
5	Tribune	26	30.24	40.58
6	ABC	10	23.55	23.79
7	Univision	37	22.88	43.90
8	Gannett	20	17.89	18.06
9	Trinity	23	17.10	34.20
10	Hearst-Argle	27	16.35	17.67
11	E.W. Scripps	15	14.14	22.09
12	Belo Corp.	20	13.26	13.98
13	Sinclair	57	12.82	22.58
14	Cox	15	10.13	10.26
15	Clear Channel	31	8.68	12.58
16	Pappas Telecasting	21	7.78	12.56
17	Raycom	30	7.75	10.32
18	Meredith	12	7.58	9.07
19	Post-Newsweek	6	7.39	7.39
20	Media General	23	7.17	8.06
21	Entravision	19	6.44	12.78
22	Emmis	16	6.12	7.00
23	Lin TV	25	6.07	7.21
24	Young	11	5.87	5.92
25	Gray Television	31	5.14	5.46

*Total coverage area for UHF stations is discounted by the FCC. Thus, group owners with a number of UHF stations may have significant differences between FCC coverage limits and actual contour coverage areas.

Sources: *Broadcasting and Cable*, BIA Financial Network, Nielsen Media Research 2005 (from *Broadcasting and Cable Magazine*, April 18, 2005).

Fox is the second-largest station owner, with 35 stations reaching the cap of 38.27 percent of TV households. The leading Fox-owned stations include New York's WYNY and WWOR, Los Angeles's KTTV and KCOP, and Chicago's WFLD. Fox also owns stations in Philadelphia, Boston, Dallas, Atlanta, Houston, and even Birmingham, Alabama, and Austin, Texas.

In contrast, Ion Media Networks (*i*), formerly Paxson Communications, has a fleet of 52 stations that form the backbone of the *i* network. They have a combined reach about 32 percent of TV households, making it the fourth-largest TV group. However, none of these stations has a dial position lower than 14 (WPXA in Atlanta). Paxson has UHF stations in New York, Los Angeles, Chicago, and Philadelphia, but many Pax-owned stations are in smaller cities, like San Antonio, Texas; Knoxville, Tennessee; and Cedar Rapids, Iowa.

Other leading TV group owners include Tribune, NBC, ABC, Gannett, A. H. Belo, Sinclair, and Cox. Each of these companies, and the others in Table 5–1, also hold other diversified media interests, including networks, newspapers, and cable systems.

PUBLIC TELEVISION

Not all TV stations are in it for the money (at least not overtly). Nearly 400 TV stations are considered noncommercial operations. These stations, owned primarily by governmental organizations, universities and school boards, and religious organizations, form the backbone of an often-struggling but ongoing alternative to commercial TV, the public television service.

In 2004, the Public Broadcasting Service (PBS) celebrated its 35th anniversary. There was much to celebrate. At its launch, PBS provided programming to 169 licensees operating 348 member stations serving the United States, Puerto Rico, the Virgin Islands, Guam, and Samoa. Nearly 90 million people in the United States watch PBS in a typical week, including about 35 million children. The fiscal year 2005 budget for PBS was $340 million. Approximately 75 percent of the budget goes to programming and promotion, while another 7 percent is spent on satellite distribution.

In some ways, PBS operates as commercial networks do. It provides a means of national distribution of programs (its satellite distribution network was operational in 1978, before those of NBC, CBS, and ABC). Its national programs attract a loyal following, from *Sesame Street* to *Nova* and *Masterpiece Theater*. But PBS differs from the commercial networks in some important ways.

Public TV programs rarely match the ratings of those on commercial TV. In fact, the PBS audience is typically 2 percent of the homes in the United States; however, while that seems small, remember that

PBS kids' series *Between the Lions* is one of many educational shows on public television.

The new president of the nation's Public Broadcasting Service, Paula Kerger, has many obstacles to conquer over the next few years to ensure that PBS survives. Kerger, a veteran of one of the nation's largest PBS stations, WNET in New York, took the reins of PBS in 2006 amid a scandal that rocked CPB (the Corporation for Public Broadcasting) and PBS (see Chapter 9).

Finding funding for public television has always been a struggle. Outgoing PBS chief Pat Mitchell had to struggle to keep funding levels from being cut. In recent years, a more conservative Congress has questioned its investment in a TV service whose output has been accused of being decidedly liberal. Despite studies that indicated that PBS was balanced in programming, Congress slashed 30 percent of the recommended PBS budget. One of the first things Kerger did was to dismiss the notion that PBS would bow to political pressure, saying it was unrealistic "to expect that every single program will represent all points of view."

Corporate underwriting for public television programs has similarly faced a decline. Large corporate sponsors General Motors, IBM, and others have faced rounds of belt-tightening, mergers, and acquisitions. Support for the arts is often a casualty of such events, under the banner of "downsizing." Like Congress, large corporations are not fond of funding programs they sometimes find are at cross-purposes with their lobbying activities or their corporate agendas.

Keeping PBS free from outside political influences while maintaining a sufficient budget to develop important new programs will be part of Kerger's responsibilities. New media, the growth of alternative cable programming, and a traditional struggle from PBS stations for more say in decision making will pose significant challenges as well.

For her part, Kerger has said that she wants to strengthen public TV's offerings on new media platforms but acknowledges that PBS doesn't have the same deep pockets as the media conglomerates, which control most of the broadcasting and cable networks. Experts think that PBS will have to push past "survival mentality" mode and into establishing an interactive relationship with its audience. Whether PBS can thrive in the new digital environment is perhaps the issue that will determine Paula Kerger's success.

2 percent equals the size of the audiences for TLC, Bravo, MSNBC, PAX, and CNBC combined! The highest-rated PBS series of all time, Ken Burns's *The Civil War*, attracted an average of just under 9 percent of U.S. homes, a figure that would probably have led to its quick cancellation were it a series on ABC, CBS, or NBC.

While small in aggregate size, the audience for public TV reflects the overall U.S. population demographically. However, PBS viewers tend to be important opinion leaders in their communities. A high proportion have college and advanced degrees and hold key leadership positions in government, business, education, and the arts in their communities.

Surveys find that the viewing audience has come to rely on public television for some of its programs, particularly its news reports (especially the highly regarded nightly *NewsHour*) and children's programs (*Sesame Street, Between the Lions,* and the like). That the public supports public television is borne out by the fact that viewers pledge nearly $500 million each year to local public TV stations.

Public television was an early advocate of digital television. In 2006, there were 331 PBS member stations offering digital broadcasts. Indeed, in some large cities, the PBS stations were broadcasting in high definition before local commercial stations. Over the last few years, PBS seems to be locked in a perennial battle with Congress for a stable source of funding with house Republicans leading an effort to reduce monies for public broadcasting. PBS leaders express concern that loss of federal funding would hamper the transition to digital broadcasting and cut into children's programming.

CABLE TELEVISION

As we all know, there is a lot more to TV than can be tuned in with a pair of rabbit-ear antennas atop the TV set. In fact, for most television viewers, the set-top or rooftop antenna has become a relic of the past. With its impressive roster of program services; its multiplicity of channels; and its promise of better pictures, better sound, and even Internet access and other services, cable TV today has become a strong competitor to the traditional TV networks and their affiliated stations.

Over the years, cable has grown in gross revenues, from small mom-and-pop operations carrying local channels to a huge business in its own right. In 1980, for example, cable was a $3 billion business—about a fourth the size of the TV business. Today, cable revenues hover around $70 billion annually, placing the cable business revenues on a par with the total revenues of all over-the-air TV.

At one time virtually all cable systems were 12-channel operations. Attaching the TV set to the cable generally filled most of the channels from 2 to 13. In the mid-1970s new cable systems offered 35 channels, requiring most TV homes to have a converter box. By the 1980s many older systems were upgraded, and new franchises were awarded to companies providing 54 or more channels. New technologies like fiber optics and digital compression enabled many cable systems in the 1990s to boast well over 100 channels as the number of cable networks exploded. By 2003, there were nearly 280 nationally distributed cable networks available to cable operators. Today digital cable and pay-per-view offerings have made the cable universe even larger.

Nationwide, more than two-thirds of the cable systems, representing three-fourths of all cable viewers, provide over 60 different channels of programming. The average subscriber can view 80 or more cable channels.

Clearly cable provides more viewing alternatives. Whether more TV is better TV is an important question that we address in some detail in a later chapter.

Cable Programming

The cable business today is something like a shopping mall. There may be room for 100 retail stores in a new mall, but how many will actually sign a lease? Which stores will be most popular with shoppers and thereby take the lion's share of the profits? While some stores will be mass merchandisers, attempting to bring in lots of customers with discounting practices and volume sales, others will be specialty stores or boutiques, aiming at a narrowly selected clientele (like teens for Old Navy, college students for Abercrombie, young adults for the Gap, and professional males for Brookstone). The same situation applies in the quest for cable audiences.

There are well over 300 national and 80 regional program services available to cable, with more in the planning stages. Some are mass marketers appealing to a diverse audience, like Sears or Macy's; others are boutiques, like Banana Republic or the Sharper Image.

For convenience, cable programming can be divided into three broad classifications: basic cable services, pay cable services, and specialty services. Let's examine each in detail.

Basic Cable Services   The backbone of cable is its lineup of basic services. These are the program services available for the lowest subscription charge. There are two main types of programming found in basic services: local and regional broadcast signals and advertiser-supported cable services.

From "must carry" to "retransmission consent": Local/ regional broadcast signals   For years cable systems were obligated to provide space on their systems to retransmit local TV stations within their communities. Such rules, known as "must carry," were declared unconstitutional in 1985.

As a result, cable operators were able to retransmit the TV signals of stations in and near their communities without compensating those stations or simply choose to delete low-rated broadcasters from the cable lineup. Local broadcasters fought diligently in the ensuing years to reinstate the rules and to receive some form of compensation for cable carriage of their services. In 1993, new regulations were implemented by the FCC to resolve this dispute after Congress passed the Cable Television Consumer Protection and Competition Act of 1992. Broadcasters were instructed to choose either "must carry" or "retransmission consent." With a selection of must carry, the cable company was required to air the local TV station's program schedule in its entirety, but the broadcaster was not entitled to any form of compensation. Broadcasters choosing retransmission consent were required to negotiate some form of compensation from the cable system in return for their signals being carried on the cable.

In the wake of the new rules, the leading station groups generally made their stations available free to local cable operators. In return, as compensation, some were provided channel space on cable systems for new services, such as regional news channels (see Chapter 9). Networks negotiated for retransmission consent and received new space on cable systems. They created secondary services like ESPN2, the FX network, and MSNBC.

The Daily Show with Jon Stewart garners a large 18- to 24-year-old audience.

The net effect of the rules is that most cable systems continue to carry the programming of most TV stations in their service area. Local and regional broadcast channels remain the backbone of basic cable programming.

Digital technology then threw a monkey wrench into the uneasy peace established in 1993. You'll recall from Chapter 3 digital television makes it possible to broadcast one high-definition stream or several streams of standard-definition television. Cable companies have maintained that must-carry simply requires them to carry one stream of the broadcast signal. Broadcasters have maintained that cable should be required to carry all the signals contained in the 6-megahertz channel, something called *multicast must carry.* In late 2005, the FCC decided that cable is only required to carry the primary video channel, but as the book went to press, there was speculation that the FCC could reconsider its ruling.

Advertiser-supported basic cable services The second classification of basic cable services is advertiser-supported cable networks, program services specifically designed to reach cable audiences. Like the broadcast networks (ABC, CBS, NBC, and Fox), they carry national advertising. They also provide

opportunities for local cable systems to place their own advertising spots.

Topping the list of the leading ad-supported cable networks are USA and TNT. Also highly rated are TBS, Fox News, ESPN, CNN, Cartoon Network, the Arts and Entertainment Network (A&E), Nickelodeon, and the Lifetime Channel. Some basic services are dedicated to women (Lifetime and Oxygen), while others are geared toward sports fans (ESPN), some to education (The Learning Channel), and some to genres of music (Country Music Television).

The Home and Garden Channel (HGTV), Food Network, Versus (formerly OLN), CNBC, The Weather Channel, Court TV, and many others succeed reaching niche audiences by providing specialized fare to the cable viewer.

The Disney Channel is frequently rated among the top cable nets, although it is not ad-supported. However, it is usually included in the extended basic tier on most cable systems.

Pay Services Pay services became popular in cable in the 1970s as a source of home viewing of theatrical motion pictures, major sports events, and entertainment specials. They are called pay services because subscribers must pay an additional fee to receive the service. Their selling feature is original programming that is not available on broadcast TV, most typically commercial-free movies and home-team sports.

The giant of pay cable is Time Warner's Home Box Office. HBO boasts 28 million households, about one in three TV homes in the United States. It easily leads all pay services in the number of subscribers. Time Warner also owns Cinemax, present in about 9 million homes. Viacom's two services, Showtime and The Movie Channel, are chief competitors to HBO and Cinemax. Showtime serves about 9 million homes; The Movie Channel about 4 million; and Starz with about 3.5 million. Other pay services with a movie emphasis include Encore, The Sundance Channel, FLIX, and BET Movies. Remember these are not discrete subscriber numbers; many families have movie "packages" that may provide more than one pay movie service.

Regional sports services represent a strong and growing segment of pay cable programming. Fox scion Rupert Murdoch has made a specialty in recent years of acquiring regional sports channels around the country (as well as owning teams, like the L.A. Dodgers and the Manchester United soccer club). Viewers pay an extra fee each month to watch the exploits of their favorite teams on Fox Sports Chicago or Fox Sports New York and more than a dozen other regional Fox outlets. However, Fox hasn't bought them all (at least not yet). New York sports fans can subscribe to Yankees Entertainment and Sports (YES) Network, unless they're Mets fans, of course, and people in the Boston area can see their beloved Red Sox, Celtics, and Bruins on New England Sports Network (NESN).

Not all the battles are played on the field, however; a number of skirmishes over who will control the rights to broadcast high-profile teams seem to be brewing. The ruckus off the field is most intense in large cities like New York, Philadelphia, Washington, and Los Angeles. Comcast, which runs regional sports channels on its cable systems, has refused to share regional programming with satellite providers; it has the cable franchises in many of the top 25 markets, giving it special access to sports in these cities. Industry analysts note that sports programming is very lucrative, generating high profit margins for cable operators as the primary reason for the dispute.

Specialty Services   Some additional services available from cable include public service channels like C-SPAN, regional news channels, electronic program guides (EPGs), local governmental channels, jukebox-style music channels (like Music Choice), many shopping channels, even a channel devoted to state lotteries (The Lottery Channel), and local weather.

Over the last 5 years noncable services have really taken off. Today cable is the largest supplier of broadband Internet services and is beginning to provide full telephone services (VoIP). While most people pick cable because of its television implications of more channels, broadband services are rapidly expanding (see Chapter 6) by providing video downloads to mobile devices and home computers. Before we look at the Internet, let's look at how the cable industry prices and packages its program offerings.

Packaging Cable Services: The Trail of "Tiers"

Cable is marketed to attract different types of customer households. The monthly charge for basic service has been regulated by the FCC to keep cable affordable to most homes in the United States and to guarantee carriage of most popular services (including local broadcast services and some of the ad-supported basic services discussed above). These regulations were eliminated in 1999, amid a loud outcry from consumer groups concerned about escalating cable rates.

While the majority of revenue to cable companies is provided by basic subscribers, profitability in the cable business is often based on the number of homes that upgrade to higher levels of service. To create different service levels, cable operators package their offerings in groups, with each succeeding level costing more per month. This process is known as **tiering**. Let's trace the trail of "tiers," from initial wiring of a home for cable to attracting the most-lucrative cable households.

Types of Cable Households   In the cable business not all homes are created equal. Cable companies make clear distinctions between the types of households in their service areas, on the basis of which program options they elect. The various types of TV homes in the United States can be viewed as a pyramid, as illustrated in Figure 5–3.

Issues: Is Big Cable the Place to Be?

Cable has been getting good news over the last few seasons. In 2006, cable snagged a little over a 60 percent share of the prime-time audience over the summer. This was a healthy lead during a time when broadcast networks usually program reruns. But could it be that not all is perfect in the land of cable?

Some analysts caution that the big cable advertising-supported networks such as TBS, USA, and Arts and Entertainment may face the same nibbling away of audience shares that broadcasters have suffered over the past two decades.

Where's the competition coming from? More cable. Smaller, more niche-oriented programmers like Food Network, HGTV, and Comedy Central could threaten big cable operations the same way TBS and USA have challenged over-the-air broadcasters for viewers. According to John Higgins at *Broadcasting and Cable* magazine, much of cable's newfound audience has been fueled by new viewers across the breadth of cable programming. It means that new, smaller networks have picked up substantial viewership. A look at the figures is illuminating. While subscriber growth rates for the large nets like Spike, CNN, ESPN, and USA have hovered around the 15 percent range, upstarts like Hallmark, Court TV, Fox News, and Bravo have averaged between 80 and 150 percent.

Since it is generally agreed in the industry that the number of subscribers for cable and DBS, pegged at 95 of the 110 million homes in the United States, has probably leveled off, the large networks have little room for growth; they're already on the dial of most of the 8,000 cable and DBS systems in the country. However, smaller networks can increase substantially by gaining access to more cable systems in the ad-supported basic service level. For example, Bravo and Oxygen could gain new viewers simply by gaining access to more cable basic tiers on cable systems, but since ESPN, Spike, and USA are already on most basic tiers, they can only increase viewership by making their offerings more attractive, and that means by spending more money on programming.

Sanford Bernstein and Company, a media research firm, looked at April 2005 as an example and found some interesting trends. If viewership for the big cable networks increased by an average of 11 percent, but their distribution (the number of homes available to the service) increased by 15 percent, would that indicate that their popularity actually decreased by 4 percent? Will the big cable networks need to keep their distribution and their viewership stable in order to maintain their shares of the cable universe? As the number of cable choices expands, the large cable networks may find themselves in the same situation as their broadcast counterparts. New upstart networks may nibble away at their share of the audience.

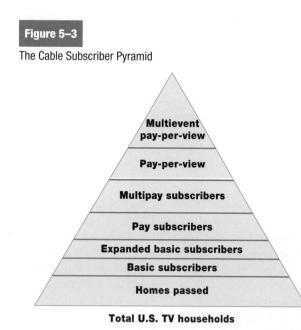

Figure 5–3

The Cable Subscriber Pyramid

Total U.S. TV households

Homes passed The base of the pyramid consists of those households in the United States that are in an area served by cable TV. This statistic is known as **homes passed (HP).** Homes passed are all households that could subscribe to a cable system if they wanted to. The cable literally passes by these households.

In real numbers, there are more than 110 million homes with TV in the United States. About 98 million homes are located in an area served by cable, for an HP figure of about 97 percent.

Cable households The next level of the pyramid includes those HPs that decide to subscribe to cable TV. This figure can be calculated as the ratio of subscriber households to HPs. The resulting percentage is sometimes called the cable system's **basic penetration.** For example, if a cable system passes 100 homes and 85 take the cable, the basic penetration rate is 85 percent. Obviously, a cable operator would like all HPs to take cable service—that is, a penetration rate of 100 percent. This ideal world does not exist. The percentage of households that elect to subscribe varies widely in cable areas. Some suburban systems have enough "upscale" consumer households to boast over 90 percent basic penetration. Other systems, including many in poor inner-city and rural areas, report penetration rates below 50 percent. Industrywide, about 60 percent of all HPs are cable subscribers, about 66 million homes.

Digital cable is the newest wrinkle in cable programming. Because it uses compression technology, digital cable can provide many more channels than standard analog cable. Some digital basic systems provide special services and demand services along with the basic channels.

Pay households Those cable homes that pay an additional fee for the pay services listed earlier (such as HBO or Showtime) are known as **pay households.** Through the period of cable's massive growth—from the mid-1970s to the mid-1980s—as many as 90 percent of all cable subscribers also took a pay service. Faced with competition from new media outlets (mainly video stores, DVDs, and the Internet), the percentage of pay units began to drop in the late 1990s. Today about 52 million homes have some sort of premium cable service, representing about three-quarters of cable homes and almost 50 percent of all TV households in the United States.

Multipay households There are two types of pay cable households: those that elect just one pay service and those that subscribe to more than one. The homes that take more than one service are known as **multipay households.**

Multipay subscribers pay the biggest cable bills—$75–$100 per month or more—much of which is additional profit for the cable company, since it can negotiate reduced rates from pay services to "bundle" its program offerings and since pay tiers are not regulated by the FCC.

Pay-per-view Near the top of the subscriber pyramid are those households that can choose their pay programming selectively by ordering it as desired from the cable company. This is known as **pay-per-view (PPV).**

PPV requires special cable technology. Pay-per-view homes require cable boxes that can be isolated by the cable company and separately programmed (so that only the home that orders the event will receive it). Such devices are known as **addressable converters.** Addressable converters are available in about two-thirds of cable homes.

New digital technology gives subscribers many more options to choose which services they would like. These services may include premium movie channels, regional sports networks, as well as specialty program services (such as BBC America, high-definition channels, Music Choice, and on-demand services). Digital on-demand services require addressability at the cable headend.

At the top of the cable pyramid is **multievent PPV,** also known as *impulse PPV.* As digital cable channel capacity increases and addressability spreads, cable executives expect consumers to buy on impulse, to purchase many different events each month on a PPV basis. This optimism is based on the great success of boxing matches, wrestling events, concerts, and other events offered on a PPV basis in recent years.

Cable and MSO Ownership

Cable TV is different from broadcasting in one important respect. Whereas there is a history of federal caps on the number of broadcast stations that can be owned by a single entity, no such limits have been imposed on cable ownership. In other words, a cable entrepreneur can own as many systems and boast as many subscribers as can be amassed, subject to antitrust law and a rarely enforced cap of 30 percent of national households. Consequently, the cable business is marked by a concentration of ownership by a large number of **multiple-system operators (MSOs).** Owners of only one system are known as **single-system operators (SSOs),** or simply **cable system operators (CSOs).** The MSOs dominate the business, as depicted in Table 5–2.

The largest cable MSO is Comcast with more than 21 million subscriber households. Next we find the two DBS providers, DirecTV and EchoStar. (While they're not cable, you get a sense of the size of DBS.) The second-largest cable MSO is Time Warner Cable, a subsidiary of the entertainment giant, which also owns HBO and Cinemax. Time Warner's cable systems amount to nearly 11 million homes. Comcast and Time Warner account for roughly 33 million

Table 5–2	Top 15 Cable and Satellite Operators	
Rank	**MSO**	**Subscription Households**
1	Comcast Cable Communication	21,448,000
2	DirecTV*	14,670,000
3	EchoStar*	11,455,000
4	Time Warner Cable	10,905,000
5	Cox Communications	6,283,000
6	Charter Communications	5,943,000
7	Adelphia Cable†	5,130,900
8	Cablevision Systems	3,005,600
9	Bright House Networks	2,180,000
10	Mediacom LLC	1,446,000
11	Insight Communications	1,257,200
12	CableOne	702,800
13	Cebridge Connection	449,200
14	RCN Corp.	371,000
15	Bresnan	300,000

*Direct broadcast satellite provider.

†Aldephia is being merged with both Comcast and Time Warner.

Source: *Broadcasting and Cable Yearbook 2006.*

subscriber households. This means that roughly 45 percent of all cable bills in the country are paid to one of these two huge companies. Other major MSOs include Charter, Cox, Cablevision Systems (the owner of the MSG Network, as well as the New York Knicks and the New York Rangers), Mediacom, and CableOne. Adelphia, which suffered from corporate scandals and bankruptcy in 2002, is in the process of being absorbed by Comcast and Time Warner.

The largest individual cable systems are located in major suburban areas and range from about 250,000 to about 3 million subscriber households. The largest systems are Cablevision's sprawling operation for the Greater New York area; followed by Comcast in Boston; Time Warner in Los Angeles; and Comcast's operations in Philadephia and Chicago. Table 5–3 shows the 10 largest systems.

Cable Economics

Unfortunately, it is difficult to evaluate cable systems using a five-star rating system like we did for the various types of television stations. But some industry rules of thumb can apply.

With high up-front capitalization and operations costs, it might appear that making money in cable is difficult, if not impossible. But the truth is that cable can be an enormously profitable enterprise. After all, few businesses find subscribers writing a check to them every month, year after year, "just for TV." While there will be an increase in revenues from advertising, the rise of PPV and DVRs, many cable executives think that the largest share of additional revenue will come from broadband Internet and telephone services. The result is a rosy outlook for cable economics.

Despite enormous construction costs, cable systems can come quickly to profitability. Once systems pass the construction phase, expenses tend to become controllable, if not constant. For example, adding a new broadband or telephone service to an existing household might bring in $25 per month in fees but might cost only $5 to provide the service. Simple arithmetic indicates an 80 percent profit margin!

For these reasons cable operations have received particularly glowing reports from financial analysts. The increasing value of cable systems is driven home by a key industry indicator: cost per subscriber. When a cable system is sold, cable investors and industry observers divide the sales price by the number of subscriber households to arrive at this figure. It is a good measure of how much a cable system is truly worth.

In 1977, the typical cable system sold for under $400 per subscriber. By 1980 the figure had risen to

Table 5–3	Top 10 Cable Clusters	
Rank	**System**	**Subscribers**
1	Cablevision—Greater New York	2,963,001
2	Comcast—Boston	1,937,608
3	Time Warner—Los Angeles	1,918,746
4	Comcast—Philadephia	1,906,925
5	Comcast—Chicago	1,760,735
6	Comcast—San Francisco Bay area	1,608,716
7	Time Warner—New York City	1,379,086
8	Comcast—Seattle	1,030,982
9	Bright House Networks—Tampa Bay	1,011,169
10	Comcast—Detroit	981,693

Source: *Broadcasting and Cable Yearbook 2006.*

about $650. By 1985 cable systems were selling for over $1,000 per subscriber household. In 2005, Time Warner offered $3,500 per subscriber to take over Adelphia customers! Few industries can match the pace of this economic growth.

DIRECT BROADCAST SATELLITES (DBS)

In less than a decade, direct broadcast satellite television service has grown to become an important competitor to cable television. Most people originally expected DBS to be a premium service for the video aficionado or a delivery vehicle for rural viewers who are unable to get cable. But since its inception in 1994, DBS has grown at a remarkable pace to serve nearly one of every four subscription television families in the United States. That translates into 26 million television homes. Some predict that DBS is poised to continue its rapid expansion through the end of the decade.

Two DBS companies provide satellite television service in the United States: one provider is DirecTV, whose controlling interest is Fox Broadcasting's Rupert Murdoch, and the second service, Dish Network, is owned by EchoStar Communications. Both DBS services provide a wide variety of programming from high-powered Ku-band satellites in geostationary orbits.

DBS Programming

DBS provides subscribers with a wide range of programming and pricing options. The number of channels available to the subscriber is tied to a monthly subscription fee, and satellite packages resemble cable tiers in the way program selection is accomplished. In addition, premium services like STARZ and HBO can be ordered to enhance the regular tier offering. At the low end, a subscriber will receive approximately 30 channels of service, with higher-priced services delivering up to more than 220 channels of programming.

One of the things that differentiated cable from satellite service was the carriage of local television channels. Advances in technology and changes in FCC rules made it possible for DBS to offer viewers local television channels in addition to the national programming services. At the moment satellite service provides local television channels to about 135 of the 210 television markets in the United States. For those who do not live in those markets, subscribers must use an outside television antenna and an A/B switch to receive local television service (including over-the-air network channels such as NBC and Fox). It should come as no surprise that an FCC study shows that where DBS provides local television service, satellite service penetration is much

A small satellite receiving dish. Over the past 10 years DBS penetration has increased. Today more than 25 million homes receive satellite TV.

greater than in those markets that don't offer local channels.

Importantly, DBS tends to be priced less than cable for comparable services. This price advantage has helped entice some cable subscribers to switch to satellite service in recent years. In the last few years both DirecTV and Dish Network have been adding local television stations and DVRs to their systems. These services and aggressive pricing propelled sizable growth, but DBS providers are worried that bundled broadband and VoIP services will entice many consumers to stay with cable instead of switching to satellite.

DBS Today and Beyond

Satellite television has been a leader at using innovative technology. Currently DBS transmission standards are already digital, meaning that satellite pictures are pristinely clear. In addition, satellite television offers HD programming for subscribers with the necessary digital equipment while HDTV-compatible boxes are just being introduced for cable.

Some of the other innovative services that direct broadcast satellite has introduced include digital video recorders (DVRs) that allow users to record programming directly to a computer hard disk and innovative satellite-to-home broadband Internet service. And, unlike cable, DBS providers sell their hardware directly to customers at retail operations such as Best Buy, Radio Shack, and Wal-Mart or via the Internet.

A research study done by the Carmel Group predicted that the growth rate for DBS would average about 19 percent for the next few years. However, in an effort to stave off the loss of customers, cable has moved quickly to bundle digital television services with high-speed broadband and telephone. DBS has only been able to offer DSL broadband by linking satellite TV to high-speed DSL phone services. Signs that this renewed competition between cable and DBS was slowing satellite growth emerged in 2006, as satellite subscription rates fell below analysts' expectations.

Looking for new ways to compete with cable, DirecTV began offering early downloads of popular FX programming into set-top DVRs in 2006. Subscribers can get early viewing of popular shows like *The Shield* before they are aired on the network. Subscribers can also download shows from Fox and NBC. DirecTV also announced that its new set-top boxes will allow shows to be downloaded to a media player called "PocketDish."

WORKING IN TELEVISION

We close this chapter with a look at television stations and cable operations as places to work and build careers. First, we look at how television facilities are organized and staffed. Second, we take a look at salaries. In short, where are the jobs and how much do they pay?

TV Station Organization

The organizational structure of a TV station varies according to the size of the organization. There is no specific way in which all stations are organized, but there are some general areas common to most TV stations. Figure 5–4 presents a typical organizational structure for a station in a large community.

At the top of the organizational ladder is the general manager (GM), or station manager—two different names for the same job. This person is ultimately responsible for the operation of the station. If the station is part of a group of stations, the GM usually is a vice president in the parent organization.

TV stations are generally divided into five divisions, each division having its own head who reports directly to the station manager. The five areas are sales, engineering, business, programming, and news. Each of these areas is vital for the efficient operation of a TV station.

Sales   Sales is the most important part of the TV station—at least according to anyone in the sales department. This division of the TV station is headed by a general sales manager. It is her or his job to oversee the sales staff—both local and national. The salespeople for the station are called account executives or sales representatives.

The sales department is also in charge of **traffic** and **continuity.** Traffic is not the helicopter reports but that part of the station that schedules commercials and verifies that scheduled commercials are aired properly. Traffic departments are responsible for the program logs that tell the people in the control room when each video event is to occur. The continuity department makes sure the station's schedules have no interruptions between commercials and programs.

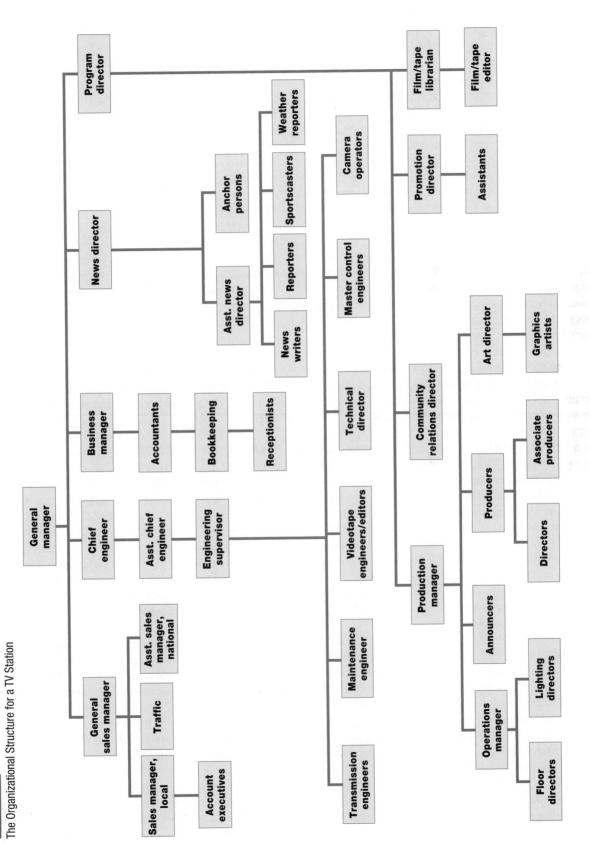

Figure 5–4

The Organizational Structure for a TV Station

The verification that an advertisement was played is just as important as scheduling it. If the scheduled commercial doesn't air or only partially airs (say, because of an equipment malfunction), then the sponsor is entitled to a **make-good**—a free commercial in the same time category—to replace the commercial that didn't air. Make-goods are given in lieu of returning the advertiser's money.

Engineering   The second major division in a TV station is engineering. Engineering is the most important part of the TV station—just ask any engineer.

The engineering department is responsible for the maintenance of the equipment, including the transmitter. If there is an equipment failure, it is up to a member of the engineering department to find the problem and correct it.

In sufficiently large or unionized stations engineers run the audio/video equipment. People who load the video machines, edit, run the audio board, and push the buttons on the switchers are from the engineering department. Camera operators are also usually from this department. In smaller stations or nonunion shops there may be no hard-and-fast rules about who uses what equipment.

Business   The third area of the TV station is the business division. The business division is usually headed by the business manager. Most business managers feel that they run the most important division of the station. Accounts payable (money owed by the station) and accounts receivable (money owed to the station) are handled in this division. Everyone who is owed money by the station and everyone who owes money to the station has his or her paperwork go through this division. Receptionists and secretaries are also a part of the business division.

Programming   The fourth and, according to the people who work there, the most important area of a TV station is programming. The program director, often abbreviated PD, oversees a number of subdivisions and, in consultation with the station manager, is responsible for the purchase of all new programming for the station and the scheduling of the programming during the broadcast day.

Under the program director, three subdivisions can be identified at most stations. Usually the largest subdivision is run by the production manager, who oversees studio workers such as floor managers and lighting directors, art directors and videographers, producers, directors, and production assistants. In small markets the crew may double up on many activities.

The second subdivision is headed by the community relations director and her or his staff. This division is usually in charge of public service announcements. The community relations director may also be in charge of TV programs examining minority interests at the station or may be the official spokesperson for the station at community events.

The third subdivision is run by the promotion director, who typically has three duties. First, the promotion director oversees the creation and placement of messages that promote programs, movies, specials, and the station's image. Second, she or he plans and runs activities designed to gain publicity—such as sponsoring a local charity road race. Third, the promotion director is responsible for the purchase of advertising in other media. This person is in charge of the commercial aspects of promoting the station, whereas the community relations director is usually seen as being in charge of the altruistic side of the station.

News   The fifth division is news, which, as any newsperson will tell you, is the most important part of the station. The news division is headed by the news director, who is in charge of the reporters, news writers, anchors, sportscasters, and weather forecasters. The news division of a station is supposed to operate independently of influences from the other divisions and so is separate from all other divisions. The smaller the station is, the harder it is to maintain this independence. As with the other division heads, the news director reports directly to the station manager.

News has a special place in broadcasting. Stations with active news departments become more important to—and are viewed more favorably by—the communities they serve. The overall quality of a station is often judged by how good its news department is. The value of a station during a sale can be affected by the reputation of the news department; a good news department is considered an asset to a station.

Today with the number of duopolies of stations increasing in major markets (a duopoly is where one company owns more than one station), the news department in the larger station may produce a news

It was ferocious. Some called it a doomsday scenario. It was the country's worst natural disaster. Evidently the storm was beyond the capabilities of our state and federal relief agencies, but television covered the story with compassion and clarity.

NBC news anchor Brian Williams was packing to go on vacation when he got the call to head to New Orleans. Williams went into the city Sunday before the storm hit. He and his NBC crew parked their satellite truck next to the Superdome. He recalls that they knew the superstructure of the dome would hold against the storm, but they didn't know if the roof of the Superdome would stay on. The nation found out Monday morning when Williams used the picture capabilities in his cell phone to transmit pictures of holes in the roof to viewers of the *Today Show.*

But Katrina was no ordinary storm. Even professional journalists were not prepared for the pictures their cameras recorded later when the storm passed: desperate people clinging to their roofs, miles and miles of flooding and devastation, water pouring over the levees, families separated, and thousands of people crying for help. These were the first images sent back to America from helicopters that flew over the region that Monday.

Some broadcasters stayed on the air to relay vital information to the people hit by the storm. WLOX in Biloxi had to evacuate the newsroom and the control room when massive pieces of concrete were thrown through the second story of the building. Throughout the storm and at great peril, WLOX stayed on the air.

In New Orleans, CBS affiliate WWL had a plan readied for such an emergency. Five years earlier the station had worked with Louisiana State University to use its TV studios in case of such a disaster. The station also built a concrete bunker, able to withstand category 5 winds, for the transmitter and generator. Throughout the ordeal WWL produced more than 200 hours of live coverage.

Some say the media went too far. CNN was criticized for showing pictures of bloodied bodies lying on the floor of the New Orleans Convention Center, while Geraldo Rivera was accused of nudging relief workers out of the way. Overall, however, most critics agreed that television did an outstanding job of covering one the most difficult stories in recent times.

show for the smaller station. Thus some stations may not have news departments.

Departmental Evaluation   As indicated, each department thinks it is the most important department at the station. Which department is really the most important? Are the sales executives right that the station would close its doors if they were not finding sponsors? Are the programming and production people right when they argue that without them there would be nothing to sponsor? Or do the engineers, who insist that without them there wouldn't be any signal, have the better claim?

Cable System Organization

Cable systems have an organizational structure similar to that of TV stations, but use slightly different names to denote the major functions. Figure 5–5 provides an organizational chart for a typical cable television system.

First, in cable, the manager of the cable system may be known as the general manager, as in broadcast TV, or as the system manager. At one time, these executives were called "sysops" (short for "system operators"). Today, that designation is more common to computer networks.

The technical side of the cable business is handled by the chief technician (chief tech, in cable parlance). Roughly equivalent to the chief engineer on the broadcast side, the chief tech supervises cable plant as well as installation and maintenance. The chief tech has the additional burden of coordinating and dispatching field crews to maintain and improve cable service throughout the system.

The sales function in cable includes advertising sales, but it also involves the important task of recruiting and retaining subscribers. Thus, the promotion function in cable is a bit broader than on the broadcast side. For this reason, cable promotion executives tend to be called **marketing managers** (rather than promotion directors). Similarly, office management requires more people than is common in broadcast TV. Cable systems often have more than one retail location, at which numerous **customer service representatives (CSRs)** process bills, hand out converters, and take complaints from subscribers.

Figure 5–5

Cable System Organizational Chart

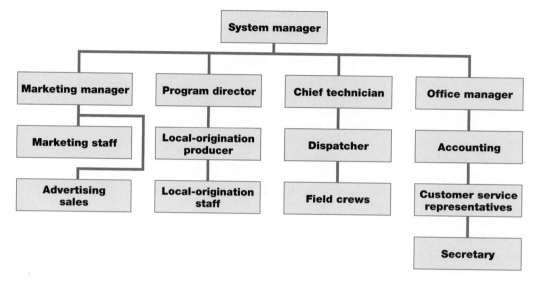

Finally, the programming department in cable is slightly different from its counterpart in broadcast TV. In cable, the program director is the liaison between the various program services and the local system. Locally produced programs (such as home shopping and local call-in programs) typically fall under the aegis of the **local-origination (LO) producer,** the rough equivalent of the community affairs director in broadcasting. Cable systems with full-fledged local news operations (see Chapter 9) may also boast a separate news director and production staff.

All told, however, cable systems and TV stations are staffed and managed in similar ways. Critical departments include general operations, programming, sales, and engineering.

THE JOB OUTLOOK

Before we look at the job picture, remember that broadcast and cable television are part of the larger information industry sector, and some general observations can be made. While the U.S. Bureau of Labor is predicting growth, the first line of this chapter stated that TV is an industry going through a transformation. That means that the jobs (and salaries) described below are frequently changing—as are technology, ownership, programming, and distribution.

So one kernel of good advice is to keep an open mind about your career choice. The job you seek today may not even exist when you graduate. If it does, it's apt to require a set of skills other than those you acquired in the classroom or on an internship.

A second thing is true about a career in television—whether broadcast or cable: Both are "cottage industries"—that is to say, despite the power and influence of their programming, the industries are in fact quite small. All told, the combined television and cable workforce represents about 325,000 people, including all employees of both commercial and nonprofit TV stations and networks and of cable systems and headquarters. As in other small industries, a move up the career ladder requires skill, dedication, and perseverance. Employers frequently look for someone with a good work ethic and a large dose of creativity. Too, much like the popular game "six degrees of Kevin Bacon," you'll find it quite easy to find a link between your current employer or co-workers and other managers and employees from other stations, networks, or organizations. Thus, it is good advice to maintain positive relationships as you move along the career path and not to "burn bridges" by exhibiting the kind of workplace behaviors apt to catch up with you later on. As the old saying goes, it's not what you know, but who you know (and what they think of you as a co-worker or boss).

The job outlook in television has brightened, especially for women and minorities.

Finally, the trend toward industry concentration and automation traced throughout this text has had great impact on the media workforce. Generally speaking, there are fewer jobs in areas like television production, and the power of trade associations, unions, and guilds has diminished. At the same time, the competition for audiences and from new media has led to job growth in other areas, like Web site development, sales, marketing, and promotion. Workforce growth in the news area has also occurred, as more and more TV stations and cable systems look to TV news as a means of driving viewer interest and attention.

Broadcast TV Job Trends

About 120,000 people work in one of the broadcast TV professions (e.g., camera, editors, reporters, engineers)—nearly 80 percent work in commercial TV, with the remainder in public TV. The highest earnings tend to be in the northeastern and northern states; the lowest are in the South. Salaries depend on a number of factors: the size of the community in which the station is located, whether the workers at the station are unionized, the dominance of a station in its market, and so on.

Sales executives are usually paid on a commission basis. To survive, they must sell time. If they are not good at selling time, they rarely make enough to live on and so move on to a different field. If they can sell, then TV can be very lucrative. There is always a strong demand for good salespeople in broadcasting, and TV is no exception.

Production crews and those who appear on the air are represented by unions at some stations. Organized, that is, unionized, stations almost without exception pay their employees better than nonunion stations in the same area. There are several different unions representing workers at a station. Generally performers are represented by AFTRA, the American Federation of Television and Radio Artists. Engineers and production people are usually represented by NABET, the National Association of Broadcast Engineers and Technicians; IATSE, the International Alliance of Theatre and Screen Employees; and/or IBEW, the International Brotherhood of Electrical Workers.

Unions usually represent the workers at contract renewal time, when management and union come to agreement on compensation and work responsibilities.

Reflecting national trends, unions have been in decline in TV. Whereas nationwide the number of employees belonging to a union was once as high as one in three, today fewer than one in six workers belongs to a union. This trend has also been felt in TV, as the power of NABET, IATSE, and other organizations is much less today than it was in the 1960s and 1970s.

Pay in TV is largely determined by the size of the market one works in. Simply put, the larger the city, the more money you will earn. In addition, on average, VHF stations pay more than UHF stations, and network affiliates pay better than do independents. Commercial TV tends to pay better than public television, although public broadcasters tend to have higher job security than their counterparts at commercial stations.

As is true for most businesses, managers make the most money in TV. Nationwide, the typical GM earns over $100,000 per year, over $177,000 in the nation's top 50 TV markets. As in radio, sales managers make the most money. In fact, you would be hard-pressed to find a sales executive in a top 10 TV market earning less than $150,000 per year.

Next to sales, salaries in the news department are the highest in TV. In the top 10 markets, anchors and reporters can earn six-figure salaries. The downside is that salaries slip significantly in smaller markets.

Engineering and programming positions, from the video editor to the camera operator, tend to provide steady employment at stable but lower salaries than high-profile sales and news jobs offer. For example, the National Association of Broadcasters says the average annual salary for camera operators was $30,000 in 2005. There is less volatility from market to market in salaries and employee benefits.

Cable TV Job Trends

During the era of cable's great expansion, from the late 1970s to the mid-1980s, it was estimated that the cable industry was expanding by an average of 1,000 new jobs per month. This was an astonishingly high figure, particularly since this expansion coincided with an era of high national unemployment and a serious economic recession.

Cable employment slowed in the late 1980s and early 1990s, as most systems completed their construction, and many cable networks faced cost-cutting due to increasing competition. Today there are nearly 10,000 cable systems in the United States employing 130,000 people. About 1 in 10 cable employees is found at network or MSO headquarters; the remainder at local cable systems around the country.

Whereas the size of the staff in a radio and TV station is usually based on the size of the station's home city, in cable, the number of employees is based on the number of subscriber households. That is, systems with more homes hire more people. This makes sense: Large systems are more likely to sell advertising and to program their own channels. They also need more customer service representatives, installers, and technicians. A large system (more than 300,000 subscriber households) is about the size of a large TV station, with 75 or more full-time employees. Midsized systems (100,000 to 300,000 subscribers) are more like large radio stations, with 30 to 50 people on staff. Small cable systems (under 100,000 households) are run like small-market broadcast stations, both radio and TV, with fewer than 30 total employees.

Unlike broadcasting, cable is a decidedly blue-collar industry. Most jobs fall into the technical or office/clerical category. Technical jobs generally require training in fields like electronics and engineering. Cable recruits its technicians from trade schools, community college electronics programs, and vocational-technical (vo-tech) schools. Job applicants are also sought from related communications fields, including the telephone and data-processing industries, and the Society of Cable Telecommunications Engineers (SCTE) offers certification programs for a number of technician positions.

Because of its history and tradition as a service business (and not "show business"), cable salaries have typically lagged behind those in broadcasting. One reason for lower salaries and wages is the relative lack of union membership in the cable business. Whereas most telephone employees and many broadcast technicians belong to unions, less than 10 percent of the cable workforce is unionized. However, as cable operations become more profitable, they are also becoming more like broadcast stations. As we have seen, many cable systems are actively seeking advertising dollars.

Nationwide, the typical general manager of a cable system earns about $80,000. Other high-paid positions in cable include treasurer or finance director ($70,000), human resources director ($55,000), program manager ($58,000), and marketing director ($60,000). Lower-paying positions include office manager ($32,000) and cable service and technical operators ($40,000).

Women and Minorities in TV

Like many other industries in the United States, TV has been, historically, primarily a white, male-dominated industry. Steps were taken in the late 1960s and early 1970s to begin to rectify the imbalance, but changes have been slow in coming.

Overall, women hold about 4 in 10 jobs in television today, and members of minority groups (including African Americans, Hispanic Americans, Asian Americans, and Native Americans) represent nearly 30 percent of TV employees. The good news is that those percentages have been on a slow and steady increase in recent years.

On the negative side, women still tend to find themselves in office positions. More than 87 percent of office and secretarial staffs remain female. Ethnic minorities tend to find themselves in technical and operations positions. However, gains for both women and members of minority groups have been seen in recent years in the more lucrative areas of sales and news. Today, more than half the broadcast sales workforce, and 45 percent of the cable sales force, is female. On the news side, about one in two news anchors and reporters is a woman, reflecting the population. One in five TV newspersons is a member of a minority group. However, entry into management is another matter. Less than one in five TV news directors is a woman, and only 1 in 10 minorities heads a TV news department.

Like much of American industry, there remains a rather large gender gap. Men make more than women in both broadcast and cable TV. All told, women's salaries lag about 10 percent behind those for men in similar positions. Some good news for women is that they have tended to get larger pay increases than men in recent years. However, the gender gap remains real and persistent.

In 2005, the leading trade magazine, *Broadcasting and Cable,* noted that of the top 25 broadcast station groups, only one (Young Broadcasting) was headed by a woman. Those trends were among the reasons that FCC Chairman Michael Powell (himself an African American) was pushing hard to increase opportunities in television for female and nonwhite owners, operators, and employees.

SUMMARY

- The popularity of television with American viewers has made it an important and highly profitable business. However, it is also a business in transition, facing new competition for viewers and from new technologies.

- More than 1,700 TV stations compete for audiences. Commercial stations earn their revenue primarily from advertising sales. Noncommercial stations rely on government funds, grants, and donations from viewers. Television stations are of two main types: VHF stations (channels 2–13) and UHF stations (channels 14 and above). VHF stations are generally more watched and more profitable. In 2009, all full-time TV stations will be digital (DTV).

- Network television is a segment of the TV business in which local TV stations agree to carry programs from a major network in return for a share of their advertising slots. In recent years, compensation paid by the network has declined for network affiliates. The network business was dominated for many years by ABC, CBS, and NBC. Newer networks are now on the scene, including Fox, CW, and Pax TV.

- The local television business relies on sales to local and regional advertisers. The most-successful local TV stations are those owned and operated by a major network, or those owned and managed by a large-TV-station group owner. Weaker TV stations include independents and low-power operations.

- About 400 stations are public television operations. PBS provides programming to most of these stations, and its children's shows, news, and documentaries have attracted viewers and continuing government support.

- Cable television has grown in recent years to become an important component of the television landscape. Cable is in more than two-thirds of America's TV homes, and more than 300 different national program services compete for space on the cable. The cable business makes its money by marketing and selling to different levels of customer homes. Revenues are enhanced by moving customers from basic service to pay, multipay, and new services, including Internet access and local telephone service. The cable business is dominated by large, multiple-system operators, most of whom also have ownership interest in cable programming services, telephone services, and broadcast TV services.

- Both broadcast and cable television facilities are organized into separate staffs, which typically include general management; programming; sales, marketing and promotion; and engineering. Job growth has been noted in the marketing and sales areas, as well as in local news, as cable systems and local TV stations aggressively court viewers faced with more and more options.

- In general, the best salaries are earned by employees of large TV stations and cable systems, and by employees in sales or general management. While opportunities for women and members of ethnic minority groups have risen in recent years, the television industry still lags behind other industries in employment and salary equity.

KEY TERMS

VHF; very high frequency   104
UHF; ultra-high frequency   104
network television   105
local television   105
affiliates   108
independent TV station   109
low-power television
    (LPTV)   109
tiering   115
homes passed (HP)   116

basic penetration   116
pay households   117
multipay households   117
pay-per-view (PPV)   117
addressable converters   117
multievent PPV   117
multiple-system operators
    (MSOs)   117
single-system operators
    (SSOs)   117

cable system operators
    (CSOs)   117
traffic   120
continuity   120
make-good   122
marketing managers   123
customer service representatives
    (CSRs)   123
local-origination (LO)
    producer   124

SUGGESTIONS FOR FURTHER READING

Blumenthal, H., & Goodenough, O. (2006). *This business of television* (2nd ed.). New York: Billboard Books.

Day, J. (1995). *The vanishing vision: The inside story of public television.* Berkeley: University of California Press.

Ellis, E. (2004). *Opportunities in broadcasting careers.* New York: McGraw-Hill.

Engleman, R. (1996). *Public radio & television in America: A political history.* Thousand Oaks, CA: Sage.

Jessell, H. (2006). *Broadcasting and cable yearbook 2006.* New Providence, NJ: R.R. Bowker.

Parsons, P., & Frieden, R. (1998). *The cable and satellite television industries.* Boston: Allyn & Bacon.

Sherman, B. (1995). *Telecommunications management* (2nd ed.). New York: McGraw-Hill.

———. (1999). *The television industry standard.* New York: Gerson-Lehrman.

Vogel, H. (2001). *Entertainment industry: A guide for financial analysis.* Cambridge, UK: Cambridge University Press.

Walker, J., & Ferguson, D. (1998). *The broadcast television industry.* Boston: Allyn & Bacon.

Waterman, D., & Weiss, A. (1997). *Vertical integration in cable television.* Cambridge, MA: MIT Press.

Weaver, D. (1998). *Breaking into television: Proven advice from veterans and interns.* Princeton, NJ: Peterson's.

INTERNET EXERCISES

Visit our Web site at **www.mhhe.com/dominick6** for study-guide exercises to help you learn and apply material in each chapter. You will find ideas for future research as well as useful Web links to provide you with an opportunity to journey through the new electronic media.

The Internet and New Media Today   6

Quick Facts

 Number of Internet users worldwide in 2006: 1,022,863,307 (estimated)

 Most popular Web site worldwide: Yahoo (2006)

 Number of Americans with broadband Web access: 84,000,000 (2006)

 Number of iPods sold since being introduced in October 2001: 60,000,000 (2006)

 Fastest-growing Web site in 2005: MySpace.com

 Percent of Americans who cite the Internet as their main source for news: 24 (2006)

It is clear from the content of the previous chapter that the television industry today can be summed up with one word: *transformation*. Now for something completely different: The language of the Internet is quite different from that of traditional broadcasting—surfing, routers, ISPs, portals, podcasts, and domain names. The history of information services reinforces this notion. The development of the Internet occurred among people with specific interests, such as computer hobbyists (geeks?), businesspeople, and scientists. Discussions on early bulletin boards often centered on computers and software usage. These services weren't anything at all like the mass media. But over the last decade, the Internet has evolved rapidly, and it has changed into a mass medium. Broadcasting and cable networks all have Web sites, as do magazines and movie studios. There are sites streaming video, you can download prime-time television episodes, and radio stations are broadcasting live. The media presence on the World Wide Web is important and growing. This chapter takes a look at the new media, who's on the Net, and how choices are made about where to surf. Not to worry, though—you won't need a degree in computer science to follow this road map.

A BRIEF HISTORY

In the Beginning Was the Word: Teletext

Some of the pioneering information-based services available to the general public started first in Europe with the use of television signals or the telephone system. In America, large newspaper publishers, trying to come to grips with the new electronic communication systems, also experimented with various kinds of information services to determine whether there was a consumer market for purchasing information. These first systems were called **teletext.**

Britain pioneered an early system called CEEFAX in 1973, a one-way system that sent data to your home TV by encoding information within the television signal. Although the system could display large amounts of data, it was slow and had limited graphics capability.

Toward the end of the 1970s, U.S. newspaper giants Knight-Ridder and Times-Mirror spent millions of dollars trying to develop **videotex,** an information service designed to serve as electronic newspapers. These early services were based on essentially the same television technology as teletext, but users accessed the information via the telephone. Early experiments did not generate much interest among test-market users either, so after losing millions of dollars most American newspapers scrapped the idea and shut down the services.

Minitel

In 1980, the French telephone company introduced Minitel, a **videotext** system that connected special terminals to the telephone. Videotext systems are completely interactive. French Telecom gave terminals to customers instead of providing a printed telephone directory. Initially there were few offerings other than the telephone directory, and service was slow. But by 1984, Minitel service offerings began to

Ceefax

BBC Television Centre
Wood Lane,
London W12 7RJ
Telex: 265781

**News & general
enquiries:**
01-743 8000
Ext. 3701 or 3703

Sport & Finance:
01-580 4468
Ext. 2880

**Engineering
Information:**
01-580 4468
Ext. 2921

CEEFAX data were transmitted in the television signal's blanking pulse. It could take several minutes to update page information because data were sent out sequentially.

grow. During the first years of operation, the government heavily subsidized the service, but since it used the telephone system, there was a ready-made customer base.

As people began using the system, the number of services on Minitel grew rapidly. Escort services, interestingly, were soon available in large numbers, but, before long, other businesses began seeing opportunities. Today Minitel offers a wide gamut of services—for example, personal messaging, banking, e-mail, and ordering train tickets and even take-out food for home delivery. Since Minitel was really an extension of the phone, its ubiquity made it an enticing service, but it is facing increasing competition as the French turn toward the Net for these services.

Hometown America Gets Wired—Slowly

CEEFAX and Minitel may seem unfamiliar to you, but AOL and Prodigy are probably not. But here's a point that needs to be made: Commercial development of information services occurred differently in America. While many foreign governments actively promoted their information and computer industries—such as CEEFAX and Minitel—most communication innovations in America have tended to occur because of the efforts of private entrepreneurs. Even though the U.S. government built the original communications network (ARPANET), access was limited to governmental, educational, scientific, and military personnel. It was entrepreneurs who used that technology to start up and build the first information services to serve businesses and the home consumer in the United States.

In 1978, William Von Meister, an entrepreneur, envisioned a "home information utility" linked by computers and started a computer bulletin board service called The Source. Meister's brainchild became the first home computer network, providing news and financial information, but he quickly ran into financial trouble. Publishing giant Reader's Digest decided it couldn't ignore this potential area, and 2 years later it bailed out Meister in a $6 million takeover.

One year later H&R Block took over CompuServe, another pioneering information service, with the intention of linking tax services with information services. While that aspect of the business never caught on, CompuServe maintained its business focus by providing in-depth discussion areas related to business, commerce, and technology. In 1980, it became the first online service to offer real-time chat capabilities. Today CompuServe is owned by AOL.

New Markets, New Entrants: Prodigy and America Online

Two new services joined the national ranks of online service providers.

Prodigy, a joint venture between Sears, Roebuck and IBM, started in 1985. It was designed to serve as an online magazine. With flat-fee pricing, unlimited access, and e-mail all at one low price, the service looked like a real bargain to many customers. And unlike The Source and CompuServe, Prodigy provided unique content specifically geared toward its users, much the same way a magazine would. Prodigy tried to make computer networking into a mass-market service and hoped that subscribers would be enticed by the prominent on-screen advertising to request additional screens of product information. As part owner of the venture, Sears also hoped to replace its aging catalog shopping service with a modern online shopping network. The idea of generating new catalog revenue, in addition to charging a flat monthly access fee, transformed the online service provider from a bulletin board service to that of a content provider.

Also in 1985, a small start-up company, Quantum Computer Services, began operations by providing support for computer gamers. Quantum officially became America Online (AOL) in 1989 and immediately broadened its appeal beyond games by offering special areas for different communities of users. For example, it focused on special services for users of Macintosh, IBM, and Commodore computers. AOL's development of chat rooms was an important way it distinguished itself from Prodigy and other computer services. Rather than making discussion forums ancillary to other services, AOL put them out in front.

Computer services didn't take off right away. In the 1980s, **Internet service providers (ISPs)** met with opposition from many home computer owners and with varying degrees of acceptance from others for a number of reasons. Dial-up access numbers were limited mostly to large urban areas. Thus, if you lived outside that calling area, you needed to make a long-distance call to get a connection. With the per-minute telephone charge and modem speeds of only 300 or 1,200 baud per second, these services were much too slow to download any significant computer databases or visual images. Several events, however, changed the telecommunications marketplace as the 1980s came to a close, and the fortunes of AOL, CompuServe, and Prodigy changed dramatically. First, the growth of competition in the long-distance telephone business increased dramatically after the breakup of AT&T. So users who lived in suburban areas saw the price of their usage drop.

At the same time a new generation of more-powerful computers and faster modems emerged. Black-and-white screens were replaced with color displays. Users became more interested in using graphics and images with their computers. These factors, coupled with the introduction of the Macintosh and Microsoft's Windows interface, made online services much more attractive to the average user.

America Online and Prodigy took advantage of these changes and embarked on high-visibility advertising campaigns to encourage people to try their services. AOL sent out millions of trial software packages in the mail and included them in magazines, hoping to entice people to connect for a trial period. Millions of Americans signed up. But while America Online's customer base exploded, technological change was going to force all these companies to alter their business plans dramatically.

ISPs Grow and the Web Emerges

Recall from Chapter 2 that ARPANET demonstrated that networked computers could be made to share complex information. By 1988, more than 100,000 host computers were interconnected, and the growth in the number of users spurred tremendous innovation in computer networking services. In 1989, both CompuServe and MCI provided gateways making it possible to send e-mail to locations around the globe. Because e-mail could now move between different commercial providers through the Internet, usage exploded among business users. But it was Tim Berners-Lee's development of the **World Wide Web** and the introduction of the Mosaic browser in 1993 that spurred the growth of local Internet service providers. Almost overnight the general population began talking about the new communications revolution. Small Internet service providers sprang up in cities like neighborhood convenience stores. Frequently these ISPs offered easy, unlimited access to the Internet, e-mail, and the

necessary software for accessing net services tools for a set monthly fee.

The sudden growth of the Internet and the new World Wide Web challenged AOL, Prodigy, and CompuServe. Newspapers and magazines began to experiment by putting portions of their content on the Web. Since ISPs were frequently local or regional, there were no more long-distance charges and fewer repeated busy signals. In comparison, AOL, Prodigy, and CompuServe provided their customers with many useful and unique services but initially gave them very limited access to the World Wide Web. For example, AOL customers who wanted to use the Web found that America Online's system didn't work well with browsers. Some people began predicting the demise of AOL and CompuServe, claiming that customers would leave these services once they became sophisticated Web users.

The Growth of the World Wide Web and What Came After

The phrase "surfing the Net," coined by a librarian, Jean Armour Polly, sums it all up. The relative ease of searching for information and the ability to link from one page to another halfway around the world put incredible power into the hands of the user. The World Wide Web became a "killer application": something that convinced many people that they should buy personal computers.

In 1993, Mosaic became the first browser for personal computers, and, if you can imagine it, there were only about 50 locations around the world with Web pages running. That changed quickly. Though few companies and universities had Web pages initially, there were nearly 2 million computer hosts already attached to the Internet worldwide, and each one of those sites had the capability of becoming a Web site immediately. The only thing a site administrator needed to do was to set up an index page in the **HyperText Markup Language (HTML).** Once content pages were linked to that index, a new Web site was born. Fairly soon after the release of the Mosaic browser, many universities started experimentally displaying pages with this new form of hypertext media. Large publishing companies also started sites immediately. The Web spread like wildfire.

By fall 1994, there were more than 3 million Internet host sites connected worldwide, and new domain names were being added at a rate of 2,000 a

Figure 6–1

Internet Growth 1988–2005

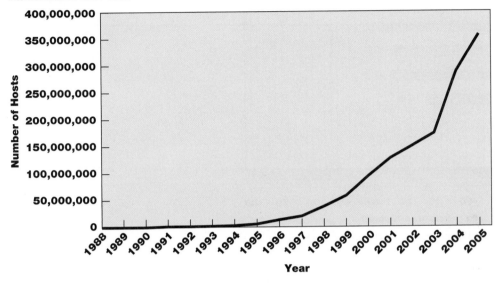

month. Within 2 years the number of Internet hosts tripled again to nearly 9 million (see Figure 6–1).

Innovations at both the user and corporate levels changed the Web very quickly. Online publications blossomed, and personal Web pages started popping up everywhere. College professors put their syllabi on the Internet for students to access, cooks posted their favorite recipes, and Web soap operas started up—as did thousands of different small enterprises directly related to a new concept called *e-commerce*. In the early days, few people made any money except those sites that charged a fee for the titillating views of sex that they offered.

As with any great new invention, new industries are created to support previously unrealized needs. Now that information was being added to the World Wide Web quickly, user-friendly **search engines** became very important. Early programs such as Hot Bot and AltaVista sent "Web crawlers" around the net during off-peak hours of the night cataloging pages. Between 1993 and 1996 there were dozens and dozens of search engines being developed. Among those was one called BackRub that looked at ways of linking to Web sites and another called Yahoo! that cataloged sites on the web. Two years later BackRub became Google, and Yahoo! became an important portal.

The growth of the Internet has elicited all kinds of speculation about what the Net will look like in the future. The current growth of the Internet shows few signs of slowing down. ComScore Networks

estimates that in 2006 there were about 150 million Americans age 15 and over regularly using the Web and about 700 million people worldwide. Perhaps more important to note, however, is that the fastest growth taking place is now outside the United States.

Advertising revenues for the Internet are increasing rapidly. Veronis Suhler Stevenson's Communication Industry Forecast estimates that ad revenue will total $9.3 billion in 2006 and will continue to grow. (See Figure 6–2.)

INTERNET BASICS—WHO OWNS THE WEB?

The Internet is cyberspace; there's no one place where it resides. But that's the point. Although it represents intellectual property, the Internet is not real estate. It's not owned or managed by any one person, or government, or company. A number of different groups have the responsibility for coordinating the Internet and setting specifications to make it work. Among the different groups charged with managing cyberspace is the Internet Society, a nonprofit organization that helps promote global connectivity. Membership to the Internet Society is open to anyone.

Several other organizations play important roles in making the Internet work efficiently. The Internet Engineering Task Force (IETF), for example, was formed to support responsible and effective use of

Figure 6–2

Internet Advertising Growth 2000–2006

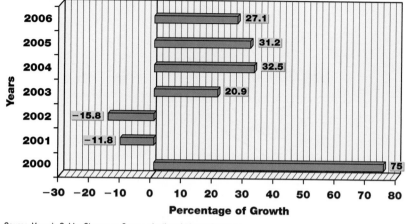

Source: Veronis Suhler Stevenson Communications Industry Forecast.

the network. The Internet Assigned Numbers Authority (IANA) has the overall responsibility for managing Internet protocol, and this organization delegates the daily responsibilities to regional organizations. In North America that task is given to the American Registry for Internet Numbers.

Tim Berners-Lee, the inventor of the Web, heads the **World Wide Web Consortium (W3C),** which is run jointly by the MIT Laboratory for Computer Science, the European Research Consortium for Informatics and Mathematics, and Keio University in Japan. Together these organizations provide the guidance necessary for work on the standards related to Web architecture.

How Standards and Protocols Make the Web Work

While Internet standards and protocols are decided upon by the various voluntary standards groups, no single organization has control or say as to how the network can be used or what can be sent over the network. An individual user selling old records on eBay has as much right to use the Web as a public library or a government agency. Corporations have the same rights too. The question of knowing where and to whom to send a message or where to locate specific information on the Web is resolved by giving a unique address to each site. If your computer is connected to an Internet service provider or network, you are part of the Internet. When you type an address or link to a Web page, a request for

information is made through the ISP gateway to the specific server housing the requested information. A router computer keeps tabs and sends the information packets to the correct destinations.

A **uniform resource locator (URL)** provides the key to retrieving the correct information and then getting it delivered to the requester's address. Each URL is hierarchical, designating a specific protocol (such as www for World Wide Web or ftp for file transfer protocol). Next is a secondary **domain name** and then a primary domain name. Secondary domains are usually the company or institutional name (such as NBC or IBM). Top-level domains such as

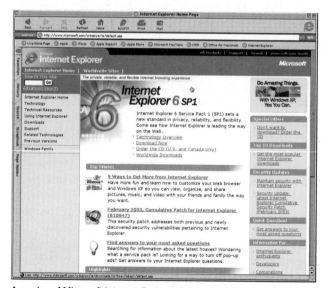

A version of Microsoft Internet Explorer. Courtesy of Microsoft Corp.

Is Steve Jobs a brilliant seer into the future or just plain lucky? Is he a rude, charismatic, power-hungry corporate executive? Is he the yin to Bill Gates's yang or just the most astute marketing man of the last decade? Actually while many books and articles have been written about Jobs, his portrait frequently seems unclear. What we do know is that after founding Apple Computer 30 years ago, Jobs has altered the media business forever.

Steve, the adopted son of Paul and Clara Jobs, grew up in the nascent Silicon Valley, surrounded by engineers who worked for tech companies like Hewlett-Packard. As a teen he hooked up with an engineering wizard, Steve Wozniak, and the two of them developed a small computer in Jobs's garage.

The Apple II may have been the product that made the home computer industry take off, but it was really the Macintosh's introduction in 1984 that signaled a change in what we thought about computers. With its sleek design and an amazing, intuitive graphical interface (soon copied by Microsoft), the Mac ignited the desktop publishing industry. Interestingly, while Jobs brought the innovative computer to the market, he lost control of his own company because investors thought him too young to be CEO of Apple. In 1985, at the age of 30, Jobs was both a millionaire and unemployed.

Jobs kicked around for a new project and founded another computer company called NeXT. The computer did not succeed, but Jobs, looking for other ventures, purchased a small animation studio called Pixar from George Lucas in 1991. Within the next few years *Toy Story* had developed into the first computer-animated feature film to become a huge breakthrough success. Ironically, Apple Computer, losing market share and money, was looking around for a new operating system for the aging Macintosh platform. It chose NeXT, and in 2000, Jobs found himself back at the helm of his former company.

Back at Apple, Jobs looked for new directions for a company that had lost its way. One year later iPod was born, soon followed by iPhoto, iMovie, and iTunes, a suite of software that made it possible for anyone to develop digital media. Many also credit Jobs with the ability to talk the languishing music industry into taking a chance on selling music downloads by creating the iTunes Music Store. Thus iPods, iMovie, and the music store have become huge successes for Apple, burnishing its tarnished image. Suddenly Apple is cool again.

Pixar's unbroken string of hit film successes like *Toy Story 2, Finding Nemo,* and *The Incredibles* gave Jobs the muscle to negotiate a sale of the animation studio to Disney, and in 2005, Jobs was given a seat on the Disney board. Using that leverage, he talked ABC (a Disney subsidiary) into selling downloads of popular television shows like *Lost,* starting the video downloading craze. Movie downloads soon followed.

Thirty years after the introduction of the Apple II, Jobs has helped make desktop publishing, podcasting, computer animation, and now video downloads part of the everyday experience. Products like iMovie, Garageband, and iPhoto have made media creation easy. Criticized for his notoriously bad temper, driving nature, and large ego, Jobs is also seen as a visionary. In Jobs's own words: "Don't let the noise of others' opinions drown out your own inner voice."

.com (pronounced "dot-com") in the United States help provide a unique address or destination. Outside the United States, the top-level domain names also reflect a geographical region of the world. Messages emanating out of Great Britain have a .uk domain, while .ca indicates a domain in Canada.

Top-level domains also provide a context for the site that we access or send messages to. For example, dot-com (.com) is usually a commercial establishment, while dot-org (.org) is usually a nonprofit institution. National Public Radio is .org, for example. Recently, additional domain names such as .biz for business and .tv for rich media content have been added to accommodate future growth of the Internet. As more and more people began to use the Internet, companies started putting their URLs in their television advertising. It's quite common now to see www.saturn.com, for example, at the bottom of the television screen within a Saturn commercial.

E-mail, Browsers, Downloading, and Messaging

The most popular services on the Internet are e-mail, the World Wide Web, instant messaging services, and file sharing. There are many different e-mail packages that offer various levels of functionality. A number of Web browsers, such as Mozilla Firefox, Opera, and Internet Explorer are the most popular applications that run on today's personal computers. Currently

Microsoft's Explorer seems to have won the browser wars, with approximately 70 percent of all Web users having a version installed on their computer hard drives. Firefox claims most of the rest of the market.

Browsers allow us to communicate with various public Web sites anywhere in the world by interpreting and displaying the contents of an HTML document. Browsers follow a set of standards as to what can be displayed based on protocols defined by the World Wide Web Consortium (W3C). These standards are constantly evolving too. As protocols become more refined, the capability of browsers to provide higher levels of functionality for the user will increase. However, as smart as browsers are, they are mostly just fancy text-reading programs. It is the program within the frame of the browser that provides real functionality.

Instant messaging services have taken off in the last few years. They differ from e-mail because they provide instantaneous chat capability. Currently AOL's Instant Messenger (IM), Microsoft's Messenger, and Yahoo!'s Messenger services account for most of the estimated 250 million users worldwide. AOL's IM allows users to chat, send links, and share files, but some new messaging programs are experimenting with avatar-inspired programs.

Plug-ins

An HTML page may contain, in addition to text, many different types of files that can display unique graphics, photographs, music, or animations. The trick is to get your browser to correctly identify the file type and start up the appropriate "plug-in" or helper application to handle the file. Plug-in software can be downloaded from Web sites for the browsers or from third-party software companies, usually for free.

Audio, video, and interactive applications can also be displayed on your browser page with the plug-in helper applications. For example, Quicktime or Media Player, applications that allow the playback of video files, start up when the browser senses a .mov or .mpg (Moving Picture Experts Group) suffix tag at the end of a file. Similarly, a program such as Real Audio begins to run when the browser encounters a .ram file suffix, assuming that your browser has the needed plug-in stored in the necessary folder on the hard drive.

Newer versions of multimedia plug-ins such as Quicktime allow your computer to display "streaming" audio or video. That means the file will start playing before the file has been fully transmitted. At times, there may be a delay in the downloading of a

mediated file, and you may see a "rebuffering" message. This happens when the network gets jammed with Internet traffic. During peak times data traffic jams are quite common.

Plug-ins extend the capabilities of browsers beyond audio and video. Adobe's Acrobat Reader makes it possible to read documents and see them as they were created. Macromedia's Flash Player and Java, from Sun Microsystems, provide interactive experiences by creating subprogram routines that run in the background or concurrently within the browser environment. Both programs are being used at game sites to allow the computer to load and display interactive graphics and audio quickly and seamlessly. Other scripting programs, such as PHP (Hypertext Preprocessor), provide data collection and other forms of interactivity for both the user and the Web host.

Pulling an Elephant Through a Straw— Downloading the New Media

Almost as soon as the World Wide Web came into existence, entertainment and information executives began looking for ways to use the new medium to deliver content and to charge the user for it (of course). In 1995, big newspapers created Web sites; then television and cable networks started sites hoping to lure demographically attractive Web surfers.

Modem connection speeds in 1995 were much slower than they are today. As a result, the "wait period" or download time for audio/video entertainment material was just too long for real media downloads. Ed Bennett, who had spent years involved in electronic media as head of VH-1, was quoted once as saying that "downloading music and video on the Web was like pulling an elephant through a straw." That changed with the introduction of MP3, broadband service, and other new technologies.

Long download times still discourage some people with modems from using the multimedia capabilities, but this is changing. Overall the speed of the Internet has dramatically increased over the last 5 years. That's because most computers have ethernet ports now and cable modems or DSL connections have improved our ability to download large files quickly. Today the majority of American households have high-speed Internet access.

In addition to faster broadband connections, streaming technology, and newer video codecs (*compressor-dec*ompressor programs that reduce the size of media files) used by Windows Media Player

Events: Students Took Control of the Web

In 1994, Jerry Yang and David Filo, two graduate students at Stanford, were doing what students all over the world do when faced with a seemingly impossible amount of work to finish. They were goofing off! Both students were several months away from finishing their dissertations in engineering. Instead of studying, they were spending most of their time surfing the new World Wide Web. In 1993, Web sites began springing up all over. Yang and Filo took notice and began to keep track, listing them in a hierarchical order. Working out of their trailer, they spent days—then weeks—indexing. To speed the process along, they wrote a software program to locate, identify, and index the various sites. As the Web began to grow bigger, their list began to grow quickly.

Those in the know say that if Yang and Filo had started 2 years earlier it would have been a silly exercise, but 2 years later major competitors were playing catch-up. So Yahoo! started just at the right time. Along the way they were assisted by Marc Andreesen, founder of Netscape Communications, who as a graduate assistant created the Web browser. The rest, as they say, is history, but the history of these student upstarts would be incomplete if we stopped here.

A year later grad student Sergey Brin was assigned the task of showing Larry Page around the Stanford campus. The two didn't like each other at first, but eventually found a common point of interest trying to solve a huge challenge in computing: retrieving appropriate data from massively large databases. By 1996, Larry and Sergey developed a search engine called BackRub, so named because the software could analyze back links to Web sites.

Larry and Sergey were ready to start experimenting with their search engine, but being poor grad students limited their resources, Larry set up the first computers in his dorm room. Then the two set about trying to sell their ideas. Unable to interest others, they developed a business plan and in 1998 gave the pitch to Andy Bechtolsheim, one of Sun Microsystems' founders. He immediately wrote out a check to Google for $100,000. The problem was that while Sergey and Larry had chosen the name, they hadn't formed the company yet. They couldn't cash the check!

Several weeks later they did manage to cash the check, and Google opened its door (a garage door at that) for business; they were up and running. The rest is history; within months *PC Magazine* named Google one of the Top 100 Web sites. Soon after, Google was handling hundreds of millions of search requests per day. Over the next few years Google's operations grew and grew and grew.

Today both Yahoo! and Google are worth billions of dollars and are among the top Web sites. Four students set the world ablaze with their visions.

---

and Quicktime have made it possible to watch video successfully today.

Portals

When surfing the World Wide Web, a user needs to start someplace. As the browser opens, it goes to a designated "home" location. Subscribers who join an ISP such as Road Runner will find the company's home page loads into the computer automatically. After a bit of use, some people change their home pages because they find a preferred location. Search engine sites (e.g., Google.com), news sites (e.g., CNN.com), and other sites that have a full range of search/news/chat/shopping options (e.g., Yahoo.com) frequently are chosen by users as their default browser page. These all-in-one starting places are called *portals*.

Portal is defined as an entrance or doorway. It's one of the many new words that have entered the Internet lexicon. Portals are important to the Web becaus[e] they've become the starting place for people to beg[in] their cyberjourney. When the Web was introduced [to] the general public in 1994, people surfed around in th[e] experimental medium. However, today the Wor[ld] Wide Web is vast with tens of millions of pages; ho[w] does one know where to begin? The notion of begi[n]ning a cyberjourney at a comprehensive starting pla[ce] that offers good suggestions is increasingly importa[nt].

Yahoo!, Microsoft MSN, and Google are amo[ng] the largest Web sites. In 2006, Yahoo! was the mo[st] popular destination for news, entertainment, trav[el] maps, weather reports, shopping, and more. Porta[ls] serve a number of functions. They provide a means [of] searching for information, but they also may provi[de] free e-mail, photo storage, Internet chat, shoppin[g] directory services, and reference materials as we[ll]. But an increasingly important function is to provide [a] way for users to get links and recommendatio[ns]

Table 6–1	Top Web Sites in March 2006		
Rank	**Site**	**Audience (000s)**	**Time Spent**
1	Yahoo!	105,027	3:28:39
2	Microsoft	99,368	0:50:16
3	MSN	95,124	1:52:10
4	Google	93,244	1:00:56
5	AOL	75,348	6:13:54
6	eBay	55,573	1:59:18
7	MapQuest	40,809	0:12:05
8	Amazon	40,721	0:23:21
9	Real Networks	36,961	0:43:00
10	MySpace	36,373	2:09:04

Source: ZDNet IT facts; Nielsen/NetRatings.

about other Web sites they could visit. This search function allows portals to recommend other businesses with whom they have established business relationships. One vital commercial aspect of having a successful site is that it is able to attract advertisers who want to reach a large number of eyeballs to view their Web announcements. Table 6–1 illustrates the fact that millions of people visit portals each month.

Communities Come and Go

Another popular model for the Web is the **virtual community,** a place where people can congregate (in cyberspace), chat, and share ideas and common interests. Net researchers have posited many ideas about what constitutes a virtual community. Does a community accept all the postings of its members, their lifestyles, and opinions, like Craigslist? Or does a community revolve around frequent interaction, even when that interaction sometimes causes strife or confrontation? Or do virtual communities develop over time by having their members interact regularly around shared experiences, like Facebook? Perhaps defining a cybercommunity is more difficult than we thought, but we're virtually certain we'll know one when we see one.

There are many different kinds communities available on the Web. MySpace and Craigslist are two examples, but they are different in many ways. MySpace originally started in 2003 as a venue for independent musicians. Big-name bands like Weezer and Nine-Inch Nails debuted music on the site. Today, though, MySpace has turned into a sprawling public forum/meeting space where users can share photos, journals, and music and socialize with friends. News Corporation (same company that owns Fox) purchased MySpace in 2005 for $580 million.

People congregate in many ways on MySpace. By posting a profile regarding one's musical interests, for example, one may draw viewers to the page, but it might also be a poem or an unusual self-portrait that entices someone. Perhaps the thing that's so interesting about MySpace is its level of interactivity and the amorphous way it is possible to move from pictures, to words, to music, to people. If you'll accept a city street analogy, each click takes the viewer down a new street with new sights, sounds, and people to meet. Along the way, banner ads change as a new link is made. Over the last year, the Web site's membership has skyrocketed, and it currently boasts some 50 million users. However, not all is completely serene in the virtual world. There are concerns with MySpace and other virtual communities like it. Recently stories have surfaced about minors posting dangerously personal information like addresses and telephone numbers on their pages. Parents have complained about incidents of bullying from classmates, and there have been reports of sexual predators enticing minors into meeting for sexual encounters. Evidently a virtual community may pose the same risks as a real one.

Craigslist is quite different. No animations or flashy graphics and no music, yet the site is among the most frequently visited Web sites in the nation. Craig Newmark, a former IBM programmer, observed the behavior of people using community bulletin boards (such as San Francisco's famous The WELL) helping one another. In 1995, Newmark began posting information about events and cool things in the San Francisco area. Craig's e-mail list spread by word of mouth, and soon people began posting job openings, items for sale, apartments, and more. As more and more people got interested in the postings, the Web site grew into Craigslist.

Today, the site is completely supported by job posting ads (more than 500,000 listings in 2005), which generated $25 million. The revenue is used to support the operations. Every Craigslist site looks the same, and every page is devoid of banners trying to sell something. The site is the epitome of minimalist, but people click on it in droves. Every month users view nearly 4 billion pages on the different Craigslist sites, making it among the top Web sites in the United States. Today it serves 52 countries and hundreds of cities around the world. Because each location's page listings are unique,

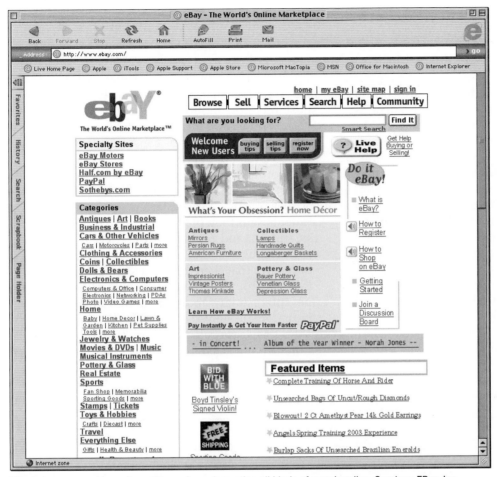

EBay's home page. Every day millions of people auction all kinds of merchandise. Courtesy-EBay, Inc.

many users comment on the feeling of community they experience when using the site.

Electronic and Interactive Gaming

If you thought it started with games like Space Invaders and Pac-Man back in the 1970s, the Stone Age of electronic arcade games, you would be wrong. It started when Harvard researcher Stephen Russell and friends developed a computer game called Spacewar way back in 1962. Supposedly he was using the computer for statistical calculations, but Russell and friends were fans of science fiction and the thought of developing an action game was too tempting. Spacewar was crude and simplistic by today's standards, but it signaled the beginning of the start of a huge industry. Other computer games followed. The first adventure game (called Adventure, oddly enough) was born in 1976, along with other games like Pong and Pac-Man. These early attempts signaled

the beginning of what was to come. Today's gaming industry is very large, challenging the movie industry in size and scope. Some analysts pegged the interactive entertainment industry at more than $28 billion worldwide with more than $10 billion generated in the United States in 2005.

While millions of people play games on their computers and their cell phones, it is the gaming console that is propelling the industry. Gaming consoles were introduced in the 1970s by Magnavox and Atari, but it was the introduction of Nintendo Entertainment System (NES) in 1985 that really made game consoles take off. The Nintendo system revolutionized the concept of gaming by introducing the controller instead of a joystick. The controller gave home games the same capabilities as arcade games. NES also priced the hardware below cost and then made profit by selling games (a practice that still holds true today). Nintendo followed the success of its home console soon after with a portable version called Gameboy. Sega and Sony soon followed with their own systems, but each new game system was incompatible with other systems.

The home game industry soon developed action—adventure games that allowed players to weave an adventure through sophisticated story-lines. Games such as Legend of Zelda, Resident Evil, Gran Turismo, and Grand Theft Auto have become huge sellers. With a solid base of users, game manufacturers have increased the power and capability of new consoles. Software developers have increased the sophistication of games, too. In 2000, Sony's PlayStation 2 (PS2) revolutionized gaming by providing superior graphics, DVD capabilities, and the ability to play games across a computer network. Then software giant Microsoft followed soon after with its Xbox, which was well received in the gaming community. Industry researchers peg game saturation at 40 percent of all U.S. households, and that means there's room for substantial growth.

Currently, most of the excitement in the gaming community revolves around a new generation of video game consoles, including the Xbox 360, the PlayStation 3, and Nintendo Wii. These machines boast incredible graphics power and other features such as built-in hard drives, wireless capability, and high-definition television capability. Most industry analysts think that online connectivity will play a substantial role in future hardware and software releases. While the core of the industry is centered around high-powered game consoles, wireless gaming is also gaining in popularity.

According to a Pew Internet and American Life Project, gaming will continue to be very popular. In 2006, nearly three-quarters of current college students said they played console, computer, or online games, and 65 percent describe themselves as either regular or occasional players, but an MIT study says that there is also a significant number of male players who are older than the typical college age. Interestingly, too, not enough is really known about female gamers. The Sims, a popular game of the 1990s, appealed to a largely untapped female audience; focus groups showed that 50 percent of

Issues: The Network Neutrality Debate—Live Free or Pay a Toll

The World Wide Web is a bit like the old wild west that we've all read about. The west was an unsettled place and many experiments in living were tested. Some worked and some didn't. To a large extent the World Wide Web is like that. It's a bit like a new frontier. But have you ever asked yourself why one Web site becomes popular and another fails? For example, Google has emerged as the largest search engine because more and more people keep choosing to use it. Is that because its technology is better than that of other search engines? Probably.

But what would happen if your Internet service provider received a fee every time you used Excite instead of Google? The technology exists to provide you with better (faster) access to one site and not another. Suppose your service provider made the connection to Excite work 10 times faster than Google's? It's likely that pretty soon you would migrate your search to the faster site and away from the slower one.

In the next few years a major issue will be decided about whether the Internet should remain neutral, thereby allowing all Web sites equal access and speed across the network, or whether the some sites should be favored over another. The issue is called *network neutrality*.

On the one hand companies like Yahoo! and Google, travel services, and news media organizations have asked Congress and the FCC to write rules that would guarantee network neutrality. On the other hand, service providers like AT&T and Verizon say that they need to find a way for paying the cost of building new networks that will provide customers with faster service. If you decide to download video from a place like iTunes, Apple collects $1.99 for the download, but AT&T, which delivers the data to your computer, doesn't make anything extra for that use of bandwidth. Telecommunications companies say that's not fair, and one executive went so far as to suggest a surcharge for every download.

Congress has begun to take the first steps toward updating the Telecommunications Act of 1996, the key bill that governs much of modern network services. It may be that within the next few years Congress will decide whether the network remains neutral or becomes a toll road.

Sims audience are teenage girls. Industry leaders see the connectivity of new game consoles and computers as extremely important to building a female audience.

Business analysts are bullish about the potential for growth in the electronic game market, but researchers at the National Institute on Media and Family are not. In the 10th Annual MediaWise Video Game Report Card, the nonpartisan, nonsectarian group claimed that the industry efforts to be good corporate citizens have largely failed, as few games receive appropriate ratings. The Video Game Report Card suggests that ever more aggressive and violent games get M ratings each year. (See Chapter 13 for a discussion about the effects of video games.)

The Bottom Line

The Web differs from other electronic media because there are many different ways in which to make money. Traditional media, such as broadcast and cable, use advertising and subscription services as the primary mechanism for revenue, but the Web is different. Telecommunications and cable companies sell connections to the Web as Internet service providers. Portals can sell space and sponsorships for ads on their pages, or they may sell goods via online catalogs or auctions. Retail businesses can sell any of their regular merchandise and services on the Web. Of course, a company could offer any combination of these services.

Revenues from the Internet are growing. If we were to look at spending patterns, we'd see that Americans spend the majority of that money on travel-related purchases such as airline tickets and hotel reservations. Next come computer hardware and software purchases followed by home products. Total online retail sales is growing rapidly and is estimated to be over $170 billion for 2006. To put these figures into perspective, we need to remember that total Internet revenues were only $550 million in 1997.

During its period of initial growth, several different kinds of companies viewed the Internet as a gold mine for generating revenue. Some have made money; others have not. Originally content service providers charged users on a per-hour basis. Prodigy thought that users would pay a monthly subscriber fee that could be supplemented by advertising and online sales. Overall, these plans have not worked out. Small ISPs wanted to charge a per-hour connect

fee to generate revenue, but many switched over to a flat fee under increasing competitive pressures. The high cost of network expansion, development of the World Wide Web, and the growing competition from companies such as Microsoft Network and Yahoo! have made it difficult for ISPs to make substantial profits.

Search engine companies and portals have found that advertising can be successful when used properly. Search engine marketing is the fastest-growing sector in online marketing. Banner ads or the first link sponsorships are often tied to the user's search request. Based on the keyword from the user, a related banner is displayed. For example, a person searching for information on cars could pull up a link to a Ford site. Banners are potential revenue streams for these companies, but few companies have shown both substantial profits and the likelihood of long-term growth based solely on banner revenues. The Internet Advertising Bureau reports that banners represent about 50 percent of all Web ads, followed by sponsorships, **interstitials** (ad pages that appear before the requested page), and other forms.

One of the real paradoxes of the new media and the information revolution is that now that all this information is available, people may be suffering from trying to interpret too much information on small computer screens. The information revolution has arrived, and many people claim that they are inundated with too much information. No doubt the way people surf the Web and use the various services available to them needs to be focused clearly. This conundrum has not been lost on Internet companies.

NAPSTER AND IPODS—ICONS AND NEW INDUSTRIAL MODELS

Technology can create new possibilities and immense problems simultaneously. Napster, a music swapping service, began operating in June 1999 and quickly revolutionized the way people sought and acquired music. Napster, created by then-college-freshman Shawn Fanning, allowed people to perform a music search and then swap music and multimedia files stored on their computers. By typing in a title or artist, the Napster user could call up a list of potential servers where a person could download the file. Clicking on the song title would cause the file to be "shared," or transferred from the host computer to the Napster user's computer. Soon (and we mean almost immediately) college students around the country started swapping songs.

By December 1999, the Recording Industry Association of America (RIAA), worried that record sales could be hurt, sued for copyright infringement. Metallica and other performers threatened suit as well, and as summer ended, a U.S. district court ordered Napster to shut down. Napster was ultimately ordered to block 100 percent of all copyrighted material, and it ceased operations in 2001, filing for bankruptcy some months later.

Today other file-sharing programs such as Morpheus and Lime Wire have replaced Napster as peer-to-peer (P2P) file-sharing programs. By 2002, more than 60 million users had downloaded Morpheus software. These products are powerful software programs that allow users to share files without needing to use a central directory, a feature that caused Napster legal problems.

Many college students have found peer-to-peer technology much to their liking, but as court actions have shown, there are numerous legal and ethical issues surrounding the free exchange of copyrighted materials. Citing decreases in CD sales, the Recording Industry Association of America began filing suits against file-sharing users. While these cases were widely publicized, the few thousand cases filed represented an infinitesimal percentage of those who downloaded music. Citizen rights groups like the Electronic Freedom Foundation have decried RIAA actions, and a war of words has been waged. Then, in 2005, the Supreme Court ruled that distributors of peer-sharing software could be held responsible for theft if they encouraged users to illegally swap files. By 2006, the RIAA and the Motion Picture Association of America had begun a new program to discourage university local area network file-sharing programs like Direct Connect, My Tunes, and OurTunes. Despite passage of the Digital Millennium Copyright Act (DMCA) and threats of lawsuits from the RIAA, file sharing seems to be a popular pastime for many users.

Just as Napster was shuttering its doors in 2001, Apple Computer introduced the **iPod,** an iconic new MP3 player, and companion software called iTunes; iTunes was designed to let users manage the music libraries on their computers and transport files to the music player. Sales for iPods were respectable, but the high cost of the device ($399) and lack of Windows compatibility were barriers to widespread adoption; however, that changed dramatically when Apple made iPod software for PCs available.

In spring 2003, Apple introduced the iTunes Music Store that allowed users to purchase songs for 99 cents each. With Windows' compatibility, lower pricing for the players, and the ability to buy music legally, sales skyrocketed. By early 2004, iPods were quickly becoming must-have devices for teenagers. Generation 5 iPods featured new color screens and the ability to play video as well as audio.

Between 2004 and 2005, iPod sales increased by over 600 percent, and by the end of 2006, Apple had sold nearly 70 million units, holding about three-quarters of the MP3 player market in the United States. As sales for iPods soared, iTunes Music Store downloads have increased dramatically. In the past 3 years more than 1 billion songs have been downloaded, and new words like "podcasting" have entered the lexicon. These numbers are significant as the RIAA began posting large increases in online sales of music, which were practically nonexistent prior to the creation of the iTunes Music Store. Competitors to iTunes have sprung up, also offering other legal music downloading schemes.

The World Wide Web, Electronic Media, and the Promise of Mobility

The Internet has changed our expectations about what broadcasting and cable services should be. Program producers can now coordinate programming both on television and on their Web sites, and then they can release the show for downloading to a portable device.

Obviously cross-promotion is already taking place. Are you a fan of *Days of Our Lives*? There's a wealth of show information on the Web site, including plot summaries, sneak peaks, photo recaps, character bios, fashion information, message boards, and fan blogs. All these features are designed to drive viewers back to the show and to maintain interest in the storylines. At the same time, top and side banner ads drive viewers to new NBC programming. *American Idol*'s Web site provides highlights of the season and recaps of Simon and Paula rants and raves, downloads of various performances, wallpaper for your computer, and a customized entry form for fans. All the while, there are links to show sponsors and *American Idol* merchandise. Clearly the interactivity of television show Web sites is an important factor in retaining interest in the program.

The potential to link services on the World Wide Web to either television or radio is common now. If you want more information on a story you've seen on

Apple's iTunes music store sells audio, videos, and movies for downloading. Since 2003 more than 2 billion songs have been downloaded.

ABC, you can go to ABCnews.com. More information is immediately available. Similarly, Web users expect services that they can't get on traditional media. For example, radio listeners who miss a segment of NPR's *All Things Considered* can go to the NPR Web site to download the segment they missed. Some people believe that synergy between traditional electronic media and the Web will make it possible to transfer viewers or listeners from a broadcast medium to the Web and vice versa. In doing so, producers keep audiences looking or listening to their product longer. Podcasts also provide a convenient way to download audio and video content and allow users to transfer that content to a portable player.

The World Wide Web is much more than a means of interlocking promotions between broadcast media and the Internet. New concepts in coordinated marketing and programming are developing rapidly as mobile computing takes off. The Web is a very powerful outlet, and it may also entice new advertisers that have not been using radio or television. More important, the Web's growth rate worldwide shows no sign of letting up. Large growth gives producers the

opportunity to expand to new audiences beyond their current geographical boundaries. Though still in the early stages, video online appears to be gaining in popularity. Many analysts predict that the future of video on the Web is very bright. According to a 2006 survey, approximately 25 percent of all Web users surveyed claim to watch some video at least once a week. At the moment, news clips are the most widely viewed, followed closely by funny videos.

Video-on-demand (VOD) is all the buzz, and while everyone is talking about it, there is little agreement as to what will become the primary mobile platform. As the growth of broadband increases, so too does the ability to view programming in different locations. Mobile services may include downloading audio and video from a home computer, or it can take other forms. Laptops provide users with bright, large screens and the ability to play most content, but they're not very convenient for a commuter who wants to view last night's episode of *The Office* while heading home from work. Video iPods, mobile phones, PlayStation portable systems (PSP), and other devices are capable of providing content to

Television programs like *24* use Web sites to keep viewers informed of current happenings, to sell DVDs and related products, and to enhance fans' knowledge of the show and its characters.

users on the go, but they all have small viewing screens. Obviously there are technical trade-offs.

In addition to the small screen, cost of service may be an issue. The survey conducted by Knowledge Networks found that half of all subscribers to mobile video services don't use the service and, when polled, it appears that cost was an issue. Of the cell phone users polled who actually pay for a video download service, only 50 percent were actually using that capability on their cell phones. Similarly only about 3 out of 10 video iPod users were using their devices for viewing. Most viewers said they would be more likely to use mobile services if they were free or if the services cost less with commercial advertisers.

Evolving Radio and Webcasting: Streaming and Royalty Rights

Over the last 80 years radio has survived the introduction of numerous forms of competition by constantly evolving and changing. Radio lost network stars and its biggest shows to television in the 1950s, leaving it to find specific niches to fill; along came

Top 40 radio. Elaborate car stereos, compact disc Walkmans, and iPods provided alternative ways for people to hear high-quality music on the go; but talk radio grew. Will the growth of Internet radio and other new media services such as satellite broadcasting create new challenges for radio? Absolutely!

It's an old comedy routine: There's good news and bad news. First the bad news: Online users appear to be listening to commercial radio less. Studies of more than 2,500 people completed in spring 2002 suggested new trends in the way people use media, and recent surveys confirm these findings. According to a 2006 Arbitron/Edison Media poll, 21 percent of Internet users aged 12 and above reportedly listened to radio online during an average month. Males aged 18–34 tend to be the predominant listeners. Heaviest user times were during traditional working hours. On the downside, as Americans go online more, radio's listenership is likely to drop. In addition, audio podcast listeners tend to skew much younger than the general population. Does this signal the end of radio? We doubt it, but the research does show youthful users have a continuing desire to use streaming media content on the Internet at the expense of traditional media like radio.

More bad news: Late in 2002, Congress approved a deal that required small Internet stations to pay lower royalties for the material they use. Some predict that 2004 would see a resurgence of radio stations on the Web, but that never materialized. While some stations returned to the Web, many decided the performance rights costs under the Digital Millennium Copyright Act of 1998 were too steep.

Now for the good news: Listeners say they want more from radio's Web sites. Local Web sites now publish updated concert information, merge promotional activities with other local online sites, and provide names of artists and titles of songs, and feedback blogs or dedication lines. In fact, the Web gives radio many new capabilities the audio medium lacks by itself.

Public radio seems to be benefiting from webcasting. Public radio listeners who streamed programs tend to listen to radio more than non-Internet listeners, and they tend to be heavy public radio listeners generally. Research suggested that tuning into Internet radio wasn't affecting public radio broadcast listening; Internet usage tended to be in addition to regular broadcast listening.

Internet radio doesn't need to rely upon an over-the-air signal to penetrate thick building walls. Webcasting just needs a computer hooked to the net; so Internet radio could build listenership during key "dayparts" when office listening is traditionally low. But what radio programming will be like both on and off the Web in the year 2010 and beyond is anyone's guess. Tables 6–2 and 6–3 highlight the top 5 Internet radio networks and top Internet formats as given by Arbitron.

Changing the Face of the Web News

9/11   First, Americans turned to radio for break-ing news. Then with ENG equipment and satellite news

Table 6–3	Top Radio Formats and Owners	
Rank	**Format**	**Owner**
1	Musicmatch	Artist Match
2	Classical	WQXR-FM / New York Times
3	AOL Smooth Jazz	AOL Radio@Network
4	Hot Adult Contemporary	Virgin Radio
5	JazzFM (London)	Jazz Guardian Media
6	Lite Rock	AOL Radio @ Network
7	Pop/Top 40	AOL Radio @ Network
8	Top Country	AOL Radio @ Network
9	Awesome 80s	AOL Radio @ Network
10	WLS Talk Radio	ABC Radio Network

Source: Arbitron, June 2003.

gathering, television started broadcasting breaking news. Then CNN came along; then the news crawl. Now news is changing again. Millions of people turn to the Web as a source of news every day. Heavy news days increase Web traffic at popular news sites. According to Google.com, news-related searches (e.g., CNN.com) were 60 times greater on September 11, 2001, than the previous day.

Americans were hungry for any news on September 11. News organizations immediately posted pictures and stories related to the attack on America. Both television and the Web became sources for up-to-the-minute information about the terrorist event. Clearly the Web has taken its place alongside television, radio, and the newspaper as a primary provider of news and information.

Public Reaction to Changes in News and Information How are Americans reacting to this new influx of information? They search for information online frequently. It's probably no great surprise that "sex" is the most frequently searched term on the Web. In 2006, "sex" "porn," and related terms were searched more frequently than "games," "music," "MySpace," and "eBay," combined. But Web users turn to news and weather sites frequently. Looking at the Google tallies for the most frequently requested terms on search engines illustrates that current events are among the top requests every week. Evidently Web users put a good deal of faith in online sources. A Pew research study completed in 2005 showed that the Internet continues to gain importance as a

Table 6–2	Top 5 Online Radio Networks—Average Quarter-Hour	
Rank	**Name**	**Listenership**
1	AOL Radio Network	79,000
2	Yahoo! Launchcast	73,000
3	Live 365	28,500
4	Musicmatch	22,000
5	Virgin Radio	5,000

Source: Arbitron Internet Broadcast Ratings, February 2004.

primary news source, particularly for people in the 18–49 age group. Nearly one in four Americans list online sources as their main source for news and information, and another 23 percent say they go online every day for news and information.

Blogs

Weblogs, generally referred to as **blogs,** are essentially journals or chat Web sites that display information in reverse chronological order. While they have exploded in popularity over the last few years, online journals can be traced back to the early 1990s. Early Web sites, such as the National Center for Supercomputing Applications, essentially started posting a what's new page as the Web began to develop. In early 1994, Justin Hall started Justin's Home Page, which later became Links from Underground. Hall's Web site was essentially a "filtered log," meaning that he made choices about what sites were posted. Two years later, the 24 Hours of Democracy Project broke ground as a shared experience. Soon after Jorn Barger coined the term *weblog,* but that was shortened to *blog.* Toward the end of the 1990s, new Web sites like LiveJournal greatly simplified the creation of blogs along with the ease of posting information to the site.

Although online journals began in the early days of the Web, it was the events of September 11 that gave rise to blogging's popularity. After the attacks on the World Trade Center and the Pentagon, many blogs gained readership among the general public searching for information to understand what motivated the attacks. Soon after, the first blog controversy to gain national attention evolved after senator Trent Lott made statements honoring Strom Thurmond, a senator who espoused white supremacist viewpoints in the 1980s. After Lott's remarks about how America would have been better if Thurmond had been elected president, bloggers kept pressure on Lott until the mainstream press picked up the story. The arguments for and against the war in Iraq made blogging part of the political mainstream, as politicians and journalists set up their own Web sites. Firsthand experiences of the war (milblogs) have given readers some unusually candid perspectives on the realities of war.

Blogging has been used to draw attention to obscure news facts and became important for both political parties during the 2004 presidential campaign. They've also been used to provide a set of checks and balances to the mainstream press. During the "Rathergate"

scandal, conservative bloggers supporting the president declared Bush's military service records shown on *60 Minutes* to be forgeries. While blogging certainly extends the notions of democracy by giving many the opportunity to speak, not all the dialogue is political. Socially, blogs such as Gawker provide daily doses of gossip and news regarding celebrities and the media.

Today blogging is very popular among young adults and teens. Many sites have become part of the mainstream, where hundreds of people read and post remarks daily.

Television on the Web and IPTV

When snippets of video started to appear on the Web, some futurists speculated that broadcast television would die out as thousands of video channels of programming became available. Rumors of television's demise seem to have been greatly overstated. While increases in computer capabilities and broadband connections have made downloading television programs feasible, it still is somewhat different from just turning on a TV and choosing from hundreds of channels immediately. Picture quality can vary from very good to poor, depending on transmission standards. Not all playback is immediate. For example, a 20-minute podcast segment downloaded from the iTunes site takes about 4 minutes over a broadband connection. A number of different playback models do exist on the Web. GUBA is a site that specializes in videos, both free and pay. Users can choose among a number of popular movie titles. Some may be rented, and some must be purchased. Once purchased, they can be played on a computer or ported to a portable video device.

Internet Protocol Television (IPTV) is a new service that is gaining attention as several large telecommunications companies like Verizon and AT&T have announced plans to provide bundled TV services along with residential telephone and broadband Internet services. In the past, slow download speeds made this impossible, but as network speeds and bandwidth increase, IPTV looks increasingly feasible. Large telecommunications companies have bet billions of dollars on this new technology.

Both live TV (multicasting) and video-on-demand services would require a set-top box connected to a television, much like a digital cable box, or a home entertainment system, but unlike cable TV the consumer would select the show, and it would be downloaded via high-speed, fiber-optic technology. Some experts say both standard and high-definition

Ethics: Technology's Dirty Little Secret—Porn

Sex sells. It is undeniable that the porn industry is a big entertainment (many would say exploitation) industry. Just how big a business is it? The *New York Times* magazine ran a cover story a few years ago, pegging it at between $10 and $14 billion annually. Those are large numbers, and Forrester Research was often credited as the source for the data. But while Forrester did publish a report in 1998, it pegged the industry at somewhere between $750 million and $1 billion. Not surprisingly, it is difficult to pin down exact numbers because many companies do not want to talk about their connection to the "adult" industry.

The pornography industry adopted the Internet very early as a technology, as it did with the VCR and DVD. With the Internet, adult entertainment companies were among the first to figure out online payment, streaming video, and other Web technologies that we take for granted. Their work paid handsomely. Today, the term "sex" is usually among the most frequently used search terms at the various Web search sites. However, as the Web grows, it is becoming less important. According to a study commissioned by Google, 20 percent of its searches were for adult-related themes. Hitwise Data USA, a company that studies Internet traffic, pegs adult entertainment at about 14 percent of all Web traffic. (The second most popular service is e-mail, with 9 percent of traffic.)

WAP (wireless application protocol) technology is now being adopted by the porn industry. According to *Electronic Business* the mobile adult content industry is developing very quickly. Adult content providers like New Frontier Media and Private Media Group have targeted mobile services. Why? New telephones have better video capabilities, making them better instruments for displaying porn. Many early adopters are willing to pay a premium to receive pornography on personal devices, such as cell phones, leaving the family's computer in the den untouched. One industry executive said that the industry is still a few years away from making profits in the area, but expects it will become a big part of its business. According to Jonathan Coopersmith, a researcher at Texas A&M University, pornography is very important for technology in the early stages of adoption. But, he concedes, it's very difficult to get accurate data. Evidently people in the technology industry are reluctant to talk about it.

signals are possible with several enhancements. For example, switching camera angles and pictures within pictures during sporting events, along with different commentary, would allow a fan to choose commentary and pictures that better represent a favorite team. And VOD services could work in conjunction with digital video recorders recording several programs simultaneously, anticipating consumer demand. Feature films could be released directly to DVRs instead of going through the intermediate step of a DVD release. Whether IPTV service delivers what it promises and moves beyond current television remains to be seen.

BEYOND

The rapid, worldwide growth of the Internet is unparalleled in the recent history of electronic media. Only radio and then television had similar adoption rates. But exactly what effect the accelerated growth of the World Wide Web will have on traditional electronic media is difficult to predict. The following are some likely scenarios.

Home electronics have become digital. Digital cameras, camcorders, and the introduction of DVD players demonstrate consumer acceptance of new technology. This equipment coupled with powerful home computer programs like iMovie and an Internet connection has helped make the individual a Web-based publisher. Today Web sites like YouTube and Flickr and MySpace provide opportunities for individual creative output to be published. Public space on the Web provides worldwide exposure to creative talents. New Web operations are not confined by geographical considerations. Networks and portals will serve tailored audiences.

Advanced technology will make the Internet an increasingly attractive place to distribute and deliver audio and video directly to the consumer, but it's not ready for prime time yet. Web delivery of MP3-quality audio, books on tape, and spoken newscasts has changed media merchandising. Other services such as Google Earth promise new views of our world, and this software can be functionally linked to database systems. The possibilities are immense.

Hard-drive digital VCRs will merge with home computers, providing us with the ability to record and play programs simultaneously and distribute that content throughout the home. While DVR penetration was less than 15 percent of all homes in 2006, some experts predict that the number could double in the next 2 years.

Because Internet radio and television do not require federal licenses, new programming will continue to develop based on specific interests. Web networks with the latest technologies that will provide users with 360-degree panoramic views, three-dimensional viewing, and automatic language translation are in the offing. High-powered computer graphics will create a new sense of realism in scenery and movement in action games, and networked gaming will enhance the level of play.

Distribution of adult-oriented material and anti-social material is likely to expand on the Web, much to the dismay of many religious, governmental, and family groups. Fringe groups and radical groups have greater access to espouse their views on blogs. Fraud and privacy issues are increasingly important in the future, as e-commerce grows. Adoption of worldwide policies for the instantaneous free flow of information and data between different countries may become a more important issue if countries place access restrictions on data flow.

CAREER PATHS: SOMEWHERE, OUT THERE . . .

Can you work in one of many new exciting career fields in cyberspace? No, sorry. You'll have to work here on earth. But as the World Wide Web continues to grow, both in the United States and around the world, job opportunities related to Web-based product creation, sales, and site management

continue to increase; people trained in computer science, programming, and in the telecommunications field are thus currently in high demand.

You don't have to be a computer genius, however. Internet growth is creating nontechnical jobs too. There are good jobs available for people who have the ability to use Web development products and desktop publishing software packages today. Industry leaders emphasize that there are jobs for people with good communication skills, the ability to follow a task through to completion, and an eagerness to learn. And many people stress the importance of doing internships as a means of gaining experience and making those valuable first connections. Take heed, and plan your internship experiences early.

At the moment, growth in Internet advertising has helped create a lucrative field in which to pursue a job. But how lucrative it is relates to the skills you bring to the job (not surprisingly). The Association of Internet Professionals (AIP) surveyed current professionals to gain some information about average salaries within several segments of the Internet industry. What it found was encouraging for individuals who want to enter some aspect of this work. According to CNNMoney.com, average salaries for Web designers and creative directors hover around $60,000.

The 2005 Network World Salary Survey puts software system programmers among those at the top of the survey, making an average of $79,000. Technical positions such as telecom managers average $81,000 yearly. Directors of online services and corporate management reported earnings around $115,000. Bear in mind that these are average salaries. Starting salaries are always lower.

SUMMARY

- The first information services were one-way text services called teletext. Britain's CEEFAX was an early version that was transmitted over the air. Minitel, a large-scale interactive text service, started in France. Although America pioneered computer networking, information services were not quick to start up. In the early 1980s, The Source and CompuServe became early information service providers. They were joined by Prodigy and America Online toward the end of the 1980s.

- In the mid-1980s, AOL and Prodigy adopted graphics interfaces that attracted many home computer users. Long-distance interconnection charges decreased, and new computers enhanced the online experience.

- The Internet is owned by no single organization. Several organizations, such as the Internet Society and the World Wide Web Consortium, set guidelines for its standards and its operation.

- When a uniform resource locator (URL) is typed into a browser, a request for information is made from the home computer to a network router to the server housing information. Domain names help provide pathways for information.

- Microsoft's Internet Explorer is the most popular browser available for the World Wide Web. Web sites that provide many customer services are called portals. Portals frequently contain banners or other forms of advertising. Yahoo!, MSM, AOL, and Google are among the largest and most popular Web sites.

- Ad revenues have begun to rise after the Internet bubble burst of 2000.

- In 2001, the courts ruled that Napster violated the copyright laws and told the service to comply with the law or stop the service. Apple Computer's highly successful iPod and iTunes Music Store has spurred the growth of legal music downloads.

- *New media* is the term applied to the convergence of audio/video technologies with the World Wide Web. Media companies use the Web as an ancillary means of reaching target audiences. Cable and DSL modems provide for much faster download times.

- Web users report a slight reduction in over-the-air radio listening; Web radio listenership, on the other hand, is on the rise. Studies point to the fact that millions of Americans turn to the Web for breaking news stories.

- Blogs have grown in popularity as people have become comfortable in sharing information and opinions.

- IPTV may provide television services that rival or exceed cable's capabilities.

- As the World Wide Web expands, so, too, do job possibilities. Jobs in desktop publishing and graphic arts are in demand, as are positions in computer programming, site management, and marketing. Because the Internet continues to grow rapidly, job prospects continue to look bright.

KEY TERMS

teletext   130
videotex   130
videotext   130
Internet service providers
    (ISPs)   131
World Wide Web   132
HyperText Markup Language
    (HTML)   132

search engines   133
World Wide Web Consortium
    (W3C)   134
uniform resource locator
    (URL)   134
domain name   134
portal   137
virtual community   138

interstitials   141
iPod   142
blogs   146
Internet Protocol Television
    (IPTV)   146

SUGGESTIONS FOR FURTHER READING

Biersdorfer, J. (2006). *iPod & iTunes: The missing manual* (4th ed.). Sebastapol, CA: O'Reilly.

Cairncross, F. (2001). *The death of distance.* Cambridge: Harvard University Press.

Dodd, A. Z. (2005). *The essential guide to telecommunications.* Upper Saddle River, NJ: Prentice Hall.

Gralla, P. (2003). *How the Internet works.* Indianapolis, IN: Cue Publishing.

Grant, A. E. (2004). *Communication technology update* (9th ed.). Boston: Focal Press.

Henry, S. (2002). *The dinner club: How the masters of the Internet universe rode the rise and fall of the greatest boom in history.* New York: Free Press.

Horak, R.; Newton, H.; & Miller, M. A. (2002). *Communication systems and networks* (3rd. ed.). New York: Wiley.

Kerland, D.; Messere, F.; & Palombo, P. (1996). *Introduction to the Internet for electronic media.* Belmont, CA: Wadsworth.

Ludlow, P. (1999). *High noon on the electronic frontier.* Boston: MIT Press.

Manovich, L. (2002). *The language of new media.* Boston: MIT Press.

Menn, J. (2003). *All the rave: The rise and fall of Shawn Fanning's Napster.* New York: Crown.

Negroponte, N. (1995). *Being digital.* New York: Vintage Books.

Sinclair, J. (1998). *Web pages with TV HTML.* Rockland, MA: Charles River Media.

Swisher, K. (1998). *AOL.com.* New York: Random House.

Winston, B. (1998). *Media technology and society.* London: Routledge.

INTERNET EXERCISES

Visit our Web site at **www.mhhe.com/dominick6** for study-guide exercises to help you learn and apply material in each chapter. You will find ideas for future research as well as useful Web links to provide you with an opportunity to journey through the new electronic media.

Part Three   How It's Done

The Business of Broadcasting, Satellite, and Cable

Quick Facts

 Average cost of 30-second Super Bowl spot in 1976: $125,000

 Average cost of 30-second Super Bowl spot in 2006: $2.5 million

 Amount of money spent on Internet display ads (2005): $8.3 billion

 Total sponsorship revenue for National Public Radio (2005): $37.7 million

 Cost of a 30-second spot on Katie Coric's final *Today Show:* $110,000

 Total spot TV advertising in Los Angeles TV market (2004): $2.1 billion

It's time for a short quiz. One question: What is the primary product that a radio or television station has to sell? Here are the choices:

a.   Entertainment.
b.   Advertising time.
c.   Listeners to advertisers.

If you answered *c*, you're right. All the other answers are less correct.

Let's dwell on this for just a minute. Commercial mass media have a unique dual nature. The mass-media technology is designed to link audiences with program suppliers and with sponsors. Broadcasting and cable operations need to provide listeners and viewers with programs that meet their tastes and needs. Stations transmit programs to attract an audience. A commercial radio station, for example, doesn't make any money unless it has an audience that some advertiser pays money to reach. Television stations that broadcast network programs make some money because an advertiser is paying the station for the time adjacent to network programming.

So while it's true that stations are attracting audiences because of their programming, it is the advertising revenue generated as a result of having a desirable audience that really pays for the programming. Mass-media technology provides a means of reaching a large number of people simultaneously, and as a result it is an economical way of linking audiences with advertisers via television and radio programming. Essentially you and your friends are the product a broadcasting station is selling to an advertiser.

In all electronic media there is this kind of interplay among the technology, the consumer, and economics. For example, there is also an interplay for the cable industry, but it works just a little differently from broadcasting. Obviously cable has advertising, and thus cable, too, must be selling the audience's attention to advertisers (unless a consumer is willing to pay extra money to receive noncommercial channels such as HBO or Showtime). But there is a difference between over-the-air broadcasting and cablecasting. Cable companies also charge viewers a monthly subscription fee for the privilege of receiving cable programming. In fact, the majority of cable's revenue is generated by the monthly franchise fee that consumers pay to receive the service. Cable thus has a dual income: Cable operators sell advertising and they collect revenues from a monthly subscription service. Some cable companies such as

Comcast and Time Warner are also offering high-speed Internet access and telephone (VoIP) as services, which would act as additional sources of income for these companies. Of course, cable operators also have a different cost structure because cable is a different technology from over-the-air broadcasting: Cable franchisers have a large video distribution network to maintain, while broadcasters just have a transmitter and studios. The business model for radio and television is thus different from that for cable; both cable and broadcasting must be technology-dependent. Web sites make money through ad placement, much like a newspaper or magazine.

This chapter will address the economics of broadcasting, cable, and the Internet, but while economics is sometimes referred to as a dismal science, advertising revenues for electronic media are anything but dismal. They've grown steadily since broadcasting's beginnings. We need to understand how a station generates revenue and spends money. Broadcasting and cable are big businesses, after all. Without profits, there would be no money for program development, and thus no programming. Exploring the relationships that exist between broadcasters and other electronic media and advertisers and within the industry will give us some insight into how the business works.

COMPETITION AND ELECTRONIC MEDIA

Radio, television, cable, and satellite broadcasters all face competition from other services. The amount of competition often helps the government determine how closely it will monitor and control the mass-media facility. Chapter 10 goes into regulation in detail, but let's discuss a few basic principles here. Generally the amount of government oversight of the electronic media is tied to how competitive those media are. If there is more competition, there is less regulation.

Radio is less heavily regulated than television, for example. There are about 11,000 commercial radio stations compared with 1,300 commercial television stations. Guess which medium has fewer regulations regarding ownership? With cable television there are different rules too. For example, there are very few places in the United States where there is more than one cable operator in a franchise area. As a result, the cable operator can be mandated to provide government and public access channels for the local municipality. How about the Internet? Isn't it more like a magazine stand with thousands of different choices and lots of competition? The point we are trying to make is simply this: The different electronic media have different levels of competition and face different amounts of government oversight as a result.

If a medium faces no competition, there is a **monopoly.** It's hard to find a place in the United States today that only receives one local radio station and no other distant radio or television signals. If there were such a town, the station in that town would have a monopoly on advertising for electronic media. If there are a limited number of competitors—say, only three national commercial television networks—we would call that an **oligopoly.** Here the limited number of competitors means that each of the networks will probably gain a share of available advertising revenue. If a market faces complete competition—say, a large radio market with 25 or more radio signals available—it is possible to let the listeners decide which stations will become popular and thereby gain a large share of the advertising dollars. We call this a "marketplace" solution, or **pure competition,** because the competitive forces within the market make each station try hard to gain a share of the advertising revenue. Within this last category, it is possible for weak stations to actually go out of business or get purchased by larger group owners when they do not succeed in gaining a sufficient audience.

Competition among Different Media Types

This may seem obvious to you, but let's state it anyway. People use the various forms of media differently. To some extent competition is defined by how people use a specific medium and what competition it faces from all other competitors. For example, the competition for specific listeners among radio stations must be different from the competition for viewers on television. As we noted in Chapter 4, radio is the most intimate of the mass media. It is a highly portable and personal medium. It is more likely to compete against other portable devices such as iPods for your attention than against cable or television. Radio programming centers around music, news, and talk. There is practically no drama. Comedy on radio is more like stand-up than situational. And radio is omnipresent. People can listen in places where watching television would be difficult.

Someone jogging or driving a car could listen to radio, but could not watch television. Workers in an office are likely to listen to the radio in the background; in fact, some have started listening on their computers via the Internet.

Television is used differently. Many people get home, kick off their shoes, and sit down to watch a little TV. The term *couch potato* engenders thoughts of someone at rest, but the term is rarely applied to radio listeners! Television is more likely to compete with cable and movie rentals for its viewers. We can compare other media too. Obviously billboards must compete with radio somewhat, but newspapers have the potential to compete with both radio and television, depending on where and when people read their papers. You get the point.

Advertisers will frequently buy different media to reach as many customers as possible. They will also frequently spread their messages over different times in the broadcast day to ensure the broadest dissemination of their message. A look at Figure 7–1 shows that time spent listening to the radio and watching television is greater than time spent with any other media; thus advertisers are particularly concerned with these two media.

Determining a Medium to Buy and Figuring Out Its Cost

There is a triangular relationship in the media business between programmers, media sellers, and media buyers. How does the advertiser actually decide to buy time from one radio station over another, or why does an appliance store use television as opposed to the local newspaper for advertising? As we learned in Chapters 4 and 5, broadcasters need to develop successful programs that certain people will want to listen to or watch. To determine just how successful a TV program is, a station needs to evaluate how many viewers watch the program. Finding out about the age, gender, and income of viewers (demographics) is important too. Stations can use that information to attract certain advertisers. Chapter 12 covers audience measurement, so this chapter will focus on how the advertiser decides to allocate advertising dollars.

Marketers and advertisers generally put together a buying plan developed on three basic elements: (1) population or market size, (2) effective buying income, and (3) retail sales for each geographical area where they sell their products. If the product is a national or regional product, advertising agencies

Figure 7–1

Media Usage Per Year Per Person–2006

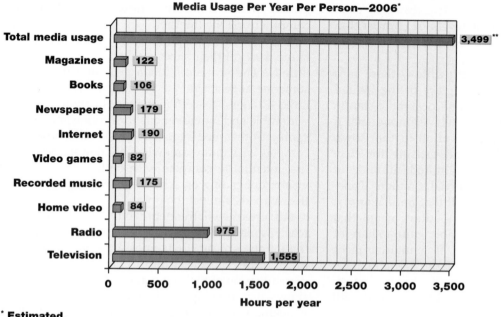

Media Usage Per Year Per Person—2006*

	Hours per year
Total media usage	3,499**
Magazines	122
Books	106
Newspapers	179
Internet	190
Video games	82
Recorded music	175
Home video	84
Radio	975
Television	1,555

Hours per year

* Estimated.

** Total time can include multitasking, such as Internet and TV.

Source: Veronis Suhler Stevenson Communications Industry Forecast 2006.

Note: Total TV includes broadcast, cable, and satellite viewing. Home video counts prerecorded VHS and DVDs. Video games include consoles and PC entertainment software.

and marketing firms collect data relevant to that product and may develop a **buying power index (BPI)** for the specific markets they're interested in. The higher the BPI, the greater buying power for that market or region. If the media plan is sizable—that is, if there is a substantial amount of money allocated for advertising the product—the advertiser may use the services of a company that provides information regarding the amount of money that competing national advertisers spend on various media. Research companies break down advertising expenditures according to specific classifications of products, such as nonprescription drugs. This information provides the advertiser with a way of gauging what the competition is spending on media.

After data collection, the advertiser will develop media plans for the product. Frequently, sophisticated analysis will be used for allocating advertising funds to buy time on broadcasting stations. For example, a national restaurant chain may target the Durham, North Carolina, market for spending because the chain is expanding the number of restaurants in that area. A brand manager will want to purchase airtime on television stations for a 2-week period prior to the opening of each new store. The time segments available for commercials in radio and TV are called *spots,* and this term is also used to refer to the commercials themselves.

Media buyers use various formulas for determining the effectiveness of ad placement. One such measure, called **gross rating points (GRPs),** gives the buyer a way to evaluate a run of *x* number of commercials over the specific time period that has a consistent rating for the target audience. **Gross impressions,** another measure, reflects the total of all persons reached by each commercial in the advertising campaign. Using this kind of information to determine audiences and effectiveness, advertisers will calculate how much money they want to spend to achieve their marketing goals.

Nationally advertised brands such as Coke or McDonald's may decide to purchase broadcasting time on national television and cable networks, or they could choose to buy time on network affiliates or independent stations on a market-by-market basis. Frequently, nationally advertised brands will also help out the local retailer through cooperative advertising. (We discuss these differences in greater detail a bit later in this chapter.) Occasionally an advertiser will select or not select specific media based solely on cost (e.g., a firm may decide it cannot afford to advertise during the Super Bowl).

Placing the Ad

Once advertisers determine the kind of media they want to buy (radio only or television only, for instance) and when (e.g., morning drive time on radio or prime time on TV), they can begin to evaluate the benefits of purchasing time on one or more specific media outlets. Generally, advertising time is sold for a specific number of spots called a *package* and covers a specific period (called *flight dates*). For example, a nursery wouldn't want its "Spring Gardening Sale" spots aired at the end of July or beginning of August. So the media buyer will specify beginning and ending dates for the advertisement to run. Time buyers want to be able to compare the cost of doing business at station A with another media facility (station B) down the road. For the sake of this example, we're going to use radio, but both radio and television stations publish rate cards (see Figure 7–2) to help time buyers evaluate the cost of advertising. The next step is to find out how many potential listeners you can reach for your money.

Frequently rate cards will reflect charges based on different numbers of spots. As an advertiser purchases more time, the cost per spot decreases.

CPM: Measuring the Cost of Advertising on Two Stations

Media buyers use a standard formula to figure out the actual cost of a commercial spot. The unit cost is expressed as the cost to reach 1,000 audience members. **Cost per thousand** is abbreviated CPM, where M is the roman numeral for 1,000. To calculate the CPM of a radio station, you need to know the cost of the spot and the size of the audience. For example, if a shoe store owner wanted to advertise on station WXXX, which charged $240 per spot and had a listening audience of 20,000 people, the CPM formula would look like this:

$$\text{CPM}_{\text{WXXX}} = \frac{\text{Cost of spot}}{\text{Audience (000s)}} = \frac{240}{20} = \$12.00$$

Thus, the CPM, or cost of reaching 1,000 listeners, would be $12.00 on WXXX. Now, compare this CPM with that of station WZZZ, a station that has a similar listenership in terms of demographics. While the cost of advertising on WZZZ is slightly higher, it also has a slightly larger audience. The cost of advertising on WZZZ is $270 per spot for reaching 30,000 listeners, so its cost per 1,000 is only $9.00:

$$\text{CPM}_{\text{WZZZ}} = \frac{\text{Cost of spot}}{\text{Audience (000s)}} = \frac{270}{30} = \$9.00$$

If the media buyer were to compare the costs per thousand for the two stations, WZZZ would be a better buy. Even though WZZZ charges slightly more per spot, the CPM is lower because it has a larger listening audience.

CPM is a good way of expressing efficiency—that is, the cost of reaching a thousand potential buyers of the product. For advertisers, the goal is generally to reach the largest potential audience for the smallest dollar investment; however, sometimes it is useful to spend more money to reach audiences with specific demographic characteristics. For example, a luxury car dealership may choose a show with a smaller audience, if the audience for that show is more affluent and likely to purchase luxury cars. Cost per point (CPP) is another good way of measuring efficiency and is similar to CPM, except that it measures a specific demographic. Let's take our luxury car dealership again. If the cost of the advertising unit (such as a 30-second spot) was divided by the average rating of males 35 years and older listening to the station, you could figure the CPP for reaching males likely to buy your automobile.

Local Markets

Obviously the scenario we described for developing a media buy doesn't apply to all situations. Many advertisers are just not large enough to hire an advertising agency or a media buyer. In many smaller markets, a station sales representative will work directly with a store owner to develop a commercial package. Once the commercial is written and approved, it will be turned over to the station's production manager to execute. The sales representative will then schedule the spot in the station's commercial rotation for play.

The sales representative and the store owner might develop a long-term contract that reflects a discount for sponsoring a specific time slot—say, the 8 A.M. news. The sales rep will place a **standing order** for the shoe store's commercial to run over a specific period (maybe several weeks or months, for example).

Figure 7–2

Figure 7–2

Radio Advertising Rate Card

RATE CARD

TIME	MONDAY–FRIDAY	SATURDAY	SUNDAY
AM DRIVE 5:30A–10A *"MARTY & PAIGE IN THE MORNING"*	$255	$90	$75
MIDDAY 10A–3P *"KEVIN"*	$255	$300	$180
PM DRIVE 3P–8P *"JAVA JOEL"*	$315	$180	$180
EVENINGS 8P–12A *"SHAWN MICHAELS"*	$180	$150	$90
OVERNIGHTS *"DANGER BOY"*	$30	$30	$30
THREE DAYPART TAP 6A–8P	$270	$225	$150
FOUR DAY PART TAP 6A–12A	$240	$180	$120
BTA MON–SUN 6A–6A	$180	$150	$105

"The supply of time is totally inelastic. No matter how high the demand, the supply will not go up. Yesterday's time is gone forever and will never come back. Time is, therefore, always in exceedingly short supply!"
—Peter Drucker

Now no other advertiser will be able to sponsor the morning newscast for the duration of the standing order. This is known as a *nonpreemptible spot* because it cannot be bumped by another advertiser. In this example, the station's sales rep is acting like an account executive by fulfilling the needs of the local shoe store. Since the time period is reserved for weeks or perhaps months, the sales representative will need to see the shoe store owner regularly to develop new ideas for the commercials that air during the news sponsorship.

Small-market radio stations frequently don't subscribe to a ratings service. As a result it may not be possible to calculate the CPM on small-market stations. In rural America, where some towns only have a weekly newspaper and one or two local radio stations, a store owner may simply work out the best deal possible with some or all of the local media available.

BROADCASTING SALES PRACTICES

Radio Sales

There are more than 13,000 radio stations in the United States. Five out of every six are commercial stations. Radio stations derive their revenues by selling listeners to potential advertisers who have products or services they want to promote. In Chapter 4, we stated that the goal of a radio station is to gain a large number of a certain type of listener. Radio sales are closely tied with demographic analysis and program planning. An all-news format radio station does not expect to have a large number of adolescents in its listening audience. An analysis of listening habits for people ages 12 to 18 would show that adolescents and young adults tend to listen to radio stations that concentrate on playing music appropriate to their age group.

The all-news radio listeners, according to research, however, will tend to be older (35+) and more affluent than listeners of most other radio formats. So while the all-news format station might actually have many fewer listeners than a station that caters to the young adults (say an urban contemporary format), it may actually charge the advertiser more for those listeners. A look at the type of sponsors might reveal that those clients interested in buying time on the all-news station are likely to be more upscale than the advertisers on a station trying to reach a much younger audience. Luxury cars, travel cruises, and commercials for brokerage houses or insurance are likely to be advertised on all-news radio.

The Search for Spots   As we mentioned earlier, there are three types of advertising purchases made in broadcasting. The term *local sales* refers to the sale of commercial advertising by stations to advertisers in their immediate service area. Auto dealers, appliance stores, and restaurants are frequent local advertisers. As we noted, salespeople will call on local businesses and attempt to sell them ad time on the station.

Station ad rates are pegged to the share of the audience that is listening to the station at a given time. Shares are determined by Arbitron (see Chapter 12), which publishes radio ratings reports. The larger the share, the more money a station can charge for its commercial spots. Most stations give discounts if an advertiser buys a large number of spots (called a package) and if the advertiser commits to buying spots that will run over an extended period of time.

Ads cost more or less depending on the time period in which they air. The rate card reflects the radio day as it is broken down into **dayparts.** The most expensive daypart in which to advertise is generally morning drive time, and afternoon drive time is the second most expensive. The largest number of listeners is found in the audience during morning and evening drives. Commuters are frequent targets of advertising; tire and battery sales, insurance, and convenience stores are frequently advertised during these time periods. Special sections of a ratings book will usually highlight average commute times for each radio market. The time between morning and evening drive is called *midday*. It is also an important advertising time. Evening is the next daypart, followed by late night or overnight. When an advertiser buys a package that will run on a station throughout the broadcast day, the term *run of schedule (ROS)* is used to designate that the spots are played during all the dayparts. Advertisers may buy time throughout the day or for specific dayparts. They will also buy time across the week or over several weeks or months, depending on the advertiser's needs.

Radio stations also make use of **cooperative advertising,** or simply co-op. Many local retail stores sell items made by national manufacturers. In a co-op arrangement, the national firm will share the cost of advertising with the local business. Thus the Maytag Company might pay part of the cost of local radio time purchased by Green's Appliance Store. Local retailers like co-ops because, in addition to helping Green's pay for the ads, the ads are often produced by national ad agencies and are high in production value. Co-ops allow local retailers to tie their businesses in with a national campaign. Stations need to provide affidavits showing how many times the co-ops run. In fact, at some stations one or more members of the sales staff are assigned exclusively to deal with co-op plans.

The term *national spot sales* refers to the sale of commercial radio time to major national and regional advertisers. For example, Ford and General Motors buy national spots so that their commercials are heard all over the country but at different times and on different stations. The local dealer will participate in buying local spot sales with the manufacturer (for example, *"Your Chevy dealers have great deals on end-of-year clearance models"*). Frequently, national brands have regional managers to handle the ad campaigns, which can vary greatly from one region of the country to the next. For example, Goodyear probably won't run snow tire commercials in the South or the Southwest. The brand manager will buy time on northern stations where snow is most likely.

National spot sales are normally made on behalf of local stations by station representation firms, or reps. Reps maintain offices in the nation's biggest cities, like New York, Los Angeles, Dallas, and Atlanta, which are also home to the nation's leading advertisers and their agencies. Suppose Coke's media buyers want to buy spots on classic rock stations all over the United States. They will contact rep firms that may handle many different stations in markets around the country. The Coke media buyer places one order but buys airtime for many different individual stations in many different markets using this technique.

The third type of radio advertising is *network sales,* which is the sale of commercial advertising by regular networks, such as ABC, or CBS, or special radio networks that carry specific programs such as a local college football game. Network commercials are aired within the programs and carried on each station in the network. Although local stations receive no revenue for carrying the program, there may be some available time within the programs allocated for local spot sales. Network programs and sporting events can usually be sold locally at a premium, making carriage of the game a lucrative event for the local station. Some specialized programs, such as *American Top 40,* are distributed via CD or satellites to local stations with national spots embedded within the program. Local spots may be inserted at the top or bottom of the hour for these weekly specials.

Table 7–1	Radio Advertising Volume, 1965–2005 (in $ millions)			
Year	Network	National Spot	Local	Total
1965	$ 60	$ 275	$ 582	$ 917
1970	56	371	881	1,308
1975	83	436	1,461	1,980
1980	183	779	2,740	3,702
1985	365	1,335	4,790	6,490
1990	433	1,626	6,780	8,839
1995	512	1,741	7,987	10,240
2001	893	3,036	13,932	17,861
2005	1,050	3,380	15,509	19,939

Source: Universal McCann and Radio Advertising Bureau.

The Future of Radio Sales   Take a look at Table 7–1. It displays radio revenues reaped by advertising agencies since 1965; the revenues are broken down by type of expenditure. In 1970, about 30 percent of all radio buys were national spot sales. Local sales accounted for about two-thirds of all revenue. Network radio was in substantial decline at this time (before satellite distribution), with advertisers spending less than 4 percent of their radio budgets on network programs. Today, nearly 80 percent of all radio sales are local. National spot sales account for only $1 out of every $6 of radio advertising. The majority of these sales go to the top-rated stations in the largest markets. But in the last few years, network radio has rebounded thanks to diverse personalities such as Rush Limbaugh, Don Imus, and Dr. Joy Browne. We will trace this trend in more detail in Chapter 8.

How does advertising affect radio's future? Radio, along with other advertising media, was hurt by the events of 9/11, and sales declined in its aftermath. However, radio is poised to grow slightly over the next few years. During the previous two decades, radio garnered only about 7 percent of all advertising dollars. Some radio group owners have started consolidating with billboard advertisers, making the radio-billboard combination a more attractive place for ad dollars, but while billboard and out-of-home advertising are growing, radio has largely stagnated. National spot advertising has grown now that group owners have the ability to market broadly through the multiple station groups that were created during the consolidation after the Telecommunications Act of 1996. High-definition radio may offer some new opportunities for radio groups, but it will be several years before there are enough stations and receivers in the field.

As in the TV business, national spot advertising is usually sold on the basis of station popularity, as measured by ratings. Almost without exception the highest-rated stations will get the majority of advertising expenditures. Media buyers usually go with these higher-ranking stations, leaving the other stations out of the huge advertising expenditure. Stations ranking considerably above their competition thus outbill and outearn their competition, usually by a wider margin than their ratings advantage. Consequently, a station's share of the audience is an extremely important sales tool for a media rep. The higher-ranking stations are much easier to sell to media buyers.

Public Radio Stations Public, educational, and noncommercial radio stations are difficult to categorize. There are many noncommercial radio stations that operate on tiny budgets, frequently operating as part of a high school or college communications program. Some of these stations operate on a part-time basis, while others are full-service stations. It is possible for the FCC to require a part-time, noncommercial station to share its frequency with other noncommercial entities in an urban area.

Public radio stations are affiliated with National Public Radio. These stations carry network and syndicated programs reflecting the entire range of programming from news to classical music, from *Car Talk* to *Prairie Home Companion* to *Talk of the Nation*. Many are well financed by local educational or community entities. Other stations rely heavily on listener support. Unlike PBS, which acts as a television program distributor and syndicator, National Public Radio is a program producer and supplier. NPR uses underwriting to help defray the cost of programming, but it also receives money from its affiliated stations, which purchase programming, and from the Corporation for Public Broadcasting (CPB). NPR has embraced some new technologies as a way of expanding programming and revenue. It has two satellite channels on Sirius Satellite Radio and provides a wide range of podcasts on iTunes Music Store, which are sponsored. NPR's budget was approximately $150 million in 2006.

Many NPR stations ask for listener support as part of their way to raise the funds necessary to buy programming. Some local and state governments support public radio stations through grants, although grant monies have been in decline since the mid-1990s. Because educational and noncommercial radio stations run the gamut from extremely small to very large, it is difficult to generalize about personnel and budgets. Noncommercial stations can solicit corporate or advertiser support through underwriting. Unlike commercial advertising, underwriting cannot make a call to action, such as "To order yours call 555-XXXX now."

Television

America's 1,600 full-time television stations are much more complex structurally than radio stations. Television stations have a greater reliance on outside programming sources than radio. Radio stations rely either on local talent for playing music for a local audience or satellite programming that is demographically targeted to that audience. Television network programming is primarily based on shows of a fixed length that are meant to reach very large audiences. It makes sense, therefore, that television programming is acquired, aired, and sold rather differently from most radio programming.

In small- to medium-sized television markets, almost all the stations are affiliated with one of the four big television networks, or with one of the smaller networks like Pax or CW. Affiliates downlink the network feed off a geostationary satellite. During those times when the network is supplying programs, the television station is responsible for retransmission of the network programs for that market and for station breaks at designated times. Station breaks between network programs allow the local stations to sell advertisers **adjacencies,** lucrative local spots that are aired next to prime-time, daytime, late-night, and weekend network programming. Those few minutes adjacent to network programs usually command a premium and are very lucrative for affiliated stations.

The amount of money that a particular station or network can charge sponsors is influenced by several factors, such as the number of people predicted to watch a given program or to watch during a given time period and the number of commercials the advertiser wishes to place with the station or network. In general, the cost charged to the advertiser is based on the estimated number of people viewing a program. The larger the ratings estimate, the more a station or network will charge for the spot.

Several economic factors affect the way the industry works, but competitive programming is the primary factor (see Chapter 9). Networks are important producers of programming. They develop different kinds of shows to cover many time slots throughout the broadcast day, including the crucial prime-time hours between the evening news and late news. But when there is no network feed, television stations turn to the **syndication** market for programs. Shows that were once successful on the network are frequently syndicated to local stations. These former prime-time reruns compete with other syndicated programming produced exclusively for local distribution, such as the popular game show *Jeopardy,* talk shows like *The View,* or magazines such as *Entertainment Tonight,* and other first-run syndication. Last, all these shows compete with locally produced programming. Local news and information shows are also important programs for television

stations. As you can see, television programming is quite different from that of radio.

Network Sales—Getting Things Upfront   Even though audiences for the television networks have slipped below the 50 percent mark, network television is still a cost-effective way to reach large numbers of Americans at one time. Advertisers buy time slots within individual programs on the networks to reach the large mass audience. Television viewing is heaviest during the fall and spring; it's lightest during the summer. Media buyers purchase network time to meet the specific needs of their client's products, frequently paying more for special times of the year, such as the pre-Christmas selling season or special occasions such as the Olympics.

The television advertising year is broken down into a number of different sales periods, but most networks like to see **upfront** revenue. This sales

Profile: *Wheel of Fortune* and *Jeopardy*—The Grand Daddies of Quiz Shows

The 1950s had game show scandals with programs like *Twenty-One* and the *$64,000 Question.* Since then game shows have come and gone: *Concentration, $20,000 Pyramid,* and *Family Feud.* Some new shows like *Deal or No Deal* do very well for several seasons, but *Wheel of Fortune* and *Jeopardy* continue to reign supreme in the hotly contested first-run syndication market. Both shows are produced by King World Productions.

Even though *Wheel* and *Jeopardy* have distinctive sets, you may have noticed that both shows go "on the road" every season. Harry Friedman, executive producer for the two shows, took *Jeopardy* on the road for the first time in November 1997. Since then the shows have traveled extensively. Friedman says that even though producing a game show on location is expensive, taking the shows around the country creates a buzz in the local markets where the shows stop and this frequently causes ratings to jump in those regions of the country.

Both shows, despite having been on the air for many years, still rank high in syndicated ratings, though *Wheel* consistently ranks higher than *Jeopardy,* particularly in the important women 25–54 audience.

Wheel has been the top-rated game show since it premiered in 1983. Perhaps one of the reasons that *Wheel* attracts such a large audience year after year is that the show's two stars seem real and down to earth. Pat Sajak, the host, says the show's neither hip nor too young. "It's a diverting half-hour and that's all it's supposed to be."

Every season brings something new to the shows. In its 20th season, *Wheel* fine-tuned its format by adding a "mystery round." The change adds two mystery wedges to the wheel; if the player lands on one, he or she needs to decide whether to take the money or choose the mystery prize on the back of the wedge. Just one hitch, though. The back of the wedge could be either a prize or a bankrupt, forfeiting the winnings up to that point.

Jeopardy has seen some revamping, too. All the dollar amounts of the questions have been doubled, and contestants can stay on the show as long as they win. In 2005, *Jeopardy's* ratings skyrocketed when Ken Jennings won for 74 consecutive days. Whew!

Friedman expects both shows to continue their popularity, and they're scheduled to run through the 2009–2010 television season. Friedman says, "It's okay to change the show, but we never change the game." He must know what he's talking about. Friedman's worked on 30 game shows during his career.

period begins in late spring and ends in the summer before the fall television season begins. National advertisers buy time on the new season before it starts because this assures advertisers that they control time slots within the popular program time periods or program nights. Upfront is an important time. Network sales produce the revenue stream that they use to pay for the cost of programming, to pay the costs of distribution, and to pay the creative talent to develop new programs. In other words, when a network sells more inventory before the season starts, it is better able to gauge revenues for the upcoming season, something Wall Street seems to appreciate. Cable networks sell upfront inventory for their programs too.

National advertisers also use **scatter buying,** which involves buying time over several time slots during the broadcast day, to purchase network time. The four quarters in the scatter buying market correspond to the seasons of the year. Buying time this way can be very cost-effective for advertisers. If the actual audience share does not meet preseason estimates, the cost for buying that time slot will decrease in the scatter market. The reverse can be true too. For example, if analysis of a new television show's audience reveals a greater viewership, particularly strong among females aged 25 to 45 (a very attractive demographic), advertising agencies may decide to buy time during that show in the scatter market even though the rates increase. Buying time in the scatter market allows an advertiser to use a planning cycle more effectively, and some networks give ratings guarantees for these purchases since hard numbers can be ascertained from overnight ratings. But broadcast networks also offer guaranteed audience targets in the upfront market to protect the incentive to buy time early. This strategy seems to be working less well in recent years; upfront sales for the 2006–2007 television season were estimated to net $9.05 billion, down slightly from the previous years. Some networks sell as much as 60 percent of their available time in the upfront market.

Networks collect large sums of money from advertisers because they offer buyers the promise of reaching large audiences, but they must rely on affiliates to carry their programming to make good on delivering the numbers. Fox sells time to Chevy and promises that the ad can be seen by 95 percent of the total U.S. population. However, the guarantee for 95 percent of the population is based on all Fox affiliates carrying the specific program where the ad is

placed. The relationship is symbiotic both for advertising and programming. For example, Fox and its affiliates agreed to share the costs for NFL programming in 2005. In return, Fox and its affiliates both get a program that targets a desirable population (males) that's hard to reach with regular programming.

Some networks use **compensation** as an incentive for affiliates to carry their programs. Networks and affiliates negotiate for the rights to sell additional local inventory in return for carrying programs. Usually this means that affiliates can make additional revenue since CPMs in prime time are much higher than other parts of the broadcast day. Remember that most five-star stations are actually owned and operated by the networks. In essence, networks help themselves when they carry their own programs, along with all the other group owners who have affiliated stations. Networks sometimes make very little money on their network operations; but they make a tremendous amount of money on their owned-and-operated stations. KNBC in Los Angeles and WNBC in New York are among the most profitable stations in the country. They're owned by NBC Universal.

The Economics of Networking   The finances of network television programming are very complex. In the 1970s, when the networks were at the peak of their power, the government barred them from owning financial interests in their programs (financial syndication rules). These government regulations, which allowed independent producers to develop, were relaxed in recent years as more competitors have entered the television marketplace. Today television networks can own their own programming, and they can develop new programming with the intention of profiting from the show when it is placed into the syndication marketplace (reruns). Conversely a network's parent company may produce programs for competitors. For example, Warner Brothers, which owned WB, produced *The West Wing* for NBC Universal.

Television programs, particularly dramas and high-profile situation comedies, are very expensive to produce. The per-episode cost for a drama can be in the millions of dollars. Much of the cost is personnel, but the cost of production has escalated over the years. Programs that survive the first few weeks of a television season sometimes go on to become hits and run for years. Programs such as *Friends* and *Frasier* are prime examples. However, it is not unusual for networks to lose money the first season that a program airs. That's because the cost of production, promotion, and compensation can exceed the revenue the networks derive from the sale of time until a new show finds its audience and starts making money. Some expensive shows do not make enough advertising revenue to pay for production because their ratings are not high enough.

To make network television profitable, networks charge a large amount of money for a 30-second spot during the most popular programs. Table 7–2 shows the costs to advertise on some popular network programs. Even though costs are high, particularly for *American Idol* and *Desperate Housewives,* the CPM for these shows is only about $27.00 because the shows garner such high ratings. The CPM for advertising on a network television is actually in line with many national brands' advertising budgets and generally lower than buying time on local television stations individually. Network television still provides a truly mass audience, even though audiences are getting smaller.

Networks usually negotiate to broadcast the program at least twice: once in either the fall or spring 11-week season and one rerun in the summer or in the holiday season. Television producers share the costs with the network. Producers, too, may actually lose money in the first showing of a hit series, but they tend to make money in the *back-end* market. This means that when a program gets sold for distribution in syndication, the show can make a tremendous amount of money for the producers because it is sold to television stations on a market-by-market basis or to a cable network on a per-episode basis.

Sports provide a real dilemma for television networks. Televised professional sporting events are becoming increasingly expensive as the salaries for sports stars rise to astronomical levels. Sports leagues demand increasing revenue for broadcast rights for a number of reasons. Some sports teams do not make sufficient revenues from gate sales to pay the athletes' salaries. Team owners rely on royalties from the broadcast of games and merchandising to supplement the gate receipts. Since sporting events have little potential as reruns, there are very few ways for networks to recoup the cost for the rights to air the event (especially with declining viewership). When costs exceed the ability to charge advertisers for the product, they lose money. Networks continue to ante up for large sporting events to capture male viewers aged 18 to 49. In recent years, some networks have lost money broadcasting certain professional sports. Industry analysts pegged ABC's losses on *Monday Night Football* at $150 million during the 2006 season. When asked to pony up more, ABC and its affiliates, which had helped pay for NFL rights, passed. As a result, *Monday Night Football* moved to ESPN, which has two revenue streams: advertising and franchise fees. ESPN is paying $1.1 billion for the multiyear contract.

Syndications and Local Sales Stations will fill non-network time with TV shows that have been purchased in the syndication market. Syndicated programming may be composed of off-network syndications (reruns) such as *Seinfeld, Everybody Loves Raymond,* and *CSI,* or the shows could be developed specifically as first-run syndication. First-run syndications such as *Jeopardy, Entertainment Tonight,* and *Access Hollywood* are shown directly on local television stations, usually in *early fringe* (the hour before prime time).

When a television station licenses a syndicated show package, it obtains the rights to show each episode a certain number of times in the local market. For example, suppose WEEE-TV decided to pay $10,000 per episode for the rights to show 150 episodes of *CSI: Crime Scene Investigation* three times each. (Striped across the 5-day week, 150 times 3 is 450 daily showings; this will provide approximately 1½ years of local programming for the station.) This deal, worth $1.5 million for the program producer, would be based (1) on the size of the market and (2) on how much other TV stations in that market might be willing to bid for the rights to the show. If

Table 7–2	Cost of 30-Second Time Slot for Prime-Time Programs (2005 Season)	
American Idol (Tuesday)	$660,000	FOX
Desperate Housewives	560,000	ABC
Survivor	425,000	CBS
Invasion	240,000	ABC
Everybody Hates Chris	179,000	UPN
Wife Swap	105,000	ABC
Ghost Whisperer	100,000	CBS
Gilmore Girls	96,000	WB

Source: *The Hollywood Reporter,* September 13, 2005.

Issues: Changing the Way Networks Do Business

In earlier chapters, you read about the growth of the networks and how this growth made both David Sarnoff and William Paley wealthy, famous, and powerful. Today, the economic situation is different from the heady days when networks commanded 90 percent of the viewing audience. In 2006, network audience shares combined were less than 45 percent, and only two of the four major television networks reported profits for the year (ABC and CBS).

The reality of the business today is that making money in network television has never been harder. Cable is an increasingly competitive player, and DVDs and the Internet compete for the eyes and ears of the audience. This new reality has prompted some within the industry to change the way the networks do business.

First, there seems to be more schedule juggling than in the past. There was speculation during the 2006 upfront sales season that ABC would switch *Gray's Anatomy,* and Fox watched eagerly, contemplating a change in its schedule if ABC switched from Sunday to another night. Was ABC going to try to counter program crime drama with lighter romance and dramedy fare during the week?

Second, program costs are causing networks to reevaluate their costs versus audience return. Disney decided to move *Monday Night Football* to ESPN, which has a dual revenue stream, and off ABC, where it was dragging down network profits.

Today the first showing for a program in prime time is considered a starting point for the networks. Networks are interested in providing viewing opportunities anywhere and at any time. Thus, program repurposing is likely to increase. Every time a consumer downloads an episode of *Lost* or *24,* the networks recoup a little of their outlay. Mobile downloads are likely to grow too.

Even as the nature of programming changes, networks are looking to find new opportunities to promote product lines. For example, the ABC daytime soap *All My Children* ran a 3-month storyline revolving around Erica Kane trying to infiltrate a well-known cosmetics company that was sponsoring the show. And judges on Fox's megahit *American Idol* are seen frequently with soft drinks from one of the show's sponsors.

Studios are scrambling to cover the costs of shows that don't succeed with the few new shows that become hits, but even this has changed. *Variety* quoted Dick Wolf, creator of NBC's *Law and Order,* saying, "You take a business that didn't make much sense—namely, 97 percent of everything fails—and now, on the back end, the pot of gold, you've got a partner. It's a daunting model to penetrate."

But even as studios and networks complain about the high costs of producing and complain about each other, old habits die hard. Steven Bochco, producer of *NYPD Blue,* says the process is like major league baseball: "Everyone tries to police themselves [regarding costs], but when there's a free agent on the market, they all break the bank."

the producers were able to strike similar deals in just 80 of the 240 television markets in the United States, they would be very happy and very rich. To carry this example to a conclusion, WEEE-TV sells the number of commercial minutes available within each *CSI* episode locally or in national spot sales. The station must make back the cost of syndication plus enough money to cover station overhead, station commissions, and still meet a profit target. You can see that the amount of money needed to support showing network reruns, particularly big hits, on the local station can be very high. Because costs for quality programming can be so high, many shows are offered as barter syndication.

Syndicated programming runs the gamut from sophisticated coproductions to quiz shows to dramas to fairly vulgar talk shows. Some programs don't cost any money at all, while some are expensive; barter syndication programs may be provided to television stations for little or no money, but if the station uses barter, it offers the distributor a certain amount of its commercial time to sell within the program. As we noted with radio, stations are obliged to carry the spots if they carry the programs. Frequently these shows will include a couple of 30-second "holes" in which local spots can be inserted by the local station. On some quiz shows, viewers will see product placements (that is, where the items are given away as prizes). These products are given by sponsors as consideration for the promotional value of having them seen on the show, making quiz shows relatively inexpensive to produce. Next time you watch *Wheel of Fortune,* note how many automobiles are on the floor as grand prizes.

Commercials provide revenue for broadcast stations. National brands may buy time on the TV networks or they may use a representative firm to place ads in local TV markets.

News and informational programs are extremely important local products for the station to sell. Many stations operate large and sophisticated news departments capable of programming several hours per day on the station. Time sold during and adjacent to highly rated local news programming often generates large percentages of the TV station's revenue. A 2004 study indicated that time sales during local news programming generate as much as 40 percent of a station's total revenue. Networks encourage affiliates to have strong local news since they often run directly before the network news. A good local newscast can provide a strong lead-in for the network newscast. With the higher ratings numbers, higher spot prices can be charged.

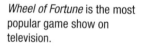

Wheel of Fortune is the most popular game show on television.

Spot Advertising   Spot advertising consists of commercials that national advertisers place on selected stations across the nation. For example, makers of harvesting equipment might wish to purchase ads in a large number of rural markets. Buying time on the network would be inefficient for them since it would be unlikely that many people in New York City or Los Angeles would be shopping for harvesters. Local advertising consists of commercials that are shown on the broadcast station in your area and that feature products and services in the local community served by the TV station.

Most spot buying is handled by a local station's national representative (or simply rep) firm. The rep represents local stations to national and regional buyers. National reps make it easier for buyers to purchase time by being a central contact point for a given station. A national rep may represent only one station in a given market or all the stations of a group owner. This prevents a conflict of interest.

Reps will also offer programming advice and market research to help the station increase its viewership. This advice is not altruistic, however; an increase in viewer numbers means better ratings. Reps have an easier time selling time at higher rates to national advertisers for stations that have the highest ratings in their areas. More time sold at a higher

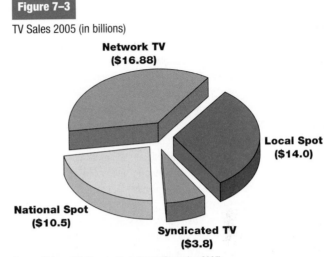

Figure 7–3

TV Sales 2005 (in billions)

Network TV
($16.88)

Local Spot
($14.0)

National Spot
($10.5)

Syndicated TV
($3.8)

Source: Universal McCann Insider's Report (December 2005).

CPM means more profit for the rep (whose fee is a percentage of sales) as well as for the station. Since the goal of the rep is to sell commercials on each of the many stations he or she represents in a given market or region, this kind of advertising is usually known as the spot business.

As Figure 7–3 indicates, the national spot business today is a sizable advertising segment, totaling about

QVC is one of the most profitable cable networks, generating billions in revenue each year.

Events: Gillette, Sports Networks, and Super Events

In 1939, the Gillette razor company paid $200,000 for the rights to broadcast the World Series by radio. Paying this sum of money, large for 1939, established the facts that sponsoring sports was both costly and profitable. This event triggered the beginning of a relationship between sports teams, players, and the product sponsors that like to be associated with them. The target was to reach males in the audience. Over the years, costs and technology have changed the way the game is played.

Networks quickly realized there was money to be made by selling advertising within these mega-events. Today Rupert Murdoch, Disney, and Comcast all want to exercise control over sports broadcasting. By 2000, Murdoch's News Corporation, the parent company of Fox, purchased a financial stake in 19 of the 23 networks that broadcast regional sporting events. These deals did not include teams in the National Football League that already play games seen over the Fox television network. Murdoch wanted to offer advertisers the convenience of one-stop spot shopping. Buyers can go to one organization and make buys on most teams in the three primary professional sports. News Corporation became the first real competition to ABC/ESPN, which has long dominated professional sports. However, there is a difference. While advertisers buy network time on ESPN, spots shown on News Corporation are primarily purchased regionally as spot sales. There's more flexibility.

Comcast, the nation's largest cable company, created the Outdoor Life Network (OLN) to compete with ESPN and other sports venues in 1995 with a mere 4.8 million subscribers. OLN started life a few years earlier as the Outdoor Channel, an offshoot of a successful infomercial called *The Gold Prospecting Show*. In its early days the network's offers were limited to smaller sports venues. The growing popularity of events like the National Hockey League games, the Tour de France, and the Boston Marathon have helped the network grow. OLN became Versus in 2006.

Regional and specialized sports networks have also developed for cable viewers. Comcast started four regional sports networks to compete with Fox. Comcast offers different regions Sports West, Philadephia, Baltimore-Washingon, and Chicago. All provide regional games to Comcast viewers. These regional venues are joined by networks like YES and the New England Sports Network.

Today the NFL dominates the sports scene. In the 2006 football season, ABC, CBS, NBC, ESPN, Fox, and DirecTV all carried NFL action and aired thousands of spots promoting various NFL games. Media experts say that all the various deals will yield revenues of $2.6 billion in 2006–2007 for the NFL. But of all sporting events, the Super Bowl is king. Each year a handful of advertisers ante up a royal sum for 30 seconds of time in the most coveted of advertising time periods.

The 2006 Super Bowl's advertising time raked in a cool $2.5 million for ABC and yielded 90.7 million viewers for advertisers. Viewers wait eagerly to see the commercials. High-profile advertising has become a tradition during the Super Bowl since Apple Computer ran a now-famous commercial introducing the Macintosh in 1984. Consumers wait to see what ad agencies have cooked up for the show. In 2006, advertising was decidedly more tame, reflecting the feeling that previous years' ads may have offended some viewers.

As a new twist, the NFL provided multimedia distribution for just the TV commercials, allowing viewers to see them again on cable video-on-demand or by having them downloaded to cell phones.

10 billion annually in billings. National or local spot advertising is the lifeblood of many TV stations, especially those in major markets. Automotive retailers, national restaurant chains, movie studios and entertainment enterprises, and computer/office equipment suppliers tend to use national spot sales heavily. Firms with a particularly impressive track record for their clients include Katz, Telerep, and Blair.

Local Sales Today an increasing amount of the advertising revenue of a local station comes from the sale of advertising time to local merchants. Local car dealerships, appliance stores, lawyers, laser hair removal services, and others seek to tell people about their services and products through advertising on the local station.

Stations employ salespeople called *account executives* to visit potential advertisers and to demonstrate how advertising on their TV station will increase business. As we noted earlier, a good account executive will help the client develop an advertising strategy based on the amount of money the advertiser has to spend. Like the radio example we used earlier, the account executive should help the client plan the time of the year in which to advertise and the time of the broadcast day during which to advertise and may, particularly in smaller markets, help write commercials. Account executives are usually paid a commission, a percentage of the value of advertising they sell.

The primary tools of the account executive are the ratings and the list of prices for advertising, which are on the rate card. The cost of advertising is based on the show the client chooses to advertise in.

In terms of advertising revenues, local businesses are increasingly important to local stations. In the last 30 years, local advertising from local merchants and service providers has increased from 35 to nearly 50 percent of total sales. Local spot sales totaled more than $14 billion in 2005.

Cable Television Sales   National cable television sales are similar to that of network television, and it is becoming an increasingly important venue for advertisers (see Table 7–3). National advertisers buy time both upfront and in the scatter markets, although at a considerable discount from network television rates. That's because cable is still very much a niche medium and there are many cable channels. The Cable Advertising Bureau projected that the growth of advertising for cable will remain strong. Basic cable network advertising was approximately $15.6 billion in 2005, and total cable ad revenue was about $21.2 billion. Car manufacturers, media companies, telecommunications, and general merchandise retailers tend to be cable's largest advertisers (see Table 7–4). Cable's ability to target very specific audiences is a real plus, but some cable networks that target broad audiences are doing very well. Today, some cable network ratings exceed the lower-rated broadcast networks. In addition, cable has a very strong children's television audience. These

Table 7–4	Top Cable Product Catagories
1	Auto, Auto Accessories, & Equipment
2	Medicine
3	Telecommunications
4	Financial
5	Restaurants

Source: Advertising Age Fact Pack 2006.

factors point to the prospect of steady growth in national cable sales. Comparatively speaking, cable sales have grown more rapidly than those of over-the-air television.

Local cable television spots air across many different basic ad-supported cable networks simultaneously. Over the last few years, many different cable systems have interconnected, allowing cable ads to be sold over entire geographic regions. Cable spot advertising firms provide clients with the ability to buy nationally, regionally (called multimarket), locally, or even in a portion of a market. By coordinating the station break times on different cable networks, local franchisers are able to show commercial **pods** of local spot sales. In addition, many larger cable franchises now cover large urban and metropolitan areas of major U.S. cities. Local cable revenue is expected to become much more important in the next few years.

Public Television   Public television stations can be small or large, depending on the markets that they serve. Funding for a public station comes from a variety of sources. Fewer federal and state dollars are available for public stations than in the past, and as a result underwriting rules for television were relaxed in the mid-1980s. They cannot "sell" time as commercial stations do, so public stations generally rely upon underwritings and local revenue-raising promotions for a portion of their budget. Underwritings for public television are much more commercial-like than they were 10 years ago. Stations will now show the corporate logo of the underwriter, in addition to noting the specifics of its goods or service.

Public television stations also rely upon corporate and individual members to help pay for the costs of programming. At the station level, corporate underwriting usually means that a local company will help pay for the cost of the specific programming. Shows

Table 7–3	Top Cable Advertisers, 2004	
Rank	**Advertiser**	**Expenditure in Millions**
1	Procter and Gamble Company	$704.7
2	General Motors Corporation	303.9
3	Time Warner	209.4
4	Glaxo Smith Kline	202.9

Source: Advertising Age Fact Pack 2006.

Ethics: Radio Promotion—Chaos Out of Control?

While promotion is increasingly important in the hotly competitive environment of radio today, there are indications that some stations are going overboard in their efforts to lure audiences. Some examples:

- A morning DJ for a Phoenix station pogo-sticked the entire 26-mile route of the Boston Marathon—it took him 2 days—and he wound up with severe knee damage.

- An Abilene, Texas, DJ tried to raise money for the United Way by spending 81 straight hours on a Ferris wheel. One night, while adjusting his sleeping bag, he fell off. Lucky for him, he was at the bottom of the wheel at the time. The Ferris wheel attendant who immediately rushed to his aid, however, was not so lucky; he was hit by the wheel and suffered a concussion.

- In Jacksonville, North Carolina, Fat Boy, the morning shock jock, sent his sidekick Waffleman covered in mud to ring the doorbells at people's homes, asking if he could take a shower at their homes. Numerous residents called the cops and complained. The shock jock resigned, but we don't have any details of what became of the sidekick and whether he came clean on the promotion.

- Two DJs in Miami almost caused an international incident when they telephoned Fidel Castro and pretended to be Venezuelan president Hugo Chavez. Castro was not amused.

Listeners are well aware of the treasures to be had in radio promotion. Sometimes they listen just for a chance to win. Sometimes the promotion goes wrong. T-Bone of Kansas City's *The Rock* taped 100 Powerball lottery tickets to his naked body and then stood on a median strip at an intersection of the Shawnee Mission Parkway, encouraging listeners to drive by and take tickets off him. T-Bone, using his cell phone, described his exploits to his listeners until the police picked him up for public nudity and disorderly conduct. Evidently none of the tickets was a winner for the lottery, which was worth $250 million that week.

such as *The Antiques Roadshow* will have both a national and local underwriter. The show's production costs are partially underwritten by the national sponsor, while the local PBS affiliate may use a local retail store to pay for the rights to air the program. Membership drives usually occur twice each year, the goal of which is to resubscribe current station members and add new ones to the roster. During these membership periods the station will run a heavy schedule of specials and promotions.

Promotions tend to center around art auctions, community fund-raising events, and similar activities that raise revenue for the station. PBS also makes substantial use of its image as the place for quality programming in order to raise funds. During special membership drives, local stations will broadcast concerts and specials by noted performers as a way of generating new station members. Concert specials will often be followed by the star herself or himself asking for your pledge of support. In the same vein, PBS stations use their children's television stars, such as Big Bird, to help raise funds for the station.

Today, federal funding for public television is approximately 17 percent of its $330 million operating budget. PBS and others have criticized the low government funding levels, but Congress has not seemed especially interested in increasing levels for noncommercial television programming. During the 2005 legislative session there was a reduction in PBS funding as a result of looming federal budget deficits.

OTHER ASPECTS OF BROADCAST SALES

Station Identification and Promotion

Station identification is extremely important since the sale of time is directly related to the number of listeners the station has, and generally, the greater the listenership, the greater the potential number of sponsors. So stations try to make themselves identifiable to their listeners and sponsors through the use of slogans and promotional contests.

Radio stations will use a combination of call letters and their frequency (location on the radio dial) as a means of promoting themselves. Number and letter combinations like "95X" often connote music preference in the same way that "Lite 102" has meaning for the listener. Other stations use slogans like "the Nerve" or "the River," as a way to make themselves more identifiable. These combinations are recorded in diaries at "sweeps" times, and a rating for the station is determined. Stations will adopt slogans that help identify them to their listeners. For example, stations that call themselves "your news leader" will place heavy emphasis on their information and news services.

Promotions are very important for a station, especially before or during a sweeps period. Frequently, a radio station will trade out commercial time for products or services that the station can give away. For example, a station may give away a luxury car and trade the equivalent value of the car for air time that the dealership can use. Contests are used as a way to build listenership and loyalty. Promotions vary greatly based on the size of the market and the station.

Good ratings are vital. Just one ratings point can translate into thousands of dollars in extra sales for a station. In the last few years, many stations have increased the value of the prizes given away during sweeps in an effort to raise the diary numbers and ultimately their ratings. Expensive sports cars and cash prizes in excess of $10,000 or $20,000 are not unusual prizes.

Radio stations also use another type of promotion to raise listenership: Commercial-free rides encourage extended listening. Commercials are then clustered together at the end of, say, "20 minutes of nonstop music." When the 20-minute ride extends past the 15-, 30-, or 45-minute mark, that listener is counted in the ratings for that average quarter hour. (See Chapter 12.)

When a station changes its overall format, it may change just prior to a ratings period. After an advertising blitz, stations might begin a "commercial-free" month during that period. The commercial-free month may boost ratings, and the station's sales for the next quarter or half of year will be set by the numbers garnered during that ratings period. Frequently listeners are drawn to the station during the commercial-free month but often revert back to old listening habits when commercials resume. Most stations realize that they need good numbers all year long, so promotion tends to be an ongoing process. Other promotional vehicles may include station events within the community.

Television has a great need for promoting programs and personalities. Television promotion tends to be somewhat different from that of radio. You'll see few contests and even fewer opportunities to win the sports car of your dreams. Instead, television promotion tends to be divided into two specific categories: the promotion of specific shows or the copromotion of events in coordination with a sales event.

Promotional announcements, or promos, are short announcements that publicize a program on the station. These messages remind you of the content of a show—"Tomorrow on *Maury:* Satanic transvestite drug-abusing prostitutes who want to adopt"—or they may just remind the viewer of an upcoming program—"All the latest breaking news tonight at 11." The process of promoting a television show is important and costly for broadcasters. Remember that every 10- or 20-second promotion is time that a television station cannot sell. Obviously a station must make a commitment to promote itself and its shows. Viewers won't immediately know when they can watch *Judge Judy* unless the station tells them (although some viewers do use the TV listings!).

Local television news is another area in which stations need to promote themselves. Does the station have a particular focus on local government? A special investigative team? Or special "family healthcasts" or a "Your Stories" feature? Does the station specialize in covering a particular local sports team? Viewers will need to know what distinguishes one station's news programming from that of the competition. (One station in Southern California touts the fact that it is the only station in the market with Doppler radar even though it rarely rains in that part of the country!) Solid promotions are necessary to build audience and, as a result, revenue through high-priced advertising. Usually television stations will need to use cross-promotion (such as billboards) in order to reach those potential viewers who normally don't watch that newscast.

Station Web sites are increasingly important to building strong ties to listeners or viewers in the community. As a result Web sites are important promotional vehicles for broadcast stations. A good broadcast Web site provides important linkages to the station's programming and news departments. Many stations are providing extended coverage for local news stories on the Web. Frequently there are resources linking people to community service organizations, expanded weather and sports coverage, particularly for television stations which have significant news organizations.

Web sites are usually linked to the station's public service initiatives and can provide important

Dr. Phil started by giving advice to Oprah's viewers. Now he hosts his own talk show.

information for members of the community. In the aftermath of the Hurricane Katrina disaster, many broadcast stations in southern states provided information on their Web sites about how to get help, look for missing persons, and apply for disaster relief. The outreach programs that broadcasters provide build important linkages between the stations and their listeners.

Other Announcements

The second type of announcement aired on broadcast stations is the *public service announcement (PSA)*. These announcements, as the term implies, are unpaid. Every year broadcasters perform millions of dollars' worth of public service by offering timely announcements to their audience without charge. At the national level, PSA campaigns are organized and managed by the National Association of Broadcasters and the Advertising Bureau.

Local radio and television stations frequently donate airtime and talent to produce or cosponsor local events that raise millions of dollars for local charities and people in need. In the aftermath of Hurricane Katrina broadcast stations around the county began collecting donations for the relief effort. KWCH-TV in Wichita held a clothing drive to replenish needed clothing for Goodwill Industries, which was emptied after the hurricane, while WMZO-FM and WRC-TV in Washington, D.C., raised $500,000 for relief efforts, and 12 radio stations in West Virginia organized a 12 hour fund-raiser to help the Red Cross. These are a few of the hundreds of events that broadcasters around the country organized as part of the relief efforts.

THE FUTURE OF BROADCASTING AND CABLE/SATELLITE SALES

Good is an appropriate word. It describes the current general outlook for electronic media. The attacks on the World Trade Center and the Pentagon in 2001, coupled with the war in Iraq, caused many advertisers to pull back. Revenues in 2001 and 2003 shrank. However, media research analysts from Veronis, Suhler and Associates and Universal McCann point to an annual growth of more than 6 percent and predict that this rate will continue through 2009. That's good news for those readers hoping to get a job in one of the electronic media fields after graduation.

Sales managers for television and radio stations usually like to point out that sales are among the top-paying jobs in the field. Further, they insist that as sales managers, they hold the most important jobs in broadcasting. If the salespeople didn't do their job well, there would be little money for programming. We think there's something to what they say.

SUMMARY

- Electronic media outlets such as radio, television, and cable sell audiences to advertisers. The audience gains entertainment or information, and media outlets sell the audience's attention to advertising agencies.
- Different media outlets compete for audience attention. For example, television competes against video outlets such as cable and video rentals. Radio competes against audio competitors and outdoor advertising. Cable gets revenue through advertising but makes the majority of its income charging subscribers access fees.
- The amount of competition in the marketplace frequently defines the kind of regulation that is appro-

priate for that medium. In a monopoly there is no effective competition, and government regulation is likely to be greater. When there is a great amount of competition, ratings define the leading media outlets.

- Advertising effectiveness is measure in cost per thousand (CPM). Advertisers usually look to buy at the lowest CPM.

- In comparing the various outlets to place an advertisement, media buyers look at the cost of advertising on the different media. Cost per thousand is a way to compare the cost of advertising on different media.

- Both radio and television have different ways of selling time to advertisers. Local, spot, and network sales provide venues for advertisers to focus in on specific audiences or to advertise broadly. Television networks are complicated media outlets. Networks develop compensation agreements with affiliates for carrying their programs or give affiliates time in which to advertise.

- Stations fill their broadcast times with syndication and local programming when networks do not provide programming.

- There are several types of announcements on radio and television. Promotions help to provide excitement for the station or its programming. Public service announcements (PSAs) provide free announcements and publicity to nonprofit organizations or to help with appropriate charity causes.

KEY TERMS

monopoly 153	cost per thousand (CPM) 155	upfront (sales) 160
oligopoly 153	standing order 155	scatter buying 161
pure competition 153	dayparts 157	compensation 161
buying power index (BPI) 154	cooperative advertising 157	pods 167
gross rating points (GRPs) 154	adjacencies 159	station identification 168
gross impressions 154	syndication 160	

SUGGESTIONS FOR FURTHER READING

Alexander, A.; Owers, J.; Carveth, R.; & Hollifield, C. A., eds. (2003). *Media economics: Theory and practice.* Hillsdale, NJ: Lawrence Erlbaum.

Cave, M., ed. (2002). *Handbook of telecommunications economics.* Amsterdam: North-Holland.

Dizard, W. (1994). *Old media/new media.* White Plains, NY: Longman.

Gross, L.; Gross, B., & Perebinossoff, P. (2005). *Programming for TV, radio & the Internet* (2nd ed.). Boston: Focal Press.

Hoskins, C.; McFadyen, S.; & Finn, A. (2004). *Media economics: Applying economics to new and traditional media.* Thousand Oaks, CA: Sage.

Jessell, H. (2006). *Broadcasting and cable yearbook 2006.* New Providence, NJ: R.R. Bowker.

Parsons, P., & Frieden, R. M. (1998). *The cable and satellite television industries.* Needham Heights, MA: Allyn & Bacon.

Shane, Ed. (1999). *Selling electronic media.* Boston: Focal Press.

Sherman, B. L. (1995). *Telecommunications management* (2nd ed.). New York: McGraw-Hill.

Goodrich, W. B., & Sissors, J. (2001). *Media planning workbook* (3rd ed.). New York: McGraw-Hill.

Tapscott, D. (1996). *The digital economy: Promise and peril in the age of networked intelligence.* New York: McGraw-Hill.

Walker, J., & Ferguson, D. (1998). *The broadcast television industry.* Needham Heights, MA: Allyn & Bacon.

Wimmer, R., & Dominick, J. R. (2005). *Mass media research* (8th ed.). Belmont, CA: Wadsworth.

INTERNET EXERCISES

Visit our Web site at www.mhhe.com/dominick6 for study-guide exercises to help you learn and apply material in each chapter. You will find ideas for future research as well as useful Web links to provide you with an opportunity to journey through the new electronic media.

8 Radio Programming

Quick Facts

 Number of Americans who listen to radio each week: 280 million (2005 est.)

 Number of hours per week subscribers spend with XM satellite radio (average): 22 (2006)

 Number of hours per week terrestrial listeners spend with traditional radio (average): 19 hours, 15 minutes (2006)

 Radio's most important time of day: 6 to 10 A.M. (morning drive)

 Number of direct broadcast radio satellites in U.S. orbit: 5

 Estimated number of podcast listeners in the United States (2006 estimate): 22 million

To unlock the secret of radio programming today, it's helpful to turn to the biological sciences. Biologists define *symbiosis* as "the living together in intimate association or close union of two organisms," especially if mutually beneficial—like silverfish and army ants or coral and sea creatures.

Symbiosis is also an especially good term to use to describe radio programming today. Radio enjoys a close and mutually beneficial relationship with a variety of other "organisms." The popularity of music from feature films (from *Saturday Night Fever* in 1975 to *Dirty Dancing* in 1987 to *Pulp Fiction* in 1994 to *Garden State* in 2004) illustrates how radio is intertwined today with the movie business. The rise of MTV and its host of imitators (such as Country Music Television and VH-1) points to radio's interrelationship with TV, especially cable. But radio's most symbiotic relationship is with the popular music business: the world of CDs and iTunes. Since radio is more than an electronic jukebox, we will also examine the dynamics of information programming on radio: the nature of news radio and talk radio.

RADIO REGULATION AND FORMAT DESIGN

For this symbiotic relationship to work, it's necessary for radio stations to have the freedom to choose the programming they want to provide to their communities. Section 326 of the Communications Act, the law that empowered the FCC to govern broadcast operations, states:

> Nothing in this Act shall be understood or construed to give the Commission the power of censorship over the radio communications or signals transmitted by any radio station, and no regulation or condition shall be promulgated or fixed by the Commission which shall interfere with the right of free speech by means of radio communication.

In short, the FCC has neither the right nor the power to control radio programming. Radio stations are free to program their airtime however they may. In certain specific areas, such as political advertising, obscenity, and indecency, Congress has directed the FCC to promulgate programming rules (see Chapter 10). However, the bulk of radio programming—music, news, and information—is largely free of governmental intrusion. In fact, this characteristic is one of the fundamental distinctions between the sound of American radio and that of

the rest of the world. Basically, American radio is programmed to satisfy listener tastes and not, as in government-owned systems, to serve political or bureaucratic interests.

We call this situation "format freedom." Faced with the task of filling 24 hours per day, 365 days a year, radio programmers are on their own. Their task is simple: to provide attractive programming to meet the informational and/or entertainment needs of an audience. In commercial radio, the audience must be large or important enough to be of interest to advertisers. Public stations must entertain and inform their listeners to an extent that justifies financial support from government agencies, foundations, business underwriters, and the listeners themselves. If the task seems especially formidable, generally programmers don't have to worry about direct governmental intrusion.

A MATRIX OF RADIO PROGRAMMING

Figure 8–1 maps the types of radio programming today. Across the top of the matrix of radio programming are the sources of radio programming. **Local programming** is original programming produced by the radio station in its studios or from locations in its immediate service area. **Prerecorded or syndicated programming** is programming obtained by the station from a commercial supplier, advertiser, or program producer from outside the station. The most common sources of programming of this type are compact discs from record companies. Prerecorded programs may also be received by stations through telephone lines or by microwave relay, but most commonly from a satellite, as a download or distributed via CD. Stations that belong to a network such as ABC, CBS, or National Public Radio are permanently interconnected, usually by telephone lines or satellite transponders. Unlike syndication, **network programming** is regularly scheduled; that is, with

Figure 8–1

Types of Radio Programming

		Source		
		Local	Prerecorded/ Syndicated	Network
Type	Music	1	2	3
	News/Talk	4	5	6

few exceptions, network programs run the same time each day at every station on the network.

Top to bottom in Figure 8–1 are the two main types of radio programming. Most plentiful in radio today is music programming, from opera to country, from "adult standards" to progressive jazz. News/talk covers the broad spectrum from news, sports, and traffic reports to sexual advice, from stand-up comedy to stock tips.

Music

Now, let's examine the kinds of radio programs that fall into each box of Figure 8–1. In box 1 is locally produced music programming. Once a staple of radio programming, when many stations employed their own orchestras, original music emanating from studios or area concert halls is heard today on only a few stations (mostly noncommercial). Some rock stations have had success promoting the music of local bands. For example, WNNX (99X) in Atlanta, a modern rock station, has broadcast numerous live performances from its studios and has successfully marketed these performances on disc and tape. Since 1979, Classic Rocker WTKW (TK99) in Syracuse has featured the latest releases of local bands along with interviews every Sunday night on *Soundcheck.* Some programs heard nationally today began as local productions. American Public Radio's *Prairie Home Companion,* hosted by affable Garrison Keillor, started in this fashion. However, locally produced music is becoming increasingly rare and is thus the smallest segment of the matrix.

The biggest element of radio programming today is box 2, prerecorded and syndicated music. Nearly 9 of 10 radio stations rely on some kind of music as the backbone of their schedule, and that music is most likely coming from a CD, a computer hard drive, or a satellite transponder. This is the high-intensity world of format radio, described in detail later.

Profile: Unvarnished Advice from the Queen of Talk Radio

America's most popular female radio talk-show host, Dr. Laura Schlessinger, is the second-most-listened-to radio personality. Currently heard on nearly 300 radio stations from coast to coast, Dr. Laura's show isn't all love and roses. She's made a name for herself dispensing unvarnished moral advice to her listeners. In fact, one critic has labeled her "the Village Scold" of talk radio. For Dr. Laura, that may be both a problem and a virtue.

Recently *Talkers* magazine, a trade publication in the radio industry, estimated Schlessinger's audience at around 8 million listeners but shrinking. While that's enough to put Dr. Laura in the top 5 after talk leaders Rush Limbaugh and Sean Hannity, over the last few years she has lost several million listeners as her show was dropped by big stations in New York, Boston, Chicago, and elsewhere. A number of stations dropped or bumped Dr. Laura after the 9/11 attack, putting on programs that were more news oriented.

On December 13, 2000, Schlessinger's show made headlines when a caller, identified as "Chris," admitted that he was the shooter in a murder-for-hire plot and was now thinking about telling his family.

Schlessinger built a large and loyal audience as her sharp-tongued lectures were something of a novelty. Dr. Laura's voice resonates with sternly worded strong medicine. During the mid-1990s, she was radio's hottest property, but problems began when she became embroiled in a public dispute with the gay community by calling homosexuality "a biological mistake." Gay advocacy groups started a nationwide advertising boycott campaign against her, and then her newly launched syndicated TV show quickly went sour.

After the TV show failed, she has claimed that TV has more froufrou and celebrity but was not as meaningful as radio. Even though she's made millions from radio, Schlessinger has said that she thinks radio has become too narrow and that it needs to move back to becoming more full service.

A native New Yorker, Schlessinger made her name as an alternative to the frequently male-dominated world of talk radio. While Dr. Laura holds a PhD, it's not in either psychology or psychiatry. Her graduate degree is actually in physiology, but her advice is followed by millions of listeners. At her peak, she was heard on nearly 400 stations and claimed nearly 15 million listeners.

Pronounced dead and buried by industry observers just a few years ago, network music programming (box 3) has undergone a renaissance in
recent years. Joining the long-running orchestral and
opera broadcasts (such as the Texaco-sponsored
Metropolitan Opera, and the New York Philhar-
monic, Philadelphia Orchestra, and Chicago Symphony broadcasts) have been the live broadcasts of
popular music formats from Westwood One, the
Los Angeles–based radio network. Rock-and-roll
music has been the network's strong suit, featuring
live national broadcasts of concerts by the Rolling
Stones, Eric Clapton, the Red Hot Chili Peppers,
and the Dixie Chicks. More recently, Westwood
One created *Absolutely Live,* a new series of hour-
long concerts featuring premier rock artists like
Linkin Park, Foo Fighters, Dave Matthews Band,
and Radiohead.

ABC Radio 24-hour format services and the Jones
Radio Networks also provide full-time programming via satellite in many popular formats. These
program services can be fully automated so that the
local station can run with a minimum of personnel
or they can be integrated into local operations.

News/Talk

Locally produced news/talk programming (box 4)
includes the many news, sports, weather, and traffic
reporters at work in radio today, as well as a range of
local hosts of political, civic, medical, and financial
information shows. As we saw in Chapter 4, news
and talk stations have the largest staffs in radio, including hosts, anchors, reporters, producers, and
many technicians.

You will note from Figure 8–1 that there is a
dashed line between boxes 5 and 6: syndicated and
network radio. This is because the two forms are
combining into similar services.

For example, many popular talk personalities
who have been successful in one market are now being syndicated via satellite to many other markets.
Howard Stern of WXRK in New York was aired in
about 20 markets until he moved to satellite radio in
2006. A popular syndicated talker is WFAN (New
York) personality Don Imus. Imus is heard on 100
stations around the nation, including WTKK-FM in
Boston, WTNT-AM in Washington, and KOTK-AM
in Portland.

Other leading syndicated radio talkers are Jim
Bohannon, Tom Leykis, Sean Hannity, Bill O'Reilly,

Howard Stern, one of the personalities behind the growth of radio
syndication. Stern's sometimes controversial show is now on
satellite radio.

Dr. Dean Edell, Doug Stephan, and Dr. Laura
Schlessinger, the most listened-to woman on American radio. Even if you are not familiar with these
personalities, you've probably heard of the reigning
king of talk radio: Rush Limbaugh.

Limbaugh, a conservative commentator, is heard
on about 600 stations, with a weekly cumulative
audience of more than 13 million Americans. While
many listeners disagree with his politics, there is no
denying his contribution to the radio business.
When his program began to attract attention about
13 years ago, AM radio was in decline. Most AM
stations were bankrupt or near bankrupt. The AM
listening audience was shrinking. Thanks to the popularity of Limbaugh, his legion of imitators, and his
ideological opposites (like liberal Tom Leykis),
the AM band rebounded. By 1998, talk radio was

the leading format in many of the top 25 metropolitan areas, reaching a daily audience of more than 10.5 million adults, most on their way to or from high-paying jobs.

MODES OF RADIO PRODUCTION

Just as radio programmers have a full menu of types and sources of programming, they likewise have a range of ways to produce those programs for their audiences. This is just one example of the many decisions that have to be made by radio managers. We call these choices modes of radio production. Figure 8–2 depicts the various modes.

At the left end of the continuum is local, live production. When radio stations employ their own announcers or newscasters locally and play music that they themselves own, they are using this mode of production.

Live-assist production occurs when radio managers use syndicated programming, such as satellite-delivered music services, but retain local announcers and DJs as the backbone of their program schedule. In this case the live air personality assists in the implementation of the syndicated schedule, hence live-assist.

Semiautomation refers to the reliance of the local station on the services of the syndicated program producer. For example, the music typically comes in via satellite. When a break point for a commercial or program announcement is reached, a digital cart machine or a computer is triggered to play an announcement by a subaudible cue tone triggered in the satellite transmission. In a semiautomated system the station occasionally inserts live personalities, perhaps in the morning drive program or for news and local weather breaks. But the backbone of the programming is the syndicated music schedule.

At the far end of the radio production continuum is **turnkey automation.** This refers to fully automated radio stations that take one of two main forms. Some automated stations consist largely of a satellite dish and a control board. The satellite dish downlinks a radio program service, such as country, rock, or beautiful music. ABC Radio, for example, offers 11 different formats from Jack FM to traditional country to oldies. These formats are programmed 24/7 and require very little local talent. In some cases the service has been made to sound so localized that time, weather, and news information are sent by satellite or computer to the program producer in time for the announcers thousands of miles away to prepare the inserts.

Other turnkey automation systems rely on hard drives and digital cart machines that interface with a computer console. The program director uses a computer program to prepare the logs, schedule all the music, information, and commercial elements, including their order, length, and frequency. Once the manager has approved the logs, the same or another computer at the station controls the program schedule, playing the music, commercials, and sound files with news and weather from a number of computer hard drives or other recording media.

New developments in radio automation rely on the enhanced audio-processing capabilities of today's computers. It is now possible to have a music radio station without a single record, tape, or compact disc. All the different sound elements needed to make the station's format work can be stored in digital computer format and played on demand from a computer in the station's control booth. **Voice-tracking** is a program wrinkle that surfaced as computers offered program directors more options and features. With automation software, a jock can record all the "intros" and "outros" to songs, along with additional banter for an entire airshift in less than an hour. The computer can integrate the voice and music portions of the show to provide the listener with a seamless show. While automation makes it possible for a station group owner to hire one jock to do the voice tracks for several different stations around the country, it reduces the spontaneity of live radio.

The task facing radio program managers is formidable. They must decide whether to emphasize talk or music or strive to operate a full-service station. Having made that decision, they must determine where the programming should come

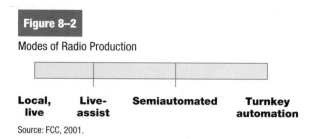

Figure 8–2

Modes of Radio Production

| Local, live | Live-assist | Semiautomated | Turnkey automation |

Source: FCC, 2001.

Dr. Laura Schlessinger's talk show has millions of loyal listeners.

from. Will it all emanate locally? Should the station acquire a music library? If not, which program sources should be used? Should the station purchase a satellite dish? For what services? Should it affiliate with a network? If so, which one(s)? And to what degree of commitment? In addition, the programmer must decide on how the programs will be produced for the audience. Will format freedom reign, giving local control to program directors and disc jockeys? Will outside consultants make many program decisions, with the goal of assisting local announcers and personalities? Will the station use programming from afar via satellite, with only occasional local break-ins? Or will the station be essentially a radio music box, completely automated and controlled by management personnel and their desktop computers?

CREATING THE RADIO FORMAT

The myriad of options facing radio management regarding programming can be answered by the process of creating and refining a format. In radio terminology, the format is the overall sound and image of the radio station: its comprehensive approach to its

talk, music, advertisements, promotional strategies, community relations, personalities, and other factors. There are three keys to a successful format:

1. To identify and serve a predetermined set of listeners.
2. To serve those listeners better than the competition.
3. To reward those listeners both on and off the air, so they become consistent customers for the products and services advertised on the station.

In radio today, the format reigns supreme. It is both an art and a science, combining such artistic expressions as the musical talents of singers and groups and the diverse personalities of DJs and talk-show hosts with the social and behavioral sciences, including polls, surveys, and focus groups.

RADIO MUSIC FORMATTING

Today, more than 8 of 10 radio stations overall, and 9 of 10 on FM, choose some form of music as the backbone of their programming. Figure 8–3 details the process of developing a radio music format.

Figure 8–3

Developing the Music Format

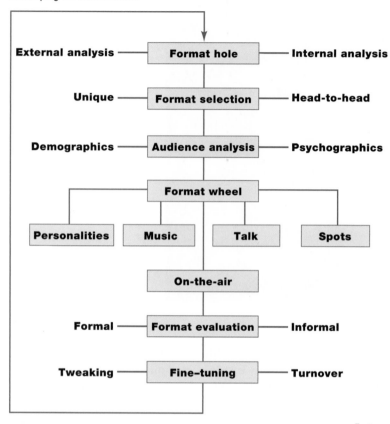

THE "FORMAT HOLE"

Whether placing a new station on the air, acquiring an established station, or reevaluating the programming of an existing station, radio broadcasters have two main choices about how to fill their airtime. They may try to outdo the competition in a given service by programming the same format—most of the nation's largest markets boast at least two of radio's major formats, from contemporary hit radio, to urban, country, and rock—or the station may decide instead to inventory and analyze radio programming in the market in search of an unfulfilled programming need. Managers may decide to try the Jack FM format, modern rock, progressive jazz, or other formats in areas where these services were previously not heard.

Whatever the choice, the secret to successful radio programming is to carve a unique niche, one that will deliver a large enough audience to attract advertising revenues to that station. In the radio business the phrase used is "find the format hole." The process is dependent on two sets of factors: internal and external.

Internal factors affecting the analysis include the ownership of the station, its dial location, power, technical facilities, and management philosophy. For example, it would not make much sense for a station at 99.5 on the FM dial to play contemporary music if a competitor is already playing this format at 101 FM. It would not be wise for a 5,000-watt AM station at 1570 on the dial, with a full-service country format, to compete against a 50,000-watt powerhouse in that format at 720 on the dial. The more powerful station with better dial position will win.

The process of external analysis begins with a competitive market study, which examines the existing stations, including their technical properties, their ownership, their financial performance, their ratings, and, of course, their current formats. If there are competitors, are they strong? Or do they have program weaknesses (bad musical selection, poor announcers, weak promotions, bad dial location, too much clutter, and so on) that make them vulnerable to competitive attack?

Other external factors include geography and population characteristics (country/western in Wichita, laid-back new age in Los Angeles, urban contemporary for Baltimore, or nostalgia for the aging population of West Palm Beach, for instance).

The search for the format hole yields one of two outcomes: the station selects a new or different format that is unavailable in the market, or it decides to compete in the same format with one or more existing stations. The former choice makes the station unique; the latter we refer to as becoming a head-to-head competitor.

Audience Analysis

The goal of radio programming is to attract and maintain an audience. So it makes sense that one of the primary steps in creating a music format is audience identification. In format radio, every station must ascertain its **target audience,** the primary group of people sought by the station's programming. As we traced briefly in Chapter 4, the target audience is usually defined by its principal **demographics,** including age, gender, racial/ethnic background, income, and other descriptors.

The radio audience can also defined by listeners' attitudes, beliefs, values, hobbies, lifestyle choices, and motivations for listening. These kinds of audience attributes are known collectively as **psychographics.** Following are some industry rules of thumb regarding demographics and psychographics.

Listener Demographics One reason radio has remained and even rebounded in the TV, cable, and Internet eras is its phenomenal reach. As we have seen, radio is an intensely personal medium that reaches almost all Americans on a daily basis. All told, radio reaches over 280 million people each week. Just under half of all Americans over the age of 12 listen to radio between 6 and 10 A.M. on weekdays. From 6 A.M. to 6 P.M., radio reaches more people than TV, cable, newspapers, magazines, and computers and online services. In short, radio has excellent demographics.

Anthony Kiedis, front man for the Red Hot Chili Peppers, inspired a new generation of musicians and helped the modern rock format on the radio.

Radio managers divide the U.S. population into standard demographic categories. Gender is demographically defined in terms of men and women (naturally enough). Combined, men and women over age 12 are considered "persons." Those 18 and above are "adults" in a radio ratings book. The standard age cutoffs (known as "age breakouts," or simply "breaks," in the radio business) are tots (ages 2–11), teens (12–17), 18–24, 18–34, 18–49, 25–34, 35–54, and 55 and above (the growing audience of "senior adults"). Demographic research indicates that radio is primarily a "young" medium (even though radio is over 100 years old): Nearly 55 percent of the radio audience is under the age of 45; more than a third of the radio audience falls into the 25–44 age range, and the largest groups of female listeners (who make most consumer purchases) are in the 18–54 age range. This may change as the population ages.

Currently, the ideal radio format appeals to women, especially those in their mid-30s—hence the popularity of country, oldies, and adult contemporary (soft rock), three of the leading radio formats. Radio stations attracting males would be wise to seek an older, professional audience (oldies/news), aging "baby boomers" in their late 40s (news/talk or

classic rock), or younger (18 to 24) music aficionados (modern rock or urban).

Nationally, the black and Hispanic audience together represent about 26 percent of all listeners—a large and growing group. Thus, there has been the rapid rise of Hispanic, black/urban/contemporary, hot AC, and other radio formats described back in Chapter 4.

Radio programming begins with an analysis of these demographics, but not on a national basis. The first step is to look at these and other descriptive characteristics as they occur in a station's local market. Younger demographics might send a program director toward a younger format; older, to an older sound. But at best, demographics provide only a partial picture of the radio audience.

Listener Psychographics   With about 15 distinct format categories (and several subcategories within specific formats) competing for a share of the radio audience, and with more than one station and as many as five or six programming similar formats in many cities, stations have tried to develop more detailed methods of identifying their audiences. The current rage in radio research is listener psychographics (see Chapter 12), also known as *values and lifestyle* or *qualitative research.* *Psychographic research* is an attempt to understand radio listeners according to their attitudes, values, beliefs, leisure pursuits, political interests, and other factors. For many radio programmers today, the age and gender of the audience are insufficient data: They need to know how their listeners view the world (and how their selected radio stations fit into that world).

Since the late 1980s radio stations have amassed volumes of research about what works and what doesn't. But as consumer tastes and behaviors change, lifestyles and attitudes research frequently gives radio program directors better insights into trends than simply playing the demographic numbers game.

America's tastes and interests are constantly changing, and psychographic studies try to get at these changes in taste. Consider the growth in popularity of the Jack FM radio format in 2006, for example. The idea behind Jack FM was to break out of the normal radio mold of tightly controlling the music selections in favor of developing a much deeper and more diverse playlist. Was the desire for new musical choices the result of the growth in the use of MP3 players? Or has the growth in MP3 players occurred because listeners were tired of hearing the same songs on the radio? To answer these questions, program directors needed more sophisticated research than simple demographic information. Psychographic information about consumer behavior and attitudes provide program directors with insights about how to arrange music and program segments to please the listening audience.

A senior executive for Edison Research notes that by properly using focus groups station managers can develop an understanding of consumer viewpoints that are difficult to get elsewhere. Previous qualitative studies have provided data that have helped provide differentiation among formats. Let's take a look at some of the results.

Contemporary hit radio (CHR)   Research has revealed that listeners to Top 40 stations tend to fall into two main psychographic groups. One group listens primarily to hear new music with an up-tempo beat and a lot of urban rhythms (the kind of music heard blaring from cars with their windows rolled down). In the 1980s, Radio W.A.R.S., a classic series of studies done for the National Association of Broadcasters, called these listeners "new music trendies" and "get-me-up rockers." Another subset of the format seemed attracted to CHR, however, because it returned them to the format's heyday in the late 1950s

and early 1960s. For them, listening to CHR was motivated by the desire to be put into a romantic, nostalgic mood. Songs about young love, funny DJs, and lots of oldies are what they want. Images of Wolfman Jack playing "Teen Angel" late on a Saturday night in southern California come to mind (think *American Graffiti* and you'll have the correct image).

As the 1990s ended, this research seemed quite predictive. Even today, multiple forms of CHR are very popular. The "urbanized" approach has led to the rap, Latin, and dance-influenced CHR, known in the trade as "churban" (CHR + urban contemporary). The nostalgia-fed CHR that treasures older standards led to the rise of the "arrow" format (arrow = all rock-and-roll oldies) developed by the influential CBS radio group.

Research conducted in 2006 conducted by Arbitron shows CHR listeners to be overwhelmingly female (62 percent), with the primary listener being under 30. These listeners are avid Web surfers who look for social information such as movie listings, dating services, and games.

In addition, CHR listeners are also more likely to listen to Spanish, alternative, urban, and modern rock stations than are listeners to other formats like country, adult standards, and news/talk.

Modern rock   Rock listeners are among radio's most "socially motivated" listeners, considering themselves music experts. Arbitron's 2006 study found active rockers were slightly older than alternative rock listeners and were more likely to be married and hold down a steady job. Alternative listeners are overwhelmingly male (67 percent) and are the most active Web surfers polled. You're likely to find most alternative listeners clustered around larger radio markets in the West, the Northeast, and the South. Both alternative and active rock listeners are slightly more likely to vote Republican than Democrat in national elections, but while the two groups may share the same political preferences, alternative rock listeners are much more likely to shop at Target.

Again, trends in radio programming today reveal the predictive nature of psychographic research. Modern rock stations tend to reflect the worldview of the "plugged-in smarts." Many listeners to this format see themselves on the cutting edge, especially with music. Most modern rock stations capitalize on this perception: Their disc jockeys affect a certain "insider" attitude; station promotions, slogans, and even buttons and bumper stickers usually have a decidedly modern and antiestablishment look. Other

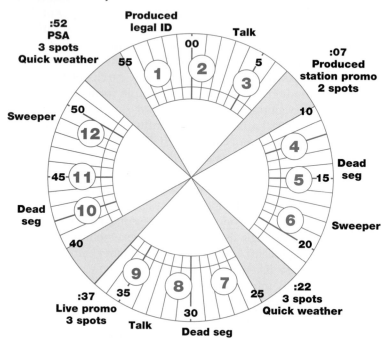

Figure 8–4

Hot Clock for a Country Station

According to Arbitron research, women who listen to country music don't want the DJ to waste their time. Talk is kept to a minimum with an emphasis on music.

rock stations target the "uninvolved" or the "mindless loyalists." For them, playing familiar mainstream music is complemented by uninterrupted musical sweeps, inoffensive DJs, and a more traditional graphical identity (think Grateful Dead T-shirts).

Of course, both of these studies mentioned represent samples that were national in scope; thus it is entirely possible (and likely) that listener motivations are different in Keokuk, Iowa, and Honolulu, Hawaii. For this reason many stations conduct their own psychographic listener studies. We examine those modes of research in Chapter 12.

The Hot Clock

The next step in radio music programming involves the implementation of the schedule: the planning and execution of the station's sound. Most radio programmers today employ a version of a useful chart known as the **hot clock,** "format wheel," or "sound hour." Figures 8–4 and 8–5 are sample hot clocks.

Radio Dayparts   The format wheel looks like the face of a clock, with each element of the station's on-air sound—music, commercials, news, sports, promotions, and so on—scheduled at its precise interval in

the programming hour. The hot clock performs two main functions. First, it enables programmers to get a visual image of an otherwise invisible concept, their "sound." Second, it enables programmers to compare their program proposals with the competition. In this way programmers make sure that at the time they air music, the other station plays its commercials; that the news does not air on both stations at the same time; that it is unlikely that the same song will air simultaneously on both stations; and so on.

Normally programmers use a different clock for each important scheduling period. Figure 8–6 illustrates how radio use varies throughout the day from Monday to Friday and on weekends. Find the peaks on each chart, and you have discovered the medium's key **dayparts** (important time periods).

Morning drive   Let's examine the Monday-to-Friday graph first. The highest point on the graph is radio's most important time period: Monday to Friday in the early morning. For convenience, programmers usually identify the boundaries of this time period as 6 A.M. to 10 A.M. Since most listeners are preparing to commute or are commuting to work and school, this is known as morning drive time. In most radio markets this is *prime time*. This is where radio managers in the major

Figure 8–5

Hot Clock for a Rock Station

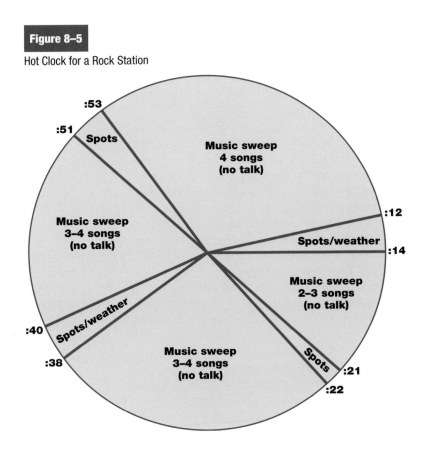

Figure 8–6

Radio Listening Throughout the Day

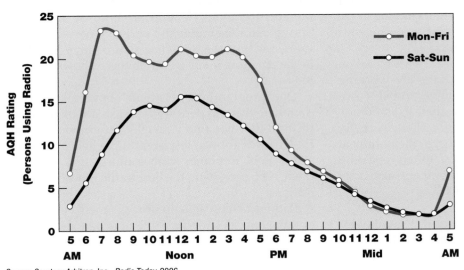

Source: Courtesy Arbitron, Inc., *Radio Today,* 2006.

In the late 1950s, the DJ became "king" of the radio business. Big-name DJs in major markets, like Allen Freed in Cleveland, Howard Miller in Chicago, and Murray the K in New York, had become well known to thousands of loyal listeners, and they exerted considerable influence in the record business. Simply put, if they liked a song and played it over the air, the song had a good chance of success.

This fact did not go unnoticed by the record industry, which showered DJs and music directors with gifts and gratuities, known as *payola*. Lucky "jocks" received cars, golf clubs, vacation trips—you name it. But the gravy train ground to a halt in 1960, when, following a series of highly publicized hearings, Congress enacted legislation making the acceptance of payola a criminal offense, punishable by a $10,000 fine. Since then, many stations have had their DJs and PDs (program directors) sign affidavits guaranteeing compliance with the payola statutes.

However, payola has never really vanished. In 2005, New York Attorney General Elliot Spitzer took the music industry to task for misconduct. Succeeding where federal prosecutors had failed previously, Spitzer sued Sony, Universal, EMI, and Warner Music Group for pay-for-play activities, including bribing station personnel and providing benefits for listeners in exchange for airplay. But payola can take several forms. Spitzer was also concerned about the practice that pays independent promoters who are hired to promote specific songs. These "indies" then approach radio stations to get them to play certain releases. They're paid by the record company when a song is added to the station's playlist, but here's where the problem develops: The indie may then turn around and pay the radio station for promotional expenses such as concerts or provide trips for the disc jockeys and music directors for promotional tours. Opponents of this practice say it shuts out recording artists who aren't paying the independent promoter or other spokespersons.

While none of the record companies admitted to wrongdoing, the four paid nearly $28 million in settlements. Spitzer's not done with the radio business yet. He has turned his attention to major radio broadcasters Entercom, Clear Channel, and Citadel. At issue is the practice of repeatedly playing certain songs in the graveyard shifts so the songs would get counted by charting agencies. Record companies have been doing this by sponsoring the overnight programs. Even though the programs contain sponsorship announcements that comply with federal law, New York's attorney general thinks the practices mislead the listening audience. Evidently the FCC agrees with Spitzer. In April 2006, the FCC opened a new series of inquiries into payola. What do you think?

---

markets commit their greatest program resources. The highest-paid radio personalities toil in this time period, frequently earning salaries in the mid- to high-six-figure range. Stations go to great expense and effort to have the top-rated morning show. Beginning in the 1990s the competitive battle has taken outrageous turns, leading to the rise of "shock jocks."

Another recent trend in morning drive is based on trends in the population. Americans are working longer and longer hours. As you've probably noticed, traffic is generally worse than ever before. Thus, morning drive has begun earlier. In many large cities, the top radio talents begin their shifts at 5 A.M. Some still work until 10 A.M. (often repeating elements from their earliest hours); others make way for the midday team at 8:30 or 9:00 A.M.

Evening drive The next "hump" in the Monday-to-Friday graph is seen in the late afternoon. This is radio's second-most-important time slot: 3 P.M. to 7 P.M., evening drive time.

The audience for evening drive radio is only about two-thirds the size of that for morning drive. This is because not everyone who commutes to work goes directly home. Also, the attractiveness of late-afternoon TV (Oprah Winfrey and Jerry Springer, for example) and early TV newscasts captures much of the audience at this time. People at home are more likely to watch these shows than listen to radio.

One programming element above all tends to dominate this daypart: traffic. Take a look skyward the next time you find yourself in afternoon city traffic. Chances are you'll spot multiple helicopters and a few light airplanes with radio station logos on them, each promising the best traffic reports for their stations.

Ratings books can help programmers develop the optimal hot clock for the drive time periods since the book will show listener trends, including information about the time spent listening and the time spent commuting in the specific market.

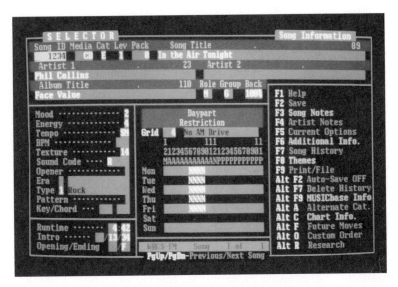

While hot clocks help programmers visualize the sound of their radio stations, most make use of computers to program their airtime.

Daytime There is a nice plateau in the weekday chart where radio listening holds steady at this time. This is the fast-growing daytime period, from 10:00 A.M. to 3:00 P.M. The popularity of portable radios in the home and workplace makes this one of radio's most important time periods.

The noon hour is especially critical to radio programmers in daytime. This is because of the popularity of listening to radio on lunch breaks. Many music stations air special programs designed for their target audiences at this time. AC stations may feature an "oldies café"; CHR stations may feature a "danceteria"; and an album-rock station may run a "metallic lunchbox."

Evening and late night Note how radio listening slides in the early evening (as America turns on its TV sets and PCs) and continues to plummet through the night until dawn. Thus two less important Monday-to-Friday dayparts for programmers are evening (7:00 P.M. to midnight) and overnight, or graveyard, from midnight to 6:00 A.M.

Most stations revert to format in the evening and late-night hours. That is, they play long, extended versions of the preferred programming for their most-dedicated listeners. Since it is harder to sell commercials in these dayparts (due to the comparatively small audience), the loyal listener is rewarded with longer musical programs, specials, and other extended programming.

Weekend radio Looking at the weekend plots on Figure 8–6 immediately reveals the most important time period to programmers and advertisers: Saturday and Sunday in the late morning and early afternoon. This is when we are most likely to turn the radio on, as we clean the house, wash the car (or the dog), and head to the park or beach. There is a slow and steady decline from about 2 P.M. on through the rest of the day on weekends as we turn our attention elsewhere.

Note that at no time on the weekend does radio listening exceed levels achieved on Monday to Friday. The best time on weekend seems to be between 10 A.M. and 2 P.M. But with many listeners attending church, shopping at the mall, or sleeping late, this time slot is usually not a prime programming period.

Filling the Clock: Radio Programming Terminology

At minimum, stations will use a hot clock for their Monday-through-Friday schedule in the morning drive time period, the midday time slot, the afternoon drive slot, and the evening schedule. Stations may also employ a weekend clock for the daytime slots comprising late morning through the early afternoon.

Of course, these days radio hot clocks are rarely constructed with a compass or by outlining a paper pie plate, as was common "back in the day." Instead, program directors plot their show elements on their desktop PCs using software that tracks music rotation and schedules breaks and fine-tunes the station's sound. Still, the process is the same, as is the terminology. Here's how the hot clock is put together.

There are three main types of information depicted in the hot clock: commercial and promotional matter, music, and news/talk segments. The number and location of the commercial positions normally are set first by the general manager in consultation with the sales and program managers. Their job is to decide how many commercials will run and in which parts of the hour. While some adult contemporary or "lite" music stations run as few as 8 or 9 commercial minutes per hour, some rock stations run as many as 15 or 16, and up to 20 or more in peak seasons such as the Christmas rush. The FCC has no strict limit on the number of commercial minutes per hour, but many stations hold the line at 16. The decision on number and placement of commercials is crucial. Although commercials pay for everything else on the station, too many spots—a situation called advertising **clutter**—may cause listeners to tune out or, worse, to tune elsewhere. (In 2005, one of the largest group station owners cut commercial minutes by 20 percent in an attempt to reduce clutter on its stations.)

In addition to scheduling commercial matter, stations will also use the format wheel to schedule their promotional announcements, including contests and giveaways. The commercial and promotional segments of the hot clock are normally known as *spot sets*. Somewhat confusingly, they may also be called *stop sets* since the music stops during these breaks.

The musical segments of the hot clocks are typically broken down into two or three subcategories, such as current hits (given the most airplay); recurrents, recent hits that are still popular; and gold, for golden oldies. Sometimes programmers use keywords to denote the various song categories, such as "power cuts" or "prime cuts" for the most popular current songs, "stash" or "closet classics" for obscure oldies, and "image cuts" for songs that seem to match the format perfectly, such as Billy Joel songs for adult contemporary. Some programmers use color-coding schemes. Red typically denotes power cuts, green may identify a new song in heavy rotation, and gold is used to signify an oldies set.

The area of overlap on the format wheel, where one program element ends and another begins, is known as a **segue,** pronounced "segway." The purest segue is one in which the musical segments blend from one song into another, without DJ interruption. But there are other options. The transition may be made by naming the artists and saying something about the previous song, a procedure known

as a "liner." The station identification (ID) may be made. The announcer might give the time and temperature (T&T). She might promote an upcoming feature ("teaser") or highlight a list of program and promotional activities ("billboard"). A promotional announcement ("promo") might be made. The air personality might promote the next artist or album ("front-sell") or announce the performers of the last set of songs ("back-announce" or "back-sell"). Or the DJ might cover the time to the next musical set ("sweep") with comedy, ad libs, or listener call-ins ("fill"). With this glossary in mind, see if you can determine the program "sound" of the stations depicted in Figures 8–4 and 8–5.

Once the hot clock has been set, the format is in motion and the station is on the air! But the programming process is far from over.

Format Evaluation

Music programming is a particularly dynamic task. Audience tastes are constantly changing. A new pop star is always appearing on the charts. Listeners tire quickly of some songs. Others remain in our ears and minds seemingly forever. So how does the music programmer select the songs for the wheel? When does a song get pulled? This is the difficult process of format evaluation, the next step in radio programming.

One good way to start is by keeping track of song popularity by using Web services like iTunes Music Store or by reading influential industry publications like *Billboard* magazine and *Radio and Records.* Leading stations in the major formats provide a report of the songs they are featuring, known as a playlist, on Apple's iTunes Web site. In return they get "intelligence" about what popular songs and artists are being featured around the nation by other radio stations playing similar formats. The major record labels use these report cards to make sure their artists are receiving airplay and can gauge their appeal since each music download is tracked. *Radio and Records,* an influential trade publication, lists top songs in the different popular formats on its Web site. Student radio stations find the *College Music Journal* an indispensable guide to breaking musical acts.

Most stations also keep track of what their listeners are telling them about their format. **Call-ins,** telephone calls to the station, are logged to determine how listeners feel about the songs, artists, and personalities on the station. Stations use lists of contest

Events: You Don't Know Jack

Calling a radio station Jack or Mike or Bob or Dave may not sound like a really great promotional scheme, but it began happening all over the country in 2005. When venerable WCBS-FM in New York City, long the nation's premier oldies station, changed to the iPod-inspired Jack FM format, things got interesting. The station immediately fell from 8 to 22 in the ratings, and WCBS had to give advertisers additional airtime to make up for losses in ratings. Former Monkees rock-and-roll star turned disc jockey Mickey Dolenz and other highly paid radio legends were sent packing. But ratings did not improve in the next ratings period; evidently Jack was having a difficult time making friends in the Big Apple.

What would convince highly paid program executives at WCBS-FM, part of the Infinity broadcasting empire, to desert a popular format with well-liked, established personalities for a brand-new format? One word: age. WCBS-FM listeners (like your authors) had grown up on 60s rock-and-roll and were approaching 60 themselves. Radio managers and advertisers seem to covet youth or, more specifically, younger audiences, and WCBS's managers were no exception. Over the years, WCBS listeners had begun to drop out of that core of 25- to 54-year-old listeners.

All over the country Jack FM format stations have been sprouting up in the last 2 years. To put it simply, Jack is a radio format that disdains the conventional wisdom that most listeners respond well to lots of repetition and station self-promotion. Infinity was convinced that the new format could work in New York as it had for its stations in Los Angeles and Houston.

The Jack FM format, which started in Canada, plays a wider range of adult hits than tightly formatted radio stations. According to Arbitron there's a much broader playlist. When a station changes to Jack FM, the frequency of rotation songs drops from 7 to 10 plays per week to 4 or fewer, and the playlist may double in size. While the format appeals to 25–54, the largest part of the audience (60 percent) leans toward the younger part of the demographic. Additionally, gains in the listening audience appear without regard to station personalities, and that makes the format cheaper to produce. Where the format had been tried, it had gained market share for listeners 12+ and 25–54. Additionally Jack FM format stations tend to hold on to listeners, meaning listeners stay with the station longer.

Whether Jack FM will work for WCBS-FM is an issue. New York has a highly diverse audience, and the market has many different stations. In the meantime, to make up for the change, WCBS-HD (the digital channel) has gone back to the oldies format, while the analog station continues to run with Jack.

entrants and telephone directories to conduct **call-outs:** Short (5- to 10-second) selections of the music, known as *hooks,* are played over the phone, and listeners are typically asked to rate the song as one they like a little, are unsure about, or like a lot.

Stations also assemble groups of their listeners in large rooms and conduct **auditorium tests.** In this forum up to 200 or 300 songs can be "hook-tested." Or stations may select a small group of listeners (from 3 to 15) and conduct in-depth interviews about their musical preferences; this is a **focus group study.**

If the task of evaluating the format sounds complex, that's because it is. For this reason many stations hire outside experts to help select their music, conduct their audience research, train their DJs, organize their promotions, and perform similar programming tasks. Such services are provided by program and research consultants.

There are essentially two main types of radio consultants. *Specialized consultants* provide expertise in one particular area, such as research, music selection, promotion, or financial management. *Full-service consultants* provide "soup-to-nuts" services, from how to decorate the radio station to how to deal with crank phone callers. Some industry leaders are the Randy Lane Company; Media Strategies; Shane Media of Houston, headed by program guru Ed Shane; and Wimmer Research, based in Denver.

Fine-Tuning the Format

The final phase of radio format evolution is fine-tuning. Using data based on listener reaction—as indicated by audience ratings, station research, phone calls, and other means—the program manager makes changes in the schedule. The changes can range from minor to drastic. Minor changes involve substitutions in the musical mix, reformatting the various time periods, moving personalities around throughout the day, and so on. Major adjustments include replacing air personalities (most typically in morning drive); developing new promotional campaigns, including occasional call-letter changes; and firing music directors (a relatively common occurrence). The most drastic change is to abandon the format altogether and to try a new type of music, targeted to a different audience demographic. In recent years "format turnover" has been increasing at a spectacular rate. In the late 1990s some estimates indicated that as many as 20 percent of radio stations change formats in a given year.

Despite the apparent complexity of the process of radio music formatting, it remains popular and rewarding work. Major-market program and music directors can look forward to high incomes, great visibility in the high-gloss world of popular music, and excellent "perks," like backstage passes to concerts and limo rides with the stars. Of course, some of these perks approach the limits of legality, which brings us to the problem of payola (see box on page 184).

NEWS/TALK AND SPORTS FORMATTING

On the surface it might appear that programming a radio station without music is a simpler task than formatting the latest in rock-and-roll or figuring out who will be the next country legend. The format strategies of talk radio, however, are just as complex as those in the various music formats. How much news? How much telephone interview? What types of personalities? Sports? Which and how much? And like the music formats, how many commercials? When?

The first consideration for a station planning a spoken-word service is to determine the type and amount of talk. While there are really four common programming elements (news, talk, business, and sports), there are two extremes in the format. At one end is the all-news operation, providing summaries and spot news reports around the clock. Leading the way in this format are such classic all-news operations as WINS in New York, WBBM in Chicago, KFWB in Los Angeles, KYW in Philadelphia, and KIRO in Seattle. At the other extreme are all-talk stations, which lean heavily on the concept of the telephone call-in as the basis for their programming schedule. On this list are such stalwarts as New York's WOR and Los Angeles's KABC and KFI. Of course, some stations like WBEN in Buffalo combine news and talk in their market.

Talk-show host Bill O'Reilly.

Just like their musical counterparts, most news/talk radio stations use a format wheel to schedule their programming. Examine the clocks for an all-news station and an all-talk station in Figures 8–7 and 8–8.

All News

First, let's look at the all-news wheel. There are three basic elements in the sound hour: news segments, feature segments, and commercial matter. Typically news stations provide network news at or near the top of the hour. This provides the audience broad national and international coverage, which the station can interpret or "localize" for its audience in other news segments. Some all-news stations break for network news reports at other times, typically at the 30-minute mark (the "bottom of the hour"). Other stations use a different cycle. For example, WINS has

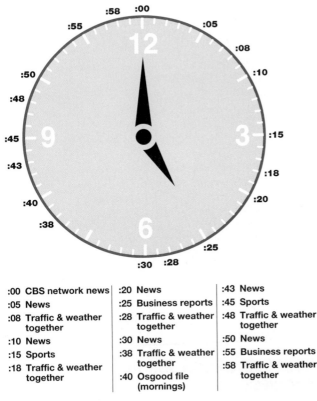

Figure 8–7

Hot Clock for an All-News Station

:00	CBS network news	:20	News	:43	News
:05	News	:25	Business reports	:45	Sports
:08	Traffic & weather together	:28	Traffic & weather together	:48	Traffic & weather together
:10	News	:30	News	:50	News
:15	Sports	:38	Traffic & weather together	:55	Business reports
:18	Traffic & weather together	:40	Osgood file (mornings)	:58	Traffic & weather together

Source: Courtesy CBS Radio.

made a slogan of its cyclical format: "Give us 22 minutes and we'll give you the world."

Credible announcers are a critical ingredient to the success of the all-news operation. Announcers must sound confident and authoritative. For this reason many all-news operations prohibit announcers from delivering commercial "pitches." This is to avoid hurting the newscaster's credibility, which might result from the announcer's reporting a natural disaster, for example, and then segueing to a used-car spot.

Feature programming at an all-news station runs the gamut from the expected (weather, sports, and traffic) to the more specialized (political, economic, and health reports). These reports usually are presented in a streamlined fashion—in units of 3 minutes or less.

By definition, all-news stations need to be bright, brisk, and dependable. News listeners tend to be "no-nonsense" information seekers. When they tune in to an all-news station, they expect to become well informed quickly. For this reason the format wheel in

all-news tends to spin rapidly; time checks are frequent; and program elements are repeated regularly throughout the day. Phrases such as "around the globe in 15 minutes" and "traffic and weather next" give evidence of this speedy rotation, especially in key dayparts like morning and evening drive. In this regard, the programming pace at an all-news station is similar to that at a Top 40 station.

News/Talk

Compared with all-news stations, those emphasizing talk tend to be "laid-back." News segments are common, particularly at the top and bottom of the hour, with the remainder of the program hour filled by features, interviews, and telephone call-in segments. As an example, inspect the hot clock for an all-talk station (Figure 8–8).

Note the more leisurely pace of the talk format. Talk segments of 5 to 7 uninterrupted minutes are commonplace, like the "music sweeps" in adult contemporary and adult standards. These are presided over by talk-show hosts. Unlike the announcers on all-news stations, who tend to be interchangeable (credibility, rather than individuality, is the key for them), talk hosts are distinct personalities. Some boast political beliefs on the left of the political spectrum; others at the far right.

Feature elements are more commonplace in the talk format. Many stations have "resident experts" in such fields as medicine, psychiatry, finance, law, economics, and politics.

The prohibition of the reading of commercials by the announcer in the all-news format rarely extends to talk radio. In fact, talk-show hosts tend to be expert "pitchmen" (and women) who frequently give broad testimonials for their sponsors' products, sometimes longer than the 30 or 60 seconds the sponsor paid for.

Both news and talk tend to carry play-by-play sports on their schedule. In large markets there is considerable competition to land the broadcast rights to professional and major college sports in those cities. Smaller news and talk operations sign on to carry regional professional teams, as part of a network. Many also carry local college and high school games.

Talk radio is still in a growth phase, fueled by the war on terror, sensational scandals, and politically charged news events. Research on the audience, conducted in 2005 by the trade magazine *Talkers,* is informative. The talk radio garners about 17 percent of the total radio audience. Listeners are mostly male

Figure 8–8

Format Wheel for an All-Talk Station

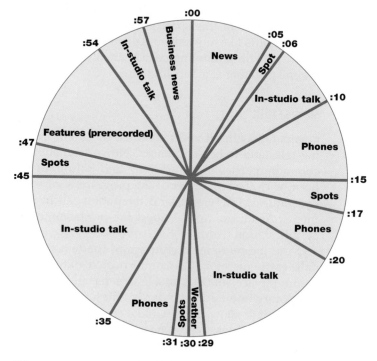

(55 percent, compared to 45 percent female); mostly mature (54 percent are aged 45 or older); mostly white (19 percent African American and 9 percent Hispanic American); and mostly smart (70 percent with more than a high school education). Republicans outnumber Democrats (23 to 14 percent), while the majority of talk radio listeners describe themselves as independents (57 percent). For what it's worth, Fox is the most watched TV news source, while few claim to read either *Time* or *Newsweek*. Football (34 percent) and baseball (29 percent) are their favorite sports, and their music formats of choice are country (22 percent) and oldies (19 percent each). Table 8–1 shows the top 5 syndicated talk shows.

Table 8–1	Top 5 Syndicated Talk Shows

Talk Show Host	Weekly Cume (in millions)
1 Rush Limbaugh	13.50+
2 Sean Hannity	12.50+
3 Michael Savage	8.25+
4 Dr. Laura	7.75+
5 Laura Ingraham	5.00+

Source: *Talkers Magazine*, Fall 2005.

NONCOMMERCIAL RADIO PROGRAMMING

As we traced briefly in Chapter 4, noncommercial radio programming is a mixed bag, depending largely on the type of facility. Recall that there are three main classes of noncommercial facilities: public, university, and community.

Public Radio Stations

Public radio stations are those that meet guidelines for federal grant assistance through the Corporation for Public Broadcasting. CPB-qualified stations must employ at least five full-time employees, must broadcast at least 18 hours per day, and must develop good quality programming to serve a demonstrated need in the community. These so-called CPB-qualified stations, numbering about 276 member stations and more than 400 associates nationwide, are the backbone of the National Public Radio network, which boasts the well-known programs *All Things Considered, Morning Edition, Performance Today, The Diane Rehm Show,* and *Car Talk.*

CPB-qualified stations may also feature the programs offered by a smaller competing networks such as Public Radio International (PRI) and American

Public Media. PRI produces programming and distributes programs produced by other organizations. Some of its most popular shows include *This American Life,* produced by Chicago Public Radio, and *BBC World Service.* American Public Media distributes programs such as *Marketplace* and CBC's long-running *As It Happens,* but it is probably best known for distributing *A Prairie Home Companion,* the venerable variety show hosted by Garrison Keillor. Today, *Prairie Home Companion* is heard on more than 500 radio stations by an estimated 4 million listeners weekly.

Typically, CPB-qualified stations rely on NPR, PRI, and American Public Media for about a quarter of their daily schedule. The remainder of the schedule is filled with locally originated music and public affairs programs. The overwhelming majority of classical music stations in the United States today are CPB-qualified. Other forms of music receiving airplay include jazz, opera, folk, and show tunes.

Public radio is following some of the same trends as commercial radio. During the 2-year period 2003–2005, public radio audiences fell about 2 percent. While this decline is relatively small, it represents a change from the unprecedented 22 percent

growth experience since the 1980s and 1990s. Jackie Nixon, NPR's director of audience research, speculates that some of the leveling off may be due to "news fatigue" as news coverage expanded during the height of the war on terror and the war in Iraq. In 2005, NPR estimated that nearly 2 million individuals listened to NPR during at least one quarter hour (AQH) each week. (See Chapter 12 for more information on ratings.)

In concert with expanded audience research, public radio has been diversifying its programs and distribution networks. With the advent of new technologies, public radio has been eager to make programs and show segments available to the listening audience via Web sites and through podcasting technology. But it's not all wine and roses for public radio. Federal funding continues to be an important concern as the government representatives look for ways to cut the looming federal deficit, and some colleges and community license holders have considered selling their licenses to Christian broadcasting organizations.

College Radio

Although over 150 NPR-affiliated stations are operated by universities, we do not mean these stations when we speak of "college radio." Instead, we are referring to about 800 stations licensed to American colleges (and some high schools) that do not meet the CPB criteria. Many are operated as student activities or training centers; most feature "alternative" programming schedules to both NPR and commercial radio. The musical mix at most college stations is eclectic and mostly progressive. For example, examine the program schedule for WUOG, the student station at the University of Georgia (Figure 8–9). The schedule illustrates both block and strip programming techniques. Progressive rock is striped across the weekday, with special blocks of programming on weekends and evenings.

As we have seen, commercial radio formatting is tightly structured and controlled. For this reason, college radio has served both as a place where new music is likely to be played first and where there is likely to be less structured programming. During the 1980s and 1990s college radio pioneered what is now commonly called *alternative rock,* and it's always served as a place where many new performers received their initial airplay. Venerable rockers like U2, the Police, and R.E.M. started out

One of the most popular programs on National Public Radio is *Car Talk,* hosted by Tom and Ray Magliozzi.

Figure 8–9

WUOG Program Guide (Used with permission)

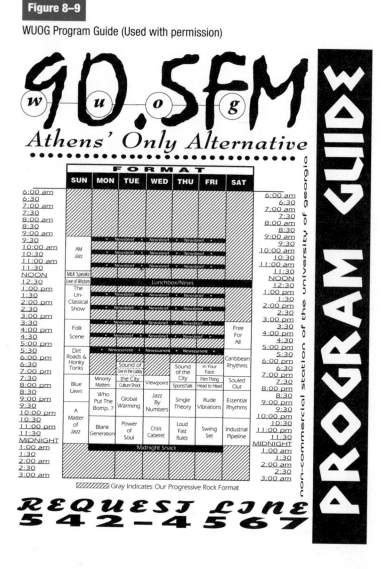

on college radio, and more recently, The Shins, Death Cab for Cutie, White Stripes, and Franz Ferdinand have made the transition from indie bands to major artists.

Many college stations are active in news and public affairs programming. Again, the structure and approach of these services is an amalgam. Stations affiliated with journalism and mass communications programs may have news and public affairs schedules that emulate those at a commercial operation. Others rely for news programming upon volunteer efforts by their staffers. In such cases schedules tend to be sporadic and content varied, to say the least.

Community-Station Programming

If *diversity* is the word to describe college radio, the term is equally suited to the broad category of community radio stations. Community stations are operated by civic associations, school boards, charitable foundations, and, increasingly, religious organizations.

Most community stations use a **block programming** approach. Unlike commercial formats, where the music, talk, and commercial elements are generally consistent throughout the day, in the block scheme, programming is divided into 2- or 3-hour blocks appealing to different audiences at different

Most people associate the name *Muzak* with lush stringed instrumental versions of pop standards. You may remember when you were growing up, standing in line at a bank, wondering why the store piped in a bland instrumental version of a great Beatles song.

Muzak was founded by George Squier in 1922. The company, called Wired Radio, delivered music and news to homes in Staten Island through telegraph wires. Needless to say, broadcasting quickly supplanted the need for a wired programming service in the home, so Squier's company began concentrating on delivering background music to restaurants, hotels, and other businesses.

In 1934, Wired Radio became Muzak, and the programming we fondly called "elevator music" was piped into buildings in and around New York City. The company pioneered a concept called "stimulus progression," 15-minute music cycles gradually increasing and decreasing in intensity. The concept worked pretty well through the mid-1960s, but then a musical revolution began. Muzak's playlist and rock music began to diverge; people began to use the name derisively to refer to anything bland. Muzak updated its concepts some in the 1970s and 1980s, but it wasn't until the 1990s that things really changed.

VP for programming, Alvin Collis, a former sound engineer and self-proclaimed musician and storyteller, had a revelation. Modern stores are like theatrical sets (think Old Navy or Banana Republic). Music needs to meet the expectations of the customer, and that means programming specifically to the store's demographics and psychographics. Music played for British Airways will be different from the music chosen for the Charlotte Russe or Gold's Gym.

Today Muzak employs 22 program designers, mostly musicians or people with deep musical background. They develop programs for customers from a fairly vast library of digital recordings including every popular genre from jazz to heavy metal to country. Today Muzak is as likely to program a cut by Velvet Revolver as it is Kenny G. There might be a broad playlist or a fast rotation of top 40 songs, depending on the client. (Some clients actually specify which artists they want on their programs.) Muzak programs to meet the tastes of the customers whose clients choose the programming service. Not so different from radio. When you think about it, it's a lot like programming a radio station.

---

times. Educational outlets, for example, may begin the day with a 2-hour block appealing to elementary-age students. Midday might be used for in-home college-level instruction, and the afternoon dedicated to social studies programming for secondary schoolers.

The trend toward diversity in programming at noncommercial stations extends to the religious stations. While virtually all religious operations make live broadcasts of church sermons and activities a vital part of their programming day, beyond that there is great variation. Among Christian stations, for example, at various times one can hear old-time Gospel (like "The Old Gospel Ship"), solemn hymns, or "contemporary Christian" rock. And within the religious radio milieu, there are "networks." For example, the Salem Radio Network programs three full-service different Christian music formats for stations as well as specialty programs. Its programs are heard on more than 1,500 stations around the country each week.

Micro-Broadcasting and Low-Power FM   In the 1960s and 1970s, the FCC allocated low-power licenses to educational institutions and community groups. However, in 1978, the commission stopped the practice and required all 10-watt stations to increase power to a minimum of 100 watts. In January 2000, the FCC began authorizing new, very low power FM stations again. Former FCC chairman William Kennard began this new service as a way of providing options for small community organizations that were not being served by current commercial and public services. These new stations are typically 100 watts or less, and have an average listening radius of about only 4 miles. These stations are only available for noncommercial entities including public safety organizations and public transportation facilities.

Low-power stations are developing around the country, but they are still in their infancy regarding programming and direction. What new radio services will develop as an outgrowth of this public service initative? It's too early to tell. As they say in radio, "Stay tuned."

SUMMARY

- There are strong ties between radio and the music business: It is evident that airplay means higher record sales. The advent of MTV, CDs, and MP3 has also reinforced the interdependence of these businesses with radio.

- Radio programming can derive from local, prerecorded or syndicated, and network sources. Radio shows can be produced in four ways: local live, live-assist, semiautomation, and turnkey automation.

- Stations strive to make their formats unique. One way of achieving this is to analyze the market of a particular city and to find a format hole or a niche that is not being well served.

- When a station attempts to choose a format, internal factors that are considered include ownership, dial location, power, technical facilities, and management philosophy. External factors such as strength of competitors, geography, and demographics also need to be analyzed. The new trend is toward psychographic research, which tells programmers the type of listener each musical category attracts.

- Station managers plan their programs on a hot clock. This helps them visualize the sound of a station. A program schedule is divided into dayparts, including morning drive, daytime, evening drive, evening, and overnight.

- Talk radio has seen spectacular growth in recent years, resuscitating the AM band and providing its listeners a range of services, from all-news to sports, financial advice, and psychological counseling.

- On the nonprofit side, public radio stations receive programming from three major network sources: National Public Radio (NPR), Public Radio International (PRI), and American Public Media. College stations tend to emphasize diversity and block programming; religious and community stations offer everything from chapel broadcasts to Christian rock-and-roll. Low-power FM stations will provide programming opportunities for religious and community groups in the future.

KEY TERMS

local programming 173
prerecorded or syndicated
    programming 173
network programming 173
turnkey automation 176
voice-tracking 176

target audience 179
demographics 179
psychographics 179
hot clock 182
dayparts 182
clutter 186

segue 186
call-ins 186
call-outs 187
auditorium tests 187
focus group study 187
block programming 192

SUGGESTIONS FOR FURTHER READING

Clark, L. (1998). *Shock radio.* New York: Forge.

Eastman, S., & Ferguson, D. (2005). *Media programming: Strategies and practices* (7th ed.). Belmont, CA: Wadsworth.

Glass, Ira, & Able, J. (1999). *Radio: An illustrated guide.* Chicago: WBEZ Alliance.

Gross, L.; Gross, B.; & Perebinossoff, P. (2005). *Programming for TV, radio & the Internet* (2nd ed.). Boston: Focal Press.

Hausman, D., Benoit, P., Messere, F., & O'Donnell, L. (2007). *Modern radio production* (7th ed.). Belmont, CA: Wadsworth.

Hillard, R., & Keith, M. (2003). *Dirty discourse: Sex and indecency on American radio.* Ames: Iowa State University Press.

Keith, M. (2003). *The radio station* (6th ed.). Boston: Focal Press.

Laufer, P. (1995). *Inside talk radio: America's voice or just hot air?* Secaucus, NJ: Carol Publishing Group.

Looker, T. (1995). *The sound and the story: NPR and the art of radio.* Boston: Houghton Mifflin.

Lynch, J. (1998). *Process and practice of radio programming.* Lanham, MD: University Press of America.

MacFarland, D. T. (1997). *Future radio programming strategies: Cultivating leadership in the digital age* (2nd ed.). Mahwah, NJ: Erlbaum.

INTERNET EXERCISES

Visit our Web site at www.mhhe.com/dominick6 for study-guide exercises to help you learn and apply material in each chapter. You will find ideas for future research as well as useful Web links to provide you with an opportunity to journey through the new electronic media.

TV Programming 9

Quick Facts

 Percent of Americans who cite network TV as credible: 64 (2006)

 Percent of Americans who think network news organizations are more interested in ratings than generally informing the public: 66 (2005)

 Percent of Americans who think the press is too critical of America: 40 (2006)

 Cost per episode of *Seinfeld* in cable syndication: $1 million

 Number of new program ideas pitched to TV networks each year: 5,000 (est.)

 Number of successful new TV series each year: 1–3 (average)

We study television for a lot of reasons: its social impact; its effect on politics; its influence on modes of conversation, fashion, and relationships; and on and on. Throughout this book, we've looked at its ownership, its financial structure, its employment patterns, and the like. But for the majority of the public, television is really only about one thing: programming. And that programming, whether it's found on the broadcast networks, local TV stations, cable, satellite, or the Internet, has only two main functions: information and entertainment. Simply put, people watch TV programs for either news or entertainment. In this chapter, we examine how television programming is made. First, we look at information programming—the often-controversial topic of television news. Second, we examine the field of entertainment television—how TV manufactures "stars and stories" for the entertainment of a large, loyal, and eager public. But first, we bring you the news.

THE RISE OF TELEVISION NEWS

The Roper and Pew Studies

Every few years various research organizations conduct surveys asking people to identify (1) their main source of news and (2) the news source that they perceive to be the most credible. From 1963 through 2005, TV was named most frequently as the primary source of news. Its lead over second-place newspapers increased through 2000, although that's leveled over over the last 5 years. The big change is how many people now use the Internet. The proportion of people naming radio fell steadily from the 1960s, as did the magazine category (which was never named by more than 1 in 10 people to begin with). Few people over the years named "other people" as their primary news source. Today, however, the news business is changing as people can now access their news from more sources and on more platforms than ever before.

Still, television news also has received high marks on credibility. Since 1961 TV has been cited as the most believable source of news. By 1992 TV was named as most credible more than two to one over newspapers.

While the war in Iraq and Hurricane Katrina riveted our attention to the television screen during the past couple of years, it was the terrorist attacks on September 11, 2001, that shaped our view that television delivers information into our homes better than any other news source. During the 24 hours following the attacks, 9 out of every 10 homes in America watched the unfolding events on television. For many Americans television is an electronic hearth during times of crisis; it's where we congregate to hear vital news.

While TV news credibility has taken some hits lately (we'll get to that later), the Pew study showed that when Americans were asked to name their top two sources of news, TV was named more often by nearly three-quarters of those responding. Newspapers were named most often by 44 percent of those polled. The Internet made the list originally in 1997 with a mere 2 percent, but now 24 percent of Americans surveyed named it as a primary source. That figure is expected to continue to rise as networks and newspapers put more and more resources online.

A BRIEF HISTORY OF TV NEWS

Although the wording of the questions has caused some debate about the validity of the original Roper findings, they clearly indicate the rise of TV as a news source in our era. How did this happen? When did TV become our eyes on the world? The Roper studies suggest that it happened in the early 1960s— November 22, 1963, to be exact.

The Kennedy Assassination: The Death of Camelot and the Birth of Television News

President John F. Kennedy had been warned by his advisers not to go to Dallas. Like many places in the South, the city was torn by political and racial unrest. The press hinted that there might be trouble when a president perceived as a liberal traveled to a staunchly conservative city, but Kennedy could not be dissuaded from going. A large contingent of the media was on hand as the president's motorcade passed the Texas School Book Depository. Shots rang out. The president was mortally wounded.

Within 5 minutes, news of the shooting moved on the United Press wire service. Within 10 minutes the three TV networks had interrupted their afternoon lineups of game shows and soap operas. Receiving the news from a young Dallas reporter named Dan Rather, an emotional Walter Cronkite told the nation on CBS that its president had been slain.

On his third birthday, John F. Kennedy, Jr., salutes the casket bearing his father's body. More than 500 million people worldwide watched the events of that weekend in November of 1963.

Assassinations in other nations might have led to governmental chaos and public violence, but in the United States it turned people to their TV sets. For 4 days all regular programming was suspended and people sat, seemingly transfixed by the story unfolding on TV. The full resources of the TV medium were turned to this one event. Television was there when President Kennedy's widow, Jacqueline, returned with the coffin to Washington and when the accused assassin, Lee Harvey Oswald, was himself gunned down by a Dallas nightclub owner, Jack Ruby. And TV permitted the nation to attend the funeral, as world leaders came to pay their respects.

Like the events of 9/11, more than 9 in 10 Americans were said to have watched the TV coverage that fateful weekend. Watching, too, were over 500 million people in 23 countries, as the coverage was fed to a new device that had recently been launched: the communications satellite.

Network news had just been expanded from 15 to 30 minutes. It consisted mostly of silent newsfilm and "talking heads." Local news was even more primitive: Many stations focused their efforts on sassy "weather girls"; their anchors would read a national story and a dog food commercial with the same officious presentation that they had employed

in radio. But those days were over. In one weekend, TV news had seized the public consciousness. Things would never be the same.

No longer was TV news the stepchild of print or of its progenitor, radio. As 1963 drew to a close, both NBC (with the formidable team of Chet Huntley and David Brinkley) and CBS (with the "most trusted man in America," Walter Cronkite) were telecasting 30 minutes of nightly news. By 1965 the national news was in color. This became important as events both at home and abroad began to capture and command the TV news eye.

Television News Comes of Age

Today there is a certain nostalgia for the era of the 1960s and early 1970s, a period in history bounded by the Kennedy assassination in 1963 and the Watergate scandal, which ended in 1974 with the resignation of President Richard Nixon. Aging "baby boomers" (people born after World War II and who reached adolescence in the 1960s) tend to recall the time as a period of playful experimentation, blue jeans, rock-and-roll, and "flower power." There certainly were moments of fun, but the decade was marked by violent confrontations, social upheavals, and cultural change. And for the first time in history it all happened in front of the TV cameras. Three major events occurred in this period. Each event became forever intertwined with the growth of TV journalism.

Television and Civil Rights

In 1962, Dr. Martin Luther King, Jr., outlined a new strategy:

> We are here today to say to the white men that we will no longer let them use their clubs in dark corners. We are going to make them do it in the glaring light of television.[1]

And it worked—TV was there. It was in Little Rock in 1957 to capture the violence following the integration of Central High School. It was in Montgomery, Birmingham, and other southern cities to witness sit-ins at lunch counters and bus stations. It was in Washington to cover the hundreds of thousands who rallied for civil rights in 1963. Television was in Detroit, Watts, and Newark to cover civil disorders, presenting searing images of white police chiefs turning dogs and fire hoses onto defenseless demonstrators. It revealed the hatred of white supremacists, including the Ku Klux Klan, as throngs of peaceful protesters filed through their towns. Later it demonstrated black anger and frustration, as TV turned its cameras on arsonists and looters in the summer riots of 1965 and 1967 and following the assassination of Dr. King in 1968.

Television in Vietnam

A second major news event of the 1960s took place thousands of miles away. But it, too, harnessed the power of TV—particularly its ability to bring distant events into America's living rooms. The event was the war in Vietnam. Although Vietnam has been called "the first television war," TV had gone to Korea in the early 1950s. This early coverage, however, lacked the immediacy that would characterize Vietnam reporting. The years in which the war was actively fought by Americans (1961–1975) were indeed the "television years." During this period, TV news made virtually all its major advances: portable cameras, satellite relay systems, color, videotape replay, and on and on. This was the era when TV's first generation of reporters (Eric Sevareid, Chet Huntley, Charles Collingwood, and others), who had been trained in radio or print journalism, gave way to a new wave

of youthful reporters who had grown up in the age of TV. In this group were Ed Bradley, Ted Koppel, Steve Bell, and Liz Trotta, the first woman to cover war for television.

Like the civil rights movement, the war in Vietnam provided a training ground for the new people and techniques coming to TV. As a result, the public was deluged with daily reports, with illustrations of American and enemy dead, with dramatic "point-of-view" shots from cameras mounted on helicopter gun ships, and later in the bellies of evacuation aircraft.

For many who lived through those years, the war is remembered as a series of indelible TV images: the whirr of engines as choppers evacuated wounded soldiers; GIs "torching" a village with their Zippo lighters (reported first by Morley Safer on CBS in 1965); antiwar demonstrators chanting "the whole world is watching" as they clashed with police during the 1968 Democratic National Convention in Chicago; the execution of a prisoner by Saigon police chief Lo An (aired on NBC in 1968); panic-stricken South Vietnamese clutching the landing gear of evacuation aircraft in 1975; and flotillas of rafts and fishing boats crammed with refugees as the "boat people" fled their country in the late 1970s.

One Small Step

TV news grew concurrently with the U.S. space program. Beginning with Alan Shepard's space flight in 1961, "space shots" became a major focus on TV news, leading up to the lunar landing of *Apollo 11*.

In the summer of 1969 Neil Armstrong set foot on the moon, an event witnessed by the largest global TV audience up to that time, an estimated 600 million people on six of the seven continents. NASA had carefully orchestrated the event as a TV program, having mounted a small camera (provided by RCA) on the steps of the landing craft, in front of which astronauts Armstrong and Edwin "Buzz" Aldrin would cavort. The two unfurled and planted an American flag, stiffened by an aluminum rod to give the appearance that it was fluttering in some imaginary lunar breeze. Within minutes President Nixon was on a split screen to talk to the astronauts by telephone. Two hours later the world audience watched as the astronauts blasted off for the return trip to earth. The astronauts had provided for this unique TV angle (the first point-of-view shot from outer space) by setting up another RCA camera in the lunar soil.

---

[1] In David J. Garrow, *Protest at Selma* (New Haven, CT: Yale University Press, 1978), p. 111.

TV News Becomes Big Business

Civil rights; Vietnam; the space race; and subsequent events like the Watergate scandal (in 1974 and 1975), the hostage crisis in Iran (in 1980), the disasters involving space shuttles *Challenger* (1986) and *Columbia* (2003) and the aftermath of Hurricane Katrina (2005) brought TV news to the forefront. The major networks expanded their news coverage (ABC's *Nightline*, for example, began as a nightly update of the hostage situation). Local television news also grew. And for good reason. It had become a profit center for television stations, accounting for as much as one-third to one-half of all advertising revenues. Following are some major trends in TV news in its growth period of the 1970s and 1980s.

"Happy Talk"   Throughout its history, TV news had been identified with its anchors and reporters. Newscasters, at both the national networks and local stations, tended to appear strong, serious, some would say staid, and conservative. At the networks there were Walter Cronkite, Eric Sevareid, John Chancellor, David Brinkley, Nancy Dickerson, and many others. In New York there were Bill Beutel and Jim Jensen; in Chicago, Fahey Flynn; in Los Angeles, Clete Roberts; in Miami, Ralph Renick. In every major city there were established figures in news, each with impeccable credentials and an aura of journalistic integrity and self-assurance.

In the late 1970s, a new breed of newscaster began to appear. Men were younger, more daring, and even dashing, frequently dressed in the most modern clothing styles, many with facial hair (previously avoided—except for the stately mustache sported by Cronkite).

For the first time women began to appear in the anchor position. Like the new breed of male newscasters, they were young and attractive. On-camera looks, charisma, charm, and sex appeal became at least as important as journalistic training and ability.

Not only did this new breed look different, but they also acted different from their predecessors. They talked to each other on the air. Sometimes they talked about the news reports they had just seen; sometimes they just seemed to be engaging in the

Neil Armstrong walking on the moon.

kind of gossip and repartee found in most offices. This new approach to TV news was lambasted by the more serious print media, which called it "happy talk." There was concern that TV news was moving away from issues toward personalities, away from information to entertainment, and away from serious news to "sleaze." Research seemed to support these claims. Studies found that stations with the happy-talk format featured more sensational and violent content than did traditional newscasts. They also had higher ratings.

ENG and SNG   Another new trend in TV news was its dependence on new communications technologies. The trend can be summed up in two three-letter abbreviations: ENG and SNG.

Electronic news gathering (ENG) emerged in the mid-1970s, when portable video cameras and

recorders became commercially available. The basic elements of ENG included a lightweight TV camera and small videotape recorder, which could be handheld by the cameraperson. Today's ENG equipment includes camera-recorder combinations, known as camcorders.

ENG revolutionized TV news. Prior to the introduction of ENG, TV news relied on cumbersome and costly film equipment. Film stock needed to be processed and physically assembled or edited. It could not be reused. Film cameras required unwieldy and obtrusive lights. With ENG, cameras and recorders could go anywhere. Events could be recorded in full, with natural sound, and the most important parts could be edited together electronically, in a speedy and cost-efficient manner.

Several years later, the dawn of **satellite news gathering (SNG)** had arrived. Satellite news gathering

Ethics: Branded Journalism

It's 8:30 P.M. You may have seen this and mistaken it for something else: "Now . . . the latest in high-tech gadgets that may help adults who are cannot get around easily. I'm Joel Frank with News Break."

With this opening it sounds like a newsbreak from the local station or from the network. Then the report continues as it talks about the growing number of adults who have mobility problems each year. The piece ends with an interview of an expert from a company with a solution to the problem. During the interview portion, the company's name is featured in the lower third of the screen. The talent, who is seated in front of what appears to be an authentic-looking news set, looks like a bona fide news reporter. Actually this is a 60-second commercial.

The company that produced the spot is probably a public relations or advertising firm and has purchased time on the local station just as it would purchase a standard commercial. Only this is not played like a commercial; it looks to be news.

Fast-forward to the 11:00 P.M. news. After the first 11 minutes, in which the station does a rundown of top local stories and highlights of the national and international news, a feature is introduced. A piece of video is rolled and a good-looking reporter says, "It's one of the most remarkable campaigns in aviation history, thousands leaving impressive careers . . . to take up the front lines in the war against terrorism." The report tells of a success story in the Bush administration's drive to shore up aviation security and ends with "This is Jennifer Morrow reporting." (Jennifer Morrow is a made-up name as it turns out.) The 90-second feature wasn't produced by either the local station or its network affiliate. It was produced by the Transportation Security Administration and was designed to fit seamlessly into an evening newscast.

Today the lines between commercial message and propaganda and news appear to be blurring. Some in Congress worry that it is an improper use of government funds (and possibly illegal) for the U.S. government to dispense covert propaganda to the American people. Why? Because government gets to deliver an unfiltered message in the trappings of a legitimate news story. The story is sent into the ether like so many transmissions and comes out looking like news. But it's not. Earlier during the commercial illustration, the company sponsoring the newsbreak gets the same pass. There's no journalist who has scrutinized the story for legitimacy or truthfulness. Is it ethical for an unsuspecting public to receive such messages?

refers to the use of mobile trucks mounted with satellite communications equipment to report local, national, and international events. SNG trucks and vans could transmit up to communications satellites the pictures and sounds gathered by ENG. The satellites sent the signal back down to local stations and networks to use in their news programs. It was thus possible to obtain live news pictures from virtually anywhere in the world.

Today many stations own "flyaway uplink" vans, capable of transmitting events live to a satellite and back to earth, to the studio. CNN and the major networks have access to satellite uplink equipment small enough to cram into a suitcase.

The News as Showbiz With increasing profitability inevitably came the "ratings war." News directors began to follow ratings with at least as much concern as their counterparts in the sales and programming departments. At local stations the competition for audiences was most intense during the periods when the Nielsen ratings company conducted surveys of local TV viewing (see Chapter 12). These periods are known as **sweeps.**

In TV the sweep periods occur four times a year—in February, May, July, and November. In a quest for "number-one" status, many local news operations took to programming series of short documentaries, known as **minidocs,** during these times. Many minidocs aired during the sweeps focused on sensational topics, including teenage prostitution, spousal and child abuse, and religious cults. They were accompanied by extensive advertising campaigns on the air and in print, on billboards and buses. In many ways the hoopla surrounding news was not unlike that which accompanied the premiere of a new motion picture. In fact, TV news became the stuff of movies and TV shows—*Broadcast News, Switching Channels, Max Headroom, Murphy Brown*—suggesting that the TV newsperson had become a modern icon.

A number of **news consultants** emerged to provide the expertise required of news managers in this competitive environment. Leading news consultants included such firms as Frank Magid, Reymer and Gersin, and McHugh-Hoffman. Consultants provided advice to stations to use in selecting their talent, designing their sets, using graphics, devising sweeps-weeks promotions, and other areas. Their research techniques, ranging from focus-group tests to viewer surveys, are analyzed in Chapter 12.

All News, All the Time The cable industry began C-SPAN in 1979. The public service operation provides gavel-to-gavel coverage of congressional hearings, political party conventions, and other public affairs programming. However, on June 1, 1980, brash cable-TV entrepreneur Ted Turner started CNN, a 24-hour news service. *CNN Headline News* started 18 months later, and both services struggled for several years before attaining widespread coverage on cable systems. But the Persian Gulf War in 1991 changed CNN's fortunes and its stature as a major news provider. Within minutes of the beginning of the war, CNN cameras in Baghdad showed the nighttime air raid and Iraqi antiaircraft fire. During the next 24 hours, CNN correspondents Peter Arnett and Bernard Shaw provided continuous coverage of the early days of the war. The Gulf War marked a turning point for cable news, as research showed that during the early days of the war CNN had more viewers than any of the three television networks.

Other cable information services sprang up during this period. In 1991, CNBC was forged by NBC when it acquired Financial News Network, and Bloomberg Information Television was inaugurated in 1995. However, the creation of Fox News Channel and MSNBC, both started in 1996, demonstrated that news had become an important source of programming for cable providers.

TV NEWS TODAY

As television stations, networks, and cable systems face increasing competition—from each other, from the Internet, from radio, from magazines, and even from some "smart" mobile pagers and phones—news has become increasingly important. Following are some key trends in television journalism.

Coventuring

One important trend has been the development of cooperative ventures by television news outlets with other stations in their market, with their arch-rival cable systems, and even with their oldest competitors, the local newspapers. As the costs of the new toys of TV news mount, and as new means of delivering information become increasingly available to consumers (such as computer online services and interactive cable), news managers have recognized that coventuring makes good business sense.

News operations can be excellent sources of revenue for local television stations. Moreover, news sets and news anchors build an image for the station.

Coventuring with other TV stations in the market usually occurs between a local news leader at a network affiliate and an independent station. Today, many station groups own more than one station in the same market. Often the news organization from the larger station will provide a separate service to the second station. In other instances, the news leader buys time on the independent station to program an alternative version of its local news.

Television news outlets are also coventuring with news/talk radio stations. For example, in Washington, D.C., ABC's WJLA-TV and all-news station WTOP-AM (a Bonneville station) have entered into a news partnership. WJLA's weathercast Web sites are linked to the WTOP Web site.

If cooperation with competing independent TV stations and radio wasn't shocking enough, in the 1990s some local TV stations began to sleep with the enemy—local cable systems. The idea is to use the resources of local affiliates to feed specially customized newscasts to cable subscribers in a given community. Typically, special short newscasts, known as *inserts,* are produced for the residents served by a local cable company. These air only in the cable area; over-the-air viewers stay with the affiliate newscast. The phenomenon is known as **local-local news,** since the cable subscriber receives an even more localized version of a local newscast. One particularly successful local-local venture is based in San Francisco. NBC affiliate KRON-TV provides local news segments to more than a dozen cable systems in the Bay Area. Segments are updated three or four times a day and are broadcast twice an hour. The newscasts are specially targeted for the region that each cable system operates, including the city of San Francisco, the east Bay, south Bay, and Marin County areas.

At the corporate level, coventuring has become commonplace. CNN, for example, uses a distribution system, called Pathfire, in conjunction with other distribution and financial partners. CNN segments are downloaded via satellite to Pathfire servers to affiliated stations and news outlets. CNN and *Sports Illustrated* (both owned by Time Warner) have partnered to develop SI.com, a sports Web site. A coventure with *Time* magazine got off to an inauspicious start in 1998, when CNN and *Time* combined for an apparently fallacious report called "Operation Tailwind," which claimed that the U.S. military had pursued and released poison gas on American deserters during the Vietnam War.

Regional and Local Cable News

Another significant trend in the 1990s has been the rise of regional cable-news channels. Unlike local-local news, which offers quick cut-ins or news summaries to cable viewers, **regional cable-news services** are 24-hour localized versions of CNN.

The pioneer in regional cable news is News12 Long Island, created by Cablevision to serve subscribers in Nassau and Suffolk counties, suburbs of New York City. Today News12 is part of a regional interactive service run by Comcast. Different news services provide local news for suburban New Yorkers in the Long Island, Westchester, Connecticut, and Hudson Valley regions. Inside the city limits, Time Warner's NY1 provides news around the clock to

Events: The Best of Television in the Worst of Times

8:49 A.M. CNN: "Obviously, a very disturbing live shot of the World Trade Center, and we have unconfirmed reports that a plane has crashed into one of the towers."

Just 4 minutes after the first plane slammed into the World Trade Center (WTC) on that bright, beautiful September morning, the nation's broadcast news organizations did what they do—and they did it brilliantly. They brought live, nonstop coverage of the attacks on the WTC and the Pentagon into American homes, providing breaking news as they tried to sort fact from fiction.

For years, television networks had seen their viewership decline, but during the crisis nearly 80 million viewers tuned in to one or more of the Big Four networks. Despite that huge audience the networks weren't selling anything. All commercials had been suspended for the remainder of the week. Instead, America got continuous news, and the coverage presented a clear example of programming that was in the nation's "public interest."

The major television networks agreed to suspend competition and to share footage. News crawls appeared at the bottom of the screen trying to summarize the events as they unfolded. News was everywhere. ESPN carried ABC; MTV and VH1 carried CBS; TNT and TBS carried CNN; C-Span carried CBC Canada; and TLC picked up BBC World Service. The nation was glued to the television screen.

Throughout the next several days network news organizations mustered all their resources to provide outstanding coverage. Network anchors, reporters, and engineers worked exceedingly long hours providing the longest unbroken string of coverage for a single story in the history of television.

The terrorist attacks gave broadcast news organizations one of the biggest challenges in the history of journalism. How did they do? Tom Brokaw was quoted as saying, "I have never seen NBC News or any other organization respond as well to a story of this complexity and magnitude." But maybe *Washington Post* columnist Tom Shales said it best when he said, "They proved how indispensable they can be in times of national crisis, informing and enlightening and merely by the fact that they keep going, consoling."

cable viewers in Brooklyn, Queens, the Bronx, Manhattan, and Staten Island. Suburban Los Angeles is served by Orange County Newschannel, a venture of Orange County *Register* and *Freedom* newspapers. Similarly, Chicagoland Television (CLTV) uses the resources of the *Chicago Tribune* to provide regional cable news to the second city and its suburbs.

Smaller regional news channels have emerged in the last few years. News 10 Now serves the Central New York region, including the cities of Syracuse, Ithaca, and Watertown. Six New Now serves Sarasota, Florida. In 2005, more than 40 regional cable-news services were operating in all parts of the United States.

Global News

Ironically, at the same time TV news delivery becomes more and more localized through regional cable and news-on-demand, it is also moving in an opposite direction. The success of Cable News Network has generated competition in serving the global news audience.

BBC World competes worldwide with CNN and broadcasts to more than 200 countries and territories around the world. In fact, the service became available in the United States in February 1995, as BBC Americas, and is found on many U.S. cable channels. News Corporation's Sky News offers an alternative to CNN in Europe, in parts of Southeast Asia on Star TV, in Australia, and other regions of Rupert Murdoch's considerable reach.

International news channels are not limited to the English language. France's TF-1 and Canal Plus have teamed to create an all-news service for the French-speaking world. Not to be outdone, Televisora de Costa Rica created Telenoticias, a Latin American service entirely in Spanish. The Arab news service, Al-Jazeera, also began a world news service. Operating out of Qutar and other major capitals, the Arab news service in available in about 40 million homes worldwide.

So television news remains an important part of the media landscape. For local TV stations, it is a profit center and a critical source of viewer attention, identification, and loyalty. For networks, like CNN, ABC, NBC, CBS, and Fox, news is more than a necessary evil. It helps them earn and retain credibility, especially in the eyes of those viewers who tend to distrust what they hear on talk radio or read on the Internet. Speaking of the Internet, reliable and credible news helps Web surfers separate the few grains of wheat from the tons of chaff available on the World Wide Web. News-based pages help the new medium earn the trust (and the business) of many consumers put off by the vitriolic—and often downright scurrilous—content of many Web pages. The news for TV news is mostly good. Now let's see how TV news gets made.

THE TV NEWS TEAM

TV News Command Structure

Television news is a collaborative craft. It is not unusual for a large-market station to boast more than 100 people in the news department. The major networks still maintain hundreds of news personnel. CNN alone employs over 1,000 people at its Atlanta headquarters and nearly 4,000 people worldwide. Coordinating the efforts of these small armies is no easy task, especially with the pressures of both the deadline and the bottom line. Thus TV news organizations tend to follow rigid command structures, outlined in Figure 9–1.

The News Director   Overall responsibility for the news department falls to the news director. News directors tend to have a solid background in TV news, many as former reporters or anchors. The news director hires news personnel, establishes news and editorial policy, and evaluates the newscast in post-mortem screenings with the staff of the news department. Today's news directors are increasingly concerned with budgets, making sure the news is produced at a profit. The exciting, high-pressure nature of the job has led to a typical job tenure in the range of about 3 years.

News Producer   If the news director is the boss of the day-to-day news operation, the news producer is the czar of any given newscast, such as the "11 o'clock Report" or "The Noon News." The producers maintain editorial control over the stories that make up their individual TV newscasts. The producers prepare the story lineup, determine the stories' lengths, and decide how they will be handled. The producer of each newscast will proofread all copy, select the graphics, and be present in the control room to make last-minute changes during the newscast.

Most news operations have special segments, or "beats," such as consumer affairs, health, arts and

Figure 9–1

TV News Command Structure

entertainment, and, of course, sports and weather. These beats are headed by unit producers, who assume overall responsibility for these segments.

Assignment Editor The main job of the assignment editor is to dispatch reporters and photographers to cover news stories. The job requires great organizational skills. At a local station, as many as five different crews may be out in the field at one time. At a network, literally dozens of crews need to be dispatched and returned to the studio for editing and other production tasks. To assist in this complex task, assignment editors maintain a **future file.** This is an annotated listing of upcoming news stories, scheduled as many as 30 or 60 days in advance. Traditionally a series of file folders is each labeled with upcoming dates and filled with events for each day; many future files today are stored in computers. Of course, the future file is useless when breaking news occurs: A plane crash, flooding in nearby areas, or a tornado really taxes the skills of the assignment editor.

Field Producer If there is sufficient lead time to prepare for a story, such as a space shuttle launch or a murder trial, it may be assigned to a field producer. The field producer will prepare research and background information, scout locations, and perform other valuable advance functions for the reporter and photographer, who will be busy working on other stories. On breaking stories of great magnitude (an assassination attempt or a skyjacking, for example), the news director may assign a field producer to coordinate the coverage.

Reporters Reporters receive their orders from the assignment desk and begin their research, usually on the telephone. They set up interviews and determine shooting locations. Typically the reporter has been teamed with a photographer. At small stations, regional news channels, and some budget-conscious large stations, the reporter may be a one-person band, responsible for shooting her own stories. The reporter proceeds to the scene, obtains interviews and other video, and returns to the studio to supervise the editing, write and announce the voice-over and lead-in copy, and, if part of the newscast, get dressed and made up for the newscast.

Writers It is a sad fact that many of today's reporters may be selected for their on-camera appearance rather than their journalistic skills. For this reason many stations and networks employ newswriters to help script the newscast. Writers may prepare some material for reporters and anchors (although most anchors like to write their own material). They frequently prepare the clever lines used to introduce the newscast (teasers) or to attract the audience to return after commercial breaks (bumpers).

Editors Most newscasts consist of separate stories, called *packages,* linked by the anchors and reporters. Each package is a complete story, edited together with its own voice-over and graphic material. The editor is the person who puts the package together. Typically the reporter returns from the field with too much material, all of it shot out of sequence. He may have done the introduction to the story six or seven times; there may be dozens of separate pieces to an interview. The reporter (and sometimes the field producers, unit producer, producer, or news director as well) retreats with the editor to a small editing room to make sense of the mayhem of the typical field report. In many small news operations, reporters edit their own packages.

TV news has benefited greatly in recent years by the development of digital editing systems, such as Avid's Newscutter and Apple's Final Cut Pro (see Chapter 3).

CRUMBLING CREDIBILITY? ISSUES IN TV NEWS

We opened the chapter with the famous Roper polls, which suggest that TV is the most credible source of news for the American public. Take a look at Table 9–1. According to a Pew research study, news credibility has steadily declined between 1996 and 2004.

Table 9–1	Decline in News Credibility since 1996*			
Network	**1996**	**2000**	**2002**	**2004**
NBC News	29%	29%	25%	24%
CBS News	32	29	26	24
ABC News	31	30	24	24
CNN	38	39	37	32
NPR	—	25	23	23

*For respondents who could rate each news source.

Source: The Pew Research Center for the people and the press, June 8, 2004.

Events: The Demise of the Evening New Anchor?

For more than two decades, the majority of Americans heard about the day's events by tuning in Rather, Brokaw, or Jennings. All three anchors spent years honing their journalistic skills covering everything from the civil rights movement of the 1960s to the Arab-Israeli 6 Day War to the fall of the Berlin Wall to the attacks on the World Trade Center. Rather, Brokaw, and Jennings inherited their seats from notables: Cronkite, Chancellor, and Reynolds. In taking over their seats, the anchors inherited the power to shape opinion by insisting on the coverage of certain stories. They spoke with almost God-like authority.

But now many media experts say that their departures signal a change in the news business and the way news is digested in America. In 1970, the combined ratings for the three newscasts stood at approximately 48.* Today those ratings stand at 18 percent of the population, and they're falling.

News choice has exploded since 1995. Americans are as likely to tune into Fox News or CNN as to watch ABC. Younger Americans are comfortable choosing Internet news sources for a quick look at world events, and many college students frequently say they get their news from shows like the *Daily Show*. But isn't that really a comedy show? Some media experts think that this change in viewing represents a sea change in the news business. For example, during the 1970s and 1980s, the evening news was appointment television for many families. The news came on during the dinner hour and gave us a digest of the important stories of the day. According to the Pew Center for Research, 46 percent of those who responded in the annual news survey described themselves as news "grazers."

There may be other changes as well. Former CBS News president Andrew Heyward said that the anchors "used their extraordinary power to fight for serious and important stories." Heyward wonders if the next set of anchors will have the clout to battle corporate executives for coverage of serious issues. Other journalists share Heyward's concerns. In a poll conducted by Public Perspective, half the journalists responding to a survey said that the most important problems facing journalism were quality, standards of reporting, and journalistic ethics.

The face of the evening news has changed. Brian Williams, Charlie Gibson, and Katie Couric now represent the faces of the evening news. Will audience share continue to dwindle, or will a new generation of Americans consume the daily digest as part of the evening entrée?

*Each rating point equals approximately 1 percent of the total U.S. population.

One of the main reasons for this decline is the perceived preoccupation with scandal, known variously as the "tabloidization" of news, "pack journalism," or the TV news "feeding frenzy." The seemingly limitless and boundless coverage of violent or sexy (or both) stories began with the O. J. Simpson arrest and trials, which began in 1994, and has since led to coverage of the JonBenet Ramsey killing, the "nanny murder" trial of Louise Woodward, the murder trial of Robert Blake, and trial of Michael Jackson. Critics claim the legitimate news organizations are spending too much time and effort on these stories, at the expense of other, more important topics. Faced with increasing competition and driven by profit, managers of major media outlets point to the ratings this coverage creates. They can also make a strong claim, at least in the case of the Bill Clinton impeachment attempt, that such scandals represent legitimate news. However, sensationalized news gathering does not always bring higher ratings. In fact, a 5-year study, concluded in 2002 by the Project for Excellence in Journalism, found that the size of local news audiences has been in decline for the last few years, despite the events of 9/11 and the coverage that followed. Half of the 103 local news directors surveyed believe that the industry is heading down the wrong path with regard to local news coverage.

For many years the National Opinion Research Center has conducted surveys tapping the degree of confidence the public has in various American institutions, including the press.

In the early 1970s (the height of the press's triumphant Watergate period) confidence in the press was high. One in four Americans expressed great confidence in the press; only 15 percent expressed little or no faith in it. Today the situation has reversed. A quarter of the population has little confidence in the American press; less than one in five places great faith in it.

The medium may not be helping its own cause. With an emphasis on ratings, developing stories about satanism, cult worship, prostitution, gambling, and aliens replacing investigative reports and public service efforts, today's news has become just another form of TV entertainment, which brings us to our next topic.

TV ENTERTAINMENT PROGRAMMING

Most of us use the mass media for relaxation, escape, and diversion—in a word, entertainment. Entertainment does not come cheap in TV and cable. A major TV network might spend more than $25 million a week on nonnews programming. The entertainment programming business is an integral part of modern broadcasting and cable.

There are three basic ways in which a TV station or cable company can acquire programs: network, syndication, and local origination. First, we provide brief definitions of these terms. Then we examine each major program source in detail.

As you might expect, **network programming** refers to original programming funded by, produced for, and distributed by the major TV and cable networks. Recent popular broadcast network programs include *Lost* and *Grey's Anatomy* on ABC, *My Name Is Earl* and *The Office* on NBC, *CSI* and *Two and a Half Men* on CBS, and *House* and *24* on Fox.

Cable works differently since its programming originates via the network directly to cable franchises around the country. There are no affiliates, and clearance is not an issue. In recent years cable has offered more competitive original programming such as *The Sopranos* on HBO or Nick's *SpongeBob*, but some insights into how much ground cable has gained in the last few years can be realized by looking at original cable programming. *Nip/Tuck* on FX, *Project Runway* on Bravo, and *Monk* on USA all gained national viewing audiences in their first season.

Syndication refers to TV programming sold by distribution companies to local TV stations and cable services. Syndication companies sell two kinds of shows: off-network (series that have appeared first on the networks and are being rerun by local stations or cable systems) and first-run (shows expressly produced for syndication). Some off-net successes in syndication include *Everybody Loves Raymond*, *Seinfeld*, and *That 70s Show*.

First-run powerhouses are mostly talk and game shows, like *Oprah*, *Wheel of Fortune*, and *Entertainment Tonight*. However, some dramatic programs in past years have been successfully marketed through syndication, led by the crew of MGM's *Stargate SG1*.

Local origination refers to programs produced by local TV stations (or cable companies) for viewers in their own communities. The most common forms of

My Name Is Earl, a quirky NBC comedy, uses a single-camera technique to tell the story. *Earl* was one of the few comedy hits of the 2005 television season.

local origination programs are the local news and talk shows that most TV stations and cable systems carry daily. Larger-market television stations tend to develop more local programming than medium- and small-market stations. In the 1950s and 1960s many stations also featured cartoon programs for kids hosted by "talent" from the station (typically a cameraman or technician frustrated in an earlier career in vaudeville or theater). If you don't remember these local shows from your youth, your parents probably do.

NETWORK TELEVISION: THE BIG FOUR, PLUS THREE

From the beginnings of TV in the late 1940s to the late 1970s, TV programming was dominated by three commercial networks: CBS, NBC, and ABC. For more than a generation these networks were America's great entertainers. Their programs, ranging from variety shows like Ed Sullivan's *Toast of the Town* to comedies like *I Love Lucy* and *Mork and Mindy*, dramas like *The Fugitive* and sports programs like the Super Bowl, attracted millions of viewers. In the 1980s, a new service emerged as a fourth network: Rupert Murdoch's Fox Broadcasting Corporation. In the mid-1990s, two newer networks struggled for a share of television's huge audience: Paramount (UPN) and Warner Brothers (WB). They were joined in 1998 by broadcaster Lowell "Bud" Paxson's Pax TV network. Recently WB and UPN merged into the CW network (see Chapter 5).

Affiliation

The backbone of any network is the group of stations that carries its programs. Stations that receive network programming are known as **affiliates.** Traditionally, roughly 200 stations were affiliated with each of the Big Three of ABC, CBS, and NBC. Following its major expansion in 1994 (with the acquisition of New World and its investment in other properties), the Fox lineup approached parity with ABC, CBS, and NBC, at about 200 stations.

With roughly 200 stations each, the major networks cover nearly all the U.S. homes with TV. This is critical, because national coverage enables them to sell the nation's leading advertisers commercials within their programs.

The newer networks are at a comparative disadvantage, each launching with about 100 affiliated stations. By 2000, the WB network boasted the widest coverage, with about 90 percent of TV households in areas served by WB affiliates. UPN and Pax covered less than 9 in 10 U.S. households but were distributing their programs on local cable in some areas to boost their coverage. Nevertheless, neither UPN or WB could muster sufficient profits to continue operation.

To become an affiliate, the local TV station signs a contract, known as an **affiliation agreement,** with the network. Historically, the major networks paid stations a fee for broadcasting network programs. This fee is known as **network compensation.** The fee has ranged from under $500 to more than $10,000 per hour, depending on the station's coverage area, market size, and popularity.

The television business had become increasingly competitive in recent years, and things have changed dramatically in network compensation. The high costs of original programming (like $13 million per episode for *ER*) and rights to sports events have caused the major networks to rethink their affiliation agreements. Today compensation does not exist in this form. Networks and affiliates have partnered to bring expensive programming (such as the NFL) to broadcast television. Today compensation occurs when networks provide affiliates with more time within network programs for local sales. Local affiliates can charge higher CPMs in prime-time programs because the audience is fairly large.

Affiliates may elect to carry the network shows, or they may refuse them. Programs that are carried by the station are said to have **cleared;** those that are refused are known as **preemptions.** In recent years many affiliates, especially those of the Big Four, have exercised their right to refuse network programs, thereby producing some strained network-affiliate relationships and some widely publicized defections to other networks.

In return for their investment in programming and their affiliation agreements, the networks gain access to the mass audience. Through their system of local affiliates, the networks have the potential to pull together a huge simultaneous audience, which they can sell to a national advertiser for a concomitantly large price. The name of the game is the audience. Networks try to attract either a large, undifferentiated audience, as is the case with *American Idol*, or a relatively smaller audience that has the demographic profile that advertisers find attractive, as is the case with *Everybody Hates Chris*, with its 18- to

34-year-old audience. It's a high-stakes game. The network with the most successful programs will make the most money (or lose the least money). The one with fewer viewers or the wrong kind of viewers will have bad news for its shareholders, and its suffering affiliates will respond appropriately.

The Network Programming Process

Network programming is cyclical: Like baseball, it has its own seasons, pennant races, winners, and losers. First, let's examine the ground rules.

Financial Interest and Syndication Rules   With the exception of news, sports, and a limited number of other programs, historically the networks did not own the shows that filled their nightly schedules. Fearing monopoly in entertainment production by the Big Three, in the early 1970s the FCC adopted a set of regulations known as the **financial interest and syndication rules.** In showbiz jargon the regulations were known as "fin-syn." In a nutshell, the rules limited network participation in the ownership of programs produced for them and in subsequent syndication. Rather than paying outright for their shows, the networks paid **license fees** to production companies for the rights to show them. After the network run, programs were sold into syndication, but not by the networks. After nearly two decades of legal wrangling, the fin-syn rules were substantially modified by the FCC in 1993 and were abandoned entirely by the end of 1995.

The net effect was that after 1995 networks were allowed to own their own shows and to sell them in syndication following the completion of their network runs.

By the late 1990s, the networks were actively involved in the production of their own programs. CBS was a partner in *King of Queens* and *Everybody Loves Raymond.* NBC Universal owns the *Law and Order* franchise along with shows like *Will & Grace* and *Las Vegas.* As owners of studios (see the section on studios that appears a bit later in the chapter), ABC (Disney), Fox (Twentieth Century), NBC (Universal), and WB (Warner Brothers) are likewise directly involved in program development as well as ownership.

Prime-Time Access Rule   The FCC implemented the **prime-time access rule (PTAR)** in 1971. The rule restricted the amount of time an affiliate could accept

from the network, in effect allowing networks to control no more than 3 hours of the 4-hour prime-time nightly schedule (with some exceptions). Since TV viewing increases through the evening, naturally the networks maintained control of the 3 hours from 8:00 P.M. to 11:00 P.M. (7:00 P.M. to 10:00 P.M. in the central time zone). This created *early fringe*, a 1-hour segment for local affiliated stations to fill by themselves. PTAR further prohibited network affiliates in the top 50 markets from filling this time (known today as "prime access" or simply "access") with off-network syndicated reruns.

Although the intent of the rule was to encourage production by non-Hollywood companies and maybe even stimulate local production, the reality is that most stations turned to first-run syndication in this time period. Evening game shows, especially *Wheel of Fortune* and *Jeopardy,* became very popular as did shows like *Entertainment Tonight* and *Access Hollywood.*

PTAR had another lasting effect: It enabled independent stations to compete on more equal terrain with network affiliates in the very important hour when people were sampling the TV schedule to make their nightly viewing choices. By programming their best shows here (ironically, a lot of popular old network shows that could not be shown on some network stations), many new independent stations were able to siphon viewers from affiliates to themselves.

As with fin-syn, there was great pressure to modify or abandon PTAR. The FCC scrapped most of the PTAR requirements at the end of 1996. Still, "access" survives as an important lead-in to network prime-time programming as it is very lucrative for local affiliates.

Network Seasons   Network programming is organized around two seasons. The fall premiere season begins in late September and runs through the middle of December. This is when new programs are launched and returning programs begin showing new episodes. The so-called second season runs from the end of January through the beginning of May. This is when the networks replace low-rated programs with specials and new series.

At one time the two seasons were distinct. The three networks premiered their new shows in one week around late September; the second season almost always occurred in early February. Today, however, there seems to be more variability. Some shows will take a hiatus midseason in the fall and return in the spring. Some important network shows, such as *24*, don't have a fall season at all.

Fox was especially instrumental in this trend. Fox staggered the introduction of its new programs, sprinkling premieres throughout the year. A particularly effective strategy included running new episodes of hit shows, like *The Simpsons* and *American Idol*, in the summer, when ABC, NBC, and CBS were in reruns. The same strategy has been pursued by the newer networks, UPN, WB, and Pax. In 2005, ABC tried a similar strategy with *Dancing with the Stars*.

In past years the network season lasted 39 weeks. As many as 32 episodes of a new show would be ordered, with the remaining 20 weeks occupied by specials and reruns. Today escalating production costs, competition, and a declining success rate have led the networks to order as few as 8, 10, or 11 new episodes of a series, with an option to repeat at least two. This is one reason the season has shrunk (or expanded to year-round, depending on one's point of view).

Who gets the orders? Production of TV series is dominated by a few large studios, increasingly enough owned by the huge communications conglomerates which also own many of the television networks. These are the major studios, or "the majors," for short. However, some hit shows come from outside these huge conglomerates. A small number of independent producers ("independents," for short) exert important influence over the network programs we see. Let's start with the majors.

The major studios   The major studios in TV production are familiar names, although their ownership may be less familiar. Longtime television heavyweight Columbia/Tri-Star, which produced such shows as *Dawson's Creek* for WB, *The Nanny* and *L.A. Doctors* for CBS, and *Dilbert* for UPN, was purchased in 1989 by Sony Pictures for $3.4 billion. Today Sony produces shows like *The Shield* and *Day of Our Lives*.

Another foreign-owned major is Twentieth Television, part of Rupert Murdoch's News Corporation empire. While Twentieth produces some programs for its own Fox network (*Malcom in the Middle* and *The Simpsons*), it also provides programming to its competitors such as *My Name Is Earl* for NBC and *Judging Amy* for CBS.

Not all the programming majors are foreign-owned. Warner Brothers, owned by Time Warner, is the home studio of such recent hit shows as *Without a Trace, The West Wing, Two and a Half Men*, and *Smallville*. Paramount, a part of the CBS conglomerate, is the source of such shows as *Frasier* and CBS's *Survivor* and *CSI* series, *Diagnosis Murder* for PAX, plus its own enormously successful *Star Trek* series.

Another firm with major studio status in Hollywood is NBC Universal. In 2004 NBC purchased Vivendi-Universal, gaining access to thousands of movie and television titles. Recent TV shows produced by Universal include all the different variations of *Law and Order, Crossing Jordan*, the cable favorite *Monk*, and the recent Fox hit *House*.

The TV programming arm of the Mickey Mouse media empire, Disney, is its Hollywood-based Walt Disney Studios, Touchstone, and Buena Vista Television divisions. Such shows as *Alias* and *Home Improvement* as well as current hits *Scrubs* for NBC and the syndication *Who Wants to Be a Millionaire* come from the Mouse house. Disney has also partnered in other series, like the animated *PJs* on Fox and the WB youth drama *Felicity*.

Independent producers   The networks also order programs from a small number of independent producers that have had a series of network successes. One of these is Stephen J. Cannell, whose success with *The Rockford Files, Baretta*, and *The A-Team* led to network orders for *Wiseguy, 21 Jump Street, Hunter*, and *Marker*, one of the first shows on the UPN network.

Carsey-Werner (formerly Carsey-Werner-Mandabach) was founded by former ABC programmers Tom Werner and Marcy Carsey. Their first show, *Oh! Madeline!* was forgettable. Their second was not: *Cosby*. Carsey-Werner was one of the few TV independents left, responsible for such successes as *Roseanne, 3rd Rock from the Sun*, and *That 70s Show*. In 2006, Carsey-Werner announced that it would stop producing prime-time television, essentially shuttering the last major independent television production house.

Stephen Bochco is another influential independent, with a track record on network TV, including *Hill Street Blues, Doogie Houser, M.D.*, and series creator of *L.A. Law*. Bochco's megahit *NYPD Blue* is one of the most respected shows ever produced for television. One of his most spectacular failures was *Commander in Chief*, which started with top 10 ratings and then went into a death spiral, on ABC. Bochco currently has several shows in development for the networks.

Aaron Spelling, another famous independent producer, died in 2006. His two monster hits *Dynasty* and *Hotel* were preceded by *Love Boat* and *Fantasy Island.* His recent efforts include *Beverly Hills 90210, Melrose Place,* and *7th Heaven.*

Dreamworks, the film studio created by Steven Spielberg, David Geffen, and Jeffrey Katzenberg, entered television in a big way. With former ABC programmer Ted Harbert at the helm, Dreamworks has produced the ABC comedy *Spin City* and the less successful *Undeclared* for Fox. Dreamworks also produced *Band of Brothers* for HBO and its 2002 project *Taken,* which aired on the Sci-Fi channel. In 2006 the studio was purchased by Paramount.

Other well-known independents are Witt-Thomas-Harris (*Beauty and the Beast, It's a Living,* and *Everything's Relative*); Mozark Productions (*Designing Women, Hearts Afire,* and *Delta*), the company of Linda Bloodworth Thomason and Harry Thomason (famous friends of Bill Clinton); and Regency Television, which coproduces *Malcolm in the Middle* with Fox television.

The independent television market is now a relatively small community as the major studios essentially control all the major prime-time television shows.

The significance of the sale of television programming on Hollywood is vital to understand. In 2004, the major studios collected more than $17 billion in revenues and royalties for the sale of TV productions. Ironically, some industry analysts claim Hollywood makes a bigger share of its profits from television than from the feature film industry, since the costs of promotion and distribution of films are so high. In television, these costs are borne by the networks. Thus, it is little wonder that the relationship between major studios and the television networks has become more important in recent years.

Pitching a Program   Programs get on the air through two primary means. Some are commissioned by the network, whose research and development discovers public interest in a particular program concept. It is said that the late NBC program executive Brandon Tartikoff ordered *Miami Vice* by telling producer Michael Mann to "give me MTV with cops!" Similarly, after meeting Mr. T at a Hollywood party, Tartikoff is reported to have handed Stephen J. Cannell a piece of paper reading: " 'The A-Team,' 'Mission Impossible,' 'The Dirty Dozen,' and 'The Magnificent Seven,' all rolled into one, and Mr. T drives the car!"

More commonly, new program ideas are introduced, or "pitched," to the networks by their producers. The pitch can be based on an idea or **concept,** a short story narrative, known as a **treatment,** or a sample script. It is estimated that the networks are presented with as many as 5,000 new program ideas each year in one form or another. About 500 are chosen for further development.

At this point a development executive begins working with others in the producing field. Lawyers, accountants, and agents get involved in the **development process.** Most commonly, the program (by now known as a "property") is developed under the terms of a **step deal**—an arrangement by which the property is put together in a series of distinct phases spelled out step by step in a contract. The network will "front" the major portion of the development money for the program, in return for creative control over the show's content. The network gets **right of first refusal,** the contractual right to prohibit the production company from producing the program for another client. In some instances, the deal also enables the network to appoint additional writers to develop the concept or "punch up" the script.

At this time fewer than one-half of the optioned ideas will lead to a deal or fully scripted stage. From this pool the networks will order about 30 or 35 **pilots,** or sample episodes, each costing in the range of $750,000 to $1.5 million to produce. Just because the network has ordered a sample episode, this does not guarantee that the show will find a place in a network's schedule. Usually the networks will show the pilot to test audiences and program executives for their reactions. More changes may be ordered, or the development may be canceled. By early spring about a dozen of these pilots will result in series orders. The shows that did make it through the step-by-step process are placed in the networks' schedules and will be shown to advertising executives during the upfront selling season. (See Chapter 7.) Ten of these twelve are likely to be canceled before the second season. Often, in the late spring or summer, networks will run pilots that didn't make it, in an effort to recover some of their production costs.

Network program costs   While the concept of a show, its location, and its stars are certainly important, for TV executives perhaps most important is its cost. As you see, the network business is highly speculative because it's difficult to predict which shows will succeed; nevertheless, a network needs to develop a cost

Table 9–2	Typical Costs for Network Programs
Program Type	**Cost per Episode ($ millions)**
Major miniseries	$4–7
Movie of the week	3–5
Adventure/mystery/drama	2–4
Situation comedy	0.9–2.0
Reality/newsmagazine	0.75–1.5

target for each episode. Table 9–2 presents typical production costs for various program types.

The most expensive program type is the lavish, multipart network miniseries, which can cost more than $7 million per hour to produce. With profits declining and competition increasing, you might think that these high production costs have made the networks avoid the production of miniseries. But the opposite has been the case. High-concept miniseries create "event" programming for the major networks, giving them programming to promote, and giving viewers a reason to watch them, instead of one of the "upstart" networks or, heaven forbid, cable. In recent years, both broadcast and cable have developed high-ticket programming. Several seasons ago NBC offered the $30 million *Merlin,* which followed in the wake of the successful *Gulliver's Travels* and *The Odyssey.* Recently HBO and the BBC teamed up to relive the glories and debauchery of ancient Rome. The 12-episode series cost a cool $100 million to produce.

The next-most-expensive program type is movies made for TV. In industry parlance, these are referred to as *movies of the week* (MOWs), "made-fors," or more cynically "disease of the week" shows. Typically these shows are contemporary dramas revolving around personal relationships, tragedy, domestic strife, or recent criminal cases. Some made-fors receiving attention recently were those based on the O. J. Simpson and Menendez brothers murder cases; Amy Fisher's adventures with Joey Buttafuoco; and the tragic flight of United 93. Today, very few movies of the week are produced for television; most made-for-television movies are aired on cable channels like Lifetime, USA Networks, and the Hallmark Channel.

Adventure, mystery, and drama series are the next most expensive, costing, on average, between $2 and $4 million on a weekly basis. *ER* broke the bank on this form of television production in 1998,

when NBC agreed to renew the show from Warner Brothers for $13 million per episode. This deal sent shock waves through the industry, with producers of other popular dramas pressing their networks for more money for big-name stars, exotic locations, and expensive sets and special effects. Shows like *24,* which have a large number of remote locations week after week, can be very expensive to shoot. The cash-strapped networks have responded as you might think: by seeking less expensive shows to offset the high cost of miniseries, made-fors, and action hours.

Fortunately for the networks, the most popular program type is also one of the least costly. Situation comedies cost about $900,000 to $2 million per episode. Sitcoms can hold the line on cost since most are shot in a studio as opposed to an expensive location; they are recorded in real time before an audience, which keeps the need for editing and special effects to a minimum; and today some are shot on videotape, which is cheaper than using film. Most dramas, on the other hand, continue to use film, and many are shot in wide-screen high definition.

If a situation comedy becomes a true hit and lasts several seasons, its costs can increase dramatically, mainly in the area of star salaries. By the end of its run in 1998, *Seinfeld* was costing NBC about $3 million per program. Similarly, Paul Reiser and Helen Hunt were persuaded to continue on *Mad about You* for another season (1998–1999) with the promise of $1 million each per episode (bringing the show's total cost to $3.25 million per half-hour).

The bargain basement of network TV are so-called reality shows, including game shows, news documentaries, and "infotainment" series. For example, CBS's highly rated *60 Minutes* costs about $900,000 per hour, and ABC's *20/20* is budgeted in the $750,000 range. *Dateline NBC* is a bargain for NBC, budgeted at only $650,000 per hour. The low cost of reality shows is one reason for their proliferation in recent years. However, not all reality shows are inexpensive. Both *Survivor* and *The Amazing Race* are fairly expensive (for reality shows) because of the costs associated with shooting on location.

Cable Network Programming

We covered the programming of cable and pay-cable networks in Chapter 5. However, it is useful to note here how these networks are programmed in comparison with the broadcast networks.

Larry David, co-creator of *Curb Your Enthusiasm,* shoots the comedy without a script. The cast is given a scene outline and frequently improvises their lines.

When Steve York took his clothes off on Koala TV, the student government organization of the University of California at San Diego (UCSD) that funded the programs on SRTV (student-run TV) threatened legal action if the program wasn't pulled off the closed-circuit cable channel. Then, in protest, the senior went one step further. In November 2005 Koala TV aired a 10-minute video of himself engaged in sex with an adult film actress. According to the *San Diego Union Tribune*, York blocked the face of the actress and superimposed the image of a student senator who had voiced support for a ban on nudity and sex.

York said his actions were prompted by the student senate voting in the ban on nudity. Program managers at SRTV said that they had a policy of remaining content-neutral regarding the programming on the station. And while the station insisted that it had not received any complaints, student government leaders said they received hundreds of complaints. Reacting to demands from the university administration, student government took control of the station and shut it down. They found out later that starting the station back up took more effort. As the issue dragged on from March 2005 into the fall semester, station managers and university officials disagreed about the ban on graphic sexual content and the need for a review board to approve new programs. University officials maintain that airing such content violated the station's charter.

York, claiming a First Amendment issue, called for a referendum, and 2,600 students (about 16 percent of the student body) signed a petition to put the station back on the air. Andrew Tess, a student manager for the station, said, "We want our media to produce discussions and campus dialogue." However, some students have argued that if campus residents were going to be required to pay the mandated student fees that fund the station, then there should be a way to opt out of the service if they're offended by it. Meanwhile, UCSD officials said that they were concerned about Koala TV damaging the university's reputation by airing more pornographic content.

The issue has received widespread coverage in the media, including the local San Diego media, the university's alumni publication, but also Fox's *O'Reilly Factor* and the adult entertainment industry's lobby organization, the Free Speech Coalition. York, who allegedly received several offers from the adult film industry, says he wants to go to law school instead. In an interview in *Vyuz San Diego* York described himself as a Larry Flint kind of liberal. "Pornography is the sharpest political tool you can use, and I don't mind using it in that regard."

Theatrical Motion Pictures As we have seen, the bulk of the program schedule (over 80 percent of airtime) on the major pay-cable services, including HBO/Cinemax and Showtime/The Movie Channel, consists of theatrical motion pictures. Most of these are licensed to the pay services by the "majors," Hollywood's largest studios.

The studios normally make their films (known as "titles" in the trade) available to pay cable a year after their first theatrical release. There is a narrower release window for pay per view (PPV) of 6 months or less. Sometimes studios will delay the pay release of major box office hits to continue to reap profits at the box office. Occasionally a theatrical release may be so disappointing that the studio will release the film to cable and home video within weeks of its theatrical debut.

Some distributors make their films available to multiple pay services simultaneously. However, to offset viewer dissatisfaction with pay services ("they all play the same movies"), there has been a trend toward studios' signing **exclusivity deals** with pay services. Such contracts guarantee first cable release to one pay service.

Theatrical motion pictures are also the backbone of a number of the advertiser-supported cable networks, including the USA Network, TBS Superstation, and Lifetime. These films are normally sold in packages, series of titles made available by a distribution company for sale to cable networks and local TV stations. In fact, it was Ted Turner's acquisition of virtually the entire MGM film library (including *Gone with the Wind*) that enabled his launch of Turner Network Television (TNT) and Turner Classic Movies (TCM). American Movie Classics (AMC) has also carved its niche by acquiring distribution rights to large packages of film titles.

Cable-Original Movies In their quest to keep pay cable attractive to consumers despite competition from video stores and other sources, cable programmers are producing their own movies. Some have been released for theatrical distribution first, to be followed by a pay-cable run. Others have been produced for a premiere on the cable network, to be followed by theatrical or home video release.

The typical made-for-cable movie today has a budget in the range of $4 million to $8 million. This is less than a third of the typical budget of a feature film but about a third higher than the cost of a "movie of the week" on one of the broadcast networks. For the extra cost, the cable "made-for" can typically attract a better-known cast and high production values and take on more delicate or controversial subject matter than is the norm on broadcast TV.

HBO has been a leader in the production of cable original movies, producing between 10 and 15 each year, many based on real-life stories. *Elizabeth I*, for example, which portrayed the life of the legendary queen, received 13 Emmy nominations, including nominations for outstanding miniseries, best director, and outstanding lead actress. Among its recent offerings were the space epic *From the Earth to the Moon* (budgeted at $65 million), *Band of Brothers*, and *Empire Falls*, based on Richard Russo's Pulitzer Prize–winning novel. Showtime is also committed to original films, with the critically acclaimed *Our Fathers*, *Behind the Red Door*, and *Mandela and de Klerk*, among its recent productions.

Cable Series   In their early days, cable and pay cable relied almost exclusively on movies, sports, and concerts for their programming. The few cable series that did run tended to be the low-budget, easy-to-film variety (Las Vegas acts, stand-up comedy, showbiz chatter, and so on). One sign of the maturity of the cable business is the emergence of regularly scheduled high-profile series from many cable networks. In fact, more TV programming is produced today for cable networks than for the traditional broadcast networks.

Some recent cable-original series of note were *Six Feet Under*, *Sex and the City*, and *The Sopranos* on HBO; *Brotherhood* on Showtime; VH-1's *Behind the Music*; and MTV's *The Real World*. Dozens of others like *Monk*, *Psych*, *The 4400*, *Nip/Tuck*, and *The Shield* (to mention a few) have sprung up on advertiser-supported cable networks.

Generally, cable services produce their original programs at lower cost than do the commercial TV networks. This cost savings is achieved in a variety of ways. First, smaller independent production companies are often used instead of the costly major studios. To cut overhead expenses that pile up while shooting in a big studio lot, many series are shot on location or in major cities outside the United States, where the dollar is stronger than local currency. Canada and England have become very popular production sites, with Toronto and London standing in for Los Angeles and New York.

In addition, cable networks often engage in coproduction ventures with foreign networks and production companies, many of which have had trouble getting their programs into the lucrative American market. For example, the HBO miniseries *Elizabeth I* was a coproduction with England's Channel 4.

Public Television Programming

Although the dominant networks (in terms of audience size and budget) are the major commercial broadcast and cable firms, public TV remains a vital source of national programming. PBS reaches nearly 90 million Americans each week through its on-air and online programming. Today some 350 full-power noncommercial TV stations have the same needs as their commercial counterparts: to fill their schedule with programming attractive to audiences. To do so, these stations rely on the Public Broadcasting Service (PBS). Generally public television does not strive for the large audience by providing popular programming for the masses. Public television stations frequently try to identify underserved audiences and develop specific programs for those audiences.

PBS operates in reverse fashion from the commercial networks. Whereas NBC, CBS, ABC, and Fox funnel money to production companies and pay stations to carry their programs, PBS charges membership dues to its affiliates (over 90 percent of all public TV stations). In return, PBS provides programs funded by pooled station funds, the CPB, foundations, individual contributions, and other sources. PBS itself produces no programs. Instead, through its National Program Service (NPS), it serves as a conduit to program producers, usually avoiding the suppliers common to network scheduling.

A key difference between the commercial networks and PBS is that the stations (not the network) decide when to carry national programs. The most popular programs on PBS form the "core schedule," which is designated for same-night carriage. PBS recommends but cannot require stations to air these shows the same night that they are fed by satellite

Most cable networks aim for niche audiences, such as this program about Thomas Edison on the History Channel.

to member stations. Same-night carriage helps PBS promote its shows nationally. Although most PBS affiliates air the core schedule the same day, many PBS shows are taped and delayed for days or weeks. And within limits, which vary from show to show, stations frequently rerun PBS shows. Thus, unlike CBS or NBC, a PBS show may or may not air nationally in a given day, and when it finally does run, a show may be rerun long before the summer. Like cable shows, however, rerunning programming can build the cumulative audience.

On average, PBS today distributes about 1,500 hours of programming per year to its member stations (about 4 hours per day). The bulk of PBS programming consists of news and public affairs (about 40 percent). This includes programs like *Frontline, NOVA, Washington Week,* and *The News Hour.* Next most common are cultural programs, such as *Masterpiece Theater, The American Experience, Dance in America,* and *Live from Lincoln Center.* Children's programs make up just over 1 in 10 PBS shows, from *Sesame Street* to *Teletubbies* to *Between the Lions.* How-to shows and special-interest programs are nearly as common, from *Motorweek* to *This Old House* to *Antiques Roadshow.* Filling out the PBS schedule are shows that are strictly educational (like *Newton's*

Apple and *Reading Rainbow*) and a very small sprinkling of sports (mostly tennis and soccer).

PBS strives to avoid the producers that are common to commercial TV. Nearly 40 percent of producers for public TV consider themselves independent. Just over one in four programs on the network come from one of its member stations, and about 7 percent emanate from international producers. The remaining shows are developed and funded by unique consortiums of stations, philanthropic groups, corporations, foundations; you name it! The idea of providing the public with an independent point of view is sometimes controversial.

Because part of PBS funding emanates out of the Corporation for Public Broadcasting, a government-funded entity, PBS has always had to walk a line that avoids taking a partisan viewpoint, something commercial networks are free to do. In February 2005, PBS Chairman Kenneth Tomlinson, a Bush appointee, questioned whether PBS and NPR programming was impartial. Without CPB knowledge, Tomlinson hired an outside firm to monitor weekly PBS news programs. Some months later an internal audit critical of these actions was released, and Tomlinson resigned from CPB. However, responding to the notion that PBS was bias in its presentation of public affairs programming, network president Pat Mitchell appointed former *Washington Post* journalist Michael Getler, the PBS ombudsman. Whether PBS will continue to receive pressure about its programming content remains to be seen. Nevertheless, one of television's most important investigative programs, *Frontline*, illustrates the fact that PBS frequently will cover issues that are all but ignored by commercial broadcasters.

Locally PBS-affiliated stations provide a wide range of local programming from talk to sports to cultural events. Local programs are usually funded by underwriters from the community of license. To fill out the local schedule, public television stations frequently rely on British-imported comedy and drama series, produced by the BBC or Independent Television (see Chapter 14).

THE WORLD OF TV SYNDICATION

After the networks (broadcast, cable, and PBS), the largest purveyors of programming are the **syndicators:** the companies that sell programs directly to TV stations and cable services. The growth in the number of TV stations, the arrival of cable and new broadcast networks, and the growth of the home video market have created tremendous new demands. Where once syndication meant only two things—movies and network reruns—the syndication universe today ranges from films to talk shows, music videos, and adventure yarns, to how-to shows on everything from exercise to hunting water buffalo. Today TV syndication is about a $9 billion annual business.

The Syndication Market

There are two primary buyers or markets for syndicated programming. The traditional market for syndication is local TV. Today over 1,300 local TV stations obtain syndicated programming to fill their program schedules during time periods without network programs or local programs (mainly news).

The second market for syndicated programming is the cable networks. The chief cable buyers of syndication are the advertiser-supported services, like TBS Superstation, the USA network, Lifetime, TNT, and others. Syndicators also sell their product to international broadcasters, but the revenue for this market is much smaller than for domestic syndication.

The Syndication Bazaar

In 1963, a small group of TV programmers got together with an equally small group of syndicators to pool their resources and streamline their efforts. From those humble beginnings has come an annual showbiz extravaganza known as NATPE International. (NATPE stands for National Association of Television Program Executives.)

In 2001, a total of 20,000 TV executives—including programmers, syndicators, and even some stars—attended NATPE International. Part Hollywood hype and part consumer trade show, the convention is the place where new syndicated programs are unveiled and, most of all, plugged. Syndication programmers lure buyers to screening rooms. Liquor flows. Premiums—like cowboy hats from producers of westerns—abound. And sometimes deals were made. Local television stations could pick and choose programming to fill the time between local programming and network programs.

Fast-forward to 2006, and we find that the syndication market has evolved. Many of the people who attend NATPE now are international customers who are shopping around for American programming to fill their schedules. In 2006, attendance had shrunk to 8,000 and most Hollywood studios had moved their screening rooms off the convention floor to hotel suites. But syndication is a viable competitor to prime time for advertisers. With more than 132 weekly shows being offered, the syndication market is important to broadcast and cable.

Over the past few years increased competition for viewers and quality programming has changed the face of syndication. Now it appears that new mobile video devices may spark additional ways to screen syndicated programming, bypassing both broadcasters and cable programmers.

Types of Syndicated Programming

What does one see at NATPE? Despite the vast array of programming available, it is possible to classify syndicated programming into three main types: motion pictures that have completed their theatrical run, whose home video and pay-cable releases are sold to stations in movie packages; programming originally produced for one of the major TV networks, sold to stations as off-net syndication; and original programming produced expressly for syndication, known as first-run. Each type of syndication is distributed in a unique way.

Movie Packages   Movies are a mainstay of the program schedule for the pay-cable networks (from HBO and Showtime to Encore and Starz), many TV stations, and many basic cable networks (including USA, Lifetime, American Movie Classics, Turner Classic Movies and the Sci-Fi channel). Even network affiliates need movies for parts of their daytime, late-night, and weekend programming. There are lots of movies out there: It is estimated that since the sound era began in 1927, over half a million films have been produced in the United States alone. Keep that figure in mind when you get the feeling in a video store that you have seen everything.

From the earliest days of TV, movies have been the backbone of syndication. The new TV stations needed something to show; facing declining atten-

dance, the motion picture business needed a new revenue source. The venture was a match made in heaven (if not Hollywood). Early on, it became unwieldy to sell movies one at a time. Thus the distribution companies (originally subsidiaries of the major studios) began to package the movies as a collection of titles. Today, with the exception of a very few blockbusters (such as *Spider-Man 2* or *Pirates of the Carribean*), movies sold in syndication are packaged.

Stations acquire the rights to movies under license agreements. The agreements generally run from 3 to 6 years and allow the station to show a movie up to six times or more during the period covered. Typically packages of recent box office successes (known as A movies) cost stations more than older and less popular films (known as B movies). In a market like New York City, *Happy Gilmore* may license for as much as $500,000, whereas *I Was a Teenage Werewolf* can run for as little as $50.

The annual NATPE programming bazaar attracts thousands of TV executives and producers from around the globe.

Off-Net Syndication Say what you will about the commercial broadcast networks—their imitative schedules, their lowest-common-denominator programs, and their so-called demise in recent years. The fact remains that network programs enjoy great popularity, which sustains over time. In the jargon of syndication, network shows have "staying power" and "legs." Old network programs never die: They are sold to stations and cable services as **off-net syndication.** In 2005, the 1950s sitcom *I Love Lucy* still generated millions of dollars for CBS.

Off-net series are packaged for syndication in a manner similar to motion-picture packaging. The station or cable service pays for a certain number of episodes in the series and gets the right to show each title a number of times. Six runs over a period of 6 years is commonplace. The price per episode for off-net programs varies widely. It depends on the size of the TV market, the popularity of the show in its first run, the number of programs available, and so on.

Normally at least 100 episodes of a network show are needed to launch it in off-net syndication. The ideal number of episodes is 130. Why? Since there are 260 weekdays in a year, an off-net episode can run exactly twice annually when programmed in a time period each Monday to Friday. This process of scheduling a show to run in the same daypart each weekday is known as **stripping.**

Shows that have recently eclipsed the magic number and scored a hit in off-net syndication include *Seinfeld, Friends, Everybody Loves Raymond,* and *The Simpsons.*

Even as the 100-episode rule works for broadcast television, the syndicated market is evolving. Some experts regard video-on-demand and downloading off sites like Apple's iTunes as an opportunity to market programs that don't make the 100-episode mark. Interestingly, providing these download opportunities may provide ratings bumps for shows, extending the possibility of making it to 100 shows. Ratings for *Lost* and *Desperate Housewives* actually increased slightly after they became available on iTunes.

First-Run Syndication Programs that make their debut in syndication, without a prior network life, are known as **first-run syndication.** Traditionally first-run syndication has been characterized by cheap, easy-to-produce programs designed to be strip-programmed.

Game shows and talk programs have fit the bill perfectly over the years and have been the bulk of first-run syndication. Today's dominating syndicated quiz programs are *Jeopardy* and *Wheel of Fortune.* The queen of syndicated talk is Oprah Winfrey. She has been joined in first-run syndication by Ellen DeGeneres, Jerry Springer, Dr. Phil, Maury, and a host of others. Court TV shows such as *Judge Judy, Cristina's Court,* and *Divorce Court* are also popular syndicated fair.

Not all syndicated originals are cheap quiz and talk programs. Off-network drama such as *CSI: Crime Scene Investigation, Law and Order, 24,* and *Smallville* have all worked successfully. And buoyed by Paramount's success with *Star Trek: The Next Generation* and *Deep Space Nine,* as well as the worldwide appeal of *Baywatch,* first-run action/adventure proliferated in the late 1990s. Some of these shows were long on action, short on dialogue, and skimpy on costuming. This category that included such first-run epics as *Xena* and *Hercules* now includes shows like *Farscape.*

Cable Syndication Cable networks have entered the off-network syndication market in a substantial way. High-profile programs are being purchased by cable networks to provide a unique flavor to their offerings, making cable the largest single buyer of syndicated programming. As the viewer shift from network television to cable continues, cable has a stronger base to build advertising revenues. (Remember that local cable franchises pay a monthly subscription fee per subscriber that makes up the bulk of cable's revenue.) Not surprisingly, the cost-per-episode fees are much higher than usual for cable programming.

Barter Syndication

At one time, TV stations would purchase syndicated programming on a cash-and-carry basis. However, for a number of reasons cash sales of syndicated programming have declined in recent years. For one thing, the bottom-line consciousness of the TV industry has made station managers reluctant to take million-dollar gambles on syndicated programs. Station mergers and buyouts along with increased competition from cable have left little cash to speculate in program investment. And syndicators have had difficulty extracting payments from stations on installment plans. In the past some stations have been late in paying their bills; some (especially UHF stations with huge inventories) have defaulted altogether.

Thus, high prices have combined with low cash flows to create a new form of syndication finance. Just as the term was used in the days of fur trappers and Indian agents, barter refers to the trading of one commodity for another of similar value. In TV, the valuable commodity offered by the syndicator is programming; the item of value at the station is its airtime. In **barter syndication** the syndicator provides the program to the station free or at a substantially reduced cost per episode (cash plus barter). In return, the station sacrifices some of the advertising slots in the show. The syndicator can integrate its own ads into the show, or the syndicator can act like a TV network, calling on major advertisers to place ads in each of the markets in which the program plays. Recently more and more stations have negotiated barter arrangements for syndicated programming.

In barter syndication, the key to the syndicator is market clearance. The more markets the program plays in, the larger is the national audience that can be offered to advertisers. Clearing 80 percent of the nation's TV markets is considered good; over 90 percent clearance is excellent.

Advertising revenues from barter syndication have increased dramatically in recent years. In 1988 barter revenues to syndicators represented about $800 million. Today barter syndication is a $4 billion business.

LOCAL TELEVISION PROGRAMMING

The last piece of the programming puzzle is provided by individual TV stations and cable systems through their original, locally produced programs.

Local programming has been a growth area in recent years as TV stations and cable systems have sought a unique identity when faced with new competitors like satellite DBS and the Internet.

Local Television Stations

Faced with escalating syndication costs, lagging network performances, and the loss of local advertising dollars to barter, TV stations are placing increasing emphasis on their own local programming. As we saw in a previous section, the bulk of the local TV budget goes to local news and talk.

Many TV stations have expanded their local news "hole" from early fringe and late night to include morning, which is at the forefront of expanding local production. Studies indicate that commuting times are increasing and Americans are rising earlier. Many stations are now programming earlier hours before network morning magazine shows in attempts to reach these commuters. According to a Gallup poll conducted in 1999, 58 percent of American adults say they watch local news in the morning for information, traffic, and weather reports. Overall, viewership for morning news programs reflects a younger audience than the evening news, an attractive demographic for advertisers.

But local news is not the only programming produced by local stations. In virtually all large cities, there are locally produced alternatives to *Today* and *Good Morning, America*. Some local stations are moving from news and talk to comedy, drama, and music programming. Diversity is the key word in local TV production. Surveys of general managers and program directors suggest that local production of everything from situation comedies to dramas will increase in larger television markets.

Local Cable Programming

Just as the future of TV stations may lie in their ability to develop local programming, the cable industry is making similar forecasts.

As we documented earlier in this chapter, cable systems have been especially vigorous in developing news and sports programs as an alternative to local affiliates in their service areas. The rise of regional cable news has been a boon to local cable channels.

Other community channel services on the rise include on-screen TV program guides, electronic bulletin boards that feature classified and personal advertising, regional weather services, and electronic "tours of homes" offered by area realtors.

PROGRAMMING STRATEGIES

Now that we understand the various types and sources of TV programming today, we close this chapter by providing a taste of the techniques of TV programming. Space precludes a full discussion of how TV programmers determine their schedules. This process fills entire books and full-semester courses at many institutions. The books listed at the end of the chapter provide a good beginning point to an understanding of TV programming in practice. Now, on to the "taste test."

There is an old saying in television: "People don't watch stations; they watch programs." This means we select the station to watch based on programming rather than selecting the program because of the station that transmits it. It is also a reminder of the importance of programming to the success of TV.

The first step in programming is to define the potential audience. Cartoons shown while children are in school or a football broadcast while men are at work may attract small audiences, but not the numbers possible if the cartoons are run after school or the football games are shown on Sundays when most men aren't working.

Programmers must also have some idea about which groups prefer the shows that are available to be used. *Murder She Wrote* generally attracted women and older men as its main group of viewers. To have optimum viewership it was necessary to schedule *Murder She Wrote* at a time when these people would be in front of their TV sets. Sunday evenings following *60 Minutes* seemed like a good idea to CBS. The show was a mainstay in that time period for over a decade. The time period was inherited by shows with appeal to a similar demographic: first *Touched by an Angel* and then *Cold Case*.

Obviously, programming must entail more than merely placing a program that appeals to a particular audience at a time when that audience may view it. There are a number of techniques that programmers use to maximize viewership. Once you have viewers, you want to hang on to them.

Audience Flow

Audiences will tend to stay with the TV station they are watching until something they dislike shows up on the screen. In some ways audiences exhibit inertia, viewing the same station until forced to change. The proliferation of remote controls has changed this tendency, since viewers no longer are required to get out of their chairs to change the channel, but inertia still influences viewing. The movement of audiences from one program to another is called **audience flow.**

The successful programmer will build and hold an audience from show to show. This means putting together programs that generally attract the same audience.

One reason for the continuing success of *Oprah* is that this issues-based talk program provides the perfect lead-in to local news. At the network level, programmers try to build their evenings around a core audience. CBS's powerful Monday evening block was designed to keep and attract women 25–49, flowing nicely from *King of Queens* to *How I Met Your Mother* to *Two and a Half Men* in 2005. Similarly, a few seasons ago Fox had arranged its schedule on Monday nights to hook younger women, with a block of *Melrose Place* and *Ally McBeal.*

Counterprogramming

Counterprogramming is a technique wherein the programmer decides to go for an audience different from the audience that competing stations or networks are trying to attract.

Independent TV stations have long counterprogrammed network affiliates in their market by programming children's programs when their competitors carried local news, or male-oriented local sports when affiliates were in the female-oriented prime-time blocks. Cable networks have also been master counterprogrammers. One example is the success of ESPN's *Sportscenter,* which comes on at 11 P.M., when many local TV stations go to their news programming. CNN carries its most popular talk program, *Larry King Live,* when the major networks go to their dramas and situation comedies. Two more examples: CBS programs Monday nights with *King of Queens, Two and a Half Men,* and *Out of Practice.* It should come as no surprise that this was a counterprogram strategy to ABC's *Monday Night Football.* Finally, NBC counterprograms *Survivor* on Thursday with two situation comedies: *My Name Is Earl* and *The Office.*

Challenge Programming

Challenge programming is the opposite of counterprogramming. In **challenge programming,** the TV network or station goes head to head with the same type of programming as a major competitor, or goes after the same demographic with a different program with similar audience appeal. Local stations often go head to head with their afternoon talk shows, such as *Oprah* against *Jerry Springer.* They do this in local news and may also compete with morning talk and noontime information shows.

One famous example of challenge programming concerned the decision by CBS and NBC in 1994 to go head to head with high-profile medical dramas. CBS sought to win Thursday evenings at 10 (9 central) with *Chicago Hope*. NBC set its sights on the same time period with *ER*. ABC was happy to stay on the sidelines by counterprogramming with *Prime Time Live*. When the smoke cleared, NBC had won the battle; by winter 1995, CBS had moved *Chicago Hope* to Monday nights. By 1999, *ER* was a staple of NBC's Thursday schedule and frequently in the Top 10 programs. The 2006–2007 season saw another example of challenge programming when ABC's *Grey's Anatomy* went against CBS's *CSI*.

A FINAL WORD

Programming is the fun part of TV. It is what attracts viewers so that the station or network can sell time to advertisers, to make money. A great deal of thought and effort is put into deciding which programs fit where. The reason for this concern in programming is not primarily that the station or network cares whether viewers are entertained or informed but that this is how they make their money.

SUMMARY

- TV programming takes two major forms: news and entertainment.

- Television news is the nation's primary source of news and is regarded as credible by a large portion of the public.

- Television news reached maturity when President Kennedy was assassinated. The 1960s events such as the civil rights movement, the Vietnam War, and Neil Armstrong's first step on the moon came to life in people's living rooms.

- The 1970s and 1980s were marked by money and machines. Television news became a significant profit center for local TV stations and cable. Anchor salaries rose. Electronic news gathering and satellite news came on the scene.

- The 1990s saw growth in TV news due to new networks, regional cable news, and more global competition.

- Many people are involved in the preproduction stage of the newscast. They are the news director, news producer, assignment editor, field producer, reporter, writers, and editors.

- Television stations can obtain entertainment programming through networks, syndication, and local origination. The commercial networks—ABC, CBS, NBC, and Fox—provide broad, mass-appeal programming.

- Historically, networks have relied on outside sources for their programs—in particular, the major Hollywood studios and a cluster of well-known independent producers. Recently, the networks have expanded the scope of their own in-house productions and in some cases have merged with studios. The networks receive a great number of suggested storylines. Because the number is so large, there is only a slight chance that any one idea will be accepted.

- Miniseries and made-for-TV and cable movies are the most expensive types of programming. Situation comedies and reality programs, on the other hand, are the cheapest to produce.

- As cable matures, it has directly affected the networks. Cable has been producing higher-quality shows, and the effects can be seen in the ratings.

- Syndication has become a popular source of programming. To understand fully the syndication business, one must be aware of NATPE trade shows and types of syndication.

- Cable syndication is growing as the audience watching cable continues to expand.

- Local TV stations achieve an identity by producing local shows; therefore, many community and cable stations are trying this technique. Because they will be saving money and providing original programming, these stations are likely to survive in the future.

- TV programming strategies include audience flow, counterprogramming, and challenge programming.

KEY TERMS

electronic news gathering
   (ENG)   200
satellite news gathering
   (SNG)   200
sweeps   201

minidocs   201
news consultants   201
coventuring   202
local-local news   202
regional cable-news services   202

future file   205
network programming   207
syndication   207
local origination   207
affiliates   208

SUGGESTIONS FOR FURTHER READING

Auletta, K. (1998). *The Highwaymen*. Wilmington, CA: Harvest Press.

Barkin, S. (2002). *American television news: The media marketplace and the public interest*. Armonk, NY: M. E. Sharpe.

Block, A. B. (1990). *Outfoxed: Marvin Davis, Barry Diller, Rupert Murdoch and the inside story of America's fourth television network*. New York: St. Martin's.

Blumenthal, H., & Goodenough, O. (2006). *This business of television* (2nd ed.). New York: Billboard Books.

Boyd, A. (1997). *Broadcast journalism: Techniques of radio and TV news* (4th ed.). Oxford; Boston: Focal Press.

Cremer, C. (1996). *ENG: Television news* (3rd ed.). New York: McGraw-Hill.

Ferguson, D., & Eastman, S. (2001). *Broadcast/cable/web programming: Strategies and practices* (6th ed.). Belmont, CA: Wadsworth.

Medoff, N., & Kaye, B. (2005). *Electronic Media: Then, now and later*. Boston: Pearson.

Parson, P., & Frieden, R. (1997). *The cable and satellite television industries*. Boston: Allyn & Bacon.

Walker, J., & Ferguson, D. (1997). *Broadcast television industry*. Boston: Allyn & Bacon.

INTERNET EXERCISES

Visit our Web site at www.mhhe.com/dominick6 for study-guide exercises to help you learn and apply material in each chapter. You will find ideas for future research as well as useful Web links to provide you with an opportunity to journey through the new electronic media.

Part Four | How It's Controlled

Rules and Regulations 10

Quick Facts

 License terms for TV and radio stations: 8 years

 FCC has five commissioners, six bureaus, and about 2,200 employees

 Number of states that permit cameras in the courtroom: 50

 Amount of fines levied against CBS for indecent programming in 2006: $3.3 million

 Percent of high school students who think the First Amendment "goes too far in the rights it guarantees" (Knight Foundation Poll, 2005): 35

The electronic media are regulated by federal and state laws, by rules enacted by the FCC and other regulatory agencies, and by a system of self-regulation. This chapter looks at the formal system of rules and regulations that have an impact on broadcasting, satellites, cable, and the Internet; the next chapter examines self-regulation.

RATIONALE

Unlike many other industries, broadcasting has always had special requirements and special responsibilities placed on it by government. What makes it different? There have been two main rationales for treating broadcasting as a special case: (1) the scarcity theory and (2) the pervasive presence theory.

The **scarcity theory** notes that the electromagnetic spectrum is limited. Only a finite number of broadcast stations can exist in a certain place in a certain time; too many stations can interfere with one another. This means that only a limited number of aspiring broadcasters can be served and that the government must choose from among the potential applicants.

In addition, the scarcity theory holds that the spectrum is such a valuable resource that it should not be privately owned. Instead, it is treated like a public resource, owned by all, like a national park. The government treats those fortunate enough to broadcast as trustees of the public and imposes special obligations on them, such as requiring that they provide candidates for public office equal opportunities to use their stations.

Recent technological advances such as cable TV, which offers would-be broadcasters a large number of channels, have prompted a reevaluation of the scarcity theory. Many critics would argue that it is outmoded. Others, however, point out that, as long as the number of people wishing to broadcast exceeds the available facilities, scarcity still exists.

The **pervasive presence theory** is of more recent origin. It holds that broadcasting is available to virtually all of the population and, once the TV or radio set is turned on, offensive messages can enter the home without warning, reaching both adults and children. This situation is fundamentally different from encountering an offensive message in a public forum. If you're out in public, you're on your own.

You might encounter things that offend your sensibilities. Should you meet someone wearing a T-shirt with an offensive word printed on it, your only recourse would be to turn away. The home, however, is not the same as a public place; you should not expect to encounter unwanted offensive messages there. Consequently, the pervasive presence theory holds that you're entitled to some protection. Thus the basic intrusiveness of broadcasting allows the government to regulate it.

HISTORY

How did the government get involved with broadcasting regulation in the first place? In 1910 Congress passed the Wireless Ship Act. Only four paragraphs long, it basically mandated that large oceangoing passenger ships must be equipped with wireless sets. It had little relevance to broadcasting, primarily because broadcasting as we know it did not yet exist. Two years later the Radio Act of 1912 was passed. Spurred by the sinking of the *Titanic* and the need to ratify international treaties, the 1912 act required those wishing to engage in broadcasting to obtain a license from the secretary of commerce. Further, to prevent interference among maritime stations, it provided for the use of call letters and established the assignment of frequencies and hours of operation. The law also strengthened the regulations concerning the use of wireless by ships. As was the case with the earlier law, the 1912 act still envisioned radio as point-to-point communication, like the telegraph, which uses the spectrum only sporadically, and did not anticipate broadcasting, which uses the spectrum continuously. Consequently, for the next 8 years or so, when most wireless communication was of the point-to-point variety, the law worked reasonably well. As the 1920s dawned, however, and radio turned into broadcasting, the 1912 act quickly broke down.

As related in Chapter 1, the number of broadcast stations greatly increased and available spectrum space could not accommodate them. Interference quickly became a serious problem. By 1926 the interference problem had gotten so bad that many parts of the country could no longer get a consistently clear broadcast signal. Consequently, after prodding from President Calvin Coolidge, Congress finally passed a new law—the Radio Act of 1927.

The 1927 Radio Act

Although more than 80 years old, the **Radio Act of 1927** still demonstrates the basic principles that under lie broadcast regulation. Embracing the scarcity argument, the key provisions of the act were the following:

1. The recognition that the public owned the electromagnetic spectrum, thereby eliminating private ownership of radio frequencies.

2. The notion that radio stations had to operate in the "public interest, convenience or necessity."

3. A prohibition against censorship of broadcast programs by the government.

4. The creation of a five-member **Federal Radio Commission (FRC),** which would grant licenses, make rules to prevent interference, and establish coverage areas with its decisions subject to judicial review.

Over the next few years, the FRC enacted technical standards that eliminated the interference problem and further elaborated the concept of the public interest. In one case, the FRC denied the license of a station in Kansas because it broadcast prescriptions for bogus patent medicines (See box on page 229). The federal court system affirmed this decision, thus demonstrating that the FRC was not restricted to an examination of solely technical matters and could indeed look at content.

The Communications Act of 1934

The 1927 act was superseded 7 years later when President Franklin Roosevelt streamlined the government's regulatory operations concerning communication. In response to Roosevelt's recommendations, Congress passed a new communications act **(The Communications Act of 1934),** which expanded the membership of the FRC from five to seven members and gave the organization a new name—the **Federal Communications Commission (FCC).** The powers of the new commission were broadened to include all wireless and wire forms of communication (including the telephone), except for those used by the military and the government. The 1927 law was regarded so highly that much of it was rewritten into the new legislation and the key provisions previously outlined were left unchanged.

The Communications Act of 1934 and related pieces of legislation are found in Title 47 of the U.S.

Code. Title 47 is divided into chapters. The chapter most pertinent for our purposes is Chapter 5, "Wire and Radio Communication." Chapter 5 is further divided into subchapters which incorporate the 1934 act. Subchapter 3 contains provisions relating to radio and TV, and it is this part of the act that has most relevance for broadcasters. Some of the key sections most often mentioned in the trade press are:

- *Section 301.* Users of the electromagnetic spectrum must be licensed by the FCC.

- *Section 312.* Candidates for federal office must be given reasonable access to broadcast facilities.

- *Section 315.* Use of broadcast facilities by candidates for public office is outlined. (This provision is so important that an entire section is devoted to it later in this chapter.)

- *Section 326.* The FCC is forbidden to censor the content of radio and TV programming.

Like most laws, the 1934 Communications Act has been amended and reshaped, usually in response to a current problem or to changing technology. For example, in 1959, Congress amended the act to make it illegal for people to rig quiz shows. Three years later, Congress passed the **Communications Satellite Act,** which expanded the regulatory powers of the FCC. With all of its various revisions, the 1934 law remained the nation's most influential broadcasting law for six decades.

Cable Regulation

The history of cable regulation has been marked by major changes of direction. When cable first came on the scene in the 1950s, the FCC refused to regulate it since cable didn't use over-the-air frequencies. By the 1960s, however, cable became a viable competitor to broadcast stations and the FCC responded to pressure from broadcasters and enacted regulations that effectively hampered cable's growth in large markets. By the 1970s, cable operators were exerting their own pressure on the commission, which eventually issued a new set of rules that were somewhat more favorable to cable.

While all of this was going on at the federal level, cable systems were also bound by regulations at the state and local levels. Thus a company that owned cable systems in 20 communities might be faced with 20 different sets of local rules. The most important local rule established exclusivity. Local governments awarded an exclusive franchise to a single cable company to serve a community or neighborhood in exchange for the provision of specialized community channels, payment of a franchise fee, and maintenance of low rates. Many companies, in their zeal to obtain a franchise, overpromised and had to scale down their systems, creating some bad feelings between them and the local governments.

Reexamination

The 1980s saw a general trend toward deregulation. The FCC abolished many regulations that pertained to radio, simplified license renewal applications, and eased operating regulations for TV stations. Congress got into the spirit by extending the license terms for both radio and TV stations and by passing the **Cable Communications Policy Act of 1984,** which allowed cable systems the freedom to set their own rates.

By the 1990s, advances in technology and changes in the business arena prompted Congress to take another look at regulation. New communication technologies such as direct-to-home broadcasting via satellite and the Internet presented new opportunities and challenges. Telephone companies were interested in providing video programming, and some cable companies were actively exploring the possibility of offering phone services. In response to these and other forces, Congress passed the **Telecommunications Act of 1996,** which had a major impact on all areas of electronic media.

The Telecommunications Act of 1996 was the most significant piece of electronic media legislation in more than 60 years. One of the main goals of the act was to foster competition between cable companies and phone companies by allowing phone companies to provide cable TV services and by allowing cable companies to offer local phone service. This competition, it was hoped, would result in more consumer choices, better service, and lower bills.

The act was slow to produce its desired results, but by 2006 competition between cable and phone companies was heating up. Several telecommunications companies began to offer video services. Verizon, for example, offered one community in Texas 180 digital video and music channels for about $40 per month. AT&T was testing a video service that was delivered over the Internet. Thanks to a new technology called Voice over Internet Protocol (VoIP), traditional cable companies were also offering phone service. Cablevision and Cox Cable both offered plans that included local and long-distance phone service, high-speed Internet access, and digital cable for about $90 per month. Experts predict that this competition will become even more intense as technology companies such as Microsoft and Intel also offer movies and television programming over the Internet. The evolving technology and fast-changing business climate prompted Congress in 2006 to begin a reexamination of the 1996 act. Some of the issues that were being discussed included problems caused by the move to digital television (see Chapter 5) and *network neutrality,* a provision that would block Internet service providers from favoring one Web company over another. Under network neutrality, for example, an Internet service provider could not charge an additional fee to Google so that Google's search engine would run faster than its competitors'.

The act also had a significant impact in several other areas, as discussed in Chapters 4, 5, and 6. It removed the cap on the number of radio stations that one person or organization could own. It also liberalized the rules concerning local ownership. In large markets, one organization can own as many as eight radio stations. Concerning television, one person or organization can now own as many stations as she wants as long as the combined reach of the stations does not exceed 39 percent of the nation's homes (the old law set a 25 percent cap). The law also extended the license renewal term to 8 years for both radio (7 years under the old law) and television stations (5 years under the old law). The law further gave cable systems more leeway in setting the rates they charge their subscribers. Finally, the act required new TV sets to be equipped with a **V-chip,** a device that enables parents to control access to programs that they consider objectionable. More on the V-chip in the next chapter.

REGULATORY FORCES

Broadcast and cable policy results from the interaction of several factors. Legislative, administrative, judicial, political, and economic forces are all important determiners of regulation. Drawing upon the model used by Krasnow, Longley, and Terry in *The Politics of Broadcast Regulation*, this section examines eight key components in the process: the FCC, Congress, the courts, the White House, industry lobbyists, the public, state and local governments, and the marketplace.

One of the key cases decided by the new Federal Radio Commission concerned station KFKB ("Kansas Folks Know Best") in tiny Milford, Kansas. Licensed to Dr. John R. Brinkley, KFKB ("The Sunshine Station in the Heart of the Nation") became one of the most popular stations in America during the 1920s, primarily because of the notoriety surrounding its owner. John Romulus Brinkley was the son of a medical doctor. At an early age he decided to follow in his father's footsteps and entered medicine. Young Brinkley graduated, if that's the right word, from the Eclectic Medical University of Kansas City. (He apparently finished his course of study in a few weeks, paid $100, and received a diploma.) Forty states did not recognize degrees from his college, but that left "Dr." Brinkley eight others he could practice in. He eventually wound up in Milford and opened a modest hospital, which he immodestly named after himself. If that wasn't enough, he also set up the Brinkley Research Laboratories and the Brinkley Training School for Nurses.

Brinkley had studied a little bit about the workings of human glands. He also was a shrewd judge of human nature. Consequently, he began to advertise his rejuvenation operations over KFKB. Designed to restore sexual drive in middle-aged men, the actual operation consisted of grafting or injecting material from the sexual organs of male goats into his human patients. The operation was done under local anesthesia and took only 15 minutes. The cost was a rather significant sum in those days—$750. (The goats, of course, paid a much higher price.) One interesting touch introduced by the doctor: Patients could pick their own goat in advance from the doctor's private herd, sort of like picking out a lobster for your dinner from a tank at a seafood restaurant. As time passed, Brinkley was touting his operation as a cure-all for skin diseases, high blood pressure, insanity, and paralysis.

KFKB was the perfect medium for Brinkley's advertising. At the time, thanks to the doctor's investment, it was one of the most powerful stations in North America. Twice a day, people from Saskatchewan to Panama could hear the doctor's own radio talk show, in which he promoted his operation, gave precise instructions on how to get to Milford, and even advised prospective patients on how to transport the $750 safely.

People flocked to Milford and Brinkley became a rich man. In an era when legitimate doctors were making an annual salary of about $5,000 Brinkley was pulling in about $125,000 a year. He owned his own airplane, his own yacht, and a fleet of cars, and usually wore a couple of 12-carat diamond rings.

In addition to his gland operations, Brinkley also started selling his own prescription drugs. On a show called *The Medical Question Box* Brinkley would read letters people had written him about their ailments. He would then prescribe his medicines by number. Pharmacists all over the region were supplied with the Brinkley formulas, which usually consisted of ingredients such as alcohol and castor oil. For each bottle that was sold, the pharmacist would give a cut to Brinkley.

Not all was rosy, however. Kansas City newspapers attacked the doctor's methods, the American Medical Association exposed Brinkley's quackery, and the Federal Radio Commission eventually revoked his broadcast license and further defined the principle that programming must be in the public interest. Undaunted, Brinkley ran for governor of Kansas as a write-in candidate and nearly won. Since KFKB was no longer open to him, Brinkley bought a station in Mexico, XER, 500,000 watts strong, and kept his messages blanketing North America. Eventually the doctor moved to Del Rio, Texas, across the border from XER, and continued his medical practice there, this time specializing in cures for enlarged prostate glands. When a competing doctor opened up a similar practice in Del Rio, Brinkley moved to Little Rock, Arkansas.

Once in Arkansas, Brinkley's troubles began. Malpractice awards to discontented patients, back taxes, legal fees, the costs of running his Mexican station, and his extravagant lifestyle soon exhausted even Brinkley's sizable bank account. The doctor had to declare bankruptcy. As if that wasn't bad enough, the U.S. government finally persuaded Mexico to ease international radio interference problems by shutting down XER and similar stations. Less than a year later, at 56, J. R. Brinkley succumbed to a heart attack, thus ending the career of one of early radio's unsavory but colorful broadcasters.

The Federal Communications Commission

The FCC currently consists of five commissioners, one of whom serves as chair, appointed by the president and confirmed by the Senate, for staggered 5-year terms. Political balance is achieved by requiring that no more than three members be from one political party.

Serving the commissioners are six bureaus, as shown in Figure 10–1.

1. The Consumer and Government Affairs Bureau informs consumers about telecommunications goods and services and coordinates policy efforts with other governmental agencies.

2. As the name suggests, the Enforcement Bureau is responsible for upholding FCC rules and regulations.

3. The International Bureau represents the FCC in satellite and other matters that involve the United States and other countries.

4. The Wireless Telecommunications Bureau regulates cellular phones, pagers, two-way radios, and similar devices.

5. The Wireline Competition Bureau regulates telephone companies.

6. Of most importance to broadcasting and cable is the Media Bureau, which oversees AM and FM radio, broadcast TV, cable, and satellite services.

The FCC uses a variety of methods to regulate broadcasting and cable, and satellites. These methods are examined in detail below. For now, keep in mind that the FCC is a major force in the development and application of electronic media policy.

Congress

The FCC regulates broadcasting with Congress looking over its shoulder. The FCC is a creature of Congress. Congress created the FCC, and, if it wished, Congress could abolish the FCC. (In fact, in 1982 Congress changed the status of the FCC from a permanent agency to one that had to be reauthorized every 2 years.) The U.S. Congress is an important part of broadcasting and cable regulation because of its power to enact and amend laws. It was Congress that passed the Communications Act of 1934 and the Telecommunications Act of 1996.

In addition to these two essential communication laws, Congress has enacted other legislation that has had an impact on broadcasting and cable. For example, in 1969, it prohibited cigarette advertising on TV and radio, and in 1990 it passed a law that concerned children's television programming.

Moreover, although it sounds odd, Congress can affect regulatory policy by doing nothing. If it so chooses, Congress can terminate pending legislation or postpone it indefinitely by tabling it. It did this in 1994 when it failed to act on a bill designed to set up the new "information superhighway" and forced its sponsors to resubmit it.

Congress can also exert pressure in nonlegislative ways. First, Congress controls the budget of the FCC. If the FCC has acted in a way that displeases the

Figure 10–1

Structure of the Federal Communications Commission

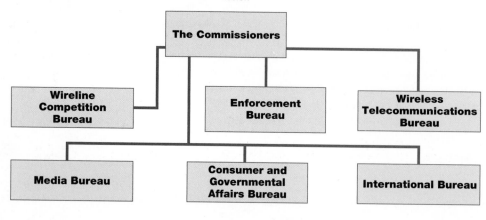

Congress, the commission may find its budget reduced. Further, all presidential appointments to the FCC must be approved by Congress. This gives Congress the opportunity to delay or block a particularly sensitive appointment. Finally, Congress can hold public hearings that highlight, at least in general terms, how Congress feels about a topic. The FCC, in turn, may get the message and shape its policies accordingly.

The Courts

If Congress looks over one shoulder of the FCC, the federal court system looks over the other. If a broadcaster, cable operator, or a citizen disagrees with an FCC decision, he or she appeals it to the federal courts. Most cases concerning broadcasting are decided by the U.S. Court of Appeals for the District of Columbia, whose decisions are subject to review by the Supreme Court only. Courts, however, do not act on their own. They wait for others to initiate actions. If a complaint is raised, courts do not normally reverse an agency's decision if the agency acted in a fair, nonarbitrary way and if the FCC actually has jurisdiction over the matter in question.

Although it does not get involved in many of the decisions of the FCC, when the judicial system does get a chance to speak, it has shown itself to be an important factor in determining broadcast policy. It was a court decision that articulated the pervasive presence rationale behind broadcasting regulation and affirmed the FCC's right to regulate indecent programming. Another court decision totally revamped the renewal hearing process. Before 1966, only those who would be affected by technical interference or economic hardship caused by the renewal or granting of a station's license could appear and offer evidence and testimony at a hearing. Then, in the WLBT case, the Court of Appeals ruled that private citizens had the right to participate in the process and citizen involvement grew rapidly in succeeding years. Deregulation has somewhat diminished citizen involvement, but the WLBT case established the right of citizens to intervene.

Of course, courts do not exist in a vacuum; they interact with many of the other forces active in regulating broadcasting. Federal judges are appointed by the president with the approval of the Senate. Congress writes and rewrites the laws that the courts interpret. Court decisions, as with WLBT, alter, for some groups, the ease of access into the regulatory process. Broadcasters and citizens can bring lawsuits to attract judicial attention. All in all, courts play a pivotal role in the regulatory process.

The White House

If it were possible for the FCC to have a third shoulder, the White House would be watching over it. The influence of the executive branch may not be as visible as that exerted by the Congress and the courts, but it is nonetheless potent.

In the first place, the president has the power of appointment over both FCC commissioners and judges. With regard to the FCC, since many members do not serve out their full terms, the president can fairly quickly establish a slate of congenial commissioners. President George W. Bush, for example, was able to appoint three FCC commissioners during the first 20 months of his first term. Although the Communications Act limits the number of commissioners from one political party to no more than three, most presidents are able to find people who express the administration's prevailing political philosophy. Furthermore, the president can designate any of the sitting commissioners as chair at any time, without congressional intervention or approval. As a result, the president can set the regulatory tone of the FCC.

Second, the White House has its own agency that specializes in the broad field of telecommunications— the **National Telecommunications and Information Administration (NTIA).** Housed in the Commerce Department, the NTIA allocates radio frequencies that are used by the federal government, makes grants to public telecommunications facilities, advises the administration on telecommunications matters, and represents the administration's interests before the FCC and the Congress. The NTIA is one of those organizations that will play as big a role in broadcasting and cable policymaking as the president desires.

Third, the various cabinet offices can also influence broadcasting and cable policy. The Department of Justice can prevent mergers that might result in antitrust problems, and the State Department represents the United States in international matters dealing with satellite orbital slots and mass communication–related businesses. The State Department's role will become more important in the future thanks to the growth of international communication systems.

Finally, the White House can influence policy by initiating communication legislation. Although the president cannot introduce bills in Congress, the

Kevin J. Martin was named
chairman of the FCC in 2005.

White House can draft a bill and usually find a friendly member of Congress to propose it. In that same connection, the president also has the power to veto any unfavorable communication laws passed by Congress. Of course, Congress can also override a presidential veto.

Industry Lobbyists

A lobbyist is a person who represents a special interest and tries to influence legislators' voting behavior. Some people regard lobbyists as a negative force in policymaking, but it should be pointed out that they serve a necessary information function. Many lawmakers regard lobbyists as an asset; they help the lawmaker learn about the impact of pending bills on various segments of society. Lobbying has gone on in Washington for more than 200 years and is a deeply ingrained part of the political process. It comes as no surprise, then, that the broadcasting and cable industries maintain extensive lobbying organizations whose task is to make the industry's wishes known to the FCC, Congress, the courts, and the president.

Each of the major networks maintains its own lobbyists, as do a host of trade associations: the National Association of Broadcasters (traditionally the most influential for the broadcasting industry), the National Cable Television Association (the NCTA—the NAB's rival in the cable industry), the Association of Independent TV Stations, the National Association

of Public TV Stations, the National Religious Broadcasters Association, and the National Association of Farm Broadcasters—to name just a few.

Lobbying tends to work best in a negative sense. It seems easier for lobbyists to stop something they consider bad from happening than it is for them to get something good to happen. Some of the biggest lobbying successes stem from the blockage of proposed legislation. In 2004, for example, broadcast lobbyists defeated an attempt by Congress to tax broadcasters' analog spectrum space for as much as $500 million.

Finally, the expense and energy that must be expended to support lobbying groups mean that one key player in the policy arena is underrepresented— the general public. Most citizens' groups lack the expertise, time, and money to maintain full-time lobbyists. As a result, policymaking tends to be influenced far more by the industry than by the average citizen. There are, however, a few ways in which citizens get involved in the process, and this is the focus of the next section.

The Public

Citizen involvement in broadcasting policy was at its high point in the 1970s. Citizen interest or media reform groups were active in more than 30 states in 1974 and had filed almost 300 petitions to deny the licenses of stations coming up for renewal. By the early 1980s, however, dwindling financial support, longer license terms, and a general emphasis on deregulation combined to weaken the power of these groups.

This decline does not mean that members of the public are shut out of the regulatory process. Some public interest groups still remain, most notably the Media Access Project and Parents Television Council. These groups generally try to put pressure on Congress and the broadcasters by generating favorable public opinion for their causes. Finally, the public influences policy in a more general manner through its election of both the president and members of Congress, who in turn help shape communications policy.

State and Local Governments

Federal laws supersede state and local regulations, but many states have legislation that covers areas not specifically touched on in federal communications law. For example, almost every state has a law dealing with defamation (injuring a person's reputation) and/or reporters' rights to keep sources confidential. Many states have their own laws covering lotteries (the conduct of contests and promotions) and statutes

covering fraudulent or misleading ads. Public broadcasting, moreover, is regulated by many states through acts that spell out the ownership, operation, and funding of educational radio and TV stations. And, of course, broadcasters must comply with local law governing taxation and working conditions.

States and cities can also enact laws that protect the privacy of subscribers to local stations. Information about personal viewing habits cannot be released to unauthorized persons or organizations (this prevents, for example, a political candidate from obtaining from a cable company the information that his rival subscribes to an adult movie channel). Communities can also collect a franchise fee, subject to limitations, from a cable operator and determine the duration of the franchise agreement.

The Marketplace

In its move toward deregulation the FCC has often used the phrase "let the marketplace decide." It follows, then, that the marketplace has become an important factor in determining broadcasting policy.

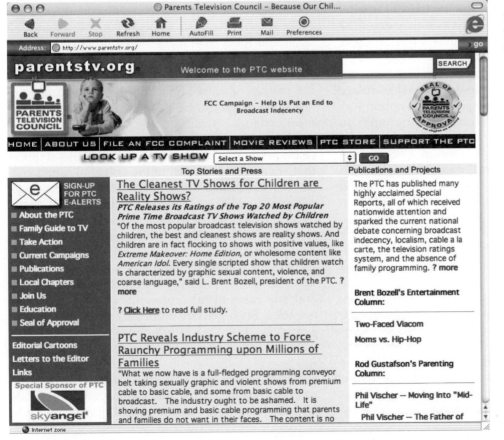

The Parents Television Council was influential in persuading the FCC to take a stronger stand against indecency.

But what exactly is "the marketplace"? Broadly speaking, it's a place where buyers and sellers freely come together to exchange goods or services. Obviously, with regard to broadcasting and cable, there is no single place where buyer and seller are physically present. In this circumstance the marketplace notion refers to general economic forces, like supply, demand, competition, and price, that shape the broadcasting and cable industries.

The attitude of the FCC toward the marketplace varies with different administrations and with different commissioners. Over the years, however, the general trend has been for the FCC to rely more on the marketplace as an important determinant of the public interest. The philosophy underlying this position views the electromagnetic spectrum as an economic asset that is utilized best when the government steps back and lets the laws of economics take over. In short, it is hoped that the marketplace will encourage those services that the public wants.

The marketplace has its advantages. It can promote efficiency, encourage the creation of new services, and encourage diversity. On the downside, the marketplace is only responsive to economic forces and is not sensitive to social needs. Moreover, the real marketplace seldom approaches the ideal model posited by economic textbooks. Once they enter the market, for example, big companies exert far more clout than smaller companies.

At the midpoint of the decade, both Congress and the FCC were taking a close look at the marketplace approach. In some areas the marketplace notion was abandoned in favor of regulation. For example, in an effort to speed up the transition to digital television, Congress passed legislation in 2006 that set February 17, 2009, as the final date when television broadcasting must switch from analog to digital transmission. In other areas, such as the competition between phone companies and cable operators, the impetus seems to be in the other direction. In any case, it seems likely that the marketplace will continue to be an important factor in broadcasting and cable in the years to come.

Now that the general forces that influence broadcasting and cable regulation have been introduced, the remainder of this chapter focuses on more-specific regulatory issues: (1) the FCC's regulatory responsibilities; (2) political broadcasting; (3) other federal laws that apply to the area; (4) laws affecting electronic journalism; and (5) advertising regulations. A note of caution: This is a turbulent area; by the time you read this section, things may have changed. Like industry professionals, students, publishers, and textbook authors face the task of keeping up with this dynamic area. Check the book's Web site for recent developments.

THE ROLE OF THE FCC

Licensing is the primary function of the FCC and the most important method of regulation. The FCC grants new licenses and renews existing ones. Let's first examine how the FCC makes decisions about granting a license. Note that the FCC grants licenses only to stations; it does not license networks. Each of the networks, however, owns local stations that must have their licenses renewed.

License Granting

Applying for a license to operate a new station is a fairly complicated process. (In fact, since there are so few radio and TV frequencies available that would not cause interference problems with existing stations, most persons who get into broadcasting do so by purchasing an existing facility. Many rules mentioned below would also apply to this situation.) After finding a suitable radio frequency or TV channel, all applicants must meet some minimum qualifications.

Personal Qualifications   First, the applicant must be a U.S. citizen or an organization that is free from significant foreign control. Next, the applicant must meet certain character qualifications, but the law is vague on what exactly constitutes a "good" or "bad" character. In practice, the FCC usually looks at things that are directly relevant to the potential future conduct of a potential broadcaster, although recent developments suggest that the commission has begun to look more closely at general character qualifications as well. In 1990 the FCC required broadcasters to report all convictions for felonies, all convictions for serious misdemeanors, any adverse civil judgments involving antitrust or anticompetitive activity, and any cases of misrepresentation to government agencies. Such activity, said the commission, could jeopardize the broadcaster's ability to hold or acquire a license.

Financial and Technical Considerations   The new applicant must assert the financial capability to build and operate a new station. In addition, as might be expected, all applicants must demonstrate that they can meet all of the technical requirements set forth in commission rules concerning equipment operation. The applicant must also propose an affirmative action employment plan to assure the hiring of minority group members and women.

Diversity of Ownership

Throughout its history of granting licenses, the FCC has generally endorsed the philosophy that diversity of ownership was a desirable social goal. Recently, however, under pressure from the courts and Congress, the commission has relaxed many of its rules limiting ownership.

As mentioned above, the 1996 Telecommunications Act permitted one organization to own an unlimited number of radio stations nationwide and as many as eight radio stations in a single market. In 1999, the FCC loosened its rules to permit under certain conditions one company to own two TV stations in the same market (a duopoly). Further, the

Telecommunications Act provided that any organization could own an unlimited number of TV stations provided that the total audience reach of the station does not exceed 35 percent of U.S. TV households. After much controversy, Congress raised the cap to 39 percent in 2004.

License Renewal

In addition to approving applications for new stations' licenses and requests for transfer of ownership to a new license, the FCC must approve license renewals.

Each radio and TV station must apply for a license renewal every 8 years. When a license comes up for renewal, the FCC must determine whether the station has operated in the public interest. In past years, the FCC required stations to submit sizable amounts of information along with their renewal applications. The current renewal application for most stations is only a few pages long (some supporting documentation, however, is also required). Cable TV

The Web site of the FCC contains current news releases, facts about the commissioners, and consumer information, as well as reports on numerous other topics.

systems are not licensed by the FCC. Instead, this is the responsibility of the local governments that grant the franchise.

Renewal Forms   What does the FCC look for in a license renewal? The renewal form gives a pretty good idea. The form makes sure that the station's most recent Ownership Report, which lists owners and shareholders, is on file with the commission. The form also makes sure the licensee is an American citizen, checks for the extent of foreign control, and asks if the station has maintained for public inspection a file that contains those documents required by commission rules. Commercial TV stations must also report their programs that address the educational needs of children.

Competing Applications

What happens when there is more than one applicant for a license? This situation commonly occurs when a license for an existing station is contested by one or more competitors. On the one hand, giving preference to the current license holder might close out newcomers who could do a better job. On the other hand, ignoring past performance could be unfair to a station that had served the public well and ought not be replaced by an untested newcomer. After wrestling with this question for many years, the FCC settled on a method called **renewal expectancy.** If an incumbent station had provided substantially sound and favorable past service, it would be difficult for a challenger to be granted the license over the established station. The Telecommunications Act strengthened this philosophy so that currently a station can expect to have its license renewed unless it has committed some serious violation.

License Denials   What must a station do to have its request for license renewal denied? One big reason for denial is lying to the FCC. If a licensee knowingly gives false information to the commission (such as concealing the actual owners of the station), the license is in jeopardy. Unauthorized transfer of control is another serious offense. Programming violations alone, such as violating the indecency rules, have rarely led to nonrenewal. Moreover, the FCC is unlikely to deny a license renewal on its own initiative. Cases that are not routinely passed (perhaps 2 to 3 percent of the total) are brought to the commission's attention by private citizens who file a petition to

deny. Of these, only a tiny fraction of licenses (less than 1 percent of the total) are not approved at renewal time. Nonetheless, the threat of nonrenewal is perceived as real by many broadcasters and is a potent weapon in the FCC's enforcement arsenal.

Enforcement   The FCC has several different methods it can use to enforce its decisions, ranging from a slap on the wrist to a virtual death sentence. At the mildest level, the FCC can issue a letter of reprimand that scolds a station for some practice that is not in the public interest. Usually, unless the station persists in provoking the FCC, that ends the matter. Other legal remedies include a cease-and-desist order (which makes a station halt a certain practice) or a fine (called a forfeiture). For example, in 2006 the FCC levied a $32,500 fine against each of 103 CBS-affiliated stations that aired an episode of *Without a Trace* that the FCC declared indecent.

The FCC, in effect, can put a station on probation by failing to renew a license for its full term. This is called short-term renewal and usually ranges from 6 months to 2 years. The idea behind short-term renewal is to give the commission a chance to take an early look at a station to determine if past deficiencies have been corrected. Infractions likely to bring short-term licenses involve deceptive promotions, lack of supervision of station facilities, and violation of equal employment practices.

The FCC can sound a death knell for stations by refusing to renew a license or revoking one currently in force. Although this action is used sparingly, it does occur. Since 1990 the FCC has denied the renewals of TV stations in Chicago and San Francisco and a radio station in Ohio for misrepresentation.

Policymaking   Another regulatory tool is policymaking. Under the public interest guidelines, the FCC can enact rules governing some aspect of broadcasting and/or cable. To enact a rule, the commission must announce a proposal and allow for public comments. Moreover, the FCC can't put most new rules and regulations into effect until it publishes a summary, usually in a publication called the *Federal Register.*

Another component of the policy process involves planning for the future. The FCC maintains an Office of Strategic Planning and Policy Analysis, which analyzes trends and attempts to anticipate future policy problems. A recent paper, for example, examined how the FCC could create a deregulated environment in which the Internet could flourish.

The FCC, Cable TV, Satellite TV, and the Internet

The FCC does not license cable TV systems. Instead, state and local governments grant franchises. The length of the franchise period is also set at the local level, usually at some period between 10 and 15 years. When a franchise comes up for renewal, the local franchising authority examines the cable system's performance. Unless the cable system has failed to live up to the franchise terms or has provided unacceptable service, there is a strong presumption that the franchise will be renewed.

The local franchise authority has the power to regulate the rates charged for basic cable service, the lowest level of service that a subscriber can buy. Aside from that, cable systems set their own rates for other tiers of service. Pay-per-view rates and rates charged per channel or per program service (such as HBO) are not regulated by the FCC or by the local franchise authority.

Although the FCC does not license cable systems, it is responsible for enforcing a number of laws and regulations. For example, the Cable Television Consumer Protection and Competition Act of 1992 required that cable systems must carry the signals of broadcast stations that served the cable system's market. The commission would also examine complaints about violations of the Equal Employment Opportunities regulations. In addition, cable operators are required to keep certain documents in a file that is open to the public.

The Communications Satellite Act of 1962 gave the FCC the power to regulate technical issues concerning satellite TV. More recently, the 1999 **Satellite Home Viewer Improvement Act (SHVI)** permitted satellite carriers, such as EchoStar or the Dish Network, to transmit local broadcast TV signals into local markets (sometimes referred to as "local into local"). It also allowed satellite services to provide distant stations (stations not in the subscriber's local market). The SHVI mandated that the FCC establish rules for mandatory carriage of broadcast signals and to determine which consumers are eligible to receive distant stations. In general, the law attempts to put satellite carriers on an equal footing with cable companies, thus increasing competition and giving more choices to consumers.

The FCC does not regulate the Internet or Internet service providers (ISPs). The FCC does, however, regulate telephone and cable and thus has an influence on how you connect to the Internet. In 2005, for example, the FCC did away with regulations that treated broadband services provided by telephone companies differently from broadband offered by cable companies.

Equal Opportunities: Section 315

From radio's earliest beginnings Congress recognized that broadcasting had tremendous potential as a political tool. A candidate for political office who was a skilled demagogue might use the medium to sway public opinion. By the time the 1927 Radio Act was written, Congress had already seen how some skilled communicators could use the medium for their own advantage. Consequently, what would eventually be known as **section 315** was incorporated into the 1927 act.

The crux of section 315 in the current act is the following:

> If any licensee shall permit any person who is a legally qualified candidate for any public office to use a broadcasting station, he shall afford equal opportunities to all other such candidates for that office in the use of such broadcasting station.

Sounds simple enough, but, in operation, section 315 can prove complicated. Note that section 315 talks about equal *opportunities* as opposed to equal *time*. If a station provides a candidate with 30 minutes of prime time, it cannot offer an opponent 30 minutes at 3:00 A.M., nor can it offer the second candidate 30 one-minute spots throughout the day. The station would have to provide 30 minutes in prime time. Note further that section 315 does not obligate a station to provide free time to a candidate unless free time was first offered to an opponent.

Also note that the section is not self-triggering. A station is under no obligation to tell opponents that a candidate has used its facilities. The station is required to keep political files, however, and a candidate can easily examine these to see whether any of the other candidates had made use of the station. The opponent must request equal time within a specified time interval. Also keep in mind that section 312 of the Communications Act requires broadcasters to provide reasonable access for candidates for federal office. They can, however, require candidates to pay for this time.

In addition, there are rules governing how much stations can charge candidates for purchased time.

Although the **fairness doctrine** no longer officially exists, from time to time someone in Congress talks about resurrecting it. Consequently, it's helpful to know something about its history and constitutional implications.

In the late 1940s, the fairness doctrine was born when the FCC encouraged broadcasters to comment on controversial issues of public importance, provided they covered all sides of the issues. Broadcasters thought the doctrine was unconstitutional, and a case eventually reached the Supreme Court. In response, the Court relied on the scarcity principle to justify more regulation for broadcasting than for newspapers and ruled that the right of the public to receive information was paramount and took precedence over the rights of the broadcasters. Thus, the fairness doctrine was constitutional.

The controversy didn't end there, however, and broadcasters continued to pressure the FCC to clarify or modify the doctrine. For its part, the FCC was never an enthusiastic supporter of the doctrine, and in 1981 the commission asked Congress to repeal it. Many members of Congress, however, favored the doctrine and refused to act. In 1985, the FCC released a study which concluded that the fairness doctrine was not serving the public interest and once again asked Congress to abolish it. Once again, Congress refused.

Finally, after a federal court ruled that the fairness doctrine was not part of statutory law but was simply a regulation of the FCC, the commission went ahead and abolished the doctrine on its own. Several efforts by Congress during the 1980s and 1990s to write the doctrine into federal law were unsuccessful, and as of this writing the doctrine is still defunct; that is no guarantee, however, that things will stay that way in the future.

When it was in force, the doctrine imposed a duty on broadcasters to identify controversial public issues and present balanced programming to address those issues. Broadcasters were under special obligation to seek out opposing viewpoints. Note that, unlike section 315, the fairness doctrine never said that opposing views were entitled to equal time; the doctrine simply stated that some reasonable amount of time should be devoted to these views.

Broadcasters are prohibited from charging more for political time than they do for other kinds of commercials. The rules also make sure that a station doesn't charge candidate A $1,000 for a spot while charging candidate B $5,000 for an equivalent spot.

Other complications also arise. Who is a legally qualified candidate? According to the commission, there are three criteria:

1. The candidate must have announced publicly an intention to run for office.

2. The candidate must be legally qualified for the office (to run for president, you must be a U.S. citizen and at least 35 years old).

3. The candidate must have taken the steps spelled out by law to qualify for a place on the ballot or have publicly announced a write-in candidacy.

This means that if a highly popular president nearing the end of a first term in office, generally expected to seek reelection, appears on TV and harshly criticizes a likely opponent, section 315 will not be triggered because, technically speaking, the president has not announced publicly for the office. Similarly, suppose the 30-year-old leader of the Vegetarian party announced plans to run for the presidency. The law would not apply since a 30-year-old is not legally qualified for the office.

Section 315 applies only among those candidates actually opposing each other at that moment. This means that it works differently during a primary than it works during a general election. During a primary, an appearance by a candidate for the Democratic nomination to an office would not create equal opportunity rights among those running for the Republican nomination. Once the primaries are over, however, an appearance by the Democratic nominee would mean the Republican nominee would probably be entitled to an equal opportunity to appear.

Section 315 raises a question regarding the definition of "use" of a broadcasting facility. Broadly speaking, a use occurs when the candidate's voice or picture is included in a program or commercial spot. A program or commercial about a candidate in which the candidate does not appear would not qualify. Most of the time, a use is fairly easy to recognize. Sometimes, however, it's trickier. What happens if the candidate appears in a role that is totally different from that of candidate? How about the candidate who makes a guest appearance in a skit on *Saturday Night Live*? Or what about a candidate for the U.S. Senate who appears on a wildlife program and discusses his love for fishing? Could his opponents claim equal time under section 315? The commission has ruled that a candidate's appearance is a use even if the candidate is appearing for a completely unrelated purpose and never mentions his or her candidacy. Thus if the host of a children's show on a local station becomes a legally qualified candidate, each time he or she appears on the kiddie show the opposition is entitled to a comparable amount of time for free.

But what about the situation where an incumbent president who has already announced for reelection holds a press conference? Does this mean that all the other candidates are entitled to equal time? A similar situation occurred in 1959 when a minority party candidate for mayor of Chicago requested equal time because the current mayor who was running for reelection was shown in a series of film clips used on the evening news. Congress reacted by amending section 315 and providing these exceptions. Section 315 does *not* apply to the following:

1. Bona fide newscasts.

2. Bona fide news interviews.

3. Bona fide news documentaries in which the appearance of the candidate is incidental to the subject of the documentary.

4. On-the-spot coverage of bona fide news.

Questions can also be raised about exactly how much time an opponent is entitled to. Usually if the candidate appears or the audience hears the candidate's voice in a 30- or 60-second spot, opponents are entitled to 30 or 60 seconds, even if the candidate was on screen for a few seconds only. But, if the candidate was on screen or on mike for only a portion of an interview show, opponents are entitled to an amount of time equal only to that featuring the candidate. For example, if a candidate appears for 15 minutes on an hour-long *Late Show with David Letterman*, opponents are entitled to 15 minutes, not a whole hour.

OTHER FEDERAL LAWS COVERING BROADCASTING AND CABLE

In addition to the provisions of the Communications Act of 1934 and the Telecommunications Act of 1996, broadcasters and cable operators must abide by other relevant statutes that relate to their operations.

This section discusses five topics to which such laws apply: children's TV, copyright, obscenity, equal employment opportunities, and antitrust.

Children's Television

The **Children's Television Act of 1990** imposed an obligation on TV stations to serve the informational and educational needs of children through programming designed especially to serve those needs. The legislation also put a cap on the number of commercial minutes allowed in children's programs (10½ minutes per hour on weekends and 12 minutes per hour on weekdays) and established a multimillion-dollar endowment for the funding of children's educational programs. The FCC also ruled that, starting in 1997, TV stations had to present a minimum of 3 hours per week of educational programs. Failure to provide such programming would result in additional scrutiny by the FCC when the station's license came up for renewal. The commission has taken an active role in enforcing these provisions and many stations have received fines for exceeding the commercial-minute guidelines.

Copyright: Trying to Keep Up

Copyright law protects intellectual property; it allows creative people, such as writers, photographers, and painters, to control the commercial copying and use of intellectual property they create, such as books, films, phonograph records, audio- and videotapes, and sculptures.

In its simplest terms, the current copyright law protects works that are "fixed in any tangible means of expression." This includes CDs and DVDs, dramatic works, motion pictures, TV programs, computer programs, and sculpture. Ideas and news events are not copyrightable (you could, however, copyright your particular written or recorded version of a news story). For a work created during or after 1978, copyright protection lasts for the life of the author plus 70 years. For works created before that date, the period of copyright protection will vary. Frequently the creator of a work transfers the copyright so that in some cases the owner is not necessarily the creator. To be *fully* protected a work must contain notice of the copyright (usually consisting of the letter *C* in a circle, the copyright owner's name, and the date of origination) and must be registered and deposited with the Copyright Office in Washington, D.C. Nonetheless, any fixed form of an idea is now granted some protection from the moment that it is fixed in a tangible form.

Once a work is copyrighted, the owner has the right to authorize works derived from the original (for example, a novelist could authorize a movie script based on the book), to distribute copies of the work, and to display and/or perform the work publicly. Even though a work has been copyrighted, others can borrow limited amounts from the material under the doctrine of *fair use.* Critics, for example, can quote from a work without needing permission.

Let's take a closer look at how copyright laws apply to broadcasting and cable, starting first with performance rights. An author is entitled to a royalty payment when his or her work is performed publicly. When a copyrighted work is broadcast over the air—that is, when a radio station plays a record, *that* constitutes public performance. The broadcasters pay royalties for such performances. The audience for the material pays nothing.

Music Licensing   There are more than 13,000 radio stations and 1,700 TV stations in the United States, and it would obviously be difficult for composers and song writers to negotiate a royalty agreement each time their songs were played on the air. Accordingly, private music licensing organizations were established to grant the appropriate rights and to collect and distribute royalty payments. In this country, performing rights are handled by the **American Society of Composers, Authors and Publishers (ASCAP), Broadcast Music Incorporated (BMI),** and **SESAC.**

The major licensing firms grant what is known as **blanket rights,** whereby media firms pay a single fee to the licensing agency. In return the stations get performance rights to the agency's entire music catalog. These rights do not come cheaply. To illustrate, in 2004 the radio industry agreed to pay ASCAP $1.7 billion over 6 years for performance rights. The licensing agencies distribute this money to composers and publishers.

Copyright and the Internet

The Internet, of course, has raised new and thorny issues with regard to copyright. The most celebrated case involved Napster, a music file-sharing service that allowed subscribers to download free music from the Internet. In 1999, the recording industry

reacted by filing a lawsuit against Napster for copyright infringement. The industry argued that Napster was facilitating the illegal distribution of copyrighted material. Napster argued that it was protected by the fair use provision of the copyright law. The court ruled against Napster and put the service out of business in 2002. (Napster was later resurrected as a pay-for-download service.) Napster's demise did not stop illegal file sharing, as other services, such as Grokster and Kazaa, took its place.

The music industry responded by filing lawsuits against several hundred individuals who had illegally downloaded thousands of songs. Many of those targeted by the recording industry ended up paying large sums of money to settle their suits. These lawsuits appeared to have at least some success in curbing illegal downloading. One 2004 survey noted that illegal file sharing had dropped more than 50 percent among those 18 and older. Other data, however, suggested that the drop was temporary and that file sharers simply moved to other services where they were more difficult to track.

The recording industry then escalated the battle by filing suit against the file-sharing services themselves, such as Grokster, that made the illegal downloading possible. In 2005, the Supreme Court ruled that Grokster induced and encouraged its members to violate copyright law and could be sued for the copyright infringement of its customers. This was good news to the recording industry, which hailed it as the beginning of the end of illegal file sharing. The industry may have celebrated too soon, however, as file sharing continued to flourish in 2006. In fact, in addition to music files, pirated movies and TV programs were also widely traded. It is apparent that illegal file sharing is one problem that will not be easily solved.

Copyright issues also affected Internet radio stations. The 1998 Digital Millennium Copyright Act mandated that record companies and artists have the right to be paid an additional royalty when their music is played on the Internet. Internet radio stations could pay .076 cents per song per listener, or 1.17 cents per listener, or 10.9 percent of their subscriber revenues. As of 2006, these rates were being renegotiated for the next 4 years.

Obscenity, Indecency, and Profanity

Section 1464 of the U.S. Criminal Code states that anybody who utters profane, indecent, or obscene

Issues: The "Napsterization" of TV

When the original Napster music file-sharing program was at its peak during the 1990s, television executives looked on with interest but felt they were not at risk from the new technology because video files of TV shows took unreasonably long times to download over a dial-up connection. Their sanguine feelings were short-lived, however, when broadband connections became popular in American homes and download speeds increased. Nonetheless, the download times for TV programs were still long enough to discourage some people. Then came BitTorrent, a file-sharing program that drastically reduced the time needed to download files. All of a sudden, the TV industry was facing the same illegal downloading problems that vexed the recording industry.

Illegally swapping TV programs hurts the bottom line of the TV industry in a couple of ways. First, people who watch illegally downloaded programs aren't counted in the Nielsen ratings. Second, they don't have to subscribe to HBO or Showtime to get premium programs. Third, they can damage the market for DVD compilations of TV series. Why spend $49 for a season of *Seinfeld* when you can download it for free with BitTorrent?

Like the music industry, the television industry, along with the movie industry, combated file sharing on several levels. They filed copyright infringement suits against people who operate servers that encourage illegal downloading. They also began "spoofing," sending copies of what appear to be legitimate TV shows to BitTorrent sites that contain digital gibberish or directions on how to legally acquire copies of the shows. The television industry is also developing technological weapons. Cable and satellite companies have agreed to include in their set-top boxes software that makes it more difficult to illegally share programs.

Another solution is for the industry to come up with a legal alternative that is convenient and reasonably priced. Several cable and broadcast networks have a deal with Apple's iTunes that lets consumers download episodes of TV shows for $1.99 each.

Despite the potential problems raised by illegal file sharing, the television industry is unlikely to be as seriously affected as the recording industry. Music files can be easily downloaded and transferred to other devices. Downloaded TV programs are less convenient. They have to be viewed on a computer screen, a small iPod screen, or burned to a DVD in order to be watched on a conventional TV screen. Of course, this may change as more technological advances take place. Not surprisingly, TV executives will be paying close attention.

Five Most Pirated TV Shows—2005
1   *The Simpsons*
2   *Family Guy*
3   *Friends*
4   *The O.C.*
5   *American Idol*

Source: *New York Times*, Arts Section, January 30, 2005.

language over radio or TV is liable to fine or imprisonment. Both the FCC and the Department of Justice can prosecute under this section. If found guilty, violators face a fine of up to $10,000, possible loss of license, or even jail. This seems clear enough. A couple of problems, however, quickly surface. First, remember that the FCC is prohibited from censoring broadcast content. Second, how exactly do you define obscenity, indecency, and profanity?

Let's take profanity first. *Profanity* is technically defined as the irreverent or blasphemous use of the name of God. In the past the FCC has been reluctant to punish stations that have accidentally aired the occasional profanity. That position is subject to change, however, depending upon the political philosophy of the current administration and the FCC membership. A 2004 FCC ruling, for example, basically prohibited the use of expletives that might be considered profane or indecent. In 2006, a conservative

The home page of Kazaa, one of the many Napster successors. Despite the efforts of the music industry, more people are downloading music from file-sharing sites like Kazaa than ever before.

FCC let it be known that the airing of objectionable content might bring about stiff fines. Consequently, in the future stations that air profanity might face the ire of the FCC.

Obscenity is another matter. The struggle to come up with a workable definition of obscenity has been long and tortuous and will not be repeated here. The definition that currently applies to broadcasting is the definition spelled out by the Supreme Court in the *Miller v. California* (1973) case. To be obscene, a program, considered as a whole, must (1) contain material that depicts or describes in a patently offensive way certain sexual acts defined in state law; (2) appeal to the prurient interest of the average person applying contemporary local community standards (*prurient* is one of those legal words the courts are fond of using; it means tending to excite lust); and (3) lack serious artistic, literary, political, or scientific value. Obviously, most radio and TV stations would be wary of presenting programs that come anywhere near these criteria for fear of alienating much of their audience. Consequently, the FCC tends not to issue too many decisions based on the obscenity criterion alone.

But what about cable? Some of the movies commonly shown on certain cable channels go much further than what is shown on traditional TV. The 1984 cable act made it a crime to transmit obscenity over cable. Further, state and local franchise agreements can prohibit obscene programming. Even though cable content is far more daring than over-the-air TV, subscribers are unlikely to see the kind of movies that would be defined as legally obscene. In fact, most hard-core or XXX-rated films are released in two versions, one for theatrical or DVD release and a less explicit version for cable. In practice, then, obscenity, as legally defined, is seldom at issue in broadcasting and cable.

This leaves the area of indecent programming—the area in which the FCC has chosen to exercise vigilance. Indecent content refers to content that is not obscene under the *Miller* standards but still contains potentially offensive elements. To be more specific, here's the common legal definition of broadcast indecency:

> Something broadcast is indecent if it depicts or describes sexual or excretory activities or organs in a fashion that's patently offensive according to contemporary community standards for the broadcast media at a time of day when there is a reasonable risk that children may be in the audience.

For example, a program that simply contains nudity is not obscene, although some people might be offended. Further, four-letter words that describe sexual or excretory acts are not, by themselves, obscene. They may, however, be classified as indecent.

The Seven Dirty Words Case George Carlin is probably the only comedian ever to have his act reviewed by the Supreme Court. Here's how it happened. On the afternoon of October 30, 1973, WBAI-FM, New York City, a listener-sponsored station licensed to the Pacifica Foundation, announced that it was about to broadcast a program that would contain sensitive language that some might find offensive. The WBAI DJ then played all 12 minutes of a George Carlin routine entitled "Filthy Words." Recorded live before a theater audience, the routine analyzed the words that "you couldn't say on the public airwaves." Carlin then listed seven such words and used them repeatedly throughout the rest of his monologue.

A man and his teenage son heard the broadcast while driving in their car and complained to the FCC; it was the only complaint the commission received about the monologue. The FCC decreed that the station had violated the rules against airing indecent content and put the station on notice that subsequent complaints about its programming might lead to severe penalties. Pacifica appealed the ruling, and an appeals court sided with WBAI and chastised the FCC for violating section 326 of the Communications Act, which prohibits censorship. Several years later, however, the case made its way to the Supreme Court, and the original FCC decision was reaffirmed. The Court said, among other things, that the commission's actions did not constitute censorship since they had not edited the monologue in advance. Further, the program could be regulated because the monologue was broadcast at a time when children were probably in the audience. Special treatment of broadcasting was justified because of its uniquely pervasive presence and because it is easily accessible to children. Thus the FCC could regulate indecent programming.

In the years following the *Pacifica* decision, many radio broadcasters pushed the limits by developing a new format called "raunch radio" or "shock radio." The FCC warned stations of possible fines for this content and suggested it might be more appropriate if presented after midnight when fewer children were in the audience. Congress got into the act in 1988 when it ordered the FCC to enforce a 24-hour ban on indecency, but this ban was overturned by a

court decision. After several years of political and legal wrangling, the FCC and the courts have agreed to a "safe harbor" provision that protects indecent material if aired between 10 P.M. and 6 A.M.

In 2001 the FCC issued a policy statement that attempted to clarify its policy regarding broadcast indecency. A 2002 decision by the FCC's Enforcement Bureau seemed to suggest that the context surrounding the use of indecent language was an important factor. Despite these efforts, what is or isn't indecent continued to be a vexing problem for broadcasters and the FCC.

The issue gained even more attention thanks to Janet Jackson's famous wardrobe malfunction during the 2004 Super Bowl halftime show. The FCC received more than 1.4 million complaints in the year following Jackson's overexposure and eventually wound up fining CBS more than a half million dollars for airing the event.

In 2006, with the FCC under pressure from conservative groups, FCC chair Kevin Martin served notice that the agency was cracking down on what it perceived to be indecent programming. It fined CBS and its affiliate stations more than $3 million for carrying an episode of *Without a Trace* that the contained scenes of what the FCC called a teenage orgy. An episode of *The Surreal Life 2* was fined $27,500 for showing pixilated scenes (where the actual picture is obscured) of nudity. A PBS station was fined $15,000 for airing a documentary about blues musicians that used what the FCC termed the "f-word" and the "s-word." (This fine illustrated some of the confusion over the indecency standards since the FCC did not fine stations that aired an unedited version of *Saving Private Ryan*, which also contained the f-word, because the commission determined that the word was not indecent because of its context.) Broadcasters announced plans to appeal the fines, arguing that the FCC overstepped its authority and that its regulations concerning indecency were unconstitutional.

Congress joined the campaign against indecency by passing new legislation that significantly increased the FCC's clout when dealing with indecent content. Under the new 2006 law, a broadcaster could be fined up to a maximum of $325,000 for airing indecency, 10 times the previous maximum. Although many big city stations could probably absorb such a fine with only a minor impact on their bottom lines, many stations in smaller communities might be put out of business.

Indecent Content and Cable   Cable channels generally have a much wider latitude with programming that might be considered indecent. In fact, the 1984 cable act did not authorize the regulation of indecent material. The act differentiated between obscene and indecent material and permitted regulation of the former only. In addition, federal and state courts have found that the FCC's *Pacifica* ruling does not apply to cable. (George Carlin was able to perform his "Filthy Words" routine on HBO without incident.) The courts argue that cable is not as pervasive as broadcasting (you have to order it and pay additional fees for it) or as easily accessible to children (subscribers could buy and use lock boxes to limit viewing).

Nonetheless, the mid-decade controversy over indecency spilled over onto the cable and satellite industries. Citizens' groups such as the Parents Television Council argued that for the average viewer, there is little difference between broadcast and cable/satellite channels so that provisions against indecency should affect all content providers. This view found some support among members of Congress, and there was talk of legislation that would hold cable and satellite networks to the same standards as broadcasters. In response, the cable/satellite industry made it clear that any such attempt would trigger a court battle over First Amendment rights.

Additionally, FCC chair Kevin Martin endorsed a new policy that would allow consumers to choose precisely which channels they want to buy. This "à la carte" option would do away with the traditional programming bundles or tiers of channels that were currently offered by cable and satellite providers and would allow subscribers to avoid those cable networks that had the potential to carry indecent programs. Responding to this pressure from Congress and the FCC, some cable companies voluntarily offered "family-friendly" packages that they hoped would ward off more stringent regulations.

Indecency and the Internet   There are probably more than 10,000 sites on the Internet that contain sexually oriented material. The ubiquity of this material and the ease with which it could be accessed by minors prompted Congress to include the Communications Decency Act as part of the Telecommunications Act of 1996. Basically, the law made it a crime to transmit indecent and obscene material over the Net to anybody under 18 years of age.

The constitutionality of this act was immediately called into question, and the case went to the Supreme Court. The Court ruled that the Internet was entitled to the highest degree of First Amendment protection, similar to that afforded books and magazines, and ruled the act unconstitutional. Congress responded with the 1998 Child Online Protection Act, which required commercial Web sites to secure a credit card number or other proof of age before allowing Internet users to view sites with adult content. The law would impose a $50,000 fine and a jail term on operators of Web sites that publish content harmful to children. Portions of this law were immediately appealed and the appeals set off an 8-year legal battle. The Supreme Court twice has issued injunctions against enforcing the act until all the legal issues are resolved. As this book went to press, the case was still unresolved.

In 2000, Congress passed the Children's Internet Protection Act, requiring public libraries to install filters on their computers to block access to adult sites. A federal court ruled against this law, but the Supreme Court ruled in 2003 that the act was constitutional and that filters could be installed in those libraries that accept federal funding. As is obvious, Congress has yet to find a way to protect children from Internet obscenity that also protects the free speech rights of adults.

Equal Employment Opportunities

Broadcasters and cablecasters are bound by federal law prohibiting job discrimination based on race, color, sex, religion, or national origin. Further, they must adhere to regulations set down by the Equal Employment Opportunity Commission. Although not directly responsible for enforcing all equal employment opportunity (EEO) provisions, the FCC has made it clear that it will assert jurisdiction over this area in broadcasting and cable.

THE LAW AND BROADCAST JOURNALISM

There are several areas of law that are most relevant to the news-gathering and reporting duties of broadcast and cable channels. Some of these laws cover topics that are common to both print and electronic journalists (such as libel and invasion of privacy). Other laws are more relevant to video reporters (such as the restrictions on cameras in the courtroom).

Further, many of these laws vary from state to state, but some have raised constitutional issues that have been addressed by the Supreme Court.

This section covers four areas that are highly relevant to the broadcast press: (1) defamation, (2) privacy, (3) protection of confidential sources, and (4) use of cameras and microphones in the courtroom.

Defamation

The law regarding **defamation** is concerned with the protection of a person's reputation. A defamatory statement injures the good name of an individual (or organization) and lowers his or her standing in the community. The law of defamation makes sure that the press does not act in an irresponsible and malicious manner. As we shall see, erroneous stories that damage the reputations of others can bring serious consequences.

There are two kinds of defamation: libel and slander. **Slander** comes from spoken words; in other words, slander is oral defamation. **Libel** is defamation stated in a tangible medium, such as a printed story or a photograph, or in some other form that has a capacity to endure. Since libel exists in a medium that can be widely circulated, the courts treat it more seriously than slander, which evaporates after it is uttered. Broadcast defamation is usually regarded as libel rather than slander.

Broadcast journalists have become particularly wary of suits alleging libel because they can carry sizable cash awards to the victims if the media are found at fault.

Elements of Libel   If someone brings a libel suit, he or she must prove five different things to win. First, the statement(s) in question must have actually defamed the person and caused some harm. The material must have diminished the person's good name or reputation or held the person up to ridicule, hatred, or contempt. Harm can be such things as lost wages or physical discomfort or impairment in doing one's job. A prime example of a defamatory statement would be falsely reporting that a person has been convicted of a crime. The second element is publication. This usually presents no ambiguities; if a story was broadcast, then it fulfills the publication criterion. The third element is identification. A person must prove that he or she was identified in a story. Identification does not necessarily have to be by name. A nickname, a cartoon, a description, or anything else that pinpoints someone's identity would suffice.

The fourth element is fault or error. To win a libel suit, a party must show some degree of fault or carelessness on the part of the media organization. The degree of fault that must be established depends on who's suing, what they are suing about, and which state's laws are being applied. As we shall see, certain individuals have to prove greater degrees of fault than others. Finally, in most instances the individual has to prove the falsity of what was published or broadcast.

Defenses against Libel   When a libel suit is filed against a broadcast reporter and/or station, several defenses are available. The first of these is truth. If the reporter can prove that what was broadcast was true, then there is no libel. This sounds a lot easier than it is since the burden of proving truth, which can be an expensive and time-consuming process, falls on the reporter. Moreover, when the alleged libel is vague and doesn't deal with specific events, proving truth may be difficult. Finally, recent court decisions suggest that in many circumstances people who bring libel suits against the media must bear the burden of proving the defamatory statement false. All of these factors diminish the appeal of truth as a defense.

Note that libel suits concern defamatory statements of fact only. There is no such thing as libelous *opinion,* since no one can prove that an opinion is true or false. In 1990, however, the Supreme Court ruled that expressions of opinion can be held libelous if they imply an assertion of fact that can be proven false. Labeling a statement as an opinion does not necessarily make it immune from a libel suit.

A second defense is privilege. Used in its legal sense, privilege means immunity. There are certain situations in which the courts have held that the public's right to know is more important than a person's reputation. Courtroom proceedings, legislative debates, and public city council sessions are examples of areas that are generally conceded to be privileged. If a broadcast reporter gives a fair and accurate report of these events, the reporter will be immune to a libel suit even if what was reported contained a defamatory remark. Keep in mind, however, that accurately quoting someone else's libelous remarks outside an official public meeting or official public record is not a surefire defense against libel.

The third defense is fair comment and criticism. People who thrust themselves into the public arena are fair game for criticism. The performance of public officials, pro sports figures, artists, singers, columnists, and others who invite public scrutiny is open to the fair comment defense. This defense, however, applies to opinion and criticism; it does not entitle the press to report factual matters erroneously. A movie critic, for example, could probably say that a certain actor's performance was amateurish and wooden without fearing a libel suit. If, however, the critic went on and falsely reported that the bad acting was the result of drug addiction, that would be a different story.

In 1964, in the pivotal *New York Times v. Sullivan* case, the Supreme Court greatly expanded the opportunity for comment on the actions of public officials. The Court ruled that public officials must prove that false and defamatory statements were made with "actual malice" before a libel suit could be won. The Court went on to state that actual malice meant publishing or broadcasting something with the knowledge that it was false or with "reckless disregard" of whether it was false. In later years the Court ruled that public figures also must prove actual malice to win a libel suit.

In effect, two different degrees of fault are used as standards in libel cases. In many states a private citizen must simply prove that the media acted with negligence. For some states negligence means that accepted professional standards were not followed. Other states take negligence to mean that a reporter did not exercise reasonable care in determining whether a story was true or false. A few states define negligence in relation to whether the reporter had reason to believe that material that was published or broadcast was true. Public figures and public officials are held to a higher standard; they must also prove actual malice. (Note that the really big financial awards in libel cases come from what are called "punitive damages"—awards levied by juries to punish the offending media outlet. To win punitive damages, even a private citizen must prove actual malice.)

Invasion of Privacy

The right to privacy is a relatively new area of media law. Stated simply, it means that the individual has a right to be left alone—not to be subjected to intrusions or unwarranted publicity. The right to privacy is not specifically found in the Constitution,

although many have argued that the right is implied in several amendments. Like defamation, laws concerning privacy differ from state to state.

Not surprisingly, invasion of privacy is a complicated topic. In fact, legal experts suggest that it actually covers four different areas. The right of privacy protects against (1) unwarranted publication of private facts, (2) intrusion upon a person's solitude or seclusion, (3) publicity that creates a false impression about a person (called "false light"), and (4) unauthorized commercial exploitation of a person's name or likeness.

Private Facts   Disclosure of private facts occurs when a broadcast station or cable channel reports personal information that the individual did not want to make public. Disclosure resembles libel in that the individual must be identifiable and the facts must cause the individual humiliation or shame. Unlike libel, however, the facts revealed are true and may not necessarily damage a person's reputation. For example, suppose that a TV station shot footage of you in a hospital bed after cosmetic surgery when your face was swollen, black and blue, and generally ugly-looking. The station then ran the tape without your consent on the six-o'clock news with your name prominently mentioned as part of a series it was doing on the hospital. It's possible you might have a case for invasion of privacy. To qualify as the basis for a suit, private facts must be highly offensive to a person of "reasonable sensibilities."

When faced with an invasion-of-privacy suit, the media have several defenses. The reporter might argue that consent was obtained before the information was released. Information obtained from a public record is generally immune to invasion-of-privacy actions. Last, the reporter could argue that the information was released in connection with a newsworthy event.

Intrusion and Trespass   **Intrusion** is an invasion of a person's solitude or seclusion without consent. The intrusion may or may not include **trespass,** which is defined as physical presence on private property without the consent or approval of the property's owner. Thus using a telephoto lens to secretly take pictures through a person's bedroom window could constitute intrusion. Secretly sneaking through the yard to take pictures through the bedroom window with a regular lens would probably constitute trespass and intrusion. Problems with intrusion and trespass generally crop up in the news-gathering stage. In fact, a reporter can be sued for trespass or intrusion even if he or she never broadcasts the information that was gathered.

Whether some news-gathering technique violates a person's right of privacy depends on how much privacy a person should normally expect in the particular situation involved. For example, people in their living rooms have a right to expect that they will not be secretly photographed or have their words recorded. People walking down a public street have less expectation of privacy.

Broadcast journalists can generally avoid charges of trespass by securing the consent of the owner of private property before entering it. In some limited instances during fires and natural disasters police or fire officials might control property and can grant consent to reporters to enter. Reporters, however, do not have the right to follow an unruly crowd onto private property without the consent of the owner or the police. In addition, TV reporters might be guilty of trespass if they enter, with cameras rolling, private property that is open to the public—like a place of business.

The concept of trespass assumed greater importance in a 1996 case involving the Food Lion grocery store chain and the ABC newsmagazine *Prime Time Live* over a report that Food Lion was violating health standards. Rather than sue for defamation, Food Lion charged that ABC had committed trespass when it gained access to nonpublic areas of a grocery store under false pretenses and taped employees with a concealed camera. The jury agreed with Food Lion and brought back a $5.5 million judgment against the network for committing fraud and trespass. A judge later reduced the amount for the fraud offense to $315,000. The jury awarded Food Lion only $1 for the trespass offense. In 1999, a U.S. Court of Appeals threw out the $315,000 fraud award. Even though the trespass verdict did not amount to much, it set a precedent and made investigative reporters reexamine some of their journalistic techniques.

False Light   A reporter can cast a person in a **false light** in several ways: omitting pertinent facts, distorting certain information, falsely implying that a person is other than what he or she is, or using a photograph out of context. A suit that alleges invasion of privacy through false light is similar to one brought for defamation (in fact, the two are often brought at the same time). A person can't be put in false light by the truth. Thus, like libel, there must be a false assertion of fact. In addition, the misin-

formation must be publicized. Finally, to win a false light suit, some people might have to prove actual malice on the part of the media. Unlike libel, in false light suits the false assertion is not defamatory. In fact, suits alleging false light have been brought over the publicizing of incorrect information that was flattering to the person. People who bring false light suits seek compensation not for harm to their reputation—how others feel about them—but for the shame, humiliation, and suffering they *feel* because of the false portrayal.

Commercial Exploitation   This area tends to be more of a problem area for advertisers, promoters, agents, and public relations practitioners. Basically, it prohibits the unauthorized use of a person's name or likeness in some commercial venture. Thus it would be an invasion of privacy if you walked into a supermarket and found that a pickle manufacturer had, without your permission, put your face on a whole shelf of pickle jars. The best way for broadcasters to avoid privacy invasion suits based on unauthorized exploitation is to obtain written consent from subjects.

Well-known individuals, of course, can have more of a stake in these matters. In fact, over the last several years an offshoot of the commercial appropriation area known as the "right of publicity" has been articulated by the courts. In contrast with the traditional privacy area, which is based on the right to be left alone, the right of publicity is concerned with who gets the financial rewards when the notoriety surrounding a famous person is used for commercial purposes. In this regard, the right of publicity resembles a property right rather than a personal right and bears a little resemblance to copyright. In essence, the courts have ruled that famous people are protected against the unlawful appropriation of their fame. For example, model Christy Brinkley was successful in her suit against stores that were selling posters of her without her permission.

Protecting Sources

Since 1950 a conflict has developed between courts and reporters over the protection of news sources, notes, and news footage. Some background will be useful before we discuss the specifics.

There are two basic types of litigation. In a criminal trial the government seeks to punish someone for illegal behavior. Murder, rape, and robbery are examples of proceedings that would be covered by criminal law. Civil law involves a dispute between two individuals for harm that one has allegedly caused the other. Breach of contract, claims of overbilling, disputes between neighbors over property rights, defamation, and invasion of privacy are examples of civil suits. In a criminal or civil trial it is necessary for the court to have at its disposal any and all evidence that bears directly on the outcome of the trial in order to assure a fair decision.

Courts have the power to issue subpoenas, official orders summoning witnesses to appear and testify, to make sure all who have information come forth and present what they know. There are only a few exceptions to this principle, called *privileges*. No person is forced to testify against himself or herself. Husband–wife communication is also considered privileged. Other common areas of privilege are lawyer–client communication and doctor–patient conversations. For many years journalists have argued that their relationship with a news source qualifies as the same type of privilege. They argue that without a promise of confidentiality, many sources would be reluctant to come forward and the news-gathering process would be severely hindered. In fact, many journalists have been fined and sent to jail for failure to disclose the names of sources or for failing to turn over to the court notes, photos, and videotapes.

Before the 1970s the courts were reluctant to grant any privileges to journalists. Since then, however, journalists are in a better position thanks to several court decisions and the passage of state "shield laws," which offer limited protection for journalists. The landmark decision was handed down by the Supreme Court in 1972 in *Branzburg v. Hayes*. Originally regarded as a defeat for the principle of journalistic privilege, the decision actually spelled out guidelines that covered when a reporter might legally refuse to testify. To make a reporter reveal confidential sources and information, the government must pass a three-part test. The three-part test listed below is often used in civil proceedings but seldom used in criminal trials. The government must prove the following:

1. That the journalist has information that bears directly on the case.

2. That the evidence cannot be obtained from any other sources.

3. That the evidence is crucial in the determination of the case.

The government's success in passing this test varies with the legal context. Reporters are most likely to be required to testify before grand juries, particularly if the reporter witnessed criminal activity; they are least likely to be compelled to testify when the defense in a civil trial is trying to obtain information. Civil libel actions where the medium is the defendant create special problems. Some states don't permit the protection of a shield law if it would frustrate a plaintiff's effort to show actual malice.

Thirty-one states have granted limited protection to journalists by enacting shield laws. These laws, of course, vary from state to state. In some states, protection is given to a journalist who refuses to reveal a source, but protection does not extend to notes, tape, and other media used in the news-gathering process. Moreover, some states have strict definitions as to who exactly is a journalist and is covered by the shield law. Several states require the journalist to prove that a source was actually promised confidentiality. Some states require that the information be published before the shield law is triggered. Other state laws list exceptions where the protection is not granted.

Cameras in the Courtroom

The controversy over cameras in the courtroom highlights an area where two basic rights come into conflict: the right of a defendant to a fair trial and the right of a free press to report the news.

The controversy began in 1932 during the trial of the man accused of kidnapping and murdering the infant son of national hero Charles Lindbergh. Newspaper, radio, and newsreel reporters helped turn the trial into a media circus, and a special committee of the American Bar Association (ABA) was created after the trial to draw up media guidelines. This group recommended that a canon (labeled **Canon 35**) be added to the code of conduct of the ABA which would prohibit the broadcasting and taking of photographs of a trial. Many states enacted Canon 35 into law.

In 1962, the Supreme Court affirmed the ban on cameras and microphones in the courtroom, but several justices noted that future technological advances in TV and radio might make broadcasting a trial less disruptive and suggested that it would one day be permissible. This prediction came true in 1981 when the Court ruled that televising a trial was not inherently prejudicial and left it up to the states to come up with systems to implement trial coverage.

Since that time, the trend has been toward more access. As of 2006, all 50 states allowed some form of coverage. In most states, the consent of the presiding judge is required and the judge controls the coverage. Currently, a cable network, Court TV, specializes in televising trials. Cameras are still not allowed in federal district courts; Supreme Court proceedings are not televised either.

REGULATING ADVERTISING

Advertising is a big business: about $80 billion was spent on broadcasting and cable advertising in 2004. Since advertising is such an influential industry, the government has enacted laws and regulations that deal with advertising messages.

Recent decisions by the Supreme Court have established that advertising does deserve some protection under the First Amendment. The Court, however, was unwilling to grant advertising the degree of protection that it gave to other forms of speech. Advertising that is accurate and truthful can be regulated by the state provided the state's regulation passes a three-part test: The regulation must serve a substantial government goal, advance the interests of the state, and be narrowly drawn.

The above paragraph refers to ads that are accurate and truthful. But what about false and deceptive advertising? How is that controlled? The agency most visible in this area is the **Federal Trade Commission (FTC).**

Congress set up the FTC in 1914 to regulate unfair business practices. In 1938 its power was broadened to include jurisdiction over deceptive advertising. Nonetheless, as far as advertising was concerned, the FTC remained an obscure institution until the consumer movement of the 1960s and 1970s when it became highly active in regulating questionable ads. (It even ordered some companies to run "corrective" ads to counteract any misunderstanding caused by their original ads.) After the move toward deregulation in the 1980s, the FTC assumed a much lower profile.

Like the FCC, the FTC is an independent regulatory agency with five commissioners appointed by the president for renewable 7-year terms. The FTC's Bureau of Consumer Protection handles advertising complaints. The FTC is charged with regulating false, misleading, and/or deceptive advertising and may investigate questionable cases on its own or respond to the complaints of competitors or the gen-

eral public. The FTC may hold formal hearings concerning a complaint and issue a decision. Again, like the FCC, the FTC's decision can be appealed through the federal courts.

The FTC guards mainly against deceptive advertising, and over the years the commission has developed a set of guidelines that define *deception.* Taken as a whole, the ad must have deceived a reasonable person. Any kind of falsehood constitutes deception. For example, a broadcast ad promising buyers a genuine diamond is deceptive if, in fact, what the consumer receives is a zirconium. Even a statement that is literally true might be judged deceptive. Wonder Bread ads claimed that the bread was fortified with vitamins and minerals that are necessary for healthy growth. Although literally true, the ad was ruled deceptive because it did not point out that every fortified bread contained the same vitamins and minerals.

The FTC, however, does recognize that there is room for reasonable exaggeration in advertising. Consequently, the commission permits "puffery" in subjective statements of opinion that the average consumer will probably not take seriously. Thus it would probably be OK for a restaurant to claim that it serves "the world's best coffee" or for a repair shop to advertise the "friendliest service in town." Puffery crosses over into deception when exaggerated claims turn into factual assertions of superiority.

The FTC has several enforcement means at its disposal. At the mildest level, the FTC can simply express its opinion about the questionable content of an ad, as it did in 1988 when it notified aspirin manufacturers that they should not promote aspirin as a preventive for heart attacks. Further, it can require that certain statements be carried in the ads to make the ads more accurate. For example, when some Listerine ads claimed the product killed germs that caused sore throats that came with a cold or fever, the FTC ordered the makers of Listerine to include a statement in their ads to the effect that Listerine was not a *cure* for sore throats associated with colds or fever. An appeals court upheld the right of the FTC to order advertisers to engage in such corrective campaigns even though the advertiser objected.

The FTC also can notify an advertiser that its ads are deceptive and ask that the advertiser sign a **consent decree.** By agreeing to a consent decree, the advertiser removes the advertising in question but does not admit that the ad was in fact deceptive. More than 90 percent of all FTC cases are settled by consent decrees. A stronger weapon is a **cease-and-desist order.** In this

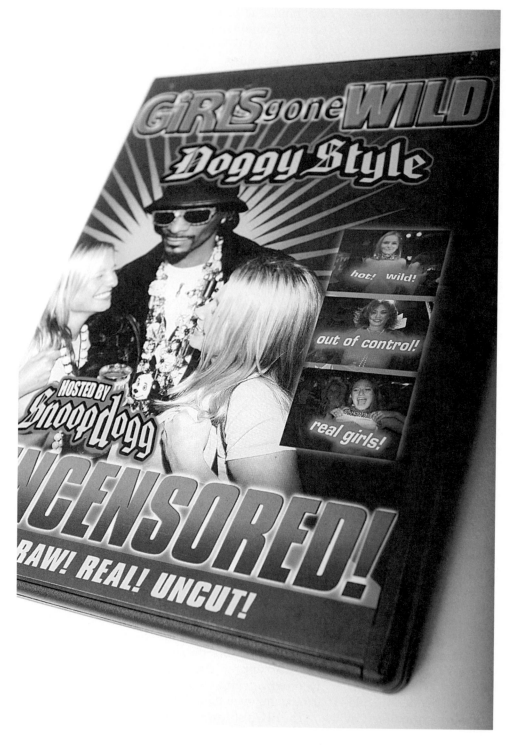

The company selling the *Girls Gone Wild* series of DVDs agreed to pay a $1.1 million fine to settle an FTC lawsuit that charged it with deceptive billing and shipping practices.

The shift from analog to digital video transmission has opened up several new regulatory issues. One of the most contentious may concern the FCC's new regulations for children's television. An existing FCC regulation from the 1990 Children's Television Act requires that stations present 3 hours of educational and informational programming directed at children each week. The new rule requires broadcasters who multicast programs on their digital channels to provide additional children's programming in proportion to the overall total of new programming that they carry. The broadcasters argued that the new channels might be used for such services as 24-hour news or weather channels, where children's programming seems out of place.

Another existing regulation sets a limit to the number of commercial minutes on children's shows on broadcast and cable channels. The new regulation would make broadcasters and cablecasters count most promotional announcements, including those for Web site addresses, toward the commercial limit. Moreover, another rule would prohibit networks from displaying the Web site addresses where characters from the TV show are used to sell products. These latter provisions have especially disturbed the industry since the networks are eager to attract children to their various Web sites, where FCC rules don't apply and where the networks expect to make an increasing amount of advertising revenue. Opposition to the new rules was immediate as the networks argued that the regulations were violations of their First Amendment rights. On the other hand, children's advocacy groups, such as Children Now, argued that the regulations didn't go far enough.

In early 2006, the broadcast and cable industry and the advocacy groups reached a compromise deal. The networks agreed to the provision for additional children's programs in their new digital channels and to restrict the use of characters, such as Sponge Bob, to sell products to kids on Web sites whose addresses are shown on-screen during a program. In return, the nets would not be required to count promotional announcements as commercial time. As this book went to press, the FCC was seeking comments on the proposed agreement before it makes a decision.

situation, the FTC issues a formal complaint against an ad and a formal hearing is scheduled. If after the hearing it is ruled that the ad was deceptive, a judge issues a cease-and-desist order and the company must stop airing the offending ad. Failure to do so results in a fine. In rare cases, when an ad might have injurious effects on the public, the FTC can seek an injunction to stop the offending ad quickly.

In practical terms, broadcasters and cable system operators should be encouraged to know that very few of the ads aired in any given year are likely to raise legal questions. In addition, since the advertising industry conducts most of its business in public, it is concerned with the harmful effects that might follow the publication or broadcast of any false or misleading ad. Consequently, the advertising profession has developed an elaborate system of self-regulation (see next chapter) that prevents most deceptive ads from being released. Networks also have departments that screen ads before they are accepted. Nonetheless, an occasional problem ad might crop up, which makes a knowledge of FTC rules and regulations helpful.

Ads for prescription drugs have become common on TV. Thirty-second spots for Prilosec, Lipitor, and other prescription drugs accounted for more than $2.5 billion in advertising revenue in 2004. The **Food and Drug Administration (FDA)** is responsible for regulating these ads. In fact, it was a change in the FDA's advertising policy that opened the door for TV prescription drug advertising. For many years pharmaceutical companies were permitted to advertise only to physicians and not to the general public. The FDA changed that rule in 1997 and allowed direct-to-consumer advertising. Current regulations require that drug ads contain information about the drug's safety and side effects.

SUMMARY

- Broadcasting and cable regulation is based on two rationales: the scarcity theory and the pervasive presence theory. The regulation of the electronic media is influenced by the FCC, Congress, the courts, the White House, industry lobbyists, the public, state and local governments, and the operation of the marketplace.
- The Communications Act of 1934 and the Telecommunications Act of 1996 provide the groundwork for

the regulation of the electronic media. The FCC implements these acts by assigning and renewing licenses. Although it does not license cable systems, the FCC does have some regulatory power over the industry. Section 315 of the Communications Act provides equal opportunities for political candidates on television stations.

• Copyright laws are important in broadcasting and cable. Music licensing is the method by which performers and composers are paid for the use of their work by broadcasters and cable operators. VCR owners can tape a program off the air for their personal use without violating copyright laws. The Internet has raised new issues about copyright protection.

• Federal laws pertaining to obscenity apply to broadcasting and cable. In addition, the FCC has drafted special provisions that deal with indecent content on radio and TV.

• Cablecasters and broadcasters are bound by the regulations set down by the Equal Employment Opportunity Commission.

• Several legal areas touch upon the practice of broadcast journalism: defamation, invasion of privacy, protecting sources, and using cameras and microphones in the courtroom.

• Advertising qualifies for protection as free speech under the First Amendment. The FTC is the main agency that regulates false and deceptive advertising. Drug advertising is regulated by the FDA.

KEY TERMS

scarcity theory   226
pervasive presence theory   226
Radio Act of 1927   227
Federal Radio Commission
  (FRC)   227
Communications Act
  of 1934   227
Federal Communications
  Commission (FCC)   227
Communications Satellite Act   227
Cable Communications Policy Act
  of 1984   228
Telecommunications Act
  of 1996   228
V-chip   228

National Telecommunications and
  Information Administration
  (NTIA)   231
renewal expectancy   236
Satellite Home Viewer
  Improvement Act (SHVI)   237
section 315   237
fairness doctrine   238
Children's Television Act
  of 1990   239
American Society of Composers,
  Authors and Publishers
  (ASCAP)   240
Broadcast Music Incorporated
  (BMI)   240

SESAC   240
blanket rights   240
defamation   245
slander   245
libel   245
intrusion   246
trespass   246
false light   247
Canon 35   248
Federal Trade Commission
  (FTC)   249
consent decree   249
cease-and-desist order   249
Food and Drug Administration
  (FDA)   251

SUGGESTIONS FOR FURTHER READING

Carter, T. B.; Franklin, M. A.; & Wright, J. B. (1997). *The First Amendment and the Fourth Estate.* Westbury, NY: Foundation Press.

———. (1996). *The First Amendment and the Fifth Estate.* Westbury, NY: Foundation Press.

Creech, K. (2003). *Electronic media law and regulation.* Boston: Focal Press.

Krasnow, E.; Longley, L.; & Terry, H. (1982). *The politics of broadcast regulation.* New York: St. Martin's Press.

Middleton, K., & Lee, W. (2006). *The law of public communication.* Boston: Allyn & Bacon.

Overbeck, W. (2003). *Major principles of media law.* New York: HBJ College Division.

Pember, D., & Calvert, C. (2005). *Mass media law.* New York: McGraw-Hill.

Sadler, R. (2005). *Electronic media law.* Thousand Oaks, CA: Sage.

Spitzer, M. (1986). *Seven dirty words and six other stories.* New Haven, CT: Yale University Press.

INTERNET EXERCISES

Visit our Web site at **www.mhhe.com/dominick6** for study-guide exercises to help you learn and apply material in each chapter. You will find ideas for future research as well as useful Web links to provide you with an opportunity to journey through the new electronic media.

Self-Regulation and Ethics 11

Quick Facts

 Date of first National Association of Broadcasters code for broadcasting: 1929

 Date code abolished: 1983

 Most influential citizens' group in TV history: Action for Children's Television

 Number of scenes containing sexual content in a week of TV in 1998: 1,930

 Number of scenes containing sexual content in a week of TV in 2005: 3,783

Graphic scenes, such as this one from *CSI*, can cause problems for broadcasters.

The preceding chapter dealt with laws regarding broadcasting and cable. There are many situations, however, that laws or FCC regulations do not cover. In these circumstances, broadcasting and cable professionals must rely on their own ethics, internal standards, and/or organizational operating policies for guidance.

Consider the following. During prime time in 2005 and 2006 you could have seen contestants eating a nasty-looking insect called a camel spider and dunking their heads into a sludge-filled sink to retrieve keys with their teeth (*Fear Factor*); gross autopsies and program episodes that dealt with sadomasochism and other sexual fetishes (*CSI*); and scenes of scantily clad Paris Hilton suggestively cavorting in soap suds as she washes a Bentley in a hamburger commercial (courtesy of Carl's Jr.).

There's nothing illegal about putting scantily clad models, repulsive food items, or sexual references on TV. The decision to air this type of content boils down to a consideration of individual principles, professional standards, and personal ethics. In short, it's a matter of **self-regulation.** A consideration of self-regulation is important because the trend toward fewer formal regulations means that more and more decisions are being left to the discretion of individual broadcasters and program producers. Accordingly, this chapter focuses on (1) the major factors that influence self-regulation in broadcasting and cable and (2) ethics and its relationship to self-regulation.

SELF-REGULATION IN BROADCASTING AND CABLE

This section examines (1) codes of responsibility and/or good practice, (2) departments devoted to maintaining proper standards, (3) the V-chip, (4) professional groups and organizations, and (5) citizens' groups.

Codes

Codes are written statements of principle that guide the general behavior of those working in a profession. Code statements can be prescriptive—"Thou shalt do this"—or proscriptive—"Thou shalt not do this." At one end of the spectrum they imply the minimum expectations of the profession (journalists should not plagiarize); at the other they embody the ideal way of acting (journalists should tell the truth). Professional codes are common in medicine, law, pharmacy, and journalism.

The NAB Code Although many group-owned broadcasting stations adopted strict codes, probably the most famous of all in broadcasting was that developed by the National Association of Broadcasters (NAB). The NAB established the first radio code in 1929, just 2 years after the FRC was founded. In 1952, as TV was growing, the NAB adopted a code for it too. By 1980 the two codes had been amended many times to keep up with the changing social climate. Adherence to the code was voluntary, and figures from 1980 show that about one-half of all radio stations and two-thirds of all TV stations were code subscribers. The NAB had a code authority with a staff of about 33 people who made sure that stations followed the codes. The only punishment the NAB could dish out to the violator, however, was revocation of the right to display the seal of good practice, a penalty that hardly inspired fear among station owners.

A glance at the codes themselves showed that they covered both programming and advertising. Included in the programming area were such diverse topics as news presentation, political broadcasting, religion, community responsibility, and programming aimed at children. The advertising section of the codes contained, among other items, guidelines about what products were acceptable, rules for the presentation of broadcast ads, and time standards suggesting limits on the time per hour that should be devoted to commercials.

The time standard provisions ultimately got the codes into trouble with the Department of Justice, which claimed in an antitrust suit that broadcasters were keeping the prices of ads high by artificially restricting the amount of commercial time available. The NAB, after a negative court decision, suspended the advertising portion of its code. Later, upon advice of lawyers, the NAB revoked the programming sections as well. By 1983 the codes ceased to exist.

Nonetheless, the codes still have some lingering impact. Although the courts said it was anticompetitive for groups of broadcasters to get together to produce common codes, it was still permissible for individual stations and group-owned stations to maintain their own codes. As a result, many stations still informally follow code provisions.

In 1990 the NAB's Executive Committee developed new voluntary programming principles. In order to avoid any of the legal complications that surrounded the original code statements, the NAB's legal department generated the principles and emphasized that there would be no enforcement of these provisions by the NAB or other groups. The new principles were entirely consistent with the philosophy of the original code but were restricted to four key areas: children's TV, indecency and obscenity, violence, and drug abuse. They urged special care in children's programming and that violence should not be portrayed excessively or in a gratuitous

manner. Further, the guidelines noted that obscenity was never acceptable for broadcast and that all sexually oriented material should be presented with particular care. Finally, the principles recommended that glamorization of drug use should be avoided.

The government has recently pressured the broadcasting and cable industry to resurrect a more formal code of good behavior. In 1997 a bill was introduced in Congress that would have allowed members of the broadcasting and cable industries to develop a new code without fear of antitrust laws. The bill did not pass. In 1998, the Advisory Committee on Public Interest Obligations of Digital Television Broadcasters recommended that the NAB draft an updated voluntary code of conduct for broadcasters. Two years later four senators asked the FCC to examine whether current broadcast programming was actually serving the public interest and suggested that an industrywide code be reestablished.

The issue surfaced again in 2004 after Janet Jackson's wardrobe malfunction during the Super Bowl's halftime show. As the FCC and various lawmakers considered legislation that would crack down on indecent broadcasts (see previous chapter), the NAB announced the formation of a task force that would consider an industrywide code and other options for self-regulation that would address concerns over potentially offensive content. As of 2006 no new code had been proposed. Many NAB members opposed such an effort on First Amendment grounds.

Other Codes and Policies There are other noteworthy industrywide guidelines that deal with broadcast journalism and advertising.

The Radio and Television News Directors Association (RTNDA) has an six-article Code of Broadcast News Ethics that covers items ranging from courtroom coverage to privacy invasions. The Society of Professional Journalists (SPJ) also has a code of ethics that covers all media including broadcasting. This code covers such topics as fair play, accuracy, objectivity, and press responsibility. The language of both codes is general and far-reaching. For example, from the SPJ code: "Seek truth and report it" and "Be accountable."

In the advertising area, the American Advertising Federation and the Association of Better Business Bureaus International have developed a nine-item code that deals with such topics as truth in advertising ("Advertising shall tell the truth . . ."), taste and decency ("Advertising shall be free of statements . . .

which are offensive to good taste"), and responsibility ("Advertisers shall be willing to provide substantiation of claims made"). This code has been endorsed by the NAB and many other industry groups.

The absence of a general code of behavior for broadcasting and cable has given station managers and program directors a great deal of discretion in such matters as children's programming, artistic freedom, religious shows, programs devoted to important local issues, and acceptable topics. Management must be sensitive to the political, social, and economic sensibilities of the community; otherwise, a bad decision can cost a radio, TV, or cable organization credibility, trust, and, in the long run, dollars.

To help guard against bad decisions, many stations have developed their own policy guidelines covering sensitive issues. These station policies generally complement and expand the industrywide codes of conduct. Not surprisingly, the broadcast newsroom is the place where a written policy is most often found.

Written codes, however, are not without controversy. On the one hand, proponents of codes argue that they indicate to the general public that the media organization is sensitive to its ethical duties. Moreover, written codes of conduct ensure that every employee understands what the company views as proper or correct behavior; ethical decisions are not left to the whim of each individual. On the other hand, opponents argue that any company policy statement that covers the entire workings of the organization will have to be worded so vaguely that it will be of little use in specific day-to-day decision making. Further, opponents fear that a written code or policy statement might actually be used against a radio or TV station in court. For example, a private citizen who's suing a TV station for libel might argue that the station was negligent because it failed to follow its own written guidelines.

Many of the company codes that exist today tend to be proscriptive in nature and narrow in focus. Basically, they tend to spell out the minimum expectations for an individual employee. For example, many TV station policies forbid journalists from taking gifts from their news sources, or program directors from accepting gifts from program suppliers. Stations also have policies that bar employees from accepting free sports tickets and junkets or from holding outside employment that might conflict with their job at the station.

It's apparent that written guidelines can't do the whole job. In fact, most policy statements and codes fail to address the number-one ethical problem revealed by a survey conducted by *Electronic Media:* the conflict between making money and serving the public. Three out of four media executives agreed that the goals of making money and public service were sometimes in conflict. This is not surprising since most policy statements and guidelines are directed at the individual, whereas ethical problems are increasingly originating at the corporate level. For example, many stations and cable systems are owned by groups. How much of the profit made by a local operation should be reinvested back into the station and how much should go to shore up unprofitable operations in other communities or to finance new acquisitions? Should a TV station run sensational stories on its TV newscasts during sweep weeks to inflate its ratings? How much local news should be carried on a radio station if it means losing some money in the process? These are questions that codes seldom deal with.

Departments of Standards and Practices

The major broadcast and cable networks maintain staffs to make sure that their commercials and programs do not offend advertisers, affiliated stations and cable systems, audience members, and the FCC. In prior years these departments, usually called standards and practices (S&P) or something similar, were large and influential. In recent years, however, they have been cut back and the producers of the various programs now make many of the decisions about what is or is not acceptable.

It's obvious that standards concerning what's acceptable on television have changed dramatically over the years. Back in the 1960s, S&P executives at the TV networks decreed that Barbara Eden of *I Dream of Jeannie* couldn't reveal her navel and that Rob and Laura of the *Dick Van Dyke Show* couldn't be shown in bed together even though they were married. Standards became more liberal in the early 1970s with such shows as *All in the Family* and *Maude*. This trend continued through the 1980s and 1990s. As of 2006, standards had relaxed even more. The Fox series *24* featured heroin use, underage sex, rape, and male prostitution. A made-for-TV movie about basketball coach Bobby Knight used the f-word 15 times in the first 15 minutes. Comedy Central's *South Park* used another well-known four-letter word 162 times in a half-hour episode. The *CSI* series of programs dealt with a number of themes that would never have aired in the 1970s or 1980s.

Ethics: Miracles or Exploitation?

In spring 2006, the ABC television network presented a new reality series called *The Miracle Workers*. The concept behind the series was to select patients with serious disorders and match them with expert physicians who would use cutting-edge techniques to try to cure them. Or as the tag line for the show summed it up, "When a person's life is on the line and doctors insist that nothing more can be done, it's time to turn to the Miracle Workers." The pilot show, for example, featured a man getting a cornea transplant and a woman with a spine defect who gets a titanium disc implant.

At first glance, the show seemed to be an extension of previous ABC "makeover" hits, such as *Extreme Makeover* and *Extreme Makeover: Home Edition*. A closer look, however, suggested that the show raised troubling ethical issues for both doctors and the television industry.

First, there was the question of exploitation. Is it ethical to play upon the suffering and hardships of others in order to entertain people? Ethical theories suggest that a person should not treat others as a means to an end. Did this show use human beings simply to generate sensationalism and pathos in order to get good ratings? Does it turn the audience into voyeurs intrigued by another person's ordeals?

Second, there is the issue of selection. Ideally, the decision to offer medical care should be based on need and not on whether a patient is photogenic or has a compelling story that would make good television. To complicate the issue even further, for some patients ABC will help pay some of the medical bills and the CVS pharmacy chain will add a $25,000 gift card. Is it morally correct to give extraordinary medical care as a prize?

Third, there is the issue of privacy. Doctor–patient relationships have always been confidential, and privacy is one of the fundamental principles of medicine. In order to receive these cutting-edge medical treatments, patients have to agree to be televised and give up their rights. Granted, the patients have knowingly consented to these conditions, but is their consent voluntarily given or is it in reality consent coerced by their overwhelming desire to get better?

The producers counter some of these arguments by using the utilitarian argument. The good that the show does for these patients outweighs any of the harm done by possible ethical breaches. As an ABC executive put it: "We help a lot of people. In a day and age of mean-spirited, bug-eating shows, we've done something good."*

*Quoted in the *Ottawa Citizen*, February 1, 2006, p. A1.

What's behind this trend toward greater liberalization? First of all, society's standards have become more tolerant. Language that was once considered offensive in radio or TV broadcasts (such as *hell* or *damn*) now hardly raises an eyebrow. Programs about homosexuality, abortion, and child pornography generate few complaints from the viewing audience. Second, the success of such premium cable series as HBO's *The Sopranos* and *Sex and the City* have encouraged broadcasters and other cable networks to push the envelope even further to compete with the pay channels. Audiences don't seem too disturbed by this trend toward more realistic dialogue and content. Finally, the V-chip (discussed in more detail below) has helped accelerate this development. The chip works with a rating system that allows programmers to alert the audience to possible offensive content. Program creators are apparently using a label such as "For Mature Audiences" to include more adult themes in their programs. In short,

the V-chip relieves programmers of some of the burden of self-regulation and passes it on to parents. As mentioned in Chapter 10, however, the FCC under Kevin Martin has begun a concentrated effort to curb indecency on the broadcast networks. Whether this campaign has any long-lasting effect on the content of TV shows remains to be seen.

A network's competitive position also influences its standards. The newer Fox network, for example, in an attempt to catch viewers' attention, allowed shows such as *Married . . . with Children, The Simpsons, King of the Hill*, and *When Animals Attack* to venture into areas that the older, more-established networks might have avoided.

Cable networks, of course, have a little more leeway when it comes to controversial content but they also follow standards. Comedy Central, for example, runs the crude *South Park* late in the evening, when fewer young children are in the audience, and FX does the same with *The Shield*. MTV has demanded cuts in

Cable series, such as Fx's *The Shield*, push the limits of what's acceptable TV content.

music videos the network deemed too controversial in their original form. Premium cable channels, such as HBO and Showtime, have the greatest amount of latitude when it comes to presenting mature and sexual content. HBO's *Sex and the City,* for example, came to broadcast TV only after extensive editing.

At the local level both broadcasting and cable operations pay close attention to questions of taste and appropriateness, but they do not have formalized departments that handle the task. Some group owners of stations have codes that they try to apply to all the stations they own, but most standards-and-practices decisions are made by managers or program executives. Further, not all decisions will be the same. The acceptability of certain TV or radio messages depends on several factors: (1) the size of the market, (2) the time period, (3) the station's audience, and (4) the type of content involved.

To elaborate, what's acceptable in New York City might not be appropriate for Minot, North Dakota. Standards vary widely from city to city and from region to region. The local radio, TV, or cable executive is usually the best judge of what his or her community will tolerate. For example, in 2006 seven NBC affiliates refused to carry *The Book of Daniel,* a series about a drug-addicted priest with a gay son. The show was canceled soon after.

The time period also has a lot to do with acceptability. Stations tend to be more careful if there's a good chance that children will be in the audience. Programs and films with adult themes are typically scheduled late in the evening, when few children are presumed to be listening. Cable movie channels generally schedule their racier films after 10:00 P.M.

The audience attracted by a station's programming is another important factor. Radio stations that feature a talk format with controversial topic usually spark few protests because their listeners know what to expect. Listener-sponsored Pacifica radio stations routinely program material that other stations would heartily avoid. Although they do get into occasional trouble (for example, the *Pacifica* case), the audience for Pacifica stations rarely complains.

Finally, the kind of program also makes a difference. Rough language and shocking pictures are sometimes OK for a news or public affairs program.

The V-chip

The **V-chip** represents an intriguing blend of legal regulation and self-regulation. Section 551 of the Telecommunications Act of 1996 requires TV set manufacturers to install a V-chip content-blocking device in every TV set that is 13 inches or larger.

The V-chip works in concert with the voluntary program rating system developed by the television industry that identifies programs with sexual, violent, or indecent content. After much discussion, the industry came up with a rating system that initially classified TV content according to its acceptability for various age levels:

"TV-Y"—programs suitable to "all children."

"TV-Y7"—programs "directed to older children," ages 7 and above.

"TV-G"—general audience.

"TV-PG"—parental guidance suggested.

"TV-14"—parents strongly cautioned for children under 14.

"TV-M"—mature audience only.

After complaints from public interest groups that this system was not informative enough, the ratings were later amended to include special advisories for specific content: "S" for sexual content; "L" for profanity and other strong language; "V" for excessive violence; and "D" for sexually suggestive dialogue. Thus, a program could be rated "TV-14—SLD." The ratings for each program are assigned by members of the television industry. The rating itself is electronically encoded in the program's transmission signal and appears on the screen at the beginning of the program.

Parents can program the V-chip to block out content that they deem inappropriate for their children. For example, if parents are concerned about televised violence, they can use the chip to block any program that has a "V" in its rating.

There were many uncertainties following the introduction of the V-chip. Broadcasters feared that a "TV-M" or a "V" rating might discourage advertisers from purchasing commercial time. Some suggested that the V-chip might be used as an excuse for programmers to push the envelope and develop even more controversial content. Critics of the V-chip argued that most Americans would ignore it. Now that the V-chip has been around for more than 6 years, some conclusions seem apparent:

- Most parents aren't aware of the V-chip or what it does. A 2001 survey by the Kaiser Family Foundation revealed that only 17 percent of the 40 percent of the families who owned TV sets equipped with the V-chip (that's about 7 percent of all families) used the technology to block objectionable programs. In fact, about half the parents didn't know that their new sets even had a V-chip.

- Parents have more awareness of the ratings system. The same survey noted that more than half

of the parents used the program ratings to make decisions about what their children watched. The age-based ratings were better known than the specific content ratings. Only 5 percent of the parents, for example, knew that a "D" rating indicated sexually suggestive dialogue.

- Most advertisers continued to purchase commercial time with little regard for a program's rating.

- Programming content, as mentioned above, has become more risqué and coarse, and many believe that the V-chip has contributed to that trend.

In response to the FCC's crackdown on indecent content and in an attempt to head off restrictive legislation, the television industry has changed its attitude toward the V-chip. Broadcasters and cablecasters announced plans in 2006 to launch a $300 million publicity campaign to educate parents about the V-chip. In addition, the industry supported the formation of TV Watch, a coalition of industry and citizens' groups, to promote the use of the chip and to lobby Congress against increased government control of TV content.

Professional Groups

Professional groups are trade and industry organizations that offer their members advice about research, technical, legal, and management issues. The best known of these for broadcasters is the **National Association of Broadcasters (NAB).** The NAB has about 6,000 radio-station and 1,100 TV-station members, along with more than 1,500 individual members in the broadcasting industry. We have already examined the lobbying component of the NAB; its other services include designing public service campaigns, offering legal advice, conducting technology research, and maintaining an information library. In cable, the **National Cable Television Association (NCTA)** is the most influential group, with a range of services that parallels the NAB's. Other professional groups include the Radio Television News Directors Association, the National Association of Television Program Executives, the National Association of Farm Broadcasters, the Association of Maximum Service Telecasters, the National Association of Public Television Stations, and the National Association of Black-Owned Broadcasters, to name a few. A recent issue of *Broadcasting-Cablecasting Yearbook* listed about 175 national associations concerned with cable and broadcasting.

Professional groups contribute to self-regulation in both formal and informal ways. On the informal level, each group sponsors conventions and meetings where members exchange relevant business and professional information. These meetings offer ways for managers from one part of the country to learn how managers from other regions are handling similar problems. A station in Maine might find that a policy or set of guidelines used by a station in Ohio solves its problem. Organizational meetings let professionals get feedback from their peers. Professional organizations also set examples and demonstrate standards of meritorious behavior that members can emulate. The NAB, for example, reported that in 2003 radio and TV stations nationwide contributed more than $9 billion to community service projects.

The most elaborate system of formal self-regulation by a professional group deals with national advertising. Basically, the process works like this. If a consumer or a competitor thinks an ad is deceptive, a complaint is filed with the **National Advertising Division (NAD)** of the Council of Better Business Bureaus. Most complaints are filed by competitors, but the NAD monitors national radio and TV and can initiate action itself. The NAD can either dismiss the complaint or contact the advertiser for additional information that might refute the complaint. If the NAD is not satisfied with the advertiser's response, it can ask the company to change or stop using the ad. If the advertiser agrees (and most do), then that's the end of it. On the other hand, if the advertiser disagrees with the NAD, the case can be taken to the **National Advertising Review Board (NARB).**

The NARB functions much like a court of appeals. A review panel is appointed, the case is examined again, and the complaint is either upheld or dismissed. If the complaint is upheld, the advertiser is asked once again to change or discontinue the ad. If the advertiser still refuses, the case can be referred to the FTC or another government agency for possible legal action.

One of the problems with this system is that it takes a long time. In many cases, by the time the NAD has weighed the facts of the case, decided that the ad in question was truly deceptive, and notified the company to stop, the advertising campaign has run its course and the ad is already off the air. Nonetheless, although it doesn't have any legal or formal authority, the NAD/NARB system and the implied threat of legal action are taken seriously by most people in the industry.

Last, scholarly and academic organizations, such as the Broadcast Education Association and the Association for Education in Journalism and Mass Communication, contribute to self-regulation through their work with students. These and similar organizations urge colleges and universities to emphasize ethical and professional responsibilities in their curricula. Academic organizations also study and help clarify the norms and standards of the profession so that practitioners can have some guidance in making ethical decisions.

Citizens' Groups

In addition to shaping the legal and policy environment of broadcasting, citizens' groups (or pressure groups) exert a force for self-regulation by communicating directly with broadcasters. In recent years citizens' groups have been most vocal about three areas: (1) the portrayal of minorities, (2) the presentation of sex and violence, and (3) children's programming.

Portrayal of Minorities   The concern over the portrayal of minorities began during the civil rights movement of the 1960s. African Americans correctly noted that few blacks appeared in network prime-time programming and that those few who did were usually shown in menial occupations. Their pressure on the networks for more-balanced portrayals ultimately led to more-important roles for blacks, such as Bill Cosby's in *I Spy* and Diahann Carroll's in *Julia*.

The success of these efforts prompted Latinos to campaign successfully for the removal of a commercial character known as the Frito Bandito, which many found offensive. Ethnic stereotyping in a series called *Chico and the Man* was also a target of Mexican American citizens' groups. Other groups, such as Native Americans, Italian Americans, the Gray Panthers, Arab Americans, and Asian Americans, have also pressured the networks to eliminate stereotyped portrayals. The National Gay Task Force has also lobbied the networks for a balanced portrayal of homosexuals.

A 2005 report of the Multi-Ethnic Coalition stated that television reflected diversity better in 2005 than in previous years but that it still had a long way to go. The report noted that Asian and Hispanic characters had increased the most but that Native Americans were rarely portrayed.

Presentation of Sex and Violence   The portrayal of sex and violence has been a recurring topic of concern

Issues: The Best and Worst

The Parents Television Council, a citizens' group, regularly ranks what it considers the five best and the five worst family-friendly shows. Below is a list from early 2006.

	The Best		The Worst
1	American Idol	1	Las Vegas
2	Deal or No Deal	2	The War at Home
3	Extreme Makeover—Home Edition	3	House
4	Reba	4	Supernatural
5	Get This Party Started	5	Family Guy

for citizens' groups. The Center for Media and Public Affairs reports data on trends in TV violence over the years. Similarly, the UCLA Center for Communication Policy monitors violence in network programs. The American Medial Association has joined with citizens' groups in the campaign to reduce TV violence.

Information about the sexual content of television is gathered by the Parents Television Council. Its Web site (www.parentstv.org) contains a listing of advertisers who support family-friendly programming as well as those associated with more-raunchy programs. The conservative group Morality in Media has campaigned against television content that the group considered obscene or indecent.

Children's Programming Programming for children is another recurring concern of many groups, including the national Parent Teacher Association and the National Education Association. Since the passage of the **Children's Television Act of 1990** and the

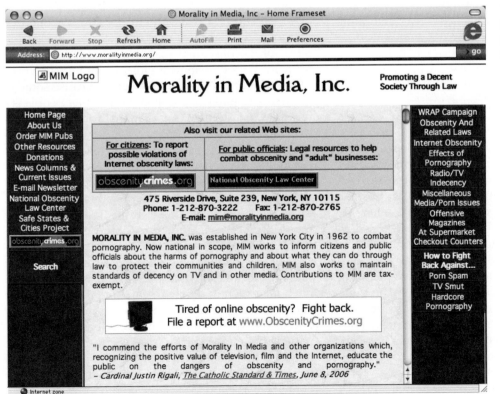

The citizens' group Morality in Media campaigns against obscene and indecent media content.

subsequent ruling by the FCC that stations devote 3 hours a week to children's programs, the major focus of children's television advocates has been the enforcement of these provisions. The Center for Media Education, for example, maintains a Web site that contains a description of the new legal regulations, a listing of what programs the networks are presenting that meet the 3-hour requirement, and information on how to read a TV station's public file to see if the station is in compliance.

Effects   Citizens' groups pose special problems for the self-regulatory attempts of the industry. They increase the sensitivity of programmers toward potentially offensive material, but at the same time they severely restrict the creative freedom of writers and producers. Their cumulative effect thus may lead to a kind of self-censorship. In addition, program producers are forced to walk a thin line between alternatives. For example, gay citizens' groups are calling for increased portrayals of homosexuals in TV drama. If the producers accede to the demands, they might risk offending a substantial part of their viewing audience. Similarly, networks and production companies are careful not to allow potentially harmful acts of violence to remain in a show, but even seemingly innocuous acts of aggression may still raise the ire of some citizens' groups. What some consider innocent sexual bantering may be offensive to others. Satisfying everybody is not an easy task.

ETHICS

All of us deal regularly with ethical problems. For example, suppose one of your teachers returns your test with a grade of 95 on it. As you look through the test, you realize your teacher made an addition mistake and your real score is 85. Do you tell your teacher? Or suppose the cashier at the bookstore gives you $25 in change when you were supposed to get only $15. Do you return the extra $10? Personal ethical principles are important in the self-regulation of broadcasting and cable, since many decision makers rely on them in situations that are not covered by codes or standards and practices. And since the many crucial ethical decisions of broadcasters and cablecasters are open to public inspection and criticism, ethical behavior is critical to those working in radio and TV. This section takes a brief look at the formal study of

ethics and then examines how ethics might apply in the day-to-day world of TV and radio.

The Greek word *ethos* originally meant an abode or an accustomed dwelling place, a place where we would feel comfortable. In like manner, the study of ethics can be thought of as helping us make those decisions with which we are comfortable. In formal terms, ethics addresses the question, Which human actions are morally permissible and which are not? Or, in more familiar terms, What is the right thing to do?

Ethics and law are related; both limit human activities. Laws, however, are enforced by sanctions and penalties, whereas ethics are enforced by our moral sense of the proper thing. In many cases the law and ethics overlap—the legally correct action is also the morally correct action. In other cases a decision that's perfectly legal may not be the best decision from an ethical standpoint.

Perhaps a brief and basic tour of the philosophical groundwork that underlies ethics might help.

Ethical Theories

Without getting too bogged down in the technical language of the philosophy of ethics, we first need to define two key concepts: teleological theories and deontological theories. A **teleological** (from the Greek, *teleos*, an end or a result) **theory** of ethics is one that measures the rightness or wrongness of an action in terms of its consequences. To say that it is unethical for a TV station to show a violent film in prime time when a lot of children are watching because some of them might imitate the film and hurt other people is a teleological judgment. A policy that forbids reporters from accepting gifts and consideration from the people they cover because it would hurt their journalistic credibility is another teleological judgment.

A **deontological** (from the Greek, *deon*, duty) **theory** does not concern itself with consequences; instead, it spells out those duties that are morally required of all of us. The source of these moral obligations can come from reason, society, the supernatural, or the human conscience. For example, a policy that forbids investigative TV journalists from assuming a false identity while researching a story because such actions constitute lying, an action forbidden by one of the Ten Commandments, is based on supernatural deontological grounds. Note that it doesn't matter if the consequences of the lying are beneficial to society. A lie is prohibited since it is counter to God's will as expressed in the commandments.

With that as a background, let's examine some specific ethical principles and see how they might relate to broadcasting and cable.

Utilitarianism   Probably the most popular and clearest ethical principle is a teleological theory, utilitarianism. **Utilitarianism** holds that a person should act in a way that produces the greatest possible ratio of good over evil. In other words, one should make the decision whose consequences will yield the greatest good for the greatest number (or the least harm for the fewest number). Under this principle the ethical person is one who adds to the goodness and reduces the evil of human life.

A broadcaster who chose to follow utilitarianism as an ethical standard would first have to calculate the probable consequences that would result from each possible course of action (this is not easy; sometimes it's impossible to predict all the consequences of a given decision). Second, the broadcaster would have to assign a positive or negative value to each probable consequence and then choose the alternative that maximizes benefit and minimizes harm.

To illustrate, suppose the sales manager asks the news director (let's assume that's you) at a given station to kill a story about health code violations at a local restaurant. The restaurant is one of the biggest advertisers on your station and has threatened to cancel if you run the story. From the utilitarian perspective you first define your possible actions: (1) run the story, (2) kill the story, and (3) run an edited

Ethics: The Dynamics of Self-Regulation—NBC and Liquor Advertising

Chapter 10 listed several forces that influence the formation of laws and regulations that govern broadcasting and cable. These same forces can also play a role in self-regulation as demonstrated by NBC's decisions regarding the advertising of hard liquor on TV.

There's no law that says you can't advertise hard liquor on television. That decision has been left to self-regulation. For many years, both the major broadcast networks and the Distilled Spirits Council of the United States had a self-imposed ban against advertising liquor on TV and radio. In 1996, however, the council ended its ban and left its members free to pursue broadcast advertising. This left individual stations and networks to decide whether they wanted to continue the ban or to accept liquor ads. Many local stations and cable networks decided to accept the ads. The major TV networks, however, decided to continue their ban.

Then, in late 2001, faced with a decline in advertising revenue, NBC announced it would start accepting ads for hard liquor, hoping to take in more than $100 million in revenue from this new source. A few months later, however, NBC reversed itself and stopped accepting liquor ads. The apparent reasons behind NBC's about-face offer some interesting insights into the workings of self-regulation.

In the first place, the decision to accept the ads caused public relations problems for NBC as citizens' groups, such as Mothers Against Drunk Driving and the American Medical Association, criticized the decision by claiming that the ads would encourage alcoholism and irresponsible drinking. Second, the decision got the attention of Congress, and several key members voiced their opposition to carrying the ads and asked NBC to reconsider. Moreover, there was talk of Congress holding hearings on whether such advertising was in the public interest. The marketplace also entered into the process. NBC evidently feared that such hearings might also consider the propriety of carrying ads for beer and wine. Beer and wine advertisers spend more than $1.8 billion a year on network ads. A congressional hearing might have led to legislation banning or restricting both hard liquor and beer and wine ads. Third, neither ABC nor CBS went along with NBC. In fact, many of the network's affiliates announced that they were against the network's decision. Industry lobby groups, such as the National Association of Broadcasters, offered little support. The network was alone at the center of the controversy.

Faced with mounting opposition, NBC followed a utilitarian philosophy. The network weighed the negative consequences that would follow from its decision to air hard liquor ads against the potential monetary gain. It evidently decided that the negative outweighed the positive and reversed its decision.

version of the story without naming the restaurant involved. The consequences of killing the story are easy to predict. Your station continues to get money and stays in business, thus keeping everyone on your staff employed. It might also help the restaurant stay in business, since consumers who are health conscious might have stayed away had the story been aired. On the other hand, failing to run the story or running it minus the name of the offending restaurant might have significant negative effects. First, it might hurt the credibility of your news operation, particularly if other local media identify the restaurant. In the long run this might cause people to stop watching your newscast and hurt your revenues. Second, the morale in your news department might be negatively affected. Third, unwary consumers who eat at the restaurant might have their health jeopardized by the unsanitary conditions. Carrying the full story would help credibility, improve station morale, and warn unsuspecting members of the general public. In short, our cursory utilitarian analysis suggests that it would be better to carry the story.

Egoism   Another teleological theory is known as **egoism.** Its basic premise is simple: act in the way that is best for you. Any action is judged to be right or wrong in terms of its consequences for one's self. If decision A is more in your self-interest than decision B, then decision A is right.

Egoism was popularized by writer-philosopher Ayn Rand, who argued that a person should not sacrifice self to others. Rather, a person should have the highest regard and owe the greatest obligation to his or her own self. (Rand's book *The Fountainhead* is a forceful interpretation of this view. Incidentally, a movie of the same name, starring Gary Cooper, was based on this book, making it probably the only motion picture ever to be based on a formal ethical theory.)

Egoism sounds like an intellectual rationalization for doing whatever you please. But it goes deeper than that. Egoism doesn't preclude kindness or thoughtfulness toward others. In fact, it requires the individual to make a thoughtful and rational analysis of each choice to determine what exactly is best for the individual. Doing what is best for you frequently also entails doing what is best for others. In any case, egoism is an interesting example of an individualistic ethic that many have criticized as being paradoxical and inconsistent.

In our restaurant example, the news director goes through the same analysis as discussed earlier, but now he or she is not concerned about the consequences for the station, the restaurant, the public, or the news staff. The news director is interested only in what will be best for himself or herself. In this case the news director might well conclude that killing the story would harm his or her reputation as an aggressive, probing journalist and thus would run the story since, in the long run, the action would be beneficial to a news director's career.

Categorical Imperative   Probably the most famous deontological theory was developed by Immanuel Kant. Our proper duty, not the consequences of our actions, must govern our decisions. Kant argued that our proper course of action must be arrived at through reason and an examination of conscience. How do we recognize our proper duty? By subjecting it to the **categorical imperative:** Act only on those principles that you would want to become universal law. This philosophy is close to the famous golden rule in Western cultures. An ethical person should perform only those behaviors that he or she would like all to perform. What is right for one is right for all. In this context, "categorical" means without exception. What's right is right and that's the end of it.

Someone following the categorical imperative might handle the restaurant news story in this manner: Since holding back important information is not something that I would want everybody to do, the story must run. In this instance there is a categorical imperative against squelching the publication of important information. Therefore, it should not be done in this or other situations. Period.

The Golden Mean   Another deontological theory stems from the writings of Aristotle. A natural scientist, Aristotle grounded his theory of ethics in natural law. He noted that too much or too little of something was harmful. A plant would wither if given too little water but would drown if given too much. The proper course of action is somewhere between these two extremes. Moderation, temperance, equilibrium, and harmony are concepts that are important in his philosophy.

When faced with an ethical dilemma, a person using this theory begins by identifying the extremes

Issues: Fake News?

A video news release (VNR) is the video equivalent of a printed press release. A VNR looks like a typical "package" in a television newscast: A reporter reads an introduction, provides a voice-over narration of relevant scenes, and closes with a summary. The big difference is that a VNR is produced by a public relations firm for a client with a message to deliver.

The use of VNRs has become more popular recently because many broadcast newsrooms are providing several hours of news a day but are also faced with reduced budgets. Consequently, news directors are on the lookout for inexpensive content that will fill time but still look professionally done. VNRs fill that need.

VNRs are are distributed to television networks and stations across the country via satellite feed by services such as CNN's NewsSource. They are sometimes used in full, but most of the time the video is used as a "B-roll" to illustrate a story produced by the local station.

VNRs generated a storm of controversy in 2003 when it was revealed that the U.S. Health and Human Services Department had produced a VNR promoting the government's new Medicare drug benefit and that many stations had aired the video without identifying its sponsor.

The debate highlighted several ethical issues. First, is it ethical for the government to produce and distribute VNRs? Critics contended that the VNRs were thinly veiled propaganda pieces pushed by the Bush administration. The government responded that it turned to VNRs since the mainstream media did a poor job reporting on the topic. In addition, as long as the VNRs were factual and did not advocate a position, then there was no ethical problem. Finally, the government noted that the report was identified as a VNR when it was sent to CNN's NewsSource.

Second, what are the obligations of the services that feed the VNR, such as CNN NewsSource, and the stations that use them? CNN pointed out that the video was labeled as a VNR in its feed, but the local stations responded that the VNR was included with other legitimate news sources and in the stress of day-to-day deadline reporting that it was easy to miss the label.

Third, what is the ethical obligation of the firms that produce VNRs? The guidelines endorsed by the Public Relations Society of America states that the distributors of VNRs and the organizations they represent should clearly and plainly identify themselves. But what does that mean? Should there simply be a brief graphic (one that can easily be missed) before the report that says who paid for it? Or should there be some internal acknowledgment within the report itself. In the VNR for the Health and Human Services Department, for example, the reporter concluded with, "In Washington, I'm Karen Ryan reporting." Should she have said, "I'm Karen Ryan reporting for the Health and Human Services Department"?

Media critics, such as the Center for Media and Democracy, argue that identifying VNRs should be more than an ethical obligation. They contend that the FCC should require on-screen disclosure of all VNRs because the audience has a right to know where the news is coming from.

In any case, VNRs have been used by public relations firms for more than 25 years. It is unlikely that their use will decrease in the future.

and then searches to find some balance point or mean that lies between them—the **golden mean.** This may be easy or hard to do, depending on the situation. In the restaurant example one extreme would be to publish everything; the other, to publish nothing. Perhaps a compromise position between the two would be to air the story completely but also to provide time for the restaurant owner to reply to the charges. Perhaps the story might note that these are the first violations in the restaurant's history or include other tempering remarks.

Cultural Ethics **Cultural ethics theory,** which is grounded in society as opposed to nature, holds that an individual is shaped by his or her culture. Our moral judgments are shaped by those we experienced when growing up and when entering other socializing environments such as school or work. Cultural ethics suggests that the individual accepts the discipline of society, adjusts to its needs and customs, and finds ethical security within it. There are no universals by which each culture is judged; each is self-legislative, determining its own rules of right and wrong. Moreover, many different subcultures within society may be relevant. An ethical problem encountered on the job might be assessed in the context of the workplace with all of its relevant norms.

In the broadcasting area, the practical application of this theory suggests that a station or cable system owner consult the norms of other media or of other businesses or of the general community before making an ethical decision. In the restaurant example the station involved might see how other stations are treating the story or have treated such stories in the past. Similarly, the way that other media, such as newspapers, handle the situation should be noted. Or the station might consult the managers of other stations throughout the area to get advice about the proper course to follow.

Situational Ethics   The theory of situational ethics also examines ethics in relative terms. Unlike cultural ethics, however, **situational ethics,** or *situationism,* argues that the traditions and norms of society provide inadequate guidance because each individual problem or situation is unique and calls for a creative solution. Decisions regarding how we ought to act must be grounded in the concrete details that make up each circumstance. Universal ethical principles like the categorical imperative might provide some guidance, but they are merely hints as to the correct course; they do not apply in every situation. A general principle that we endorse, such as "TV newscasters should always tell the truth," can be violated if the situation calls for it (such as broadcasting a false story to gain the release of hostages).

Of course, the way we see and analyze situations varies from person to person. No two individuals will define the same situation in exactly the same terms. How we perceive things depends on our moral upbringing and our ethical values. Consequently, different answers are possible depending on how one assesses the situation.

In our restaurant example the entire situation must be examined before making a decision. Was the board of health on a vendetta against this particular restaurant? Has the restaurant recently changed management? How much money will actually be lost if the restaurant cancels its advertising? Could this revenue be replaced from another source? Have all the violations been corrected? These are some aspects of the situation that might be considered before a decision is made. From a

situationist point of view there is no single "correct" answer to this problem.

"Doing" Ethics

A knowledge of ethical principles is useful for all those entering the radio and TV profession. First, it is important to have some predefined standard in place when a quick and difficult ethical call is required. Second, a personal code of ethics assures an individual of some measure of consistency from one decision to the next. Third, media professionals are often asked to explain or defend their decisions to the public. A knowledge of ethical principles and the techniques of moral reasoning can give those explanations more credibility and validity. Fourth, and most pragmatically, good ethics and good business generally go hand in hand, at least in the long run. Although short-term economic gains may result from making ethical compromises, one study done in the late 1970s showed that companies that ranked high in ethics also tended to rank high in growth and in earnings per share.

How can a person develop a set of ethical standards that will be relevant and useful in day-to-day situations? If you have read this far, you already have gotten a head start. The first step is to become familiar with enduring ethical principles, such as those just enumerated, or others that may be germane to your profession. For example, if the classical ethical theories do not seem helpful, you might want to consider the set of ethical principles proposed by Edmund Lambeth in *Committed Journalism.* Although designed for working journalists, his principles have relevance for everyone employed in broadcasting and cable. Lambeth suggests that an individual's decisions should adhere to the following principles:

1. Tell the truth.
2. Behave justly.
3. Respect independence and freedom.
4. Act humanely.
5. Behave responsibly.

Another model for journalists endorsed by many in the profession has seven principles or moral duties:

1. Don't cause harm.
2. Keep all promises.
3. Make up for previous wrongful acts.

4. Act in a just manner.

5. Improve your own virtue.

6. Be good to people who have been good to you.

7. Try to make the world better.

It matters little whether you subscribe to Aristotle's golden mean or principles suggested by Lambeth; the point is that you need to develop some underlying set of ethical principles.

Next you need to develop a model or plan of action that serves as a guide in making ethical choices. When a person is confronted with an ethical dilemma, the model serves as a blueprint for thinking. One possible model might be the following:

Stage one. Determine the situation. Compile all the facts and information that are relevant to the situation. Learn all you can about the circumstances that prompted the problems.

Stage two. Examine and clarify all the possible alternatives. Make sure you are aware of all your loyalties and possible courses of action. (If you subscribe to a teleological theory of ethics, you may also have to assess the possible consequences of each action.)

Stage three. Determine what ethical theories or principles you will follow in the situation. Try over time to develop some consistency in the choice of theories or principles.

Stage four. Decide and act accordingly.

Ethics in the Real World

We have now seen some theories and models promulgated by philosophers who have the luxury of time to reflect on their various ramifications. In the real world of TV and radio, however, rarely do professionals have the time to reflect on their decisions. For example, in New York City a convict with a gun threatened to kill hostages if his demands weren't broadcast immediately by a local TV station. The police on the scene urged the station manager to grant this request. The station involved in this dilemma had about 2 minutes to decide what to do. That's probably not enough time to do a thorough utilitarian or Kantian analysis of the situation. (In real life the TV station agreed to the request and bloodshed was averted. Subsequently, however, the station was soundly criticized by local newspapers for giving a forum to a gunman.)

Moreover, many broadcasters and cablecasters enter their profession without a personal code of ethics. Academic courses in media ethics became popular only in the early 1980s. Many current media executives were trained in selling, programming, or news but had to pick up informally along the way whatever ethical standards they have. In fact, many executives would probably be hard-pressed to articulate exactly where and how they developed their ethical standards.

Third, although some broadcast and cable organizations have codes of conduct or good practice, they are generally written in broad, general terms and may have little relevance to the individual. Companies rarely conduct education and training sessions in ethics. A new employee who expects the company to provide him or her with a ready-made set of ethics will probably be disappointed.

Finally, recent experience suggests that many ethical problems exist at the corporate level as well as at the individual level. The view that the only responsibility of business is to make a profit has come under attack by those who argue that since corporations have such a significant impact on the environment, their surrounding communities, and the individual consumer, they have an ethical obligation to serve the needs of the larger society. It is not surprising, then, that the number-one ethical problem that was cited in an *Electronic Media* survey done in 1987 was balancing corporate profits against public service. This suggests that employees of broadcasting and cable companies will be faced with ethical decisions throughout their careers. New employees will probably have to make choices about their own personal behaviors, while veterans who have risen to the managerial level will be making decisions regarding proper corporate policy. Personal codes of ethics must also accommodate the corporate situation.

In sum, a theoretical knowledge of ethical principles and analysis is helpful, but it must be tempered by an awareness of the nature of the day-to-day pressures in TV and radio.

Ethics: A Final Word

Many texts on media ethics present case studies that raise ethical problems for discussion. Students spend much time debating alternatives and find that there may be little agreement on the proper choice. Different ethical principles do indeed suggest different courses of action. Many students become frustrated by this and look upon ethics as simply a set of mental games that can be used to rationalize almost any decision. This frustration is understandable. It helps, however, to point out that ethical problems are not like algebra problems. There is no one answer that all will come up with. Ethical theories are not like a computer; they do not print out correct answers with mechanical precision. Abstract ethical rules cannot anticipate all possible situations. They necessarily leave room for personal judgment.

Ethical decision making is more an art than a science. The ethical principles and models presented here represent different perspectives from which ethical problems can be viewed. They encourage careful analysis and thoughtful, systematic reflection before making a choice. A system of ethics must be flexible, and it ought to do more than merely

rationalize the personal preferences of the person making the choice. As Edmund Lambeth says in *Committed Journalism,* an ethical system "must have bite and give direction." In sum, this brief discussion of ethics is not intended to give everybody the answers. It was designed to present some enduring principles, to encourage a reasoned approach to ethical problems, and to foster a basic concern for ethical issues, recognizing all the while that many ethical decisions have to be made in an uncertain world amid unclear circumstances and with imperfect knowledge.

SUMMARY

- Personal ethics have become an increasingly important issue for broadcasters as the competitive atmosphere, fostered by deregulation, heightens. Station managers now must be accountable for regulating themselves. Codes, departments, professional groups and organizations, and citizens' groups all help promote responsibility.

- The acceptability of a message depends on the size of a market, the time period, the station's audience, and the type of content involved.

- Ethics and law share common threads. Both are restrictive measures. The difference lies in the fact that one is enforced by the state, whereas the other is enforced by personal judgment.

- There are numerous ethical theories that attempt to explain how a person determines right from wrong. Some major theories are utilitarianism, egoism, the categorical imperative, the golden mean, cultural ethics, and situational ethics.

KEY TERMS

self-regulation   254
V-chip   258
National Association of
   Broadcasters (NAB)   259
National Cable Television
   Association (NCTA)   259
National Advertising Division
   (NAD)   260

National Advertising Review Board
   (NARB)   260
Children's Television Act
   of 1990   261
teleological theory   262
deontological theory   262
utilitarianism   263
egoism   264

categorical imperative   264
golden mean   265
cultural ethics theory   265
situational ethics   266

SUGGESTIONS FOR FURTHER READING

Christians, C.; Rotzoll, K.; Fackler, M.; & McKee, K. (2004). *Media ethics* (7th ed.). New York: Addison-Wesley.

Day, L. 2005. *Ethics in media communications.* Belmont, CA: Wadsworth.

Ethical dilemmas. (1988, February 29). *Electronic media,* p. 1.

Fink, C. (1995). *Media ethics.* New York: McGraw-Hill.

Goodwin, H. (1987). *Groping for ethics in journalism* (2nd ed.). Ames: Iowa State University Press.

Gordon, D.; Kihross, J.; Merill, J. G.; & Reuss, C. (1998). *Controversies in media ethics.* New York: Addison-Wesley.

Hausman, C. (1992). *Crisis of confidence.* New York: HarperCollins.

Klaidman, S., & Beauchamp, T. (1987). *The virtuous journalist.* New York: Oxford University Press.

Lambeth, E. (1992). *Committed journalism.* Bloomington: Indiana University Press.

Limburg, V. E. (1994). *Electronic media ethics*. Boston: Focal Press.

Merrill, J., & Odell, S. (1983). *Philosophy and journalism*. New York: Longman.

Meyer, P. (1987). *Ethical journalism*. New York: Longman.

Patterson, P., & Wilkins, L., eds. (1997). *Media ethics: Issues and cases*. New York: McGraw-Hill.

Retief, J. (2002). *Media ethics: An introduction to responsible journalism*. Oxford: Oxford University Press.

INTERNET EXERCISES

Visit our Web site at www.mhhe.com/dominick6 for study-guide exercises to help you learn and apply material in each chapter. You will find ideas for future research as well as useful Web links to provide you with an opportunity to journey through the new electronic media.

Part Five   What It Does

Ratings and Audience Feedback

Quick Facts

 Year of first national radio audience survey: 1927

 Number of U.S. households with TV: about 110 million

 Number of households in Nielsen Media Research's People Meter sample: 5,100

 Number of persons in Media Metrix's Internet ratings sample: 120,000

 Household rating of number-one show (*I Love Lucy*) in 1956: 47.5

 Household rating of number-one show (*American Idol*) in 2006: 19.2

Advertisers spend billions every year to purchase time on radio and television for their commercial messages. Not surprisingly, they like to know if their money is well-spent. For this to happen, they need information about how many and what kinds of people watch and listen. Enter the ratings.

This chapter discusses how to measure and evaluate what people are listening to or watching. The first part examines how ratings and ratings companies developed in the United States. The next sections will look at how data are collected, analyzed, and reported. The final section explores how additional feedback from the audience is gathered.

HISTORY OF AUDIENCE MEASUREMENT

Audience research first appeared in the 1920s when station owners became curious about the size of their listening audience. Early announcers requested listeners to drop a postcard to the station reporting that they had heard a particular program and indicating whether the signal was clear. The need for more-detailed data became important when advertisers, particularly those who bought time on network radio, demanded accurate estimates of audience size. Consequently, the American Association of Advertising Agencies and the Association of National Advertisers formed the **Cooperative Analysis of Broadcasting (CAB)** in 1930.

The CAB collected data on network listening in 35 cities across the United States using the **telephone recall method.** Calls were placed at different times during the day to homes selected at random from phone directories, and respondents were asked to recall the programs that they had listened to.

One problem with the credibility of the CAB ratings was in fact this use of the recall method. Although asking a person to remember what he or she had heard in the last few hours is more accurate than asking the person about listening on a previous night, human memory is still open to failure.

The CAB operated until 1946, when it fell victim to another organization with a superior way of measuring the audience. The C. E. Hooper company introduced the **telephone coincidental method,** in which respondents were asked if they were listening to the radio at the time of the call, and, if the answer was yes, they were asked to name the program or the station to which they were listening. The coincidental method is an improvement over the recall method because it does not rely on the fallible memory of the respondent. The results of the Hooper surveys, called Hooperatings, were sold to advertisers, advertising agencies, and broadcasters.

In 1942, the A. C. Nielsen Company (now Nielsen Media Research) started a ratings service that used a different method, one that did not rely on the telephone, to collect data about radio listening. Nielsen connected a mechanical device, called the **audimeter,** to the radios of a randomly selected sample of people. The audimeter consisted of a sharp stylus that made a scratch on a roll of paper tape (later replaced by 16-millimeter film) in synchronization with the radio's tuning dial. After a period of time, listeners sent back the tape or film to Nielsen, where the scratches were analyzed to reveal how long the set was on and to what station it was tuned.

Note that, whereas previous companies measured actual listening, Nielsen measured set use. The audimeter could determine only if the radio was turned on and to what station it was tuned. It could not determine who, if anyone, was listening. Nonetheless, advertisers preferred the Nielsen numbers, and in 1950 Nielsen bought out Hooperatings.

The audimeter moved to TV in the 1950s. A device was attached to every TV set in the home and families were instructed to open up the audimeter at the end of a week's viewing and send the film back to Nielsen for analysis. A Nielsen family received 50 cents per week for their cooperation. Data from the audimeters formed the basis for two Nielsen reports: the **Nielsen Television Index (NTI),** which reported the viewership of network programs, and the **Nielsen Station Index (NSI),** which did the same for local television markets.

Nielsen got a competitor in local TV ratings in 1949 when the American Research Bureau (later called Arbitron) began collecting ratings data. One of the problems with the Nielsen ratings was the lack of demographic data; the audimeter simply measured when the set was on and what channel it was tuned in to—it did not provide information about who, if anybody, was watching or listening. The Arbitron company solved this problem by using yet another data gathering technique—the **diary.** A sample of viewers was asked to record viewing in a specially prepared diary and to mail the finished diary back to Arbitron. In response, Nielsen introduced the diary as a supplement to its audimeters in 1955. Not to be outdone, Arbitron emulated Nielsen and introduced its own version of the audimeter in the 1960s.

A set-top box and a handheld keypad make up the People Meter system.

Citing increased costs, Nielsen abandoned its radio ratings service in 1963 to concentrate on television. Shortly thereafter, Arbitron announced it would use its diary method to measure local market radio. From the mid-1960s to the 1980s, Nielsen alone provided network TV ratings and competed with Arbitron for local TV market ratings. Arbitron was the dominant company in radio ratings.

The mechanical measurement devices continued to be improved. Nielsen introduced the **storage instantaneous audimeter (SIA)** in several local markets during the 1960s and 1970s. This device sent information directly from the audimeter through phone lines to Nielsen's computers. The SIA made it possible to publish ratings the day after a program was broadcast.

Yet another mechanical device for measuring the audience was introduced in the late 1980s—the **People Meter.** Developed by an English company, AGB Television Research, in an attempt to compete with Nielsen, the People Meter was connected to the TV set and automatically recorded the channel and time. But it also had a new feature—a device that resembled a remote control with a numbered keypad. Each family member was assigned a

unique code number. When he or she started watching TV, the family member was supposed to punch in his or her number on the keypad and then punch it again when they stopped watching. This information was stored in the People Meter and then transmitted via phone lines to central computers that had detailed demographic information about each family member obtained through a personal interview when the meter was installed. Thus, the People Meter could determine exactly who was in the audience. Nielsen quickly introduced its own version of the People Meter for use with its national NTI report. AGB was unable to secure enough clients for its new service and ceased operation in 1988.

People Meters have several advantages over diaries. First, they aren't affected by memory. Many people forget to fill out their diaries. Second, the data are sent electronically to Nielsen, eliminating the problem of people who don't mail back their diaries. Moreover, unlike SIAs, which measure only set usage, the People Meters report data about who is watching.

On the downside, People Meters are relatively expensive to install and maintain. This means that changing homes in the sample is difficult. Second, children's viewing is hard to measure with the People Meter. When the switch from SIAs to People Meters took place, a 22 percent drop in children's viewing was reported. Children aged 2 to 11 are apparently inconsistent in logging in with the People Meter and get bored with punching the buttons as they watch TV. Finally, like the SIAs, People Meters only measure at-home viewing. TV watching at work, in a bar, or in a college dormitory is not accounted for with the People Meter.

Arbitron, Nielsen's chief rival in providing local market TV ratings, also introduced its own version of the People Meter. The recession of the early 1990s, however, forced many local TV stations, which had previously subscribed to both Nielsen and Arbitron, to cancel one of their contracts in order to save money. The one they canceled was usually Arbitron, and in 1993 the company announced it was abandoning television ratings to concentrate on radio.

As of 2006, Nielsen had no serious competitors in the television ratings business and Arbitron dominated local market radio ratings. In addition, in 2001 Arbitron acquired **RADAR (radio's all-dimension audience research),** a service that rated network radio listening.

The need for rating the Internet audience became apparent as more and more advertisers demanded data about how many people were seeing their ads on the Web. By the mid-1990s, software programs that counted the number of visitors to a Web site were common. These programs, however, had many shortcomings and were not reliable. Companies such as Media Metrix and Nielsen//NetRatings introduced more-sophisticated measurement techniques in the late 1990s. Both firms gathered data from a panel of consumers who installed software on their computers to track the time they spend online and the various sites that they visit.

THE RATINGS PROCESS
Measuring TV Viewing

Nielsen Media Research draws two different types of samples to measure TV viewing. The national sample used for the NTI is designed to be representative of the entire U.S. population. To draw this sample, Neilsen first selects at random more than 6,000 small geographic areas, usually blocks in urban areas or their equivalent in rural areas, and lists

all households in these areas. Next, a sample of 5,100 households is drawn at random. Each household is then contacted, and, if it agrees to participate in the survey, a Nielsen representative installs a People Meter and trains household members how to use it.

For the local market NSI reports, Nielsen first divides the country into more than 200 markets. Within each market, a sample is drawn from phone books and supplemented by random digit dialing in order to obtain unlisted numbers. Sample sizes vary by market but are usually in the range of 1,000 to 2,000 households. Nielsen measures local station TV viewing using two different techniques. In 54 of the largest markets, SIAs are attached to each television in the household and viewing data are gathered about "set tuning" behavior. This information is supplemented with demographic data collected by means of a diary that is sent to participating households. Each member of the household is supposed to record what program he or she is watching and send the diary back to Nielsen at the end of a week. Four times a year (February, May, July, and November), diary measurement is used to collect information from all 210 TV markets in the United States. These measurement periods are called "sweeps," and the information from the diaries is used by local stations to determine advertising rates.

In 2002, Nielsen started to move away from its SIA plus diary data gathering method in large markets and began to replace them with the **local People Meter (LPM).** The change caused controversy (see the box "The Battle of Boston") because the LPM results were often at odds with the data gathered by the older diary method. In addition, many people protested that the new technique significantly underestimated the viewing of minority groups. In response, Nielsen made several changes to its sampling and recruiting procedures. These changes helped quiet the dispute, and as of 2006, LPMs were operating in Boston, New York, Chicago, Washington, D.C., San Francisco, and Philadelphia. Nielsen plans to have all the top 10 markets changed over to LPMs by 2007 or 2008.

The first data collected by the LPMs brought good news to cable networks and bad news to broadcast stations. In all markets, ratings of cable networks jumped anywhere from 40 to 80 percent, while broadcast ratings slipped by about 1 to 12 percent. Moreover, in the past, networks used to present some of their strongest programs during sweeps weeks to maximize the advertising rates their local affiliates would charge for the next 3 months. With the LPMs, however, audience demographic data are gathered continuously, and stations no longer have to wait 3 months for the results. It is unclear what impact this change may have on sweeps programming.

In mid-2006 Nielsen announced an ambitious plan that would ultimately lead to the phasing out of all diaries by 2011. In addition, Nielsen planned to measure out-of-home viewing on the Internet and handheld devices such as cell phones and PDAs.

Finally, in a move that might revamp the way advertising is bought, the company revealed that it will start providing ratings for commercials that air during a program. In the past Nielsen had supplied average ratings for the program, and advertisers had based their purchases on those numbers. Under the new system, advertisers will be able to determine how many viewers there were during the commercial breaks.

Processing the Data

Data from the People Meter and the SIA samples are stored in the home devices until they are automatically retrieved by Nielsen's computers. In addition, program schedules and local system cable informa-

tion are also checked to make sure the viewing data match up with the correct programs. All of this information is processed overnight and made available for customer access the next day. Diary information takes longer to process. The diaries are first mailed back to Nielsen where they are checked for legibility and consistency. The data are then entered into Nielsen computers and tabulated. It usually takes several weeks before these reports are available.

The Ratings Books

The NTI contains data on the estimated audience—divided into relevant demographic categories—for each network program broadcast during the measurement period. The report also features a day-by-day comparison of the audience for each of the major networks as well as an estimate of audience watching cable channels, independent broadcast stations, public TV, and premium channels. Nielsen has recently started reporting same-day DVR playback as well.

The NSI is a little more complicated. Each local market ratings book contains a map that divides the market into three areas: (1) the metro area, where most of the population in the market lives; (2) the

Issues: The Battle of Boston—Diaries vs. People Meters

Boston hadn't seen this kind of hostility since the Revolutionary War. In April 2002, Nielsen Media Research announced that it was making Boston a test site for its new local People Meter ratings system. Local television markets, such as Boston, were measured using a combination of audimeters and diaries. Nielsen's plans called for Boston to be the first market to rely solely upon the People Meter to measure local market viewing.

No way, said the local Boston TV stations, which promptly canceled their contracts with Nielsen.

Why the unwillingness to go with the new technology? In the first place, the local stations claimed the results were unreliable. They claimed the People Meter results were sometimes more than 40 percent different from diary results. During one test period, the People Meter combined rating for the three local station newscasts was less than what each station had gotten during a previous diary rating period. Further, the Boston stations resented being measured by a system that was out of sync with the rest of the country. In comparison to other large markets, local station viewing numbers would be down, thus potentially hurting ad sales. Finally, the new People Meter system was more expensive than the traditional audimeter and diary technique. Why, asked the Boston stations, should we pay more for a method that lowers our ratings and makes us out-of-step with the rest of the country?

Nielsen defended the People Meter technology, pointing out that the old diary technique was developed during the 1950s, when there were only three channels to view. In addition, the People Meter sample can produce overnight ratings and can provide viewing estimates among different demographic groups. In short, said the company, local People Meters were the wave of the future.

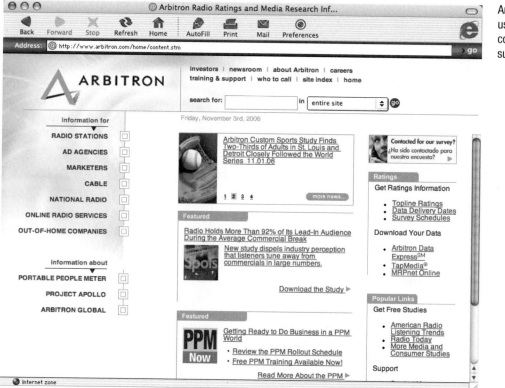

Arbitron's Web site contains useful information on how the company conducts its radio surveys.

designated market area (DMA), where the stations in that market get most of their viewers; and (3) the NSI area, that portion of the market that surrounds the DMA and accounts for 95 percent of the total viewing audience in that market. NSI areas may overlap, but DMAs do not.

The next section of the NSI contains special information, including the number of homes actually in the sample and demographic characteristics of the market. There are also notes about technical problems the stations may have had during the ratings period, such as being knocked off the air by a thunderstorm or power failure.

Audience estimates appear next. These numbers are broken down by time periods and by programs. Thus, a station manager can see how a specific program is doing against its competition and how well it maintains the audience from the program that preceded it.

Nielsen also prepares several specialized reports: The Nielsen Homevideo Index provides measurement of cable viewing, pay cable, VCRs, satellite channels, and other video services; the Nielsen Syndication Service reports viewing levels

of syndicated programs; and the Nielsen Sports Marketing Service tracks the viewing of particular sports teams. Nielsen also offers a special service that measures the Hispanic television audience.

Terms and Concepts in TV Ratings

There are three important terms in TV ratings. **Households using television (HUT)** represents the number or the percentage of households that have a TV set on during a specific time period.

The second term is **rating.** Specifically, a rating is the percentage or proportion of all households with a TV set watching a particular program at a particular time. A rating of 10 means that 10 percent of all the homes in the market were watching a specific program. Ratings consider all households in the market, not just those with TV sets in use.

The third term is *share of the audience* or **share.** The share is the total number of households watching a particular program at a specific time divided by the total number of households using TV. Thus, the share is based only on those households that actually have their TV sets turned on.

Some programs can have the same share but have different ratings. For example, let's pretend there are 1,000 households in our market. At 6 A.M., 100 of those 1,000 households have their TV sets on. Of those 100 households, 20 are watching *The Sunrise Home Shopping Show*. The rating for this program would be 20 divided by 1,000, or 2 percent. The share would be 20 divided by 100, or 20 percent. Later that night, let's say at 9 P.M., 600 households are watching TV, and of those 600, 120 are watching *Lost*. The rating for *Lost* would be 120 divided by 1,000, or 12 percent. The show's share of the audience would be 120 divided by 600, or 20 percent, exactly the same as that of *The Sunrise Home Shopping Show*.

Here are the formulas for calculating ratings and shares:

$$\text{Ratings} = \frac{\text{Number of households watching a program}}{\text{Total number of households in market}}$$

$$\text{Share} = \frac{\text{Number of households watching a program}}{\text{Total number of HUT}}$$

For another calculation example, see the box "Calculating Ratings and Shares."

Measuring Radio Listening

Arbitron is the leading company that provides ratings of local radio stations and network radio listening. Arbitron uses the diary method, and many of its procedures are similar to those used by Nielsen Media Research to measure TV viewing.

Arbitron draws its sample by randomly sampling phone numbers from a list compiled by a market research company. Numbers are also randomly generated to account for unlisted phones. The number of households drawn for the sample varies based on a statistical formula that takes into account the total number of households in the market. Sample sizes may range from 750 to 4,500 for local market surveys, with medium-sized markets having a sample size of about 1,000 diaries.

Those households that are selected by Arbitron are called and asked if they would like to participate in the survey. Arbitron mails a brightly colored package to each household that agrees. Inside the package are envelopes (for each member of the household over 11 years of age) that contain a diary, instructions, a letter of thanks, and about a dollar or so.

Diaries cover a 1-week period beginning on a Wednesday. There is one page per day with a column for indicating when a person started listening to a station and when the person stopped. Another column asks the person to write down the frequency or call letters of the station while another records where the listening took place (in a car, at the office, at home, etc.).

Some simple demographic questions are included at the end of the diary. When the diary is completed, the respondent mails it back to Arbitron, where the next phase begins.

Processing the Data

Once received by Arbitron, the diaries are subject to several review procedures. The first review removes diaries that Arbitron considers unusable: those that come in late, those that are illegible, those missing demographic information, and so forth. Other reviews look for inconsistent information (e.g., reporting listening to a station that doesn't exist) and other minor errors (e.g., transposing the call letters of a station). The data are then entered into the computer for analysis.

The Radio Ratings Book

A local market radio ratings report is similar in format to its TV counterpart. The first page contains a map that divides the market into metro, DMA, and total survey areas, much like the NSI. This is followed by general market statistics—number of automobiles, housing values, retail sales data, and the like. Another section reports whether any radio stations conducted unusual promotions designed to artificially increase their audiences during the ratings period. The next section of the book presents demographic data about listeners categorized by dayparts. A station, for example, can easily find its rating among men 12 to 24 during the Monday to Friday 6 A.M. to 10 A.M. daypart. Other sections of the book summarize total time spent listening to the station, where the listening occurred, and the average audience size per station by quarter-hour estimates.

Arbitron issues its Radio Market Reports for more than 280 local markets. Ratings reports are issued four times a year for larger markets. Smaller market reports are issued less frequently.

Arbitron also provides a service called RADAR that measures network radio listening. Network ratings are computed from a nationwide sample of 50,000 radio listening diaries.

Events: Calculating Ratings and Shares

Let's use the following hypothetical data in our calculations. A ratings company samples 24,000 households (all having TVs) in a given market and determines the following for the 7:30 to 7:45 time period.

Station	Number of Sample Households Watching
WAAA	4,800
WBBB	2,400
WCCC	1,200
Other stations	1,200
	9,600 = HUT

Let's figure out WBBB's rating:

$$\text{WBBB's rating} = \frac{2,400}{24,000} = .10, \text{ or } 10\%$$

To calculate WBBB's share of the audience, we must first determine the total number of households using TV (HUT) during the 7:30 to 7:45 time period. To do this, we add $4,800 + 2,400 + 1,200 + 1,200 = 9,600$. WBBB's share, then, is:

$$\text{Share} = \frac{2,400}{9,600} = .25, \text{ or } 25\%$$

Also note the following relationships:

$$(1) \text{ \% HUT} = \frac{\text{Rating}}{\text{Share}}$$

In our example

$$\text{\% HUT} = \frac{.10}{.25} = .40, \text{ or } 40\%$$

This means that 40 percent of all the TV homes in the sample were watching TV from 7:30 to 7:45.

$$(2) \text{ Rating} = \text{Share} \times \text{\% HUT}$$

In our example

$$\text{Rating} = .25 \times .40 = .10$$

This is simply another way to calculate the rating.

$$(3) \text{ Share} = \frac{\text{Rating}}{\text{\% HUT}}$$

In our example

$$\text{Share} = \frac{.10}{.40} = .25, \text{ or } 25\%$$

This is another way to calculate the share.

Terms and Concepts in Radio Ratings

The basic unit of measurement is different for radio and television ratings. The basic unit for most television ratings is the household. For radio, the basic unit is the person. The formulas for ratings and shares for radio listening reflect this difference. Specifically, in radio

$$\text{Ratings} = \frac{\text{Number of persons listening to a station}}{\text{Total number of persons in market}},$$

and

$$\text{Share} = \frac{\text{Number of persons listening to a station}}{\text{Total number of persons using radio}}.$$

There are two other ratings terms that are more commonly associated with radio ratings. The cumulative audience (or **cume**) is an estimate of the total number of different listeners who listen to a given station at least once during the time part under consideration. In other words, cume is a measure of how many different people listen at least once during the week during the given day part.

Average quarter-hour persons estimates the average number of persons who are listening to a station within a 15-minute period. It is calculated by dividing the estimated number of listeners in a given time period by the number of quarter hours (four per hour) in that time period.

ACCURACY OF THE RATINGS

There are more than 110 million television households in the United States. The Nielsen People Meter sample size is only 5,100, about .00005 of the total. Is it possible for a sample this small to mirror accurately the viewing behaviors of the entire population? The answer to this question is yes, within limits. A sample doesn't have to be large to represent the whole population, as long as it is *representative* of the whole population. To illustrate, when you go to the doctor for a blood test, the doctor does not draw a couple of quarts of blood from your body. A blood test uses only a few milliliters. From this small sample, the doctor can estimate your red cell count, your cholesterol, your hematocrit, and a number of other variables.

Imagine a huge container filled with thousands of coins—pennies, nickels, dimes, and quarters. Let's suppose that 50 percent of the coins are pennies but that this fact is unknown to you. The only way you could be absolutely *sure* what percentage of the coins were pennies would be to count every coin in the huge container, an arduous and time-consuming job. Suppose instead you took a random sample of 100 coins. If sampling were a perfect process, you would find that pennies accounted for 50 percent of your sample. Sometimes this happens, but more often you'll wind up with a little more or a little less than 50 percent pennies. It is also possible, but exceedingly unlikely, that you could draw a sample of 100 percent pennies or another of 0 percent pennies. The bigger the size of your sample, the more likely it is that your results will tend to cluster around the 50 percent mark.

Statisticians have studied the process of sampling and have calculated the accuracy ranges of samples of various sizes. One way of expressing accuracy is to use a concept known as the 95 percent **confidence interval.** This is an interval calculated from sample data that has a 95 percent chance of actually including the population value. For example, let's say the Nielsen People Meter sample of 5,100 homes finds that 20 percent of households watched *American Idol.* Similar to our coin example, we probably wouldn't expect that exactly 20 percent of the 110 million TV households in the United States were also watching. By using statistical formulas, however, we can estimate the 95 percent confidence interval, which in this case, ranges roughly from 19 percent to 21 percent. This means that we are 95 percent sure that, in the entire population of 110 million homes, somewhere between 19 percent and 21 percent are watching *Idol.*

To sum up this statistical discussion, Nielsen ratings are not exact estimates. They are subject to sampling error. However, when their margin of error is taken into account, Nielsen ratings (and other ratings based on a random sample) provide rather accurate estimations of audience viewing behavior.

Incidentally, there is an organization that strives to ensure reasonable accuracy in the realm of ratings: the **Media Rating Council (MRC).** (See the box "Media Rating Council.") This council periodically audits Nielsen, Arbitron, and other ratings services to check on their methods and reports. The MRC is an independent body whose fees are paid by the ratings companies.

It should also be noted here that factors other than sampling error also have an impact on accuracy. Note that the above discussion was based on the

The Media Rating Council (MRC) is an organization whose task is to make sure that audience research firms present data that are credible and valid. Formed in 1964, at the urging of the U.S. Congress in the aftermath of hearings on shortcomings in the way that radio and TV stations counted their audiences, the MRC (originally called the Broadcast Ratings Council) relies on the voluntary compliance of its members. All companies that collect audience data are invited to apply for membership.

Members are obligated to provide the MRC with full information about their data collection and analysis procedures and to submit to annual audits of their methods. The MRC hires an independent auditing firm to conduct the evaluation of the member rating services. Auditors check to see if the research company meets the MRC's standards for media research and if the company actually conducts its research in the way that it claims. If the company passes the audit, it is given the MRC's seal of good practice.

In addition to its auditing activities, the MRC also supports research that attempts to improve the quality of audience research. The MRC, for example, played a key role in improving the methods connected with the introduction of the local People Meter.

assumption that the ratings were drawn from a random sample of the population. Although both Nielsen and Arbitron go to great lengths to gather data from a truly random sample, that goal is seldom attained: When contacted, many households in the original sample may refuse to cooperate; individuals in the People Meter sample may get tired of pressing buttons and stop using it; people in the sample who agree to fill out a diary may get bored after a day or so and not return it; other diaries may be filled out illegibly; and People Meters and SIAs are subject to mechanical errors. All of these factors contribute to a **nonresponse bias.** Nonresponse is a more serious concern for diary samples. In many markets, Arbitron may be able to use 50 percent or less of all the radio diaries it sends out.

Additionally, some people may not tell the truth. During a telephone coincidental survey, one of the authors heard the audio from the TV set in the background that was tuned to a wrestling match. When asked what program he was watching, the respondent replied, "The local newscast." Individuals with SIAs might tune their sets to PBS whenever they leave the house. Diary keepers might fill in many educational programs that they did not watch. These are examples of the **social desirability bias,** or providing answers that the respondent thinks will make him or her look more refined or more educated.

Both of these factors reinforce the fact that ratings are estimates of viewing and listening behavior. They are not exact. Nonetheless, they are the best available means for the industry to determine who is watching or listening to what or which programs.

USES FOR RATINGS

Local stations and networks use the ratings to see how they are doing in terms of their total audience. Typically, the bigger the audience, the more money stations and networks can charge for advertising. This is why *American Idol,* which has a weekly audience of about 19 million households, can charge about $500,000 for a 30-second commercial, while *Cops,* which has a weekly audience of 4 to 5 million homes, charges only $65,000.

In addition, ratings can be used to determine what types of people are watching. Advertisers are interested not only in audience size but also in audience type. A show like MTV's *Laguna Beach,* for example, can charge higher rates, not because its total audience is particularly large, but because the show attracts 18- to 34-year-olds—an audience that many advertisers want to reach.

The sales staff at a station uses ratings to persuade potential advertisers that their stations attract the type of audience most likely to buy the advertiser's product. The salespeople at a radio station with a sports-talk format, for example, can show the owner of a cigar bar that an ad on their station would reach a predominantly male audience, a prime target for a cigar merchant.

The station's news department can use the ratings to see how much viewing occurs in neighboring communities. If the ratings show substantial viewing, the station might want to increase coverage of those areas to encourage continued viewing and better ratings.

These are just a few of the uses for ratings data. Keep in mind, however, that while the ratings are a handy tool, they are only one of several considerations that are used by broadcasters and cablecasters to make decisions. They are helpful, but as we have seen, they are not perfect.

NEW DEVELOPMENTS IN RATINGS TECHNOLOGY

Ratings companies are using advanced technology to help them improve their audience measurement techniques. One of the problems associated with the People Meter was the fact that many people, particularly children, forgot to push the button on the meter that recorded viewing. To overcome this problem, Arbitron developed a device that required no button-pushing. Called the **portable People Meter (PPM),** the device measures both radio listening and television viewing. The PPM is about the size of a pager and can be carried by an individual or clipped to a belt or some other article of clothing. It automatically detects an inaudible tone that TV stations, cable networks, and radio stations embed in their audio signal. At the end of each day, the audience member places the PPM in a special base that recharges the device and sends the collected data back to Arbitron for tabulation. Preliminary tests of the PPM were carried out in Philadelphia in 2002 and in Houston in 2005. In the Houston test, around 2,100 people participated and about 45 cable channels, 45 radio stations, and 16 broadcast stations encoded their signals. Preliminary results suggested that people listen to more radio stations than reported by the diary technique but their total listening time was less.

Furthermore, the growing popularity of DVRs, iPods, podcasting, video-on-demand, and cell phone video has made measuring the audience more complicated than ever before. Advertisers are also demanding more precise measurement of the impact of their media investments. Marketers were no longer satisfied with traditional viewing data but were searching for "engagement measurements," measures that show how much of a likelihood there is for a consumer to respond to an ad.

In an effort to take these factors into account, the Nielsen company started including DVR viewing in its regular People Meter reports. Additionally, Nielsen is developing Project Apollo, an ambitious project that will link product sales to media exposure. Apollo uses a panel of consumers who will wear a personal People Meter and also use a special scanning wand to scan the Universal Product Code on all items they buy at the grocery or drug stores. This provides advertisers with a single source of data for both purchase and media behavior. For example, if Crest toothpaste runs several ads on an episode of *Lost*, Apollo would tell the company how many viewers of the program actually went out and purchased the toothpaste. The costs to develop such a system, however, are considerable, and big advertisers were somewhat hesitant to commit their resources to the project.

Nielsen Media Research has developed a system, dubbed *Grabix*, that combines minute-by-minute ratings with scenes from the TV program or commercial that is being rated. Grabix uses a split-screen with the upper half displaying a line that indicates the household rating or the rating among some demographic group on a minute-by-minute basis. Video from the program or commercial that matches the data on the upper half of the screen is displayed

The personal portable People Meter comes with its own recharging stand.

During its 60 years or so in the business of measuring TV audiences, Nielsen has never measured out-of-home viewing, but starting in early 2007 the ratings company will include college students living away from home in its sample. This change by Nielsen reflects the importance that advertisers are placing on reaching young viewers and keeping an eye on what they are watching.

Only those students whose families have been chosen as part of the sample will be included. Further, only student viewing in dormitories, fraternity and sorority houses, and off-campus apartments will be tabulated. Viewing in bars, restaurants, and public TV rooms will not be counted.

Nonetheless, this innovation may have significant impact on the ratings of some programs and cable networks. A pilot study suggested that college students watched an average of more than 24 hours of TV a week.

Experts are mixed when it comes to predicting which specific shows might be affected the most. Some suggest that shows featuring teenage or college-age characters, such as *Gilmore Girls*, might get a boost. Others think that cult favorites among college students, such as *Family Guy*, will get better ratings. Almost all expect MTV and ESPN, a tuning favorite in fraternity houses, to improve.

It's probable that some shows or cable networks might get about a 0.2 to 1.0 jump in their ratings. This may not sound like much, but even an increase of a tenth of a rating point can be worth thousands of dollars in increased revenue. Or as one TV executive put it, every little bit counts.

on the bottom half. Among other things, Grabix allows an advertiser to see exactly how many viewers stay tuned for commercials during a program break. It also lets programmers see the drop in viewership that occurs after a big-name guest star finishes being interviewed on a talk show.

Finally, Nielsen is grappling with the problem posed by the switch to digital TV. In multicasting becomes common and the audience has access to hundreds of TV channels, including HDTV and video-on-demand, new devices will have to be developed to measure all of the various viewing options. Measuring the use of personal video recorders and streaming video and audio on the Internet poses additional problems for the ratings companies.

In short, the future of measuring the electronic media will be filled with challenges. It is likely that no single system of data collection will be adequate. There will probably be a combination of high-tech approaches including personal People Meters, LPMs, and SIAs along with the low-tech diary.

MEASURING THE INTERNET AUDIENCE

Reliable data on the Internet audience is important because without such data advertisers are reluctant to spend money on Net advertising. As in broadcasting and cable, advertisers want to know who is visiting a World Wide Web site, how often they visit, how long they spend at the site, and whether the cost is reasonable. Obtaining such data, however, is difficult. Despite their limits, the Arbitron and Nielsen audience data are generally accepted as industry standards. An industry standard for Internet audience measurement is still evolving.

Early attempts to measure Web page traffic were programs that measured "hits," or the number of times someone logged on to the page. A counter at the bottom of the page kept a running total of the number of visits. These numbers were notoriously unreliable since the programs measured hits in different ways depending on the server. Moreover, there were other programs that called Web sites over and over to inflate the number of hits. Advertisers preferred an independent organization that counts the numbers.

From 1996 to 1998, several companies began to offer Internet measurement services: Media Metrix, NewRatings, RelevantKnowledge, and the ACNielsen Company. By 2000, consolidation narrowed the field to two major competitors. Media Metrix merged with RelevantKnowledge and ACNielsen joined forces with NetRatings to form Nielsen//NetRatings Inc. Consequently, unlike radio and television, where one ratings company provides the definitive report, two companies provide data on the Internet audience. Nielsen//NetRatings provides a report called NetView that is based on a panel of 40,000 users in the United States. Nielsen recruits its panel members by random telephone calls. Those who agree to be in the panel install tracking software in their computers. In addition, four times a year Nielsen performs a telephone survey to project the total number of U.S. households that have Internet access.

Competing with Nielsen is comScore. ComScore also recruits its members by random phone calls and reports that it uses more than a million consumers worldwide to track Web behavior. Media Metrix, its main U.S. report, is based on a panel of 120,000 consumers who have installed special tracking software. Like Nielsen, comScore also tracks online buying and financial transactions.

Advertisers are perplexed because the two competing services sometimes provide widely conflicting reports of Web traffic. In November 2004, for example, NetRatings reported that 94 million people visited the Yahoo! Web site. For the same period, comScore credited Yahoo! with 116 million visitors. In addition, NetRatings and comScore are not consistent when it comes to aggregating numbers for related Web sites. ComScore lumps together visitors to the MSN network and other Microsoft sites, while NetRatings keep it estimates separate. Not surprisingly, as of 2006, advertisers and Web publishers were pressuring the two firms to standardize their reporting and to have their numbers audited.

Both comScore and NetRatings use a similar methodology. They recruit volunteers who agree to let the companies install software that monitors how the participants surf the Web. Measuring Web site visits, however, is much more difficult than measuring TV viewing or radio listening. A local radio market may only have a couple of dozen stations to monitor; a television market may have a hundred or so stations and networks. Web site researchers have to collect data concerning more than 300,000 sites.

In addition, much Web surfing is done at work. CNN.com and ESPN.com get most of their usage during the daytime hours. Many businesses and government organizations do not allow ratings companies to install tracking software on office computers because they fear that the software might also be used to access confidential information or sales data. As a result, daytime Web usage might be underestimated. Finally, neither company tracks usage in schools, libraries, or other public places. The next few years will probably see more refinements in the way the Internet audience is measured.

BEYOND RATINGS: OTHER AUDIENCE RESEARCH

Although audience ratings serve as the primary source of feedback for the electronic media industry, owners and managers often need additional information about who is listening and watching. This section examines two broad categories of audience research that are used to supplement ratings data.

Music Research

Most radio stations play music. All stations want to play the right mix of music so that they will attract as large an audience as possible. They want to avoid playing new songs that their listeners dislike and to avoid playing popular songs so many times that listeners get tired of them (a phenomenon called **burnout**). Broadcasters use two methods to test music: call-outs and auditorium testing.

Call-outs   **Call-out research** refers to a process whereby listeners are surveyed by telephone and asked to rate certain songs. About 20 **hooks**—5- to 10-second cuts of the most memorable parts of the songs—are played, and the listener is asked to rate each song on several rating scales. One scale measures whether the listener likes the song, while another measures whether the song has reached the burnout stage. Programmers at the station can use the results of the survey to determine those songs that their audience wants to hear as well as those that have peaked in popularity.

The biggest disadvantage of the call-out method is that it can't be used to test new or unfamiliar music. Since it depends on familiar hooks, program directors and music directors must rely upon other techniques when evaluating new releases. One possible method is auditorium testing.

Auditorium Testing   **Auditorium testing** consists of gathering a sample of 75–100 people in an auditorium or similar facility for about 60 to 90 minutes to evaluate musical selections—both new and familiar. Auditorium testing has two advantages over call-out research: It can test new songs, and it can test a much larger number of hooks. An auditorium test designed to rate familiar songs can test more than 300 hooks at a single session. Additionally, entire songs can be played so that the audience can rate music they have never heard before. Radio stations that are

Videotaping a focus group session. The moderator is leading a discussion about a commercial that the group has just watched.

considering a format change use auditorium testing to examine reactions to the new format. Instead of a series of hooks, audience members hear longer portions of the proposed format, including music, promotional announcements, and DJ patter.

Market Research

Market research covers a variety of techniques used by broadcasting and cable programmers to gain more knowledge about their audiences and their audiences' reactions to programs and personalities.

Production Research   Before spending huge sums of money to develop a new program or a TV commercial, networks, studios, and ad agencies may want to examine some early responses. **Concept testing** is used by production companies to gauge audience reactions to possible new program ideas. Audience members are given a one- or two-paragraph description of the concept behind a particular show and asked if they would watch it.

Commercials are sometimes tested with a **rough cut,** a simply produced version of the ad using

minimal sets, little editing, amateur actors, and no special effects. These rough cuts are used to get a general sense about the direction and the approach of the planned ad. Researchers realize that some low ratings of the rough cut are due to its unfinished nature.

New ads and programs may be tested by using **electronic response indicators (ERIs).** Each seat in a special auditorium is equipped with a dial or a series of buttons that enable a viewer to rate continuously what he or she sees on a screen. One button may be marked "like a lot," while another might be marked "like a little," all the way down to a button marked "don't like at all." The responses are sent directly to a computer that keeps track of the average responses. Thus an advertiser might determine that the first 15 seconds of the commercial were well liked but the rest of the ad rated poorly.

A more realistic method for analyzing viewer reactions to a program is **cable testing.** A research company recruits a sample of 500 to 600 viewers from a typical market. The members of the sample are asked to watch the new program on a cable channel that is not assigned to a broadcast or a cable network. After the show, a survey is conducted among sample members to see what viewers liked or disliked about the program and to ascertain whether they would watch the program if it were regularly scheduled.

Focus groups provide more-detailed information about how people think and feel about an ad or a program. A **focus group** is a group of 6 to 12 people and a moderator who have a focused discussion about a topic. The members of the group are screened to ensure that they are appropriate for the research. For example, a radio station conducting a focus group to find out what listeners thought of its music programming would be careful to include only regular listeners in the group. Members are generally paid between $25 and $50 to participate.

The moderator usually has a prepared list of topics for the group to discuss. It is also the moderator's job to elicit responses from everybody in the group and to make sure the group stays on the topic.

Researchers recommend that more than one focus group be conducted for a particular topic. The results from a single group might be unique or idiosyncratic and lead to wrong decisions. The total number of groups used to investigate a topic depends upon how much the sponsoring organization can afford to pay, but the typical number of groups used is between four and six per topic.

Focus groups are best thought of as a diagnostic device. Their responses can reveal the reasons behind certain attitudes or behaviors. Since focus groups comprise small, nonrandom samples, it is dangerous to generalize their results to the total population.

Audience Segmentation Research   Radio and television ratings books provide information on the different demographic segments of the audience. Programmers are able to determine whether particular programs do better among males or females and whether a show has a predominantly young or old audience. Demographic breakdowns, however, may not tell the whole story. The listening, viewing, and buying habits of a 20-year-old female living on a farm in Manhattan, Kansas, may be totally different from those of a 20-year-old female living in an apartment in Manhattan, New York City. Accordingly, many market researchers suggest classifying audience members along other dimensions.

Psychographic research segments the audience according to various personality traits. Audience members report their viewing and listening behavior and then rate their personalities on a number of different scales: independent–dependent; active–passive; leader–follower; relaxed–tense, romantic–practical, and so forth. The results can be used by program producers and advertisers. For example, if the audience for "20/20" scores high on the practical dimension, commercials that emphasize such themes as "saving money" or "seldom needs repair" might be emphasized.

Lifestyle surveys are similar to psychographic research but put more importance on values that may influence consumer behavior. There are many measurement scales used to segment audiences based on their lifestyles but the most well-known is VALS— values and lifestyle segmentation—developed at the Stanford Research Institute. The test divides people into eight groups, including "Strugglers," "Strivers," "Achievers," and "Actualizers." Advertisers use the VALS results to develop campaigns that are consistent with the values and orientations of their target audiences.

SUMMARY

- Audience estimates, expressed as ratings, are an important tool for broadcasters, cablecasters, Web site operators, and advertisers. Audience reports published by different ratings companies aid decision making in the industry.
- Early ratings companies, such as the Cooperative Analysis of Broadcasting and the C. E. Hooper Company used telephone surveys to measure radio listening. The A. C. Nielsen Company (now Nielsen Media Research) used a mechanical device attached to a radio or TV set to generate its estimates of the audience.

- Currently, the Arbitron Company uses diaries to measure radio listening, while Nielsen uses a handheld device, called a People Meter, along with set-top meters and diaries to measure TV viewing. Media Metrix and Nielsen//NetRatings use a panel of computer users to track data on Web site visits.
- Ratings companies calculate ratings, share of the audience, households using TV, people using radio, and cumulative audience figures and publish their results online and in ratings books. The reports contain maps,

demographic information, daypart results, and reports concerning specific programs. This information is used by networks, syndication companies, local stations, and advertisers.

- In addition to ratings research, radio stations use call-out research and auditorium testing to fine-tune their playlists.

- Broadcasters and cablecasters also use market research to pretest programs and commercials. Focus groups are conducted to investigate why certain programs and commercials are popular and others aren't.

- Finally, lifestyle research and psychographic research focus on personality traits and values in an effort to understand the audience further.

KEY TERMS

SUGGESTIONS FOR FURTHER READING

Beville, H. M. (1988). *Audience ratings* (2nd ed.). Hillsdale, NJ: Erlbaum.

Chappell, M. N., & Hooper, C. E. (1944). *Radio audience measurement.* New York: Stephen Daye.

Lindlof, T. (1987). *Natural audiences: Qualitative research of media uses and effects.* Norwood, NJ: Ablex.

Stewart, D. W., & Shamdasani, P. N. (1990). *Focus groups: Theory and practice.* Newbury Park, CA: Sage.

Webster, J.; Phalen, P.; & Lichty, L. (2000). *Ratings analysis: The theory and practice of audience research.* Mahwah, NJ: Erlbaum.

Wimmer, R., & Dominick, J. (2006). *Mass media research: An introduction* (8th ed.). Belmont, CA: Wadsworth.

INTERNET EXERCISES

Visit our Web site at www.mhhe.com/dominick6 for study-guide exercises to help you learn and apply material in each chapter. You will find ideas for future research as well as useful Web links to provide you with an opportunity to journey through the new electronic media.

Effects 13

Quick Facts

 Hourly rate of violence on children's TV, 2005: 8 acts

 Percent of young Americans who get political campaign news from the daily newspaper: 23

 Percent of young Americans who get political campaign news from comedy TV shows: 21

 Average length of sound bite for political candidates on TV news: 9.7 seconds

 Most researched television program in history: *Sesame Street*

Do TV and radio have an impact on our lives? Ask yourself the following questions:

1. What rights does a person have when arrested?

2. While on a date, have you ever used a line or clever remark that you heard on TV?

3. When you're preparing for an important occasion, do you worry about dandruff, acne, perspiration, bad breath, ring around the collar, yellow teeth?

4. Did you ever consciously dress like a character you saw on TV?

5. Have you ever voted for a contestant on *American Idol*?

6. Do you vote differently because of televised ads for political candidates?

The answers to these questions will tell you how much of an impact TV and radio have had on your personal life.

Now consider the global scale. What impact have the broadcast media had on society? This question is a little more difficult to answer. Nonetheless, it's an important topic. Radio and TV have been, at various times, the alleged culprits behind a host of social ills. Television, it was claimed, made us more violent and antisocial, hurt our reading skills, decreased our SAT scores, fostered sexual stereotypes, and more. From a pragmatic standpoint society needs to know if, in fact, these allegations are valid, and if so, how to correct them. Consequently, this chapter briefly examines how we go about studying the impact of radio and TV, the changing views concerning media effects over the past 70 years or so, and the most current research about the effects of broadcasting in specific areas.

STUDYING THE EFFECTS OF THE ELECTRONIC MEDIA

There are many ways to examine the social consequences of the electronic media. Some scientists employ qualitative methods, in which they make direct observations and in-depth analyses of mass communication behaviors in natural settings. Other scholars use the critical or cultural studies technique that has been long popular in the humanities to provide a more interpretive look at the process of mass communication. Both the qualitative and critical/cultural studies approaches suggest new and different ways of explaining and understanding the nature of the impact of electronic media. This chapter, however, focuses more on the traditional and pragmatic social science approach to mass media effects; it emphasizes those research questions that have implications for social policy.

In electronic media research, several techniques are used to gather data about audience effects. These techniques are wide-ranging, partly because historically the effects of mass communication have been studied by psychologists, social scientists, political scientists, and others. Not surprisingly, each discipline has relied on the technique most closely associated with it. Thus psychologists use the experimental method, whereas sociologists use surveys. There are, however, many variations on experimental and survey research. In general, it's possible to say that there are four main social scientific methods:

1. Experimental methods, which can take place either in controlled "laboratory" conditions or in more natural "field" conditions.

2. Survey methods, which can either sample the subjects one time only or continue over time.

3. Content analysis, which is a systematic method for analyzing and classifying communication content.

4. Meta-analysis, which is a method that looks at a number of existing studies about a similar topic and summarizes the main findings by using statistical procedures that highlight which results are consistently found.

Each of these four methods has its own built-in pros and cons. Knowing the advantages and disadvantages of these various techniques is important because they have an impact on the degree of confidence that we have in research results.

Laboratory experiments are done under tightly controlled conditions and allow researchers to focus on the effects of one or more factors that may have an impact on the audience. Usually at least two groups are involved; one group gets treated one way while the other is treated differently. The big advantage of lab experiments over other methods is that they allow researchers to make statements about cause and effect. In an experiment subjects are randomly assigned to experimental conditions, and the researcher has control over most external factors that might bias the results, thus making the claim of cause and effect stronger. Their big disadvantage is that they are done under artificial conditions, so behavior that occurs in the lab might not occur in real life.

Field experiments occur outside the lab. Sometimes a natural event occurs that creates the conditions necessary for an experiment, and sometimes field experiments can be set up by the researcher. To illustrate, suppose one program is fed to one-half the homes on a special cable system while the remainder sees a different program. The effects of this single program could then be examined. The advantage of field experiments is naturalness; people are studied in their typical environments. The big disadvantage is the lack of control. Unlike the lab, field experiments are subject to the contaminating influences of outside events.

Surveys generally consist of a person's answers to a set of predetermined questions. Surveys are done through the mail, over the phone, on the Internet, or in person and usually involve some kind of questionnaire or other written document. The big advantage of survey research is its realistic approach. People in natural settings are asked questions about their typical behaviors. A big disadvantage with surveys is the fact that they can't establish cause and effect. After a survey a researcher can say only that factor *A* and factor *B* are related; that researcher cannot say that *A* causes *B* or that *B* causes *A*. A survey only establishes a relationship. Another disadvantage is that surveys rely on self-reports. It can only be assumed that respondents give valid and truthful responses.

Surveys can be done one time or they can be **longitudinal** (repeated over time). A **trend study** is one in which the same question or questions are asked of different people at different times. An example of a trend study would be a poll done 6 months before an election that asks which presidential candidate people intend to vote for and is then repeated with a different group of people a week before the election.

Panel studies are a special type of longitudinal survey in which the same people are studied at different points in time. The advantage in a panel study is that some evidence of cause and effect can be established, usually through sophisticated statistical analysis. The disadvantages include the fact that panel studies take a long time to do and they suffer from attrition—respondents die, move away, or get bored and are no longer part of the study group.

Content analysis studies segments of TV and radio content in order to describe the messages presented by these media. Such studies have been useful in defining media stereotypes and establishing a gauge of the amount of violence in TV programming. The biggest problem with content analysis is that it cannot be used alone as a basis for making statements about the effects of media content. For example, just because a content analysis establishes that Saturday morning cartoons are saturated with violence, it doesn't necessarily follow that children who watch these shows will behave violently. That might be the case, but it would take an audience study to substantiate that claim—a content analysis by itself would be insufficient.

A **meta-analysis** looks at many studies in different settings and across a variety of samples. It provides a macroview of the research in a given area and gives a good synopsis of the major findings. For example, meta-analyses have been conducted on studies that have examined the effects of television violence on aggressive behavior and on the impact of playing video games. Each individual study examined in a meta-analysis provides a different estimate of the strength of the relationship that is being examined. By accumulating the results across a number of studies a more accurate picture of the relationship can be determined. Meta-analysis, however, is not without disadvantages. Critics have charged that it can oversimplify a complicated pattern of results and that any design flaws in the original studies that are reviewed will produce misleading conclusions. In any case, meta-analysis has become more popular in recent years.

THEORIES OF MEDIA EFFECTS

These methods have been used to study the impact of mass media since the early 1900s. Throughout that time our view about the power of media effects has undergone significant changes as social science learns more about the various factors that affect media impact. As we shall see, there were periods in history when the media (including broadcasting) were thought of as quite powerful and other times when they were thought to have little effect. The current thinking seems to represent a compromise between these two extreme positions. The rest of this section briefly reviews the various theories concerning the effects of mass media that have evolved over the years.

Hypodermic Needle Theory

One of the earliest theories of media effects held that mass-communicated messages would have strong and more or less universal effects on the audience they reached. It was thought that the media would "shoot" beliefs into people's minds much the same way a doctor inoculates people with a hypodermic needle. Much of this thinking was due to the apparent success of propaganda before and during World War I. For example, in 1914–1916, as World War I broke out in Europe, skillful British propaganda stories were considered responsible for bringing the United States into the war on the side of the Allies. After the war, a new medium, radio, further reinforced the hypodermic model. Successful radio rogues, such as Dr. Brinkley (see Chapter 10), and the *War of the Worlds* scare seemed to support the view that mass media can have powerful consequences.

Reexaminations of the development of this model suggest that it was not so thoroughly accepted as once believed. In addition, some social scientists of this early period also argued that other factors should be considered when discussing the impact of the media. In any case, advances in experimental and survey research began to cast serious doubt on the hypodermic needle model. By the mid-1940s it was obvious that the model's assumptions about the way communication affects audiences were too simplistic. The pendulum was about to swing in the other direction.

Limited-Effects Theory

Persuasion, especially the political kind that goes on in election campaigns, was the main focus of this new line of research. Several studies indicated that the media did not have a direct effect on the audience, as was previously believed. The newly developed two-step flow theory suggested that media influence first passed through a group of people known as opinion leaders and then on to the rest of the audience. Further research posited that media influence was filtered through a net of intervening factors, such as a person's prior beliefs and knowledge and the influence of family, friends, and peer groups. The mass media were simply one of a great many determinants of how people think or behave.

This view brought some comfort to those who feared that the public might be brainwashed by skillful ideologues and clever propaganda techniques, since it suggested that they were unlikely to succeed. It also was appealing to mass-media executives, who could use it to counter criticism that the media were the cause of various social ills.

The most complete statement of the limited-effects position (although he doesn't call it that) appears in a book by Joseph Klapper, *The Effects of Mass Communication,* published in 1960. Klapper reviewed the existing research and summed it up in a series of generalizations, the most widely quoted of which held that mass communication alone does not ordinarily cause audience effects but instead functions primarily to reinforce existing conditions.

Klapper's generalizations enjoyed popularity for nearly two decades; in fact, there are some who still subscribe to the limited-effects model even today. Nonetheless, keep in mind that the bulk of the studies reviewed by Klapper were done before TV became the dominant mass medium. In addition, although the most widely quoted of Klapper's conclusions concerned the reinforcement effect of the media, he also noted that there were occasions when the media could exert direct effects or when the mediating factors that generally produce reinforcement are absent or themselves help foster change. As TV became more prevalent and researchers discovered more areas where media effects were direct, the limited-effects model gave way to a new formulation.

Specific-Effects Theory

The most recent theory of media effects represents a middle ground. Researchers realize that media are not all-powerful; they compete with or complement other sources of influence such as friends, family, and teachers. Nonetheless, there are circumstances under which specific types of media content might have a significant effect on certain members of the audience. Although this statement might not be entirely satisfying from a scientific standpoint, in the last few years communication researchers have made great progress in identifying how and when, and sometimes even why, mass media, especially broadcasting, affect individuals and groups. Accordingly, the answer to the question, What are the effects of the mass media? has become complex, as social scientists continue to define the circumstances, the topics, and the people for whom specific effects might occur.

The remainder of this chapter examines seven of the most investigated topics in recent broadcasting research: (1) the effect of violent TV programming on antisocial behavior, (2) perceptions of social reality, (3) stereotyping, (4) TV and politics, (5) TV and educational skills, (6) prosocial behavior, and (7) social impact of the Internet.

VIDEO VIOLENCE

It is appropriate that we first examine the media violence area. This subject is the most controversial, generates the most research, utilizes all of the four research techniques mentioned earlier, illustrates some of the problems in generalizing from research data, and is the one topic about which communication researchers know the most.

History

Concern about the impact of electronic media violence first surfaced during the 1930s when parents worried that gangster movies would corrupt the morals of young people. When television became popular during the 1950s, video violence became an issue. Congressional hearings examined the topic and concluded that watching TV was an important factor in shaping the attitudes and characters of its younger audience.

The urban violence and general unrest that characterized the mid-1960s sparked a new burst of interest in the topic. A presidential commission, the National Commission on the Causes and Prevention of Violence, reviewed the existing research evidence and concluded that violent behavior as depicted on TV had a negative effect on the audience.

A few years later the U.S. Surgeon General's Office sponsored a research effort involving 50 separate studies that examined this same area. After some debate and further congressional hearings, most researchers who participated in the project agreed that their findings indicated a causal link, albeit a weak one, between watching TV violence and antisocial attitudes and behaviors. In 1982, 10 years after the release of the original Surgeon General's Report, an update reinforced the original conclusion that TV violence was a cause of aggressive behavior.

Many studies appearing since the update have changed their focus to "effect size." This approach gets away from the simple question of whether TV violence has an effect on the audience and considers instead the more complicated question of how big an effect it has. Several researchers have disagreed over

The American Psychiatric Association estimates that by the time a child is 18 he or she will have seen nearly 200,000 acts of violence on television and in motion pictures.

The newspaper headlines were certainly alarming: "Violence linked to one hour of TV"; "Hour a day the safe limit"; "More than one hour of TV a day turns teens to violence"; "Too much TV for young breeds violent adults." These headlines were typical of the news coverage that greeted the March 2002 publication of a survey in the journal *Science* that examined the link between television viewing and aggression in young people.

The study examined 700 people. It started in 1975, when most were about 14, and ended in 1993. The researchers interviewed the subjects four times during that 18-year period, grouping them into those who watched less than an hour of TV a day, 1-to-3-hour watchers, and 3-hour-plus watchers. Aggression was measured by asking the respondents and their mothers to report specific acts of violent behavior. The researchers also checked state and federal records to see whether respondents had been arrested for some violent crime.

The results noted that among those young people who watched less than an hour of TV per day when they were 14, only about 6 percent had committed aggressive acts by the ages of 16 to 22. On the other hand, among those who watched 1 to 3 hours of TV daily, the corresponding figure was nearly 23 percent. For those who watched more than 3 hours daily, the figure jumped to 29 percent.

This longitudinal panel study is impressive because it covers such a long period of time. In addition, the researchers controlled for other factors that might be related to aggression: low income, family neglect, prior history of violence, low parental education, and neighborhood violence. The link between TV watching and aggression persisted even after these factors were removed. The survey also provides evidence that the impact of viewing might extend well beyond adolescence into young adulthood.

The study's conclusions, however, should be taken with some skepticism. In the first place, the researchers measured overall TV viewing. They did not measure how many violent programs these young people watched. There's no reason to think that viewing 2 hours of situation comedy or 2 hours of the Discovery Channel should be linked to violence. The study would have been much stronger had the researchers established a link between aggression and specific programs that contained violence. Second, there were relatively few people (about 12 percent of the sample) who watched an hour or less of TV per day. This lack of viewing might be due to the fact that this group might be spending more time with their parents or who have parents who closely supervise their behavior. Those who watch a lot of TV might be spending their time away from their parents and parental supervision. In short, some other factor, not measured by the researchers, might be causing the relationship. This survey once again highlights how difficult it is to establish a causal link between TV viewing and violent behavior.

the significance of some of the relatively weak effects that have been discovered.

The issue resurfaced with the passage of the Telecommunications Act of 1996. In response to public and congressional pressure, the act contained a provision mandating that new TV sets be equipped with a V-chip that would allow parents to block out violent content (and other forms of objectionable behavior) from their TV sets. (The V-chip is discussed in more detail in Chapter 11.)

Another reincarnation of this issue occurred after the outbreaks of school violence in Littleton, Colorado; Paducah, Kentucky; and Jonesboro, Arkansas. Congress once again held hearings on media violence and yet another report, *Youth Violence,* was issued by the U.S. Surgeon General linking exposure to TV violence with some forms of aggressive behavior. A

similar conclusion was reached by a long-term, longitudinal study published in 2002 (see boxed material).

Finally, the issue surfaced again in connection with the FCC's increased concern over indecent programming. A group of lawmakers wrote the FCC and asked why the commission worried about the effects of indecent programs but paid little attention to violent programming. Accordingly, in 2004 the FCC held an inquiry about TV violence that covered a wide range of topics from the effects of fantasy violence to the efficacy of the V-chip.

So much for the history of this topic. Next, we review specific research evidence, pointing out its strengths and weaknesses, and conclude with an attempt to summarize the research consensus in this area.

Research Evidence

Experiments were one of the first methods used to investigate the impact of media violence. A series of studies done in the early 1960s documented that children could easily learn and imitate violent actions that they witnessed on screen.

A second set of experiments from the early 1960s was designed to settle the debate touched off by two competing theories of media effects. On the one hand, the **catharsis theory** posited that watching scenes of media violence would actually reduce the aggressiveness of viewers since their hostile feelings would be purged while watching the media portrayals. Not surprisingly, this viewpoint was popular with many industry executives. On the other hand, the **stimulation theory** predicted that watching scenes of violence actually prompted audience members to behave more aggressively after viewing. The experimental design used to test these competing theories is presented in simplified form in Figure 13–1. The results of these and other experiments showed little support for catharsis. In fact, the bulk of the laboratory research argues for the stimulation effect. This is not to say that the catharsis hypothesis is categorically wrong. There may be some instances where it might occur. Most of the time, however, the likely end product is increased aggression.

These early experiments were criticized for their artificiality. They were done in the lab under controlled conditions and used violent segments that were not typical of what everybody saw on TV. Later experiments used more-realistic violent segments and more-relevant aggression measures. For example, several experiments used actual programs that contained about the average number of violent acts per hour in prime-time TV (about five or six). Additional experiments used more real-life measures of aggression. Several observed the actual interpersonal aggression of children in play groups or in classrooms. These and other more-natural measures confirm that watching violence stimulates subsequent real-life aggression.

In sum, the results from laboratory experiments demonstrate that shortly after exposure to media violence, individuals, especially youngsters, are likely to show an increase in their own level of aggression. In fact, since the mid-1970s there has been a marked decrease in the number of lab experiments examining this topic partly because the results have been so consistent. More recent experiments have accepted the fact that exposure to violence facilitates subsequent aggression and have concentrated instead on factors that might increase or decrease the *amount* of aggression performed in response to media portrayals.

Laboratory studies are important because, as mentioned earlier, they help establish a plausible cause-and-effect pattern and control for the effects of extraneous factors. Still, the laboratory is not real life, and to be more sure of our conclusions we need to examine the results of research that is done outside the lab.

Surveys (also called correlational studies) are done in the real world. Although they offer little evidence of cause and effect, they do not have the artificiality of the lab associated with them. Most surveys on this topic incorporate the design of Figure 13–2. If the viewing of media violence is indeed associated

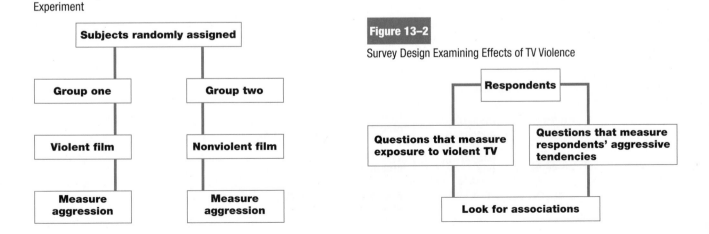

Figure 13–1

Simplified Diagram for Catharsis versus Stimulation Experiment

Figure 13–2

Survey Design Examining Effects of TV Violence

with real-world aggression, then people who watch a lot of violent TV should also score high on scales that measure their own aggressive behavior or attitudes toward aggression. The results from a large number of surveys involving literally thousands of respondents across different regions, socioeconomic statuses, and ethnic backgrounds have been remarkably consistent: There is a modest but consistent association between viewing violent TV programs and aggressive tendencies.

These results, however, are not without problems, like trying to establish cause and effect. Although viewing TV violence and aggression are related, TV viewing does not necessarily cause aggression. In fact, it's logically possible that aggressive individuals choose to watch more violent TV, which would mean that aggression could cause the viewing of violent TV. Finally, it's also possible that the relationship might be caused by some third factor. Maybe the real cause of aggression is a history of child abuse, and this in turn is associated with watching violent TV. Survey statistics would show a positive relationship between viewing violent TV and aggression, but the real cause might be something else.

Once again, to sum up, correlational studies provide another piece of the puzzle; they show that viewing TV violence and antisocial behavior are linked in the real world, but they don't tell us anything definitive about cause and effect. Remember, however, that lab studies can determine cause and effect and their results are consistent with the notion that TV viewing causes subsequent aggression. So far we have reason to be somewhat comfortable with that conclusion. But there is still other evidence to consider.

In the past 30 years or so, several field experiments were carried out to investigate the potential antisocial effects of TV violence. Recall that field experiments give us some basis for deciding cause and effect but suffer from a lack of control of other, potentially contaminating factors.

The results from field experiments are somewhat inconsistent. At least two done in the early 1970s found no effect from viewing violent TV. One of these two, however, was plagued by procedural problems and its results should be accepted cautiously. On the other hand, at least five field experiments have yielded data consonant with the lab and survey findings. The main conclusion of these studies seems to be that individuals who watch a diet of violent programs tend to exhibit more antisocial or aggressive behavior. In some studies this effect was stronger than in others, but the direction was consistent.

Figure 13–3 shows the design used in one of these field experiments. In this case the experiment was based on natural circumstances. The researchers were able to identify a Canadian town that was surrounded by mountains and was unable to receive TV signals until 1974. This town was matched with two others, one that could receive only the Canadian Broadcasting Corporation (CBC) and another that could get the CBC plus the three U.S. networks. The towns were studied in 1973 and again 2 years later. Children in the town that had just gotten TV showed an increase in the rate of aggressive acts that was more than three times higher than those for children living in the other two towns.

On balance, the results from field experiments are not so striking as those using the lab and correlational methods. On the whole, though, they

Figure 13–3

Canadian Field Experiment Design

Community	Time one		Time two	
1	No TV	Measure aggression, media exposure, and related variables	One TV channel	Measure aggression, media exposure, and related variables
2	One TV channel		Two TV channels	
3	Four TV channels		Four TV channels	

Figure 13–4

Longitudinal Design to Study TV Violence

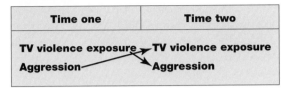

tend to support, although weakly in some cases, the notion that viewing violent TV fosters aggressive behavior.

Panel surveys, as noted earlier, are longitudinal research projects that examine the same individuals at different points in time. They are not plagued by the artificiality of the laboratory, and their design allows us to draw some conclusions about cause and effect. Since the early 1970s the results of several panel studies have become available for analysis.

The panel analysis begins with measurements of both real-life aggression and exposure to TV violence, taken at two different times. Next, the researchers determine if TV viewing as measured at time 1 is related to aggression at time 2. At the same time, the relationship between aggression at time 1 and TV viewing at time 2 is also assessed. If early TV viewing is more strongly related to later aggression than early aggression is to later TV violence viewing, then we have evidence that it's the TV viewing causing the violence and not vice versa. Figure 13–4 diagrams this approach.

Several longitudinal studies done in the United States and Europe, including both panel and trend studies, have found, with some exceptions, similar results. The majority of the studies seem to suggest that the sequence of causation is that viewing TV violence causes viewers to become more aggressive. The degree of the relationship between the two factors is small and, in a few instances, difficult to detect, but it is consistent. In addition, the process seems to be reciprocal. Watching TV violence encourages aggression, which in turn encourages the watching of more violent TV, and so on.

There is one more piece to be added to the puzzle. As mentioned above, a meta-analysis examines the results of many studies and draws general conclusions about the strength of a relationship. One meta-analysis conducted in 2002 looked at more than 280 studies—including lab experiments, field

experiments, surveys, and panel studies—concerning TV violence and aggressive behavior. The results of this analysis revealed a positive link between media violence and aggression regardless of the research method. The greatest effect was found in lab experiments, while long-term panel surveys produced the weakest.

Having reviewed evidence from four basic research methods, what can we conclude about the effects of violent TV on antisocial behavior? Laboratory experiments demonstrate that under certain conditions, TV can have powerful effects on aggressive behavior. Field experiments provide additional, although less consistent, evidence that TV can exert an impact in the real world. Surveys show a consistent but somewhat weak pattern of association between violence viewing and aggression. Longitudinal studies also show a persistent but weak relationship between the two and suggest a pattern whereby watching TV causes subsequent aggression. Meta-analysis shows consistent results across many samples using different methods. Unfortunately, few findings in areas such as this are unambiguous. Nonetheless, a judgment is in order. Keep in mind that some might disagree, but the consensus among social scientists seems to be the following:

1. Television violence is *a* cause of subsequent aggressive tendencies in viewers; it is not *the* cause since many factors besides TV determine whether people behave aggressively.

2. The precise impact of TV violence will be affected by many other factors, including age, sex, family interaction, and the way violence is presented on the screen.

3. In relative terms, the effect of TV violence on aggression tends to be small.

Does this close the case? Not quite. The third summary statement has been the focus of much current debate. The majority of researchers concede that there is some kind of causal link between viewing video violence and aggression, but several argue that the link is too weak to be meaningful. To be more specific, statisticians characterize the strength of any relationship in terms of the amount of variability in one measure that is accounted for by the other. For example, suppose a person was trying to guess your college grade point average just by looking at you. Chances are the person wouldn't do

Issues: Putting Things in Perspective

Which has more violence: TV shows or nursery rhymes? Nursery rhymes by far. A researcher in London analyzed 2 weeks of television violence and compared it to the violence in 25 popular rhymes such as "Jack and Jill" and "Simple Simon." The results showed that children's rhymes contained 10 times more violence than TV shows broadcast during the early evening hours when most children were watching.

too well. Now let's show the person your SAT scores and let the person guess again. Chances are that the person will do a little better. Why? Because there is an association (a moderate one, at least) between GPA and SAT scores. In other words, they share some variation. The more shared variability there is between two measures, the better a person can predict. If two factors are strongly related, changes in one might account for 60 to 70 percent (or higher: 100 percent if perfectly related) of the change in the other. A person could make quite accurate predictions in this instance. If two factors are not associated at all, change in one would explain 0 percent of changes in the other. In this case a person's predictions would be no better than chance. Thus the strength of a relationship is measured by the variability explained. As far as TV violence and aggression are concerned, exposure to televised violence typically explains from about 2 to 9 percent of the variability in aggression. Knowing how much TV violence you watch helps a little, but not much, in predicting your aggression level. Put another way, between 91 and 98 percent of the variability in aggression is due to other causes. Given this situation, is the effect of TV on aggression really that meaningful? Does it have any practical or social importance?

This question is more political or philosophical than scientific, but research can offer some guidelines for comparison. The usual effect size found for TV violence's impact on antisocial behavior is only slightly less than that found for the effects of viewing *Sesame Street* and *The Electric Company* on cognitive skills of the audience. It's also only slightly less than the effect that a program of drug therapy has on psychotic patients. Indeed, several drugs in widespread use have therapeutic effects about as great as the effect size of TV violence and aggression. In sum, although the magnitude of the effect may not be great, it is not that much different from effects in other areas that we take to be socially and practically meaningful. Thus even though the effect may be small, this does not mean that it should be dismissed.

Video Game Violence

The first video games emerged in the late 1970s. Early games were usually played at video arcades but Nintendo, Sony, and Sega developed versions to be played on the home television set. Eventually, these games migrated to the home computer.

By today's standards, the violence in the earlier forms of video games was mild (e.g., PacMan, Missile Command, Centipede). In the 1990s, however, a new breed of video game, the first-person shooter, came on the market. Games such as Duke Nukem, Doom, and Wolfenstein had as their main object the killing or wounding of opponents. The graphics associated with these games became even more realistic and bloodier as the new century progressed. When it was discovered that the two teenagers involved in the violence at Columbine High School were avid fans of Doom, parents, researchers, and policymakers became more interested in the impact of this kind of content on society.

Video games are popular. More than 80 percent of all U.S. households have some form of video game platform. Children spend an average of 7 hours a week playing these games, and boys play twice as much as girls. College students are no strangers to video games. One survey found that about 15 percent of male first-year students played video games more than 6 hours a week and about 3 percent played more than 20 hours per week.

Content analyses have shown that many of these games portray violence. A 2003 survey noted that 68 percent of the top 60 games contained some act of violence. As of 2006, many popular games were saturated with aggressive and antisocial behavior. In Grand Theft Auto: San Andreas, players can steal cars, beat up prostitutes, and kill police officers, and 25 to Life lets players attack police officers with guns, bats, and pipe bombs while using bystanders as human shields. In Bully, players can whack teachers and classmates with baseball bats.

Evidence about the effects of these games comes from laboratory experiments, surveys, and meta-analyses. The lab experiments have been conducted on a wide range of age groups, from elementary school children to college undergraduates. Studies that have examined the impact of playing violent video games on young children's play behavior have generally found an increase in aggression after playing the games. Experiments with older subjects have shown mixed results; the majority have found that playing violent video/computer games leads to subsequent increases in aggression, but several have failed to find such an effect.

Surveys have also been conducted across many age groups and have used a variety of methods to measure aggressive behavior, including self-reports, teacher and peer ratings, and delinquency records. The survey results are a little more consistent. They suggest that video/computer game play is linked to both increases in aggressive behavior and favorable attitudes toward aggression. There was also some evidence of a link between game playing and a decreased self-esteem and an unfavorable self-concept.

Three meta-analyses have been conducted on all the studies that examined the impact of video/computer games. Keep in mind, however, that fewer studies exist in this area when compared to studies about the impact of violent television programs. In addition, many studies were done before the current wave of ultrarealistic video games hit the market. Moreover, some studies failed to differentiate among the wide variety of violent games that were available. Playing PacMan, for example, would probably produce different effects than playing Doom. Finally, there have been no long-term longitudinal studies about the effects of playing violent games. Consequently, it is somewhat risky to draw generalizations. Nonetheless, the conclusions of the two meta-analyses are basically similar:

1. Video/computer game playing has a small effect on subsequent aggression, but this effect is smaller than the comparable impact of violent TV shows on aggression. The most recent meta-analysis, however, found that studies that used the most reliable and valid methods found stronger evidence of an effect. It's possible that previous meta-analysis had underestimated the true magnitude of the effect. Thus, the effect might actually be more powerful than the comparable effect for TV viewing.

2. The effects of game playing are the same on the young and old, but there is some evidence to suggest that older players might show more of an effect.

3. The type of violence portrayed in the game might be important. Violence against human or fantasy figures seems to produce stronger effects than sports-related violence.

In sum, research into the effects of video games is still at a formative level. Given the large amounts of time that young people spend playing these games and the number of violent themes contained in video/computer games, it is likely that the body of research surrounding this topic will increase in the next few years. It is hoped that future research will help clarify the ultimate impact of this content.

A MEAN AND SCARY WORLD? PERCEPTIONS OF REALITY

A preceding section traced the impact of TV on the behavior of the audience. This section is more concerned with the impact of TV on how the audience thinks about and perceives reality.

The media, particularly TV, are the source of much of what we know about the world. The media, however, bring us more than simply information. They also, at least to some degree, shape the way we perceive the outside world. Or, put another way, the media affect the way we construct our social reality. For instance, what is it like to live in southern New Zealand? It seems probable that very few of you reading this book have had much of a chance to experience living in southern New Zealand or to talk to people who have. Consequently, a TV show on the life of the people who live there might have tremendous influence on your perceptions in this area. This isn't much of a problem as long as the media presentations accurately represent reality.

There are, however, many areas where the world presented on TV differs greatly from reality. For example, studies of TV entertainment content have shown that far more TV characters work in crime and law enforcement than do people in the real world. Criminals on TV commit violent crime far more often than do their real-life counterparts. Trials on TV are decided by juries more often than they are in reality. Leading characters in TV shows are almost always American; people from other countries are rarely shown. More people on soap operas have affairs and illegitimate children than do real people. More unscrupulous and treacherous people are shown on TV than exist in real life. Again, this wouldn't be much of a problem if people were able to separate the two worlds, TV and reality, without any confusion. For some, however, separating the two is not easy.

This is the focus of cultivation theory. **Cultivation theory** was popularized by George Gerbner and his colleagues at the University of Pennsylvania. In simplified form, the theory suggests that the more a person is exposed to TV, the more likely that the person's construction of social reality will be more like that shown on TV and less like reality.

The procedure first used to put the theory to the test requires a content analysis of TV to isolate those portrayals that are at odds with reality. A content analysis is a systematic and objective analysis of the messages portrayed on TV. The second step requires dividing audience members into heavy-viewing and light-viewing groups and then asking for their perceptions of various social events or situations. If cultivation theory is correct, then a lot of the heavy viewers should give answers more in line with the TV world, whereas a lot of the light viewers should give answers more in keeping with the real world. Figure 13–5 shows the basic model used for analysis.

Gerbner and his colleagues have done several surveys examining the cultivation effect. In one study adolescents were asked how many people were involved in some kind of violence each year, 3 or 10 percent (the TV answer); 83 percent of the heavy viewers gave the TV answer as compared with 62 percent of the light viewers. Another question asked how often a police officer usually draws a gun on an average day. The choices were less than once a day (the real-world answer) and more than five times a day (the answer more in line with the TV world). Three times as many

heavy viewers (18 percent) as light viewers (6 percent) said more than five times a day.

Cultivation studies have received a fair amount of publicity in the popular press (*TV Guide* even carried an article by Gerbner and his colleagues), and the theory has a certain commonsense appeal. Recent research, however, suggests that the process of cultivation is much more complex than originally thought.

In the first place, remember that most of the cultivation studies relied on the survey approach. Although the survey method can establish a relationship, it cannot be used to rule out other factors that might be causing the relationship. Consequently, more-recent studies suggest that when other factors in the process (like age, sex, race, and education) are simultaneously controlled, the cultivation effect either is weakened or disappears.

In response to these findings, cultivation theory was revised to include two additional concepts—mainstreaming and resonance—that account for the fact that heavy TV viewing may have different outcomes for various social groups. **Mainstreaming** means that heavy viewers within social subgroups develop common perceptions that differ from those of light viewers in the same subgroup. For example, among light TV viewers, nonwhites are generally more distrusting than whites and are more likely to report that people will take advantage of you if they get the chance. Among heavy viewers, however, the gap between whites and nonwhites on this measure is significantly smaller. Heavy TV viewing has a homogenizing effect in this instance and brings both groups closer to the mainstream.

Resonance refers to a situation in which viewers get a "double-dose" from both TV and reality. For example, heavy TV viewers who live in a high-crime area have their belief in a scary world reinforced by both TV and their firsthand experience. They should show an exaggerated cultivation effect when compared with light viewers.

Also remember that surveys cannot establish cause and effect. Cultivation theory assumes that TV viewing is cultivating the subsequent perceptions of reality. It is possible, however, that people who are fearful of going out at night stay home and watch more TV, thus making the perception the cause of the viewing rather than the effect. Of course, the best way to sort out cause and effect would be an experiment, but since cultivation theory talks about the long-term cumulative effect of TV exposure, a definitive experiment would be difficult to design.

Figure 13–5

Design for Cultivation Analysis

TV viewing	Number giving TV answer	Number giving non–TV answer
High	A lot	A few
Low	A few	A lot

Issues: Video Games and Cultivation Analysis

Can spending long hours playing video games result in distorted images of social reality? Cultivation theory was originally formulated before playing video games became popular and dealt with exposure to recurrent themes and portrayals on television. In many ways the video game experience is similar to television exposure. The game characters are predictable, the settings are realistic, and the general messages and lessons contained in the game play are consistent. Playing video games, however, also is different from watching TV. The games are available at all times, the experience is more immersive, and the player has more control over the course of the game. All these factors make it likely that some form of cultivation is possible.

A study published in a 2006 issue of the *Journal of Communication* examined this complicated issue. The researcher examined the video game Asheron's Call 2, a game with ample amounts of violence, including featured characters using weapons. One group played the game for a month with an average of about 14 hours per week of game play. Another group did not play the game.

When the two groups were compared, males that played the game believed that people in the real world would be more likely to be robbed by somebody with a weapon than the non–game players. Females who played the game did not exhibit this difference. Perceptions of the frequency of other violent acts not contained in the video game (physical assault, rape, murder) did not differ between game players and those who did not play the game.

In short, the game did produce a specific and limited cultivation effect but only among males. The researcher noted that this finding ran counter to the notion that exposure to TV content should have broad and general cultivation effects. Nonetheless, although the study raised more questions than it answered, it does appear that cultivation can occur in other video channels in addition to TV.

Other cultivation studies have tried to specify the conditions that are most likely to foster or inhibit cultivation. Although the results are not entirely consistent, it appears that cultivation depends on the following:

1. *The motivation for viewing.* Ritualistic, low-involvement viewing appears to be more potent than planned and motivated viewing.

2. *Amount of experience with the topic.* Studies have noted that cultivation seems to work best when audience members have only indirect or distant contact with the topic. This seems to contradict the resonance notion.

3. *Perceived realism of the content.* Cultivation appears to be enhanced when the viewer perceives the content of entertainment shows to be realistic.

More recent studies of cultivation theory have demonstrated that the research itself must be done carefully to avoid spurious findings. One study found that the amount of TV viewed that divides the high TV group from the low TV group must be chosen precisely or distortions will appear in the results. Other studies have found that the way the questions are worded and the precise topics to be evaluated will also have an impact.

Finally, the results of a recent meta-analysis of more than two decades of cultivation research encompassing more than 90 studies offer a summary statement about the impact of TV on a person's view of social reality. The analysis concluded that the cultivation literature has demonstrated a weak but persistent relationship between TV viewing and beliefs about the real world. How weak? Recall that viewing TV violence explains about 2 to 9 percent of the variability in aggression level. The impact of cultivation is weaker: TV viewing accounts for about 1 percent of the variation in social perceptions. This is not to say that this is an unimportant consequence. A 1 percent effect that is constant and consistent over the years can turn out to be influential. For example, suppose you're a golfer who uses 100 strokes per 18 holes. If you improved your golf game by about 1 percent per year, at the end of 20 years you would have cut about 20 strokes off your average 18-hole score. The impact of viewing, however, may not necessarily be this predictable. In sum, long-term, cumulative exposure to TV cultivates, to some small but potentially significant degree, the acceptance of ideas and perceptions that are similar to the world portrayed on TV.

It is probably obvious that there is still a lot to learn about cultivation. It represents one of the few topics that has attracted research interest from sociologists, social psychologists, and mass communication researchers. It will likely continue to be an important research area for the foreseeable future.

Racial, Ethnic, and Sex-Role Stereotyping

Somewhat related to cultivation analysis is the research area that examines the impact of stereotyping on viewers' attitudes. The civil rights and the women's movements of the 1960s and 1970s sparked interest in the way that various minority groups and women were portrayed in TV programs.

With regard to sex roles, early content analyses disclosed that men outnumbered women two to one in starring roles and that men appeared in a far greater variety of occupational roles. When they did appear, women were likely to be housewives, secretaries, or nurses. Female characters were also portrayed as passive, deferential, and generally weak, in contrast to male characters, who, on the whole, were active, dominant, and powerful. More recent content analyses have shown that females are now portrayed in a wider range of occupations but that little else has changed.

A number of studies about the effects of exposure to this material began to surface in the early 1970s. Many of these studies used the correlational approach, and, although they were not as rigorous as they could be, their findings generally supported what the cultivation hypothesis would predict: Youngsters who watched a lot of TV should have attitudes and perceptions about sex roles that are in line with the stereotypical portrayals on TV. In one study heavy TV viewers were far more likely than moderate TV watchers to choose a sex-stereotyped profession (for example, boys choosing to be doctors or police officers and girls choosing to be housewives or nurses). Another study noted that children who were heavy viewers scored higher on a standardized test that measured sex stereotyping.

Like cultivation analysis, the major problems with this sort of research are establishing causation and sorting out the impact of TV from other sources of sex-role information (schools, peers, parents, books, and so on). In an attempt to clarify the process, panel studies have examined the correlation between viewing and stereotyping. The results suggested that the causal connection evidently works in both directions: TV viewing led to more stereotypical attitudes and people with more stereotypical attitudes watched more TV, thus reinforcing the effects.

A second popular technique for examining the effects of TV on sex-role attitudes usually takes place in the laboratory and consists of showing subjects (usually youngsters) men and women in counterstereotypical roles (for example, a male nurse, a female mechanic) and then seeing if changes in perceptions occur. Results from these studies have found that exposure to this nontraditional content does seem to decrease sex-role stereotyping. In one typical experiment a group of girls saw commercials in which a woman was shown as a butcher, a welder, and a laborer. Another group saw commercials featuring women as telephone operators, models, and manicurists. After viewing, girls who saw the nontraditional roles expressed a greater preference for traditional male jobs than did the other group. Similar results have been found in at least a half dozen other experiments.

Taken as a whole these studies demonstrate that sex-role beliefs can be affected by the mass media.

Turning to ethnic and racial portrayals, we find that numerous content analyses conducted over the past 40 years have examined the way minorities are portrayed in entertainment programming, commercials, and newscasts. The vast majority of these content analyses have examined the portrayal of African Americans on television; there are few studies that examine the depiction of other ethnic and racial groups. Studies conducted during the 1970s found that African Americans were underrepresented in prime-time TV programs. One analysis found that whites accounted for about 90 percent of characters on TV, while African Americans made up about 7 percent and other nonblack minority groups were almost nonexistent.

Recent studies have found different results. In 2005, a content analysis of five broadcast networks disclosed that whites made up 80 percent of the characters and that African Americans made up about 14 percent, about equal to the percentage of African Americans in the U.S. population. Other minorities, however, remain underrepresented. Hispanics, for example, account for approximately 14 percent of the U.S. population but made up only 4 percent of TV characters. Asians were also underrepresented, making up about 2 percent of all TV characters, and Native Americans were virtually invisible in prime time. Keep in mind that these numbers refer to the mainstream broadcast networks. Special cable networks, such as BET or Univision, will regularly feature large numbers of minority characters. A similar

Prime-time TV has been criticized many times for its stereotypical portrayal of females. Analyses have shown that women are more likely to be identified by their marital status, while men are identified by their occupation. Further, more male characters were likely to be employed in high-status positions. Females, in contrast, were more likely to be shown in relatively powerless roles, such as homemaker and student.

Are such disparities the result of the gender makeup of the creative personnel who put the show together? Do programs that have a mixed-gender creative team portray females differently from those shows put together by just males? Those were a couple of the questions asked by a 2004 study published in the *Journal of Broadcasting & Electronic Media*.

The authors analyzed on-screen portrayals of one episode of every series on the six broadcast TV networks. For each of the 1,445 characters in their sample, they examined a number of characteristics, including occupational status, success in achieving goals, and leadership activities. To establish the gender of the creative teams, the researchers examined the credits at the end of each program to determine the number of women who worked as creators, writers, or producers. (If a name was ambiguous, they contacted the production company for the correct information.)

The researchers then grouped the shows into six categories: all-male writers versus mixed-gender writers; all-male creators versus mixed-gender creators; and all-male executive producers versus mixed-gender executive producers.

Did having females on the creative team make a difference? On programs with all-male writers, 17 percent of the male characters but only 6 percent of the female characters had leadership roles. On programs with male creators, 16 percent of male characters had leadership roles but only 5 percent of the females. The same pattern was found for shows with all-male executive producers. With one exception, all-male creative teams also portrayed more males than females in positions of power and more males exhibited goal-seeking behaviors.

When it came to mixed-gender creative teams, the results were mixed, but in five of the nine possible comparisons, no meaningful gender differences were found regarding occupational power, leadership roles, or goal-seeking behaviors. As the authors concluded, the results provide evidence that women working behind the scenes were associated with more equitable portrayals of female and male characters.

---

trend has been found with TV commercials. African Americans were rarely seen in ads during the 1960s and 1970s, but their numbers have increased in recent years.

Studies looking at the impact of these portrayals on racial and ethnic stereotypes are less numerous than the content analyses, and most have focused on the impact of programs depicting African Americans. Researchers have examined the influence of TV programs that feature minorities on both minority and majority audiences. For example, the degree to which white children have personal contact with African Americans affects how white youngsters view TV shows that have black performers: Youngsters who have more personal contact with African Americans judge the TV programs to be less realistic. Moreover, long-term exposure to educational programming, such as *Sesame Street*, has been found to be associated with more positive evaluations of African Americans.

TV programs featuring black performers have an influence on the attitudes and perceptions of African American children. Black youngsters, for example, are positively influenced by ads with black characters. In addition, African American children who spend a good deal of time watching shows with black performers tended to have higher self-esteem than black children who did not view this type of programming.

In sum, these studies, like those dealing with sex-role portrayals, suggest that TV programs depicting minority characters can modify racial attitudes and perceptions.

BROADCASTING AND POLITICS

Even the most casual of political observers will concede that the broadcasting media, and TV in particular, have changed American politics. A new term, *telepolitics*, has been coined to describe the way politics is now practiced. This section looks at the obvious and not-so-obvious influences of broadcasting on the political system.

Those who have studied the impact of media on politics generally divide the field into two categories. The first has to do with the influences on the ultimate political act—voting. Studies in this category examine how media help shape our election campaigns, our images of candidates and issues, our knowledge of politics, whether we vote, and for whom we cast a ballot. The second category includes studies of how media, TV especially, are changing the basic political structure and how we perceive it. We shall examine each category, but first let's look at the media, electioneering, and voting.

Media Influences on Voting Behavior

The past 75 years have seen rather striking changes in the way political scientists and mass communication researchers have viewed the importance of media in political campaigns. Early fears about the political impact of the media were shown to be unjustified by careful studies done in the 1940s and 1950s. Most people reported that factors other than the media, such as their party affiliation and the opinions of respected others, were the most influential factors determining their vote choice. Since 1960, however, TV has assumed dominance as the most potent political medium and voters have tended to be less influenced by party ties and organizations. Accordingly, the potential for media impact may be on the increase.

One thing is certain. People get a lot of political information from the media during the course of a campaign. Candidates who get extensive coverage also show strong gains in public awareness.

Moreover, the pattern of news coverage during an election campaign can help determine what political issues the public perceives as important, a phenomenon known as **agenda setting.** For example, if the media give extensive coverage to U.S. policy in Central America, audience members may think that this is an important issue and rate it high on their own personal agenda of political issues.

Voters, of course, get more than just issue-related information from the media. Another area of research is concerned with the role of TV and other media in forming voters' images of the candidates. In particular, political ads are designed to project a coherent and attractive image to voters. Studies have suggested that a candidate's image can be the

dominant factor in many elections. As party identification weakens, voters tend to rely on a general image to help them make up their minds. This "image effect" seems strongest among uncommitted voters and is most noted during the early stages of a campaign.

When it comes down to the actual choices (1) whether to vote at all and (2) for whom to vote, the research is not so definitive as one might think. Voting behavior is a complex activity and many factors—interpersonal communication, personal values, social class, age, ethnicity, party affiliation—along with media exposure come into play. To make it even more complicated, some people are unable to distinguish exactly what factors influence their choice. Existing research, however, does offer some conclusions. Not surprisingly, voters who learn a great deal about a particular candidate are likely to vote for that candidate. Certain kinds of media exposure are also related to voter turnout. Print media readership was found to be related to greater voter participation, whereas people who were heavy TV viewers were less likely to vote. Exposure to TV ads and other political TV programs was also related to turnout and voter choices, but this effect was most pronounced among those who had little interest in the campaign.

The 1992 and 1996 presidential campaigns were significant because they both used the "new" mass communication media (Web sites, e-mail, satellite news conferences) and nontraditional media (radio talk shows, TV interview shows, MTV) to get their message across. By 2000, however, the traditional media reemerged as candidates turned to conventional television and newspapers in their efforts to reach voters. Early predictions that the Internet would increase voter interest and knowledge about political issues did not come to pass as surveys revealed that using the Internet to get news about politics was not related to issue knowledge or intention to vote.

The effects of the "new" media in the 2004 election were more easily seen. The Internet turned out to be a potent fund-raising channel. During the primaries, candidate Howard Dean financed much of his campaign through donations raised on his Web site. John Kerry, the eventual Democratic nominee, wound up raising $81 million online during the primary season. Second, political interest groups, such as Moveon.org and Swiftvets.com, used their Web sites to raise issues that might not have been covered by the traditional press. Finally, the blog emerged as a new political weapon. Liberal blog sites, such as DailyKos.com, and conservative sites, such as Powerline.com, added new voices to the political debate and were closely monitored by the mainstream media. Bloggers, for example, challenged a *60 Minutes II* report aired shortly before the 2004 election that purported to show documents that raised serious questions about incumbent candidate George W. Bush's service in the Texas Air National Guard. After much controversy, CBS admitted that it could not authenticate the documents and apologized to its viewers.

TV debates between or among presidential candidates have become a fixture of modern campaigns, and their results have been closely studied to determine what, if any, impact they have on voter preference. Numerous studies of the debates of the last six presidential elections generally agree that the debates reinforced preferences that were formed before the debates took place. Almost 6 out of 10 voters have made up their minds by the time the debates occur, and most viewers simply have their choice confirmed.

The two televised debates of the 1996 presidential campaign reinforced the above findings. Incumbent President Bill Clinton had a big lead over challenger Bob Dole going into the debates, and public opinion polls detected no change in his lead after the debates were over.

The series of presidential debates between Al Gore and George W. Bush during the 2000 election were notable because they attracted the lowest average number of viewers per debate, thanks to competition from baseball playoffs and entertainment programming on the Fox network. To illustrate, the presidential debates during the 1980s averaged about 68 million viewers per debate; in 2000, that number had dropped to about 40 million. Perhaps the novelty of the debates has worn off.

The effects of viewing the 2000 debates were hard to detect. The race was close all the way and eventually was decided by the Supreme Court. Polls taken after the debates showed small and inconsistent changes in candidate preference. Watching the debates, however, was related to gains in political knowledge and a greater understanding of the issues in the campaign.

The Daily Kos, a liberal blog authored by Markos Zúniga, is read by about 700,000 people every week.

Analysis of the impact of the 2004 debates between John Kerry and George W. Bush suggested that presidential debates may matter less than was previously thought. Almost all analysts agreed the Kerry was perceived the victor in the debates, but his performance failed to translate to the polls as Bush won with a comfortable margin.

A final area that received recent research interest relates to the impact of **exit polls** on voter behavior. Exit polls can be used by the news media to predict election results before all the votes are in and all the polls are closed. Exit polls are not as influential in statewide elections because most news organizations refrain from making predictions until all the polls are closed in the state. Presidential elections are another matter. It has been speculated that an early prediction of a winner in a presidential race might deter people from going to the polls or cause them to change their vote choice. Research findings suggest that the impact of an early "call" depends upon the perceived closeness of the race and how early the call is made.

The potential influence of exit polls was vividly demonstrated both in the 2000 and 2004 elections. In 2000, the major networks used their exit polls to incorrectly predict that Al Gore would win the key state of Florida. They later did a 180-degree turn and predicted that George W. Bush would win, only to back away from that position and finally declare the state too close too call. Both candidates argued that this flip-flopping hurt their election chances. In 2004, early exit poll results suggesting a Kerry victory were prematurely leaked on a Web site and received significant coverage in the media. The early numbers turned out to be incorrect and prompted the major media outlets to improve their methods for collecting and reporting exit poll data.

Media Impact on the Political System

Turning now to the second general area of research, the impact of the media on the political system as a whole, we find that there is less research available but the findings are no less important. One line of research suggests that political institutions and the media have become interdependent in a number of ways. Political reporters need information to do their jobs, and the government and politicians need media exposure. Thus public officials hold news conferences early enough to meet media deadlines, presidents have "photo opportunities," and correspondents accompany administration leaders on world trips.

Further, many politicians have learned to stage media events that accommodate both sides: The politician gets exposure, and the TV reporter gets a 10-second "sound bite" for the evening news. This interdependence is also demonstrated by the change in political conventions. In prior years, conventions actually selected candidates. These days conventions are more like coronation ceremonies, closely orchestrated to maximize prime-time TV coverage.

The recent trend toward negative political advertising has also been a topic of concern. Definitive results about its impact have yet to be determined. On the one hand, many political consultants point to the success of several gubernatorial and senatorial elections in the 1996 campaign that relied on negative advertising and were successful. On the other hand, several surveys and experiments have shown that negative advertising seems to make voters more cynical, less inclined to participate in political campaigns, and even less likely to vote. The level of negative advertising hit a new high in the 1998 midyear elections, and many observers suggested that it had a boomerang effect for several candidates. Negative ads were numerous during the 2004 presidential election with the most negative sponsored by political action groups.

To sum up the rather broad and complicated area of broadcasting and politics, research concerning the political impact of the media demonstrates the specific-effects viewpoint mentioned earlier. In some areas, such as building political knowledge, shaping political images, and setting agendas, the media effects are fairly direct and evident. In other areas, such as voter turnout and voter choice, the media work along with a host of other factors and their impact is not particularly strong.

TELEVISION AND LEARNING

It seems that every new medium has been indicted at one time or another for lowering the educational level of American youth. During the 1930s critics charged that radio was a negative influence on youngsters' school achievement and made it difficult for them to develop good study habits. In the mid-1950s, when TV took center stage, concern about its effects on children mounted quickly, but early studies failed to show convincing evidence that watching TV was related to poor school performance. These surveys did uncover some links between heavy viewing and poor academic performance, but the lack of conclusive evidence pushed the issue out of public focus. In the 1970s, however, the issue was rekindled, primarily as a response to an alarming dip in SAT scores. This section reviews the research on TV's effect on IQ, school achievement, and reading.

The results of the research on the relationship between TV viewing and IQ are not surprising. Heavy viewers tend to have lower IQs than light viewers, and many critics have argued that watching TV actually lowers a person's intelligence. Further research suggests that the association is not that simple. First, it appears that age is a factor. At least two studies noted that heavy viewing was actually linked to higher IQs in kids up to the age of 10 or 11 but that after 11 the relationship reverses. In sum, there appears to be a weak negative relationship between IQ and TV viewing, but age is a complicating factor. And, as is the case with surveys, the direction of causation is not clear.

When it comes to school achievement, the results are not conclusive but they also suggest a slight negative relationship. Youngsters who watch a lot of TV tend not to do so well at school as do their lighter-viewing counterparts. In one study of more than 600 sixth to ninth graders, high TV viewers tended to score lower on tests of vocabulary and language achievement than did light viewers, even when the effects of IQ were statistically controlled. Interestingly, TV viewing was not associated with math achievement scores. Surveys done among adults confirm that high TV viewers do less well on vocabulary tests, suggesting the negative relationship carries over from youth.

Another study indicated that the type of TV content viewed, along with the amount of viewing, was important in determining the precise relationship between TV and achievement. This survey found that children who watched a good deal of news and educational programs got better grades in school, whereas those who watched a lot of adventure shows got lower grades. A recent panel study among high school students, however, found no evidence of TV's effects on math and reading achievement after controlling for such confounding factors as parents' education level, IQ, race, and school attendance. In any case, virtually all of the studies showed the relationship, if one was found, to be relatively weak. In terms of the amount of variability explained, TV viewing generally accounted for about 1 to 4 percent of the variation in achievement scores, a link even weaker than that discussed between exposure to TV violence and aggression. A 2005 study done in New Zealand found that young people who finished college watched an hour less of TV per weekday than those that dropped out of high school. This relationship persisted even after the respondents' IQ, social class, and other variables were statistically controlled.

The relationship between TV and reading performance is hard to sum up. Although common sense might suggest that TV viewing has a negative influence on reading skills, the research has found no clear relationship. True, a few surveys have found a weak negative relationship between entertainment TV viewing and reading achievement scores, but other studies have found the opposite.

A large-scale study published in 1990 sheds additional light in this area. This research used data gathered from a national sample of about 1,750 children over a 4-year period. The children were first studied when they were 6 to 11 years old and then studied again 4 years later. Cross-sectional correlations done at one point in time were as expected: Negative relationships existed between the amount of TV viewing and IQ, reading skill, and arithmetic ability. When the relationships were examined longitudinally, however, the negative relationships disappeared. The best predictors of intelligence and aptitude were parents' educational level, race, size of family, and birth order.

On the more positive side, related research has shown that TV can teach youngsters specific skills that will help them develop reading competence. Research examining *Sesame Street* and *The Electric Company* showed that they helped children develop letter recognition and decoding skills, which promoted reading fluency.

Overall, the data offer some qualified support to the notion that TV viewing, at best, has a small adverse effect on IQ and school achievement. The results certainly support the conclusion that, excluding especially designed educational programs, TV offers no particular educational benefits to its young viewers; all the hours that youngsters invest in it carry no measurable scholastic rewards.

TELEVISION AND PROSOCIAL BEHAVIOR

It's tempting, of course, to blame all of society's ills on TV. To be fair, however, we should also point out that TV has had several positive or prosocial effects as well. Prosocial behavior covers a wider range of activity than does antisocial behavior. Usually a prosocial behavior is defined as one that is ultimately good for a person and for society. Some behaviors commonly defined as prosocial are learning cognitive skills associated with school achievement, cooperation, self-control, helping, sharing, resisting temptation, offering sympathy, and making reparation for bad behavior. Many of these prosocial acts are not so obvious or as unmistakable as common antisocial acts; it's a lot easier to see somebody hitting somebody else than it is to see a person resisting temptation. In any case, this section takes a look at the more beneficial results of TV viewing.

First, as noted earlier, specially constructed programs can be effective in preparing young people for school. Without a doubt, the most successful program in this area is *Sesame Street*. On the air for nearly 40 years, *Sesame Street* is viewed by nearly 6 million preschoolers every week. Further, *Sesame Street* is the most researched TV series ever, and the available data highlight the success of the series. To summarize some of the major findings:

1. Children who viewed *Sesame Street* regularly, either in school or at home, scored higher on tests measuring school readiness.

2. The more children watched the program, the better their scores were.

3. Disadvantaged children who were frequent viewers showed gains almost as great as their advantaged counterparts.

4. Frequent viewers also seemed to develop more positive attitudes toward school in general.

5. Children who were encouraged to view the program showed more gains than those who were not encouraged.

The success of *Sesame Street* brought it high visibility and criticism. First, it was noted that *Sesame Street* seemed to enlarge the skills gap between advantaged and disadvantaged children. Although disadvantaged children frequently gained as much as advantaged children, fewer disadvantaged children were frequent *Sesame Street* watchers, leading to the net result that a larger proportion of advantaged kids gained by viewing. To cope with this criticism, educators looked for ways to encourage more viewing by the disadvantaged. The second criticism charged that the show's fast-paced style might cause problems when children entered the more slow-paced school environment. It was argued that heavy *Sesame Street* viewers might be bored and/or hyperactive as a consequence. This turned out to be a false

Big Bird and his pals on *Sesame Street* are known the world over. Produced by The Children's Television Workshop, the show has been on the air for nearly 40 years.

alarm, and subsequent research has not linked these problems with frequent viewing.

Other programs that were constructed to get across prosocial about mental health or personal social adjustment have proven helpful. For example, viewers of *Mister Rogers' Neighborhood* were found to be more cooperative and more persistent than nonviewers. A 2-year study of children who were regular watchers of the Nickelodeon series *Allegra's Window* and *Gullah Gullah Island* disclosed that viewers were better able to solve problems and had more flexible thinking skills than nonviewers. Viewers of another Nickelodeon series, *Blue's Clues*, were better at problem-solving than those who didn't watch.

Surveys that link the viewing of prosocial TV with the performance of prosocial acts in real life are rare. One study done in the 1970s found a weak connection between the two, an association that was even weaker than the correlation between viewing of TV violence and aggression. A 1999 study found a relationship among first graders between watching prosocial situation comedies (*Full House* and *The Cosby Show*) and performing prosocial acts, but the relationship did not show up among third graders, perhaps due to the increased influence of other sources, such as peers. A 2005 meta-analysis of 34 studies found that those children who watched prosocial content in lab experiments were slightly more likely to exhibit prosocial behaviors than those who did not see prosocial material.

In summary, TV seems to have several effects on behaviors that most would define as prosocial:

1. Television teaches certain cognitive skills that are necessary for school success.

2. Television shows can help reduce gender-related stereotypes.

3. Laboratory experiments suggest viewing commercial TV shows with definite prosocial messages can prompt subsequent prosocial behaviors, but this link has not yet been found to carry over in any significant degree to real life.

Before closing this section we should point out that there are many more areas that might have been mentioned. For example, many communications researchers are now devoting increased attention to how individuals process messages in their brain—the study of the cognitive aspects of communication. Moreover, it should be clear by now that the research in many of these areas highlights the thinking embodied in the specific-effects theory discussed earlier in the chapter. Radio and TV usually operate along with a number of other factors to produce an effect, and trying to untangle the unique effects of the media can be quite frustrating. And although the study of media effects is still relatively new, the data are steadily accumulating. It also appears that the electronic media are not necessarily as powerful as many people have charged, although they can exert significant influence in specific instances. Finally, we have a lot more work to do, particularly since new media have transformed the media habits of the audience.

SOCIAL IMPACT OF THE INTERNET

The Internet changes so rapidly that it is difficult to make generalizations about its impact. There are, however, some preliminary findings that merit reporting.

First, surveys project that the number of Internet users is large and growing rapidly. Worldwide, about 6 billion people were online in 2006. In the United States, about 200 million people were connected to the Internet, about 67 percent of the population. Additionally, the demographics of Internet users are changing. When it first emerged, the Internet was mainly used by males and younger persons. In 2006, however, the audience was split evenly between males and females and the percentage of adults over 50 had grown by more than 50 percent between 1998 and 2004. There was also some evidence that the "digital divide," the gap in online access that separated upper-income groups from lower-incomes groups and whites from minorities, seemed to be narrowing. As of 2004, low-income users grew at twice the rate of high-income users and Latinos were the fastest-growing online ethnic group. Whites are still more likely to be online; about 75 percent of white households have Internet access compared to 46 percent of African-American homes and 44 percent of Hispanic homes.

Time spent online seems to displace time spent watching television but doesn't seem to have much impact on other media use. Television viewing apparently suffers because a great deal of Internet usage is done in the prime-time evening hours, when people traditionally have watched TV. Internet users also spend more time reading newspapers and magazines than do nonusers and are also heavier radio listeners and movie-goers.

The Internet is becoming a major source of news for some Americans. A 2005 survey by the Pew Foundation asked where Americans got their news "yesterday." About 23 percent used the Internet compared to about 60 percent for local TV news and 40 percent for the local paper. The online news audience is even bigger during periods of national breaking news, such as during the aftermath of the terrorists attacks of September 11, 2001. More than 30 million American adults went online to get news of the attacks.

Research into the behavioral effects of Internet use is still in its formative stage. Much concern has arisen about the impact of exposure to the pornographic sites on the World Wide Web. One preliminary study suggested a relationship between viewing pornographic Web content and sexual abuse of females. This will obviously be an area that will attract much research interest in the future.

Social scientists are also examining a phenomenon called **Internet addiction**—a psychological dependence on the Net that may cause people to ignore family, friends, and work as they spend most of their time surfing the Net. Students are apparently one group at risk for this malady. One study found that high Internet use was related to lower grades; another found a correlation between college drop-out rates and high Internet use.

Surveys about the Internet's impact on people's social lives have turned up some interesting results. An early 3-year survey conducted from 1995 to 1997 found that Internet use appeared to cause an increase in feelings of remoteness and isolation. Many respondents reported that even though they were frequent visitors to chat rooms and made heavy use of e-mail, their feelings of loneliness had increased and they were spending less time in face-to-face interactions with family members and friends. Subsequent surveys, however, found the opposite. One survey found that Internet users were more socially involved with their local communities. Another found that Internet users were more politically involved and had more social contacts than nonusers. A 3-year study done in England from 1999 to 2001 disclosed that Internet users were just as sociable on those who were not online. In fact, those who just recently went online reported big jumps in the amount of time devoted to outside social activities. The researchers suggested that online access to friends and those with similar interests made it easier to arrange social get-togethers. Finally, the authors of the original 1998 survey reinterviewed their respondents 3 years later and found that Internet users in their sample were now the ones with the most social contacts. The researchers concluded that the Internet had changed since the earlier survey and, thanks to innovations such as instant messages, was more likely to encourage social contacts.

Survey research about the social impact of the Internet has generally supported one main conclusion, labeled the "rich get richer" model. Internet users with extraverted personalities were the ones most likely to show increases in social activities, community involvement, and personal feelings of well-being. For these people, the Internet simply represented another channel to use to link up with friends. On the other hand, introverted individuals who were online tended to shy away from more social contact.

THE FUTURE: SOCIAL CONCERNS

New media technologies such as interactive, 500-channel cable and satellite TV systems, home computers and TV sets connected to the World Wide Web, interactive DVDs, cell phones, video conferences, and iPods raise new social concerns.

All this new hardware will increase the distance between the media-haves and the media-have-nots. New technologies slowly filter down to lower socioeconomic groups. The people who could most benefit from easy access to information are usually the last to get it because new technology is expensive. For example, computers that teach preschoolers how to read and how to count will be a tremendous education aid. They will be expensive, however, and perhaps only available to advantaged children. When these children enter school, the gap between their skills and those of disadvantaged children may be even greater than it is today.

The more money a family has to devote to entertainment and informational services, the more that will be available to them. At some point in the development of new technologies there will have to be a debate over the social issue of how to distribute equitably the informational wealth that these new technologies will bring.

With information comes political enfranchisement. The problem will not be whether a family has only 30 channels to watch or 500, but whether an individual has the ability to gather and control information. People who have little access to electronic databases will have less power than those who do.

Then there is the problem of information overload. Information overload hardly needs to be defined to college students who are studying 9 or 10 different subjects a year. The term generally refers to the feeling of confusion and helplessness that occurs when a person is confronted with too much stimulation in a limited time period. With 500 or more TV channels, video games, computers, and cell phones, the consumer of the future will have more information available than he or she could ever use.

Last, there is the problem of escapism and isolation. The term *couch potato* came into vogue during the 1980s to describe a type of person who turned away from personal interaction and merely vegetated in front of the TV. How many people will become couch potatoes in the future when 500 channels of TV and realistic video games are routinely available?

The new communication technologies will bring promise and peril. Just like the telegraph, telephone, radio, and TV that preceded them, they will bring fundamental changes to our lives. They will require difficult decisions from policymakers and from consumers alike. They will require us to learn more about them and what they can do. As Loy Singleton pointed out in his book *Telecommunications in the Information Age*, the new technologies will best serve those who know how to use them.

SUMMARY

- The social effects of broadcasting and cable have been studied by using experiments, surveys, panel studies, content analyses, and meta-analyses.

- Over the years various theories have enjoyed popularity as explanations for the effects of the media. The hypodermic needle theory considered the media a powerful persuasive force. This theory held that all people would have more or less the same reaction to a mass-communicated message. The limited-effects theory proposed just the opposite: Because of a variety of intervening variables, the media have little effect. Currently the specific-effects theory is in vogue. This theory argues that there are some circumstances under which the media have a direct effect on some people.

- The most researched topic in broadcasting is the effect of video violence on the audience. After more than 30 years of research, most scientists agree that there is little evidence to support the catharsis theory. Further, most agree that TV violence contributes, although in a small way, to the development of antisocial tenden-

cies. Research about the effects of violent video games has shown a similar pattern of results.

- There is less agreement among scientists about cultivation theory, which states that viewing large amounts of TV will distort a person's perception of reality. Evidence is mixed about this topic, and more research remains to be done. Television also seems to play a part in sex-role and racial stereotyping.

- Broadcasting has had a major effect on politics. It provides political information, sets voters' agendas, establishes candidates' images, and has some limited influence on voters' attitudes.

- Television also seems to have a slightly negative relationship with education. Youngsters who watch a lot of TV do not do as well in school as those who do not watch as much.

- Preliminary research into the impact of the Internet suggests that Internet use is generally related to more social contacts and community involvement.

KEY TERMS

laboratory experiments   288
field experiments   289
surveys   289
longitudinal   289
trend study   289
panel studies   289

content analysis   289
meta-analysis   289
catharsis theory   293
stimulation theory   293
cultivation theory   298
mainstreaming   298

resonance   298
agenda setting   302
exit polls   304
Internet addiction   308

SUGGESTIONS FOR FURTHER READING

Bryant, J., & Thompson, S. (2002). *Fundamentals of media effects.* New York: McGraw-Hill, 2002.

DeFleur, M., & Ball-Rokeach, S. (1989). *Theories of mass communication.* New York: Longman.

———. (1995). *Milestones in mass communication research.* New York: Longman.

Huesmann, L., & Eron, L. (eds.). (1986). *Television and the aggressive child.* Hillsdale, NJ: Erlbaum.

Liebert, R., & Sprafkin, J. (1988). *The early window.* New York: Pergamon.

Pearl, D., Bouthilet, L., & Lazar, J. (1982). *Television and behavior: Ten years of scientific progress and implications for the eighties* (vol. 2). Washington, DC: U.S. Government Printing Office.

Perse, E. (2001). *Media effects and society.* Mahwah, NJ: Erlbaum.

Signorielli, N., & Morgan, M. (1990). *Cultivation analysis.* Newbury Park, CA: Sage.

Sparks, G. (2002). *Media effects.* Belmont, CA: Wadsworth.

U.S. Department of Health and Human Services. (2001). *Youth violence: A report of the Surgeon General.* Washington, DC: U.S. Government Printing Office.

William, T. (1986). *The impact of television.* New York: Academic Press.

Wimmer, R., & Dominick, J. (2006). *Mass media research.* Belmont, CA: Wadsworth.

INTERNET EXERCISES

Visit our Web site at www.mhhe.com/dominick6 for study-guide exercises to help you learn and apply material in each chapter. You will find ideas for future research as well as useful Web links to provide you with an opportunity to journey through the new electronic media.

The International Scene 14

Quick Facts

 Number of languages broadcast by VOA: 44

 Annual license fee in Great Britain for owning radio and TV sets: $230 (approx.)

 Number of continents: 7

 Number of continents with MTV: 6 (all except Antarctica)

 Number of local versions of *American Idol:* 32

The accuracy of Marshall McLuhan's prediction that the mass media would turn the world into a global village could be seen during April 2005 on the French Riviera. At the Palais de Festivals in Cannes, more than a thousand production companies from all over the world gathered at the annual Mip-TV convention to sell their programs (Mip-TV is a French acronym that refers to the world's foremost audio and video market). More than 12,000 delegates attended the 5-day sales bazaar and made deals worth billions of dollars. The United States was well represented as Disney pushed its big hits, *Desperate Housewives, Lost,* and *Grey's Anatomy* to TV networks in Europe and Asia. *Desperate Housewives* alone racked up $1.2 million an episode from 130 foreign transactions. In all, the major U.S. studios made more than $6 billion worth of deals.

Although U.S. shows were popular, other countries were well represented. Korean companies marketed their programs to the United States as well as to other Asian nations. Russian companies were selling period dramas to European networks. Producers from Mexico were promoting telenovelas (prime-time soap operas) to Latin America and to the United States. Japanese companies were looking to sell their anime series to North American networks.

In addition, foreign-programming concepts are frequently imported and exported. *Dancing with the Stars* was based on a British show called *Strictly Come Dancing. Survivor* came from Sweden. The formats of *Wheel of Fortune* and *Jeopardy* have been exported to dozens of countries. In short, as far as TV is concerned, the whole world is one global marketplace.

This suggests that studying television and radio as they exist solely in the United States might be too narrow a focus. Radio and TV signals and programs do not stop at national borders. Other countries have developed systems different from ours. It is valuable to examine electronic media systems in a world context since such a perspective might give us a deeper understanding of our own system. With that in mind, this chapter examines international radio and TV.

To begin, we need to define some terms. There are two basic ways to study world broadcasting. First, there's **comparative electronic media systems,** the analysis of media systems in two or more countries. Thus if we took the U.S. system and compared it with the electronic media operations of Canada and/or Great Britain, we would be practicing comparative analysis. Next, there's the study of **international electronic media,** the analysis of radio and video services that cross national boundaries. Programs can be deliberately aimed at other countries (as is the case with the Voice of America or the Voice of Russia) or they can simply spill over from one country to its neighbor (as happens between the United States and Canada). This chapter first looks at comparative analysis and concludes with an examination of international systems.

COMPARATIVE ELECTRONIC MEDIA SYSTEMS

Let's first turn our attention to electronic media systems as they exist in other countries, recognizing that certain international factors such as geography, global politics, and culture have an influence on national systems. The study of other systems allows us to see how other countries deal with basic problems such as freedom of expression, regulation, and access. The purpose of this section is not to prove that one system is necessarily better than any other but to give us a broader perspective from which to evaluate the U.S. system.

To accomplish this purpose, we shall first present a simplified model of the major differences between national systems and then look in detail at the operations of the electronic media in four specific countries.

Differences in Electronic Media Systems: A Model

In addition to the international factors mentioned above, the arrangement of a country's media depends on the nation's political philosophy, social history, and economic system. Trying to categorize the variations that exist among countries is a difficult task. One of the earliest attempts, made in 1956, identified four main classifications based on the country's press philosophy. Authoritarian systems used the media to promote governmental goals. Libertarian systems gave great freedom to the media and promoted a free marketplace of ideas. Social responsibility systems also argued for a free press, but in return for its freedom, the press had responsibilities and obligations to fulfill for society. Finally, the communist system regarded the media as a means to transmit social policy. Another formulation classified systems into three categories: (1) paternalistic (the government or whatever agency in charge of

Figure 14–1

Typology of Broadcasting Systems

Ownership

Characteristics		Government agency	Government corporation	Private
	Goals:	Mobilization	Education/ Cultural enlightenment	Profit
	Regulation:	Strong	Moderate	Weak
	Financing:	Government	License fee/Tax Government subsidy/ Advertising	Advertising
	Programming:	Ideological/ Cultural	Cultural Educational/ Entertainment	Entertainment

broadcasting knows what is best for the people and programs their systems accordingly), with the BBC in Great Britain serving as the prime example; (2) permissive (broadcasters are allowed by the government to do pretty much what they want), with the U.S. commercial system as the best example; and (3) authoritarian (the government controls the system and uses it to achieve its objectives), with the system in the former Soviet Union as the most vivid example. Other writers have suggested additions or variations to these ideas.

Although the above notions are helpful, recent historical changes have meant that most countries now have diverse arrangements in which more than one of the above approaches is represented. The United States, for example, has a commercial system that fits the permissive approach and a public system (PBS) that is more inclined toward the paternalistic philosophy. For many years Finland had a strong state-run TV system modeled after the BBC. In 1994, however, the Finnish government licensed an advertising-supported network whose emphasis was more on entertainment than on cultural

programming or public service. This new service promptly became the most viewed network in the country. Given this growth in diversity, a more complex taxonomy might be more useful. Figure 14–1 displays a classification system that shows how ownership affects four important characteristics: (1) goals, (2) regulation, (3) financing, and (4) programming. Keep in mind this model is a simplification and many variations exist. Nonetheless, let's look at the model in more detail.

There are three main ownership patterns. A broadcasting or cable system could be operated by a government agency, as in China, where it is controlled by the Ministry of Radio, Film and TV, and in Kenya, where it is controlled by the Ministry of Information and Broadcasting. The goal of this ownership type is, generally, mobilization of the population to achieve some goal. This goal might be nation building, as in Kenya, or it might be stability and social order, as in China. Strong regulation characterizes this type of setup. Censorship, either formally by the government or informally by the members of the press themselves, is common. Financing is typically achieved

Events: The Electronic Media in Bulgaria

Bulgaria is a country about the same size as Tennessee located in Eastern Europe between Turkey and Romania and bordering on the Black Sea. It is home to about 7 million people including a sizable minority group of Turks and Roma. After World War II, Bulgaria was occupied by the Soviet Union and became a People's Republic in 1946.

From 1946 to 1989 the electronic media in Bulgaria served as the official state outlet for the ruling Communist party, an example of the government agency type of system illustrated in Figure 14–1. After the fall of communism, Bulgaria underwent tremendous social, political, and economic changes that were reflected in the country's electronic media, changes that are still going on today. Bulgaria's electronic media represent a good example of the challenges and problems faced by countries that are moving from a government-dominated system to one that is more private in nature.

As was the case for other Eastern European countries, when Communist control ended in Bulgaria there was a proliferation of media outlets trying to gain a foothold in the new free-enterprise marketplace. Some succeeded; many did not.

Perhaps radio provides the best example of this media explosion. The former state-run radio network, Bulgarian National Radio (BNR), was transformed into a public service network, somewhat similar to National Public Radio in the United States. BNR operated three national services as well as many local and regional stations, some broadcasting in a number of foreign languages. Privately owned stations and networks quickly sprang up. The most recent figures suggest that there are approximately 275 private radio stations in Bulgaria, with more than 30 FM stations in the capital city of Sofia. Smaller cities may have as many as five or six local stations in addition to BNR. A national privately owned radio network, Darik, broadcasts to the entire country. Programming on these stations is diverse, ranging from rock to news and public affairs.

The situation was somewhat different in television. For many years, the government tried to maintain control over the two national television networks run by Bulgarian National Television (BNT) while making it easier for local and regional broadcasters to start stations. Eventually, financial considerations prompted the government to put one of its networks up for sale, and the network was quickly bought by Rupert Murdoch's News Corporation and renamed bTV. A short time later, another foreign-owned television network, Nova, part of a Greek conglomerate, also started a national network. Ratings for these networks show that bTV is the most watched network, followed by Nova. BNT was in third place. The foreign ownership of TV services and their increasing popularity were trends apparent in other countries as well.

The new networks have increased the diversity of available television programming. The most popular show in Bulgaria in mid-2006 was the locally produced *Slavi Show* on Murdoch's network bTV. Slavi, the host, is a combination of Jon Stewart and Ed Sullivan who makes jokes, interviews newsmakers, and introduces variety acts including ballet. The next most popular show was the local incarnation of *Big Brother,* carried on Nova TV. An edited version runs in the early evening followed by an uncensored version at 11 P.M. As is the case in other European countries, popular American series, such as *Friends* and *Sex and the City,* also show up on Bulgarian TV. In addition, there are numerous private cable systems that offer a wide variety of programs to subscribers.

Next, the situation in Bulgaria illustrates that political forces can still cause problems with the media. Many audience members were dissatisfied with BNT because they thought its top management positions were handed out as political patronage. Some have charged that programs are produced not because of their merit but as a result of political favors and bribes. The same criticisms were leveled at BNR. In 2001 many journalists were removed from their jobs when they protested the appointment of a new director who lacked qualifications for the job. Public and international pressure ultimately led to the naming of a new director.

Finally, as is the case in other countries making the transition to a marketplace economy, the road to free expression has been bumpy. Media analysts in Bulgaria argue that political leaders put pressure on advertisers to buy time on radio and TV stations that are friendly to the government. The Council of Electronic Media (CEM), charged with regulating television and radio stations, has more power than many regulatory agencies in the United States and Europe and is susceptible to political meddling. The CEM recently tried to prevent the *Big Brother* reality series from being aired in Bulgaria because it was indecent and violated the purity of the Bulgarian language. A citizens' group, the Bulgarian Media Coalition, works to improve the operation of the media and to protect the rights of journalists. Despite these efforts, in 2005 the Freedom House organization rated the Bulgarian media as only "partly free."

Bulgaria will enter the European Union in 2007. In preparation for that event, the government is taking another look at the existing regulations that govern TV and radio. Another concern is how to finance the costs of changing from analog to a digital system. In sum, the electronic media in Bulgaria will continue to evolve as they face continuing technological, social, and cultural change.

Source: Prepared with the assistance of Dr. Stilia Felisi, UNESCO Department of Communication and Public Relations, St. Kliment Ohridski University of Sofia, Bulgaria.

through a direct grant from the national budget, as in China, or by a direct grant supplemented by another type of revenue, such as advertising in Kenya. Programming on a system run by a state agency is primarily ideological in nature and promotes a national policy. There may be, however, some cultural programming as well. Entertainment is not a priority in this system.

A broadcasting/cable system could also be operated by a government-chartered corporation, such as the British Broadcasting Corporation (BBC) or the Canadian Broadcasting Corporation (CBC) or the U.S. PBS system. The goal of this form of operation tends to be enlightenment and information. Regulation is moderate, with most laws dealing with defamation and national security. Some content regulations, as in Canada, might also be present. Financing is achieved through a license fee, as with the BBC, or by a tax or a direct government subsidy supplemented by other revenue streams, such as advertising, as with the CBC. The programming on this type of system is a mix of cultural, educational, and entertainment.

The major goal of a privately owned system, such as that in the United States, is profit. Other goals, such as enriching the cultural heritage, serving the public interest, and informing the population, are also espoused, but the profit motive tends to be paramount. Regulation in the privately owned situation is generally weak. Financing is usually done through the sale of commercial time. Most of the programming is entertainment-oriented.

Keep in mind that most countries have one or more of these three systems in operation and each influences the others. In Great Britain, for example, the success of the commercially supported and entertainment-oriented ITV channel prompted the BBC to offer more mass-entertainment programming on its channels. Also remember what was said at the beginning of this section about systems being influenced by social, economic, and political forces. The 1980s and 1990s saw the end of communism in Eastern Europe and the rise of the free-market economy. Consequently, many countries previously served by a state-run monopoly system now faced competition from privately owned stations and networks (see the box on Bulgarian media). Other countries, faced with economic problems, sold some of their state-run networks to private companies. Finally, since broadcasting signals don't stop at the border, people in countries where broadcasting was

run by a state agency or by a government corporation saw examples of popular entertainment shows on systems not previously available to them from neighboring countries. As a result, pressure began to build on governments to move toward more mass-appeal programming.

ELECTRONIC MEDIA IN OTHER COUNTRIES

This section analyzes the systems in four countries along the dimensions of structure, economics, regulation, and content. These are not the only dimensions that could be analyzed, but they are among the most seminal. Moreover, it's not possible to analyze systems in every country. For our purposes, we have chosen only four. This should not suggest that these countries are more important than others; they simply offer better examples to bring out comparisons.

The four systems that will be analyzed are those of Great Britain, the People's Republic of China, Canada, and Kenya. The British system has been praised for its excellence and has served as a model for many other systems; it is also significant because it represents a good example of a pluralistic broadcasting system in a developed country. China provides an example of a government-controlled system of broadcasting. An examination of the Canadian system will illuminate the problems of maintaining cultural autonomy in the face of broadcast spillover from the United States. In addition, Canada, as an immediate neighbor of the United States, is a good candidate for study. Kenya demonstrates the special role of broadcasting in a developing nation. It also provides us with an opportunity to discuss issues of press freedom.

The United Kingdom

Broadcasting in the United Kingdom and the United States developed at about the same time but underwent a markedly different evolution. Like many countries in Europe, Britain decided early that broadcasting should be a monopoly public service. Coupling this thought with the British tradition of strong independent public institutions, the government chartered the British Broadcasting Corporation (BBC) in 1927. The programming on this new service was essentially "highbrow," characterized by news, analysis, education shows, and classical music. Over the years, however, the BBC has diversified its radio programming by adding other, more-popular content. In the early 1970s there were four BBC radio networks in operation, one devoted entirely to rock music.

The BBC got into TV broadcasting in 1936 but, as in other countries, development was short-circuited by World War II. Television service resumed in 1946 and grew rapidly in popularity. The BBC enjoyed monopoly status until 1954 when Parliament created a competitive, commercially sponsored TV system. Further competition came about in the early 1970s when local independent radio stations were authorized. In 1995 the BBC consisted of two national and several regional TV networks, four national radio networks, and several regional and local services. The rival commercial system had two national TV networks, approximately 50 local independent radio stations, and TV and radio news services.

British broadcasting was deregulated and partially restructured in 1990. A new governing body was created for commercial TV, and more radio stations went on the air. A new commercial network, Channel 5, went on the air in 1997. British Sky Broadcasting used a direct broadcast satellite system to compete with the BBC and the commercial stations. The charter of the BBC was renewed in 1996, and despite speculation that the BBC would start accepting commercials, the system was left unchanged. The BBC added a 24-hour news channel, and, in 1998, BBC Online made its debut on the Web.

As the new century began, the BBC was taking advantage of the new digital television technology to increase the number of channels available to subscribers who own digital TV sets and digital antennas (about 60 percent of the audience as of 2005). New digital channels include two daytime kids' networks, a youth-oriented BBC 3, a cultural and arts-centered BBC 4, a 24-hour news channel, and a channel devoted to covering Parliament. In addition, the BBC is partnering with a digital TV company called Crown Castle to start a service called *Freeview,* which will be available to viewers who have conventional TV antennas. The new service will carry approximately 30 channels and increase the number of homes able to receive digital programs.

As of 2006, VCR/DVD penetration was high, more than 80 percent. Cable TV was not growing as rapidly as in the United States, primarily because of an environmental protection act that makes it necessary for all cable to be buried rather than hung from poles. As a result, cable penetration was less than 15 percent in 2006. About 30 percent of the population was equipped to receive satellite television.

The move to digital is likely to mark the beginning of a trend in Britain similar to what happened in the United States when cable TV became widely available. Large, national audiences will fracture into smaller specialized niches. In addition, a new royal charter goes into effect in 2007. The role of the BBC and independent television will doubtlessly change as Britain heads into the multichannel age.

Structure Broadcasting in the United Kingdom is organized into a **duopoly.** There are two major broadcasting entities: the noncommercial BBC and the commercial sector. The BBC is a public corporation that is ultimately responsible to Parliament but whose day-to-day operations are generally free from interference. Operating under a royal charter, the BBC oversees the noncommercial national radio and TV system, the regional radio and TV services, the BBC World Service, and BBC.com. An American parallel to the BBC is difficult to find, since most government-chartered organizations tend to be politically involved from time to time. Perhaps the Red Cross, chartered by Congress but run by its own board of trustees, comes the closest.

The commercial television network is made up of ITV 1, ITV 2, ITV 3, ITV 4, Channel 4, and Channel 5, all currently available over traditional or digital channels. In addition, commercial satellite TV is also available. The commercial radio system consists of approximately 300 national and local analog and digital radio stations.

Economic Support Since the BBC is prohibited from making money by selling commercial time, it must turn to other sources for income. The system used by the BBC is a license fee, or receiver fee, that all set owners in the United Kingdom must pay to support broadcasting. This license fee system is fairly common in Western Europe but is unfamiliar to those in the United States, who are accustomed to "free" radio and TV supported by the sale of advertising. (A variation of the license fee system has been suggested from time to time as a means of supporting the public TV system in the United States, but so far this plan has not been adopted.) As of 2006 the license fee, set by Parliament and tied to the inflation index, was about $230 per year per household for a color TV set. (License fees support both radio and TV broadcasting but are imposed only on TV receivers.) People who avoid paying it are subject to a heavy fine. About 53 percent of total license fee revenue goes to TV, about 12 percent to radio, with the remainder going for digital TV and miscellaneous expenses.

The BBC also receives income from selling program guides, books, records, and other merchandise, such as Teletubbies toys. In addition, the BBC has a commercial arm, BBC Worldwide, which exports programming. BBC America, for example, accepts advertising and is a revenue source for the BBC. The BBC was in relatively good financial health in 2006, thanks in part to cost-cutting measures, but the cost of converting to digital may mean a sharp increase in future license fees.

The commercial TV networks, on the other hand, receive no part of the license fee revenue. They pay a license fee to the Office of Communication (Ofcom), the main regulatory body in the United Kingdom, and make their money by selling advertising on their stations.

In 2004, according to Ofcom, net TV advertising revenue in the United Kingdom was about $6 billion compared to about $4 billion, the portion of the BBC license fee that went to TV. (This difference is not unusual. In other countries having similar duopolies, advertising revenue generally exceeds license income.) Note that a license fee is recession-proof. When economic conditions are poor (as they were in Great Britain in the early years of the decade), commercial broadcasters will see profit margins shrink as advertising dries up. The BBC, however, will receive steady income.

Law and Regulation   Government exercises a light hand with the BBC. Although technically the government has the final say, it has rarely exercised that power. The government, however, can exert significant pressure, as it did in the late 1980s and early 1990s when it prohibited the broadcasting of terrorist voices in connection with the violence in Northern Ireland. Moreover, in 2003 and 2004 the BBC was involved in a controversy concerning its reporting of the government's use of intelligence in the period preceding the Iraq war. After an official inquiry, a report was released that severely criticized the BBC's reporting and management structure. In the wake of the report the BBC's chair and the director general both resigned.

In 2004, the regulatory structure of British broadcasting and cable underwent a significant change as the new Office of Communications took over the duties that were formerly handled by five separate regulatory organizations. Ofcom is charged with regulating a variety of electronic services: television, radio, wireless devices, Internet providers, and telephone services (see Figure 14–2). As far as broadcasting is concerned, Ofcom has regulatory power over both the BBC and the commercial networks.

Ofcom's regulatory activities are arranged in tiers. The first tier concerns content and covers such areas as offensive or harmful material, privacy, and fairness. The second tier refers to the regulation of program production and charges Ofcom with making sure that the appropriate number of programs are produced by region or by independent companies. The third tier deals with the public service commitments of the commercial broadcaster. (The BBC public service commitments are not regulated by Ofcom; they are the responsibility of the BBC's governing body.)

Ofcom also has the responsibility of regulating advertising, but practically speaking most complaints about ads first go through the Advertising Standards Authority, an independent body set up by the advertising industry to enforce the United Kingdom's advertising codes. The codes prohibit advertising for such things as tobacco, escort agencies, and guns and direct advertisers to take special care with ads that might seen by children.

Figure 14–2

Regulation of Electronic Media in Great Britain

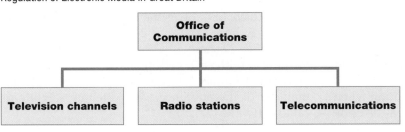

The Kumars at No. 42 is carried by BBC America.

Ofcom uses several enforcement tools. It can direct a station not to repeat a program or ad, order a station to publish a correction, fine a broadcaster, or revoke a station's license.

Within the BBC, the Governor's Programme Complaints Committee handles complaints about taste and impartiality. In 2005, the BBC received about 125,000 complaints, many of them following the airing of the controversial *Jerry Springer, the Opera,* on BBC 2. Some BBC complaints ultimately made their way to Ofcom for final resolution.

Programming   Before 1993 the BBC produced almost all of its own programming. Critics complained that the BBC could save money by using independent producers as program suppliers. Consequently, new legislation required that the BBC purchase at least 25 percent of its programs from independent suppliers. This cost-saving measure helped the BBC's financial situation. The programming on the commercial channels is all produced either by the company that holds the franchise or by independent producers. Programming on the cable and satellite networks resembles the situation in the United States. There are dozens of services available, including the Discovery Channel, CNN, and ESPN, along with movies and sports channels.

The BBC has a somewhat stodgy reputation when it comes to programming (its nickname is "Auntie Beeb"), whereas the commercial channels have a reputation for more mass-appeal programs. These images are not entirely accurate. BBC 1 airs shows that are primarily British productions, while BBC 2 relies in part on imported shows from the United States, such as *Family Guy, Monk,* and *Arrested Development.* BBC shows popular in 2005 were general-appeal shows such as *East Enders* and *Neighbours,* two long-running dramatic series, and *The Apprentice.*

The ITV commercial networks present a mixture of American and British programs. Programs airing in 2006 that would be familiar to a U.S. viewer include *Judge Judy, Surface,* and *3rd Rock from the Sun.* The locally produced shows are the most popular: *Coronation Street, Footballer's Wives,* and *Emmerdale.* Channel 4 tries to appeal to a wide audience and depends on many American-made programs, such as *My Name Is Earl, Desperate Housewives,* and *ER.* Channel 5 presents an eclectic selection of programs, including American baseball (carried live during the early morning hours) and other American programs: *House, Two and a Half Men,* and *CSI: New York.*

As of 2005, BBC 1 was the most-watched network, with an audience share of 24. ITV 1 was in second place with a 22 share. BBC 2 and Channel 4 were in a virtual tie, with each getting about 10 percent of the audience. Channel 5 trailed with 6 percent. The remainder of the audience was watching satellite or cable networks.

People's Republic of China

Broadcasting developed in China around 1940. Its development was hampered by World War II and internal fighting among China's various political factions. The first station, built with scavenged parts and utilizing a Russian transmitter, was immediately used by China's Communist party as a political tool. China's leader, Mao Zedong, decreed that the station should be used to keep in touch with areas of China that were controlled by the party and with guerrillas and armed forces in the other provinces.

After the Communists assumed power in 1949, radio became a major propaganda tool. From the beginning, the goal of Chinese broadcasting was to shape the development of Communist society. The government built new transmitting facilities and, to make up for the lack of receiving sets, installed loudspeakers for group listening in the rural sections of the country. In 1950, the Central People's Broadcasting Station (CPBS) opened in Beijing (in China, the word *broadcasting* refers to radio and not TV). China's international shortwave service, Radio Beijing, started about the same time. Local stations relayed the programming of the CPBS into the provinces. By 1960 more than 120 radio stations were providing the country with news, entertainment, public affairs, and educational and political broadcasts.

The 1960s and 1970s saw Chinese broadcasting influenced by the cultural revolution proclaimed by Mao Zedong. The programs during this period were propaganda-oriented, strident, and mostly political. Entertainment that was carried had to be in keeping with the goals of the revolution. After Mao's death in 1976, controls over the radio system were relaxed and service was eventually expanded to include six national radio channels. In the 1980s, China opened its doors to Western culture, and the CPBS even began to play American rock music (called *yaogunyue,* translated literally as "shake-roll" music). At the same time, regulation of news was eased. All of that changed in 1989 with the demonstrations in Tiananmen Square. After a few days of tolerance the government cracked down on both the TV and radio media and instituted strict censorship.

Television started in China in 1958 with one station in Beijing. Lack of hardware and technology, however, hampered the development of TV. In addition, during the cultural revolution TV development was stopped entirely. Consequently, by 1970, there were only 30 stations in the entire country. Since 1976, however, TV has been China's fastest growing medium. In 2004, there were approximately 3,000 TV, cable, and satellite stations. The audience is huge. About 400 million households have a TV set. About 30 percent of these are hooked up to cable; about 10 percent have a digital satellite dish. The Internet was also popular. In 2004, about 100 million Chinese were online, and the number was growing quickly. (Although 100 million may sound like a big number, it represents only about 8 percent of the total population of China.)

Over the last decade, the Chinese government has become more liberal in its economic philosophy and has moved toward a free marketplace. Consequently, commercials have become prevalent on Chinese TV. In 2004, advertising revenue topped the $20 billion mark. Not surprisingly, many global corporations are anxious to reach the huge Chinese market.

The Chinese government did away with many of the regulations governing the TV industry in 2004, a move that increased the total number of networks available. Most Chinese now receive about 50 national and local channels. In addition, the government ordered the national networks to improve their capabilities in preparation for the 2008 Olympics. In short, China was quickly moving from a country that was media poor to a country that is media rich.

Structure   Figure 14–3 illustrates the general structure of broadcasting in China. The State Administration of Radio, Film and Television (SARFT) makes sure that the goals of the Chinese Communist party are reflected by China's electronic media. It oversees China Central Television (CCTV), China National Radio, and China Radio International.

China is a huge country. In addition, its people speak a variety of languages and dialects. To accommodate this situation, China National Radio operates eight national networks that broadcast in eight different languages. Programming consists of news, music, sports, financial information, and lifestyle features. It is estimated that about 700 million people listen to the service.

CCTV provides 16 channels with more than 200 hours of programming every day. CCTV-1 is the primary service and carries entertainment, news, and current events. The other channels are devoted to more-specialized content: popular music, opera, science and technology, sports, and children's programming. One channel, CCTV-4, provides programs, many in English, that are geared for overseas viewers.

Figure 14–3

Organization of Chinese Broadcasting

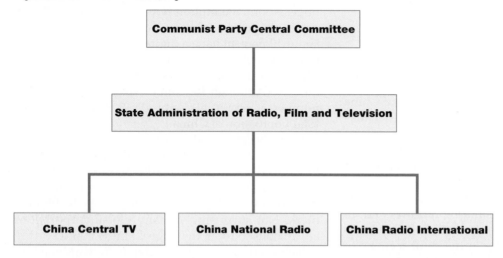

CCTV-9 is an English-language service that is seen on some cable and satellite systems in the United States. CCTV is currently changing from analog to digital transmission and experimenting with high-definition TV.

Along with CCTV, there are about 2,000 to 3,000 city and provincial stations. Local stations in the wealthier regions, such as Shanghai and Guangdong, have emerged as broadcasting leaders in their areas. Many of these local broadcasters have attracted viewers by importing Western shows and formats. Consequently, much like mass-oriented networks in other countries, CCTV-1 has seen its viewership decline.

Financing   Until the late 1980s, China's broadcasting system was supported entirely by government allocations from the national budget. The trend toward a free-market economy, however, has changed all of that, and now commercials are a common sight on Chinese TV. Eager for foreign capital, the Chinese government has opened the airwaves to commercial advertisers. As mentioned above, Chinese television collected more than $20 billion in advertising revenue in 2004. There are numerous ads for Colgate, Tide, Crest, and other American products. U.S. conglomerate Procter & Gamble spent more than $45 million on Chinese TV in 2004. China's entry into the World Trade Organization and its winning bid for the 2008 Olympics are expected to spur ad sales.

Commercials in prime Chinese programs are sold by auction. Each November CCTV holds a 2-day session in which its top 230 commercial time spots are sold to the highest bidders. Commercials in Chinese TV are grouped together and shown in 3–5-minute segments between programs. Advertising rates are much less in China than in the United States or other Western nations. In 2005, a 30-second prime-time spot on provincial broadcaster Beijing TV cost only $5,300.

Regulation   Theoretically, at least, China exemplifies the Marxist-Leninist philosophy of total integration between the government and the media. This is illustrated by the fact that ultimate control over SARFT and Chinese TV is exercised by the Central Committee of the Communist Party. According to the philosophy expressed by Mao Zedong, the functions of the media are threefold: (1) to publicize party decisions, (2) to educate the people, and (3) to form a link between the party and the people.

Censorship is a given on Chinese TV and radio. The most common type of censorship is self-censorship, since journalists and media managers know from training and experience which stories and programs might upset the government. In addition, the party monitors the content of radio and TV stations and, if it wishes, can intervene.

News coverage and programs dealing with political ideology are closely scrutinized. Government guidelines forbid the rebroadcasting of any news story other than those carried by official Chinese

Events: Not Quite a World Wide Web

Although many people in the developed countries have access to the Internet and can listen online to the various international broadcasters mentioned in the text, the table below illustrates that shortwave radio will still be an important international medium in the years to come. As of 2006, far more people had access to radio than to the Internet.

Region	Number Online (in millions)
USA and Canada	227
Europe	291
Asia/Pacific	382
Latin America	79
Africa	24
Middle East	18
World total	1,021

Source: Nielsen//NetRatings Report, March 2006.

Although 1.02 billion is a big number, it represents only about 16 percent of the world's total population. By comparison, a 2001 survey by Group France Telecomm estimated that about 50 percent of the world's population could listen to shortwave.

news agencies. In 2005, a popular series about a twelfth-century scientist was canceled by the government when one of its episodes focused on government corruption. In that same year, in order to tighten its control over popular culture, the government banned Chinese radio and TV networks from forming partnerships with other countries.

The government is particularly sensitive to illegal satellite dishes that can pick up Western shows and news programs. All individuals or organizations must get a government license before installing a satellite dish. Most licenses go to hotels that cater to a foreign clientele. Special security vans patrol urban areas looking for illegal dishes. The Chinese government also tries to regulate the flow of information over the Internet. In January 2002, China instituted controls that ordered Internet service providers to screen private e-mail for political content. A copy of those e-mails containing sensitive material was to be turned over to the government. Providers are also held responsible for monitoring chat rooms and bulletin boards and must erase prohibited content. In 2006, Google agreed to self-censor its Chinese search engine in order to expand its reach in China.

The Chinese government faces a dilemma when it comes to regulating the Internet. On the one hand, the country needs the Internet and other new media to stimulate e-commerce and other economic development. On the other hand, the government is still concerned about what effects unsupervised information might have on its citizens. As more and more media choices become available, the government may find its regulatory tasks much more difficult.

Programming Radio programming in China resembles the content of public radio in the United States. Programs consist of news, humor, storytelling, and music. AM radio is the mainstream service and has the biggest audience. FM radio tends to be localized and relies more on music. The two main China National Radio channels provide about 40 hours a day of service, two-thirds of which is general entertainment. News, features, and advertising make up the rest of the schedule. Regional stations will also carry some China National Radio programming but will originate about 12 hours per day of local programming, mainly music. Western music is played on many stations, and most Chinese are familiar with the latest trends in rock music, thanks to stations in Hong Kong.

Chinese television has seen major changes in the last two decades. CCTV no longer presents a steady diet of propaganda and programs that glorify the Communist Party. The main CCTV channel presents news, documentaries, cultural programs, and the Chinese equivalent of American soap operas. In addition, local and provincial channels are attracting viewers by importing Western shows.

State regulations limit local stations to no more than 25 percent imported programming but stations get around the rule by presenting coproductions and imitations of Western hits. MTV, for example, produces a weekly music show in cooperation with two local stations. There is also a Chinese production of *Sesame Street.*

Imitations are extensive. The top-rated show in 2005 was a Chinese version of *American Idol.* About 400 million watched the final episode, sponsored by Mongolian Cow Sour Yogurt. Talk shows, with formats similar to *Oprah,* are common. A few American shows make it to China. Some are successful; some aren't. The HBO series *Band of Brothers* aired on CCTV and got respectable ratings. On the other hand, the huge American hit *Desperate Housewives* (called *Crazy Housewives* in China) was a flop.

Canada

Broadcasting in our northern neighbor has been shaped by its geography, cultural heritage, bilingualism, and the importance of its proximity to the United States. Almost 90 percent of the Canadian population lives within range of U.S. TV signals. Because of these factors, Canadian broadcasting has had to face some unique problems.

The origins of Canadian broadcasting generally paralleled those of the United States. Experimental licensing began in 1919, and 3 years later private commercial stations began broadcasting. As radio grew, so did concern about the ultimate future of broadcasting. On the one hand, the country's British heritage suggested a model such as the BBC. On the other hand, the proximity of the commercial system in the United States suggested another approach. In 1929, a government commission recommended the creation of a national company to provide a public broadcasting service throughout the country. This ultimately led to the creation of the Canadian Broadcasting Corporation (CBC) in 1936, whose main tasks were to provide a national radio service and to regulate Canadian broadcasting. This may sound reminiscent of the BBC, but there was a well-established system of private broadcasters in operation at the time who were allowed to continue operating—but

under the regulation of the CBC. Thus, from its beginnings, Canadian broadcasting has represented a blend of the U.S. and British approaches.

Radio grew quickly, reaching 70 percent of the population by 1937. After World War II the CBC instituted FM broadcasting and started investigating the development of TV. Television became a reality in 1952, and, as in radio, both private and CBC stations were established. In 1958, after pressure from the private sector, a body separate from the CBC, known as the Board of Broadcast Governors, was established to regulate broadcasting. This in turn was followed by the Canadian Radio–Television Commission— now called the Canadian Radio–Television and Telecommunications Commission (CRTC)—which has the power over private stations and more limited authority over the CBC. Television networks, in both French and English, also started during the 1960s, as did cable TV. In fact, cable grew so rapidly in Canada, it is now one of the most "cabled" countries in the world, with about 80 percent of its homes wired. Much of this growth can be accounted for by the desire of Canadians to receive the full lineup of U.S. cable channels. The Canadians also pioneered satellite communication to cover the vast distances of their country.

The 1970s and 1980s were marked by some conflicts between the United States and Canada regarding the spillover of U.S. TV signals and lost advertising revenue. A trade agreement in 1988 finally solved most of these difficulties. Many U.S. series moved their production to Canada to save money. In the mid-1990s, the Canadian broadcasting and cable industries faced increased competition, fragmenting audiences, and dwindling advertising revenue. The CBC was particularly hard-hit. From 1990 to 2001 more than 1,700 CBC employees were laid off. The CBC budget was slashed more than $250 million from 1995 to 2000. The private sector also suffered from declining advertising revenue. The biggest commercial network, CTV, also laid off staff members and cut the budget for its news operations.

At mid-decade, Canada was moving toward a transition to digital TV. Canada adopted the same digital television technical standards as the United States but chose not to set a definite date for the changeover, preferring instead to let market forces make the decision. The CBC also announced a program to encourage the adoption of HDTV.

The CBC, similar to other public broadcasters, was facing several challenges. Its audience share was

The most popular show on the Canadian Broadcasting Corporation, *Hockey Night in Canada*, has been aired on radio and TV for more than 60 years.

down, and budget woes continued. The situation was not helped by a 2005 labor dispute when the CBC locked out members of the Canadian Media Guild, a union representing most on-air talent and many technical workers, for 7 weeks before finding a settlement.

Structure Broadcasting in Canada is officially described as a single system with two components. In practical terms, the Canadian system, like the British system, is a duopoly, a mix of the public and private, commercial and noncommercial. On the public side, as we have mentioned, the CBC is owned by the federal government and is the major broadcasting force in the country. It provides national radio and TV services through separate English and French networks. Unlike the BBC, however, the CBC relies on a number of privately owned stations that serve as affiliates and provide CBC programming to areas not served by CBC-owned stations. In addition, the CBC operates a special service for the sparsely populated north regions, an armed forces network, and Radio Canada International, its shortwave international broadcasting operation.

The private sector in Canadian broadcasting is made up of all commercial radio and TV stations that are not affiliated with the CBC. There are no privately owned radio networks in Canada, but there are private TV networks as well as several regional satellite and cable networks. Figure 14–4 provides a simplified representation of the Canadian system. Of course, as we have already mentioned, most Canadians can also pick up the major U.S. networks and many independent stations, or see American programs that are provided directly to Canadian stations.

Figure 14–4

Organization of Canadian Broadcasting

Public Sector (CBC)

1. English TV network
2. French TV network
3. French Radio network
4. English Radio network
5. Radio Canada International

Private Sector

1. English TV networks
2. French TV networks
3. Independent radio stations

Economic Support The financial system that supports Canadian broadcasting also combines elements from the British and American systems. The CBC is currently supported by funds appropriated to it by Parliament and by revenue collected from the sale of advertising on many of its stations. (True to its British heritage, from 1923 to 1953 the CBC was also supported by a license fee on receivers.) In 2005, of CBC's total $1.3 billion budget, about 70 percent came from the government and about 30 percent from ad revenue.

Some critics of the CBC have argued that the service is watched by only a small percentage of the audience, is a drain on taxpayers, and is no longer relevant in a multichannel world. Many have even suggested that Canada follow the lead of some European nations and privatize the CBC. For its part, the CBC has reaffirmed its intention to remain a public broadcasting network whose mission includes providing distinctively Canadian programming and contributing to the flow and exchange of cultural information.

The revenues of private radio and TV stations are generated primarily through the sale of advertising. Moreover, as in the United States, cable and satellite systems are supported through direct subscriber payments.

Law and Regulation Throughout the twentieth century, Canada made extensive use of independent commissions and parliamentary committees in shaping its broadcasting policy. In contrast, the United States rarely relies on this technique, preferring to use Congress and the FCC. In many instances the recommendations of these Canadian commissions and committees were enacted into law.

The current law governing Canadian broadcasting was enacted in 1976. This law established the Canadian Radio–Television Telecommunications Commission (CRTC), an independent authority charged with regulating and licensing all broadcasters and cable operators. In terms of structure and overall function, the CRTC is somewhat similar to the FCC in the United States. In 1991 Parliament revamped the Broadcasting Act and in 1993 proclaimed a new Telecommunications Act. These new laws were a recognition of the need to modernize and consolidate existing legislation in the changing world of broadcasting and telecommunications.

The one area in which Canadian regulation sharply differs from that of the United States has to do with regulation of programming. Canada does not have the equivalent of the First Amendment of the U.S. Constitution. The government, therefore, is free to take a more intrusive role into the everyday operation of radio and television stations. For example, the Broadcasting Act of 1991 emphasizes the nationalistic purposes and cultural goals of Canadian policy. It states that the broadcasting system should be owned and controlled by Canadians, should be predominantly Canadian in content and character, and should promote Canadian identity. Such language is necessary because 9 out of 10 Canadians live within 100 miles of the U.S. border and Canadians are worried that their national identity and cultural values will be overwhelmed by American broadcasting. Consequently, during the 1970s, quotas governing the minimum amount of Canadian content required to be broadcast were imposed on all domestic broadcasters. These rules are too complicated to explain in their entirety, but some specific examples will illustrate their scope and intent. For radio, 35 percent of all recorded music played between 6 A.M. and 6 P.M. on weekdays must be Canadian in origin (this means either the performer, composer, lyricist, or recording studio is Canadian). In addition, there are rules regarding diversity in radio formats. Canadian radio stations are allowed to play any kind of music but are not allowed to mix formats. For example, if a station has a country format, it has to play at least a minimum percentage of country music. There are also rules limiting how often a hit record can be played in a given time period. Many Canadian radio stations employ one full-time person just to deal with these federal regulations.

For TV, programs are scored according to a complicated point system, with points awarded to a program according to the nationality of the creative team (director, writer, performers, and so on). For private stations, 60 percent of programming must be Canadian during the day and 50 percent at night. (Keep in mind that most Canadians also have access to U.S. stations, so that, even with these regulations, about 70 percent of all English-language TV available in Canada is from the United States.) In cable, there is a rule that obligates system operators to provide one Canadian channel for every American specialty outlet on their systems.

Canada is not alone in having legislation to protect its cultural heritage (Australia and several European countries have similar rules), but few countries seem to devote as much time and energy to defending national identity. Although much of the justification for quotas is based on an appeal for cultural autonomy, it should be noted that there are economic reasons as well. If a private station is limited to importing 50 percent of its programs, the other 50 percent have to be produced in Canada, thus providing a stimulus for the Canadian economy and preventing more money from flowing out of the country. In the future Canada may have an even harder task protecting its cultural heritage as the Internet brings news and entertainment from all over the globe and Canadians can access podcasts, music downloads, and blogs. All these new channels exist beyond the reach of Canada's media regulators.

The Canadian system also has additional regulations that are not present in the American system. TV stations can carry no more than 12 minutes of commercials per hour. Furthermore, all broadcasting stations are subject to a Sex Role Portrayal Code that calls for "equitable representation of women and men in various social and occupational roles, at home and at work outside the home." With regard to the portrayal of violence, regulations prohibit the depiction of gratuitous or glamorized violence and mandate that shows with violent content are not shown before 9 P.M. In addition, Canada was the first to adopt the V-chip, a device that works with an industry rating system and allows parents to block objectionable programs from their TV screens. The United States has adopted its own version of the V-chip (see Chapter 11).

Programming   Since Canada is a multilingual nation, it must provide radio and TV programs in English, French, and other native languages. The CBC administers both an English-language all-news radio network and a French-language network that links most of the French-language stations in Montreal, Quebec, and Ottawa. In addition, the CBC provides a native-language service to residents in the far northern provinces. Network radio in Canada generally follows an eclectic approach, emphasizing music, news, and features. Private radio stations generally feature a format that emphasizes popular music and news. The CBC also operates an English and a French TV network. There are also several privately owned TV networks: CTV, an English net; SRC, broadcasting in French; Global, an English service; the Atlantic Satellite network, a regional satellite to cable service in Atlantic Canada; and CityTV, broadcasting to five of Canada's largest cities. Canada also has numerous cable systems, which reach about 30 million people, and several English and several French pay services.

Looked at in its entirety, Canadian TV tends to be entertainment-oriented, with about 75 percent of its programs in this category. News and public affairs account for about 14 percent, with sports programming (particularly hockey), making up the rest. Most of the CBC's programs are produced in Canada; it avoids American programming. The CBC's top-rated program is usually *Hockey Night in Canada*. CTV, the private network, features top-rated U.S. shows such as *Desperate Housewives, Lost,* and *Grey's Anatomy.*

Kenya

The Republic of Kenya is located on the east coast of Africa. About the same size as the state of Texas, Kenya has about 30 million people who speak either Swahili or English. The literacy rate averages about 80 percent, higher in the urban areas, particularly around Nairobi, the capital, and lower in the rural areas. Kenya was a British possession until it achieved its independence in 1963. It is a republic, although in recent years Kenya has become a rigidly controlled, one-party nation, and government power over the press has increased.

Kenya belongs to that set of nations typically described as the third world. (A third-world, or developing, country is one that is changing from an agrarian economy and colonial rule to an industrial economy and sovereignty.) The majority of countries in the world belong to the third world. As in many of these countries, the critical issue for Kenya is development. Indeed, the stress of political, economic, educational, and cultural development has strongly influenced its broadcasting system.

Radio began in Kenya in 1927 when the British East African Broadcasting Company relayed BBC broadcasts to British settlers in the area. In 1930 this company was renamed the Cable and Wireless Company and was given a monopoly on broadcasting for the East African Colony. In 1959, aided by a grant from the British government, this station was replaced by the Kenyan Broadcasting Corporation (KBC). When Kenya received its independence in 1963, the new government dissolved the KBC and turned it over to the Ministry of Information and Broadcasting, which renamed it the Voice of Kenya. The Voice of Kenya continued until 1991, when the government formed a new Kenya Broadcasting

Corporation (KBC). Today the KBC offers radio programs in Swahili and English as well as in about a dozen local languages. Several privately owned stations also broadcast in various regions of the country.

Television began in 1963 with a station in Nairobi. A second station went on the air in 1970 in Mombasa. The KBC had a monopoly on TV broadcasting until 1990 when the Kenya Television Network (KTN), a commercially supported network, went on the air. KTN went through a series of ownership changes in the 1990s and faced some financial problems but was still broadcasting as of 2006. In addition, there are three other private TV stations that serve the Nairobi area along with Stella TV, a satellite service, and Family TV, a Christian station.

The Internet has been slow to arrive in Kenya. There were about 1.5 million Kenyans online in 2006, about 4 percent of the total population. Most of these were in urban areas, and many accessed the Internet through Internet cafés. Despite the low penetration, the online community may be politically influential. During a government crackdown on Kenyan media in 2006 (see below), several bloggers provided criticism and dissenting voices to government policy.

Structure   In Kenya, as in other third world countries, radio is the primary means of mass communication. Many citizens, particularly in the rural areas, cannot read, thus limiting the impact of newspapers. As we have mentioned, TV is generally confined to the urban areas of the country. Radio is inexpensive and portable; it can run on batteries and can be understood by all residents.

As currently organized, the KBC, controlled by the Ministry of Information and Broadcasting, provides both English and Swahili programming. It also provides an educational service for schools and uses shortwave radio to reach people who live in distant villages. It has no international shortwave service. From its origin, the KBC was charged with aiding in the task of national development. Its mission statement says it is committed to "excellence in broadcast services to our audience, customers, the public and the government."

The TV system consists of one state-run network and several private stations. Like radio's, the stated goal of the state-run TV network is to encourage national development. The commercial network puts more emphasis on entertainment.

Economic Support   The state-run Kenyan radio and TV services are supported by grants from the Kenyan government. Both the TV and radio networks are permitted to accept advertising, but the revenue they collect is then turned over to the treasury. In theory, this money (and more) is returned to the stations when the government enacts its annual budget for broadcasting. The commercial TV service, as its name implies, is supported entirely by revenue raised from selling advertising time.

Law and Regulation   Kenya does not score highly when it comes to press freedom. The government-run radio and TV services are tightly controlled, and censorship is common. Print media have slightly more freedom but are still closely monitored by the government. News programs are scrutinized by the Ministry of Information and Broadcasting for stories that might reflect badly on the state. Foreign journalists must be accredited by the ministry and to maintain their accreditation are expected to report what the government defines as the "truth." Stories about the activities of the Kenyan president and the Kenyan Parliament are common features on the state-run channel.

A new political party came to power in Kenya in 2003 and promised to be more receptive to the idea of a free press, but several incidents since then have suggested otherwise. First, the government clamped down on unregistered newspapers. Second, the government put political pressure on a private radio station. Finally, in 2006 armed police wearing hoods stormed the offices of the *Standard* newspaper and KTN, its sister TV network, in retaliation for stories that criticized the government. Thousands of copies of the newspaper were burned, and the TV network was briefly knocked off the air.

Programming   Many KBC radio programs are geared for national development. Typical programs include literacy instruction, farming guidance, health education, and technological training. Privately owned stations play music, religious programs, and news. Television, centered in the urban areas, tends to be more news- and entertainment-oriented. Although many programs on the state-run KBC television network focus on national development, entertainment is not overlooked. In 2006, KBC carried the American-made *The Bold and the Beautiful, The Fresh Prince of Bel Air,* and *Walker, Texas Ranger.* KTN carries CNN International and a range of American programs.

Under Saddam Hussein television was a tightly controlled medium that was filled with propaganda. The regime kept close watch on information coming from outside the country, and satellite dishes were illegal.

In the months after Saddam's fall, 30 television and 30 radio stations went on the air. Each of the country's 18 provinces has at least one local television channel, and several more are available via satellite. The previously outlawed satellite dishes have sprouted in abundance; about 7 million were sold in the year after the repressive government lost political power.

One Iraqi broadcasting channel received help during its start-up period from an unlikely source. When coalition troops raided one of the residences of Uday Hussein, son of the Iraqi dictator, they found a huge collection of more than 3,000 VHS tapes mostly made up of Hollywood movies. The military turned the tapes over to the TV channel, where they made up much of the early programming on the new station.

Most of the top-rated programs on Iraqi TV would look somewhat familiar. There's the Arab counterpart to MTV. The local version of *Newlyweds* features young couples competing for money. *Labor and Materials* resembles *Extreme Makeover: Home Edition* except that in the Iraqi version the team rebuilds a house that was destroyed by the war. The most popular program in 2005 was *Iraqi Star,* the local version of *American Idol*. Original programs are also present, but the production values have yet to reach Western standards. The action-oriented cop show *Cobra* has a production budget of less than a thousand dollars.

Western advertisers are also taking a close look at Iraqi TV. Big ad agencies that represent multinational brands are ready to spend large sums of money once the country's future direction becomes clearer.

The big unknown is, of course, the political situation. TV stations have been the target of several violent attacks. Nonetheless, the television industry in Iraq appears to have unlimited potential, provided the opposing factions can find some way to create a stable country.

INTERNATIONAL ELECTRONIC MEDIA SYSTEMS: A HISTORICAL PERSPECTIVE

Earliest attempts at wireless broadcasting were designed to see how far a signal would go. Chapter 1 notes that one of Marconi's striking achievements was the transmission of a signal from England to Newfoundland. Thus it was only natural for other inventors to try to send their signals even farther. One of the things they quickly realized was that the frequency of the radio signal was directly related to the distance the signal would travel (see Chapter 3). For example, using reasonable power, medium-wave signals (300–3,000 kilohertz) travel a few hundred miles during the day (farther at night). This makes them appropriate for domestic radio services but not suitable for international purposes. On the other hand, shortwave signals (3,000–30,000 kilohertz) travel much farther. Using sky waves, they are reflected by the ionosphere and with the right combination of power and atmospheric conditions they can travel thousands of miles. Thus it is not uncommon for a listener in North America to be able to pick up signals from Europe and Africa. Consequently, the earliest international efforts were generally confined to this part of the spectrum. (Of course, this increased distance has its price: Shortwave signals are subject to fading and interference.)

The first radio service designed to be heard by overseas listeners was started by Holland in 1927. The program was directed at Dutch citizens in Holland's colonial empire. The purpose of this service was to keep these people in touch with what was happening back in the homeland. Germany followed suit in 1929, and Great Britain began its Empire Service in 1932.

These "colonial service" stations, however, began to attract a secondary audience of listeners who were native citizens of the country receiving the signals. This paved the way for propaganda broadcasts from one nation to another for the purpose of political persuasion. In 1929, the Soviet Union All-Union Radio, with announcers speaking in both German and French, was broadcasting appeals to the working classes of Germany and France to unite under the banner of socialism. The late 1930s brought tension and war clouds to Europe. Nazi Germany's mobilization under Hitler included an active propaganda program over shortwave. By 1939 approximately 25 nations were involved in international political broadcasting, with Germany, Italy, France, the Soviet Union, and Great Britain the most active. Note that the United States was not a leader in early shortwave broadcasting. This period was the golden age of radio (see Chapter 1), and the commercial networks gave Americans all the news and entertainment they wanted. Further, the memory of World War I was still fresh, and a mood of isolationism—of not getting involved in Europe's problems—permeated the nation. Consequently, Americans paid scant attention to shortwave. World events, however, soon changed everything.

In December 1941 the United States was swept into war against Germany and Japan. Almost immediately the U.S. government instituted a program of shortwave broadcasts to blunt the impact of German propaganda. The new U.S. service, called the **Voice of America (VOA),** made its debut February 24, 1942. VOA was quickly placed under the jurisdiction of the Office of War Information and spent the duration of the war encouraging America's allies and announcing to the rest of the world that the United States was determined to win the war.

World War II also saw a sharp increase in clandestine radio services. A **clandestine station** is an unauthorized station that broadcasts political programs, usually in the name of exile or opposition groups. The United States, Britain, and Germany all operated such stations. For example, Radio 1212 claimed to be a German station but was actually operated by the U.S. Army's Psychological Warfare Branch. The station broadcast to Germany news reports about air raids and battles that were kept secret by the Nazi high command. The real purpose of the station was to cause confusion and dissension in military ranks. On one occasion it misdirected a convoy of German trucks behind Allied lines, where they were captured. Most of these wartime clandestine stations vanished when the war ended.

Yet another type of international broadcasting also began in this era—commercially supported shortwave stations. Radio Luxembourg started sending music, news, and ads to other European countries as early as 1933 and continued to broadcast until the war erupted. Radio Monte Carlo signed on in 1943 (it derived some money from ads but was primarily supported by Italy and Germany), and even the United States got involved in broadcasting commercially sponsored shortwave radio to Latin America and Europe. The war, of course, curtailed the U.S. effort, which would resurface a few years later.

Although the shooting war stopped in 1945, the propaganda war between East and West continued. The Soviet Union established international stations in Poland, Hungary, and Bulgaria that supported international communism. Not to be outdone, the VOA stepped up its propaganda efforts. In 1952 the VOA became part of the newly formed United States Information Agency (USIA). One of the stated goals of the VOA was "to multiply and intensify psychological deterrents to communism." The BBC's External Service also entered into the propaganda fray. Broadcasts in Russian began in 1946, and the BBC was urged by many politicians to stay tough on communism. Budget cuts and aging equipment, however, plagued the service for many years.

Other countries also became involved. International operations started in Japan and West Germany in the 1950s. China increased its shortwave programming from next to nothing in 1949 to about 700 hours weekly by 1960. Fidel Castro's Radio Havana, an AM station, signed on in 1961. The Soviet Union debuted a second international service in 1964, Radio Peace and Progress. For its part, the United States answered with several new systems. Armed Forces Radio Service (AFRS), which started in 1942 to serve military forces around the world, had about 300 stations by the late 1960s and established a large foreign audience. Radio in the American Sector (RIAS), broadcasting primarily to listeners in East Germany and East Berlin, began operation in 1946 and 10 years later was one of the larger systems operating in western Europe. Radio Free Europe (RFE) and Radio Liberty (RL), founded in the early 1950s, were given the task of encouraging dissent in Communist-controlled countries. Both stations were secretly financed by the Central Intelligence Agency until 1973, when Congress approved a new governing board.

International broadcasting grew even more during the 1960s and 1970s. More than 150 countries were operating stations during these decades. Much of this increase was due to former colonies' and developing nations' starting their own external services.

The end of the Cold War during the late 1980s and early 1990s caused a fundamental change in the structure and philosophy of international broadcasting.

The democratization of many countries meant that the Voice of America and other U.S. services were no longer the only source of uncensored news. Both CNN and the BBC were available in many countries. Privately owned radio stations offering independent reports of the news cropped up in the former Soviet Union. In Africa, many FM stations were privatized and aired news unfiltered by the government. As a result, politically oriented programs decreased and were replaced by more public affairs, news, and entertainment programming. Nonetheless, the importance of the political dimensions of international radio was demonstrated by its role during the Gulf War and the attempted coup in Russia. In addition, the United States continues to operate Radio Martí and TV Martí, two broadcast services whose purpose is to provide Cubans an alternative source of news about national and international events.

Moreover, the Cold War ended just as a worldwide economic slowdown began. Consequently, many governments reexamined the goals and efficacy of their external services and took a close look at their budgets. The United States, for example, questioned whether Radio Liberty and Radio Free Europe were still necessary. After much discussion, the Clinton administration announced plans to merge the VOA, Radio Liberty, and Radio Free Europe under the United States Information Agency. The budgets of RL and RFE were cut, and, in an effort to save more money, their headquarters was moved from Munich to Prague. The German service, Deutsche Welle, also announced cuts in its budget, as did the BBC World Service, Radio Nederlands, Radio Moscow, and many others.

Only a few private international shortwave broadcasting stations were operating at the opening of the century. One of the most prominent was WRMI (Radio Miami International), whose signal covers most of Central and South America. WRMI presents a mix of Spanish-language and religious programming.

Most of the major government-sponsored international broadcasters, such as the VOA and the BBC, also make their programming available on the Internet. Keep in mind, however, that only a small percentage of the world's population is online (see box on page 321). Consequently, shortwave broadcasting will remain important for the foreseeable future.

VCR and DVD-player penetration has continued to increase both in the United States and abroad. As of 2005, about 88 percent of all TV-equipped households in Australia had a VCR or a DVD player. Japan had about 85 percent penetration, as did France. Countries in which local programming is limited, such as some in the Middle East, also have a high percentage of VCR/DVD households.

Perhaps the biggest trend in international broadcasting is the increasingly importance of television as a global medium. Although it has yet to attract the millions of people who listen to shortwave radio, there are unmistakable signs that TV is coming into its own as an international medium.

INTERNATIONAL RADIO BROADCASTERS

This section briefly examines the organization of each of the top five international radio broadcasters as of 2006.

The Voice of America

In terms of program hours per week, the United States is the most prolific international shortwave broadcaster. The most powerful U.S. system is the Voice of America (VOA), now in its sixth decade of operation. The organizational structure of the VOA has changed significantly in the last 15 years. In 1994, Broadcasting Board of Governors (BBG) was set up to streamline the operations of all nonmilitary international broadcasters. The BBG oversees VOA Radio and TV, Radio and TV Martí, and international broadcast services—Radio Free Europe/Radio Liberty (RFE/RL), Radio Free Asia (RFA), Arabic-language TV and radio services, and Radio Farda, an AM station that broadcasts in Persian.

After the collapse of communism, the role of RFE/RL was reexamined, and for a while its future was in doubt. In the wake of the September 11 attacks, however, this service gained new importance because its signal reaches Afghanistan, Iraq, and other Middle Eastern countries.

VOA radio broadcasts news, editorials, features, and music in 44 languages through a satellite-fed system of more than 100 transmitters and 28 domestic studios, most of them in Washington, D.C. Its major domestic transmitting facility occupies about 6,000 acres in Greenville, North Carolina, and other domestic transmitters are in California, Ohio, and Florida. The VOA also maintains relay stations in many foreign countries.

Reading the news at the VOA.
The VOA reaches about
100 million listeners every
week.

Profile: Al-Jazeera—Balanced or Biased?

Qatar is a small country with a lot of oil and is situated on a penisula that juts out into the Persian Gulf. Most Americans had never heard of Qatar until the days immediately following the September 11 terrorist attacks. The organization that raised public awareness of Qatar was a tiny satellite news network called Al-Jazeera ("The Peninsula").

The station was established in 1996 by a grant from the Qatari government. From its inception the station has fostered controversy. In a region where most televison stations are state-owned and programming tends to be heavily censored and dull, Al-Jazeera distinguished itself by airing uncensored newscasts, controversial talk shows, debates, and call-in programs that dealt with sensitive social, political, and even sexual issues. It didn't take long before the station offended the sensibilities of several countries. Algeria cut off the station's signal after it aired a program on that country's civil war. Egyptian media called the station's programs "sinister" and urged citizens not to watch.

The United States and the rest of the world found out about Al-Jazeera in the days following the September 11 attacks. The station had spent several years covering Afghanistan and was allowed to stay in the country after the ruling Taliban party forced all other journalists to leave. As a result, Al-Jazeera found itself with a huge exclusive story. When the United States launched air strikes into Afghanistan, Al-Jazeera had the only video. Suddenly, the little-known news station was the lead player on the global media stage. The major international media had little choice but to use Al-Jazeera's war footage.

The new prominence also brought increased scrutiny. The United States strongly criticized the station for running a tape of Osama bin Laden denouncing the United States and for rebroadcasting an earlier interview with bin Laden that praised terrorists. British newspapers charged the station with being a "mouthpiece" for bin Laden. During a meeting with the emir of Qatar, Secretary of State Colin Powell expressed concern over the station's broadcasting inflammatory rhetoric and its apparent pro-Taliban viewpoints. Al-Jazeera came under a new wave of criticism from the U.S. government for its coverage of Operation Iraqi Freedom in 2003.

For its part, Al-Jazeera rejected these charges. Station executives point out that President George W. Bush has received more of the station's news time than bin Laden. Furthermore, they note that the station has presented the American point of view through interviews with prominent leaders. Indeed, Secretary of Defense Donald Rumsfeld, National Security Adviser Condoleezza Rice, and Colin Powell appeared on the channel. Al-Jazeera contends that some of its Arab viewers accuse it of being pro-American. As one Al-Jazeera commentator put it, if the station is making both Americans and Arabs angry, it must be doing something right.

In 2006, Al-Jazeera launched an English-language network. As this book went to press, Al-Jazeera had yet to find a U.S. cable or satellite company willing to carry the new channel.

The control room of Al-Jazeera, the Qatar-based news network. Many in the United States accused Al-Jazeera of biased reporting during Operation Iraqi Freedom in 2003.

The VOA estimates that about 100 million people worldwide are regular listeners, with about 40 million of these in Eastern Europe and Russia. Programming in early 2006 included programs on health and nutrition, public affairs, and sports, as well as many programs featuring popular American music.

Radio Martí went on the air in 1984 as a special service directed toward Cuba. In 2005 it broadcast about 122 hours per week. Radio Martí's transmitter is located in the Florida Keys, and since most Cubans have conventional rather than shortwave radio receivers, it operates at 1180 kilohertz in the standard AM band. In the early 1990s Radio Martí was joined by TV Martí.

The VOA has also taken advantage of advances in technology. To overcome reception problems in the shortwave radio band, the service is also using communications satellites to beam its signal directly to more than a thousand local AM and FM stations that rebroadcast the signal to their home countries. Further, a Web site (www.voanews.com) was launched in 2000 and, as the Web address suggests, is a news-oriented site. Some VOA programs can be heard live on the Internet.

Controversy about the mission of the VOA surfaces from time to time. The latest episode involved two new services that were aimed at the Middle East. Radio Sawa began broadcasting in 2002 with programming that included American rock music. A TV service, Alhurra, followed with content that included *Great Romances, Hollywood Couples,* and the NBA game of the week. Critics argued that such programs were at odds with the local culture and could only serve to create negative feelings toward the United States.

The BBC

The BBC's World Service came into existence in 1948 when Parliament decided to merge the old Empire service with the European operations started during World War II. The BBC service is different from the VOA in that the British system is independent of government ownership. (It does, however, work closely with the British Foreign Office so that official government policies are represented accurately to the outside world.)

Programming on the BBC World Service is diverse and imaginative. Along with its highly respected news programs, there are many entertainment programs, including rock music, serious drama, sports, comedy, and features. The BBC has also introduced a series of international phone-in shows with guests ranging from Paul McCartney to the Afghan foreign minister. BBC World Service news broadcasts are carried by many public radio stations in the United States.

The BBC conducts a wide range of audience research. Data suggest that about 100 million adults regularly listen to the World Service in English and 32 other languages, including about 60 million listeners in Africa and the Middle East. The BBC has transmitters in England plus others in such places as West Berlin, Singapore, Ascension Island (in the mid-Atlantic), and Masirah Island (in the Persian Gulf). In addition, the BBC also leases time over VOA and Canadian transmitters in North America. As a result, few areas of the world are outside the BBC's range. Finally, the BBC also maintains an extensive monitoring service of international broadcasting. Both radio and TV programs from other countries are taped, translated, analyzed, and sometimes rebroadcast.

China Radio International (CRI)

The English service of the People's Republic of China got its start during the Cold War period of the late 1940s. It basically broadcast propaganda programs until the early 1970s when a thaw in U.S.–China relations caused a mellowing in its attitude toward the United States and an increase in nonpolitical content. The station now transmits more than 1,400 hours weekly in 43 foreign languages. Relay stations are located in Canada, Spain, France, French Guyana, Mali, and Switzerland. In 2005, CRI signed a deal with the PanAmSat Corporation to broadcast its programs on 36 audio channels beamed to the Americas, Europe, and Asia. CRI is also carried on a commercial AM station serving the Washington, D.C., area. CRI has a sophisticated multilingual Web site containing news headlines, schedules, and samples of its programs.

Many of CRI's programs are devoted to cultural information about China, news, analysis, and commentary. The rest is mainly music. In addition, CRI produces a half-hour program called *The Biz China,* a program designed for Western businesses interested in the Chinese market. Little is known about the audience research efforts of China Radio International, but surveys done by other international broadcasters suggest that it ranks behind the other major services in listenership. Its highest audience levels are in neighboring countries such as Thailand and India.

The Voice of Russia

During the days of the Soviet Union, this service was known as Radio Moscow and was one of the most influential international broadcasters. The demise of the Soviet Union and the resulting political turmoil have drastically reduced its importance. Renamed the Voice of Russia in 1993, the service broadcasts in 32 languages (for comparison, Radio Moscow broadcast in 82 languages) and provides a total of 98 hours of programming a day (about 80 percent of what Radio Moscow provided). Nonetheless, the Voice of Russia is still one of the five most-popular international broadcasting services.

Faced with a declining economy, the Voice of Russia now accepts advertising. Rates are extremely cheap when compared to U.S. radio. A 1-minute spot on the Voice of Russia cost only $100 in 2006.

The Voice of Russia's programming is a mixture of news, entertainment, and financial programs. The English-language service carries such programs as *Folk Box*, which features Russian folk music, *This Is Russia*, and *Moscow Mailbag*, which has been on the air more than three decades.

The large land mass of Russia enables the Voice of Russia to locate most of its transmitters on native soil and still be able to reach most of the world. Recently, in an effort to generate income, the service has been leasing its transmitters to other international broadcasters.

Like other international broadcasters, the Voice of Russia can be heard on the Internet. In addition, the Voice of Russia recently started broadcasting to the European continent via satellite.

Deutsche Welle (German Wave)

The international radio voice of Germany first signed on in 1953, with broadcasts only in German. Operations quickly expanded, and, by the 1960s, programs were broadcast in 26 languages. The service continued to grow during the last part of the century, and by 2005 Deutsche Welle (DW), which incorporated the former East German international radio service when the two Germanys merged, was broadcasting more than 1,200 hours per week in 30 languages.

DW's annual budget comes from the federal government and is funded at roughly the same level as the VOA or the BBC. It has transmitters in Europe, Africa, and Asia. In 1992 it started leasing transmitters from the Voice of Russia to improve DW's coverage of Asia. Its programs focus on news, music, and German culture, with an occasional feature on the economic and social life within the country. DW has an extensive listenership of about 65 million. Similar to other international broadcasters, DW also transmits using satellites and is available on the Internet.

Unofficial International Services: Clandestines and Pirates

As mentioned previously, a clandestine station is an unauthorized station that beams propaganda at a country for political reasons. Because of their very nature, it's hard to get authoritative data on clandestines. One source of information is www.clandestineradio.com, a Web site that tracks clandestine stations worldwide. As of 2006, this Web site contained information about clandestine activity in 50 nations, many of them in the Middle East and Africa.

Clandestine radio played a part during Operation Enduring Freedom in Afghanistan. The U.S. military set up the Radio Voice of Afghanistan, a station that broadcast news bulletins and explained the reasons behind the U.S. attack on the Taliban. During Operation Iraqi Freedom, Iraq was the target of several clandestine services. Radio al Mustaqbal (The Future) was a station located in Kuwait that was operated by an Iraqi opposition party with U.S. funding. Radio Hurriah (Freedom) was a similar station located somewhere in Iraqi Kurdistan.

In contrast to clandestine stations, **pirate radio stations,** while also unauthorized, do not devote themselves to political messages. Pirate stations generally program music and other entertainment content. Many operate outside a country (usually on a ship anchored outside territorial limits) but some can operate from within, depending on government leniency. Pirate stations broadcasting rock-and-roll from the North Sea during the late 1950s and early 1960s were credited with forcing the BBC to open the doors to rock music.

Most pirate stations are found on the shortwave band, but a few pirates can be found on the FM band. Pirate stations generally specialize in music and talk that would not be found on a traditional station. Schedules are generally erratic and the quality is highly variable. The Pirate Radio Central Web site listed reports of a half-dozen unauthorized stations in 2006.

Pirate stations can interfere with licensed stations and with air traffic communications. In 2006, airline pilots flying into Miami reported that a pirate station playing hip-hop music was interfering with their communication with the ground. Not surprisingly, the FCC does not take kindly to pirate stations. The commission shut down 20 pirate stations in Florida in late 1999. Those convicted of operating a station without a license can face hefty fines and prison terms. Rather than risk legal action, many pirate broadcasters have migrated to the Internet, where they broadcast using streaming audio.

INTERNATIONAL VIDEO

Most global video traffic consists of (1) TV signals, usually sent by satellite, designed to cross international borders, and (2) videotapes, DVDs, or films that are shipped from one country to another.

Satellite-distributed video, as has been mentioned, is one of the biggest growth areas in modern telecommunications, with both public and private broadcasters involved. On the public side, the Voice of America operates VOA-TV, a global satellite system that transmits live and taped U.S. programs in 20 languages to Europe and other parts of the world. In 1993, the BBC World Service joined British media company Pearson in a plan to broadcast a subscription-based channel first to Europe and then to other continents. The BBC channel is available on many U.S. cable and satellite systems. Of all the public broadcasters, perhaps the German international service Deutsche Welle is the most ambitious. The organization has satellite-based television channels in German, Spanish, and English. In addition, Deutsche Welle signals are also currently being beamed into the United States and carried by cable systems. China Radio International has a similar service. In the United States, the Dish Network carries the Arab-language feed of Al-Jazeera, a television network based in Qatar. In 2006, Al-Jazeera launched an English-language, 24-hour news service.

International news channels have also proliferated. CNN is seen in more than 170 million households and thousands of hotel rooms worldwide. The BBC operates a comparable service called BBC World. CNBC started international news and business reporting on its channel in 1996. MSNBC and Fox News are also distributed by satellite to other countries.

International TV is not simply confined to news. MTV is available on every continent except Antarctica and reaches 200 million homes. ESPN launched an international sports channel in 1988 and now beams its coverage into Asia, South America, Africa, Europe, and Australia. Similarly, the Cartoon Network and TNT have large global audiences. And Nickelodeon is viewed in 149 countries in 30 different languages. In Europe, BSkyB, owned in part by Rupert Murdoch, delivers satellite programming to England and the mainland. Murdoch also operates an Asian satellite system that reaches about 180 million viewers. NBC also has a satellite channel that is seen in Asia and Europe. And as mentioned earlier, live TV from around the world is available on the Internet.

Looking next at the tape, disc, and film area, the trade imbalance that characterizes much of the U.S. economy is completely reversed in TV. The United States imports only about 2 percent of its programming (mostly from Britain) while exporting a great deal. In 2005, for example, *Lost* and *Desperate Housewives* were seen in dozens of countries. As mentioned in the opening of the chapter, program concepts, however, are commonly imported into the United States. For example, Twentieth Television, the production unit of Fox Television, announced plans in 2006 to introduce an English-language version of telenovelas, a soap-opera format that is particularly successful in Latin America.

American-made programs have a difficult time being seen in some countries because of laws that put a quota on imported programming and because many countries' own domestic TV systems can now produce professional and slick programs that rival those made in the United States. In fact, in many countries, most of the top-rated prime-time shows are locally produced. The U.S. shows tend to be shown in the daytime, in the early evening, or late at night.

INTERNATIONAL OBLIGATIONS

American broadcasters follow the rules of the **International Telecommunications Union (ITU).** The ITU is a United Nations organization that is responsible for coordinating the broadcasting efforts of its member countries. The ITU tries to minimize interference between stations in different countries, regulates radio spectrum allocations, assigns initial call letters to various countries (U.S. stations begin with W or K, Canadian stations with C, and Mexican stations with X), and works to improve telecommunications services in new and developing countries. The ITU is not a regulatory body like the FCC. It does not license stations; it has only the power that its member nations allow it to have. The ITU's main purposes are to encourage cooperation and efficiency and to serve as a negotiating arena where equitable policy regulation can be worked out.

The supreme authority of the ITU is given the somewhat ungraceful name of the Plenipotentiary Conference. Composed of representatives of all member nations, it meets every 5 to 8 years. The most recent conference was held in 2002.

Over the years, the ITU has managed to concern itself largely with technical matters. Recently, however, politics have crept into ITU operations. As more third-world nations joined the organization, the role of the ITU was broadened from merely dealing with technical matters to providing technical assistance to those countries that request it. In the last 5 years, the ITU has turned its attention to the Internet and has adopted new international modem standards as well as specifications for international videoconferences. In 2006, the ITU was examining a possible future role in assigning Internet domain names and establishing standards for Internet telephone service.

SUMMARY

- A country's media system is dependent on political philosophy, social history, and economic structures. This is most evident when comparing the media systems of Great Britain, China, Canada, and Kenya since each of these countries differs greatly in these respects.

- International broadcasting started with the discovery that shortwave radio could travel long distances and could be used for propaganda. The United States did not get involved in international broadcasting until 1941, when it entered World War II. In the 1950s, the United States set up the Voice of America to counter propaganda broadcasts from the Soviet Union.

- Recent developments in the international broadcasting arena include the decrease of propaganda; cost-cutting measures going into effect at all major broadcasting organizations; the growth of television and the Internet as international media.

- The top-five international broadcasters are the Voice of America, the BBC, China Radio International, the Voice of Russia, and Deutsche Welle, the German station. International services can also be heard over the Internet. The leaders in international TV are CNN, ESPN, MTV, TNT, and the BBC. American programs are still popular in other countries despite increasing competition from local productions.

KEY TERMS

comparative electronic media
   systems   312
international electronic
   media   312

duopoly   316
Voice of America
   (VOA)   328
clandestine station   328

pirate radio stations   333
International Telecommunications
   Union (ITU)   334

SUGGESTIONS FOR FURTHER READING

British Broadcasting Corporation. (2005). *Annual report and handbook.* London: British Broadcasting Corporation.

Gross, L. S. (1995). *The international world of electronic media.* New York: McGraw-Hill.

Hachen, W. T. (1999). *World news prism.* Ames: Iowa State University Press.

Heil, A. (2003). *Voice of America: A history.* New York: Columbia University Press.

Howell, W. J. (1986). *World broadcasting in the age of the satellite.* Norwood, NJ: Ablex.

MacDonald, B. (1993). *Broadcasting in the United Kingdom.* London: Mansell.

Merrill, J. (1991). *Global journalism.* New York: Longman.

Mowlana, H. (1997). *Global information and world communication*. New York: Longman.

Soley, L., & Nichols, J. (1987). *Clandestine radio broadcasting*. New York: Praeger.

Steven, P. (2003). *The no-nonsense guide to global media*. Oxford: New Internationalist.

World Radio–TV handbook. (2005). New York: Billboard Publications.

INTERNET EXERCISES

Visit our Web site at www.mhhe.com/dominick6 for study-guide exercises to help you learn and apply material in each chapter. You will find ideas for future research as well as useful Web links to provide you with an opportunity to journey through the new electronic media.

Glossary

addressable converter   Device that allows pay-per-view cable subscribers to receive their programs.

adjacency   Commercial placement that immediately precedes or follows a specific television, cable, or radio show.

affiliate   Local radio or TV station that has a contractual relationship with a network.

American Society of Composers, Authors and Publishers (ASCAP)   Group that collects and distributes performance royalty payments to various artists.

amplifier   Device that boosts an electrical signal.

amplitude   Height of a wave above a neutral point.

ARPANET   Early version of the Internet.

audience flow   Movement of audiences from one program to another.

audimeter   Nielsen rating device that indicates if a radio or TV set is in use and to what station the set is tuned. *See also* storage instantaneous audimeter.

audion   Device invented by Lee De Forest that amplified weak radio signals.

auditorium testing   Research technique that tests popularity of records by playing them in front of a large group of people who fill out questionnaires about what they heard.

average quarter-hour persons   In radio, average number of listeners per 15-minute period in a given daypart.

barter   Type of payment for syndicated programming in which the syndicator withholds 1 or more minutes of time in the program and sells these time slots to national advertisers.

blanket rights   Music licensing arrangement in which an organization pays BMI or ASCAP a single fee that grants the organization the right to play all of BMI's or ASCAP's music.

block programming   In radio, programming to one target audience for a few hours and then changing the format to appeal to another group. Used by many community radio stations.

blog   A shared online journal where people post entries about their experiences, interests, and attitudes.

burnout   Tendency of a song to become less popular after repeated playings.

buying power index (BPI)   A weighted measurement describing a specific geographic market's ability to buy goods, based on population, effective income, and retail sales.

cable TV   Distributing television signals by wire.

call-out research   Radio research conducted by telephone to evaluate the popularity of recordings.

carrier wave   Basic continuous wave produced by a radio or TV station; modulated to carry information.

catharsis theory   Theory that suggests that watching media violence relieves the aggressive urges of those in the audience. There has been little scientific evidence for this position.

chromakey   Process by which one picture is blended with another in TV production.

clandestine radio services   Unauthorized broadcasts, usually political in nature, conducted by groups in opposition to the current government.

clutter   Commercials and other nonprogram material broadcast during program breaks.

compensation   The amount of money networks pay to their affiliates for carrying the network-fed program. Compensation rates are based on market size, ratings, and affiliate strength.

convergence   A trend whereby radio, television, and telephone communications are merged with the computer.

cooperative advertising   Arrangement in which national advertisers assist local retailers in paying for ads.

cost per thousand (CPM)   One measure of efficiency in the media. Defined as the cost to reach 1,000 people.

coventuring   Arrangement by which a TV station's news department shares its newscasts with other local TV stations, cable systems, or radio stations.

cultivation theory   Theory suggesting that watching a great deal of stereotyped TV content will cause distorted perceptions of the real world.

dayparts   A way of dividing up the broadcast day to reflect standard time periods for setting advertising rates.

demographics   Science of categorizing people based on easily observed traits. Age and sex, for example, are two common demographic categories.

digital audio broadcasting (DAB)   Broadcasting a radio signal by using a binary code (0s and 1s).

digital video disc (DVD)   Device that stores video and audio information by using laser technology.

direct broadcast satellite (DBS)   Satellite transmission designed to be received directly by the home.

diversification   Business strategy that involves spreading investments into several different areas.

downconverter Device that decodes microwave signals.

duopoly (1) System of broadcasting in which two systems, one public and one private, exist at the same time, as in Canada. (2) Owning more than one AM or FM station in the same market.

electronic news gathering (ENG) Providing information for TV news with the assistance of portable video and audio equipment. Also called electronic journalism (EJ).

electronic response indicator (ERI) Device that allows viewers to rate continuously a program or a commercial while they are viewing it.

equalizer Electronic device that adjusts the amplification of certain frequencies; allows for fine-tuning an audio signal.

exclusivity deal In cable, an arrangement whereby one premium service has the exclusive rights to show the films of a particular motion picture company.

exit poll Survey in which voters are asked about their voting decisions immediately after they leave the voting booth; used to predict the outcomes of elections before the polls close.

fairness doctrine Currently defunct policy of the Federal Communications Commission that required broadcast stations to present balanced coverage of topics of public concern.

false light A type of invasion of privacy in which media coverage creates the wrong impression about a person.

fiber-optic Cable used for transmitting a digital signal via thin strands of flexible glass.

field Half of a complete TV picture; one field is scanned every 60th of a second.

financial interest and syndication rules (fin-syn) FCC regulations limiting network participation in ownership and subsequent syndication of programs produced for the network.

focus group Small group of people who discuss predetermined topics, such as a TV newscast.

Food and Drug Administration (FDA) Federal commission that is responsible for overseeing prescription drug advertising on TV.

format The type of music or talk that a radio station chooses to program. Formats are usually targeted at a specific segment of the population. *See also* demographics.

frame Two fields or one complete TV picture; one frame is scanned every 30th of a second.

frequency Number of waves that pass a given point in a given time period, usually a second; measured in hertz (Hz).

frequency response Range of frequencies that a radio set is capable of receiving.

future file Collection of stories to be used in upcoming newscasts.

geosynchronous orbit A satellite orbit that keeps that satellite over one spot above the earth.

gross impressions The total number of advertising impressions made during a schedule of commercials. GIs are calculated by multiplying the average persons reached in a specific time period by the number of spots in that period of time.

gross rating points (GRPs) The total number of rating points gained as a result of scheduling commercials. GRPs are determined by multiplying the specific rating by the number of spots in that time period.

high-definition television (HDTV) Improved resolution TV system that uses approximately 1,100 scanning lines.

homes passed Number of homes that have the ability to receive cable TV; that is, homes passed by the cable.

hook Short, easily identifiable segment of a recording.

households using television (HUT) Number of households that are watching TV at a certain time period.

hue Each individual color as seen on color TV.

interactive television System in which TV viewers respond to programs by using a special keypad.

International Telecommunications Union (ITU) Organization that coordinates the international broadcasting activities of its members

Internet A global network of interconnected computers.

Internet service provider (ISP) A company that connects subscribers to the Internet.

inventory The amount of available advertising time a media outlet has to sell; unsold time.

kinescope Early form of recording TV shows in which a film was made of a TV receiver.

local area network (LAN) A group of computers that are linked together.

local market agreement (LMA) Arrangement whereby a company that owns one radio station can manage assets of another station without violating FCC ownership rules.

local origination Program produced by a local TV station or cable system.

low-power television (LPTV) Television stations that operate with reduced coverage and have a coverage area only 12–15 miles in diameter.

meta-analysis Research technique that summarizes the findings of many separate studies about a single topic.

minidisc (MD) A more compact version of the CD, about one-fourth the size of a standard CD.

minidoc Multipart reports that generally air Monday to Friday on local TV stations. Each minidoc segment may only be 3 or 4 minutes long.

modulation Encoding a signal by changing the characteristics of the carrier wave.

monopoly The ability to exercise unrestrained power over a market; the existence of no real or effective competition.

MP3 Recording compression technique that makes it possible to share audio files over the Internet.

multichannel, multipoint distribution system (MMDS) System using microwave transmission to provide cable service into urban areas; also called wireless cable.

multiple-system operator (MSO) Company that owns and operates more than one cable system.

multiplexing Sending different signals with the same channel.

National Association of Broadcasters (NAB) Leading professional organization of the broadcasting industry.

National Cable Television Association (NCTA) Leading professional organization of the cable industry.

network compensation Money paid by a network to one of its affiliates in return for the affiliate's carrying network shows and network commercials.

network programming Programs that are financed by and shown on TV networks.

news consultants Research companies that advise stations about ways to improve the ratings of their news programs.

noise Unwanted interference in a video or audio signal.

oligopoly In economics, a situation in which there is limited or managed competition. In broadcasting, the condition of having limited number of competitors, which ensures that every outlet will find some audience.

oscillation Vibration of a sound or radio wave.

panel method Research technique in which the same people are studied at different points in time.

pay per view (PPV) System in which cable subscribers pay a one-time fee for special programs such as movies and sporting events. *See also* addressable converter.

People Meter In ratings, handheld device that reports what TV show is being watched. People Meters also gather demographic data about who is watching.

personal People Meter (PPM) A device that is carried by an individual to measure radio listening and TV viewing by detecting subaudible tones in the stations' signals.

personal video recorder (PVR) Device that records video on hard disk, similar to a computer hard drive. TiVo is an example.

pilot Sample episode of a proposed TV series.

pirate station Unauthorized radio or TV station that generally broadcasts entertainment material.

podcasting Distributing audio and video files over the Internet for playback on iPods and similar devices.

pods A cluster of commercials, promotions, or other announcements.

portal First page opened by an Internet browser.

prime-time access rule (PTAR) In general, a regulation that limits the TV networks to 3 hours of programming during the prime-time period. Exceptions are made for news, public affairs, children's shows, documentaries, and political broadcasts.

psychographic research Research that uses personality traits to segment the audience.

pulse code modulation (PCM) Method used in digital recording and reproduction in which a signal is sampled at various points and the resulting value is translated into binary numbers.

pure competition In economics, a state where there is sufficient competition in the marketplace that prices of goods and services move toward actual cost. In broadcasting, having a sufficient number of voices in the marketplace to keep ratings and rates in a state of equilibrium.

rating In TV, the percentage of households in a market that are viewing a station divided by the total number of households with TV in that market. In radio, the total number of people who are listening to a station divided by the total number of people in the market.

right of first refusal Network's contractual guarantee to prohibit a production company from producing a specific show for another client.

rough cut Preliminary rendition of an ad or a TV show produced so that viewers can get a general idea of the content.

satellite news gathering (SNG) Use of specially equipped mobile units to transmit live and taped remote reports back to a local station.

share In radio, the number of people who are listening to a station divided by the total number of people who are listening to radio at a given time. In TV, the total number of households watching a given channel divided by the total number of households using TV.

signal-to-noise ratio Amount of desired picture or sound information that remains after subtracting unwanted interference.

single-system operator (SSO) Company that owns and operates one cable system.

standing order   A commercial order that gives a certain time in the broadcast schedule to the same customer until the order is rescinded.

station identification   Station announcement broadcast at the top or bottom of the hour telling call letters and location or having station logo superimposed on the screen.

step deal   Contractual arrangement by which TV series are produced. Production proceeds in a series of defined steps, with the network having the option to cancel after each step.

stimulation theory   Theory suggesting that watching media violence will stimulate the viewer to perform aggressive acts in real life. Opposite of the catharsis theory.

storage instantaneous audimeter (SIA)   Computer-assisted TV measurement device that makes possible overnight ratings.

storyboard   Drawings illustrating what a finished commercial or segment of a TV show will look like.

streaming   A technique that allows sound and moving pictures to be transmitted on the World Wide Web.

stripping   Scheduling the same show to run in the same time period from Monday through Friday.

supergroup   Radio companies that control large numbers of stations in several different markets.

superstation   Local TV station that is distributed to many cable systems via satellite, giving the station national exposure.

survey   Research method that uses questionnaires or similar instruments to gather data from a sample of respondents.

switcher   Device used to switch from one video signal to another. Can also be used to combine more than one video signal.

synchronization pulse   Signal that enables the output of two or more cameras and other video sources to be mixed together and also keeps the scanning process in the camera operating in time to coincide exactly with the retrace process in the TV receiver.

syndication   The sale and distribution of programming directly to the station. First-run syndication involves products that have been specifically produced for airing in the syndication marketplace.

target audience   Specific group a radio or TV program is trying to attract.

telephone coincidental interview   Method of audience research in which a respondent is asked what radio or TV station he or she is listening to at the time of the call.

teletext   Cable service that offers text and graphics displayed on the screen.

tiering   Process of selling cable subscribers increasing levels of service.

time-shifting   Recording something on a VCR to watch at a more convenient time.

treatment   Short narrative used to sell an idea for a TV show or series to a production company.

turnkey automation   Radio station that is fully automated.

TVRO   Satellite television receive-only earth station.

ultra-high frequency (UHF)   The portion of the electromagnetic spectrum that contains TV channels 14 to 69.

uniform resource locator (URL)   A unique address of an Internet site.

upfront sales   Network television time that is sold in the summer before the actual television season begins. Upfront sales are frequently for dayparts as opposed to actual programs.

V-chip   Device installed in TV sets that blocks out violent programming.

vertical integration   Process by which a firm has interests in the production, distribution, and consumption of a product.

very high frequency (VHF)   The part of the electromagnetic spectrum that contains TV channels 2 to 13.

videotex   Two-directional information service linking a data bank with computer terminals via cable or telephone lines.

voice-tracking   Radio technique in which a disc jockey records his audio for a program and all other elements are added later by a computer. Makes it possible for one DJ to do programs for several different stations.

Voice over Internet Protocol (VoIP)   Method of sending telephone calls over the Internet.

waveform   Visual representation of a wave as measured by electronic equipment.

wavelength   Distance between two corresponding points on an electromagnetic wave.

World Wide Web   Part of the Internet that contains sites featuring text and graphics.

Photo Credits

Index